# Democracy

# DEMOCRACY: A READER

Edited by

Ricardo Blaug and John Schwarzmantel

COLUMBIA UNIVERSITY PRESS

Selection and editorial material © Ricardo Blaug
and John Schwarzmantel. The texts are reprinted
by permission of other publishers.

Columbia University Press
Publishers since 1893
New York

First published in the UK by
Edinburgh University Press Ltd
22 George Square, Edinburgh

Typeset in Sabon and Gill Sans
by Bibliocraft Ltd, Dundee, and
printed and bound in Great Britain by
The University Press, Cambridge

ISBN 0-231-12480-5 (cloth)
ISBN 0-231-12481-3 (pbk.)

CIP data is on record with the Library of Congress

Casebound editions of Columbia University Press
books are printed on permanent and durable
acid-free paper.

c 10 9 8 7 6 5 4 3 2 1
p 10 9 8 7 6 5 4 3 2 1

# CONTENTS

# PREFACE

This Reader on Democracy aims to bring together as wide a range of material on democracy as can be assembled in one volume. It seeks to present both historical and contemporary analyses of democracy, and includes extracts from thinkers hostile to the democratic ideal as well as from those defending and justifying democracy. The intention is to present here sufficient material for analysis of the problems and opportunities which are faced by the practice of democratic politics in a new millennium. We hope this collection will be helpful not just to students studying the theory, history and practice of democratic politics, but to all citizens of new and established democracies who are interested in the theoretical foundations of democratic rule.

The editors are most grateful to the anonymous readers who commented on the proposal for this Reader at an early stage. They would also like to express their thanks to Mike Sullivan for photocopying a large proportion of the extracts used in this book, and for carrying out this laborious task cheerfully and efficiently. They are also very grateful to Nicola Carr of Edinburgh University Press for her support and advice throughout, and to Holly Roberts and other colleagues at Edinburgh University Press for their work in soliciting permissions to reproduce the extracts used in this Reader.

We hope that this collection will guide its users through the mass of writings seeking to analyse the democratic form of rule, and that it may be a modest aid in extending and deepening democracy in the situation of unparalled complexity which confronts the practice of democratic politics.

Ricardo Blaug, John Schwarzmantel
Leeds, June 2000

# ACKNOWLEDGEMENTS

Grateful acknowledgement is made to the following sources for permission to reproduce material in this book previously published elsewhere. Every effort has been made to trace copyright holders, but if any have been inadvertently overlooked the publisher will be pleased to make the necessary arrangement at the first opportunity.

'Funeral Oration' by Pericles, from *The History of the Peloponnesian War* by Thucydides, translated by Rex Warner (Penguin Classics, 1954). © Rex Warner, 1954, Penguin, Harmondsworth, 1972, pp. 145–8. Reproduced by permission of Penguin Books Ltd.

'The Politics' translated by B. Jowett from Aristotle's *Politics* from *The Oxford Translation of Aristotle* edited by W. D. Ross (Volume 10, 1921), reprinted by permission of Oxford University Press.

Machiavelli, *The Discourses*, translated by L. J. Walker, Routledge, 1970. Reproduced by permission of Taylor and Francis Books Ltd.

T. Hobbes from *Leviathan* edited by C. B. Macpherson, Penguin, 1968.

Jean-Jacques Rousseau, *The Social Contract*, Everyman, 1993. Reprinted by permission of Everyman Publishers Plc.

J. Madison, A. Hamilton, J. Jay, *The Federalist Papers, 10th Paper*, edited by I. Kramnick, Penguin, 1987.

'Representative Government' by J. S. Mill. © Oxford University Press, 1975. Reprinted from *Three Essays on Liberty* by John Stuart Mill (1912, reissued 1975) by permission of Oxford University Press.

*Democracy in America* by Alexis de Tocqueville, edited by J. P. Mayer and Max Lerner. Translated by George Lawrence. English translation © 1965 by Harper & Row, Publishers, Inc. Copyright Renewed. Reprinted by permission of HarperCollins Publishers, Inc.

Putney Debates, extract from *Puritanism and Liberty* (ed. A. S. P. Woodhouse), Dent, 1974, reproduced by permission of Everyman Publishers Plc.

*The Rights of Man* by Thomas Paine, edited by H. Collins, Penguin, 1969.

'French Revolution: Declaration of the Rights of Man and Citizen', from *Rights of Man* by Thomas Paine, edited by H. Collins, Penguin, 1969.

'Gettysburg Address' by Abraham Lincoln from *The Democracy Reader: Classic and Modern Speeches, Essays, Poems, Declarations, and Documents on Freedom and Human Rights Worldwide* by Diane Ravitch and Abigail M. Thernstrom (Eds.), HarperCollins, Inc., 1993.

*Capitalism, Socialism and Democracy* by J. A. Schumpeter, Allen and Unwin 1943, reproduced with permission of Taylor and Francis.

Immanuel Kant 'On the Common Saying: This may be True in Theory, but it does not Apply in Practice' in Immanuel Kant's *Political Writings* edited by H. Reiss, Cambridge University Press.

B. Constant, 'The Liberty of the Ancients compared with that of the Moderns' from *Political Writings* by B. Constant, Cambridge University Press, 1988, reproduced by permission of Cambridge University Press and Biancamaria Fontana.

'Two Concepts of Liberty' reprinted by permission of Oxford University Press. © Isaiah Berlin, 1958, 1969. Published in *Four Essays on Liberty* (Oxford University Press, 1969) and in a revised form (followed here) in *The Proper Study of Mankind* (Chatto & Windus, 1997).

*In Defense of Anarchism* by Robert Paul Wolff, University of California Press, 1998, reproduced by permission of University of California Press.

*Second Treatise on Government* by J. Locke, Cambridge University Press, 1964, reproduced by permission of Cambridge University Press.

Translation © Franklin Phillip, 1994, Editorial Matter © Patrick Coleman, 1994. Reprinted from Jean-Jacques Rousseau: *Discourse on the Origin of Inequality* translated by Franklin Phillip, edited with an introduction by Patrick Coleman (1994) by permission of Oxford University Press.

*Equality* by R. H. Tawney, Routledge, 1964. Reproduced by permission of Taylor and Francis.

B. Williams, 'The Idea of Equality' in *Philosophy, Politics and Society*: 2nd Series edited by Peter Laslett and W. G. Runciman, Blackwell, 1956 and HarperCollins NY, reproduced by permission of Blackwell Publishers.

'Speech to Bristol Electors' by Burke. © Oxford University Press 1996. Reprinted from *The Writings and Speeches of Edmund Burke*, Volume III edited by W. M. Elofson and John A. Woods (1996) by permission of Oxford University Press.

James Mill, *Political Writings: Essay on Government*, edited by Terence Ball, Cambridge University Press 1992, reprinted by permission of Cambridge University Press.

Hanna Pitkin, *The Concept of Representation*, University of California Press 1967, © 1967, The Regents of the University of California, reproduced by permission of University of California Press.

© Anne Phillips, 1995. Reprinted from *The Politics of Presence* by Anne Phillips (1995) by permission of Oxford University Press.

Young, I. M., *Justice and the Politics of Difference*. © 1990 by Princeton University Press. Reprinted by permission of Princeton University Press.

Michael Bakunin, 'Oeuvres, Vol. II' (1907) translated by George Woodcock, in G. Woodcock (ed.) *The Anarchist Reader*, Glasgow, Fontana.

Pierre-Joseph Proudhon, from 'Les Confessions d'un Révolutionnaire', 1849, in G. Woodcock (ed.) *The Anarchist Reader*, Glasgow, Fontana.

R. Wollheim 'A Paradox in the Theory of Democracy' in *Philosophy, Politics and Society*, 2nd Series, P. Laslett and W. Runciman (eds.) Blackwell, 1962, reproduced by permission of Blackwell Publishers.

'Representative Government' by J. S. Mill. This edition © Oxford University Press, 1975. Reprinted from *Three Essays on Liberty* by J. S. Mill (1975) by permission of Oxford University Press.

G. Sartori, *Theory of Democracy Revisited*, Chatham House, 1987, reproduced by permission of Chatham House.

Robert A. Dahl, *Polyarchy: Participation and Opposition*, Yale University Press, 1971 © Yale University Press, reproduced with permission of Yale University Press.

'Politics' translated by B. Jowett, from Aristotle's *Politics and Economics* from *The Oxford Translation of Aristotle* edited by W. D. Ross, Volume 10 (1921), reprinted by permission of Oxford University Press.

*Class, Citizenship and Social Class* by T. H. Marshall, © 1963 by T. H. Marshall. Used by permission of Doubleday, a division of Random House, Inc.

W. H. Sewell, Jr., 'Le Citoyen/La Citoyenne: Activity, Passivity and the Revolutionary Concept of Citizenship' in Colin Lucas (ed.), *The French Revolution and the Creation of Modern Political Culture*, Vol. 2, Pergamon Press, 1988, reproduced with permission of W. H. Sewell.

W. Kymlicka and W. Norman, 'The Return of the Citizen' from *Ethics 104:2*, University of Chicago Press. © 1994 by the University of Chicago Press. All rights reserved. Reproduced by permission of University of Chicago Press.

'On the Jewish Question' by Karl Marx, in K. Marx, *Early Writings*, ed. L. Colletti, Penguin, 1975, reprinted by permission of New Left Review.

'The Civil War in France' by Karl Marx, in K. Marx, *The First International and After*, ed. D. Fernbach, Penguin, 1974. Reprinted by permission of New Left Review.

'State and Revolution' by V. I. Lenin, in *Lenin Collected Works*, Vol. 25, Lawrence and Wishart, London, 1964. Reproduced by permission of Lawrence and Wishart.

© Ralph Miliband 1977. Reprinted from *Marxism and Politics* by Ralph Miliband (1977) by permission of Oxford University Press.

© Oxford University Press 1973. Reprinted from *Democratic Theory: Essays in Retrieval* by C. B. Macpherson (1973) by permission of Oxford University Press.

*The Republic of Plato* translated with an introduction and notes by Francis MacDonald Cornford (1941), reprinted by permission of Oxford University Press.

Edmund Burke, *Reflections on the Revolution in France*, ed. C. C. O'Brien, Penguin, 1968.

R. Scruton, *The Meaning of Conservatism*, 2nd Edition, Macmillan, London/ Basingstoke, 1984. Reprinted by permission of Macmillan Press Ltd. © Roger Scruton, 1980, 1984. All rights reserved.

B. Mussolini, extract from 'The Doctrine of Fascism', in A. Lyttelton (ed.) *Italian Fascisms from Pareto to Gentile*, Jonathan Cape, London, 1973.

*The Concept of the Political* by C. Schmitt, translated by George Schwab, University of Chicago Press, 1996, reproduced by permission of George Schwab.

Max Weber, *Economy and Society*. 2 vols., translated/edited by Roth and Wittich, © 1978 The Regents of the University of California, reproduced by permission of the University of California Press and J. C. B. Mohr.

Reprinted with the permission of The Free Press, a Division of Simon & Schuster, from *Political Parties* by Robert Michels. Translated by Eden and Cedar Paul. © 1962 by The Crowell-Collier Publishing Company.

G. Sartori, 'Anti-Elitism Revisited', *Government and Opposition*, 13:1 (1978), section on 'The Iron Law of Oligarchy', reproduced by permission of *Government and Opposition* and Giovanni Sartori.

M. Wollstonecraft, *Vindication of the Rights of Woman*, M. Kramnick (ed.), Penguin, 1975.

Diana Coole, *Women in Political Theory*, © Diana Coole, 1992, Reprinted by permission of Pearson Education Limited.

Reprinted by permission of Open University from Rowbotham, S. 'Feminism and Democracy' in Held, D. and Pollitt, C. (eds.), *New Forms of Democracy*, Open University.

S. Mendus 'Losing the Faith, Feminism and Democracy'. © Oxford University Press 1992. Reprinted from *Democracy: The Unfinished Journey* edited by John Dunn (1992).

A. Sen 'The Possibility of Social Choice' *American Economic Review*, Vol. 89, No 3, 1999, reproduced by permission of American Economic Review.

Kenneth Arrow, *Social Choice and Individual Values*, Yale University Press 1951, reproduced by permission of Yale University Press. © 1951, 1963 by Cowles Foundation for Research in Economics at Yale University.

A. Downs, *An Economic Theory of Democracy*, © 1957, 1985, Anthony Downs. Reprinted by permission of Addison Wesley Longman.

Brian Barry, *Sociologists, Economists and Democracy*, University of Chicago Press, by permission of University of Chicago Press. © 1978 by the University of Chicago Press. All rights reserved.

*The Fatal Conceit: The Errors of Socialism* by F. Hayek, edited by W. W. Bartley, Routledge and University of Chicago Press, 1988, reproduced by permission of Taylor and Francis Books Ltd, and University of Chicago Press. © 1988 by the University of Chicago. All rights reserved.

M. Friedman, *Capitalism and Freedom*, University of Chicago Press 1962, reproduced by permission of University of Chicago Press. © 1962 by The University of Chicago. All rights reserved.

D. Beetham, 'Liberalism and the Limits of Democratisation' in *Political Studies: Special Issue*, Vol. XL, 1992, © Political Studies Association, reprinted by permission of Blackwell Publishers.

H. Wainwright, *Arguments for a New Left*, Blackwell, 1994, reprinted by permission of Blackwell Publishers.

G. Nodia, 'Nationalism and Democracy' in Diamond and Plattner, *Nationalism, Ethnic Conflict and Democracy*, © 1994, Johns Hopkins University Press

© David Miller, 1995. Reprinted from *On Nationality* by David Miller (1995) by permission of Oxford University Press.

J. Schwarzmantel 'Two Concepts of the Nation' from *Socialism and the Idea of the Nation* by John Schwarzmantel, Harvester-Wheatsheaf, 1991, © J. Schwarzmantel.

Taylor, C. 'The Dynamics of Democratic Exclusion'. *Journal of Democracy*, Oct 1998 © 1998 The Johns Hopkins University Press and National Endowment for Democracy.

© Will Kymlicka 1995. Reprinted from *Multicultural Citizenship: A Liberal Theory of Minority Rights* by Will Kymlicka (1995) by permission of Oxford University Press.

Reprinted from Charles Mills, *The Racial Contract*. © 1997 Cornell University. Used by permission of the publisher, Cornell University Press.

Sen, Amartya 'Democracy as a Universal Value' from *Journal of Democracy*, Vol. 10(3), 1990. © 1990. The Johns Hopkins University Press and National Endowment for Democracy.

B. Parekh, 'The Cultural Particularity of Liberal Democracy' from *Political Studies* XL, 1992 Special Issue. © Political Studies Association. Reprinted by permission of Blackwell Publishers.

J. Silverstein, 'The Idea of Freedom in Burma and the Political Thought of Daw Aung San Suu Kyi' in Kelly and Reid (eds.), *Asian Freedoms: the Idea of Freedom in East and Southeast Asia*, Cambridge University Press, 1998, reprinted by permission of Cambridge University Press.

Extracts from *Chinese Democracy: The Individual and the State in Twentieth Century China* by Andrew J. Nathan, published by I. B. Tauris & Co Ltd, London and Alfred A. Knopf, New York. © 1986 Andrew Nathan.

Parry, G. and Moyser, G. 'More Participation, More Democracy?' in Beetham, D. *Defining and Measuring Democracy*, Sage 1994, reprinted by permission of Sage Publications Ltd.

Barber, B., *Strong Democracy: Participatory Politics for a New Age*, © 1984 The Regents of the University of California.

Pitkin, H. F. and Shumer, S. M. 'On Participation' from *Journal of Democracy* 2:4 (1982). © The Johns Hopkins University Press and National Endowment for Democracy.

M. Walzer 'A Day in the Life of a Socialist Citizen' from M. Walzer, *Obligations: Essays on Disobedience, War and Citizenship*, Harvard University Press, 1970.

*Voting: A Study of Opinion Formation in a Presidential Campaign* edited by B. Berelson, P. Lazarsfeld and W. N. McPhee, University of Chicago Press, 1954. © 1954 by the University of Chicago. All rights reserved.

C. Pateman, *Participation and Democratic Theory*, Cambridge University Press, 1970, reprinted by permission of Cambridge University Press

Jean Cohen & Andrew Arato, *Civil Society and Political Theory*, The MIT Press 1992. © 1992 Massachusetts Institute of Technology. Reprinted by permission of The MIT Press.

R. Putnam, 'Bowling Alone: America's Declining Social Capital', *Journal of Democracy* (6:1) January 1995. © 1995 The Johns Hopkins University Press and National Endowment for Democracy.

P. Hirst, 'Associational Democracy' in D. Held (ed.) *Prospects for Democracy: North, South, East and West*, Polity Press 1993, reprinted by permission of Blackwell Publishers Ltd.

Excerpted from *Prospects for Democracy: North, South, East and West*, edited by David Held with the permission of U.S. publishers, Stanford University Press. © 1993 Polity Press for the collection. Chapter Five © Paul Hirst.

Ricardo Blaug, 'New Developments in Deliberative Democracy' from *Politics* 16 (2), 1996, © 1996 Blackwell. Reprinted by permission of Blackwell Publishers.

B. Manin 'On Legitimacy and Political Deliberation' from *Political Theory* 15:3, 1987, © 1987 by Sage Publications, Inc. Reprinted by permission of Sage Publications Inc.

Jürgen Habermas, *The Public Sphere: An Encyclopedia Article* (1964), New German Critique 1974. Reprinted by permission of Telos Press Ltd.

James S. Fishkin, *The Dialogue of Justice: Toward a Self-Reflective Society*, Yale University Press 1992. © 1992 by Yale University. All rights reserved.

C. Mouffe, 'Radical Democracy: Modern or Post-modern' from *Universal Abandon? The Politics of Postmodernism*, A. Ross (ed.), Edinburgh University Press, 1988

B. Epstein, 'Radical Democracy and Cultural Politics: What About Class? What About Political Power?'. © 1995. From *Radical Democracy: Identity, Citizenship and the State*, edited by David Trend. Reproduced by permission of Taylor & Francis, Inc. / Routledge, Inc., http://www.routledge-ny.com

J. Stewart, 'Thinking Collectively in the Public Domain', *Soundings 4, The Public Good*, Autumn 1996, reprinted by permission of Lawrence and Wishart.

B. N. Hague and B. D. Loader, *Digital Democracy: Discourse and Decision Making in the Information Age*, Routledge, 1999, reproduced by permission of Taylor and Francis Books Ltd.

# INTRODUCTION
# DEMOCRACY – TRIUMPH OR CRISIS?

Democracy is everywhere praised, yet nowhere achieved. As an ideal, it has become the dominant political aspiration in the world today. As a practice it remains flawed, subject to new and serious challenges. Paradoxically it seems that democracy at the beginning of a new millennium is at one and the same time triumphant and in crisis.

Commentators such as Francis Fukuyama[1] have suggested that contemporary reality bears witness to the universal victory of democracy, at least in its liberal-democratic form. The collapse of communism and the earlier defeat of fascist regimes have removed two obstacles to the achievement of democracy. The American political scientist Samuel Huntington has written of democracy's 'third wave', in which it has challenged authoritarian and militaristic regimes in Europe (Spain, Portugal), and been invigorated, though still with uncertain outcomes, by movements of 'people power' in developing countries such as the Philippines, Indonesia and Mexico.[2] Political regimes across the world are instigating democratic reforms and joining supranational organisations such as the European Union for which democracy is an agreed condition of entry.

At the same time, the extraordinary range of theoretical work on new developments in democratic theory, deliberative democracy, feminism, the Internet and 'micro-democracy' testifies to the vitality and renewal of the democratic ideal. Freed now from the grip of the 'dead white males' who have dominated the traditional canon of democratic thought, democracy now reaches out to a host of formerly excluded groups, to new areas and places in society and even into cyberspace.

Yet running alongside this optimistic view is the growing realisation among political theorists and actors alike that several centuries of democratic striving have not succeeded in achieving the goal of a democratic society. Indeed, in the radically changed conditions of politics in a new millennium it is more difficult than ever to put into practice the core values of democratic theory, even assuming there could be agreement on what they are.

It is clear that the complexity of modern politics and the increasing globalisation of the market confront democracy with significant, and new, challenges. Democracy is faced with deep problems in both theory and practice. These difficulties arise out of the often conflicting demands of multicultural societies, the phenomenon of 'identity politics' and its sometimes divisive and particularist appeals to citizens, and, more generally, from postmodern scepticism about universal foundations. Even the hallowed canon of democratic political theory has been revealed to be culturally and economically biased, confused and inconsistent.

The twentieth century, which was supposed to see the victory of democracy, gave rise in its course to the establishment of mass totalitarian regimes of Communism and Fascism. These systems abused the name of democracy and coerced millions of people in the name of a rigid ideology. The so-called democratic century ended with manifestations of virulent ethno-nationalism within Europe itself, giving rise to the evils of 'ethnic cleansing'. There is little evidence here of any universal or inevitable trend towards democracy. Indeed, the British sociologist Michael Mann has argued that 'many modern regimes which claim to be democratic have exhibited a pronounced tendency toward ethnic and political cleansing'. Invocations of 'We the People' can lead to ideas of 'organic democracy', in which the People are defined as a unitary bloc in terms of opposition to an 'Other', which comprises minorities of an ethnic or racial or political kind. Mann goes so far as to suggest that genocide is 'the dark side of democracy'.[3]

Apart from the extremities of such a 'dark side', there seems to be widespread scepticism and cynicism, or at best indifference, to democratic politicians and to the everyday practices of contemporary liberal-democracy. While liberal-democracy is often proclaimed to be the political system held up as a universal model, this may in reality be a kind of 'democracy without democrats', where democracy has become an empty ideal with ever-decreasing relevance to the practice of politics. There is evidence that citizens feel themselves to be profoundly alienated from their representatives. It is hard to see how the manipulation of the public by 'spin-doctors' could possibly constitute good democratic practice. Ideals of popular sovereignty, of the autonomy of the democratic citizen, of informed deliberative debate leading to decisions which all can accept, these core principles of democratic politics sometimes appear as little more than intellectual abstractions with no bearing on the realities of elite-dominated societies.

There is also scepticism about the universality of democratic values. Faced with the growth of fundamentalist movements, or leaders who assert versions of democracy at odds with liberal-democratic perspectives, one possible reaction is a fear that democratic values are relative and limited to one particular epoch and geographical area. Democratic theory may just be a 'language game' played in a particular local environment, that of the West. The claim that such values are universal may be mistaken. There arises the possibility that the ideals of democracy are 'universal' merely because the Western liberal-democracies have been so effective in exporting – or imposing – their own values.

Democracy is thus at a crossroads. This Reader is intended to serve as an orientating map to the state of democratic theory and practice today. It aims to present, in a single volume, the intellectual resources necessary for citizens to themselves consider the fundamental questions posed by democracy at the start of a new millennium. It contains material both on the historical development of democratic theory and on its contemporary debates. In this Introduction, we seek to show the process of democracy as problematic, both in theory and in practice, and to analyse the difficulties and complexities that attend the realisation of the democratic ideal.

## WHAT IS DEMOCRACY?

The body of the Reader contains writings advocating, criticising and analysing the idea of democracy. This material ranges from the ancient Greeks to the present day. It begins with those writing in the context of the Greek city-state, where the exclusively male citizens met directly, without representatives, to take decisions on war and peace, life and death (literally, as in the case of Socrates). Our material ranges from those beginnings of the democratic ideal down to contemporary theory, which speculates on democracy in the framework of modern mass societies, with Internet communications instantly linking individuals with millions of people worldwide.

The Reader is intended to offer material for reflection on two key questions within this historically extended spread of writings on democracy. First, are there any core ideals of democracy that emerge from this range of democratic debate, and if so, what are they? Second, in what ways are they problematic, why has there been so much conflict, intellectual and political, over these ideals? Can there be any agreed foundation for them and are they claims of genuine universal validity? Or, on the other hand, are they merely relative to one culture, possibly to one limited time, with no more claim to truth than any other plan for organising society and political life? In other words, what precisely is the democratic ideal, and how can it be justified?

Democratic theory's long history starts with Pericles' affirmation of the value of democracy, contained in his speech given at the time when the Athenian city-state was at war with its rivals for dominance in the Peloponnese. There are two points worth noting about this long history. First, many of those who figure significantly in the traditional canon of democratic theory were not really, or fully, democrats at all. If by 'democrats' we mean those who whole-heartedly endorse a democratic society, seeing it as inclusive and based on principles of the equal worth of all human beings, then those who figure in our list of traditional affirmations of democracy (Part One below) were either hesitant or quite critical believers in democracy. It is clear that their concerns were as much about the possible degeneration of democracy into tyrannical forms (Mill, de Tocqueville) as they were affirmative of the newly emerging democratic political order. Even when political theorists sounded clear notes of a positive kind, saluting democracy as the best possible regime (Pericles and Rousseau), many commentators have noted that the form of 'democracy' being advocated was far from inclusive, keeping out slaves, women and foreigners (Pericles), and excluding women from the ranks of democratic citizens (Rousseau).

Secondly, as is made clear by our selection of critiques of democracy (Part Three below), the ideal of democracy has never been universally accepted. It has been, and this remains true, criticised both by those who welcome democracy but see existing reality as falling far short of that ideal (Marxism, Feminism), and also by those who reject the democratic ideal out of hand (elitist and authoritarian critics). The latter see it as unrealistic, as making demands on average people which they cannot live up to, as operating with an absurdly optimistic view of human nature. These criticisms are not of merely historical interest; they are echoed today by those who see democracy as unable to cope with the challenges of new technology and globalisation. Further scepticism and critical evaluation come from those who see democracy as a product of a particular civilisation, that of Western Europe and North America, one which commands no validity in other cultures, say those of Islam. The charge here is one of 'Eurocentrism', and it calls into question many of our most fundamental assumptions about individualism, rationality and the autonomy of the individual.

This Reader presents the democratic ideal as being a political system and a wider society organised on the basis of certain key principles. These principles are popular sovereignty, freedom as autonomy or self-direction, and equality. Yet focusing on these core ideas does not detract from the complexity or problematic nature of democracy in theory and practice. Over the centuries, the democratic debate continues in our own day over the precise meaning and realisation of these concepts. Popular sovereignty, for example, raises concerns over who 'the people' actually are, the question of who is to be included in the democratic community, and over the boundaries of the citizen body. Is a democratic society one in which all human beings, as rational creatures, have a claim to be included in the citizen body? This seems to be the ideal often invoked by political leaders and by contemporary citizens of democracy.

Yet not only is the ideal frequently violated in practice, for example by practices of ethnic or social exclusion, but it also raises theoretical questions which provide the stuff of contemporary debate. Are human beings rational at all? Are they *equally* rational? If there are some people better qualified and more knowledgeable in matters relevant to politics and government, then should they not be given a greater role in political life, as elitist thinkers from Plato onwards have argued? What if 'the people' (however that unit is defined) choose to exercise their sovereignty by victimising or tyrannising a minority, whether that minority is defined in ethnic or religious or cultural terms? This was a central concern of liberal thinkers like Madison, Mill and de Tocqueville. They offered a welcome, though a somewhat apprehensive one, to democratic governance, which was for them an entirely new form of government and society. De Tocqueville spoke of democracy with almost religious awe, viewing it as a new and irresistible force in the world, sweeping all before it. But from Nazi Germany to Ruanda to Kosovo, and even more recently in East Timor, the politics of the victimisation of minorities, the abuse of democracy and the perversion of the ideal of popular sovereignty have remained central to the politics of the twentieth century and beyond.

These various failures of democracy have led some, as we show in our final section on contemporary issues, to point to the need for democratic theory to take new directions. Here we encounter theories which suggest the need to respect difference and multiculturalism, to attend with greater care to more 'deliberative' forms of democracy, thereby maximising interactive discussion and reclaiming governance from what seem to be increasingly remote representatives.

Seeing the democratic ideal as a cluster of key concepts raises the question of the definition of those concepts and their justification: what is it, for example, to be 'autonomous' or self-determining? Are all people capable of this practice of self-determination, and what would its practice mean in the conditions of contemporary politics? Do democratic values rest on a particular view of human nature which is confined to particular (Western) societies? Democracy may be based on certain values, of secularism and willingness (and ability) to compromise, which in turn depend on a particular history and set of social conditions which suit Western society but do not hold true in large parts of the world today.

However, the difficulties that democratic values and practices have in establishing themselves in particular regions of the world do not necessarily undermine their claims to be a universal value. As Amartya Sen has argued, democracy has universal value because of its intrinsic importance in human life. To be prevented from participating in the political life of one's community is a major harm for all human beings. Sen further states that democracy has a universal role to play in preventing the abuse of power, and in helping people to formulate and understand their own needs, rights and duties.[4]

The ideals of democracy are, therefore, problematic, both in terms of what they mean and how they can be justified, as well as in the ways and the extent to which they can be realised in practice. The selections contained within this Reader illustrate the complex nature of democracy and the difficulty of its justification, not in order to suggest the incoherence or impossibility of democratic ideals, but to show that they need argumentation and justification.

Indeed, it is within this very process of argumentation and deliberation that a core element of a democratic society resides. In view of the pallid and debased level of political debate in those contemporary societies that call themselves democratic or 'liberal-democratic', a renewal of democratic discussion and assessment of the principles on which those societies are founded would appear to be a necessity for their health and vitality. Such debate inevitably begins with, yet goes beyond, the statements of democratic purpose that form the material of Parts One and Two of this Reader.

## DEMOCRACY AND ITS REALISATION IN PRACTICE

If democracy is far from straightforward in its theory, if the historical trajectory of democratic politics leaves large questions which have not been and cannot be finally resolved, the same is true of the problem of practice, the realisation of ideals through democratic institutions and methods. There is a large gap between the ideals of popular sovereignty and the reality of contemporary democratic societies. This Reader concentrates on the political theory of democracy, and not on the technical workings of democratic institutions. However, a central part of its purpose is to provide materials which illuminate the meaning of democracy today, and to help recognise the crucial factors which assist its realisation or, on the contrary, block its achievement. This is the focus of our fourth part, dealing with contemporary issues. It aims to present selections which link the ideals of democracy, interpreted in current conditions, to the reality of those societies claiming to be democratic. The Reader intends to shed light on these problems and here too to provide the citizens of contemporary democracies with some of the arguments and intellectual resources they need to deepen democracy.

This demand to extend democracy would seem absurd to many. Surely, some would argue, the practices and institutions of contemporary liberal-democracies exemplify what democracy is, under the conditions of large-scale political societies, which are fundamentally different from the framework of the city-states of ancient Greece. Through modern institutions of structured political parties, regular elections and the operations of pressure groups, democracy works as a mechanism, an 'institutional arrangement for arriving at political decisions by means of a competitive struggle for the people's vote'.[5]

There are two ways in which this view can be challenged, and which cast doubt on whether democracy can be seen simply as the existing practice of multi-party elections in established nation-states. The first issue is the question of the unit or framework within which democratic rule takes place. Classical democratic theory of the ancient Greek world envisaged the city-state, the *polis*, as the unit of popular rule. As Robert Dahl notes, the great transformation of modernity was the establishment of democratic rule within large nation-states.[6] However, the conditions of contemporary politics raise significant questions concerning the appropriate unit of democratic rule.

First is the problem of the nation-state itself. If the nation-state remains the unit within which citizenship rights are established and maintained, then what is the basis of the nation and who are its members or citizens? As Ghia Nodia observes, '"Nation" is another name for "We the People"',[7] but the bases of the nation can be constituted in different ways. If 'nation' is shorthand for 'ethnic group', then this can result in the exclusion from democratic citizenship of ethnic minorities and the violation of their democratic rights. Questions of nation-building and democratic citizenship, of inclusion and exclusion on national and ethnic lines, are crucial in the newly-democratising countries of post-Communism. They are also central to 'established' democracies, as our section on multiculturalism demonstrates. Does democracy require a shared culture, based on common historical experiences, and does the absence of such a common past and lack of a common language (metaphorical or literal) weaken the chances of democratic politics? Clearly, democratic theory must somehow adapt itself in order to take the problem of multiculturalism more seriously than is done in the traditional canon of democratic thought. This constitutes one of the chief challenges – but also opportunities – for democratic renewal, inside or outside the nation-state.

Beyond that, however, is the question of whether the nation-state is any longer the main, let alone the sole, framework for democratic politics. Issues of globalisation and the way in which power has shifted away from the nation-state have led some to suggest that 'cosmopolitan democracy' now provides the framework for the realisation of democracy in the contemporary world.[8] If power is organised along supranational lines, exercised through transnational organisations and institutions, then this is the appropriate terrain for democratic governance. Only in this way can autonomy be realised in the conditions of contemporary politics. Hence today's democrats must turn their attention to these institutions, as necessary elements in a programme of radical democracy.

By the same token, critics of contemporary democracy, who point out the gap between the ideal and the reality of democracy, suggest that the focus on the structured institutions of national politics is blinding citizens to other spaces and possibilities for participatory politics. In focusing on civil society, micro-democracy, the workplace, the family, in other words on the host of associations that make up a complex modern society, new areas and structures for democracy are being explored. Such new forms of democracy offer a significant challenge to existing political arrangements. These debates are captured in our sections on civil society, participation and also the market.

Debates around democracy's extended possibilities suggest one conclusion of great importance. In the nineteenth century democracy was seen as a revolutionary movement, sweeping all before it and totally transforming the structure of politics and society. Contemporary initiatives in radical democracy seek to recapture this transformative potential by freeing democracy from the somewhat restrictive framework of the nation-state and its structured, bureaucratic and representative institutions. Whether these projects fall into the category of utopian aspirations, or whether new technologies such as the Internet and new forms of direct action can 'reinvent democracy', are as yet unanswered questions. Part Four of this Reader on contemporary issues is intended to present relevant material to assess such matters.

The second issue related to the realisation of democracy is that of inclusion and exclusion. Who are the citizens? What powers should they have? How can they be empowered to make a reality of the democratic ideal? Historically, the trajectory of democratic struggle has been one of broadening the scope of the citizen body, of overcoming exclusions based on property, gender, intellectual ability, and race or ethnicity. Some critics of contemporary democracy speak of a 'racial contract' underpinning modern democracy (Mills). This 'racial contract' undermines the proclaimed inclusiveness of modern democracy. Modern liberal-democracies claim to be inclusive and universal, but if this critical reasoning is right, they are seriously impoverished by the systematic exclusion of non-whites from genuine citizenship. By the same token (though this goes beyond Mills' argument) there is a huge division between those who are in a real sense full citizens of democratic societies, sharing in its public culture and exercising its rights, and those like guest-workers, those who are 'denizens' rather than 'citizens', or those who form an underclass of marginalised people carrying out menial and degrading occupations and denied the full benefit of citizenship.[9] Can the new forms of democracy hinted at by writers whose selections we have used for the final section of this book succeed in overcoming these exclusions and divisions? If not, the future development of democracy may remain thwarted.

## DEMOCRACY: DOES IT HAVE A FUTURE?

We suggested earlier that despite the triumphalism surrounding democracy, the continuing invocations of 'the end of history' and the definitive victory of democracy in theory and practice, democratic rule may be at a crossroads. Faced with transformed conditions in which democratic ideals have to be realised, there are new obstacles to be overcome in achieving democracy, as well as new possibilities. This means that we have to read the tradition of democratic thought differently from the ways in which democracy has been hitherto conceived. All too often, the history of democracy and of democratic thought has been presented in a teleological way, as a magnificent movement starting with the Greeks, then moving inevitably through overcoming exclusions of property, gender and ethnic affiliation down to the fully-achieved democracy and citizenship of contemporary liberal-democracy, which people everywhere seek to emulate.

It would certainly be wrong to write off centuries of struggle to extend rights of popular participation, and to fail to recognise that what seems to us now a banal and uncontested right of universal suffrage was a genuinely revolutionary demand, one which opened up perspectives of radical social change and transformation of the human subject.[10] The quite recent achievement of universal suffrage in South Africa, for example, attests to the fact that struggles for this most basic of democratic rights are far from being a phenomenon of the past, consigned to a historical museum of rights accepted by all, without any of the excitement that accompanied their capture.

At the same time, we cannot merely read off the meaning of democracy from the existing practices of liberal-democracy. Democratic theory has always sought to contribute to movements for political change and to the transformation of established democracies. This Reader therefore seeks to reflect the current state of excitement that surrounds the possible resources and institutions that may deepen democracy in present conditions. It aims too to stimulate reflection on the forces that are threatening or hindering democracy, as well as on the newly emergent forms and practices that may renew democratic practice. The concluding section of the Reader seeks to provide material for citizens to make up their own minds on these issues, and we provide further reading to indicate suggestions for those who want to develop their thoughts and actions. At this point the aim is to indicate some core issues which arise from current debates about the future of democracy.

Our selection of material on contemporary issues in democratic theory in Part Four suggests that the apparently universal victory of the market and the commodification of all aspects of life have profoundly ambivalent implications for democratic politics. Ideas of consumer sovereignty suggest an anti-paternalism and provide means of holding suppliers to account.[11] Rational choice models of democracy (discussed in Part Four of this Reader) suggest that rational individuals pursuing their interests could be a good basis for democratic government, leading to the clear-headed maximisation of utilities of consumers and voters, who are one and the same. Yet by the same token, the debate on democracy and the market points out the tensions between the two: the social inequalities to which the latter gives rise undermine the equality of democratic values. This was a core point made by Marxist and socialist critics of democracy (see Part Three, Critiques of Democracy). In a society in which the market, on a global scale, is all-pervasive, can ideas of citizen equality and democratic ideas of a common good, rationally perceived, hold up? If people are participating as consumers on the basis of 'what is in it for me?', this may give rise to a purely instrumental attitude to politics, one based on sectional interest alone. Such an understanding of politics produces what Benjamin Barber calls 'thin democracy', which actively discourages the more widespread participation which some theorists see as necessary for democratic renewal.[12]

This in turn raises the question of the space within which, or the institutions through which, greater participation and 'civic virtues' could be achieved.[13] Do civil society and an active associational life provide renewed hope for democracy in contemporary conditions? Are associations the necessary factors which assist democratic renewal, and provide a framework which could supplement, if not replace, the often remote and representative-dominated structure of the nation-state? Such hopes for 'associative democracy' (Hirst) are expressed by some of the theorists represented in our 'civil society' section.[14]

Yet again, the matter is not simple: civil society can degenerate to take 'uncivil' and highly sectional forms. In any case it is not so easy to see how an active associational life can be built up quickly in societies (like Russia today?) lacking traditions of civil society and with an undeveloped infrastructure of pluralistic groups and tolerant subcultures of society. Here again, as with the market, institutions and structures which possibly assist democracy and provide chances for democratic renewal have a less positive face. What appears to be the solution may equally well be the problem with regard to democratic politics in the contemporary age. A society dominated by the market and by sectional groups may be the gravedigger of democracy rather than its midwife.

Let us deepen the gloom and pessimism by suggesting that in the present world two other factors are present which make the democratic ideal less, rather than more, likely of realisation. This Reader includes a section on nationalism, and as noted earlier in this introduction, nationalism is a malleable phenomenon, taking a multiplicity of forms. It is hard to deny the relevance and salience of this force as offering a focus for identity in today's politics. Yet what are its implications for democracy? Nationalism arose in conjunction with democracy, with both ideas appealing to the core notion of popular sovereignty. Yet we have already noted that ethno-nationalism functions as a mighty force for exclusion, denying citizenship rights to minority ethnic and national groups. We have seen recently that Western leaders were driven to use NATO bombs and highly militaristic and undemocratic forms of politics to restore democratic rights to the victims of such nationalist persecution (who thereafter take it out on remnants of the formerly dominant group, as we seem to see today in Kosovo).[15]

Traditional accounts of democracy for the most part envisaged its occurrence in a society of national homogeneity, where ethnic and national cleavages would not exist to disrupt the equality of citizen deliberation and autonomy. While this might continue to apply to some sections of the world today, this assumption of ethnic and cultural homogeneity clearly limits the practical applicability of traditional democratic theory. Some theorists, like David Miller, make a convincing case that nationality can cement democracy, and that the common 'public culture' of a nation can adapt and develop to integrate new groups.[16] Perhaps the USA would be a good example here of a form of civic nationalism which functions as a 'glue' bonding a democratic community, and fostering links of reciprocity and mutual concern which are necessary to such a society. Nationalism, however, remains in many of its forms a threatening monster devouring ideas of citizen equality and democratic rights. This was a feature which many of the classic theorists of democracy overlooked.

Classical democratic theory also failed to adequately address problems of cultural difference, group identity and pluralism. Our section on multiculturalism, and also the contributions grouped under Section 13, 'Beyond the West', offer material indicating some of the ways in which these problems are faced by democratic theory today. If a high degree of cultural homogeneity is required as the basis for democratic society, this creates problems for democracy in societies of great cultural and ethnic diversity. Democracy has to reckon with multi-cultural citizenship, but this is easier said than done.[17] It is easy to come up with platitudes on the need for democratic societies to 'recognise difference', yet in this area, democratic theory and practice encounter large problems. If parti-cular sub-groups insist on their own educational institutions, for example, will this weaken bonds of common citizen allegiance? The tradition of French republicanism saw a common schooling for all its citizens as a prerequisite for a democratic society. However, some of the most acute debates on these issues stem from the problems of reconciling this supposedly universal model with recognition of cultural differences, as in the recent case of the right of Muslim students in France to wear headscarves.[18] The classic tradition of democratic political theory may not offer many guides to action in this area.

Once again, we here confront the problem of whether democracy is genuinely a universal value. Can democratic theorists and practitioners in the contem-porary world be so sure that there is one agreed meaning of democracy that is universally valid, which can function as the model for democracy everywhere? How can one meet the relativist challenge that 'this is the way we do things here'? The Prime Minister of Malaysia, Dr Mahathir, has defended the idea of 'Asian democracy', much less open to ideas of individual rights and to values of diversity than its 'Western' component. This would, as our section on 'Beyond the West' indicates, suggest that democracy is relative to a particular time and place. If this is the case, then 'democracy' becomes a meaningless word, and so do democratic politics, since it would be a label for whatever practices are approved of in the particular society. Thus, Hitler's Germany could be con-sidered a democracy, and so too could the People's Democracies of the former Soviet Bloc. It would be difficult for democratic theory to be used in a critical and evaluative sense.

A number of attempts have been made to articulate a core meaning and definition of democracy. A number of distinguished democratic theorists have posited democracy as being based on certain fundamental principles, thus effectively countering the dangers of relativism.[19] Yet this still leaves significant problems concerning the degree to which these principles are realised in practice, the institutional requirements for their achievement, and the culturally diverse conditions in which such principles must find institutional embodiment.

## THE USES OF DEMOCRATIC THEORY

Where, then, does democratic theory stand today? What can it do both to analyse the difficult problems faced by democratic practice in the contemporary world, and to contribute, if not to their solution, then at least to preventing these difficulties from undermining the democratic ideal altogether? Perhaps our Reader can be taken as evidence for the claim by the Italian political theorist Norberto Bobbio that 'the project of political democracy was conceived for a society much less complex than the one that exists today'.[20] This leads us to take a fairly critical view of the traditional canon of democratic theory, as presented in Part One below.

Of the authors represented in Part One on 'Traditional Affirmations of Democracy', covering the period from Pericles in ancient Athens down to Joseph Schumpeter writing in 1943, several of them (Pericles, Aristotle, Machiavelli, Rousseau) envisaged democracy in a small-scale unit, city-state or small republic. As for the theorists who took a more modern perspective, seeing democracy in the context of a large nation-state (Mill, Madison, de Tocqueville), we have noted already their reservations on the subject of democracy. They were concerned that too much democracy could threaten, through the 'tyranny of the majority', the individual liberties which they as liberals held dear. As for Joseph Schumpeter, many have held that his theory of 'competitive democracy' or 'democratic elitism', as it has come to be known, provides an accurate description of what passes for democracy in contemporary liberal-democracy. Yet there is no lack of critics who suggest that his view of democracy is more elitist than democratic.[21] His focus on democracy as a method and his emphasis on 'democratic self-control' gives great autonomy to leaders: 'once they (the voters outside of parliament) have elected an individual, political action is his business and not theirs'. This seems a far cry from the ideas of popular sovereignty and active citizenship which are, we have suggested, basic democratic values.

This leads to a somewhat 'heretical' conclusion, which we put before the readers and users of this selection of classic and contemporary texts on democracy. We suggest that the canon of classical democratic theory from its origins to its mid-twentieth-century affirmations, may not be of much use in formulating directions for democratic deepening, or interpreting democratic practice, at the beginning of the twenty-first century. The range of new issues thrown up by the transformed world of politics in this new society demands a renewed democratic theory which can respond, in ways which the earlier theories could not conceive, to the new challenges of contemporary society.

Part Four on Contemporary Issues seeks to indicate both what these new challenges are and to give a sample of the way in which democratic theory in its contemporary manifestations is developing to conceptualise and respond to those challenges. While it is somewhat artificial to group a range of quite heterogeneous concerns under unifying headings, we suggest that there are three general areas of concern, three clusters of difficulties crucial to the 'reinvention of democracy' in the contemporary world. These are *citizenship*, *community* and *location*. Our concluding section aims to offer pointers in these still uncharted territories.

*First* are questions concerning the problem of how *citizenship* is to be realised. What is meant by this concept of citizenship, and can it be developed within the large-scale representative structures of the nation-state? What some have called the 'participatory turn' in recent democratic theory has pointed to a more active citizenry as a necessity for the realisation of democracy. Some commentators have suggested that this can only be achieved in more local and everyday spheres of society. A new 'micro-democracy' might supplement, or perhaps replace, a hierarchical representative democracy which leads today's citizens to manifest their scepticism and lack of trust in career politicians. Our selections give space not only to those who see a rejuvenation of democracy along these lines, but also to those who are sceptical of the possibility and of the desirability of a more active citizenry. For example, the extract by Sartori and the parody of 'a day in the life of a socialist citizen' by Walzer suggest the difficulties faced by those who want more citizen involvement. However, whatever the answer, we suggest that this area of citizenship is one of the key areas in which democratic theory can help and stimulate democratic practice. It involves reflecting on tendencies in contemporary society to manipulate or 'depoliticise' issues, to remove questions of war and peace from the arena of public debate. Was there an adequate public discussion on the recent issues of the rights and wrongs of intervention in Kosovo, for example? Do the established organs of representative liberal-democracy, like parliaments, adequately function as forums for the deliberation on issues of (literally, in some cases) life and death? If not, is it possible to envisage alternative forums of deliberation, perhaps more local, more a part of our daily lives, which could be more attractive for the mass of the citizen body?

Recent interest in deliberative democracy suggests ways in which more genuine political debate might be possible. Joshua Cohen's classic article (reproduced in part in our selections) suggests that 'the notion of a deliberative democracy is rooted in the intuitive ideal of a democratic association in which the justification of the terms and conditions of association proceeds through public argument and reasoning among equal citizens'.[22] Yet significant problems arise upon the adoption of such a view. It is not clear, for example, how deliberative democracy is to be realised, nor how it would cope with the need for effective decisions at the macro-level of the state, nor how such forums could hold any guarantee of procedural fairness. As David Miller notes, some people criticise deliberative democracy by arguing that 'deliberation is not a neutral procedure, but one that works in favour of people with certain cultural attributes, and especially white middle-class males'.[23] While we cannot resolve this debate here, we point the reader to the topic of deliberative democracy as a way of seeking to bring about the creation, in modern conditions, of a democracy worthy of the name, and the scepticism with which this aspiration is greeted in some quarters of democratic theory. It raises the fundamental questions of human nature, of what can be expected from human beings as citizens. Will transformed structures bring about more active citizens, whether in the sphere of civil society or in more traditionally political spheres, and how could such structures be brought about?

Feminist critiques of democracy, represented in our selections in Part Three below, furnish another way of approaching the theme of citizenship.[24] Such critiques suggest that democratic politics has been fundamentally flawed by its reliance on a male-dominated model of citizenship. Throughout its history, democratic politics has been seen as the preserve of males, even when the formal exclusions obstructing women from political action were removed. For this reason, Susan Mendus attributes women's loss of faith in liberal-democracy to a 'male model of normality' and a chronic refusal to pay enough attention to sexual difference.[25] Citizenship, as Sylvia Walby has suggested, is a male construct, and as long as it remains so then democracy in its present form is fundamentally flawed. How this situation can be rectified is one of the areas in which democratic theory can point to radical changes in practice.

In short, citizenship, like democracy itself, is an aspiration rather than something adequately achieved in the conditions of contemporary politics. T. H. Marshall's tripartite scheme of civil, political and social citizenship (see the extract in Section 5 below) no longer adequately captures the difficulties of what it means to be a citizen, and what it could mean, in the democracies of today. Clearly, it means more than voting at periodic elections, crucial though that is. Recent theoretical developments suggest that citizenship must also involve a process of civic identification and participation at various levels, possibly through a system of devolution or decentralised government, along with other sites of democratic involvement.

This constitutes a significant challenge to contemporary democracy. If present-day democratic systems fail to meet it, we may be left with societies beset with a deep cynicism and scepticism, not just about particular politicians and programmes, but about the democratic process in general. A society in which people are totally absorbed in their private pursuits, whether of work or leisure, is at odds with the democratic ideal of a public sphere in which deliberation on common ends takes place.

A *second* cluster of problems for democracy today centres on the issue of democratic cohesion or *community*. Community, once the very basis of democracy, now faces a proliferation of identities and affiliations in a transformed world. Madison, in his contribution to *The Federalist Papers* (see extract below in Part One), classically offered a pluralist version of democracy. He sought to tame the power of faction by proposing a large-scale republic in which the diversity of interests would find full expression, so that questions of property would not tear the republic asunder. However, while allowing for this articulation of pluralist democracy, the traditional canon of democratic thought has not given enough attention to problems of heterogeneity, difference and multiculturalism.

Broadly put, the issue relates to an age-old problem in democratic theory, but one which assumes acute forms in contemporary conditions. If democratic decision-making involves the rule of the majority, does this mean the subordination of the minority? More particularly, if there exist in contemporary democratic societies a number of identities, based on different cultures, do these undermine any shared consciousness of common democratic citizenship which could unite the citizens of a democracy? These issues are raised by the extracts in Section 12 on Multiculturalism, but are also echoed at other points in our Reader.

The sections on civil society and the market provide further contributions to this debate: the market can empower consumers, and hence endow individuals with a consciousness of their rights in the political sphere as well. Civil society can be the terrain for democratic advance, as Dryzek suggests: 'The prospects for democracy in capitalist times are better, however, in civil society than in the formal institutions of government, across rather than within national boundaries, and in realms of life not always recognised as political.'[26] Yet both the market and certain forms of associational life can, as we have already noted, take divisive, sectional and quite anti-democratic forms. Associations can be hierarchic and closed, denying their members the free choice and autonomy that are hallmarks of the democratic ideal. Similarly, civil society can breed pressure groups which are concerned to push their own interests without regard to any idea of a common good, and for some versions of democratic theory (Rousseau) this sectionalism is quite antithetical to the values of a democratic community. One of the chief problems for democratic theory and practice today is, therefore, how to reconcile the need for a common framework of democratic citizenship with the recognition of diversity and difference. It involves protection of minority rights without going to the opposite extreme of fragmentation and disassociation of democratic community.[27]

A *third* set of issues arise around the question of *location*, and also of political agency. By what means and in what 'sites' can democracy be more fully achieved in the complex conditions of the twenty-first century?[28] We have seen that neither the classic unit of the city-state nor the modern large-scale unit of the nation-state are unproblematic frameworks for the achievement of democracy. Clearly, the former is incompatible with the scale and size of modern democracy. The latter, the nation-state, is called into question by developments of globalisation and by demands for devolution, regionalisation and ideas of European citizenship for those who live in the European Union. Ideas of transnational citizenship and cosmopolitan democracy demand democracy at supranational levels of governance.[29] At the same time there are demands for democracy at lower levels of government, such as the regional level, and in some cases regions which have strong economic links may cut across national boundaries.[30]

Some commentators have expressed scepticism about the democratic potential of international associations and organisations.[31] Others see the more institutional terrains as irrelevant to the process of democratisation, preferring that we look to locations such as the workplace, the family and the associations of civil society as appropriate sites for democratic deepening. Of course, such micro-democratic initiatives are not incompatible with a more institutional or 'macro' approach, but neither can they be assumed to operate together in any simple way. Democratic theory has always struggled to adjudicate between these two rather different approaches, just as it has also found itself separated by such questions into what amounts to two opposing camps. The possibility of combining a macro-level and 'realist' approach to democracy with a 'participatory' and more idealistic one remains a central problem for democracy. It is here, surely, that progress must be made on the 'unfinished journey' (Dunn) of democracy.

## CONCLUSION: TOWARDS RADICAL DEMOCRACY?

The traditional core of democratic theory maintained that the agents of democracy are 'the people'. Yet we have seen that both in the historical canon, and in contemporary democratic theory, the notion of 'the people' is itself problematic. The political theorists of democracy operated with quite an exclusive idea of who the people were, who they comprised and what their role was. The great democrat Rousseau appears in a less rosy light when his views on women are taken into account. Current perspectives in democratic theory suggest a rather different picture, of a more diverse body of people, split into groups with different yet overlapping identities, all struggling in particular institutions. Contemporary practice indicates significant democratic experimentation among a wide range of political agents. Initiatives in 'cyberdemocracy' suggest at once a more accessible form of democracy, and at the same time threaten the creation of new exclusions. Environmental protests are exploring a more face-to-face politics and seeking to network together single-issue activism across the world. The need to claim new agents for democracy is also addressed by those who envisage an international democracy, one which spans national borders and which links like-minded citizens with others. Such an international civil society would then articulate, support and enforce democratic rights worldwide. These various initiatives see the current challenge to democracy as an opportunity. Yet different, less optimistic, scenarios are also possible. These more pessimistic possibilities include increased Foucault-type surveillance of protest groups and active citizens, fears of growing consumerism and of a dangerously depoliticised populace isolated in their privacy and indifferent to any consciousness of common citizen rights or to the public sphere in general.

The future of democracy is far from certain. Democratic theory at the moment reflects both these new opportunities and the concerns at the erosion of democracy, and trends of indifference on the part of citizens. Questions of the framework of democracy, its foundations and justification, its universalisability, and the sites or terrains for democratic action, as well as the agents and strategies for the defence and extension of democracy, all these represent exciting areas of theoretical questioning and practical experiment in new forms of democratic politics. Clearly, the key concepts highlighted in Part Two below (freedom and autonomy, equality, representation, majority rule and citizenship) provide crucial points of reference and goals for the contemporary world and its politics. There are significant difficulties in achieving such ideals in today's complex conditions. The traditional canon of democratic theory is problematic. This Reader is intended to provide its users with material to develop their own reflections on both the meaning of democracy and its prospects in the contemporary world.

NOTES

1. F. Fukuyama, *The End of History and the Last Man* (Hamish Hamilton, London, 1992).
2. S. Huntington, *The Third Wave. Democratization in the Late Twentieth Century* (University of Oklahoma Press, Norman and London, 1991).
3. Michael Mann, 'The Dark Side of Democracy: The Modern Tradition of Ethnic and Political Cleansing', *New Left Review*, no. 235, May/June 1999, pp. 18–45.
4. Amartya Sen, 'Democracy as a Universal Value', *Journal of Democracy*, Vol. 10, Number 3, July 1999, pp. 3-17.
5. J. A. Schumpeter, *Capitalism, Socialism and Democracy* (George Allen & Unwin, London, 1943), p. 269.
6. Robert A. Dahl, *Democracy and Its Critics* (Yale University Press, New Haven, CT and London, 1989), p. 23.
7. Ghia Nodia, 'Nationalism and Democracy', in L. Diamond and M. F. Plattner (eds), *Nationalism, Ethnic Conflict and Democracy* (Johns Hopkins University Press, Baltimore, MD and London, 1994), p. 6.
8. See, for example, D. Archibugi, D. Held and M. Koehler (eds), *Re-imagining Political Community. Studies in Cosmopolitan Democracy* (Polity Press, Cambridge, 1998).
9. On the idea of public culture, see David Miller, *On Nationality* (Clarendon Press, Oxford, 1995), p. 68. On questions of membership and immigration, see Seyla Benhabib, 'Citizen, Resident and Aliens in a Changing World: Political Membership in the Global Era', *Social Research*, vol. 66, no. 3, Fall 1999, pp. 709–45.
10. See Pierre Rosanvallon, *Le Sacre du Citoyen. Histoire du suffrage universel en France* (Gallimard, Paris, 1992) for an extended discussion of the history of universal suffrage in France, from the point of view of the theoretical debates for and against it.
11. David Beetham, 'Market Economy and Democratic Polity', in David Beetham, *Democracy and Human Rights* (Polity, Cambridge, 1999).
12. Benjamin Barber, *Strong Democracy: Participatory Politics for a New Age* (University of California Press, Berkeley, CA and London, 1984).
13. Richard Dagger, *Civic Virtues. Rights, Citizenship, and Republican Liberalism* (OUP, New York and London, 1997).
14. Robert D. Putnam, *Making Democracy Work. Civic Traditions in Modern Italy* (Princeton University Press, Princeton, NJ, 1993) provides a classic empirical study of the connection of group life and healthy democracy.
15. See Geoffrey Robertson, *Crimes against Humanity. The Struggle for Global Justice* (Allen Lane, The Penguin Press, London, 1999).
16. David Miller, *On Nationality* (Clarendon Press, Oxford, 1995); Maurizio Viroli, *For Love of Country. An Essay on Patriotism and Nationalism* (Clarendon Press, Oxford, 1995).
17. Will Kymlicka, *Multicultural Citizenship. A Liberal Theory of Minority Rights* (Clarendon Press, Oxford, 1995).
18. See Max Silverman, 'Citizens all?' in his *Facing Postmodernity. Contemporary French Thought on Culture and Society* (Routledge, London and New York, 1999).
19. For a discussion of problems of definition and justification, see Michael Saward, *The Terms of Democracy* (Polity, Cambridge, 1998).
20. Norberto Bobbio, *The Future of Democracy* (Polity, Cambridge, 1987), p. 37.
21. For discussions of Schumpeter, see, for example, Peter Bachrach, *The Theory of Democratic Elitism. A Critique* (University of London Press, London, 1969) and J.

Schwarzmantel, *The State in Contemporary Society. An Introduction* (Harvester-Wheatsheaf, Hemel Hempstead, 1994), chapter 4.

22. See Joshua Cohen, 'Deliberation and Democratic Legitimacy', in James Bohman and William Rehg (eds), *Deliberative Democracy, Essays on Reason and Politics* (MIT Press, Cambridge, MA and London, 1997), p. 72.

23. David Miller, 'Is Deliberative Democracy Unfair to Disadvantaged Groups?', in David Miller, *Citizenship and National Identity* (Polity, Cambridge, 2000), p. 144.

24. See J. Squires, *Gender and Political Theory* (Polity, Cambridge, 1999).

25. Susan Mendus, 'Losing the Faith: Feminism and Democracy', in John Dunn (ed.), *Democracy. The Unfinished Journey 508BC to AD1993* (Oxford University Press, Oxford, 1992).

26. J. Dryzek, *Democracy in Capitalist Times* (Oxford University Press, New York and Oxford, 1996), p. 3.

27. For an analysis of 'fragmentation' and its significance for political theory, see J.Schwarzmantel, 'Nationalism and Fragmentation', unpublished paper given to Political Studies Association conference, 1999.

28. See Danilo Zolo, *Democracy and Complexity. A Realist Approach,* trans. David McKie (Polity, Cambridge, 1992).

29. See David Held, 'Democracy and Globalisation', in D. Archibugi, D. Held and M. Koehler (eds), *Re-imagining Political Community. Studies in Cosmopolitan Democracy* (Polity, Cambridge, 1998).

30. Andrew Linklater, *The Transformation of Political Community* (Polity, Cambridge, 1999).

31. See Robert A. Dahl, 'Can International Organisations Be Democratic? A Skeptic's View', in I. Shapiro and C. Hacker-Cordon (eds) *Democracy's Edges* (CUP, Cambridge, 1999).

# PART ONE
# TRADITIONAL AFFIRMATIONS
# OF DEMOCRACY

# TRADITIONAL AFFIRMATIONS
# OF DEMOCRACY
# INTRODUCTION

---

We have called this section 'traditional affirmations of democracy', although such a title is itself problematic. It is designed to offer selections from the classic discussions of democracy through the canon of political theory, starting in the times of the ancient Greek *polis*. However, some of the extracts offer questionings rather than straightforward affirmations and celebrations of democracy. The purpose of this selection of extracts is to show how central figures in the history of political theory have analysed the nature and problematic workings of the democratic ideal.

The extract from *Pericles*' speech to his Athenian fellow-citizens, as reconstructed by the ancient historian Thucydides, is classic in two senses. First, it affirms the democratic ideals of the classic Greek city-state, or *polis*, and second, it draws attention to central features of democracy which have remained the objects of debate and criticism, as well as praise, down to our own day. Pericles acclaims democracy as being the rule of the whole people. The democracy of ancient Athens, he affirms, involves equality before the law, the choosing of people for office on grounds of ability, and tolerance for the differences of citizens in their private life. Above all, Athenian democracy involved an ideal of civic virtue. Those who were not interested in politics had no right to call themselves citizens. Conversely, the citizens of ancient Athens were distinguished by their knowledge and interest in politics. Hence they were ready to devote themselves to securing the defence of the polis when it came under attack. Pericles contrasts this civic virtue with the 'laborious training' and 'state-induced courage' of Sparta, Athens' more militaristic rival. Finally, Pericles sounded the theme of *autonomy*, a central strand of democratic theory:

each citizen of the polis could 'show himself the rightful lord and owner of his own person'.

However, as the next extract shows, from its very beginnings in the Greek *polis* democracy was faced with more sceptical analyses of its nature and implications. *Aristotle* noted what we would now call the social bases of democracy. Democracy meant the rule of the poor and free-born, as opposed to the domination of the wealthy. The rule of the poor majority, the 'demos', could easily degenerate into a form of autocracy, where the popular majority ignored the limits of laws and imposed its will regardless. The power of the masses could be whipped up by unscrupulous demagogues. This fear of the degeneration of democracy into despotism was to be echoed by many later theorists of democracy, including Alexis de Tocqueville with his fears of 'the tyranny of the majority'. Thus right from the beginning we note that political theorists have pointed out the possible corruption of democracy: rule of the people could depart from a law-governed and rational system of government into the exercise of arbitrary power.

For the period of early and later modern political theory, two antitheses dominated the debate on democracy: that between republic and monarchy, and that between liberalism, or liberal-democracy, and more participatory or direct forms of democratic politics. The extracts from *Machiavelli* and *Hobbes* illustrate the former: the selection from Machiavelli's *Discourses* reveals a belief in the superiority of popular rule over that of a monarch. Public opinion is less erratic and more reliable, especially in foreign policy, than policy made by a single person. Democracy can take the form of a republic ruled by law, which Machiavelli singles out as the best possible political form. By contrast, Hobbes argues for the exercise of power by a single ruler (monarch) as opposed to that of an assembly. To escape from the state of nature, and its 'war of all against all', sovereignty has to be located in one single locus, either that of one person (monarchy) or that of an assembly (democracy). In a passage which is astonishingly prescient and modern, Hobbes suggests that the possibility of faction, corruption and division is much greater in an assembly than in a monarchy. It is only in the latter that the public interest of the society is likely to be strong, because it is bound up with the personal interest of the ruler. Where the sovereign power is located in an assembly, by contrast, its members 'are as subject to evill Counsell, and to be seduced by Orators, as a Monarch by Flatterers; and becoming one anothers Flatterers, serve one anothers Covetousnesse and Ambition by turns'. Hobbes' analysis seems very topical in an age of parliamentary corruption, log-rolling and growing scepticism of the virtues of political representatives.

Is democracy a system meant to safeguard individual rights, above all the right of private property? Or is it a system in which individuals become, and are aware of themselves as becoming, parts of a wider collective body in which the common interest prevails over their particular interests? These themes emerge from the extracts from *Madison* and *Rousseau* which follow.

Madison envisages a democracy that is pluralist and diverse. Factions are an expression of this diversity and cannot be done away with. Yet the danger of factions are equally real: they could threaten the realisation of the common good and endanger private property. The remedy lay in the creation of a republic, distinguished from a 'pure democracy' through its large size and the device of representation. The representatives in a large-scale society would be more likely to be responsive to a wide range of concerns and interests, and less inclined to support what Madison candidly calls 'an equal division of property, or ... any other improper or wicked project'. What is envisaged by Locke and Madison is therefore a liberal democracy, based on private property, individual rights and a multiplicity of interests.

The perspective which emerges from the extracts from Rousseau is different: he depicts a democracy in which a new collective body is created, the democratic sovereign. Like Pericles, he invokes the idea of autonomy, of being bound by laws which we ourselves have made. Government, or the executive, is or should be the servant of the democratic sovereign, applying the law to particular cases. The often-quoted words that those who do not obey the general will should be 'forced to be free' have been seen by some as suggesting the emergence of an all-powerful totally sovereign body bound by no limits, and potentially overriding the particular interests of the individual. This was to be, as we shall see, the fear of liberals in the age of mass democracy. Clearly, the thought of Rousseau envisages, at least potentially, a form of democracy different from the liberal-democracy theorised by Locke and Madison. This debate about different forms of democracy, the tensions between liberalism and democracy, is central to the history of democratic theory and to democracy itself.

It is illustrated in our selections by the extracts from *John Stuart Mill* and *de Tocqueville*, extracts which exemplify the ambivalent attitude of liberals towards democracy. Both Mill and de Tocqueville see democracy as the epitome of modernity, as providing means for the development of its citizens. For Mill, extending the suffrage was a 'potent means of mental improvement'. He defends democracy on two grounds: first, an anti-paternalist argument. Each individual is the best defender of his or her interest. We cannot rely on anyone else to speak for us. Second, Mill suggests that a democratic regime creates, and is at the same time dependent on, a particular type of character. He opposes the 'passive type of character' to the 'active self-helping type', and it is the latter which is engendered by a democratic system. Hence Mill suggests that a democratic regime is best suited to lead to intellectual and moral progress.

Yet, like Aristotle many centuries before, both Mill and de Tocqueville were concerned with the possible degeneration of democracy. They feared its perversion into democratic despotism and majority tyranny, and were apprehensive that democracy could stifle individualism and diversity. Democracy might breed an intolerant system in which minorities and dissident individuals were oppressed by the conformism and mediocrity of democracy. These concerns remain relevant in an age of mass democracy, as later selections in this Reader reveal.

These liberal thinkers, especially de Tocqueville, feared the association of democracy and revolution. We reproduce in this section democratic statements emerging from the English Revolution of the seventeenth century, the French Revolution of 1789 and Paine's *Rights of Man*, a text written by a participant in both the American and French Revolutions. The text from the Putney debates of 1649 reveals the debate between those who saw democracy as involving 'the poorest he as well as the richest he', and, on the other hand, those who took a more liberal view that the purpose of the English Revolution had been to secure property rights and the rule of law. The French Revolutionary *Declaration of the Rights of Man and Citizen* invokes the connection of democracy and the nation (Article III) and the participation of all citizens, directly or indirectly, in making the law (Article VI). Similarly, both the statements of *Paine* and *Abraham Lincoln* affirm the central value of democracy as being that of popular sovereignty, an association of which, as Paine says, every citizen is a member 'and as such, can acknowledge no personal subjection; and his obedience can be only to the laws'.

Finally, this selection of traditional affirmations ends with a twentieth-century classic statement, or perhaps better a revision, of democratic ideals. In his book *Capitalism, Socialism and Democracy* the economist and social philosopher *Joseph Schumpeter* gives a critique of what he calls the classic idea of democracy, in which decisions and policies emerge from the people. For Schumpeter, the task of the people was not to decide on issues but to select a government through processes of electoral competition, and leave leadership to them. This view of democracy contrasts totally with the affirmation of civic virtue, political interest and autonomy proclaimed by Pericles in ancient Athens. Do Schumpeter's words suggest a realistic mature adaptation of democratic theory to the realities of modern mass society? Or do they represent an abandonment of the very essence of democratic politics as enunciated by Pericles and later by Rousseau?

# I

# FUNERAL ORATION

## Pericles

Let me say that our system of government does not copy the institutions of our
neighbours. It is more the case of our being a model to others, than of our
imitating anyone else. Our constitution is called a democracy because power is
in the hands not of a minority but of the whole people. When it is a question of
settling private disputes, everyone is equal before the law; when it is a question
of putting one person before another in positions of public responsibility, what
counts is not membership of a particular class, but the actual ability which the
man possesses. No one, so long as he has it in him to be of service to the state, is
kept in political obscurity because of poverty. And, just as our political life is
free and open, so is our day-to-day life in our relations with each other. We do
not get into a state with our next-door neighbour if he enjoys himself in his own
way, nor do we give him the kind of black looks which, though they do no real
harm, still do hurt people's feelings. We are free and tolerant in our private lives;
but in public affairs we keep to the law. This is because it commands our deep
respect.

We give our obedience to those whom we put in positions of authority, and
we obey the laws themselves, especially those which are for the protection of the
oppressed, and those unwritten laws which it is an acknowledged shame to
break.

And here is another point. When our work is over, we are in a position to
enjoy all kinds of recreation for our spirits. There are various kinds of contests

From Thucydides, *History of the Peloponnesian War*, trans. Rex Warner, introduction and notes M.
I. Finlay (Penguin Books, Harmondsworth, 1972), pp. 143–9. Originally written *ca.* 400 BC.

and sacrifices regularly throughout the year; in our own homes we find a beauty and a good taste which delight us every day and which drive away our cares. Then the greatness of our city brings it about that all the good things from all over the world flow in to us, so that to us it seems just as natural to enjoy foreign goods as our own local products.

Then there is a great difference between us and our opponents, in our attitude towards military security. Here are some examples: Our city is open to the world, and we have no periodical deportations in order to prevent people observing or finding out secrets which might be of military advantage to the enemy. This is because we rely, not on secret weapons, but on our own real courage and loyalty. There is a difference, too, in our educational systems. The Spartans, from their earliest boyhood, are submitted to the most laborious training in courage; we pass our lives without all these restrictions, and yet are just as ready to face the same dangers as they are. Here is a proof of this: When the Spartans invade our land, they do not come by themselves, but bring all their allies with them; whereas we, when we launch an attack abroad, do the job by ourselves, and, though fighting on foreign soil, do not often fail to defeat opponents who are fighting for their own hearths and homes. As a matter of fact none of our enemies has ever yet been confronted with our total strength, because we have to divide our attention between our navy and the many missions on which our troops are sent on land. Yet, if our enemies engage a detachment of our forces and defeat it, they give themselves credit for having thrown back our entire army; or, if they lose, they claim that they were beaten by us in full strength. There are certain advantages, I think, in our way of meeting danger voluntarily, with an easy mind, instead of with a laborious training, with natural rather than with state-induced courage. We do not have to spend our time practising to meet sufferings which are still in the future; and when they are actually upon us we show ourselves just as brave as these others who are always in strict training. This is one point in which, I think, our city deserves to be admired. There are also others:

Our love of what is beautiful does not lead to extravagance; our love of the things of the mind does not make us soft. We regard wealth as something to be properly used, rather than as something to boast about. As for poverty, no one need be ashamed to admit it: the real shame is in not taking practical measures to escape from it. Here each individual is interested not only in his own affairs but in the affairs of the state as well: even those who are mostly occupied with their own business are extremely well-informed on general politics – this is a peculiarity of ours: we do not say that a man who takes no interest in politics is a man who minds his own business; we say that he has no business here at all. We Athenians, in our own persons, take our decisions on policy or submit them to proper discussions: for we do not think that there is an incompatibility between words and deeds; the worst thing is to rush into action before the consequences have been properly debated. And this is another point where we differ from other people. We are capable at the same time of taking risks and of estimating them beforehand. Others are brave out of ignorance; and, when they stop to think, they begin to fear. But the man who can most truly be accounted brave is he who best knows the meaning of what is sweet in life and of what is terrible, and then goes out undeterred to meet what is to come.

Again, in questions of general good feeling there is a great contrast between us and most other people. We make friends by doing good to others, not by receiving good from them. This makes our friendship all the more reliable, since we want to keep alive the gratitude of those who are in our debt by showing continued goodwill to them: whereas the feelings of one who owes us something lack the same enthusiasm, since he knows that, when he repays our kindness, it will be more like paying back a debt than giving something spontaneously. We are unique in this. When we do kindnesses to others, we do not do them out of any calculations of profit or loss: we do them without afterthought, relying on our free liberality. Taking everything together then, I declare that our city is an education to Greece, and I declare that in my opinion each single one of our citizens, in all the manifold aspects of life, is able to show himself the rightful lord and owner of his own person, and do this, moreover, with exceptional grace and exceptional versatility.

[...]

# 2

# THE POLITICS

## Aristotle

§ 1. It ought not to be assumed, as some thinkers are nowadays in the habit of doing, that democracy can be defined off-hand, without any qualification, as a form of constitution in which the greater number are sovereign. Even in oligarchies – and indeed in all constitutions – the majority [i.e. the majority of those who enjoy constitutional rights] is sovereign. Similarly, oligarchy cannot be simply defined as a form in which a few persons are the constitutional sovereign. § 2. Assume a total population of 1,300: assume that 1,000 of the 1,300 are wealthy; assume that these 1,000 assign no share in office to the remaining 300 poor, although they are men of free birth and their peers in other respects. Nobody will say that here there is a democracy. § 3. Or assume, again, that there are only a few poor men, but that they are stronger than the rich men who form the majority [and are therefore sovereign]. Nobody would term such a constitution an oligarchy, when no share in honours and office is given to the majority who possess riches. It is better, therefore, to say that democracy exists wherever the free-born are sovereign, and oligarchy wherever the rich are in control. § 4. As things go, the former are many, and the latter few: there are many who are free-born, but few who are rich. [The essence, however, in either case is not the factor of number, but the factor of social position.] Otherwise [i.e. if number alone were the essence] we should have an oligarchy if offices were distributed on the basis of stature (as they are said to be in Ethiopia), or on the basis of looks; for the number of tall or good-looking men

From Aristotle, *The Politics*, ed. and trans. Ernest Barker (Clarendon Press, Oxford, 1946), Book IV, chapter IV, pp. 163–9. Originally written *ca.* 335 BC.

must always be small.   § 5. Yet it is not sufficient to distinguish democracy and oligarchy merely by the criterion of poverty and wealth, any more than it is to do so merely by that of number. We have to remember that the democratic and the oligarchical state both contain a *number* of parts; and we must therefore use additional criteria to distinguish them properly. We cannot, for example, apply the term democracy to a constitution under which a few free-born persons rule a majority who are not free-born [as if birth were the one and only criterion]. (A system of this sort once existed at Apollonia, on the Ionian Gulf, and at Thera. In both of these states honours and offices were reserved for those who were of the best birth – in the sense of being the descendants of the original settlers – though they were only a handful of the whole population.) Nor can we apply the term oligarchy to a constitution under which the rich are sovereign simply because they are more numerous than the poor [as if number were the one criterion]. (An example of such a constitution formerly existed at Colophon, where before the war with Lydia a majority of the citizens were the owners of large properties.)   § 6. The proper application of the term 'democracy' is to a constitution in which the free-born and poor control the government – being at the same time a majority; and similarly the term 'oligarchy' is properly applied to a constitution in which the rich and better-born control the government – being at the same time a minority.

§ 7. The general fact that there are a number of constitutions, and the cause of that fact, have been established. It remains to explain why there are more constitutions than the two just mentioned [i.e. democracy and oligarchy]; to indicate what they are; and to suggest the reasons for their existence. In doing so we may start from the principle which was previously stated, and which can now be assumed, that every state consists, not of one, but of many parts.   § 8. [Here we may use a biological analogy.] If we aimed at a classification of the different kinds of animals, we should begin by enumerating the parts, or organs, which are necessary to every animal. These will include, for example, some of the sensory organs: they will also include the organs for getting and digesting food, such as the mouth and the stomach; they will further include the organs of locomotion which are used by the different animals. We shall then assume that our enumeration of the necessary organs is exhaustive; and we shall proceed to the further assumption that there are varieties of these organs – or, in other words, different species of mouths, stomachs, sensory organs, and organs of locomotion. We shall thus reach the conclusion that the number of possible combinations of these varieties will inevitably produce several different kinds of animals (for the same kind of animal cannot exhibit several varieties of mouth, or of ears); and thus the whole of the possible combinations of varieties will account for the different kinds of animals, or [to put the same point in another way] the number of kinds of animals will be equal to the number of the possible combinations of the necessary organs.

§ 9. It is just the same with the constitutions which have been mentioned. [There are as many kinds of *them* as there are possible combinations of the necessary parts of the state.] States too, as we have repeatedly noticed, are composed not of one but of many parts. One of these parts is the group of persons concerned with the production of food, or, as it is called, the farming class. A second, which is called the mechanical class, is the group of persons occupied in the various arts and crafts without which a city cannot be inhabited – some of them being necessities, and others contributing to luxury or to the living of a good life. § 10. A third part is what may be termed the marketing class; it includes all those who are occupied in buying and selling, either as merchants or as retailers. A fourth part is the serf class composed of agricultural labourers; and a fifth element is the defence force, which is no less necessary than the other four, if a state is not to become the slave of invaders. § 11. How is it possible, with any propriety, to call by the name of state a society which is naturally servile? It is the essence of a state to be independent and self-sufficing; and it is the absence of independence which is the mark of the slave.

We may pause to note that this is the reason why Plato's account of the parts of the state, in his *Republic*, is inadequate, though ingenious. § 12. He begins by stating that the four most necessary elements for the constitution of a state are weavers, farmers, shoemakers, and builders. He then proceeds, on the ground that these four are not self-sufficient, to add other parts – smiths; herdsmen to tend the necessary cattle; merchants and retail dealers. These are the parts which form the whole complement of the 'first state' which he sketches – as though a state merely existed for the supply of necessities, and not rather to achieve the Good, and as though it needed the shoemaker as much as it needs the farmer. § 13. The part which serves as a defence force is not introduced till a later stage, when the growth of the city's territory, and its contact with the territory of its neighbours, result in its being plunged into war. [Nor is this all that Plato has omitted in his 'first city'.] The four original parts – or whatever may be the number of the elements forming the association – will require some authority to dispense justice, and to determine what is just. § 14. If the mind is to be reckoned as more essentially a part of a living being than the body, parts of a similar order to the mind must equally be reckoned as more essentially parts of the state than those which serve its bodily needs; and by parts of a similar order to the mind we mean the military part, the part concerned in the legal organization of justice, and (we may also add) the part engaged in deliberation, which is a function that needs the gift of political understanding. § 15. Whether these three functions – war, justice, and deliberation – belong to separate groups, or to a single group, is a matter which makes no difference to the argument. It often falls to the same persons both to serve in the army and to till the fields; [and the same may be true of these three functions]. The general conclusion which we thus reach is that if those who discharge these functions are equally parts of the state with those who supply its bodily needs, they, or at least the armed forces, are *necessary* parts ...

The seventh part is the group composed of the rich, who serve the state with their property. § 16. The eighth part is the magistrates, who serve the state in its offices. No state can exist without a government; and there must therefore be persons capable of discharging the duties of office and rendering the state that service, permanently or in rotation. § 17. There only remain the two parts which have just been mentioned in passing – the deliberative part, and the part which decides on the rights of litigants. These are parts which ought to exist in all states, and to exist on a good and just basis; and this demands persons of a good quality in matters political. § 18. [Here we begin to confront a difficulty.] The different capacities belonging to the other parts may, it is generally held, be shown by one and the same group of persons. The same persons, for example, may serve as soldiers, farmers, and craftsmen; the same persons, again, may act both as a deliberative council and a judicial court. Political ability, too, is a quality to which all men pretend; and everybody thinks himself capable of filling most offices. There is one thing which is impossible: the same persons cannot be both rich and poor. § 19. This will explain why these two classes – the rich and the poor – are regarded as parts of the state in a special and peculiar sense. Nor is this all. One of these classes being small, and the other large, they also appear to be *opposite* parts. This is why they both form constitutions to suit their own interest [that of wealth in the one case, and that of numbers in the other]. It is also the reason why men think that there are only two constitutions – democracy and oligarchy.

§ 20. The fact that there are a number of constitutions, and the causes of that fact, have already been established. We may now go on to say that there are also a number of varieties of two of these constitutions – democracy and oligarchy. This is already clear from what has been previously said [at the beginning of the previous chapter]. § 21. These constitutions vary because the people (*dēmos*) and the class called the notables vary. So far as the people are concerned, one sort is engaged in farming; a second is engaged in the arts and crafts; a third is the marketing sort, which is engaged in buying and selling; a fourth is the maritime sort, which in turn is partly naval, partly mercantile, partly employed on ferries, and partly engaged in fisheries. (We may note that there are many places where one of these subdivisions forms a considerable body; as the fishermen do at Tarentum and Byzantium, the naval crews at Athens, the merchant seamen in Aegina and Chios, and the ferrymen at Tenedos.) A fifth sort is composed of unskilled labourers and persons whose means are too small to enable them to enjoy any leisure; a sixth consists of those who are not of free birth by two citizen parents; and there may also be other sorts of a similar character. § 22. The notables fall into different sorts according to wealth, birth, merit, culture, and other qualities of the same order.

The first variety of democracy is the variety which is said to follow the principle of equality closest. In this variety the law declares equality to mean that the poor are to count no more than the rich: neither is to be sovereign, and both are to be on a level. § 23. [We may approve this law]; for if we hold, as some thinkers do, that liberty and equality are chiefly to be found in democracy, it will be along these lines – with all sharing alike, as far as possible, in constitutional rights – that they will most likely be found. A constitution of this order is bound to be a democracy; for [while all share alike] the people are the majority, and the will of the majority is sovereign. § 24. A second variety of democracy is that in which offices are assigned on the basis of a property qualification, but the qualification is low: those who attain it have to be admitted to a share in office, and those who lose it are excluded. A third variety is one in which every citizen of unimpeachable descent can share in office, but the law is the final sovereign. § 25. A fourth variety is one in which every person [irrespective of descent, and] provided only that he is a citizen, can share in office, but the law is still the final sovereign. A fifth variety of democracy is like the fourth in admitting to office every person who has the status of citizen; but here the people, and not the law, is the final sovereign. This is what happens when popular decrees are sovereign instead of the law; and that is a result which is brought about by leaders of the demagogue type. § 26. In democracies which obey the law there are no demagogues; it is the better class of citizens who preside over affairs. Demagogues arise in states where the laws are not sovereign. The people then becomes an autocrat – a single composite autocrat made up of many members, with the many playing the sovereign, not as individuals, but collectively. § 27. It is not clear what Homer means when he says that 'it is not good to have the rule of many masters': whether he has in mind the collective rule of the many, or the rule of a number of magistrates acting as individuals. However that may be, a democracy of this order, being in the nature of an autocrat and not being governed by law, begins to attempt an autocracy. It grows despotic; flatterers come to be held in honour; it becomes analogous to the tyrannical form of single-person government. § 28. Both show a similar temper; both behave like despots to the better class of citizens; the decrees of the one are like the edicts of the other; the popular leader in the one is the same as, or at any rate like, the flatterer in the other; and in either case the influence of favourites predominates – that of the flatterer in tyrannies, and that of the popular leader in democracies of this variety. § 29. It is popular leaders who, by referring all issues to the decision of the people, are responsible for substituting the sovereignty of decrees for that of the laws. Once the people are sovereign in all matters, *they* are sovereign themselves over its decisions; the multitude follows their guidance; and this is the source of their great position. § 30. But the critics of the magistrates are also responsible. Their argument is, 'The *people* ought to decide': the people accept that invitation readily; and thus the authority of all the magistrates is undermined. There would appear to be solid substance in the view that a democracy of this type is not a true constitution. Where the laws are not sovereign, there is no constitution. § 31. Law should be sovereign on every issue, and the magistrates and the citizen body should only decide about details. The conclusion which emerges is clear. Democracy may be a form of constitution; but this particular system, under which everything is managed merely by decrees, is not even a democracy, in any real sense of the word. Decrees can never be general rules [and any real constitution must be based on general rules] ... So far, then, as concerns the different forms of democracy, and the definition of those forms.

[...]

# 3

# THE DISCOURSES

## Niccolò Machiavelli

Nothing is more futile and more inconstant than are the masses. So says our author, Titus Livy, and so say all other historians. For in the records of the actions men have performed one often finds the masses condemning someone to death, and then lamenting him and ardently wishing he were alive. The Roman people did this in Manlius Capitolinus's case: first they condemned him to death, then urgently wished him back. Of this our author says that 'soon after he had ceased to be a danger, the desire for him took hold of the people'. And again, when describing the events which happened in Syracuse after the death of Hieronymus, the nephew of Hiero, he says: 'It is of the nature of the masses either servilely to obey or arrogantly to domineer.'

I know not whether the view I am about to adopt will prove so hard to uphold and so full of difficulties that I shall have either shamefully to abandon it or laboriously to maintain it; for I propose to defend a position which all writers attack, as I have said. But, however that may be, I think, and always shall think there can be no harm in defending an opinion by arguments so long as one has no intention of appealing either to authority or force.

I claim, then, that for the failing for which writers blame the masses, any body of men one cares to select may be blamed, and especially princes; for anyone who does not regulate his conduct by laws will make the same mistakes as the masses are guilty of. This is easily seen, for there are and have been any number of princes, but of good and wise ones there have been but few. I am speaking of

From Niccolò Machiavelli, *The Discourses*, ed. Bernard Crick (Penguin, Harmondsworth, 1970), pp. 252–7. Originally written 1531.

princes who have succeeded in breaking the bonds which might have held them in check; among which I do not include those kings who were born in Egypt when that most ancient of ancient realms was governed in accordance with the law, nor those born in Sparta, nor those born in France in our own times, for the kingdom of France is better regulated by laws than is any other of which at present we have knowledge. Kings who are born under such conditions are not to be classed among those whose nature we have to consider in each individual case to see whether it resembles that of the masses; for, should there be masses regulated by laws in the same way as they are, there will be found in them the same goodness as we find in kings, and it will be seen that they neither 'arrogantly dominate nor servilely obey'. Such was the Roman populace which, so long as the republic remained uncorrupt, was never servilely obsequious, nor yet did it ever dominate with arrogance: on the contrary, it had its own institutions and magistrates and honourably kept its own place. But when it was necessary to take action against some powerful person, it did so, as is seen in the case of Manlius, of the Ten, and in the case of others who sought to oppress it. Also, when it had to obey dictators or consuls in the public interest, it did so. Nor is it any wonder that the Roman populace wanted Manlius Capitolinus back when he was dead, for what they wanted was his virtues, which had been such that his memory evoked everyone's sympathy, and would have had power to produce the same effect in a prince, for all writers are of opinion that virtue is praised and admired even in one's enemies. Again, had Manlius, in response to this desire, been raised from the dead, the Roman populace would have passed on him the same sentence as it did, have had him arrested and, shortly after, have condemned him to death: though, for that matter, one also finds that reputedly wise princes have put people to death and then wished them alive again; Alexander, for instance, in the case of Cleitus and other of his friends, and Herod in the case of Mariamne. But the truth is that what our historian says of the nature of the masses is not said of the masses when disciplined by laws, as were the Romans, but of undisciplined masses, like those of Syracuse, which made the same kind of mistakes as do men when infuriated and undisciplined, just as did Alexander the Great and Herod in the cases cited.

The nature of the masses, then, is no more reprehensible than is the nature of princes, for all do wrong and to the same extent when there is nothing to prevent them doing wrong. Of this there are plenty of examples besides those given, both among the Roman emperors and among other tyrants and princes; and in them we find a degree of inconstancy and changeability in behaviour such as is never found in the masses.

I arrive, then, at a conclusion contrary to the common opinion which asserts that populaces, when in power, are variable, fickle and ungrateful; and affirm that in them these faults are in no wise different from those to be found in certain princes. Were the accusation made against both the masses and princes, it would be true; but, if princes be excepted, it is false. For when the populace is in power and is well-ordered, it will be stable, prudent and grateful, in much the same way, or in a better way, than is a prince, however wise he be thought. And, on the other hand, a prince who contemns the laws, will be more ungrateful, fickle and imprudent than is the populace. Nor is inconstancy of behaviour due to a difference in nature, for they are pretty much the same, or, if one be better than the other, it is the populace: it is due to the greater or less respect which they have for the laws under which both alike are living.

If we consider the Roman populace it will be found that for four hundred years they were enemies to the very name of king and lovers of glory and of the common good of their country. Of both characteristics the Roman populace affords numerous and striking examples. And, should anyone bring up against me the ingratitude the populace displayed towards Scipio, my answer is that I have already discussed this question – at length and have there shown the ingratitude of the populace to be less than that of princes. While in the matter of prudence and stability I claim that the populace is more prudent, more stable, and of sounder judgement than the prince. Not without good reason is the voice of the populace likened to that of God; for public opinion is remarkably accurate in its prognostications, so much so that it seems as if the populace by some hidden power discerned the evil and the good that was to befall it. With regard to its judgement, when two speakers of equal skill are heard advocating different alternatives, very rarely does one find the populace failing to adopt the better view or incapable of appreciating the truth of what it hears. While, if in bold actions and such as appear advantageous it errs, as I have said above, so does a prince often err where his passions are involved, and these are much stronger than those of the populace.

It is found, too, that in the election of magistrates the populace makes a far better choice than does the prince; nor can the populace ever be persuaded that it is good to appoint to such an office a man of infamous life or corrupt habits, whereas a prince may easily and in a vast variety of ways be persuaded to do this. Again, one finds that when the populace begins to have a horror of something it remains of the same mind for many centuries; a thing that is never observed in the case of a prince. For both these characteristics I shall content myself with the evidence afforded by the Roman populace, which in the course of so many hundreds of years and so many elections of consuls and tribunes did not make four elections of which it had to repent. So much, too, as I have said, was the title of king hated that no service rendered by one of its citizens who ambitioned it, could render him immune from the penalties prescribed. Besides this, one finds that cities in which the populace is the prince, in a very short time extend vastly their dominions much more than do those which have always been under a prince; as Rome did after the expulsion of the kings, and Athens after it was free of Pisistratus.

This can only be due to one thing: government by the populace is better than government by princes. Nor do I care whether to this opinion of mine all that our historian has said in the aforesaid passage or what others have said, be objected; because if account be taken of all the disorders due to populaces and of all those due to princes, and of all the glories won by populaces and all those won by princes, it will be found that alike in goodness and in glory the populace is far superior. And if princes are superior to populaces in drawing up laws, codes of civic life, statutes and new institutions, the populace is so superior in sustaining what has been instituted, that it indubitably adds to the glory of those who have instituted them.

In short, to bring this topic to a conclusion, I say that, just as princely forms of government have endured for a very long time, so, too, have republican forms of government; and that in both cases it has been essential for them to be regulated by laws. For a prince who does what he likes is a lunatic, and a populace which does what it likes is unwise. If, therefore, it be a question of a prince subservient to the laws and of a populace chained up by laws, more virtue will be found in the populace than in the prince; and if it be a question of either of them loosed from control by the law, there will be found fewer errors in the populace than in the prince, and these of less moment and much easier to put right. For a licentious and turbulent populace, when a good man can obtain a hearing, can easily be brought to behave itself; but there is no one to talk to a bad prince, nor is there any remedy except the sword. From which an inference may be drawn in regard to the importance of their respective maladies; for, if to cure the malady of the populace a word suffices and the sword is needed to cure that of a prince, no one will fail to see that the greater the cure, the greater the fault.

When the populace has thrown off all restraint, it is not the mad things it does that are terrifying, nor is it of present evils that one is afraid, but of what may come of them, for amidst such confusion there may come to be a tyrant. In the case of bad princes it is just the opposite: it is present evils that are terrifying, but for the future there is hope, since men are convinced that the evil ways of a bad prince may make for freedom in the end. Thus one sees the difference between the two cases amounts to the same thing as the difference between what is and what must come to be. The brutalities of the masses are directed against those whom they suspect of conspiring against the common good; the brutalities of a prince against those whom he suspects of conspiring against his own good. The reason why people are prejudiced against the populace is because of the populace anyone may speak ill without fear and openly, even when the populace is ruling. But of princes people speak with the utmost trepidation and the utmost reserve.

[...]

# 4

# LEVIATHAN

## Thomas Hobbes

---

CHAPTER XIX

*Of the severall kinds of common-wealth by institution, and
of succession to the soveraigne power*

The difference of Common-wealths, consisteth in the difference of the Soveraign, or the Person representative of all and every one of the Multitude. And
because the Soveraignty is either in one Man, or in an Assembly of more than
one; and into that Assembly either Every man hath right to enter, or not every
one, but Certain men distinguished from the rest; it is manifest, there can be but
Three kinds of Common-wealth. For the Representative must needs be One
man, or More: and if more, then it is the Assembly of All, or but of a Part. When
the Representative is One man, then is the Common-wealth a MONARCHY: when
an Assembly of All that will come together, then it is a DEMOCRACY, or Popular
Common-wealth: when an Assembly of a Part onely, then it is called an
ARISTOCRACY. Other kind of Common-wealth there can be none: for either
One, or More, or All must have the Soveraign Power (which I have shewn to be
indivisible) entire.

*The different
Formes of
Common-wealths
but three*

There be other names of Government, in the Histories, and books of Policy;
as *Tyranny*, and *Oligarchy*: But they are not the names of other Formes of
Government, but of the same Formes misliked. For they that are discontented
under *Monarchy*, call it *Tyranny*; and they that are displeased with *Aristocracy*,
called it *Oligarchy*: So also, they which find themselves grieved under a

*Tyranny and
Oligarchy, but
different names
of Monarchy,
and Aristocracy*

---

From Thomas Hobbes, *Leviathan*, ed. C. B. Macpherson (Penguin, Harmondsworth, 1968),
pp. 239–48. Originally written 1651.

*Democracy*, call it *Anarchy*, (which signifies want of Government;) and yet I think no man believes, that want of Government, is any new kind of Government: nor by the same reason ought they to believe, that the Government is of one kind, when they like it, and another, when they mislike it, or are oppressed by the Governors.

It is manifest, that men who are in absolute liberty, may, if they please, give Authority to One man, to represent them every one; as well as give such Authority to any Assembly of men whatsoever; and consequently may subject themselves, if they think good, to a Monarch, as absolutely, as to any other Representative. Therefore, where there is already erected a Soveraign Power, there can be no other Representative of the same people, but onely to certain particular ends, by the Soveraign limited. For that were to erect two Soveraigns; and every man to have his person represented by two Actors, that by opposing one another, must needs divide that Power, which (if men will live in Peace) is indivisible; and thereby reduce the Multitude into the condition of Warre, contrary to the end for which all Soveraignty is instituted. And therefore as it is absurd, to think that a Soveraign Assembly, inviting the People of their Dominion, to send up their Deputies, with power to make known their Advise, or Desires, should therefore hold such Deputies, rather than themselves, for the absolute Representative of the people: so it is absurd also, to think the same in a Monarchy. And I know not how this so manifest a truth, should of late be so little observed; that in a Monarchy, he that had the Soveraignty from a descent of 600 years, was alone called Soveraign, had the title of Majesty from every one of his Subjects, and was unquestionably taken by them for their King; was notwithstanding never considered as their Representative; that name without contradiction passing for the title of those men, which at his command were sent up by the people to carry their Petitions, and give him (if he permitted it) their advise. Which may serve as an admonition, for those that are the true, and absolute Representative of a People, to instruct men in the nature of that Office, and to take heed how they admit of any other generall Representation upon any occasion whatsoever, if they mean to discharge the truth committed to them.

The difference between these three kindes of Common-wealth, consisteth not in the difference of Power; but in the difference of Convenience, or Aptitude to produce the Peace, and Security of the people; for which end they were instituted. And to compare Monarchy with the other two, we may observe; First, that whosoever beareth the Person of the people, or is one of that Assembly that bears it, beareth also his own naturall Person. And though he be carefull in his politique Person to procure the common interest; yet he is more, or no lesse carefull to procure the private good of himselfe, his family, kindred and friends; and for the most part, if the publique interest chance to crosse the private, he preferrs the private: for the Passions of men, are commonly more potent than their Reason. From whence it follows, that where the publique and private interest are most closely united, there is the publique most advanced. Now in

*Subordinate Representatives dangerous*

*Comparison of Monarchy, with Soveraign Assemblyes*

Monarchy, the private interest is the same with the publique. The riches, power, and honour of a Monarch arise onely from the riches, strength and reputation of his Subjects. For no King can be rich, nor glorious, nor secure; whose Subjects are either poore, or contemptible, or too weak through want, or dissention, to maintain a war against their enemies: Whereas in a Democracy, or Aristocracy, the publique prosperity conferres not so much to the private fortune of one that is corrupt, or ambitious, as doth many times a perfidious advice, a treacherous action, or a Civill warre.

Secondly, that a Monarch receiveth counsell of whom, when, and where he pleaseth; and consequently may heare the opinion of men versed in the matter about which he deliberates, of what rank or quality soever, and as long before the time of action, and with as much secrecy, as he will. But when a Soveraigne Assembly has need of Counsell, none are admitted but such as have a Right thereto from the beginning; which for the most part are of those who have beene versed more in the acquisition of Wealth than of Knowledge; and are to give their advice in long discourses, which may, and do commonly excite men to action, but not governe them in it. For the *Understanding* is by the flame of the Passions, never enlightned, but dazled: Nor is there any place, or time, wherein an Assemblie can receive Counsell with secrecie, because of their owne Multitude.

Thirdly, that the Resolutions of a Monarch, are subject to no other Inconstancy, than that of Humane Nature; but in Assemblies, besides that of Nature, there ariseth an Inconstancy from the Number. For the absence of a few, that would have the Resolution once taken, continue firme, (which may happen by security, negligence, or private impediments,) or the diligent appearance of a few of the contrary opinion, undoes to day, all that was concluded yesterday.

Fourthly, that a Monarch cannot disagree with himselfe, out of envy, or interest; but an Assembly may; and that to such a height, as may produce a Civill Warre.

Fifthly, that in Monarchy there is this inconvenience; that any Subject, by the power of one man, for the enriching of a favourite or flatterer, may be deprived of all he possesseth; which I confesse is a great and inevitable inconvenience. But the same may as well happen, where the Soveraigne Power is in an Assembly: For their power is the same; and they are as subject to evill Counsell, and to be seduced by Orators, as a Monarch by Flatterers; and becoming one an others Flatterers, serve one anothers Covetousnesse and Ambition by turnes. And whereas the Favorites of Monarchs, are few, and they have none els to advance but their owne Kindred; the Favorites of an Assembly, are many; and the Kindred much more numerous, than of any Monarch. Besides, there is no Favourite of a Monarch, which cannot as well succour his friends, as hurt his enemies: But Orators, that is to say, Favourites of Soveraigne Assemblies, though they have great power to hurt, have little to save. For to accuse, requires lesse Eloquence (such is mans Nature) than to excuse; and condemnation, than absolution more resembles Justice.

Sixtly, that it is an inconvenience in Monarchie, that the Soveraigntie may descend upon an Infant, or one that cannot discerne between Good and Evill: and consisteth in this, that the use of his Power, must be in the hand of another Man, or of some Assembly of men, which are to governe by his right, and in his name; as Curators, and Protectors of his Person, and Authority. But to say there is inconvenience, in putting the use of the Soveraign Power, into the hand of a Man, or an Assembly of men; is to say that all Government is more Inconvenient, than Confusion, and Civill Warre. And therefore all the danger that can be pretended, must arise from the Contention of those, that for an office of so great honour, and profit, may become Competitors. To make it appear, that this inconvenience, proceedeth not from that forme of Government we call Monarchy, we are to consider, that the precedent Monarch, hath appointed who shall have the Tuition of his Infant Successor, either expressely by Testament, or tacitly, by not controlling the Custome in that case received: And then such inconvenience (if it happen) is to be attributed, not to the Monarchy, but to the Ambition, and Injustice of the Subjects; which in all kinds of Government, where the people are not well instructed in their Duty, and the Rights of Soveraignty, is the same. Or else the precedent Monarch, hath not at all taken order for such Tuition; And then the Law of Nature hath provided this sufficient rule, That the Tuition shall be in him, that hath by Nature most interest in the preservation of the Authority of the Infant, and to whom least benefit can accrue by his death, or diminution. For seeing every man by nature seeketh his own benefit, and promotion; to put an Infant into the power of those, that can promote themselves by his destruction, or dammage, is not Tuition, but Trechery. So that sufficient provision being taken, against all just quarrell, about the Government under a Child, if any contention arise to the disturbance of the publique Peace, it is not to be attributed to the forme of Monarchy, but to the ambition of Subjects, and ignorance of their Duty. On the other side, there is no great Common-wealth, the Soveraignty whereof is in a great Assembly, which is not, as to consultations of Peace, and Warre, and making of Lawes, in the same condition, as if the Government were in a Child. For as a Child wants the judgement to dissent from counsell given him, and is thereby necessitated to take the advise of them, or him, to whom he is committed: So an Assembly wanteth the liberty, to dissent from the counsell of the major part, be it good, or bad. And as a Child has need of a Tutor, or Protector, to preserve his Person, and Authority: So also (in great Common-wealths,) the Soveraign Assembly, in all great dangers and troubles, have need of *Custodes libertatis*; that is of Dictators, or Protectors of their Authoritie; which are as much as Temporary Monarchs; to whom for a time, they may commit the entire exercise of their Power; and have (at the end of that time) been oftner deprived thereof, than Infant Kings, by their Protectors, Regents, or any other Tutors.

Though the Kinds of Soveraigntie be, as I have now shewn, but three; that is to say, Monarchie, where One Man has it; or Democracie, where the generall

Assembly of Subjects hath it; or Aristocracie, where it is in an Assembly of certain persons nominated, or otherwise distinguished from the rest: Yet he that shall consider the particular Common-wealthes that have been, and are in the world, will not perhaps easily reduce them to three, and may thereby be inclined to think there be other Formes, arising from these mingled together. As for example, Elective Kingdomes; where Kings have the Soveraigne Power put into their hands for a time; or Kingdomes, wherein the King hath a power limited: which Governments, are nevertheless by most Writers called Monarchie. Likewise if a Popular, or Aristocraticall Common-wealth, subdue an Enemies Countrie, and govern the same, by a President, Procurator, or other Magistrate; this may seeme perhaps at first sight, to be a Democraticall, or Aristocraticall Government. But it is not so. For Elective Kings, are not Soveraignes, but Ministers of the Soveraigne; nor limited Kings Soveraignes, but Ministers of them that have the Soveraigne Power: Nor are those Provinces which are in subjection to a Democracie, or Aristocracie of another Common-wealth, Democratically, or Aristocratically governed, but Monarchically.

And first, concerning an Elective King whose power is limited to his life, as it is in many places of Christendome at this day; or to certaine Yeares or Moneths, as the Dictators power amongst the Romans; If he have Right to appoint his Successor, he is no more Elective but Hereditary. But if he have no Power to elect his Successor, then there is some other Man, or Assembly known, which after his decease may elect a new, or else the Commonwealth dieth, and dissolveth with him, and returneth to the condition of Warre. If it be known who have the power to give the Soveraigntie after his death, it is known also that the Soveraigntie was in them before: For none have right to give that which they have not right to possesse, and keep to themselves, if they think good. But if there be none that can give the Soveraigntie, after the decease of him that was first elected; then has he power, nay he is obliged by the Law of Nature, to provide, by establishing his Successor, to keep those that had trusted him with the Government, from relapsing into the miserable condition of Civill warre. And consequently he was, when elected, a Soveraign absolute.

Secondly, that King whose power is limited, is not superiour to him, or them that have the power to limit it; and he that is not superiour, is not supreme; that is to say not Soveraign. The Soveraignty therefore was alwaies in that Assembly which had the Right to Limit him; and by consequence the government not Monarchy, but either Democracy, or Aristocracy; as of old time in *Sparta*; where the Kings had a priviledge to lead their Armies; but the Soveraignty was in the *Ephori*.

Thirdly, whereas heretofore the Roman People, governed the land of *Judea* (for example) by a President; yet was not *Judea* therefore a Democracy; because they were not governed by any Assembly, into which, any of them, had right to enter; nor by an Aristocracy; because they were not governed by any Assembly, into which, any man could enter by their Election: but they were governed by one Person, which though as to the people of *Rome* was an Assembly of the people, or Democracy; yet as to people of *Judea*, which had no right at all of participating in the government, was a Monarch. For though where the people are governed by an Assembly, chosen by themselves out of their own number, the government is called a Democracy, or Aristocracy; yet when they are governed by an Assembly, not of their own choosing, 'tis a Monarchy; not of *One* man, over another man; but of one people, over another people.

Of all these Formes of Government, the matter being mortall, so that not onely Monarchs, but also whole Assemblies dy, it is necessary for the conservation of the peace of men, that as there was order taken for an Artificiall Man, so there be order also taken, for an Artificiall Eternity of life; without which, men that are governed by an Assembly, should return into the condition of Warre in every age; and they that are governed by One man, as soon as their Governour dyeth. This Artificiall Eternity, is that which men call the Right of *Succession*. Of the Right of Succession

There is no perfect forme of Government, where the disposing of the Succession is not in the present Soveraign. For if it be in any other particular Man, or private Assembly, it is in a person subject, and may be assumed by the Soveraign at his pleasure; and consequently the Right is in himselfe. And if it be in no particular man, but left to a new choyce; then is the Common-wealth dissolved; and the Right is in him that can get it; contrary to the intention of them that did Institute the Common-wealth, for their perpetuall, and not temporary security.

In a Democracy, the whole Assembly cannot faile, unlesse the Multitude that are to be governed faile. And therefore questions of the right of Succession, have in that forme of Government no place at all.

In an Aristocracy, when any of the Assembly dyeth, the election of another into his room belongeth to the Assembly, as the Soveraign, to whom belongeth the choosing of all Counsellours, and Officers. For that which the Representative doth, as Actor, every one of the Subjects doth, as Author. And though the Soveraign Assembly, may give Power to others, to elect new men, for supply of their Court; yet it is still by their Authority, that the Election is made; and by the same it may (when the publique shall require it) be recalled.

[...]

# 5

# THE SOCIAL CONTRACT

## Jean-Jacques Rousseau

[...]

### CHAPTER VI
#### THE SOCIAL COMPACT

I suppose men to have reached the point at which the obstacles in the way of their preservation in the state of nature show their power of resistance to be greater than the resources at the disposal of each individual for his maintenance in that state. That primitive condition can then subsist no longer; and the human race would perish unless it changed its manner of existence.

But, as men cannot engender new forces, but only unite and direct existing ones, they have no other means of preserving themselves than the formation, by aggregation, of a sum of forces great enough to overcome the resistance. These they have to bring into play by means of a single motive power, and cause to act in concert.

This sum of forces can arise only where several persons come together: but, as the force and liberty of each man are the chief instruments of his self-preservation, how can he pledge them without harming his own interests, and neglecting the care he owes to himself? This difficulty, in its bearing on my present subject, may be stated in the following terms:

From Jean-Jacques Rousseau, *The Social Contract and Discourses*, trans. and intro. G. D. H. Cole (Everyman's Library: Dent, London/Dutton, New York, 1968), Book I, chapters VI and VII, pp. 11–15; Book III, chapters I and IV, pp. 46–50, 54–6. Originally written 1762.

'The problem is to find a form of association which will defend and protect with the whole common force the person and goods of each associate, and in which each, while uniting himself with all, may still obey himself alone, and remain as free as before.' This is the fundamental problem of which the *Social Contract* provides the solution.

The clauses of this contract are so determined by the nature of the act that the slightest modification would make them vain and ineffective; so that, although they have perhaps never been formally set forth, they are everywhere the same and everywhere tacitly admitted and recognized, until, on the violation of the social compact, each regains his original rights and resumes his natural liberty, while losing the conventional liberty in favour of which he renounced it.

These clauses, properly understood, may be reduced to one – the total alienation of each associate, together with all his rights, to the whole community; for, in the first place, as each gives himself absolutely, the conditions are the same for all; and, this being so, no one has any interest in making them burdensome to others.

Moreover, the alienation being without reserve, the union is as perfect as it can be, and no associate has anything more to demand: for, if the individuals retained certain rights, as there would be no common superior to decide between them and the public, each, being on one point his own judge, would ask to be so on all; the state of nature would thus continue, and the association would necessarily become inoperative or tyrannical.

Finally, each man, in giving himself to all, gives himself to nobody; and as there is no associate over which he does not acquire the same right as he yields others over himself, he gains an equivalent for everything he loses, and an increase of force for the preservation of what he has.

If then we discard from the social compact what is not of its essence, we shall find that it reduces itself to the following terms:

*'Each of us puts his person and all his power in common under the supreme direction of the general will, and, in our corporate capacity, we receive each member as an indivisible part of the whole.'*

At once, in place of the individual personality of each contracting party, this act of association creates a moral and collective body, composed of as many members as the assembly contains voters, and receiving from this act its unity, its common identity, its life, and its will. This public person, so formed by the union of all other persons, formerly took the name of *city*,[1] and now takes that of *Republic* or *body politic*; it is called by its members *State* when passive, *Sovereign* when active, and *Power* when compared with others like itself. Those who are associated in it take collectively the name of *people*, and severally are called *citizens*, as sharing in the sovereign power, and *subjects*, as being under the laws of the State. But these terms are often confused and taken one for another: it is enough to know how to distinguish them when they are being used with precision.

## CHAPTER VII
### THE SOVEREIGN

This formula shows us that the act of association comprises a mutual undertaking between the public and the individuals, and that each individual, in making a contract, as we may say, with himself, is bound in a double capacity; as a member of the Sovereign he is bound to the individuals, and as a member of the State to the Sovereign. But the maxim of civil right, that no one is bound by undertakings made to himself, does not apply in this case; for there is a great difference between incurring an obligation to yourself and incurring one to a whole of which you form a part.

Attention must further be called to the fact that public deliberation, while competent to bind all the subjects to the Sovereign, because of the two different capacities in which each of them may be regarded, cannot, for the opposite reason, bind the Sovereign to itself; and that it is consequently against the nature of the body politic for the Sovereign to impose on itself a law which it cannot infringe. Being able to regard itself in only one capacity, it is in the position of an individual who makes a contract with himself; and this makes it clear that there neither is nor can be any kind of fundamental law binding on the body of the people – not even the social contract itself. This does not mean that the body politic cannot enter into undertakings with others, provided the contract is not infringed by them; for in relation to what is external to it, it becomes a simple being, an individual.

But the body politic or the Sovereign, drawing its being wholly from the sanctity of the contract, can never bind itself, even to an outsider, to do anything derogatory to the original act, for instance, to alienate any part of itself, or to submit to another Sovereign. Violation of the act by which it exists would be self-annihilation; and that which is itself nothing can create nothing.

As soon as this multitude is so united in one body, it is impossible to offend against one of the members without attacking the body, and still more to offend against the body without the members resenting it. Duty and interest therefore equally oblige the two contracting parties to give each other help; and the same men should seek to combine, in their double capacity, all the advantages dependent upon that capacity.

Again, the Sovereign, being formed wholly of the individuals who compose it, neither has nor can have any interest contrary to theirs; and consequently the sovereign power need give no guarantee to its subjects, because it is impossible for the body to wish to hurt all its members. We shall also see later on that it cannot hurt any in particular. The Sovereign, merely by virtue of what it is, is always what it should be.

This, however, is not the case with the relation of the subjects to the Sovereign, which, despite the common interest, would have no security that they would fulfil their undertakings, unless it found means to assure itself of their fidelity.

In fact, each individual, as a man, may have a particular will contrary or dissimilar to the general will which he has as a citizen. His particular interest may speak to him quite differently from the common interest: his absolute and naturally independent existence may make him look upon what he owes to the common cause as a gratuitous contribution, the loss of which will do less harm to others than the payment of it is burdensome to himself; and, regarding the moral person which constitutes the State as a *persona ficta*, because not a man, he may wish to enjoy the rights of citizenship without being ready to fulfil the duties of a subject. The continuance of such an injustice could not but prove the undoing of the body politic.

In order then that the social compact may not be an empty formula, it tacitly includes the undertaking, which alone can give force to the rest, that whoever refuses to obey the general will shall be compelled to do so by the whole body. This means nothing less than that he will be forced to be free; for this is the condition which, by giving each citizen to his country, secures him against all personal dependence. In this lies the key to the working of the political machine; this alone legitimizes civil undertakings, which, without it, would be absurd, tyrannical and liable to the most frightful abuses.

[...]

## BOOK III

Before speaking of the different forms of government, let us try to fix the exact sense of the word, which has not yet been very clearly explained.

### CHAPTER I
#### GOVERNMENT IN GENERAL

I warn the reader that this chapter requires careful reading, and that I am unable to make myself clear to those who refuse to be attentive.

Every free action is produced by the concurrence of two causes; one moral, i.e. the will which determines the act; the other physical, i.e. the power which executes it. When I walk towards an object, it is necessary first that I should will to go there, and, in the second place, that my feet should carry me. If a paralytic wills to run and an active man wills not to, they will both stay where they are. The body politic has the same motive powers; here too force and will are distinguished, will under the name of legislative power and force under that of executive power. Without their concurrence, nothing is, or should be, done.

We have seen that the legislative power belongs to the people, and can belong to it alone. It may, on the other hand, readily be seen, from the principles laid down above, that the executive power cannot belong to the generality as legislature or Sovereign, because it consists wholly of particular acts which fall outside the competency of the law, and consequently of the Sovereign, whose acts must always be laws.

The public force therefore needs an agent of its own to bind it together and set it to work under the direction of the general will, to serve as a means of communication between the State and the Sovereign, and to do for the collective person more or less what the union of soul and body does for man. Here we have what is, in the State, the basis of government, often wrongly confused with the Sovereign, whose minister it is.

What then is government? An intermediate body set up between the subjects and the Sovereign, to secure their mutual correspondence, charged with the execution of the laws and the maintenance of liberty, both civil and political.

The members of this body are called magistrates or *kings*, that is to say *governors*, and the whole body bears the name *prince*.[2] Thus those who hold that the act, by which a people puts itself under a prince, is not a contract, are certainly right. It is simply and solely a commission, an employment, in which the rulers, mere officials of the Sovereign, exercise in their own name the power of which it makes them depositaries. This power it can limit, modify, or recover at pleasure; for the alienation of such a right is incompatible with the nature of the social body, and contrary to the end of association.

I call then *government*, or supreme administration, the legitimate exercise of the executive power, and prince or magistrate the man or the body entrusted with that administration.

In government reside the intermediate forces whose relations make up that of the whole to the whole, or of the Sovereign to the State. This last relation may be represented as that between the extreme terms of a continuous proportion, which has government as its mean proportional. The government gets from the Sovereign the orders it gives the people, and, for the State to be properly balanced, there must, when everything is reckoned in, be equality between the product or power of the government taken in itself, and the product or power of the citizens, who are on the one hand sovereign and on the other subject.

Furthermore, none of these three terms can be altered without the equality being instantly destroyed. If the Sovereign desires to govern, or the magistrate to give laws, or if the subjects refuse to obey, disorder takes the place of regularity, force and will no longer act together, and the State is dissolved and falls into despotism or anarchy. Lastly, as there is only one mean proportional between each relation, there is also only one good government possible for a State. But, as countless events may change the relations of a people, not only may different governments be good for different peoples, but also for the same people at different times.

In attempting to give some idea of the various relations that may hold between these two extreme terms, I shall take as an example the number of a people, which is the most easily expressible.

Suppose the State is composed of ten thousand citizens. The Sovereign can only be considered collectively and as a body; but each member, as being a subject, is regarded as an individual: thus the Sovereign is to the subject as ten thousand to one, i.e. each member of the State has as his share only a ten-thousandth part of the sovereign authority, although he is wholly under its control. If the people numbers a hundred thousand, the condition of the subject undergoes no change, and each equally is under the whole authority of the laws, while his vote, being reduced to one hundred thousandth part, has ten times less influence in drawing them up. The subject therefore remaining always a unit, the relation between him and the Sovereign increases with the number of the citizens. From this it follows that, the larger the State, the less the liberty.

When I say the relation increases, I mean that it grows more unequal. Thus the greater it is in the geometrical sense, the less relation there is in the ordinary sense of the word. In the former sense, the relation, considered according to quantity, is expressed by the quotient; in the latter, considered according to identity, it is reckoned by similarity.

Now, the less relation the particular wills have to the general will, that is, morals and manners to laws, the more should the repressive force be increased. The government, then, to be good, should be proportionately stronger as the people is more numerous.

On the other hand, as the growth of the State gives the depositaries of the public authority more temptations and chances of abusing their power, the greater the force with which the government ought to be endowed for keeping the people in hand, the greater too should be the force at the disposal of the Sovereign for keeping the government in hand. I am speaking, not of absolute force, but of the relative force of the different parts of the State.

It follows from this double relation that the continuous proportion between the Sovereign, the prince, and the people, is by no means an arbitrary idea, but a necessary consequence of the nature of the body politic. It follows further that, one of the extreme terms, viz. the people, as subject, being fixed and represented by unity, whenever the duplicate ratio increases or diminishes, the simple ratio does the same, and is changed accordingly. From this we see that there is not a single unique and absolute form of government, but as many governments differing in nature as there are States differing in size.

If, ridiculing this system, any one were to say that, in order to find the mean proportional and give form to the body of the government, it is only necessary, according to me, to find the square root of the number of the people, I should answer that I am here taking this number only as an instance; that the relations of which I am speaking are not measured by the number of men alone, but generally by the amount of action, which is a combination of a multitude of causes; and that, further, if, to save words, I borrow for a moment the terms of geometry, I am none the less well aware that moral quantities do not allow of geometrical accuracy.

The government is on a small scale what the body politic which includes it is on a great one. It is a moral person endowed with certain faculties, active like the Sovereign and passive like the State, and capable of being resolved into other similar relations. This accordingly gives rise to a new proportion, within which there is yet another, according to the arrangement of the magistracies, till an indivisible middle term is reached, i.e. a single ruler or supreme magistrate, who may be represented, in the midst of this progression, as the unity between the fractional and the ordinal series.

Without encumbering ourselves with this multiplication of terms, let us rest content with regarding government as a new body within the State, distinct from the people and the Sovereign, and intermediate between them.

There is between these two bodies this essential difference, that the State exists by itself, and the government only through the Sovereign. Thus the dominant will of the prince is, or should be, nothing but the general will or the law; his force is only the public force concentrated in his hands, and, as soon as he tries to base any absolute and independent act on his own authority, the tie that binds the whole together begins to be loosened. If finally the prince should come to have a particular will more active than the will of the Sovereign, and should employ the public force in his hands in obedience to this particular will, there would be, so to speak, two Sovereigns, one rightful and the other actual, the social union would evaporate instantly, and the body politic would be dissolved.

However, in order that the government may have a true existence and a real life distinguishing it from the body of the State, and in order that all its members may be able to act in concert and fulfil the end for which it was set up, it must have a particular personality, a sensibility common to its members, and a force and will of its own making for its preservation. This particular existence implies assemblies, councils, power of deliberation and decision, rights, titles, and privileges belonging exclusively to the prince and making the office of magistrate more honourable in proportion as it is more troublesome. The difficulties lie in the manner of so ordering this subordinate whole within the whole, that it in no way alters the general constitution by affirmation of its own, and always distinguishes the particular force it possesses, which is destined to aid in its preservation, from the public force, which is destined to the preservation of the State; and, in a word, is always ready to sacrifice the government to the people, and never to sacrifice the people to the government.

Furthermore, although the artificial body of the government is the work of another artificial body, and has, we may say, only a borrowed and subordinate life, this does not prevent it from being able to act with more or less vigour or promptitude, or from being, so to speak, in more or less robust health. Finally, without departing directly from the end for which it was instituted, it may deviate more or less from it, according to the manner of its constitution.

From all these differences arise the various relations which the government ought to bear to the body of the State, according to the accidental and particular relations by which the State itself is modified, for often the government that is best in itself will become the most pernicious, if the relations in which it stands have altered according to the defects of the body politic to which it belongs.

[...]

## CHAPTER IV
DEMOCRACY

He who makes the law knows better than any one else how it should be executed and interpreted. It seems then impossible to have a better constitution than that in which the executive and legislative powers are united; but this very fact renders the government in certain respects inadequate, because things which should be distinguished are confounded, and the prince and the Sovereign, being the same person, form, so to speak, no more than a government without government.

It is not good for him who makes the laws to execute them, or for the body of the people to turn its attention away from a general standpoint and devote it to particular objects. Nothing is more dangerous than the influence of private interests in public affairs, and the abuse of the laws by the government is a less evil than the corruption of the legislator, which is the inevitable sequel to a particular standpoint. In such a case, the State being altered in substance, all reformation becomes impossible. A people that would never misuse governmental powers would never misuse independence; a people that would always govern well would not need to be governed.

If we take the term in the strict sense, there never has been a real democracy, and there never will be. It is against the natural order for the many to govern and the few to be governed. It is unimaginable that the people should remain continually assembled to devote their time to public affairs, and it is clear that they cannot set up commissions for that purpose without the form of administration being changed.

In fact, I can confidently lay down as a principle that, when the functions of government are shared by several tribunals, the less numerous sooner or later acquire the greatest authority, if only because they are in position to expedite affairs, and power thus naturally comes into their hands.

Besides, how many conditions that are difficult to unite does such a government presuppose! First, a very small State, where the people can readily be got together and where each citizen can with ease know all the rest; secondly, great simplicity of manners, to prevent business from multiplying and raising thorny problems; next, a large measure of equality in rank and fortune, without which equality of rights and authority cannot long subsist; lastly, little or no luxury – for luxury either comes of riches or makes them necessary; it corrupts at once rich and poor, the rich by possession and the poor by covetousness; it sells the country to softness and vanity, and takes away from the State all its citizens, to make them slaves one to another, and one and all to public opinion.

This is why a famous writer has made virtue the fundamental principle of Republics; for all these conditions could not exist without virtue. But, for want of the necessary distinctions, that great thinker was often inexact, and sometimes obscure, and did not see that, the sovereign authority being everywhere the same, the same principle should be found in every well-constituted State, in a greater or less degree, it is true, according to the form of the government.

It may be added that there is no government so subject to civil wars and intestine agitations as democratic or popular government, because there is none which has so strong and continual a tendency to change to another form, or which demands more vigilance and courage for its maintenance as it is. Under such a constitution above all, the citizen should arm himself with strength and constancy, and say, every day of his life, what a virtuous Count Palatine[3] said in the Diet of Poland: 'Malo periculosam libertatam quam quietum servitium.'

Were there a people of gods, their government would be democratic. So perfect a government is not for men.

[...]

## NOTES

1. The real meaning of this word has been almost wholly lost in modern times; most people mistake a town for a city, and a townsman for a citizen. They do not know that houses make a town, but citizens a city. The same mistake long ago cost the Carthaginians dear. I have never read of the title of citizens being given to the subjects of any prince, not even the ancient Macedonians or the English of to-day, though they are nearer liberty than any one else. The French alone everywhere familiarly adopt the name of citizens, because, as can be seen from their dictionaries, they have no idea of its meaning; otherwise they would be guilty in usurping it, of the crime of *lèse-majesté*: among them, the name expresses a virtue, and not a right. When Bodin spoke of our citizens and townsmen, he fell into a bad blunder in taking the one class for the other. M. d'Alembert has avoided the error, and, in his article on Geneva, has clearly distinguished the four orders of men (or even five, counting mere foreigners) who dwell in our town, of which two only compose the Republic. No other French writer, to my knowledge, has understood the real meaning of the word citizen.
2. Thus at Venice the College, even in the absence of the Doge, is called 'Most Serene Prince.'
3. The Palatine of Posen, father of the King of Poland, Duke of Lorraine. [I prefer liberty with danger to peace with slavery.]

# 6

# THE FEDERALIST PAPERS

## James Madison (et al.)

### NUMBER X
#### THE SAME SUBJECT CONTINUED

Among the numerous advantages promised by a well-constructed Union, none deserves to be more accurately developed than its tendency to break and control the violence of faction. The friend of popular governments never finds himself so much alarmed for their character and fate as when he contemplates their propensity to this dangerous vice. He will not fail, therefore, to set a due value on any plan which, without violating the principles to which he is attached, provides a proper cure for it. The instability, injustice, and confusion introduced into the public councils have, in truth, been the mortal diseases under which popular governments have everywhere perished, as they continue to be the favorite and fruitful topics from which the adversaries to liberty derive their most specious declamations. The valuable improvements made by the American constitutions on the popular models, both ancient and modern, cannot certainly be too much admired; but it would be an unwarrantable partiality to contend that they have as effectually obviated the danger on this side, as was wished and expected. Complaints are everywhere heard from our most considerate and virtuous citizens, equally the friends of public and private faith and of public and personal liberty, that our governments are too unstable, that the public good is disregarded in the conflicts of rival parties, and that measures are too often decided, not according to the rules of justice and the

From J. Madison, A. Hamilton and J. Jay, *The Federalist Papers*, ed. Isaac Kramnick (Penguin Books, Harmondsworth, 1987), pp. 122–8. Originally written 1787–8.

rights of the minor party, but by the superior force of an interested and overbearing majority. However anxiously we may wish that these complaints had no foundation, the evidence of known facts will not permit us to deny that they are in some degree true. It will be found, indeed, on a candid review of our situation, that some of the distresses under which we labor have been erroneously charged on the operation of our governments; but it will be found, at the same time, that other causes will not alone account for many of our heaviest misfortunes; and, particularly, for that prevailing and increasing distrust of public engagements and alarm for private rights which are echoed from one end of the continent to the other. These must be chiefly, if not wholly, effects of the unsteadiness and injustice with which a factious spirit has tainted our public administration.

By a faction I understand a number of citizens, whether amounting to a majority or minority of the whole, who are united and actuated by some common impulse of passion, or of interest, adverse to the rights of other citizens, or to the permanent and aggregate interests of the community.

There are two methods of curing the mischiefs of faction: the one, by removing its causes; the other, by controlling its effects.

There are again two methods of removing the causes of faction: the one, by destroying the liberty which is essential to its existence; the other, by giving to every citizen the same opinions, the same passions, and the same interests.

It could never be more truly said than of the first remedy that it was worse than the disease. Liberty is to faction what air is to fire, an aliment without which it instantly expires. But it could not be a less folly to abolish liberty, which is essential to political life, because it nourishes faction than it would be to wish the annihilation of air, which is essential to animal life, because it imparts to fire its destructive agency.

The second expedient is as impracticable as the first would be unwise. As long as the reason of man continues fallible, and he is at liberty to exercise it, different opinions will be formed. As long as the connection subsists between his reason and his self-love, his opinions and his passions will have a reciprocal influence on each other; and the former will be objects to which the latter will attach themselves. The diversity in the faculties of men, from which the rights of property originate, is not less an insuperable obstacle to a uniformity of interests. The protection of these faculties is the first object of government. From the protection of different and unequal faculties of acquiring property, the possession of different degrees and kinds of property immediately results; and from the influence of these on the sentiments and views of the respective proprietors ensues a division of the society into different interests and parties.

The latent causes of faction are thus sown in the nature of man; and we see them everywhere brought into different degrees of activity, according to the different circumstances of civil society. A zeal for different opinions concerning religion, concerning government, and many other points, as well of speculation as of practice; an attachment to different leaders ambitiously contending for pre-eminence and power; or to persons of other descriptions whose fortunes have been interesting to the human passions, have, in turn, divided mankind into parties, inflamed them with mutual animosity, and rendered them much more disposed to vex and oppress each other than to co-operate for their common good. So strong is this propensity of mankind to fall into mutual animosities that where no substantial occasion presents itself the most frivolous and fanciful distinctions have been sufficient to kindle their unfriendly passions and excite their most violent conflicts. But the most common and durable source of factions has been the various and unequal distribution of property. Those who hold and those who are without property have ever formed distinct interests in society. Those who are creditors, and those who are debtors, fall under a like discrimination. A landed interest, a manufacturing interest, a mercantile interest, a moneyed interest, with many lesser interests, grow up of necessity in civilized nations, and divide them into different classes, actuated by different sentiments and views. The regulation of these various and interfering interests forms the principal task of modern legislation and involves the spirit of party and faction in the necessary and ordinary operations of government.

No man is allowed to be a judge in his own cause, because his interest would certainly bias his judgment, and, not improbably, corrupt his integrity. With equal, nay with greater reason, a body of men are unfit to be both judges and parties at the same time; yet what are many of the most important acts of legislation but so many judicial determinations, not indeed concerning the rights of single persons, but concerning the rights of large bodies of citizens? And what are the different classes of legislators but advocates and parties to the causes which they determine? Is a law proposed concerning private debts? It is a question to which the creditors are parties on one side and the debtors on the other. Justice ought to hold the balance between them. Yet the parties are, and must be, themselves the judges; and the most numerous party, or in other words, the most powerful faction must be expected to prevail. Shall domestic manufacturers be encouraged, and in what degree, by restrictions on foreign manufacturers? are questions which would be differently decided by the landed and the manufacturing classes, and probably by neither with a sole regard to justice and the public good. The apportionment of taxes on the various descriptions of property is an act which seems to require the most exact impartiality; yet there is, perhaps, no legislative act in which greater opportunity and temptation are given to a predominant party to trample on the rules of justice. Every shilling with which they overburden the inferior number is a shilling saved to their own pockets.

It is in vain to say that enlightened statesmen will be able to adjust these clashing interests and render them all subservient to the public good. Enlightened statesmen will not always be at the helm. Nor, in many cases, can such an adjustment be made at all without taking into view indirect and remote considerations, which will rarely prevail over the immediate interest which one party may find in disregarding the rights of another or the good of the whole.

The inference to which we are brought is that the *causes* of faction cannot be removed and that relief is only to be sought in the means of controlling its *effects*.

If a faction consists of less than a majority, relief is supplied by the republican principle, which enables the majority to defeat its sinister views by regular vote. It may clog the administration, it may convulse the society; but it will be unable to execute and mask its violence under the forms of the Constitution. When a majority is included in a faction, the form of popular government, on the other hand, enables it to sacrifice to its ruling passion or interest both the public good and the rights of other citizens. To secure the public good and private rights against the danger of such a faction, and at the same time to preserve the spirit and the form of popular government, is then the great object to which our inquiries are directed. Let me add that it is the great desideratum by which alone this form of government can be rescued from the opprobrium under which it has so long labored and be recommended to the esteem and adoption of mankind.

By what means is this object attainable? Evidently by one of two only. Either the existence of the same passion or interest in a majority at the same time must be prevented, or the majority, having such coexistent passion or interest, must be rendered, by their number and local situation, unable to concert and carry into effect schemes of oppression. If the impulse and the opportunity be suffered to coincide, we well know that neither moral nor religious motives can be relied on as an adequate control. They are not found to be such on the injustice and violence of individuals, and lose their efficacy in proportion to the number combined together, that is, in proportion as their efficacy becomes needful.

From this view of the subject it may be concluded that a pure democracy, by which I mean a society consisting of a small number of citizens, who assemble and administer the government in person, can admit of no cure for the mischiefs of faction. A common passion or interest will, in almost every case, be felt by a majority of the whole; a communication and concert results from the form of government itself; and there is nothing to check the inducements to sacrifice the weaker party or an obnoxious individual. Hence it is that such democracies have ever been spectacles of turbulence and contention; have ever been found incompatible with personal security or the rights of property; and have in general been as short in their lives as they have been violent in their deaths. Theoretic politicians, who have patronized this species of government, have erroneously supposed that by reducing mankind to a perfect equality in their political rights, they would at the same time be perfectly equalized and assimilated in their possessions, their opinions, and their passions.

A republic, by which I mean a government in which the scheme of representation takes place, opens a different prospect and promises the cure for which we are seeking. Let us examine the points in which it varies from pure democracy, and we shall comprehend both the nature of the cure and the efficacy which it must derive from the Union.

The two great points of difference between a democracy and a republic are: first, the delegation of the government, in the latter, to a small number of citizens elected by the rest; secondly, the greater number of citizens and greater sphere of country over which the latter may be extended.

The effect of the first difference is, on the one hand, to refine and enlarge the public views by passing them through the medium of a chosen body of citizens, whose wisdom may best discern the true interest of their country and whose patriotism and love of justice will be least likely to sacrifice it to temporary or partial considerations. Under such a regulation it may well happen that the public voice, pronounced by the representatives of the people, will be more consonant to the public good than if pronounced by the people themselves, convened for the purpose. On the other hand, the effect may be inverted. Men of factious tempers, of local prejudices, or of sinister designs, may, by intrigue, by corruption, or by other means, first obtain the suffrages, and then betray the interests of the people. The question resulting is, whether small or extensive republics are most favorable to the election of proper guardians of the public weal; and it is clearly decided in favor of the latter by two obvious considerations.

In the first place it is to be remarked that however small the republic may be the representatives must be raised to a certain number in order to guard against the cabals of a few; and that however large it may be they must be limited to a certain number in order to guard against the confusion of a multitude. Hence, the number of representatives in the two cases not being in proportion to that of the constituents, and being proportionally greatest in the small republic, it follows that if the proportion of fit characters be not less in the large than in the small republic, the former will present a greater option, and consequently a greater probability of a fit choice.

In the next place, as each representative will be chosen by a greater number of citizens in the large than in the small republic, it will be more difficult for unworthy candidates to practice with success the vicious arts by which elections are too often carried; and the suffrages of the people being more free, will be more likely to center on men who possess the most attractive merit and the most diffusive and established characters.

It must be confessed that in this, as in most other cases, there is a mean, on both sides of which inconveniences will be found to lie. By enlarging too much the number of electors, you render the representative too little acquainted with all their local circumstances and lesser interests; as by reducing it too much, you render him unduly attached to these, and too little fit to comprehend and pursue great and national objects. The federal Constitution forms a happy combination in this respect; the great and aggregate interests being referred to the national, the local and particular to the State legislatures.

The other point of difference is the greater number of citizens and extent of territory which may be brought within the compass of republican than of democratic government; and it is this circumstance principally which renders factious combinations less to be dreaded in the former than in the latter. The smaller the society, the fewer probably will be the distinct parties and interests composing it; the fewer the distinct parties and interests, the more frequently will a majority be found of the same party; and the smaller the number of individuals composing a majority, and the smaller the compass within which they are placed, the more easily will they concert and execute their plans of oppression. Extend the sphere and you take in a greater variety of parties and interests; you make it less probable that a majority of the whole will have a common motive to invade the rights of other citizens; or if such a common motive exists, it will be more difficult for all who feel it to discover their own strength and to act in unison with each other. Besides other impediments, it may be remarked that, where there is a consciousness of unjust or dishonorable purposes, communication is always checked by distrust in proportion to the number whose concurrence is necessary.

Hence, it clearly appears that the same advantage which a republic has over a democracy in controlling the effects of faction is enjoyed by a large over a small republic – is enjoyed by the Union over the States composing it. Does this advantage consist in the substitution of representatives whose enlightened views and virtuous sentiments render them superior to local prejudices and to schemes of injustice? It will not be denied that the representation of the Union will be most likely to possess these requisite endowments. Does it consist in the greater security afforded by a greater variety of parties, against the event of any one party being able to outnumber and oppress the rest? In an equal degree does the increased variety of parties comprised within the Union increase this security? Does it, in fine, consist in the greater obstacles opposed to the concert and accomplishment of the secret wishes of an unjust and interested majority? Here again the extent of the Union gives it the most palpable advantage.

The influence of factious leaders may kindle a flame within their particular States but will be unable to spread a general conflagration through the other States. A religious sect may degenerate into a political faction in a part of the Confederacy; but the variety of sects dispersed over the entire face of it must secure the national councils against any danger from that source. A rage for paper money, for an abolition of debts, for an equal division of property, or for any other improper or wicked project, will be less apt to pervade the whole body of the Union than a particular member of it, in the same proportion as such a malady is more likely to taint a particular county or district than an entire State.

In the extent and proper structure of the Union, therefore, we behold a republican remedy for the diseases most incident to republican government. And according to the degree of pleasure and pride we feel in being republicans ought to be our zeal in cherishing the spirit and supporting the character of federalists.

PUBLIUS [Madison]

# REPRESENTATIVE GOVERNMENT

## John Stuart Mill

[...]

There is no difficulty in showing that the ideally best form of government is that in which the sovereignty, or supreme controlling power in the last resort, is vested in the entire aggregate of the community; every citizen not only having a voice in the exercise of that ultimate sovereignty, but being, at least occasionally, called on to take an actual part in the government, by the personal discharge of some public function, local or general.

To test this proposition, it has to be examined in reference to the two branches into which [...] the inquiry into the goodness of a government conveniently divides itself, namely, how far it promotes the good management of the affairs of society by means of the existing faculties, moral, intellectual, and active, of its various members, and what is its effect in improving or deteriorating those faculties.

The ideally best form of government, it is scarcely necessary to say, does not mean one which is practicable or eligible in all states of civilization, but the one which, in the circumstances in which it is practicable and eligible, is attended with the greatest amount of beneficial consequences, immediate and prospective. A completely popular government is the only polity which can make out any claim to this character. It is pre-eminent in both the departments between which the excellence of a political constitution is divided. It is both more

From John Stuart Mill, 'Considerations on Representative Government', in J. S. Mill, *Three Essays* (Oxford University Press, Oxford, London and New York, 1975), chapter III, pp. 186–98. Originally written 1861.

favourable to present good government, and promotes a better and higher form of national character, than any other polity whatsoever.

Its superiority in reference to present well-being rests upon two principles, of as universal truth and applicability as any general propositions which can be laid down respecting human affairs. The first is, that the rights and interests of every or any person are only secure from being disregarded, when the person interested is himself able, and habitually disposed, to stand up for them. The second is, that the general prosperity attains a greater height, and is more widely diffused, in proportion to the amount and variety of the personal energies enlisted in promoting it.

Putting these two propositions into a shape more special to their present application; human beings are only secure from evil at the hands of others, in proportion as they have the power of being, and are, self-*protecting*; and they only achieve a high degree of success in their struggle with Nature, in proportion as they are self-*dependent*, relying on what they themselves can do, either separately or in concert, rather than on what others do for them.

The former proposition – that each is the only safe guardian of his own rights and interests – is one of those elementary maxims of prudence, which every person, capable of conducting his own affairs, implicitly acts upon, wherever he himself is interested. Many, indeed, have a great dislike to it as a political doctrine, and are fond of holding it up to obloquy, as a doctrine of universal selfishness. To which we may answer, that whenever it ceases to be true that mankind, as a rule, prefer themselves to others, and those nearest to them to those more remote, from that moment Communism is not only practicable, but the only defensible form of society; and will, when that time arrives, be assuredly carried into effect. For my own part, not believing in universal selfishness, I have no difficulty in admitting that Communism would even now be practicable among the *élite* of mankind, and may become so among the rest. But as this opinion is anything but popular with those defenders of existing institutions who find fault with the doctrine of the general predominance of self-interest, I am inclined to think they do in reality believe, that most men consider themselves before other people. It is not, however, necessary to affirm even thus much, in order to support the claim of all to participate in the sovereign power. We need not suppose that when power resides in an exclusive class, that class will knowingly and deliberately sacrifice the other classes to themselves: it suffices that, in the absence of its natural defenders, the interest of the excluded is always in danger of being overlooked; and, when looked at, is seen with very different eyes from those of the persons whom it directly concerns. In this country, for example, what are called the working classes may be considered as excluded from all direct participation in the government. I do not believe that the classes who do participate in it, have in general any intention of sacrificing the working classes to themselves. They once had that intention; witness the persevering attempts so long made to keep down wages by law. But in the present day, their ordinary disposition is the very opposite: they willingly make considerable sacrifices, especially of their pecuniary interest, for the benefit of the working classes, and err rather by too lavish and indiscriminating beneficence; nor do I believe that any rulers in history have been actuated by a more sincere desire to do their duty towards the poorer portion of their countrymen. Yet does Parliament, or almost any of the members composing it, ever for an instant look at any question with the eyes of a working man? When a subject arises in which the labourers as such have an interest, is it regarded from any point of view but that of the employers of labour? I do not say that the working men's view of these questions is in general nearer to the truth than the other: but it is sometimes quite as near; and in any case it ought to be respectfully listened to, instead of being, as it is, not merely turned away from, but ignored. On the question of strikes, for instance, it is doubtful if there is so much as one among the leading members of either House, who is not firmly convinced that the reason of the matter is unqualifiedly on the side of the masters, and that the men's view of it is simply absurd. Those who have studied the question, know well how far this is from being the case; and in how different, and how infinitely less superficial a manner the point would have to be argued, if the classes who strike were able to make themselves heard in Parliament.

It is an inherent condition of human affairs, that no intention, however sincere, of protecting the interests of others, can make it safe or salutary to tie up their own hands. Still more obviously true is it, that by their own hands only can any positive and durable improvement of their circumstances in life be worked out. Through the joint influence of these two principles, all free communities have both been more exempt from social injustice and crime, and have attained more brilliant prosperity, than any others, or than they themselves after they lost their freedom. Contrast the free states of the world, while their freedom lasted, with the cotemporary subjects of monarchical or oligarchical despotism: the Greek cities with the Persian satrapies; the Italian republics, and the free towns of Flanders and Germany, with the feudal monarchies of Europe; Switzerland, Holland, and England, with Austria or ante-revolutionary France. Their superior prosperity was too obvious ever to have been gainsaid: while their superiority in good government and social relations, is proved by the prosperity, and is manifest besides in every page of history. If we compare, not one age with another, but the different governments which coexisted in the same age, no amount of disorder which exaggeration itself can pretend to have existed amidst the publicity of the free states, can be compared for a moment with the contemptuous trampling upon the mass of the people which pervaded the whole life of the monarchical countries, or the disgusting individual tyranny which was of more than daily occurrence under the systems of plunder which they called fiscal arrangements, and in the secrecy of their frightful courts of justice.

It must be acknowledged that the benefits of freedom, so far as they have hitherto been enjoyed, were obtained by the extension of its privileges to a part only of the community; and that a government in which they are extended impartially to all is a desideratum still unrealized. But though every approach to this has an independent value, and in many cases more than an approach could not, in the existing state of general improvement, be made, the participation of all in these benefits is the ideally perfect conception of free government. In proportion as any, no matter who, are excluded from it, the interests of the excluded are left without the guarantee accorded to the rest, and they themselves have less scope and encouragement than they might otherwise have to that exertion of their energies for the good of themselves and of the community, to which the general prosperity is always proportioned.

Thus stands the case as regards present well-being; the good management of the affairs of the existing generation. If we now pass to the influence of the form of government upon character, we shall find the superiority of popular government over every other to be, if possible, still more decided and indisputable.

This question really depends upon a still more fundamental one – viz. which of two common types of character, for the general good of humanity, it is most desirable should predominate – the active, or the passive type; that which struggles against evils, or that which endures them; that which bends to circumstances, or that which endeavours to make circumstances bend to itself.

The commonplaces of moralists, and the general sympathies of mankind, are in favour of the passive type. Energetic characters may be admired, but the acquiescent and submissive are those which most men personally prefer. The passiveness of our neighbours increases our sense of security, and plays into the hands of our wilfulness. Passive characters, if we do not happen to need their activity, seem an obstruction the less in our own path. A contented character is not a dangerous rival. Yet nothing is more certain, than that improvement in human affairs is wholly the work of the uncontented characters; and, moreover, that it is much easier for an active mind to acquire the virtues of patience, than for a passive one to assume those of energy.

Of the three varieties of mental excellence, intellectual, practical, and moral, there never could be any doubt in regard to the first two, which side had the advantage. All intellectual superiority is the fruit of active effort. Enterprise, the desire to keep moving, to be trying and accomplishing new things for our own benefit or that of others, is the parent even of speculative, and much more of practical, talent. The intellectual culture compatible with the other type is of that feeble and vague description, which belongs to a mind that stops at amusement, or at simple contemplation. The test of real and vigorous thinking, the thinking which ascertains truths instead of dreaming dreams, is successful application to practice. Where that purpose does not exist, to give definiteness, precision, and an intelligible meaning to thought, it generates nothing better than the mystical metaphysics of the Pythagoreans or the Vedas. With respect to practical improvement, the case is still more evident. The character which improves human life is that which struggles with natural powers and tendencies, not that which gives way to them. The self-benefiting qualities are all on the side of the active and energetic character: and the habits and conduct which promote the advantage of each individual member of the community, must be at least a part of those which conduce most in the end to the advancement of the community as a whole.

But on the point of moral preferability, there seems at first sight to be room for doubt. I am not referring to the religious feeling which has so generally existed in favour of the inactive character, as being more in harmony with the submission due to the divine will. Christianity as well as other religions has fostered this sentiment; but it is the prerogative of Christianity, as regards this and many other perversions, that it is able to throw them off. Abstractedly from religious considerations, a passive character, which yields to obstacles instead of striving to overcome them, may not indeed be very useful to others, no more than to itself, but it might be expected to be at least inoffensive. Contentment is always counted among the moral virtues. But it is a complete error to suppose that contentment is necessarily or naturally attendant on passivity of character; and unless it is, the moral consequences are mischievous. Where there exists a desire for advantages not possessed, the mind which does not potentially possess them by means of its own energies, is apt to look with hatred and malice on those who do. The person bestirring himself with hopeful prospects to improve his circumstances, is the one who feels goodwill towards others engaged in, or who have succeeded in, the same pursuit. And where the majority are so engaged, those who do not attain the object have had the tone given to their feelings by the general habit of the country, and ascribe their failure to want of effort or opportunity, or to their personal ill luck. But those who, while desiring what others possess, put no energy into striving for it, are either incessantly grumbling that fortune does not do for them what they do not attempt to do for themselves, or overflowing with envy and ill-will towards those who possess what they would like to have.

In proportion as success in life is seen or believed to be the fruit of fatality or accident, and not of exertion, in that same ratio does envy develop itself as a point of national character. The most envious of all mankind are the Orientals. In Oriental moralists, in Oriental tales, the envious man is remarkably prominent. In real life, he is the terror of all who possess anything desirable, be it a palace, a handsome child, or even good health and spirits: the supposed effect of his mere look constitutes the all-pervading superstition of the evil eye. Next to Orientals in envy, as in activity, are some of the Southern Europeans. The Spaniards pursued all their great men with it, embittered their lives, and generally succeeded in putting an early stop to their successes.[1] With the French, who are essentially a southern people, the double education of despotism and Catholicism has, in spite of their impulsive temperament, made submission and endurance the common character of the people, and their most received notion of wisdom and excellence: and if envy of one another, and of all superiority, is not more rife among them than it is, the circumstance must be ascribed to the many valuable counteracting elements in the French character, and most of all to the great individual energy which, though less persistent and more intermittent than in the self-helping and struggling Anglo-Saxons, has nevertheless manifested itself among the French in nearly every direction in which the operation of their institutions has been favourable to it.

There are, no doubt, in all countries, really contented characters, who not merely do not seek, but do not desire, what they do not already possess, and these naturally bear no ill-will towards such as have apparently a more favoured lot. But the great mass of seeming contentment is real discontent, combined with indolence or self-indulgence, which, while taking no legitimate means of raising itself, delights in bringing others down to its own level. And if we look narrowly even at the cases of innocent contentment, we perceive that they only win our admiration, when the indifference is solely to improvement in outward circumstances, and there is a striving for perpetual advancement in spiritual worth, or at least a disinterested zeal to benefit others. The contented man, or the contented family, who have no ambition to make any one else happier, to promote the good of their country or their neighbourhood, or to improve themselves in moral excellence, excite in us neither admiration nor approval. We rightly ascribe this sort of contentment to mere unmanliness and want of spirit. The content which we approve, is an ability to do cheerfully without what cannot be had, a just appreciation of the comparative value of different objects of desire, and a willing renunciation of the less when incompatible with the greater. These, however, are excellences more natural to the character, in proportion as it is actively engaged in the attempt to improve its own or some other lot. He who is continually measuring his energy against difficulties, learns what are the difficulties insuperable to him, and what are those which though he might overcome, the success is not worth the cost. He whose thoughts and activities are all needed for, and habitually employed in, practicable and useful enterprises, is the person of all others least likely to let his mind dwell with brooding discontent upon things either not worth attaining, or which are not so to him. Thus the active, self-helping character is not only intrinsically the best, but is the likeliest to acquire all that is really excellent or desirable in the opposite type.

The striving, go-ahead character of England and the United States is only a fit subject of disapproving criticism, on account of the very secondary objects on which it commonly expends its strength. In itself it is the foundation of the best hopes for the general improvement of mankind. It has been acutely remarked, that whenever anything goes amiss, the habitual impulse of French people is to say, 'Il faut de la patience;' and of English people, 'What a shame.' The people who think it a shame when anything goes wrong – who rush to the conclusion that the evil could and ought to have been prevented, are those who, in the long run, do most to make the world better. If the desires are low placed, if they extend to little beyond physical comfort and the show of riches, the immediate results of the energy will not be much more than the continual extension of man's power over material objects; but even this makes room, and prepares the mechanical appliances, for the greatest intellectual and social achievements;

and while the energy is there, some persons will apply it, and it will be applied more and more, to the perfecting not of outward circumstances alone, but of man's inward nature. Inactivity, unaspiringness, absence of desire, are a more fatal hindrance to improvement than any misdirection of energy; and are that through which alone, when existing in the mass, any very formidable misdirection by an energetic few becomes possible. It is this, mainly, which retains in a savage or semi-savage state the great majority of the human race.

Now there can be no kind of doubt that the passive type of character is favoured by the government of one or a few, and the active self-helping type by that of the Many. Irresponsible rulers need the quiescence of the ruled, more than they need any activity but that which they can compel. Submissiveness to the prescriptions of men as necessities of nature, is the lesson inculcated by all governments upon those who are wholly without participation in them. The will of superiors, and the law as the will of superiors, must be passively yielded to. But no men are mere instruments or materials in the hands of their rulers, who have will or spirit or a spring of internal activity in the rest of their proceedings: and any manifestation of these qualities, instead of receiving encouragement from despots, has to get itself forgiven by them. Even when irresponsible rulers are not sufficiently conscious of danger from the mental activity of their subjects to be desirous of repressing it, the position itself is a repression. Endeavour is even more effectually restrained by the certainty of its impotence, than by any positive discouragement. Between subjection to the will of others, and the virtues of self-help and self-government, there is a natural incompatibility. This is more or less complete, according as the bondage is strained or relaxed. Rulers differ very much in the length to which they carry the control of the free agency of their subjects, or the supersession of it by managing their business for them. But the difference is in degree, not in principle; and the best despots often go the greatest lengths in chaining up the free agency of their subjects. A bad despot, when his own personal indulgences have been provided for, may sometimes be willing to let the people alone; but a good despot insists on doing them good, by making them do their own business in a better way than they themselves know of. The regulations which restricted to fixed processes all the leading branches of French manufactures, were the work of the great Colbert.

Very different is the state of the human faculties where a human being feels himself under no other external restraint than the necessities of nature, or mandates of society which he has his share in imposing, and which it is open to him, if he thinks them wrong, publicly to dissent from, and exert himself actively to get altered. No doubt, under a government partially popular, this freedom may be exercised even by those who are not partakers in the full privileges of citizenship. But it is a great additional stimulus to any one's self-help and self-reliance when he starts from even ground, and has not to feel that his success depends on the impression he can make upon the sentiments and dispositions of a body of whom he is not one. It is a great discouragement to an individual, and a still greater one to a class, to be left out of the constitution; to be reduced to plead from outside the door to the arbiters of their destiny, not taken into consultation within. The maximum of the invigorating effect of freedom upon the character is only obtained, when the person acted on either is, or is looking forward to becoming, a citizen as fully privileged as any other. What is still more important than even this matter of feeling, is the practical discipline which the character obtains, from the occasional demand made upon the citizens to exercise, for a time and in their turn, some social function. It is not sufficiently considered how little there is in most men's ordinary life to give any largeness either to their conceptions or to their sentiments. Their work is a routine; not a labour of love, but of self-interest in the most elementary form, the satisfaction of daily wants; neither the thing done, nor the process of doing it, introduces the mind to thoughts or feelings extending beyond individuals; if instructive books are within their reach, there is no stimulus to read them; and in most cases the individual has no access to any person of cultivation much superior to his own. Giving him something to do for the public, supplies, in a measure, all these deficiencies. If circumstances allow the amount of public duty assigned him to be considerable, it makes him an educated man. Notwithstanding the defects of the social system and moral ideas of antiquity, the practice of the dicastery and the ecclesia raised the intellectual standard of an average Athenian citizen far beyond anything of which there is yet an example in any other mass of men, ancient or modern. The proofs of this are apparent in every page of our great historian of Greece; but we need scarcely look further than to the high quality of the addresses which their great orators deemed best calculated to act with effect on their understanding and will. A benefit of the same kind, though far less in degree, is produced on Englishmen of the lower middle class by their liability to be placed on juries and to serve parish offices; which, though it does not occur to so many, nor is so continuous, nor introduces them to so great a variety of elevated considerations, as to admit of comparison with the public education which every citizen of Athens obtained from her democratic institutions, must make them nevertheless very different beings, in range of ideas and development of faculties, from those who have done nothing in their lives but drive a quill, or sell goods over a counter. Still more salutary is the moral part of the instruction afforded by the participation of the private citizen, if even rarely, in public functions. He is called upon, while so engaged, to weigh interests not his own; to be guided, in case of conflicting claims, by another rule than his private partialities; to apply, at every turn, principles and maxims which have for their reason of existence the common good: and he usually finds associated with him in the same work minds more familiarized than his own with these ideas and operations, whose study it will be to supply reasons to his understanding, and stimulation to his feeling for the general interest. He is made to feel himself one of the public, and whatever is for their benefit to be for his benefit. Where this school of public spirit does not exist, scarcely any sense is entertained that private persons, in no eminent social situation, owe any duties to society, except to obey the laws and submit to the government. There is no unselfish sentiment of identification with the public. Every thought or feeling, either of interest or of duty, is absorbed in the individual and in the family. The man never thinks of any collective interest, of any objects to be pursued jointly with others, but only in competition with them, and in some measure at their expense. A neighbour, not being an ally or an associate, since he is never engaged in any common undertaking for joint benefit, is therefore only a rival. Thus even private morality suffers, while public is actually extinct. Were this the universal and only possible state of things, the utmost aspirations of the lawgiver or the moralist could only stretch to making the bulk of the community a flock of sheep innocently nibbling the grass side by side.

From these accumulated considerations it is evident, that the only government which can fully satisfy all the exigencies of the social state, is one in which the whole people participate; that any participation, even in the smallest public function, is useful; that the participation should everywhere be as great as the general degree of improvement of the community will allow; and that nothing less can be ultimately desirable, than the admission of all to a share in the sovereign power of the state. But since all cannot, in a community exceeding a single small town, participate personally in any but some very minor portions of the public business, it follows that the ideal type of a perfect government must be representative.

[...]

NOTE

1. I limit the expression to past time, because I would say nothing derogatory of a great, and now at last a free, people, who are entering into the general movement of European progress with a vigour which bids fair to make up rapidly the ground they have lost. No one can doubt what Spanish intellect and energy are capable of; and their faults as a people are chiefly those for which freedom and industrial ardour are a real specific.

# 8

# DEMOCRACY IN AMERICA

## Alexis de Tocqueville

### Author's Introduction

No novelty in the United States struck me more vividly during my stay there than the equality of conditions. It was easy to see the immense influence of this basic fact on the whole course of society. It gives a particular turn to public opinion and a particular twist to the laws, new maxims to those who govern and particular habits to the governed.

I soon realized that the influence of this fact extends far beyond political mores and laws, exercising dominion over civil society as much as over the government; it creates opinions, gives birth to feelings, suggests customs, and modifies whatever it does not create.

So the more I studied American society, the more clearly I saw equality of conditions as the creative element from which each particular fact derived, and all my observations constantly returned to this nodal point.

Later, when I came to consider our own side of the Atlantic, I thought I could detect something analogous to what I had noticed in the New World. I saw an equality of conditions which, though it had not reached the extreme limits found in the United States, was daily drawing closer thereto; and that same democracy which prevailed over the societies of America seemed to me to be advancing rapidly toward power in Europe.

It was at that moment that I conceived the idea of this book.

From Alexis de Tocqueville, *Democracy in America*, trans. G. Lawrence, eds J. P. Mayer and Max Lerner (Harper & Row, New York, 1966; Collins/Fontana Library, London, 1968), Vol. I, pp. 9–19. Originally written 1835.

A great democratic revolution is taking place in our midst; everybody sees it, but by no means everybody judges it in the same way. Some think it a new thing and, supposing it an accident, hope that they can still check it; others think it irresistible, because it seems to them the most continuous, ancient, and permanent tendency known to history.

I should like for a moment to consider the state of France seven hundred years ago; at that time it was divided up between a few families who owned the land and ruled the inhabitants. At that time the right to give orders descended, like real property, from generation to generation; the only means by which men controlled each other was force; there was only one source of power, namely, landed property.

But then the political power of the clergy began to take shape and soon to extend. The ranks of the clergy were open to all, poor or rich, commoner or noble; through the church, equality began to insinuate itself into the heart of government, and a man who would have vegetated as a serf in eternal servitude could, as a priest, take his place among the nobles and often take precedence over kings.

As society became more stable and civilized, men's relations with one another became more numerous and complicated. Hence the need for civil laws was vividly felt, and the lawyers soon left their obscure tribunals and dusty chambers to appear at the king's court side by side with feudal barons dressed in chain mail and ermine.

While kings were ruining themselves in great enterprises and nobles wearing each other out in private wars, the commoners were growing rich by trade. The power of money began to be felt in affairs of state. Trade became a new way of gaining power and financiers became a political force, despised but flattered.

Gradually enlightenment spread, and a taste for literature and the arts awoke. The mind became an element in success; knowledge became a tool of government and intellect a social force; educated men played a part in affairs of state.

In proportion as new roads to power were found, the value of birth decreased. In the eleventh century, nobility was something of inestimable worth; in the thirteenth it could be bought; the first ennoblement took place in 1270, and equality was finally introduced into the government through the aristocracy itself.

During the last seven hundred years it has sometimes happened that, to combat the royal authority or dislodge rivals from power, nobles have given the people some political weight.

Even more often we find kings giving the lower classes in the state a share in government in order to humble the aristocracy.

In France the kings proved the most active and consistent of levelers. When they were strong and ambitious they tried to raise the people to the level of the nobles, and when they were weak and diffident they allowed the people to push past them. The former monarchs helped democracy by their talents, the latter by their vices. Louis XI and Louis XIV were at pains to level everyone below the throne, and finally Louis XV with all his court descended into the dust.

As soon as citizens began to hold land otherwise than by feudal tenure, and the newly discovered possibilities of personal property could also lead to influence and power, every invention in the arts and every improvement in trade and industry created fresh elements tending toward equality among men. Henceforward every new invention, every new need occasioned thereby, and every new desire craving satisfaction were steps towards a general leveling. The taste for luxury, the love of war, the dominion of fashion, all the most superficial and profound passions of the human heart, seemed to work together to impoverish the rich and enrich the poor.

Once the work of the mind had become a source of power and wealth, every addition to knowledge, every fresh discovery, and every new idea became a germ of power within reach of the people. Poetry, eloquence, memory, the graces of the mind, the fires of the imagination and profundity of thought, all things scattered broadcast by heaven, were a profit to democracy, and even when it was the adversaries of democracy who possessed these things, they still served its cause by throwing into relief the natural greatness of man. Thus its conquests spread along with those of civilization and enlightenment, and literature was an arsenal from which all, including the weak and poor, daily chose their weapons.

Running through the pages of our history, there is hardly an important event in the last seven hundred years which has not turned out to be advantageous for equality.

The Crusades and the English wars decimated the nobles and divided up their lands. Municipal institutions introduced democratic liberty into the heart of the feudal monarchy; the invention of firearms made villein and noble equal on the field of battle; printing offered equal resources to their minds; the post brought enlightenment to hovel and palace alike; Protestantism maintained that all men are equally able to find the path to heaven. America, once discovered, opened a thousand new roads to fortune and gave any obscure adventurer the chance of wealth and power.

If, beginning at the eleventh century, one takes stock of what was happening in France at fifty-year intervals, one finds each time that a double revolution has taken place in the state of society. The noble has gone down in the social scale, and the commoner gone up; as the one falls, the other rises. Each half century brings them closer, and soon they will touch.

And that is not something peculiar to France. Wherever one looks one finds the same revolution taking place throughout the Christian world.

Everywhere the diverse happenings in the lives of peoples have turned to democracy's profit; all men's efforts have aided it, both those who intended this and those who had no such intention, those who fought for democracy and those who were the declared enemies thereof; all have been driven pell-mell along the same road, and all have worked together, some against their will and some unconsciously, blind instruments in the hands of God.

Therefore the gradual progress of equality is something fated. The main features of this progress are the following: it is universal and permanent, it is daily passing beyond human control, and every event and every man helps it along. Is it wise to suppose that a movement which has been so long in train could be halted by one generation? Does anyone imagine that democracy, which has destroyed the feudal system and vanquished kings, will fall back before the middle classes and the rich? Will it stop now, when it has grown so strong and its adversaries so weak?

Whither, then, are we going? No one can tell, for already terms of comparison are lacking; in Christian lands now conditions are nearer equality than they have ever been before at any time or in any place; hence the magnitude of present achievement makes it impossible to forecast what may still be done.

This whole book has been written under the impulse of a kind of religious dread inspired by contemplation of this irresistible revolution advancing century by century over every obstacle and even now going forward amid the ruins it has itself created.

God does not Himself need to speak for us to find sure signs of His will; it is enough to observe the customary progress of nature and the continuous tendency of events; I know, without special revelation, that the stars follow orbits in space traced by His finger.

If patient observation and sincere meditation have led men of the present day to recognize that both the past and the future of their history consist in the gradual and measured advance of equality, that discovery in itself gives this progress the sacred character of the will of the Sovereign Master. In that case effort to halt democracy appears as a fight against God Himself, and nations have no alternative but to acquiesce in the social state imposed by Providence.

To me the Christian nations of our day present an alarming spectacle; the movement which carries them along is already too strong to be halted, but it is not yet so swift that we must despair of directing it; our fate is in our hands, but soon it may pass beyond control.

The first duty imposed on those who now direct society is to educate democracy; to put, if possible, new life into its beliefs; to purify its mores; to control its actions; gradually to substitute understanding of statecraft for present inexperience and knowledge of its true interests for blind instincts; to adapt government to the needs of time and place; and to modify it as men and circumstances require.

A new political science is needed for a world itself quite new.

But it is just that to which we give least attention. Carried away by a rapid current, we obstinately keep our eyes fixed on the ruins still in sight on the bank, while the stream whirls us backward – facing toward the abyss.

This great social revolution has made more rapid progress with us than with any other nation of Europe, but the progress has always been haphazard.

The leaders of the state have never thought of making any preparation by anticipation for it. The progress has been against their will or without their knowledge. The most powerful, intelligent, and moral classes of the nation have never sought to gain control of it in order to direct it. Hence democracy has been left to its wild instincts; it has grown up like those children deprived of parental care who school themselves in our town streets and know nothing of society but its vices and wretchedness. Men would seem still unaware of its existence, when suddenly it has seized power. Then all submit like slaves to its least desires; it is worshiped as the idol of strength; thereafter, when it has been weakened by its own excesses, the lawgivers conceive the imprudent project of abolishing it instead of trying to educate and correct it, and without any wish to teach it how to rule, they only strive to drive it out of the government.

As a result the democratic revolution has taken place in the body of society without those changes in laws, ideas, customs, and mores which were needed to make that revolution profitable. Hence we have our democracy without those elements which might have mitigated its vices and brought out its natural good points. While we can already see the ills it entails, we are as yet unaware of the benefits it might bring.

When royal power supported by aristocracies governed the nations of Europe in peace, society, despite all its wretchedness, enjoyed several types of happiness which are difficult to appreciate or conceive today.

The power of some subjects raised insuperable obstacles to the tyranny of the prince. The kings, feeling that in the eyes of the crowd they were clothed in almost divine majesty, derived, from the very extent of the respect they inspired, a motive for not abusing their power.

The nobles, placed so high above the people, could take the calm and benevolent interest in their welfare which a shepherd takes in his flock. Without regarding the poor as equals, they took thought for their fate as a trust confided to them by Providence.

Having never conceived the possibility of a social state other than the one they knew, and never expecting to become equal to their leaders, the people accepted benefits from their hands and did not question their rights. They loved them when they were just and merciful and felt neither repugnance nor degradation in submitting to their severities, which seemed inevitable ills sent by God. Furthermore, custom and mores had set some limits to tyranny and established a sort of law in the very midst of force.

Because it never entered the noble's head that anyone wanted to snatch away privileges which he regarded as legitimate, and since the serf considered his inferiority as an effect of the immutable order of nature, one can see that a sort of goodwill could be established between these two classes so differently favored by fortune. At that time one found inequality and wretchedness in society, but men's souls were not degraded thereby.

It is not exercise of power or habits of obedience which deprave men, but the exercise of a power which they consider illegitimate and obedience to a power which they think usurped and oppressive.

On the one side were wealth, strength, and leisure combined with farfetched luxuries, refinements of taste, the pleasures of the mind, and the cultivation of the arts; on the other, work, coarseness, and ignorance.

But among this coarse and ignorant crowd lively passions, generous feelings, deep beliefs, and untamed virtues were found.

The body social thus ordered could lay claim to stability, strength, and above all, glory.

But distinctions of rank began to get confused, and the barriers separating men to get lower. Great estates were broken up, power shared, education spread, and intellectual capacities became more equal. The social state became democratic, and the sway of democracy was finally peacefully established in institutions and in mores.

At that stage one can imagine a society in which all men, regarding the law as their common work, would love it and and submit to it without difficulty; the authority of the government would be respected as necessary, not as sacred; the love felt toward the head of the state would be not a passion but a calm and rational feeling. Each man having some rights and being sure of the enjoyment of those rights, there would be established between all classes a manly confidence and a sort of reciprocal courtesy, as far removed from pride as from servility.

Understanding its own interests, the people would appreciate that in order to enjoy the benefits of society one must shoulder its obligations. Free association of the citizens could then take the place of the individual authority of the nobles and the state would be protected both from tyranny and from license.

I appreciate that in a democracy so constituted society would not be at all immobile; but the movements inside the body social could be orderly and progressive; one might find less glory there than in an aristocracy, but there would be less wretchedness; pleasures would be less extreme, but well-being more general; the heights of knowledge might not be scaled, but ignorance would be less common; feelings would be less passionate, and manners gentler; there would be more vices and fewer crimes.

Without enthusiasm or the zeal of belief, education and experience would sometimes induce the citizens to make great sacrifices; each man being equally weak would feel a like need for the help of his companions, and knowing that he would not get their support without supplying his, he would easily appreciate that for him private interest was mixed up with public interest.

The nation as a body would be less brilliant, less glorious, and perhaps less strong, but the majority of the citizens would enjoy a more prosperous lot, and the people would be pacific not from despair of anything better but from knowing itself to be well-off.

Though all would not be good and useful in such a system of things, society would at least have appropriated all that it could of the good and useful; and men, by giving up forever the social advantages offered by aristocracy, would have taken from democracy all the good things that it can provide.

But in abandoning our ancestors' social state and throwing their institutions, ideas, and mores pell-mell behind us, what have we put in their place?

The prestige of the royal power has vanished but has not been replaced by the majesty of the law; nowadays the people despise authority but fear it, and more is dragged from them by fear than was formerly granted through respect and love.

I notice that we have destroyed those individual powers which were able singlehanded to cope with tryanny, but I see that it is the government alone which has inherited all the prerogatives snatched from families, corporations, and individuals; so the sometimes oppressive but often conservative strength of a small number of citizens has been succeeded by the weakness of all.

The breakup of fortunes has diminished the distance between rich and poor, but while bringing them closer, it seems to have provided them with new reasons for hating each other, so that with mutual fear and envy they rebuff each other's claims to power. Neither has any conception of rights, and for both force is the only argument in the present or guarantee for the future.

The poor have kept most of the prejudices of their fathers without their beliefs, their ignorance without their virtues; they accept the doctrine of self-interest as motive for action without understanding that doctrine; and their egotism is now as unenlightened as their devotion was formerly.

Society is tranquil, but the reason for that is not that it knows its strength and its good fortune, but rather that it thinks itself weak and feeble; it fears that a single effort may cost its life; each man feels what is wrong, but none has the courage or energy needed to seek something better; men have desires, regrets, sorrows, and joys which produce no visible or durable result, like old men's passions ending in impotence.

Thus we have abandoned whatever good things the old order of society could provide but have not profited from what our present state can offer; we have destroyed an aristocratic society, and settling down complacently among the ruins of the old building, we seem to want to stay there like that forever.

What is now taking place in the world of the mind is just as deplorable.

French democracy, sometimes hindered in its progress and at others left uncontrolled to its disorderly passions, has overthrown everything it found in its path, shaking all that it did not destroy. It has not slowly gained control of society in order peacefully to establish its sway; on the contrary, its progress has ever been amid the disorders and agitations of conflict. In the heat of the struggle each partisan is driven beyond the natural limits of his own views by the views and the excesses of his adversaries, loses sight of the very aim he was pursuing, and uses language which ill corresponds to his real feelings and to his secret instincts.

Hence arises that strange confusion which we are forced to witness.

I search my memory in vain, and find nothing sadder or more pitiable than that which happens before our eyes; it would seem that we have nowadays broken the natural link between opinions and tastes, acts and beliefs; that harmony which has been observed throughout history between the feelings and the ideas of men seems to have been destroyed, and one might suppose that all the laws of moral analogy had been abolished.

There are still zealous Christians among us who draw spiritual nourishment from the truths of the other life and who no doubt will readily espouse the cause of human liberty as the source of all moral greatness. Christianity, which has declared all men equal in the sight of God, cannot hesitate to acknowledge all citizens equal before the law. But by a strange concatenation of events, religion for the moment has become entangled with those institutions which democracy overthrows, and so it is often brought to rebuff the equality which it loves and to abuse freedom as its adversary, whereas by taking it by the hand it could sanctify its striving.

Alongside these religious men I find others whose eyes are turned more to the earth than to heaven; partisans of freedom, not only because they see in it the origin of the most noble virtues, but even more because they think it the source of the greatest benefits, they sincerely wish to assure its sway and allow men to taste its blessings. I think these latter should hasten to call religion to their aid, for they must know that one cannot establish the reign of liberty without that of mores, and mores cannot be firmly founded without beliefs. But they have seen religion in the ranks of their adversaries, and that is enough for them; some of them openly attack it, and the others do not dare to defend it.

In past ages we have seen low, venal minds advocating slavery, while independent, generous hearts struggled hopelessly to defend human freedom. But now one often meets naturally proud and noble men whose opinions are in direct opposition to their tastes and who vaunt that servility and baseness which they themselves have never known. Others, on the contrary, speak of freedom as if they could feel its great and sacred quality and noisily claim for humanity rights which they themselves have always scorned.

I also see gentle and virtuous men whose pure mores, quiet habits, opulence, and talents fit them to be leaders of those who dwell around them. Full of sincere patriotism, they would make great sacrifices for their country; nonetheless they are often adversaries of civilization; they confound its abuses with its benefits; and in their minds the idea of evil is indissolubly linked with that of novelty.

Besides these, there are others whose object is to make men materialists, to find out what is useful without concern for justice, to have science quite without belief and prosperity without virtue. Such men are called champions of modern civilization, and they insolently put themselves at its head, usurping a place which has been abandoned to them, though they are utterly unworthy of it.

Where are we, then?

Men of religion fight against freedom, and lovers of liberty attack religions; noble and generous spirits praise slavery, while low, servile minds preach independence; honest and enlightened citizens are the enemies of all progress, while men without patriotism or morals make themselves the apostles of civilization and enlightenment!

Have all ages been like ours? And have men always dwelt in a world in which nothing is connected? Where virtue is without genius, and genius without honor? Where love of order is confused with a tyrant's tastes, and the sacred cult of freedom is taken as scorn of law? Where conscience sheds but doubtful light on human actions? Where nothing any longer seems either forbidden or permitted, honest or dishonorable, true or false?

Am I to believe that the Creator made man in order to let him struggle endlessly through the intellectual squalor now surrounding us? I cannot believe that; God intends a calmer and more stable future for the peoples of Europe; I do not know His designs but shall not give up believing therein because I cannot fathom them, and should prefer to doubt my own understanding rather than His justice.

There is one country in the world in which this great social revolution seems almost to have reached its natural limits; it took place in a simple, easy fashion, or rather one might say that that country sees the results of the democratic revolution taking place among us, without experiencing the revolution itself.

The emigrants who colonized America at the beginning of the seventeenth century in some way separated the principle of democracy from all those other principles against which they contended when living in the heart of the old European societies, and transplanted that principle only on the shores of the New World. It could there grow in freedom and, progressing in conformity with mores, develop peacefully within the law.

It seems to me beyond doubt that sooner or later we, like the Americans, will attain almost complete equality of conditions. But I certainly do not draw from that the conclusion that we are necessarily destined one day to derive the same political consequences as the Americans from the similar social state. I am very far from believing that they have found the only form possible for democratic government; it is enough that the creative source of laws and mores is the same in the two countries, for each of us to have a profound interest in knowing what the other is doing.

So I did not study America just to satisfy curiosity, however legitimate; I sought there lessons from which we might profit. Anyone who supposes that I intend to write a panegyric is strangely mistaken; any who read this book will see that that was not my intention at all; nor have I aimed to advocate such a form of government in general, for I am one of those who think that there is hardly ever absolute right in any laws; I have not even claimed to judge whether the progress of the social revolution, which I consider irresistible is profitable or prejudicial for mankind. I accept that revolution as an accomplished fact, or a fact that soon will be accomplished, and I selected of all the peoples experiencing it that nation in which it has come to the fullest and most peaceful completion, in order to see its natural consequences clearly, and if possible, to turn it to the profit of mankind. I admit that I saw in America more than America; it was the shape of democracy itself which I sought, its inclinations, character, prejudices, and passions; I wanted to understand it so as at least to know what we have to fear or hope therefrom.

Therefore, in the first part of this book I have endeavored to show the natural turn given to the laws by democracy when left in America to its own inclinations with hardly any restraint on its instincts, and to show its stamp on the government and its influence on affairs in general. I wanted to know what blessings and what ills it brings forth. I have inquired into the precautions taken by the Americans to direct it, and noticed those others which they have neglected, and I have aimed to point out the factors which enable it to govern society.

I had intended in a second part to describe the influence in America of equality of conditions and government by democracy upon civil society, customs, ideas, and mores, but my urge to carry out this plan has cooled off. Before I could finish this self-imposed task, it would have become almost useless. Another author is soon to portray the main characteristics of the American people and, casting a thin veil over the seriousness of his purpose, give to truth charms I could not rival.

[...]

# 9

# THE PUTNEY DEBATES

[...]

*Rainborough:* I desired that those that had engaged in it [might be included]. For really I think that the poorest he that is in England hath a life to live, as the greatest he; and therefore truly, sir, I think it's clear, that every man that is to live under a government ought first by his own consent to put himself under that government; and I do think that the poorest man in England is not at all bound in a strict sense to that government that he hath not had a voice to put himself under; and I am confident that, when I have heard the reasons against it, something will be said to answer those reasons, insomuch that I should doubt whether he was an Englishman or no, that should doubt of these things.

*Ireton:* That's [the meaning of] this, ['according to the number of the inhabitants']?

Give me leave to tell you, that if you make this the rule I think you must fly for refuge to an absolute natural right, and you must deny all civil right; and I am sure it will come to that in the consequence. This, I perceive, is pressed as that which is so essential and due: the right of the people of this kingdom, and as they are the people of this kingdom, distinct and divided from other people, and that we must for this right lay aside all other considerations; this is so just, this is so due, this is so right to them. And that those that they do thus choose must have

From *Puritanism and Liberty. Being the Army Debates (1647–9) from the Clarke Manuscripts with Supplementary Documents*, selected, edited and introduction by A. S. P. Woodhouse, 2nd edn (J. M. Dent & Sons, London, 1974; simultaneous publication by the University of Chicago Press, Chicago, 1974), pp. 33–58. Originally written 1647.

such a power of binding all, and loosing all, according to those limitations, this is pressed as so due, and so just, as [it] is argued, that it is an engagement paramount [to] all others: and you must for it lay aside all others; if you have engaged any otherwise, you must break it. [We must] so look upon these as thus held out to us; so it was held out by the gentleman that brought it yesterday. For my part, I think it is no right at all. I think that no person hath a right to an interest or share in the disposing of the affairs of the kingdom, and in determining or choosing those that shall determine what laws we shall be ruled by here – no person hath a right to this, that hath not a permanent fixed interest in this kingdom, and those persons together are properly the represented of this kingdom, and consequently are [also] to make up the representers of this kingdom, who taken together do comprehend whatsoever is of real or permanent interest in the kingdom. And I am sure otherwise I cannot tell what any man can say why a foreigner coming in amongst us – or as many as will coming in amongst us, or by force or otherwise settling themselves here, or at least by our permission having a being here – why they should not as well lay claim to it as any other. We talk of birthright. Truly [by] birthright there is thus much claim. Men may justly have by birthright, by their very being born in England, that we should not seclude them out of England, that we should not refuse to give them air and place and ground, and the freedom of the highways and other things, to live amongst us – not any man that is born here, though by his birth there come nothing at all (that is part of the permanent interest of this kingdom) to him. That I think is due to a man by birth. But that by a man's being born here he shall have a share in that power that shall dispose of the lands here, and of all things here, I do not think it a sufficient ground. I am sure if we look upon that which is the utmost (within [any] man's view) of what was originally the constitution of this kingdom, upon that which is most radical and fundamental, and which if you take away, there is no man hath any land, any goods, [or] any civil interest, that is this: that those that choose the representers for the making of laws by which this state and kingdom are to be governed, are the persons who, taken together, do comprehend the local interest of this kingdom; that is, the persons in whom all land lies, and those in corporations in whom all trading lies. This is the most fundamental constitution of this kingdom and [that] which if you do not allow, you allow none at all. This constitution hath limited and determined it that only those shall have voices in elections. It is true, as was said by a gentleman near me, the meanest man in England ought to have [a voice in the election of the government he lives under – but only if he has some local interest]. I say this: that those that have the meanest local interest – that man that hath but forty shillings a year, he *hath* as great voice in the election of a knight for the shire as he that hath ten thousand a year, or more if he had never so much; and therefore there is that regard had to it. But this [local interest], still the constitution of this government hath had an eye to (and what other government hath not an eye to this?). It doth not relate to the interest of the kingdom if it do not lay the foundation of the power that's given to the representers, in those who have a permanent and a local interest in the kingdom, and who taken all together do comprehend the whole [interest of the kingdom]. There is all the reason and justice that can be, [in this]: if I will come to live in a kingdom, being a foreigner to it, or live in a kingdom, having no permanent interest in it, [and] if I will desire as a stranger, or claim as one freeborn here, the air, the free passage of highways, the protection of laws, and all such things – if I will either desire them or claim them, [then] I (if I have no permanent interest in that kingdom) must submit to those laws and those rules [which they shall choose], who, taken together, do comprehend the whole interest of the kingdom. And if we shall go to take away this, we shall plainly go to take away all property and interest that any man hath either in land by inheritance, or in estate by possession, or anything else – I say], if you take away this fundamental part of the civil constitution.

*Rainborough:*   Truly, sir, I am of the same opinion I was, and am resolved to keep it till I know reason why I should not. I confess my memory is bad, and therefore I am fain to make use of my pen. I remember that, in a former speech [which] this gentleman brought before this [meeting], he was saying that in some cases he should not value whether [there were] a king or no king, whether lords or no lords, whether a property or no property. For my part I differ in that. I do very much care whether [there be] a king or no king, lords or no lords, property or no property; and I think, if we do not all take care, we shall all have none of these very shortly. But as to this present business. I do hear nothing at all that can convince me, why any man that is born in England ought not to have his voice in election of burgesses. It is said that if a man have not a permanent interest, he can have no claim; and [that] we must be no freer than the laws will let us be, and that there is no [law in any] chronicle will let us be freer than that we [now] enjoy. Something was said to this yesterday. I do think that the main cause why Almighty God gave men reason, it was that they should make use of that reason, and that they should improve it for that end and purpose that God gave it them. And truly, I think that half a loaf is better than none if a man be anhungry: [this gift of reason without other property may seem a small thing], yet I think there is nothing that God hath given a man that any [one] else can take from him. And therefore I say, that either it must be the Law of God or the law of man that must prohibit the meanest man in the kingdom to have this benefit as well as the greatest. I do not find anything in the Law of God, that a lord shall choose twenty burgesses, and a gentleman but two, or a poor man shall choose none: I find no such thing in the Law of Nature, nor in the Law of Nations. But I do find that all Englishmen must be subject to English laws, and I do verily believe that there is no man but will say that the foundation of all law lies in the people, and if [it lie] in the people, I am to seek for this exemption.

And truly I have thought something [else]: in what a miserable distressed condition would many a man that hath fought for the Parliament in this quarrel, be! I will be bound to say that many a man whose zeal and affection to God and this kingdom hath carried him forth in this cause, hath so spent his estate that, in the way the state [and] the Army are going, he shall not hold up his head, if when his estate is lost, and not worth forty shillings a year, a man shall not have any interest. And there are many other ways by which [the] estates men have (if that be the rule which God in his providence does use) do fall to decay. A man, when he hath an estate, hath an interest in making laws, [but] when he hath none, he hath no power in it; so that a man cannot lose that which he hath for the maintenance of his family but he must [also] lose that which God and nature hath given him! And therefore I do [think], and am still of the same opinion, that every man born in England cannot, ought not, neither by the Law of God nor the Law of Nature, to be exempted from the choice of those who are to make laws for him to live under, and for him, for aught I know, to lose his life under. And therefore I think there can be no great stick in this.

Truly I think that there is not this day reigning in England a greater fruit or effect of tyranny than this very thing would produce. Truly I know nothing free but only the knight of the shire, nor do I know anything in a parliamentary way that is clear from the height and fulness of tyranny, but only [that]. As for this of corporations [which you also mentioned], it is as contrary to freedom as may be. For, sir, what is it? The King he grants a patent under the Broad Seal of England to such a corporation to send burgesses, he grants to [such] a city to send burgesses. When a poor base corporation from the King['s grant] shall send two burgesses, when five hundred men of estate shall not send one, when those that are to make their laws are called by the King, or cannot act [but] by such a call, truly I think that the people of England have little freedom.

*Ireton:* I think there was nothing that I said to give you occasion to think that I did contend for this, that such a corporation [as that] should have the electing of a man to the Parliament. I think I agreed to this matter, that all should be equally distributed. But the question is, whether it should be distributed to all persons, or whether the same persons that are the electors [now] should be the electors still, and it [be] equally distributed amongst *them*. I do not see anybody else that makes this objection; and if nobody else be sensible of it I shall soon have done. Only I shall a little crave your leave to represent the consequences of it, and clear myself from one thing that was misrepresented by the gentleman that sat next me. I think, if the gentleman remember himself, he cannot but remember that what I said was to this effect: that if I saw the hand of God leading so far as to destroy King, and destroy Lords, and destroy property, and [leave] no such thing at all amongst us, I should acquiesce in it; and so I did not care, if no king, no lords, or no property [should] be, in comparison of the tender care that I have of the honour of God, and of the people of God, whose [good] name is so much concerned in this Army. This I did deliver [so], and not absolutely.

All the main thing that I speak for, is because I would have an eye to property. I hope we do not come to contend for victory – but let every man consider with himself that he do not go that way to take away all property. For here is the case of the most fundamental part of the constitution of the kingdom, which if you take away, you take away all by that. Here men of this and this quality are determined to be the electors of men to the Parliament, and they are all those who have any permanent interest in the kingdom, and who, taken together, do comprehend the whole [permanent, local] interest of the kingdom. I mean by permanent [and] local, that [it] is not [able to be removed] anywhere else. As for instance, he that hath a freehold, and that freehold cannot be removed out of the kingdom; and so there's a [freeman of a] corporation, a place which hath the privilege of a market and trading, which if you should allow to all places equally, I do not see how you could preserve any peace in the kingdom, and that is the reason why in the constitution we have but some few market towns. Now those people [that have freeholds] and those [that] are the freemen of corporations, were looked upon by the former constitution to comprehend the permanent interest of the kingdom. For [first], he that hath his livelihood by his trade, and by his freedom of trading in such a corporation, which he cannot exercise in another, he is tied to that place, [for] his livelihood depends upon it. And secondly, that man hath an interest, hath a permanent interest there, upon which he may live, and live a freeman without dependence. These [things the] constitution [of] this kingdom hath looked at. Now I wish we may all consider of what right you will challenge that all the people should have right to elections. Is it by the right of nature? If you will hold forth that as your ground, then I think you must deny all property too, and this is my reason. For thus: by that same right of nature (whatever it be) that you pretend, by which you can say, one man hath an equal right with another to the choosing of him that shall govern him – by the same right of nature, he hath the same [equal] right in any goods he sees – meat, drink, clothes – to take and use them for his sustenance. He hath a freedom to the land, [to take] the ground, to exercise it, till it; he hath the [same] freedom to anything that any one doth account himself to have any propriety in. Why now I say then, if you, against the most fundamental part of [the] civil constitution (which I have now declared), will plead the Law of Nature, that a man should (paramount [to] this, and contrary to this) have a power of choosing those men that shall determine what shall be law in this state, though he himself have no permanent interest in the state, [but] whatever interest he hath he may carry about with him – if this be allowed, [because by the right of nature] we are free, we are equal, one man must have as much voice as another, then show me what step or difference [there is], why [I may not] by the same right [take your property, though not] of necessity to sustain nature. It is for my better being, and [the better settlement of the kingdom]? Possibly not for it, neither: possibly I may not have so real a regard to the peace of the kingdom as that man who hath a permanent interest in it. He that is here to-day, and gone to-morrow, I do not see that he hath such a permanent interest. Since you cannot plead to it by anything but the Law of Nature, [or for anything] but for the end of better being, and [since] that better being is not certain, and [what is] more, destructive to another; upon these grounds, if you do, paramount [to] all constitutions, hold up this Law of Nature, I would fain have any man show me their bounds, where you will end, and [why you should not] take away all property.

[...]

# 10

# THE RIGHTS OF MAN

## Thomas Paine

[...]

From the Revolutions of America and France, and the symptoms that have appeared in other countries, it is evident that the opinion of the world is changed with respect to systems of Government, and that revolutions are not within the compass of political calculations. The progress of time and circumstances, which men assign to the accomplishment of great changes, is too mechanical to measure the force of the mind, and the rapidity of reflection, by which revolutions are generated: All the old Governments have received a shock from those that already appear, and which were once more improbable, and are a greater subject of wonder, than a general revolution in Europe would be now.

When we survey the wretched condition of man under the monarchical and hereditary systems of Government, dragged from his home by one power, or driven by another, and impoverished by taxes more than by enemies, it becomes evident that those systems are bad, and that a general revolution in the principle and construction of Governments is necessary.

What is government more than the management of the affairs of a Nation? It is not, and from its nature cannot be, the property of any particular man or family, but of the whole community, at whose expense it is supported; and though by force or contrivance it has been usurped into an inheritance, the usurpation cannot alter the right of things. Sovereignty, as a matter of right, appertains to the Nation only, and not to any individual; and a Nation has at all

From Thomas Paine, *The Rights of Man*, ed. Henry Collins (Penguin, Harmondsworth, 1969), pp. 164–9. Originally written 1791.

times an inherent indefeasible right to abolish any form of Government it finds inconvenient, and establish such as accords with its interest, disposition, and happiness. The romantic and barbarous distinction of men into Kings and subjects, though it may suit the condition of courtiers, cannot that of citizens; and is exploded by the principle upon which Governments are now founded. Every citizen is a member of the Sovereignty, and, as such, can acknowledge no personal subjection; and his obedience can be only to the laws.

When men think of what Government is, they must necessarily suppose it to possess a knowledge of all the objects and matters upon which its authority is to be exercised. In this view of Government, the republican system, as established by America and France, operates to embrace the whole of a Nation; and the knowledge necessary to the interest of all the parts, is to be found in the centre, which the parts by representation form: But the old Governments are on a construction that excludes knowledge as well as happiness; Government by monks, who know nothing of the world beyond the walls of a convent, is as consistent as government by Kings.

What were formerly called Revolutions, were little more than a change of persons, or an alteration of local circumstances. They rose and fell like things of course, and had nothing in their existence or their fate that could influence beyond the spot that produced them. But what we now see in the world, from the Revolutions of America and France, are a renovation of the natural order of things, a system of principles as universal as truth and the existence of man, and combining moral with political happiness and national prosperity.

'I. *Men are born and always continue free, and equal in respect of their rights. Civil distinctions, therefore, can be founded only on public utility.*

'II. *The end of all political associations is the preservation of the natural and imprescriptible rights of man; and these rights are liberty, property, security, and resistance of oppression.*

'III. *The Nation is essentially the source of all Sovereignty; nor can any* INDIVIDUAL, *or* ANY BODY OF MEN, *be entitled to any authority which is not expressly derived from it.*'

In these principles, there is nothing to throw a Nation into confusion by inflaming ambition. They are calculated to call forth wisdom and abilities, and to exercise them for the public good, and not for the emolument or aggrandizement of particular descriptions of men or families. Monarchical sovereignty, the enemy of mankind, and the source of misery, is abolished; and sovereignty itself is restored to its natural and original place, the Nation. Were this the case throughout Europe, the cause of wars would be taken away.

It is attributable to Henry the Fourth of France, a man of an enlarged and benevolent heart, that he proposed, about the year 1610, a plan for abolishing war in Europe. The plan consisted in constituting an European Congress, or as the French Authors style it, a Pacific Republic; by appointing delegates from the several Nations, who were to act as a Court of arbitration in any disputes that might arise between nation and nation.

Had such a plan been adopted at the time it was proposed, the taxes of England and France, as two of the parties, would have been at least ten millions sterling annually to each Nation less than they were at the commencement of the French Revolution.

To conceive a cause why such a plan has not been adopted, (and that instead of a Congress for the purpose of *preventing* war, it has been called only to *terminate* a war, after a fruitless expense of several years), it will be necessary to consider the interest of Governments as a distinct interest to that of Nations.

Whatever is the cause of taxes to a Nation, becomes also the means of revenue to a Government. Every war terminates with an addition of taxes, and consequently with an addition of revenue; and in any event of war, in the manner they are now commenced and concluded, the power and interest of Governments are increased. War, therefore, from its productiveness, as it easily furnishes the pretence of necessity for taxes and appointments to places and offices, becomes a principal part of the system of old Governments; and to establish any mode to abolish war, however advantageous it might be to Nations, would be to take from such Government the most lucrative of its branches. The frivolous matters upon which war is made, show the disposition and avidity of Governments to uphold the system of war, and betray the motives upon which they act.

Why are not Republics plunged into war, but because the nature of their Government does not admit of an interest distinct from that of the Nation? Even Holland, though an ill-constructed Republic, and with a commerce extending over the world, existed nearly a century without war: and the instant the form of Government was changed in France, the republican principles of peace and domestic prosperity and economy arose with the new Government; and the same consequences would follow the same causes in other Nations.

As war is the system of Government on the old construction, the animosity which Nations reciprocally entertain, is nothing more than what the policy of their Governments excites, to keep up the spirit of the system. Each Government accuses the other of perfidy, intrigue, and ambition, as a means of heating the imagination of their respective Nations, and incensing them to hostilities. Man is not the enemy of man, but through the medium of a false system of Government. Instead, therefore, of exclaiming against the ambition of Kings, the exclamation should be directed against the principle of such Governments; and instead of seeking to reform the individual, the wisdom of a Nation should apply itself to reform the system.

Whether the forms and maxims of Governments which are still in practice, were adapted to the condition of the world at the period they were established, is not in this case the question. The older they are, the less correspondence can they have with the present state of things. Time, and change of circumstances and opinions, have the same progressive effect in rendering modes of Government obsolete, as they have upon customs and manners. – Agriculture, commerce, manufactures, and the tranquil arts, by which the prosperity of Nations is best promoted, require a different system of Government, and a different species of knowledge to direct its operations, than what might have been required in the former condition of the world.

As it is not difficult to perceive, from the enlightened state of mankind, that hereditary Governments are verging to their decline, and that Revolutions on the broad basis of national sovereignty, and Government by representation, are making their way in Europe, it would be an act of wisdom to anticipate their approach, and produce Revolutions by reason and accommodation, rather than commit them to the issue of convulsions.

From what we now see, nothing of reform in the political world ought to be held improbable. It is an age of Revolutions, in which everything may be looked for. The intrigue of Courts, by which the system of war is kept up, may provoke a confederation of Nations to abolish it: and an European Congress, to patronize the progress of free Government, and promote the civilization of Nations with each other, is an event nearer in probability, than once were the Revolutions and Alliance of France and America.

# 11

# DECLARATION OF THE RIGHTS OF MAN AND CITIZEN

## The National Assembly of France

The Representatives of the people of FRANCE, formed into a NATIONAL ASSEMBLY, considering that ignorance, neglect, or contempt of human rights, are the sole causes of public misfortunes and corruptions of Government, have resolved to set forth, in a solemn declaration, these natural, imprescriptible, and inalienable rights: that this declaration being constantly present to the minds of the members of the body social, they may be ever kept attentive to their rights and their duties: that the acts of the legislative and executive powers of Government, being capable of being every moment compared with the end of political institutions, may be more respected: and also, that the future claims of the citizens, being directed by simple and incontestible principles, may always tend to the maintenance of the Constitution, and the general happiness.

For these reasons, the NATIONAL ASSEMBLY doth recognize and declare, in the presence of the Supreme Being, and with the hope of his blessing and favour, the following *sacred* rights of men and of citizens:

I. *Men are born, and always continue, free, and equal in respect of their rights. Civil distinctions, therefore, can be founded only on public utility.*

II. *The end of all political associations, is, the preservation of the natural and imprescriptible rights of man; and these rights are liberty, property, security, and resistance of oppression.*

---

From the 'Declaration of the Rights of Man and Citizen, 1789', in Thomas Paine, *The Rights of Man*, ed. Henry Collins (Penguin, Harmondsworth, 1969), pp. 132–4. Originally issued August 1789.

III. *The nation is essentially the source of all sovereignty; nor can any* INDIVIDUAL, *or* ANY BODY OF MEN, *be entitled to any authority which is not expressly derived from it.*

IV. Political Liberty consists in the power of doing whatever does not injure another. The exercise of the natural rights of every man, has no other limits than those which are necessary to secure to every *other* man the free exercise of the same rights; and these limits are determinable only by the law.

V. The law ought to prohibit only actions hurtful to society. What is not prohibited by the law, should not be hindered; nor should any one be compelled to that which the law does not require.

VI. The law is an expression of the will of the community. All citizens have a right to concur, either personally, or by their representatives, in its formation. It should be the same to all, whether it protects or punishes; and *all being equal in its sight, are equally eligible to all honours, places, and employments, according to their different abilities, without any other distinction than that created by their virtues and talents.*

VII. No man should be accused, arrested, or held in confinement, except in cases determined by the law, and according to the forms which it has pre-scribed. All who promote, solicit, execute, or cause to be executed, arbitrary orders, ought to be punished; and every citizen called upon, or apprehended by virtue of the law, ought immediately to obey, and renders himself culpable by resistance.

VIII. The law ought to impose no other penalties but such as are absolutely and evidently necessary: and no one ought to be punished, but in virtue of a law promulgated before the offence, and legally applied.

IX. Every man being presumed innocent till he has been convicted, whenever his detention becomes indispensable, all rigour to him, more than is necessary to secure his person, ought to be provided against by the law.

X. No man ought to be molested on account of his opinions, not even on account of his *religious* opinions, provided his avowal of them does not disturb the public order established by the law.

XI. The unrestrained communication of thoughts and opinions being one of the most precious rights of man, every citizen may speak, write, and publish freely, provided he is responsible for the abuse of this liberty in cases determined by the law.

XII. A public force being necessary to give security to the rights of men and of citizens, that force is instituted for the benefit of the community, and not for the particular benefit of the persons with whom it is entrusted.

XIII. A common contribution being necessary for the support of the public force, and for defraying the other expenses of government, it ought to be divided equally among the members of the community, according to their abilities.

XIV. Every citizen has a right, either by himself or his representative, to a free voice in determining the necessity of public contributions, the appropriation of them, and their amount, mode of assessment, and duration.

XV. Every community has a right to demand of all its agents, an account of their conduct.

XVI. Every community in which a separation of powers and a security of rights is not provided for, wants a constitution.

XVII. The right to property being inviolable and sacred, no one ought to be deprived of it, except in cases of evident public necessity, legally ascertained, and on condition of a previous just indemnity.

12

# THE GETTYSBURG ADDRESS

## Abraham Lincoln

Four score and seven years ago our fathers brought forth on this continent, a new nation, conceived in Liberty, and dedicated to the proposition that all men are created equal.

Now we are engaged in a great civil war, testing whether that nation, or any nation so conceived and so dedicated, can long endure. We are met on a great battle-field of that war. We have come to dedicate a portion of that field, as a final resting place for those who here gave their lives that that nation might live. It is altogether fitting and proper that we should do this.

But, in a larger sense, we can not dedicate – we can not consecrate – we can not hallow – this ground. The brave men, living and dead, who struggled here, have consecrated it, far above our poor power to add or detract. The world will little note, nor long remember what we say here, but it can never forget what they did here. It is for us the living, rather, to be dedicated here to the unfinished work which they who fought here have thus far so nobly advanced. It is rather for us to be here dedicated to the great task remaining before us – that from these honored dead we take increased devotion to that cause for which they gave the last full measure of devotion – that we here highly resolve that these dead shall not have died in vain – that this nation, under God, shall have a new birth of freedom – and that government of the people, by the people, for the people, shall not perish from the earth.

From A. Lincoln, 'The Gettysburg Address', in D. Ravitch and A. Thornstrom (eds). *The Democracy Reader. Classic and Modern Speeches, Essays, Poems, Declarations and Documents on Freedom and Human Rights Worldwide.* (HarperCollins, New York, 1992), pp. 166–7.

# 13

# CAPITALISM, SOCIALISM AND DEMOCRACY

## Joseph A. Schumpeter

[...]

It will be remembered that our chief troubles about the classical theory centered in the proposition that "the people" hold a definite and rational opinion about every individual question and that they give effect to this opinion – in a democracy – by choosing "representatives" who will see to it that that opinion is carried out. Thus the selection of the representatives is made secondary to the primary purpose of the democratic arrangement which is to vest the power of deciding political issues in the electorate. Suppose we reverse the roles of these two elements and make the deciding of issues by the electorate secondary to the election of the men who are to do the deciding. To put it differently, we now take the view that the role of the people is to produce a government, or else an intermediate body which in turn will produce a national executive or government. And we define: the democratic method is that institutional arrangement for arriving at political decisions in which individuals acquire the power to decide by means of a competitive struggle for the people's vote.

Defense and explanation of this idea will speedily show that, as to both plausibility of assumptions and tenability of propositions, it greatly improves the theory of the democratic process.

First of all, we are provided with a reasonably efficient criterion by which to distinguish democratic governments from others. We have seen that the

From Joseph A. Schumpeter, *Capitalism, Socialism and Democracy* (Unwin University Books, George Allen & Unwin, London, 1943), pp. 269–73. Originally written 1943.

classical theory meets with difficulties on that score because both the will and the good of the people may be, and in many historical instances have been, served just as well or better by governments that cannot be described as democratic according to any accepted usage of the term. Now we are in a somewhat better position partly because we are resolved to stress a *modus procedendi* the presence or absence of which it is in most cases easy to verify.

For instance, a parliamentary monarchy like the English one fulfills the requirements of the democratic method because the monarch is practically constrained to appoint to cabinet office the same people as parliament would elect. A "constitutional" monarchy does not qualify to be called democratic because electorates and parliaments, while having all the other rights that electorates and parliaments have in parliamentary monarchies, lack the power to impose their choice as to the governing committee: the cabinet ministers are in this case servants of the monarch, in substance as well as in name, and can in principle be dismissed as well as appointed by him. Such an arrangement may satisfy the people. The electorate may reaffirm this fact by voting against any proposal for change. The monarch may be so popular as to be able to defeat any competition for the supreme office. But since no machinery is provided for making this competition effective the case does not come within our definition.

Second, the theory embodied in this definition leaves all the room we may wish to have for a proper recognition of the vital fact of leadership. The classical theory did not do this but, as we have seen, attributed to the electorate an altogether unrealistic degree of initiative which practically amounted to ignoring leadership. But collectives act almost exclusively by accepting leadership – this is the dominant mechanism of practically any collective action which is more than a reflex. Propositions about the working and the results of the democratic method that take account of this are bound to be infinitely more realistic than propositions which do not. They will not stop at the execution of a *volonté générale* but will go some way toward showing how it emerges or how it is substituted or faked. What we have termed Manufactured Will is no longer outside the theory, an aberration for the absence of which we piously pray; it enters on the ground floor as it should.

Third, however, so far as there are genuine group-wise volitions at all – for instance the will of the unemployed to receive unemployment benefit or the will of other groups to help – our theory does not neglect them. On the contrary we are now able to insert them in exactly the role they actually play. Such volitions do not as a rule assert themselves directly. Even if strong and definite they remain latent, often for decades, until they are called to life by some political leader who turns them into political factors. This he does, or else his agents do it for him, by organizing these volitions, by working them up and by including eventually appropriate items in his competitive offering. The interaction between sectional interests and public opinion and the way in which they produce the pattern we call the political situation appear from this angle in a new and much clearer light.

Fourth, our theory is of course no more definite than is the concept of competition for leadership. This concept presents similar difficulties as the concept of competition in the economic sphere, with which it may be usefully compared. In economic life competition is never completely lacking, but hardly ever is it perfect. Similarly, in political life there is always some competition, though perhaps only a potential one, for the allegiance of the people. To simplify matters we have restricted the kind of competition for leadership which is to define democracy, to free competition for a free vote. The justification for this is that democracy seems to imply a recognized method by which to conduct the competitive struggle, and that the electoral method is practically the only one available for communities of any size. But though this excludes many ways of securing leadership which should be excluded, such as competition by military insurrection, it does not exclude the cases that are strikingly analogous to the economic phenomena we label "unfair" or "fraudulent" competition or restraint of competition. And we cannot exclude them because if we did we should be left with a completely unrealistic ideal. Between this ideal case which does not exist and the cases in which all competition with the established leader is prevented by force, there is a continuous range of variation within which the democratic method of government shades off into the autocratic one by imperceptible steps. But if we wish to understand and not to philosophize, this is as it should be. The value of our criterion is not seriously impaired thereby.

Fifth, our theory seems to clarify the relation that subsists between democracy and individual freedom. It by the latter we mean the existence of a sphere of individual self-government the boundaries of which are historically variable – *no* society tolerates absolute freedom even of conscience and of speech, *no* society reduces that sphere to zero – the question clearly becomes a matter of degree. We have seen that the democratic method does not necessarily guarantee a greater amount of individual freedom than another political method would permit in similar circumstances. It may well be the other way round. But there is still a relation between the two. If, on principle at least, everyone is free to compete for political leadership by presenting himself to the electorate, this will in most cases though not in all mean a considerable amount of freedom of discussion *for all*. In particular it will normally mean a considerable amount of freedom of the press. This relation between democracy and freedom is not absolutely stringent and can be tampered with. But, from the standpoint of the intellectual, it is nevertheless very important. At the same time, it is all there is to that relation.

Sixth, it should be observed that in making it the primary function of the electorate to produce a government (directly or through an intermediate body) I intended to include in this phrase also the function of evicting it. The one means simply the acceptance of a leader or a group of leaders, the other means simply the withdrawal of this acceptance. This takes care of an element the reader may have missed. He may have thought that the electorate controls as well as installs. But since electorates normally do not control their political leaders in any way except by refusing to reelect them or the parliamentary majorities that support them, it seems well to reduce our ideas about this control in the way indicated by our definition. Occasionally, spontaneous revulsions occur which upset a government or an individual minister directly or else enforce a certain course of action. But they are not only exceptional, they are, as we shall see, contrary to the spirit of the democratic method.

Seventh, our theory sheds much-needed light on an old controversy. Whoever accepts the classical doctrine of democracy and in consequence believes that the democratic method is to guarantee that issues be decided and policies framed according to the will of the people must be struck by the fact that, even if that will were undeniably real and definite, decision by simple majorities would in many cases distort it rather than give effect to it. Evidently the will of the majority is the will of the majority and not the will of "the people." The latter is a mosaic that the former completely fails to "represent." To equate both by definition is not to solve the problem. Attempts at real solutions have however been made by the authors of the various plans for Proportional Representation.

These plans have met with adverse criticism on practical grounds. It is in fact obvious not only that proportional representation will offer opportunities for all sorts of idiosyncrasies to assert themselves but also that it may prevent democracy from producing efficient governments and thus prove a danger in times of stress. But before concluding that democracy becomes unworkable if its principle is carried out consistently, it is just as well to ask ourselves whether this principle really implies proportional representation. As a matter of fact it does not. If acceptance of leadership is the true function of the electorate's vote, the case for proportional representation collapses because its premises are no longer binding. The principle of democracy then merely means that the reins of government should be handed to those who command more support than do any of the competing individuals or teams. And this in turn seems to assure the standing of the majority system within the logic of the democratic method, although we might still condemn it on grounds that lie outside of that logic.

[...]

# PART TWO
# KEY CONCEPTS

# SECTION I
# FREEDOM AND AUTONOMY

# FREEDOM AND AUTONOMY
## INTRODUCTION

Our collection of extracts on key concepts of democracy starts with the related ideas of freedom and autonomy. These are the fundamental concepts of democracy: a democratic system is justified because it creates and guarantees human beings their freedom. But what is the democratic concept of freedom? For many writers on democracy it has been bound up with an idea of autonomy or self-determination, being one's own master. As *Rousseau* puts it in the first of these extracts, through the social contract we gain civil liberty and moral liberty: the former involves being ruled by the general will instead of following our individual self-interest. The latter means obedience to rules which we, in association with our fellow citizens, have made. These rules or laws regulate our actions, instead of 'the mere impulse of appetite'.

This line of reasoning is followed by *Kant* in the somewhat complex extract which follows. For Kant, autonomy involves deciding our plan of life for ourselves. Even a benevolent paternalist government would be 'the greatest despotism imaginable', because it would take away our right to decide what is best for ourselves. Kant also invokes ideas of equality, by which he means equality of opportunity and equality under the law. No legal transaction, he argues, can ever make us cease to be our own master. He also appeals to an ideal of independence, 'the independence of each member of the commonwealth as a citizen'. However, Kant makes it clear that this is the independence of male property owners, who alone can be citizens. He sees it as obvious that citizens have to be adult males, who own some property, even if it is only property in terms of some skill, capacity or knowledge. Here we can see some of the limits on the apparent universality of the democratic ideal, as expressed in Kant's formulation of it. Autonomy is the preserve of a restricted group of citizens (male, property-owning, socially independent and self-reliant): they alone are capable of acting autonomously.

The democratic concept of freedom is different from the liberal concept of freedom. In his classic lecture distinguishing the liberty of the ancients from that of the moderns, the Swiss liberal thinker Benjamin *Constant* suggested that ancient liberty involved direct participation in making the law. This could not be realised in the modern world, where freedom meant 'peaceful enjoyment and private independence'. To seek to recreate direct participation in politics in the conditions of modern society risked the crushing of individual liberty.

A similar distinction between liberal and democratic concepts of freedom emerges in the thought of the celebrated twentieth-century liberal thinker Isaiah Berlin. He distinguishes between the two in his lecture on 'Two Concepts of Liberty': liberalism involves freedom *from* – freedom from coercion by the state or the tyranny of majority opinion. This is contrasted with positive freedom, freedom to be one's own master or to be autonomous. This (says Berlin) can justify some higher power claiming to liberate people by acting in the way that they would choose if they were not slaves to their lower natures or immediate desires. This suggests that the concept of autonomy is highly problematic: can democracy justify coercion (forcing people to be free) by some body, or group, which subordinates individual desires to some higher collective interest? Does 'being one's own master' open the way to the domination of the collective over the individual?

Finally, *Robert Paul Wolff* endorses ideas of autonomy, which for him involve the need for moral deliberation, and the idea of people taking responsibility for their own actions. For Wolff, this means that for the autonomous person there is, as he puts it, 'no such thing as a command'. We might entrust some decisions in limited spheres to the judgement of experts in that particular field. But as democratic citizens we cannot or should not abrogate the responsibility for taking decisions, and for the deliberative process of arriving at decisions. This anticipates some of the material on 'deliberative democracy' (see Section 16 on this below).

Two problems are raised by these extracts: is the criterion of autonomy and democratic deliberation too high a standard for citizens to aspire to? And can the idea of autonomy be perverted or distorted to create a situation in which individual freedom is suppressed in the name of some higher good, as Berlin warns?

# 14

# THE SOCIAL CONTRACT

## Jean-Jacques Rousseau

### CHAPTER VIII
#### THE CIVIL STATE

The passage from the state of nature to the civil state produces a very remarkable change in man, by substituting justice for instinct in his conduct, and giving his actions the morality they had formerly lacked. Then only, when the voice of duty takes the place of physical impulses and right of appetite, does man, who so far had considered only himself, find that he is forced to act on different principles, and to consult his reason before listening to his inclinations. Although, in this state, he deprives himself of some advantages which he got from nature, he gains in return others so great, his faculties are so stimulated and developed, his ideas so extended, his feelings so ennobled, and his whole soul so uplifted, that, did not the abuses of this new condition often degrade him below that which he left, he would be bound to bless continually the happy moment which took him from it for ever, and, instead of a stupid and unimaginative animal, made him an intelligent being and a man.

Let us draw up the whole account in terms easily commensurable. What man loses by the social contract is his natural liberty and an unlimited right to everything he tries to get and succeeds in getting; what he gains is civil liberty and the proprietorship of all he possesses. If we are to avoid mistake in weighing one against the other, we must clearly distinguish natural liberty, which is

From Jean-Jacques Rousseau, *The Social Contract and Discourses*, trans. and intro. G. D. H. Cole (Everyman's Library: Dent, London/Dutton, New York, 1968), Book I, chapter VIII, pp. 15–16. Originally written 1762.

bounded only by the strength of the individual, from civil liberty, which is limited by the general will; and possession, which is merely the effect of force or the right of the first occupier, from property, which can be founded only on a positive title.

We might, over and above all this, add, to what man acquires in the civil state, moral liberty, which alone makes him truly master of himself; for the mere impulse of appetite is slavery, while obedience to a law which we prescribe to ourselves is liberty. But I have already said too much on this head, and the philosophical meaning of the word liberty does not now concern us.

# 15

# ON THE COMMON SAYING: 'THIS MAY BE TRUE IN THEORY BUT IT DOES NOT APPLY IN PRACTICE'

## Immanuel Kant

[...]

The civil state, regarded purely as a lawful state, is based on the following *a priori* principles:

1. The *freedom* of every member of society as a *human being*.
2. The *equality* of each with all the others as a *subject*.
3. The *independence* of each member of a commonwealth as a *citizen*.

These principles are not so much laws given by an already established state, as laws by which a state can alone be established in accordance with pure rational principles of external human right. Thus:

1. Man's *freedom* as a human being, as a principle for the constitution of a commonwealth, can be expressed in the following formula. No-one can compel me to be happy in accordance with his conception of the welfare of others, for each may seek his happiness in whatever way he sees fit, so long as he does not infringe upon the freedom of others to pursue a similar end which can be reconciled with the freedom of everyone else within a workable general law – i.e. he must accord to others the same right as he enjoys himself. A government might be established on the principle of benevolence towards the people, like that of a father towards his children. Under such a *paternal government* (*imperium paternale*), the subjects, as immature children who cannot distinguish what is truly useful or harmful to themselves, would be obliged to behave

From Immanuel Kant, 'On the Common Saying: "This May Be True in Theory but It Does not Apply in Practice"', in *Political Writings*, ed. with intro. and notes by Hans Reiss, 2nd enlarged edn (Cambridge University Press, Cambridge, 1977), pp. 74–9. Originally written 1793.

purely passively and to rely upon the judgement of the head of state as to how they *ought* to be happy, and upon his kindness in willing their happiness at all. Such a government is the greatest conceivable *despotism*, i.e. a constitution which suspends the entire freedom of its subjects, who thenceforth have no rights whatsoever. The only conceivable government for men who are capable of possessing rights, even if the ruler is benevolent, is not a *paternal* but a *patriotic* government (*imperium non paternale, sed patrioticum*). A *patriotic* attitude is one where everyone in the state, not excepting its head, regards the commonwealth as a maternal womb, or the land as the paternal ground from which he himself sprang and which he must leave to his descendants as a treasured pledge. Each regards himself as authorised to protect the rights of the commonwealth by laws of the general will, but not to submit it to his personal use at his own absolute pleasure. This right of freedom belongs to each member of the commonwealth as a human being, in so far as each is a being capable of possessing rights.

2. Man's *equality* as a subject might be formulated as follows. Each member of the commonwealth has rights of coercion in relation to all the others, except in relation to the head of state. For he alone is not a member of the commonwealth, but its creator or preserver, and he alone is authorised to coerce others without being subject to any coercive law himself. But all who are subject to laws are the subjects of a state, and are thus subject to the right of coercion along with all other members of the commonwealth; the only exception is a single person (in either the physical or the moral sense of the word), the head of state, through whom alone the rightful coercion of all others can be exercised. For if he too could be coerced, he would not be the head of state, and the hierarchy of subordination would ascend infinitely. But if there were two persons exempt from coercion, neither would be subject to coercive laws, and neither could do to the other anything contrary to right, which is impossible.

This uniform equality of human beings as subjects of a state is, however, perfectly consistent with the utmost inequality of the mass in the degree of its possessions, whether these take the form of physical or mental superiority over others, or of fortuitous external property and of particular rights (of which there may be many) with respect to others. Thus the welfare of the one depends very much on the will of the other (the poor depending on the rich), the one must obey the other (as the child its parents or the wife her husband), the one serves (the labourer) while the other pays, etc. Nevertheless, they are all equal as subjects *before the law*, which, as the pronouncement of the general will, can only be single in form, and which concerns the form of right and not the material or object in relation to which I possess rights. For no-one can coerce anyone else other than through the public law and its executor, the head of state, while everyone else can resist the others in the same way and to the same degree. No-one, however, can lose this authority to coerce others and to have rights towards them except through committing a crime. And no-one can voluntarily renounce his rights by a contract or legal transaction to the effect that he has no rights but only duties, for such a contract would deprive him of the right to make a contract, and would thus invalidate the one he had already made.

From this idea of the equality of men as subjects in a commonwealth, there emerges this further formula: every member of the commonwealth must be entitled to reach any degree of rank which a subject can earn through his talent, his industry and his good fortune. And his fellow-subjects may not stand in his way by *hereditary* prerogatives or privileges of rank and thereby hold him and his descendants back indefinitely.

All right consists solely in the restriction of the freedom of others, with the qualification that their freedom can co-exist with my freedom within the terms of a general law; and public right in a commonwealth is simply a state of affairs regulated by a real legislation which conforms to this principle and is backed up by power, and under which a whole people live as subjects in a lawful state (*status iuridicus*). This is what we call a civil state, and it is characterised by equality in the effects and counter-effects of freely willed actions which limit one another in accordance with the general law of freedom. Thus the *birthright* of each individual in such a state (i.e. before he has performed any acts which can be judged in relation to right) is absolutely *equal* as regards his authority to coerce others to use their freedom in a way which harmonises with his freedom. Since birth is not an act on the part of the one who is born, it cannot create any inequality in his legal position and cannot make him submit to any coercive laws except in so far as he is a subject, along with all the others, of the one supreme legislative power. Thus no member of the commonwealth can have a hereditary privilege as against his fellow-subjects; and no-one can hand down to his descendants the privileges attached to the rank he occupies in the common-wealth, nor act as if he were qualified as a ruler by birth and forcibly prevent others from reaching the higher levels of the hierarchy (which are *superior* and *inferior*, but never *imperans* and *subiectus*) through their own merit. He may hand down everything else, so long as it is material and not pertaining to his person, for it may be acquired and disposed of as property and may over a series of generations create considerable inequalities in wealth among the members of the commonwealth (the employee and the employer, the landowner and the agricultural servants, etc.). But he may not prevent his subordinates from raising themselves to his own level if they are able and entitled to do so by their talent, industry and good fortune. If this were not so, he would be allowed to practise coercion without himself being subject to coercive counter-measures from others, and would thus be more than their fellow-subject. No-one who lives within the lawful state of a commonwealth can forfeit this equality other than through some crime of his own, but never by contract or through military force (*occupatio bellica*). For no legal transaction on his part or on that of anyone else can make him cease to be his own master. He cannot become like a domestic animal to be employed in any chosen capacity and retained therein without consent for any desired period, even with the reservation (which is at times sanctioned by religion, as among the Indians) that he may not be maimed or killed. He can be considered happy in any condition so long as he is aware that, if he does not reach the same level as others, the fault lies either with himself (i.e. lack of ability or serious endeavour) or with circumstances for which he cannot blame others, and not with the irresistible will of any outside party. For as far as right is concerned, his fellow-subjects have no advantage over him.[1]

3. The *independence* (*sibisufficientia*) of a member of the commonwealth as a *citizen*, i.e. as a co-legislator, may be defined as follows. In the question of actual legislation, all who are free and equal under existing public laws may be considered equal, but not as regards the right to make these laws. Those who are not entitled to this right are nonetheless obliged, as members of the commonwealth, to comply with these laws, and they thus likewise enjoy their protection (not as *citizens* but as co-beneficiaries of this protection). For all right depends on laws. But a public law which defines for everyone that which is permitted and prohibited by right, is the act of a public will, from which all right proceeds and which must not therefore itself be able to do an injustice to any one. And this requires no less than the will of the entire people (since all men decide for all men and each decides for himself). For only towards oneself can one never act unjustly. But on the other hand, the will of another person cannot decide anything for someone without injustice, so that the law made by this other person would require a further law to limit his legislation. Thus an individual will cannot legislate for a commonwealth. For this requires freedom, equality and *unity* of the will of *all* the members. And the prerequisite for unity, since it necessitates a general vote (if freedom and equality are both present), is independence. The basic law, which can come only from the general, united will of the people, is called the *original contract*.

Anyone who has the right to vote on this legislation is a *citizen* (*citoyen*, i.e. citizen of a state, not *bourgeois* or citizen of a town). The only qualification required by a citizen (apart, of course, from being an adult male) is that he must be his *own master* (*sui iuris*), and must have some *property* (which can include any skill, trade, fine art or science) to support himself. In cases where he must earn his living from others, he must earn it only by *selling* that which is his,[2] and not by allowing others to make use of him; for he must in the true sense of the word *serve* no-one but the commonwealth. In this respect, artisans and large or small landowners are all equal, and each is entitled to one vote only. As for landowners, we leave aside the question of how anyone can have rightfully acquired more land than he can cultivate with his own hands (for acquisition by military seizure is not primary acquisition), and how it came about that numerous people who might otherwise have acquired permanent property were thereby reduced to serving someone else in order to live at all. It would certainly conflict with the above principle of equality if a law were to grant them a privileged status so that their descendants would always remain feudal landowners, without their land being sold or divided by inheritance and thus made useful to more people; it would also be unjust if only those belonging to an arbitrarily selected class were allowed to acquire land, should the estates in fact be divided. The owner of a large estate keeps out as many smaller property owners (and their votes) as could otherwise occupy his territories. He does not vote on their behalf, and himself has only *one* vote. It should be left exclusively to the ability, industry and good fortune of each member of the commonwealth to enable each to acquire a part and all to acquire the whole, although this distinction cannot be observed within the general legislation itself. The number of those entitled to vote on matters of legislation must be calculated purely from the number of property owners, not from the size of their properties.

Those who possess this right to vote must agree *unanimously* to the law of public justice, or else a legal contention would arise between those who agree and those who disagree, and it would require yet another higher legal principle to resolve it. An entire people cannot, however, be expected to reach unanimity, but only to show a majority of votes (and not even of direct votes, but simply of the votes of those delegated in a large nation to represent the people). Thus the actual principle of being content with majority decisions must be accepted unanimously and embodied in a contract; and this itself must be the ultimate basis on which a civil constitution is established.

[…]

## NOTES

1. If we try to find a definite meaning for the word *gracious*, as distinct from kind, beneficent, protective etc., we see that it can be attributed only to a person to whom no *coercive rights* apply. Thus only the head of the *state's government*, who enacts and distributes all benefits that are possible within the public laws (for the *sovereign* who provides them is, as it were, invisible, and is not an agent but the personified law itself), can be given the title of *gracious lord*, for he is the only individual to whom coercive rights do not apply. And even in an aristocratic government, as for example in Venice, the *senate* is the only 'gracious lord'. The nobles who belong to it, even including the *Doge* (for only the *plenary council* is the sovereign), are all subjects and equal to the others so far as the exercise of rights is concerned, for each subject has coercive rights towards every one of them. Princes (i.e. persons with a hereditary right to become rulers) are themselves called gracious lords only with future reference, an account of their claims to become rulers (i.e. by courtly etiquette, *par courtoisie*). But as owners of property, they are nonetheless fellow-subjects of the others, and even the humblest of their servants must possess a right of coercion against them through the head of state. Thus there can be no more than one gracious lord in a state. And as for gracious (more correctly *distinguished*) ladies, they can be considered entitled to this appellation by their *rank* and their *sex* (thus only as opposed to the *male* sex), and this only by virtue of a refinement of manners (known as gallantry) whereby the male sex imagines that it does itself greater honour by giving the fair sex precedence over itself.
2. He who does a piece of work (*opus*) can sell it to someone else, just as if it were his own property. But guaranteeing one's labour (*praestatio operae*) is not the same as selling a commodity. The domestic servant, the shop assistant, the labourer, or even the barber, are merely labourers (*operarii*), not *artists* (*artifices*, in the wider sense) or members of the state, and are thus unqualified to be citizens. And although the man to whom I give my firewood to chop and the tailor to whom I give material to make into clothes both appear to have a similar relationship towards me, the former differs from

the latter in the same way as the barber from the wig-maker (to whom I may in fact have given the requisite hair) or the labourer from the artist or tradesman, who does a piece of work which belongs to him until he is paid for it. For the latter, in pursuing his trade, exchanges his property with someone else (*opus*), while the former allows someone else to make use of him. – But I do admit that it is somewhat difficult to define the qualifications which entitle anyone to claim the status of being his own master.

# 16

# THE LIBERTY OF THE ANCIENTS COMPARED WITH THAT OF THE MODERNS

## Benjamin Constant

[...]

It follows from what I have just indicated that we can no longer enjoy the liberty of the ancients, which consisted in an active and constant participation in collective power. Our freedom must consist of peaceful enjoyment and private independence. The share which in antiquity everyone held in national sovereignty was by no means an abstract presumption as it is in our own day. The will of each individual had real influence: the exercise of this will was a vivid and repeated pleasure. Consequently the ancients were ready to make many a sacrifice to preserve their political rights and their share in the administration of the state. Everybody, feeling with pride all that his suffrage was worth, found in this awareness of his personal importance a great compensation.

This compensation no longer exists for us today. Lost in the multitude, the individual can almost never perceive the influence he exercises. Never does his will impress itself upon the whole; nothing confirms in his eyes his own cooperation.

The exercise of political rights, therefore, offers us but a part of the pleasures that the ancients found in it, while at the same time the progress of civilization, the commercial tendency of the age, the communication amongst peoples, have infinitely multiplied and varied the means of personal happiness.

It follows that we must be far more attached than the ancients to our indi-

From Benjamin Constant, *Political Writings*, ed. Biancamaria Fontana (Cambridge University Press, Cambridge, 1988), pp. 316–18. Originally written 1819.

vidual independence. For the ancients when they sacrificed that independence to their political rights, sacrificed less to obtain more; while in making the same sacrifice, we would give more to obtain less.

The aim of the ancients was the sharing of social power among the citizens of the same fatherland: this is what they called liberty. The aim of the moderns is the enjoyment of security in private pleasures; and they call liberty the guarantees accorded by institutions to these pleasures.

I said at the beginning that, through their failure to perceive these differences, otherwise well-intentioned men caused infinite evils during our long and stormy revolution. God forbid that I should reproach them too harshly. Their error itself was excusable. One could not read the beautiful pages of antiquity, one could not recall the actions of its great men, without feeling an indefinable and special emotion, which nothing modern can possibly arouse. The old elements of a nature, one could almost say, earlier than our own, seem to awaken in us in the face of these memories. It is difficult not to regret the time when the faculties of man developed along an already trodden path, but in so wide a career, so strong in their own powers, with such a feeling of energy and dignity. Once we abandon ourselves to this regret, it is impossible not to wish to imitate what we regret. This impression was very deep, especially when we lived under vicious governments, which, without being strong, were repressive in their effects; absurd in their principles; wretched in action; governments which had as their strength arbitrary power; for their purpose the belittling of mankind; and which some individuals still dare to praise to us today, as if we could ever forget that we have been the witnesses and the victims of their obstinacy, of their impotence and of their overthrow. The aim of our reformers was noble and generous. Who among us did not feel his heart beat with hope at the outset of the course which they seemed to open up? And shame, even today, on whoever does not feel the need to declare that acknowledging a few errors committed by our first guides does not mean blighting their memory or disowning the opinions which the friends of mankind have professed throughout the ages.

But those men had derived several of their theories from the works of two philosophers who had themselves failed to recognize the changes brought by two thousand years in the dispositions of mankind. I shall perhaps at some point examine the system of the most illustrious of these philosophers, of Jean-Jacques Rousseau, and I shall show that, by transposing into our modern age an extent of social power, of collective sovereignty, which belonged to other centuries, this sublime genius, animated by the purest love of liberty, has nevertheless furnished deadly pretexts for more than one kind of tyranny. No doubt, in pointing out what I regard as a misunderstanding which it is important to uncover, I shall be careful in my refutation, and respectful in my criticism. I shall certainly refrain from joining myself to the detractors of a great man. When chance has it that I find myself apparently in agreement with them on some one particular point, I suspect myself; and to console myself for appearing for a moment in agreement with them on a single partial question, I need to disown and denounce with all my energies these pretended allies.

[...]

# 17

# TWO CONCEPTS OF LIBERTY

## Isaiah Berlin

### VII
### *Liberty and sovereignty*

The French Revolution, like all great revolutions, was, at least in its Jacobin form, just such an eruption of the desire for 'positive' freedom of collective self-direction on the part of a large body of Frenchmen who felt liberated as a nation, even though the result was, for a good many of them, a severe restriction of individual freedoms. Rousseau had spoken exultantly of the fact that the laws of liberty might prove to be more austere than the yoke of tyranny. Tyranny is service to human masters. The law cannot be a tyrant. Rousseau does not mean by liberty the 'negative' freedom of the individual not to be interfered with within a defined area, but the possession by all, and not merely by some, of the fully qualified members of a society of a share in the public power which is entitled to interfere with every aspect of every citizen's life. The liberals of the first half of the nineteenth century correctly foresaw that liberty in this 'positive' sense could easily destroy too many of the 'negative' liberties that they held sacred. They pointed out that the sovereignty of the people could easily destroy that of individuals. Mill explained, patiently and unanswerably, that government by the people was not, in his sense, necessarily freedom at all. For those who govern are not necessarily the same 'people' as those who are governed, and democratic self-government is not the government 'of each by himself' but, at best, of 'each by the rest'. Mill and his disciples spoke of the tyranny of the

From Isaiah Berlin, 'Two Concepts of Liberty', in *Four Essays on Liberty* (Oxford University Press, Oxford, 1969), pp. 162–6.

majority and of the tyranny of 'the prevailing feeling and opinion', and saw no great difference between that and any other kind of tyranny which encroaches upon men's activities beyond the sacred frontiers of private life.

No one saw the conflict between the two types of liberty better, or expressed it more clearly, than Benjamin Constant. He pointed out that the transference by a successful rising of the unlimited authority, commonly called sovereignty, from one set of hands to another does not increase liberty, but merely shifts the burden of slavery. He reasonably asked why a man should deeply care whether he is crushed by a popular government or by a monarch, or even by a set of oppressive laws. He saw that the main problem for those who desire 'negative', individual freedom is not who wields this authority, but how much authority should be placed in any set of hands. For unlimited authority in anybody's grasp was bound, he believed, sooner or later, to destroy somebody. He maintained that usually men protested against this or that set of governors as oppressive, when the real cause of oppression lay in the mere fact of the accumulation of power itself, wherever it might happen to be, since liberty was endangered by the mere existence of absolute authority as such. 'It is not the arm that is unjust', he wrote, 'but the weapon that is too heavy – some weights are too heavy for the human hand.' Democracy may disarm a given oligarchy, a given privileged individual or set of individuals, but it can still crush individuals as mercilessly as any previous ruler. In an essay comparing the liberty of the moderns with that of the ancients he said that an equal right to oppress – or interfere – is not equivalent to liberty. Nor does universal consent to loss of liberty somehow miraculously preserve it merely by being universal, or by being consent. If I consent to be oppressed, or acquiesce in my condition with detachment or irony, am I the less oppressed? If I sell myself into slavery, am I the less a slave? If I commit suicide, am I the less dead because I have taken my own life freely? 'Popular government is a spasmodic tyranny, monarchy a more efficiently centralized despotism.' Constant saw in Rousseau the most dangerous enemy of individual liberty, because he had declared that 'by giving myself to all I give myself to none'. Constant could not see why, even though the sovereign is 'everybody', it should not oppress one of the 'members' of its indivisible self, if it so decided. I may, of course, prefer to be deprived of my liberties by an assembly, or a family, or a class, in which I am a minority. It may give me an opportunity one day of persuading the others to do for me that to which I feel I am entitled. But to be deprived of my liberty at the hands of my family or friends or fellow citizens is to be deprived of it just as effectively. Hobbes was at any rate more candid: he did not pretend that a sovereign does not enslave: he justified this slavery, but at least did not have the effrontery to call it freedom.

Throughout the nineteenth century liberal thinkers maintained that if liberty involved a limit upon the powers of any man to force me to do what I did not, or might not, wish to do, then, whatever the ideal in the name of which I was coerced, I was not free; that the doctrine of absolute sovereignty was a tyrannical doctrine in itself. If I wish to preserve my liberty, it is not enough to say that it must not be violated unless someone or other – the absolute ruler, or the popular assembly, or the King in Parliament, or the judges, or some combination of authorities, or the laws themselves – for the laws may be oppressive – authorizes its violation. I must establish a society in which there must be some frontiers of freedom which nobody should be permitted to cross. Different names or natures may be given to the rules that determine these frontiers: they may be called natural rights, or the word of God, or Natural Law, or the demands of utility or of the 'permanent interests of man'; I may believe them to be valid *a priori*, or assert them to be my own ultimate ends, or the ends of my society or culture. What these rules or commandments will have in common is that they are accepted so widely, and are grounded so deeply in the actual nature of men as they have developed through history, as to be, by now, an essential part of what we mean by being a normal human being. Genuine belief in the inviolability of a minimum extent of individual liberty entails some such absolute stand. For it is clear that it has little to hope for from the rule of majorities; democracy as such is logically uncommitted to it, and historically has at times failed to protect it, while remaining faithful to its own principles. Few governments, it has been observed, have found much difficulty in causing their subjects to generate any will that the government wanted. 'The triumph of despotism is to force the slaves to declare themselves free.' It may need no force; the slaves may proclaim their freedom quite sincerely: but they are none the less slaves. Perhaps the chief value for liberals of political – 'positive' – rights, of participating in the government, is as a means for protecting what they hold to be an ultimate value, namely individual – 'negative' – liberty.

But if democracies can, without ceasing to be democratic, suppress freedom, at least as liberals have used the word, what would make a society truly free? For Constant, Mill, Tocqueville, and the liberal tradition to which they belong, no society is free unless it is governed by at any rate two interrelated principles: first, that no power, but only rights, can be regarded as absolute, so that all men, whatever power governs them, have an absolute right to refuse to behave inhumanly; and, second, that there are frontiers, not artificially drawn, within which men should be inviolable, these frontiers being defined in terms of rules so long and widely accepted that their observance has entered into the very conception of what it is to be a normal human being, and, therefore, also of what it is to act inhumanly or insanely; rules of which it would be absurd to say, for example, that they could be abrogated by some formal procedure on the part of some court or sovereign body. When I speak of a man as being normal, a part of what I mean is that he could not break these rules easily, without a qualm of revulsion. It is such rules as these that are broken when a man is declared guilty without trial, or punished under a retroactive law; when children are ordered to denounce their parents, friends to betray one another, soldiers to use methods of barbarism; when men are tortured or murdered, or minorities are massacred because they irritate a majority or a tyrant. Such acts, even if they are made legal by the sovereign, cause horror even in these days, and this springs from the recognition of the moral validity – irrespective of the laws – of some absolute barriers to the imposition of one man's will on another. The freedom of a society, or a class or a group, in this sense of freedom, is measured by the strength of these barriers, and the number and importance of the paths which they keep open for their members – if not for all, for at any rate a great number of them.

This is almost at the opposite pole from the purposes of those who believe in liberty in the 'positive' – self-directive – sense. The former want to curb authority as such. The latter want it placed in their own hands. That is a cardinal issue. These are not two different interpretations of a single concept, but two profoundly divergent and irreconcilable attitudes to the ends of life. It is as well to recognize this, even if in practice it is often necessary to strike a compromise between them. For each of them makes absolute claims. These claims cannot both be fully satisfied. But it is a profound lack of social and moral understanding not to recognize that the satisfaction that each of them seeks is an ultimate value which, both historically and morally, has an equal right to be classed among the deepest interests of mankind.

18

# IN DEFENSE OF ANARCHISM

## Robert Paul Wolff

[...]

The fundamental assumption of moral philosophy is that men are responsible for their actions. From this assumption it follows necessarily, as Kant pointed out, that men are metaphysically free, which is to say that in some sense they are capable of choosing how they shall act. Being able to choose how he acts makes a man responsible, but merely choosing is not in itself enough to constitute *taking* responsibility for one's actions. Taking responsibility involves attempting to determine what one ought to do, and that, as philosophers since Aristotle have recognized, lays upon one the additional burdens of gaining knowledge, reflecting on motives, predicting outcomes, criticizing principles, and so forth.

The obligation to take responsibility for one's actions does not derive from man's freedom of will alone, for more is required in taking responsibility than freedom of choice. Only because man has the capacity to reason about his choices can he be said to stand under a continuing obligation to take responsibility for them. It is quite appropriate that moral philosophers should group together children and madmen as beings not fully responsible for their actions, for as madmen are thought to lack freedom of choice, so children do not yet possess the power of reason in a developed form. It is even just that we should assign a greater degree of responsibility to children, for madmen, by virtue of their lack of free will, are completely without responsibility, while children,

From Robert Paul Wolff, *In Defense of Anarchism* (A Torchbook Library Edition, Harper & Row, New York, Evanston, IL and London, 1970), pp. 12–14.

insofar as they possess reason in a partially developed form, can be held responsible (i.e., can be required to take responsibility) to a corresponding degree.

Every man who possesses both free will and reason has an obligation to take responsibility for his actions, even though he may not be actively engaged in a continuing process of reflection, investigation, and deliberation about how he ought to act. A man will sometimes announce his willingness to take responsibility for the consequences of his actions, even though he has not deliberated about them, or does not intend to do so in the future. Such a declaration is, of course, an advance over the refusal to take responsibility; it at least acknowledges the existence of the obligation. But it does not relieve the man of the duty to engage in the reflective process which he has thus far shunned. It goes without saying that a man may take responsibility for his actions and yet act wrongly. When we describe someone as a responsible individual, we do not imply that he always does what is right, but only that he does not neglect the duty of attempting to ascertain what is right.

The responsible man is not capricious or anarchic, for he does acknowledge himself bound by moral constraints. But he insists that he alone is the judge of those constraints. He may listen to the advice of others, but he makes it his own by determining for himself whether it is good advice. He may learn from others about his moral obligations, but only in the sense that a mathematician learns from other mathematicians – namely by hearing from them arguments whose validity he recognizes even though he did not think of them himself. He does not learn in the sense that one learns from an explorer, by accepting as true his accounts of things one cannot see for oneself.

Since the responsible man arrives at moral decisions which he expresses to himself in the form of imperatives, we may say that he gives laws to himself, or is self-legislating. In short, he is *autonomous*. As Kant argued, moral autonomy is a combination of freedom and responsibility; it is a submission to laws which one has made for oneself. The autonomous man, insofar as he is autonomous, is not subject to the will of another. He may do what another tells him, but not *because* he has been told to do it. He is therefore, in the political sense of the word, *free*.

[...]

# SECTION 2
# EQUALITY

# EQUALITY
# INTRODUCTION

Equality is certainly one of the key concepts of democratic theory, and one of the basic values which it is claimed a democratic society realises. The English Utilitarian philosopher Jeremy Bentham asserted as a maxim that 'Everyone should count for one, and no-one for more than one'. This has been seen as one of the foundations for the theory and practice of democracy.

But what is equality? How can it be justified? In what ways is it connected with the democratic ideal? The classic and deeply-felt analysis of the concept of inequality by *Rousseau* is a central point of reference here. As the extracts in this section reveal, Rousseau distinguishes between natural inequality and the inequality created by political and social institutions. Like other egalitarians, he does not deny that people are different, and have varying characteristics and abilities. Yet a democratic society, created, as he puts it, by the 'fundamental compact', achieves a situation of legitimate moral equality. All are equal as citizens in the newly-created democratic society. Of course individual citizens will differ in terms of their strength, intelligence or other capacities. This is irrelevant to their equal status as members of a democratic community. In the same way, in his 'Discourse on the Origin of Inequality among Men', Rousseau makes the crucial distinction between natural inequality and moral and political inequality. To assert that the former types of inequality justify the latter is a false argument.

Yet the egalitarian implications of Rousseau's philosophy are contradicted by the historically earlier position of *Locke* and his defence of private property. Locke explains that the use of money allows people to accumulate property beyond the limits of what is perishable and needed for people's immediate use.

This implies, suggests Locke, a 'tacit and voluntary consent' to inequality. It involves 'an inequality of private possessions'. Following on from Locke, contemporary philosophers like Nozick have seen in such arguments the foundations and justification of inevitable inequality in society. Others, of more egalitarian disposition, have seen in private property and the inequalities of market society, a potential undermining of the democratic ideal.

The argument in defence of equality, as a constituent element of a democratic society, has continued from Rousseau's time to contemporary debates. Twentieth-century egalitarians, like the English socialist *Tawney* and the philosopher *Bernard Williams*, seek to defend equality as a coherent ideal. In line with Rousseau, Tawney criticises the 'religion of inequality' which he sees as characterising the English society of his day. Equality is based, he argues, on ideas of a common humanity, which is perfectly compatible with recognition of individual diversity and difference: equality of provision does not mean identity of provision. He lays down the challenge that a tradition of economic equality needs to be created, one which is lacking from market-dominated societies. This contrast between the equality which liberal-democratic societies proclaim in the political sphere, and the inequality which exists in the socio-economic sphere, is a core theme of the Marxist and socialist critiques of democracy which we reproduce in the Section 6 on these critiques in Part Three below.

Williams seeks to explore the validity of the arguments in defence of equality. He invokes ideas of common humanity, and the acknowledgement that every person is a rational moral agent. This latter Kantian argument is based on the idea that as rational individuals we each have our plans of life and purposes. Williams also discusses the idea of equality of respect, looking at individuals irrespective of the particular role they play in society, and ignoring the 'labels' which describe those roles. These are all aspects of the egalitarian position and its philosophical defence.

Yet these egalitarian ideals come under sustained criticism from those who see them as unrealisable, or only attainable at the expense of other desirable values. Such arguments often come from those who see the market, and the inherent inequalities stemming from a market-dominated society, as fundamental to a free society. We reproduce some arguments to this effect in Section 10 on the market in Part Four below.

In sum, the extracts in this section suggest that while equality is a core concept of democracy, it is far from unproblematic. Critics from the Left suggest that a truly democratic society would be one for which social, as well as political, equality would be a necessary condition. Critics from the Right maintain that equality is an incoherent ideal, at least if it is extended beyond equal right to vote and equality under the law. And both feminist and postmodern critics suggest that some forms of equality can be oblivious to the importance of *difference* between citizens, between men and women, for example. Hence some forms of equality might involve the suppression of difference. A democratic society could be a homogeneous one, which represses or ignores the diversity of citizens.

# 19

# THE SECOND TREATISE
# OF GOVERNMENT

## John Locke

[...]

44. From all which it is evident, that though the things of Nature are given in common, yet Man (by being Master of himself, and *Proprietor of his own Person*, and the Actions or *Labour* of it) had still in himself *the great Foundation of Property*; and that which made up the great part of what he applyed to the Support or Comfort of his being, when Invention and Arts had improved the conveniencies of Life, was perfectly his own, and did not belong in common to others.

45. Thus *Labour*, in the Beginning, *gave a Right of Property*, where-ever any one was pleased to imploy it, upon what was common, which remained, a long while, the far greater part, and is yet more than Mankind makes use of. Men, at first, for the most part, contented themselves with what un-assisted Nature offered to their Necessities: and though afterwards, in some parts of the World, (where the Increase of People and Stock, with the *Use of Money*) had made Land scarce, and so of some Value, the several *Communities* settled the Bounds of their distinct Territories, and by Laws within themselves, regulated the Properties of the private Men of their Society, and so, *by Compact* and Agreement, *settled the Property* which Labour and Industry began; and the Leagues that have been made between several States and Kingdoms, either expressly or tacitly disowning all Claim and Right to the Land in the others

From John Locke, *Two Treatises of Government*, ed. P. Laslett (Cambridge University Press, Cambridge, 1988), pp. 298–302. Originally written 1689.

Possession, have, by common Consent, given up their Pretences to their natural common Right, which originally they had to those Countries, and so have, by *positive agreement, settled a Property* amongst themselves, in distinct Parts and parcels of the Earth: yet there are still *great Tracts of Ground* to be found, which (the Inhabitants thereof not having joyned with the rest of Mankind, in the consent of the Use of their common Money) *lie waste*, and are more than the People, who dwell on it, do, or can make use of, and so still lie in common. Tho' this can scarce happen amongst that part of Mankind, that have consented to the Use of Money.

46. The greatest part of *things really useful* to the Life of Man, and such as the necessity of subsisting made the first Commoners of the World look after, as it doth the *Americans* now, *are* generally things of *short duration*; such as, if they are not consumed by use, will decay and perish of themselves: Gold, Silver, and Diamonds, are things, that Fancy or Agreement hath put the Value on, more then real Use, and the necessary Support of Life. Now of those good things which Nature hath provided in common, every one had a Right (as hath been said) to as much as he could use, and had a Property in all that he could affect with his Labour: all that his Industry could extend to, to alter from the State Nature had put it in, was his. He that *gathered* a Hundred Bushels of Acorns or Apples, had thereby a *Property* in them; they were his Goods as soon as gathered. He was only to look that he used them before they spoiled; else he took more then his share, and robb'd others. And indeed it was a foolish thing, as well as dishonest, to hoard up more than he could make use of. If he gave away a part to any body else, so that it perished not uselessly in his Possession, these he also made use of. And if he also bartered away Plumbs that would have rotted in a Week, for Nuts that would last good for his eating a whole Year, he did no injury; he wasted not the common Stock; destroyed no part of the portion of Goods that belonged to others, so long as nothing perished uselessly in his hands. Again, if he would give his Nuts for a piece of Metal, pleased with its colour; or exchange his Sheep for Shells, or Wool for a sparkling Pebble or a Diamond, and keep those by him all his Life, he invaded not the Right of others, he might heap up as much of these durable things as he pleased; the *exceeding of the bounds of his just Property* not lying in the largeness of his Possession, but the perishing of any thing uselessly in it.

47. And thus *came in the use of Money*, some lasting thing that Men might keep without spoiling, and that by mutual consent Men would take in exchange for the truly useful, but perishable Supports of Life.

48. And as different degrees of Industry were apt to give Men Possessions in different Proportions, so this *Invention of Money* gave them the opportunity to continue and enlarge them. For supposing an Island, separate from all possible Commerce with the rest of the World, wherein there were but a hundred

Families, but there were Sheep, Horses and Cows, with other useful Animals, wholsome Fruits, and Land enough for Corn for a hundred thousand times as many, but nothing in the Island, either because of its Commonness, or Perishableness, fit to supply the place of *Money*: What reason could any one have there to enlarge his Possessions beyond the use of his Family, and a plentiful supply to its Consumption, either in what their own Industry produced, or they could barter for like perishable, useful Commodities, with others? Where there is not something both lasting and scarce, and so valuable to be hoarded up, there Men will not be apt to enlarge their *Possessions of Land*, were it never so rich, never so free for them to take. For I ask, What would a Man value Ten Thousand, or an Hundred Thousand Acres of excellent *Land*, ready cultivated, and well stocked too with Cattle, in the middle of the in-land Parts of *America*, where he had no hopes of Commerce with other Parts of the World, to draw *Money* to him by the Sale of the Product? It would not be worth the inclosing, and we should see him give up again to the wild Common of Nature, whatever was more than would supply the Conveniencies of Life to be had there for him and his Family.

49. Thus in the beginning all the World was *America*, and more so than that is now; for no such thing as *Money* was any where known. Find out something that hath the *Use and Value of Money* amongst his Neighbours, you shall see the same Man will begin presently to *enlarge* his *Possessions*.

50. But since Gold and Silver, being little useful to the Life of Man in proportion to Food, Rayment, and Carriage, has its *value* only from the consent of Men, whereof Labour yet makes, in great part, *the measure*, it is plain, that Men have agreed to disproportionate and unequal Possession of the Earth, they having by a tacit and voluntary consent found out a way, how a man may fairly possess more land than he himself can use the product of, by receiving in exchange for the overplus, Gold and Silver, which may be hoarded up without injury to any one, these metalls not spoileing or decaying in the hands of the possessor. This partage of things, in an inequality of private possessions, men have made practicable out of the bounds of Societie, and without compact, only by putting a value on gold and silver and tacitly agreeing in the use of Money. For in Governments the Laws regulate the right of property, and the possession of land is determined by positive constitutions.

51. And thus, I think, it is very easie to conceive without any difficulty, *how Labour could at first begin a title of Property* in the common things of Nature, and how the spending it upon our uses bounded it. So that there could then be no reason of quarrelling about Title, nor any doubt about the largeness of Possession it gave. Right and conveniency went together; for as a Man had a Right to all he could imploy his Labour upon, so he had no temptation to labour for more than he could make use of. This left no room for Controversie about

the Title, nor for Incroachment on the Right of others; what Portion a Man carved to himself, was easily seen; and it was useless as well as dishonest to carve himself too much, or take more than he needed.

# 20

# THE SOCIAL CONTRACT

## Jean-Jacques Rousseau

[...]

### CHAPTER IX
#### REAL PROPERTY

Each member of the community gives himself to it, at the moment of its foundation, just as he is, with all the resources at his command, including the goods he possesses. This act does not make possession, in changing hands, change its nature, and become property in the hands of the Sovereign; but, as the forces of the city are incomparably greater than those of an individual, public possession is also, in fact, stronger and more irrevocable, without being any more legitimate, at any rate from the point of view of foreigners. For the State, in relation to its members, is master of all their goods by the social contract, which, within the State, is the basis of all rights; but, in relation to other powers, it is so only by the right of the first occupier, which it holds from its members.

The right of the first occupier, though more real than the right of the strongest, becomes a real right only when the right of property has already been established. Every man has naturally a right to everything he needs; but the positive act which makes him proprietor of one thing excludes him from everything else. Having his share, he ought to keep to it, and can have no further right against the community. This is why the right of the first occupier, which in the state of nature is so weak, claims the respect of every man in civil

From Jean-Jacques Rousseau, *The Social Contract and Discourses*, trans. and intro. G. D. H. Cole (Everyman's Library: Dent, London/Dutton, New York, 1968), Book I, chapter IX, pp. 16–19. Originally written 1762.

society. In this right we are respecting not so much what belongs to another as what does not belong to ourselves.

In general, to establish the right of the first occupier over a plot of ground, the following conditions are necessary: first, the land must not yet be inhabited; secondly, a man must occupy only the amount he needs for his subsistence; and, in the third place, possession must be taken, not by an empty ceremony, but by labour and cultivation, the only sign of proprietorship that should be respected by others, in default of a legal title.

In granting the right of first occupancy to necessity and labour, are we not really stretching it as far as it can go? Is it possible to leave such a right unlimited? Is it to be enough to set foot on a plot of common ground, in order to be able to call yourself at once the master of it? Is it to be enough that a man has the strength to expel others for a moment, in order to establish his right to prevent them from ever returning? How can a man or a people seize an immense territory and keep it from the rest of the world except by a punishable usurpation, since all others are being robbed, by such an act, of the place of habitation and the means of subsistence which nature gave them in common? When Nuñez Balbao, standing on the seashore, took possession of the South Seas and the whole of South America in the name of the crown of Castille, was that enough to dispossess all their actual inhabitants, and to shut out from them all the princes of the world? On such a showing, these ceremonies are idly multiplied, and the Catholic King need only take possession all at once, from his apartment, of the whole universe, merely making a subsequent reservation about what was already in the possession of other princes.

We can imagine how the lands of individuals, where they were contiguous and came to be united, became the public territory, and how the right of Sovereignty, extending from the subjects over the lands they held, became at once real and personal. The possessors were thus made more dependent, and the forces at their command used to guarantee their fidelity. The advantage of this does not seem to have been felt by ancient monarchs, who called themselves King of the Persians, Scythians, or Macedonians, and seemed to regard themselves more as rulers of men than as masters of a country. Those of the present day more cleverly call themselves Kings of France, Spain, England, etc.: thus holding the land, they are quite confident of holding the inhabitants.

The peculiar fact about this alienation is that, in taking over the goods of individuals, the community, so far from despoiling them, only assures them legitimate possession, and changes usurpation into a true right and enjoyment into proprietorship. Thus the possessors, being regarded as depositaries of the public good, and having their rights respected by all the members of the State and maintained against foreign aggression by all its forces, have, by a cession which benefits both the public and still more themselves, acquired, so to speak, all that they gave up. This paradox may easily be explained by the distinction between the rights which the Sovereign and the proprietor have over the same estate, as we shall see later on.

It may also happen that men begin to unite one with another before they possess anything, and that, subsequently occupying a tract of country which is enough for all, they enjoy it in common, or share it out among themselves, either equally or according to a scale fixed by the Sovereign. However the acquisition be made, the right which each individual has to his own estate is always subordinate to the right which the community has over all: without this, there would be neither stability in the social tie, nor real force in the exercise of Sovereignty.

I shall end this chapter and this book by remarking on a fact on which the whole social system should rest: i.e. that, instead of destroying natural inequality, the fundamental compact substitutes, for such physical inequality as nature may have set up between men, an equality that is moral and legitimate, and that men, who may be unequal in strength or intelligence, become every one equal by convention and legal right.[1]

### NOTE

1. Under bad governments, this equality is only apparent and illusory; it serves only to keep the pauper in his poverty and the rich man in the position he has usurped. In fact, laws are always of use to those who possess and harmful to those who have nothing: from which it follows that the social state is advantageous to men only when all have something and none too much.

# 21

# A DISCOURSE ON THE ORIGIN
# OF INEQUALITY

## Jean-Jacques Rousseau

[...]

I conceive that there are two kinds of inequality among the human species; one, which I call natural or physical, because it is established by nature, and consists in a difference of age, health, bodily strength, and the qualities of the mind or of the soul: and another, which may be called moral or political inequality, because it depends on a kind of convention, and is established, or at least authorized, by the consent of men. This latter consists of the different privileges which some men enjoy to the prejudice of others; such as that of being more rich, more honoured, more powerful, or even in a position to exact obedience.

It is useless to ask what is the source of natural inequality, because that question is answered by the simple definition of the word. Again, it is still more useless to inquire whether there is any essential connection between the two inequalities; for this would be only asking, in other words, whether those who command are necessarily better than those who obey, and if strength of body or of mind, wisdom, or virtue are always found in particular individuals, in proportion to their power or wealth: a question fit perhaps to be discussed by slaves in the hearing of their masters, but highly unbecoming to reasonable and free men in search of the truth.

The subject of the present discourse, therefore, is more precisely this. To mark, in the progress of things, the moment at which right took the place of violence and nature became subject to law, and to explain by what sequence of

From Jean-Jacques Rousseau, *The Social Contract and Discourses*, trans. and intro. G. D. H. Cole (Everyman's Library: Dent, London/Dutton, New York, 1968), pp. 160–2. Originally written 1754.

miracles the strong came to submit to serve the weak, and the people to purchase imaginary repose at the expense of real felicity.

The philosophers, who have inquired into the foundations of society, have all felt the necessity of going back to a state of nature; but not one of them has got there. Some of them have not hesitated to ascribe to man, in such a state, the idea of just and unjust, without troubling themselves to show that he must be possessed of such an idea, or that it could be of any use to him. Others have spoken of the natural right of every man to keep what belongs to him, without explaining what they meant by 'belongs.' Others again, beginning by giving the strong authority over the weak, proceeded directly to the birth of government, without regard to the time that must have elapsed before the meaning of the words 'authority' and 'government' could have existed among men. Every one of them, in short, constantly dwelling on wants, avidity, oppression, desires, and pride, has transferred to the state of nature ideas which were acquired in society; so that, in speaking of the savage, they described the social man. It has not even entered into the heads of most of our writers to doubt whether the state of nature ever existed; but it is clear from the Holy Scriptures that the first man, having received his understanding and commandments immediately from God, was not himself in such a state; and that, if we give such credit to the writings of Moses as every Christian philosopher ought to give, we must deny that, even before the deluge, men were ever in the pure state of nature; unless, indeed, they fell back into it from some very extraordinary circumstance; a paradox which it would be very embarrassing to defend, and quite impossible to prove.

Let us begin then by laying facts aside, as they do not affect the questions. The investigations we may enter into, in treating this subject, must not be considered as historical truths, but only as mere conditional and hypothetical reasonings, rather calculated to explain the nature of things, than to ascertain their actual origin; just like the hypotheses which our physicists daily form respecting the formation of the world. Religion commands us to believe that God Himself having taken men out of a state of nature immediately after the creation, they are unequal only because it is His will they should be so: but it does not forbid us to form conjectures based solely on the nature of man, and the beings around him, concerning what might have become of the human race, if it had been left to itself. This then is the question asked me, and that which I propose to discuss in the following discourse. As my subject interests mankind in general, I shall endeavour to make use of a style adapted to all nations, or rather, forgetting time and place, to attend only to men to whom I am speaking. I shall suppose myself in the Lyceum of Athens, repeating the lessons of my masters, with Plato and Xenocrates for judges, and the whole human race for audience.

O man, of whatever country you are, and whatever your opinions may be, behold your history, such as I have thought to read it, not in books written by your fellow-creatures, who are liars, but in nature, which never lies. All that comes from her will be true; nor will you meet with anything false, unless I have involuntarily put in something of my own. The times of which I am going to speak are very remote: how much are you changed from what you once were! It is, so to speak, the life of your species which I am going to write, after the qualities which you have received, which your education and habits may have depraved, but cannot have entirely destroyed. There is, I feel, an age at which the individual man would wish to stop: you are about to inquire about the age at which you would have liked your whole species to stand still. Discontented with your present state, for reasons which threaten your unfortunate descendants with still greater discontent, you will perhaps wish it were in your power to go back; and this feeling should be a panegyric on your first ancestors, a criticism of your contemporaries, and a terror to the unfortunates who will come after you.

[...]

# 22

# EQUALITY

## R. H. Tawney

[...]

It is obvious, indeed, that, as things are today, no redistribution of wealth would bring general affluence, and that statisticians are within their rights in making merry with the idea that the equalization of incomes would make everyone rich. But, though riches are a good, they are not, nevertheless, the only good; and because greater production, which is concerned with the commodities to be consumed, is clearly important, it does not follow that greater equality, which is concerned with the relations between the human beings who consume them, is not important also. It is obvious, again, that the word 'Equality' possesses more than one meaning, and that the controversies surrounding it arise partly, at least, because the same term is employed with different connotations. Thus it may either purport to state a fact, or convey the expression of an ethical judgment. On the one hand, it may affirm that men are, on the whole, very similar in their natural endowments of character and intelligence. On the other hand, it may assert that, while they differ profoundly as individuals in capacity and character, they are equally entitled as human beings to consideration and respect, and that the well-being of a society is likely to be increased if it so plans its organization that, whether their powers are great or small, all its members may be equally enabled to make the best of such powers as they possess.

If made in the first sense, the assertion of human equality is clearly untenable. It is a piece of mythology against which irresistible evidence has been accumulated by biologists and psychologists. In the light of the data presented – to

From R. H. Tawney, *Equality* (Allen & Unwin, London, 1964), pp. 46–51.

mention only two recent examples – in such works as Dr Burt's admirable studies of the distribution of educational abilities among school-children, or the Report of the Mental Deficiency Committee, the fact that, quite apart from differences of environment and opportunity, individuals differ widely in their natural endowments, and in their capacity to develop them by education, is not open to question. There is some reason for holding, for instance, that, while eighty per cent of children at the age of ten fall within a range of about three mental years, the most backward may have a mental age of five, while the most gifted may have one of as much as fifteen.

The acceptance of that conclusion, nevertheless, makes a smaller breach in equalitarian doctrines than is sometimes supposed, for such doctrines have rarely been based on a denial of it. It is true, of course, that the psychological and political theory of the age between 1750 and 1850 – the theory, for example, of thinkers so different as Helvétius and Adam Smith at the beginning of the period, and Mill and Proudhon at the end of it – greatly underestimated the significance of inherited qualities, and greatly overestimated the plasticity of human nature. It may be doubted, however, whether it was quite that order of ideas which inspired the historical affirmations of human equality, even in the age when such ideas were still in fashion.

It is difficult for even the most sanguine of assemblies to retain for more than one meeting the belief that Providence has bestowed an equal measure of intelligence upon all its members. When the Americans declared it to be a self-evident truth that all men are created equal, they were thinking less of the admirable racial qualities of the inhabitants of the New World than of their political and economic relations with the Old, and would have remained unconvinced that those relations should continue even in the face of proofs of biological inferiority. When the French, who a century and a half ago preached the equalitarian idea with the same fervent conviction as is shown today by the rulers of Russia in denouncing it, set that idea side by side with liberty and fraternity as the motto of a new world, they did not mean that all men are equally intelligent or equally virtuous, any more than that they are equally tall or equally fat, but that the unity of their national life should no longer be torn to pieces by obsolete property rights and meaningless juristic distinctions. When Arnold, who was an inspector of schools as well as a poet, and who, whatever his failings, was not prone to demagogy, wrote 'choose equality', he did not suggest, it may be suspected, that all children appeared to him to be equally clever, but that a nation acts unwisely in stressing heavily distinctions based on birth or money.

Few men have been more acutely sensitive than Mill to the importance of encouraging the widest possible diversities of mind and taste. In arguing that 'the best state for human nature is that in which, while no one is poor, no one desires to be richer', and urging that social policy should be directed to increasing equality, he did not intend to convey that it should suppress varieties of individual genius and character, but that it was only in a society marked by a large measure of economic equality that such varieties were likely to find their full expression and due meed of appreciation. Theologians have not, as a rule, been disposed to ignore the fact that there are diversities of gifts and degree above degree. When they tell us that all men are equal in the eyes of God, what they mean, it is to be presumed, is what Jeremy Taylor meant, when he wrote, in a book today too little read, that 'if a man be exalted by reason of any excellence in his soul, he may please to remember that all souls are equal, and their differing operations are because their instrument is in better tune, their body is more healthful or better tempered; which is no more praise to him than it is that he was born in Italy'. It is the truth expressed in the parable of the prodigal son – the truth that it is absurd and degrading for men to make much of their intellectual and moral superiority to each other, and still more of their superiority in the arts which bring wealth and power, because, judged by their place in any universal scheme, they are all infinitely great or infinitely small. And, when observers from the Dominions, or from foreign countries, are struck by inequality as one of the special and outstanding characteristics of English social life, they do not mean that in other countries differences of personal quality are less important than in England. They mean, on the contrary, that they are more important, and that in England they tend to be obscured or obliterated behind differences of property and income, and the whole elaborate façade of a society that, compared with their own, seems stratified and hierarchical.

The equality which all these thinkers emphasize as desirable is not equality of capacity or attainment, but of circumstances, institutions, and manner of life. The inequality which they deplore is not inequality of personal gifts, but of the social and economic environment. They are concerned, not with a biological phenomenon, but with a spiritual relation and the conduct to be based on it. Their view, in short, is that, because men are men, social institutions – property rights, and the organization of industry, and the system of public health and education – should be planned, as far as is possible, to emphasize and strengthen, not the class differences which divide, but the common humanity which unites, them.

Such a view of the life which is proper to human beings may, of course, be criticized, as it often has been. But to suppose that it can be criticized effectively by pointing to the width of the intellectual and moral differences which distinguish individuals from each other is a solecism, an *ignoratio elenchi*. It is true, of course, that such differences are important, and that the advance of psychology has enabled them to be measured with a new precision, with results which are valuable in making possible both a closer adaptation of educational methods to individual needs and a more intelligent selection of varying aptitudes for different tasks. But to recognize a specific difference is one thing; to pass a general judgment of superiority or inferiority, still more to favour the first and neglect the second, is quite another. The nightingale, it has been remarked, was placed in the fourth class at the fowl show. Which of a number of varying individuals is to be judged superior to the rest depends upon the criterion which is applied, and the criterion is a matter of ethical judgment. That judgment will, if it is prudent, be tentative and provisional, since men's estimates of the relative desirability of initiative, decision, common sense, imagination, humility and sympathy appear, unfortunately, to differ, and the failures and fools – the Socrates and St Francis – of one age are the sages and saints of another. Society would not be the worse, perhaps, if idiots like Dostoevsky's were somewhat less uncommon, and the condemnation passed on those who offend one of these little ones was not limited to offenders against children whose mental ratio is in excess of eighty-five.

It is true, again, that human beings have, except as regards certain elementary, though still sadly neglected, matters of health and development, different requirements, and that these different requirements can be met satisfactorily only by varying forms of provision. But equality of provision is not identity of provision. It is to be achieved, not by treating different needs in the same way, but by devoting equal care to ensuring that they are met in the different ways most appropriate to them, as is done by a doctor who prescribes different regimens for different constitutions, or a teacher who develops different types of intelligence by different curricula. The more anxiously, indeed, a society endeavours to secure equality of consideration for all its members, the greater will be the differentiation of treatment which, when once their common human needs have been met, it accords to the special needs of different groups and individuals among them.

It is true, finally, that some men are inferior to others in respect of their intellectual endowments, and it is possible – though the truth of the possibility has not yet been satisfactorily established – that the same is true of certain classes. It does not, however, follow from this fact that such individuals or classes should receive less consideration than others, or should be treated as inferior in respect of such matters as legal status, or health, or economic arrangements, which are within the control of the community.

It may, of course, be deemed expedient so to treat them. It may be thought advisable, as Aristotle argued, to maintain the institution of slavery on the ground that some men are fit only to be living tools; or, as was customary in a comparatively recent past, to apply to the insane a severity not used towards the sane; or, as is sometimes urged today, to spend less liberally on the education of the slow than on that of the intelligent; or, in accordance with the practice of all ages, to show less respect for the poor than for the rich. But, in order to establish an inference, a major premise is necessary as well as a minor; and, if such discrimination on the part of society is desirable, its desirability must be shown by some other argument than the fact of inequality of intelligence and character. To convert a phenomenon, however interesting, into a principle, however respectable, is an error of logic. It is the confusion of a judgment of fact with a judgment of value – a confusion like that which was satirized by Montesquieu when he wrote, in his ironical defence of slavery: 'The creatures in question are black from head to foot, and their noses are so flat that it is almost impossible to pity them. It is not to be supposed that God, an all-wise Being, can have lodged a soul – still less a good soul – in a body completely black'.

Everyone recognizes the absurdity of such an argument when it is applied to matters within his personal knowledge and professional competence. Everyone realizes that, in order to justify inequalities of circumstance or opportunity by reference to differences of personal quality, it is necessary, as Professor Ginsberg observes, to show that the differences in question are relevant to the inequalities. Everyone now sees, for example, that it is not a valid argument against women's suffrage to urge, as used to be urged not so long ago, that women are physically weaker than men, since physical strength is not relevant to the question of the ability to exercise the franchise, or a valid argument in favour of slavery that some men are less intelligent than others, since it is not certain that slavery is the most suitable penalty for lack of intelligence.

Not everyone, however, is so quick to detect the fallacy when it is expressed in general terms. It is still possible, for example, for one eminent statesman to ridicule the demand for a diminution of economic inequalities on the ground that every mother knows that her children are not equal, without reflecting whether it is the habit of mothers to lavish care on the strong and neglect the delicate; and for another to dismiss the suggestion that greater economic equality is desirable, for the reason, apparently, that men are naturally unequal. It is probable, however, that the first does not think that the fact that some children are born with good digestions, and others with bad, is a reason for supplying good food to the former and bad food to the latter, rather than for giving to both food which is equal in quality but different in kind, and that the second does not suppose that the natural inequality of men makes legal equality a contemptible principle. On the contrary, when ministers of the Crown responsible for the administration of justice to the nation, they both took for granted the desirability and existence at any rate on paper of legal equality. Yet in the eighteenth century statesmen of equal eminence in France and Germany and in the nineteenth century influential thinkers in Russia and the United States, and, indeed, the ruling classes of Europe almost everywhere at a not very distant period, all were disposed to think that, since men are naturally unequal, the admission of a general equality of legal status would be the end of civilization.

[...]

# 23

# THE IDEA OF EQUALITY

## Bernard Williams

[...]

I. *Common humanity*. The factual statement of men's equality was seen, when pressed, to retreat in the direction of merely asserting the equality of men as men; and this was thought to be trivial. It is certainly insufficient, but not, after all, trivial. That all men are human is, if a tautology, a useful one, serving as a reminder that those who belong anatomically to the species *homo sapiens*, and can speak a language, use tools, live in societies, can interbreed despite racial differences, etc., are also alike in certain other respects more likely to be forgotten. These respects are notably the capacity to feel pain, both from immediate physical causes and from various situations represented in perception and in thought; and the capacity to feel affection for others, and the consequences of this, connected with the frustration of this affection, loss of its objects, etc. The assertion that men are alike in the possession of these characteristics is, while indisputable and (it may be) even necessarily true, not trivial. For it is certain that there are political and social arrangements that systematically neglect these characteristics in the case of some groups of men, while being fully aware of them in the case of others; that is to say, they treat certain men as though they did not possess these characteristics, and neglect moral claims that arise from these characteristics and which would be admitted to arise from them.

From Bernard Williams, 'The Idea of Equality', in P. Laslett and W. G. Runciman (eds), *Philosophy, Politics and Society*, 2nd series (Blackwell, Oxford, 1962), pp. 112–17.

Here it may be objected that the mere fact that ruling groups in certain societies treat other groups in this way does not mean that they neglect or overlook the characteristics in question. For, it may be suggested, they may well recognize the presence of these characteristics in the worse-treated group, but claim that in the case of that group, the characteristics do not give rise to any moral claim; the group being distinguished from other members of society in virtue of some further characteristic (for instance, by being black), this may be cited as the ground of treating them differently, whether they feel pain, affection, etc., or not.

This objection rests on the assumption, common to much moral philosophy that makes a sharp distinction between fact and value, that the question whether a certain consideration is *relevant* to a moral issue is an evaluative question: to state that a consideration is relevant or irrelevant to a certain moral question is, on this view, itself to commit oneself to a certain kind of moral principle or outlook. Thus, in the case under discussion, to say (as one would naturally say) that the fact that a man is black is, by itself, quite irrelevant to the issue of how he should be treated in respect of welfare, etc., would, on this view, be to commit to oneself to a certain sort of moral principle. This view, taken generally, seems to me quite certainly false. The principle that men should be differentially treated in respect of welfare merely on grounds of their colour is not a special sort of moral principle, but (if anything) a purely arbitrary assertion of will, like that of some Caligulan ruler who decided to execute everyone whose name contained three 'R's.

This point is in fact conceded by those who practice such things as colour discrimination. Few can be found who will explain their practice merely by saying, 'But they're black: and it is my moral principle to treat black men differently from others'. If any reasons are given at all, they will be reasons that seek to correlate the fact of blackness with certain other considerations which are at least candidates for relevance to the question of how a man should be treated: such as insensitivity, brute stupidity, ineducable irresponsibility, etc. Now these reasons are very often rationalizations, and the correlations claimed are either not really believed, or quite irrationally believed, by those who claim them. But this is a different point; the argument concerns what counts as a moral reason, and the rationalizer broadly agrees with others about what counts as such – the trouble with him is that his reasons are dictated by his policies, and not conversely. The Nazis' 'anthropologists' who tried to construct theories of Aryanism were paying, in very poor coin, the homage of irrationality to reason.

The question of relevance in moral reasons will arise again, in a different connexion, in this paper. For the moment its importance is that it gives a force to saying that those who neglect the moral claims of certain men that arise from their human capacity to feel pain, etc., are *overlooking* or *disregarding* those capacities; and are not just operating with a special moral principle, conceding the capacities to these men, but denying the moral claim. Very often, indeed, they have just persuaded themselves that the men in question have those capacities in a lesser degree. Here it is certainly to the point to assert the apparent platitude that these men are also human.

I have discussed this point in connexion with very obvious human characteristics of feeling pain and desiring affection. There are, however, other and less easily definable characteristics universal to humanity, which may all the more be neglected in political and social arrangements. For instance, there seems to be a characteristic which might be called 'a desire for self-respect'; this phrase is perhaps not too happy, in suggesting a particular culturally-limited, bourgeois value, but I mean by it a certain human desire to be identified with what one is doing, to be able to realize purposes of one's own, and not to be the instrument of another's will unless one has willingly accepted such a role. This is a very inadequate and in some ways rather empty specification of a human desire; to a better specification, both philosophical reflection and the evidences of psychology and anthropology would be relevant. Such investigations enable us to understand more deeply, in respect of the desire I have gestured towards and of similar characteristics, what it is to be human; and of what it is to be human, the apparently trivial statement of men's equality as men can serve as a reminder.

2. *Moral capacities.* So far we have considered respects in which men can be counted as all alike, which respects are, in a sense, negative: they concern the capacity to suffer, and certain needs that men have, and these involve men in moral relations as the recipients of certain kinds of treatment. It has certainly been a part, however, of the thought of those who asserted that men were equal, that there were more positive respects in which men were alike: that they were equal in certain things that they could do or achieve, as well as in things that they needed and could suffer. In respect of a whole range of abilities, from weight-lifting to the calculus, the assertion is, as was noted at the beginning, not plausible, and has not often been supposed to be. It has been held, however, that there are certain other abilities, both less open to empirical test and more essential in moral connexions, for which it is true that men are equal. These are certain sorts of moral ability or capacity, the capacity for virtue or achievement of the highest kind of moral worth.

The difficulty with this notion is that of identifying any purely moral capacities. Some human capacities are more relevant to the achievement of a virtuous life than others: intelligence, a capacity for sympathetic understanding, and a measure of resoluteness would generally be agreed to be so. But these capacities can all be displayed in non-moral connexions as well, and in such connexions would naturally be thought to differ from man to man like other natural capacities. That this is the fact of the matter has been accepted by many thinkers, notably, for instance, by Aristotle. But against this acceptance, there is a powerful strain of thought that centres on a feeling of ultimate and outrageous absurdity in the idea that the achievement of the highest kind of moral worth should depend on natural capacities, unequally and fortuitously distributed as they are; and this feeling is backed up by the observation that these natural capacities are not themselves the bearers of the moral worth, since those that have them are as gifted for vice as for virtue.

This strain of thought has found many types of religious expression; but in philosophy it is to be found in its purest form in Kant. Kant's view not only carries to the limit the notion that moral worth cannot depend on contingencies, but also emphasizes, in its picture of the Kingdom of Ends, the idea of *respect* which is owed to each man as a rational moral agent – and, since men are equally such agents, is owed equally to all, unlike admiration and similar attitudes, which are commanded unequally by men in proportion to their unequal possession of different kinds of natural excellence. These ideas are intimately connected in Kant, and it is not possible to understand his moral theory unless as much weight is given to what he says about the Kingdom of Ends as is always given to what he says about duty.

The very considerable consistency of Kant's view is bought at what would generally be agreed to be a very high price. The detachment of moral worth from all contingencies is achieved only by making man's characteristic as a moral or rational agent a transcendental characteristic; man's capacity to will freely as a rational agent is not dependent on any empirical capacities he may have – and, in particular, is not dependent on empirical capacities which men may possess unequally – because, in the Kantian view, the capacity to be a rational agent is not itself an empirical capacity at all. Accordingly, the respect owed equally to each man as a member of the Kingdom of Ends is not owed to him in respect of any empirical characteristics that he may possess, but solely in respect of the transcendental characteristic of being a free and rational will. The ground of the respect owed to each man thus emerges in the Kantian theory as a kind of secular analogue of the Christian conception of the respect owed to all men as equally children of God. Though secular, it is equally metaphysical: in neither case is it anything empirical *about* men that constitutes the ground of equal respect.

This transcendental, Kantian conception cannot provide any solid foundation for the notions of equality among men, or of equality of respect owed to them. Apart from the general difficulties of such transcendental conceptions, there is the obstinate fact that the concept of 'moral agent', and the concepts allied to it such as that of responsibility, do and must have an empirical basis. It seems empty to say that all men are equal as moral agents, when the question, for instance, of men's responsibility for their actions is one to which empirical considerations are clearly relevant, and one which moreover receives answers in terms of different degrees of responsibility and different degrees of rational control over action. To hold a man responsible for his actions is presumably the central case of treating him as a moral agent, and if men are not treated as equally responsible, there is not much left to their equality as moral agents.

If, without its transcendental basis, there is not much left to men's equality as moral agents, is there anything left to the notion of the *respect* owed to all men?

This notion of 'respect' is both complex and unclear, and I think it needs, and would repay, a good deal of investigation. Some content can, however, be attached to it; even if it is some way away from the ideas of moral agency. There certainly is a distinction, for instance, between regarding a man's life, actions or character from an æsthetic or technical point of view, and regarding them from a point of view which is concerned primarily with what it is *for him* to live that life and do those actions in that character. Thus from the technological point of view, a man who has spent his life in trying to make a certain machine which could not possibly work is merely a failed inventor, and in compiling a catalogue of those whose efforts have contributed to the sum of technical achievement, one must 'write him off': the fact that he devoted himself to this useless task with constant effort and so on, is merely irrelevant. But from a human point of view, it is clearly not irrelevant: we are concerned with him, not merely as 'a failed inventor', but as a man who wanted to be a successful inventor. Again, in professional relations and the world of work, a man operates, and his activities come up for criticism, under a variety of professional or technical titles, such as 'miner' or 'agricultural labourer' or 'junior executive'. The technical or professional attitude is that which regards the man solely under that title, the human approach that which regards him as *a man who has* that title (among others), willingly, unwillingly, through lack of alternatives, with pride, etc.

That men should be regarded from the human point of view, and not merely under these sorts of titles, is part of the content that might be attached to Kant's celebrated injunction 'treat each man as an end in himself, and never as a means only'. But I do not think that this is all that should be seen in this injunction, or all that is concerned in the notion of 'respect'. What is involved in the examples just given could be explained by saying that each man is owed an effort at identification: that he should not be regarded as the surface to which a certain label can be applied, but one should try to see the world (including the label) from his point of view. This injunction will be based on, though not of course fully explained by, the notion that men are conscious beings who necessarily have intentions and purposes and see what they are doing in a certain light.

[. . .]

# SECTION 3
# REPRESENTATION

# REPRESENTATION
## INTRODUCTION

Representation is one of the more problematic concepts in the vocabulary of democratic theory. The antithesis between direct and representative democracy has been a constant theme in its history. If democracy involves the ideal of popular sovereignty, of 'people power', then how can the people rule themselves? Do considerations of scale, available time and perhaps also differential expertise and knowledge of political matters make representation inevitable in any large-scale political community? If so, does this then open up the danger of a gap between representatives and represented? Could the former usurp power, speaking in the name of the people but in practice disregarding their will?

On this point, as on so many others, *Rousseau* vehemently stakes out a clear position. He argues that sovereignty cannot be delegated. In his stark words, once a people allows itself to be represented, it is no longer free. In fact for Rousseau the people would then no longer exist. On this line of thought, representation and popular sovereignty are mutually incompatible. The English people are free only at election time, says Rousseau. The election of representatives puts an end to their liberty.

The eighteenth-century philosopher and politician *Edmund Burke* advocates the opposite point of view in his equally classical speech to the electors of Bristol. He rejects the idea that the representatives are or should be bound by instructions or a mandate from their constituents. Parliamentary representatives cannot be so bound, and must decide on issues according to their own judgement, after hearing the debate in the representative arena and making up their mind accordingly. Burke's views have been taken as the clear statement of the role of the parliamentary *representative*, as opposed to that of a *delegate*, constrained to keep strictly to the views of those whom they represent, irrespective of their personal judgements.

The Utilitarian philosopher *James Mill*, in his essay 'On Government', salutes representation as 'the grand discovery of modern times'. He sought to reconcile the conundrum that this great discovery could give rise to new problems. If representation was a necessity of modern politics, then how is it possible to prevent the representatives from themselves following their 'sinister interest' at the expense of the interests of the community? His solution lay in the institution of checks and controls over the representatives. They should be allowed to hold office only for limited periods, though this would not preclude representatives being re-elected repeatedly if they showed themselves competent and honest. Mill thus places his faith in what his friend and contemporary Jeremy Bentham called the 'dislocative power', or what in more popular contemporary language might be called the power to 'throw the rascals out'. James Mill is thus highlighting a central strand of democratic theory and practice, the principle of accountability of representatives to represented, and the need for institutions to put this principle into practice.

More contemporary discussion has also grappled with the problem of what it is to represent, and how this should be done, whether the bases of representation should be individual or group-based. The contemporary American political philosopher *Hannah Pitkin* argues that representation in a democratic system must involve ideas of responsiveness. The people must not be passive objects of manipulation, nor would it be enough for a government to be responsive to public opinion and initiative only on occasions when it suited it to respond. There have to be institutions to secure this governmental responsiveness, and these commonly include elections to create a representative body. But, as Pitkin interestingly observes, there could be a tension between the practice of representation, its embodiment in certain institutional bodies (like parliaments), and the democratic principles of accountability and control which those bodies are meant to realise. Some of these problems were highlighted by elitist theorists (see the extract by *Michels* in Part Three, Section 7 below), who drew the conclusion that representative bodies would inevitably give rise to the domination of the few over the many. Representative democracy would give way to oligarchy and elitism.

The debate about representation also involves the problem of inclusion and exclusion. Who is being represented, and on what terms? Should representation be of individuals, as in the classic liberal tradition? In that case, this may lead to the exclusion of particular groups, and especially of marginalised or oppressed minorities. *Anne Phillips* suggests the need for a 'politics of presence' which would give voice to groups hitherto excluded or marginalised by the individualist representation of liberal-democracy. New social movements have, she suggests, put this question on the agenda. This raises the question that the traditional modes of representation in parliamentary democracy (voting for members of a representative legislature or parliament) may not be adequate to ensure reflection of different groups and identities in the political system.

Similar concerns are articulated by *Iris Marion Young*. She argues for representation not of individuals but of groups. This would prevent the exclusion of disadvantaged interests from the political system. She suggests the possibility of a 'Rainbow Coalition' articulating the interests of 'Blacks, Hispanics, women, gay men and lesbians, poor and working class people, disabled people, students', which would enrich the quality of democratic politics. The debate thus involves the problem of whether representation is, as the Utilitarian philosopher James Mill suggested, 'the grand discovery of modern times'. Others take a more sceptical view, fearing that representation can at best weaken genuine democracy, at worst lead to its destruction. For some political theorists, it spells the death knell of any genuine forms of participation.

Some of the most vehement criticisms of representation have come from thinkers within the tradition of anarchism. In this section we provide two brief extracts from *Bakunin* and *Proudhon*, two of the most prominent figures in nineteenth-century anarchism. For both of them, representation can never be anything but a fraud. A representative system cannot realise the freedom it promises, because representatives inevitably become distant from those they represent. Whatever their intentions, they grow out of touch with the daily life of citizens, and become prone to corruption and ambition. Parliamentary politics in their day (and in ours?) provides classic examples of this integration of radical politicians into the existing order. For anarchists, this scepticism of representative politics stems from a wider rejection of organisation and power as by their very nature negating freedom. This raises the question of whether the popular participation and spontaneous forms of politics advocated by anarchists are possible in large-scale and complex contemporary democracies. Is their rejection of *all* forms of organisation and representation too sweeping, and is their alternative a feasible one?

The debate on some of these issues in a contemporary setting is taken up in the concluding section on the future of democracy. Can democracy develop new forms and modes of representation that are open and participatory, which avoid the dangers which traditional forms of representation may entail?

# 24

# THE SOCIAL CONTRACT

## Jean-Jacques Rousseau

[...]

### CHAPTER XV
#### DEPUTIES OR REPRESENTATIVES

As soon as public service ceases to be the chief business of the citizens, and they would rather serve with their money than with their persons, the State is not far from its fall. When it is necessary to march out to war, they pay troops and stay at home: when it is necessary to meet in council, they name deputies and stay at home. By reason of idleness and money, they end by having soldiers to enslave their country and representatives to sell it.

It is through the hustle of commerce and the arts, through the greedy self-interest of profit, and through softness and love of amenities that personal services are replaced by money payments. Men surrender a part of their profits in order to have time to increase them at leisure. Make gifts of money, and you will not be long without chains. The word 'finance' is a slavish word, unknown in the city-state. In a country that is truly free, the citizens do everything with their own arms and nothing by means of money; so far from paying to be exempted from their duties, they would even pay for the privilege of fulfilling them themselves. I am far from taking the common view: I hold enforced labour to be less opposed to liberty than taxes.

The better the constitution of a State is, the more do public affairs encroach on private in the minds of the citizens. Private affairs are even of much less

From Jean-Jacques Rousseau, *The Social Contract and Discourses*, trans. and intro. G. D. H. Cole (Everyman's Library: Dent, London/Dutton, New York, 1968), Book III, chapter XV, pp. 77–80. Originally written 1762.

importance, because the aggregate of the common happiness furnishes a greater proportion of that of each individual, so that there is less for him to seek in particular cares. In a well-ordered city every man flies to the assemblies: under a bad government no one cares to stir a step to get to them, because no one is interested in what happens there, because it is foreseen that the general will will not prevail, and lastly because domestic cares are all-absorbing. Good laws lead to the making of better ones; bad ones bring about worse. As soon as any man says of the affairs of the State *What does it matter to me?* the State may be given up for lost.

The lukewarmness of patriotism, the activity of private interest, the vastness of States, conquest, and the abuse of government suggested the method of having deputies or representatives of the people in the national assemblies. These are what, in some countries, men have presumed to call the Third Estate. Thus the individual interest of two orders is put first and second; the public interest occupies only the third place.

Sovereignty, for the same reason as makes it inalienable, cannot be represented; it lies essentially in the general will, and will does not admit of representation: it is either the same, or other; there is no intermediate possibility. The deputies of the people, therefore, are not and cannot be its representatives: they are merely its stewards, and can carry through no definitive acts. Every law the people has not ratified in person is null and void – is, in fact, not a law. The people of England regards itself as free; but it is grossly mistaken; it is free only during the election of members of parliament. As soon as they are elected, slavery overtakes it, and it is nothing. The use it makes of the short moments of liberty it enjoys shows indeed that it deserves to lose them.

The idea of representation is modern; it comes to us from feudal government, from that iniquitous and absurd system which degrades humanity and dishonours the name of man. In ancient republics and even in monarchies, the people never had representatives; the word itself was unknown. It is very singular that in Rome, where the tribunes were so sacrosanct, it was never even imagined that they could usurp the functions of the people, and that in the midst of so great a multitude they never attempted to pass on their own authority a single *plebiscitum*. We can, however, form an idea of the difficulties caused sometimes by the people being so numerous, from what happened in the time of the Gracchi, when some of the citizens had to cast their votes from the roofs of buildings.

Where right and liberty are everything, disadvantages count for nothing. Among this wise people everything was given its just value, its lictors were allowed to do what its tribunes would never have dared to attempt; for it had no fear that its lictors would try to represent it.

To explain, however, in what way the tribunes did sometimes represent it, it is enough to conceive how the government represents the Sovereign. Law being purely the declaration of the general will, it is clear that, in the exercise of the legislative power, the people cannot be represented; but in that of the executive power, which is only the force that is applied to give the law effect, it both can and should be represented. We thus see that if we looked closely into the matter we should find that very few nations have any laws. However that may be, it is certain that the tribunes, possessing no executive power, could never represent the Roman people by right of the powers entrusted to them, but only by usurping those of the senate.

In Greece, all that the people had to do, it did for itself; it was constantly assembled in the public square. The Greeks lived in a mild climate; they had no natural greed; slaves did their work for them; their great concern was with liberty. Lacking the same advantages, how can you preserve the same rights? Your severer climates add to your needs;[1] for half the year your public squares are uninhabitable; the flatness of your languages unfits them for being heard in the open air; you sacrifice more for profit than for liberty, and fear slavery less than poverty.

What then? Is liberty maintained only by the help of slavery? It may be so. Extremes meet. Everything that is not in the course of nature has its disadvantages, civil society most of all. There are some unhappy circumstances in which we can only keep our liberty at others' expense, and where the citizen can be perfectly free only when the slave is most a slave. Such was the case with Sparta. As for you, modern peoples, you have no slaves, but you are slaves yourselves; you pay for their liberty with your own. It is in vain that you boast of this preference; I find in it more cowardice than humanity.

I do not mean by all this that it is necessary to have slaves, or that the right of slavery is legitimate: I am merely giving the reasons why modern peoples, believing themselves to be free, have representatives, while ancient peoples had none. In any case, the moment a people allows itself to be represented, it is no longer free: it no longer exists.

All things considered, I do not see that it is possible henceforth for the Sovereign to preserve among us the exercise of its rights, unless the city is very small. But if it is very small, it will be conquered? No. I will show later on how the external strength of a great people may be combined with the convenient polity and good order of a small State.

## NOTE

1. To adopt in cold countries the luxury and effeminacy of the East is to desire to submit to its chains; it is indeed to bow to them far more inevitably in our case than in theirs.

# 25

# SPEECH AT THE CONCLUSION OF THE POLL, 3 NOVEMBER 1774

## Edmund Burke

[...]

I am sorry I cannot conclude, without saying a word on a topick touched upon by my worthy Colleague. I wish that topick had been passed by; at a time when I have so little leisure to discuss it. But since he has thought proper to throw it out, I owe you a clear explanation of my poor sentiments on that subject.

He tells you, that "the topick of Instructions has occasioned much altercation and uneasiness in this City;" and he expresses himself (if I understand him rightly) in favour of the coercive authority of such instructions.

Certainly, Gentlemen, it ought to be the happiness and glory of a Representative, to live in the strictest union, the closest correspondence, and the most unreserved communication with his constituents. Their wishes ought to have great weight with him; their opinion high respect; their business unremitted attention. It is his duty to sacrifice his repose, his pleasures, his satisfactions, to theirs; and, above all, ever, and in all cases, to prefer their interest to his own. But, his unbiassed opinion, his mature judgement, his enlightened conscience, he ought not to sacrifice to you; to any man, or to any sett of men living. These he does not derive from your pleasure; no, nor from the Law and the Constitution. They are a trust from Providence, for the abuse of which he is deeply answerable. Your Representative owes you, not his industry only, but his judgement; and he betrays, instead of serving you, if he sacrifices it to your opinion.

From Edmund Burke, 'Speech at the Conclusion of the Poll, 3 November 1774', in W. M. Elofson and John A. Woods (eds), *The Writings and Speeches of Edmund Burke*, Vol. III: *Party, Parliament and the American War* 1774–80 (Clarendon Press, Oxford, 1996), pp. 68–70.

My worthy Colleague says, his Will ought to be subservient to yours. If that be all, the thing is innocent. If Government were a matter of Will upon any side, yours, without question, ought to be superior. But Government and Legislation are matters of reason and judgement, and not of inclination; and, what sort of reason is that, in which the determination precedes the discussion; in which one sett of men deliberate, and another decide; and where those who form the conclusion are perhaps three hundred miles distant from those who hear the arguments?

To deliver an opinion, is the right of all men; that of Constituents is a weighty and respectable opinion, which a Representative ought always to rejoice to hear; and which he ought always most seriously to consider. But *authoritative* instructions; *Mandates* issued, which the Member is bound blindly and implicitly to obey, to vote, and to argue for, though contrary to the clearest conviction of his judgement and conscience; these are things utterly unknown to the laws of this land, and which arise from a fundamental Mistake of the whole order and tenour of our Constitution.

Parliament is not a *Congress* of Ambassadors from different and hostile interests; which interests each must maintain, as an Agent and Advocate, against other Agents and Advocates; but Parliament is a *deliberative* Assembly of *one* Nation, with *one* Interest, that of the whole; where, not local Purposes, not local Prejudices ought to guide, but the general Good, resulting from the general Reason of the whole. You chuse a Member indeed; but when you have chosen him, he is not Member of Bristol, but he is a Member of *Parliament*. If the local Constituent should have an Interest, or should form an hasty Opinion, evidently opposite to the real good of the rest of the Community, the Member for that place ought to be as far, as any other, from any endeavour to give it Effect. I beg pardon for saying so much on this subject. I have been unwillingly drawn into it; but I shall ever use a respectful frankness of communication with you. Your faithful friend, your devoted servant, I shall be to the end of my life: A flatterer you do not wish for. On this point of instructions, however, I think it scarcely possible, we ever can have any sort of difference. Perhaps I may give you too much, rather than too little trouble.

From the first hour I was encouraged to court your favour to this happy day of obtaining it, I have never promised you any thing, but humble and persevering endeavours to do my duty. The weight of that duty, I confess, makes me tremble; and whoever well considers what it is, of all things in the world will fly from what has the least likeness to a positive and precipitate engagement. To be a good Member of Parliament, is, let me tell you, no easy task; especially at this time, when there is so strong a disposition to run into the perilous extremes of servile compliance, or wild popularity. To unite circumspection with vigour, is absolutely necessary; but it is extremely difficult. We are now Members for a rich commercial *City*; this City, however, is but a part of a rich commercial *Nation*, the Interests of which are various, multiform, and intricate. We are Members for that great *Nation*, which however is itself but part of a great

*Empire*, extended by our Virtue and our Fortune to the farthest limits of the East and of the West. All these wide-spread Interests must be considered; must be compared; must be reconciled if possible. We are Members for a *free* Country; and surely we all know, that the machine of a free Constitution is no simple thing; but as intricate and as delicate, as it is valuable. We are Members in a great and ancient *Monarchy*; and we must preserve religiously, the true legal rights of the Sovereign, which form the Key-stone that binds together the noble and well-constructed Arch of our Empire and our Constitution. A Constitution made up of balanced Powers must ever be a critical thing. As such I mean to touch that part of it which comes within my reach. I know my Inability, and I wish for support from every Quarter. In particular I shall aim at the friendship, and shall cultivate the best Correspondence, of the worthy Colleague you have given me.

I trouble you no farther than once more to thank you all; you, Gentlemen, for your Favours; the Candidates for their temperate and polite behaviour; and the Sheriffs, for a Conduct which may give a Model for all who are in public Stations.

# 26

# ESSAY ON GOVERNMENT

## James Mill

### CHAPTER VI
#### IN THE REPRESENTATIVE SYSTEM ALONE THE
#### SECURITIES FOR GOOD GOVERNMENT ARE TO BE FOUND

What then is to be done? For, according to this reasoning, we may be told that good Government appears to be impossible. The people, as a body, cannot perform the business of Government for themselves. If the powers of Government are entrusted to one man, or a few men, and a Monarchy, or governing Aristocracy, is formed, the results are fatal: And it appears that a combination of the simple forms is impossible.

Notwithstanding the truth of these propositions, it is not yet proved that good Government is impossible. For though the people, who cannot exercise the powers of Government themselves, must entrust them to some one individual or set of individuals, and such individuals will infallibly have the strongest motives to make a bad use of them, it is possible that checks may be found sufficient to prevent them. The next subject of inquiry, then, is the doctrine of checks. It is sufficiently conformable to the established and fashionable opinions to say, that, upon the right constitution of checks, all goodness of Government depends. To this proposition we fully subscribe. Nothing, therefore, can exceed the importance of correct conclusions upon this subject. After the developments already made, it is hoped that the inquiry will be neither intricate nor unsatisfactory.

From James Mill, *Political Writings*, ed. Terence Ball (Cambridge University Press, Cambridge, 1992), sections VI–VII, pp. 21–4. Originally written 1819–23.

In the grand discovery of modern times, the system of representation, the solution of all the difficulties, both speculative and practical, will perhaps be found. If it cannot, we seem to be forced upon the extraordinary conclusion, that good Government is impossible. For as there is no individual, or combination of individuals, except the community itself, who would not have an interest in bad Government, if entrusted with its powers; and as the community itself is incapable of exercising those powers, and must entrust them to some individual or combination of individuals, the conclusion is obvious: The Community itself must check those individuals, else they will follow their interest, and produce bad Government.

But how is it the Community can check? The community can act only when assembled: And then it is incapable of acting.

The community, however, can chuse Representatives: And the question is, whether the Representatives of the Community can operate as a check?

## CHAPTER VII
### WHAT IS REQUIRED IN A REPRESENTATIVE BODY TO MAKE IT A SECURITY FOR GOOD GOVERNMENT?

We may begin by laying down two propositions, which appear to involve a great portion of the inquiry; and about which it is unlikely that there will be any dispute.

I. The checking body must have a degree of power sufficient for the business of checking.

II. It must have an identity of interest with the community; otherwise it will make a mischievous use of its power.

I. To measure the degree of power which is requisite upon any occasion, we must consider the degree of power which is necessary to be overcome. Just as much as suffices for that purpose is requisite, and no more. We have then to inquire what power it is which the Representatives of the community, acting as a check, need power to overcome. The answer here is easily given. It is all that power, wheresoever lodged, which they, in whose hands it is lodged, have an interest in misusing. We have already seen, that to whomsoever the community entrusts the powers of Government, whether one, or a few, they have an interest in misusing them. All the power, therefore, which the one or the few, or which the one and the few combined, can apply to insure the accomplishment of their sinister ends, the checking body must have power to overcome, otherwise its check will be unavailing. In other words, there will be no check.

This is so exceedingly evident, that we hardly think it necessary to say another word in illustration of it. If a King is prompted by the inherent principles of human nature to seek the gratification of his will; and if he finds an obstacle in that pursuit, he removes it, of course, if he can. If any man, or any set of men, oppose him, he overcomes them, if he is able; and to prevent him, they must, at the least, have equal power with himself.

The same is the case with an Aristocracy. To oppose them with success in pursuing their interest at the expense of the community, the checking body must have power successfully to resist whatever power they possess. If there is both a King and an Aristocracy, and if they would combine to put down the checking force, and to pursue their mutual interest at the expense of the community, the checking body must have sufficient power successfully to resist the united power of both King and Aristocracy.

These conclusions are not only indisputable, but the very theory of the British Constitution is erected upon them. The House of Commons, according to that theory, is the checking body. It is also an admitted doctrine, that if the King had the power of bearing down any opposition to his will that could be made by the House of Commons; or if the King and the House of Lords combined had the power of bearing down its opposition to their joint will, it would cease to have the power of checking them; it must, therefore, have a power sufficient to overcome the united power of both.

II. All the questions which relate to the degree of power necessary to be given to that checking body, on the perfection of whose operations all the goodness of Government depends, are thus pretty easily solved. The grand difficulty consists in finding the means of constituting a checking body, whose powers shall not be turned against the community for whose protection it is created.

There can be no doubt, that if power is granted to a body of men, called Representatives, they, like any other men, will use their power, not for the advantage of the community, but for their own advantage, if they can. The only question is, therefore, how they can be prevented? in other words, how are the interests of the Representatives to be identified with those of the community?

Each Representative may be considered in two capacities; in his capacity of Representative, in which he has the exercise of power over others, and in his capacity of Member of the Community, in which others have the exercise of power over him.

If things were so arranged, that, in his capacity of Representative, it would be impossible for him to do himself so much good by misgovernment, as he would do himself harm in his capacity of member of the community, the object would be accomplished. We have already seen, that the amount of power assigned to the checking body cannot be diminished beyond a certain amount. It must be sufficient to overcome all resistance on the part of all those in whose hands the powers of Government are lodged. But if the power assigned to the Representative cannot be diminished in amount, there is only one other way in which it can be diminished, and that is, in duration.

This, then, is the instrument; lessening of duration is the instrument, by which, if by any thing, the object is to be attained. The smaller the period of time during which any man retains his capacity of Representative, as compared with the time in which he is simply a member of the community, the more difficult it will be to compensate the sacrifice of the interests of the longer period, by the profits of misgovernment during the shorter.

This is an old and approved method of identifying as nearly as possible the interests of those who rule with the interests of those who are ruled. It is in pursuance of this advantage, that the Members of the British House of Commons have always been chosen for a limited period. If the Members were hereditary, or even if they were chosen for life, every inquirer would immediately pronounce that they would employ, for their own advantage, the powers entrusted to them; and that they would go just as far in abusing the persons and properties of the people, as their estimate of the powers and spirit of the people to resist them would allow them to contemplate as safe.

[...]

# 27

# THE CONCEPT OF REPRESENTATION

## Hannah Fenichel Pitkin

[...]

It seems to me that we show a government to be representative not by demonstrating its control over its subjects but just the reverse, by demonstrating that its subjects have control over what it does. Every government's actions are attributed to its subjects formally, legally. But in a representative government this attribution has substantive content: the people really do act through their government, and are not merely passive recipients of its actions. A representative government must not merely be in control, not merely promote the public interest, but must also be responsive to the people. The notion is closely related to the view of representing as a substantive activity. For in a representative government the governed must be capable of action and judgment, capable of initiating government activity, so that the government may be conceived as responding to them. As in nonpolitical representation, the principal need not express his wishes, or even have formulated any, but he must be capable of doing so; when he does, his wishes should be fulfilled unless there is good reason (in terms of his interest) to the contrary. Correspondingly, a representative government requires that there be machinery for the expression of the wishes of the represented, and that the government respond to these wishes unless there are good reasons to the contrary. There need not be a constant activity of responding, but there must be a constant condition of responsive*ness*, of potential readiness to respond. It is not that a government represents only when

From Hannah Fenichel Pitkin, *The Concept of Representation* (University of California Press, Berkeley, CA, 1967), pp. 232–6.

it is acting in response to an express popular wish; a representative government is one which is responsive to popular wishes when there are some. Hence there must be institutional arrangements for responsiveness to these wishes. Again, it is incompatible with the idea of representation for the government to frustrate or resist the people's will without good reason, to frustrate or resist it systematically or over a long period of time. We can conceive of the people as "acting through" the government even if most of the time they are unaware of what it is doing, so long as we feel that they could initiate action if they so desired.

Because this kind of political representation requires only potential responsiveness, access to power rather than its actual exercise, it is perfectly compatible with leadership and with action to meet new or emergency situations. It is incompatible, on the other hand, with manipulation or coercion of the public. To be sure, the line between leadership and manipulation is a tenuous one, and may be difficult to draw. But there undoubtedly *is* a difference, and this difference makes leadership compatible with representation while manipulation is not. This is because leadership is, in a sense, at the mercy of the led. It succeeds only so long as they are willing to follow. Thus it is not incompatible with our requirement that the represented be able to get their way when they have an explicit will. Manipulation by a ruler, on the other hand, is imposed on the ruled, and threatens their capacity to reject a policy or initiate a new one. A person can be led and yet go of his own free will; something that is manipulated does not move itself. An inanimate object can be manipulated, but it cannot be led. Again, these are not just verbal games, but the right terms for naming a distinction in reality: the difference between democratic and dictatorial relationships between ruler and ruled. Only if it seems right to attribute governmental action to the people in the substantive sense do we speak of representative government.

But all this makes the notion of representative government seem far more impressionistic, intuitive, and temporary than it really is when we use it. Judging a government to be representative is not merely a matter of a sort of over-all esthetic impression one has formed; though there may be difficult borderline cases, not all cases are borderline. Nor does this kind of representativeness fade in and out periodically. We do not say that a government is representative today, because it happens to be responding to popular wishes, and stops being representative the next day because it is frustrating them. Representative government is not defined by particular actions at a particular moment, but by long-term systematic arrangements – by institutions and the way in which they function. No particular act of compliance with popular demands is proof of a representative government, although a few serious cases of the frustration of legitimate popular demands will serve as counterevidence. John Plamenatz points out that a dictator might choose to do what his subjects want and nevertheless not be a representative. Only if he institutionalizes this decision, so that there is not merely occasional response when he pleases, but regular, systematic responsiveness, does he become a representative. And we tend to feel that this is impossible without elections. Our concern with elections and electoral machinery, and particularly with whether elections are free and genuine, results from our conviction that such machinery is necessary to ensure systematic responsiveness. Our concern with the popularity of a regime is an attempt to find an operational measure for potential responsiveness. The fact that the people have no unfulfilled demands is an indication that they can get their demands fulfilled whenever they wish, but it is not conclusive proof. This is why a manipulated or coerced acquiescence does not satisfy us.

And here the formalistic accountability view, the descriptive view, and perhaps others as well become relevant to representative government. For only certain kinds of institutional arrangements will satisfy our requirement. An absolute monarch or dictator who chooses, for a reason of his own, to take public opinion polls and do whatever the people seem to want is not yet a representative government. We require functioning institutions that are designed to, and really do, secure a government responsive to public interest and opinion. Such a government may have a president, it may be headed by a prime minister, or it may be an assembly government. It may have geographic constituencies, proportional representation, or some other system of apportionment. It may have no political parties, weak ones, strong ones, many or few. All these forms may be representative governments; some are more successful than others.

For this purpose, our basic prerequisites seem very few. We would be reluctant to consider any system a representative government unless it held regular elections, which were "genuine" or "free." We would be reluctant, further, to consider a government representative unless it included some sort of collegiate representative body in a more than advisory capacity. We would not readily accept a system as representative in which the entire government was in the hands of a single ruler, even if he was subject to re-election at regular intervals. Perhaps it is merely historical tradition that there should be a collegiate body composed of representatives of the various "parts" of the society. Perhaps it has to do with the persistent element of isomorphism or one-to-one correspondence in descriptive representation. Or perhaps it is simply that we cannot conceive that a political system could be truly responsive unless a number of minority or opposition viewpoints are officially active in its government.

Our notion of representative government thus seems to incorporate both a very general, abstract, almost metaphorical idea – that the people of a nation are present in the actions of its government in complex ways – and some fairly concrete, practical, and historically traditional institutions intended to secure such an outcome. The notion has both substantive and formal components. In this way, representative government is an excellent illustration of a phenomenon that seems to be very common in human practices and their corresponding concepts: the duality and tension between purpose and institutionalization.

The sequence of events may be somewhat like this: men have a purpose or goal in mind, the substance of which they want to achieve. In order to achieve it, particularly if it will take time and involve many people, perhaps several generations, they establish institutions – write laws, set up administrative bodies, arrange training programs, and so on. But institutions develop a momentum or an inertia of their own; they do not always work as intended, and they may not produce the result for which they were established. Thus men may find themselves torn between commitment to the original purpose and commitment to the agreed and established channels for achieving it. Or, alternatively, the causal sequence may run the other way around. For whatever reasons, and with no deliberate, common purpose, men may gradually develop fixed ways of doing something – institutionalized behavior which has become habitual. From this patterned behavior they may begin to abstract express ideas about what it is for, how it is to be done, what principles and purposes underlie it. And, in due time, those principles may themselves come to be used as new aims for revising the institution, as critical standards for assessing the way in which it functions and improving it. Again a tension between practice and principle can arise.

[...]

# 28

# THE POLITICS OF PRESENCE

## Anne Phillips

[...]

Many of the current arguments over democracy revolve around what we might call demands for political presence: demands for the equal representation of women with men; demands for a more even-handed balance between the different ethnic groups that make up each society; demands for the political inclusion of groups that have come to see themselves as marginalized or silenced or excluded. In this major reframing of the problems of democratic equality, the separation between 'who' and 'what' is to be represented, and the subordination of the first to the second, is very much up for question. The politics of ideas is being challenged by an alternative politics of presence.

The novelty in this is not the emphasis on difference, for notions of diversity and difference have been central to liberalism from its inception and to liberal democracy throughout its formation. The defining characteristics of liberal democracy, as Robert Dahl among others has clarified, are grounded in the heterogeneity of the societies that gave it birth. It was the diversity of the citizenry, as much as its absolute size, that made the earlier (more consensual) practices of Athenian democracy so inappropriate to the modern world. Lacking any half-credible basis for seeing citizens as united in their goals, theorists of liberal democracy took issue with the homogenizing presumptions of a common good or common purpose, and made diversity their central organizing theme. John Stuart Mill's famous vacillations over democracy

From Anne Phillips, *The Politics of Presence* (Clarendon Press, Oxford, 1995), pp. 5–9.

derived from a double sense of democracy as both impetus and threat to diversity: something that breaks the hold of any single notion of the good life, but can also encourage a deadening conformity. In more straightforwardly confident vein, George Kateb has presented constitutional and representative democracy as that system *par excellence* that encourages and disseminates diversity. The procedures of electoral competition do not merely chasten and circumscribe the powers of government. By promoting a more sceptical attitude towards the basis on which competing claims are resolved, they also cultivate 'a general tolerance of, and even affection for diversity: diversity in itself, and diversity as the source of regulated contest and competition'.

Difference is not something we have only just noticed. What we can more usefully say is that difference has been perceived in an overly cerebral fashion as difference in opinions and beliefs, and the resulting emphasis on the politics of ideas has proved inadequate to the problems of political exclusion. The diversity most liberals have in mind is a diversity of beliefs, opinions, preferences, and goals, all of which may stem from the variety of experience, but are considered as in principle detachable from this. Issues of political presence are largely discounted, for when difference is considered in terms of intellectual diversity, it does not much matter who represents the range of ideas. One person may easily stand in for another; there is no additional requirement for the representatives to 'mirror' the characteristics of the person or people represented. What concerns us in the choice of representative is a congruity in political beliefs and ideals, combined perhaps with a superior ability to articulate and register opinions. Stripped of any pre-democratic authority, the role of the politician is to carry a message. The messages will vary, but it hardly matters if the messengers are the same. (Those who believe that men have a monopoly on the political skills of articulating policies and ideas will not be surprised that most messengers are men.)

Once difference is conceived, however, in relation to those experiences and identities that may constitute different kinds of groups, it is far harder to meet demands for political inclusion without also including the members of such groups. Men may conceivably stand in for women when what is at issue is the representation of agreed policies or programmes or ideals. But how can men legitimately stand in for women when what is at issue is the representation of women *per se*? White people may conceivably stand in for those of Asian or African origin when it is a matter of representing particular programmes for racial equality. But can an all-white assembly really claim to be representative when those it represents are so much more ethnically diverse? Adequate representation is increasingly interpreted as implying a more adequate representation of the different social groups that make up the citizen body, and notions of 'typical' or 'mirror' or 'descriptive' representation have then returned with renewed force. This time they have the added attraction of appearing severely practical. Contemporary concerns over fair representation often translate into immediately achievable reforms, as with the quota systems that have been adopted by a number of European political parties to deliver gender parity in elected assemblies, or the redrawing of boundaries around black-majority constituencies to raise the number of black politicians elected in the USA. This is not the world of mind-stretching political utopias, but one of realistic – often realized – reforms.

The precursor to this politics was the movement for the 'representation of labour', which swept across the fledgling democracies of Europe in the late nineteenth and early twentieth centuries, and created what are today's labour or social democratic parties. The representation of labour was often a short-hand for two, potentially contradictory, notions, one of which looked to the increased representation of working-class men inside the legislative assemblies, the other of which pursued the representation of a labour *interest*, which might be carried by people other than workers themselves. At a time when labour politics held relatively few attractions for those not of labouring origin, the tension between these two was less discernible than it is today. But those involved in socialist and social democratic parties still argued fiercely over the relationship between intellectuals and the 'authentically' working class, some feeling that a socialist politics should privilege the voices and presence of workers, others that class origins or identities should signify less than adherence to socialist ideas.

In *What Is To Be Done*, Lenin offered one classic refutation of the politics of presence, and the basic premiss of his argument came to be widely agreed by people who had no time for the rest of his views. Stressing the multiplicity of arenas within which the power of capital was exerted, he argued the limits of an experience that was confined to any one of these, and the overriding importance of strategic links between one set of struggles and another. This privileged the all-seeing intellectual (who might in principle originate from any class position or fraction), the political activist who could look beyond each specific struggle or campaign to fit the various pieces of the jigsaw together. When socialist feminists challenged such arguments in the 1970s, one of the things they noted was that they denied legitimacy to women's self-understandings; another was that they presumed an objectivity on the part of these activists that raised them to a God-like level. As Sheila Rowbotham remarked in her critique of Leninist conceptions of the vanguard party, '[t]he Party is presented as soaring above all sectional concerns without providing any guarantees that this soaring will not be in fact an expression of the particular preoccupations of the group or groups with power within it.' Part of what sustained the development of an autonomous women's movement was the arrogance of those who thought that ideas could be separated from presence.

I

Contemporary demands for political presence have often arisen out of the politics of new social movements, and they all reflect inequalities other than social class. This is an important point of distinction, for as long as social class was regarded as the pre-eminent group inequality, arguments could divide relatively neatly between the liberal position, which sought to discount difference (we should be equal *regardless* of difference), and the socialist position, which aimed at elimination (we cannot be equal until the class difference has gone). Once attention shifts to forms of group difference that are not so amenable to erasure, these alternatives no longer seem so plausible. Women do not want to change their sex, or black people the colour of their skin, as a condition for equal citizenship; nor do they want their differences discounted in an assimilationist imposition of 'sameness'. The politics around class always led back to those social and economic conditions in which class differences were grounded. Subsequent developments around race or gender or ethnicity lead more directly to the political level.

The politics that characterizes this is determinedly anti-paternalist, and reflects that explosion of self-confident and autonomous organization which developed in the civil rights movement in the USA, and the women's movements of the 1960s and 1970s. The question of who could best speak for oppressed or disadvantaged groups became a central concern within these movements; and in each case, an earlier unity that was premised on shared ideas gave way to alternative unities forged around shared experience. When a political movement sees itself as based on shared ideals and goals (combating racism, securing civil rights, achieving sexual equality), then commitment to these goals seems the only legitimate qualification for membership. But divergence over strategy and objectives soon combined with growing resentment over the organizational dominance of groups already dominant in the wider society to disrupt these earlier unities. This generated a more identity-based politics which stressed the self-organization of those most directly oppressed.

In the subsequent development of feminist politics, the question of who can best speak for or on behalf of another became a major source of tension, for once men were dislodged from their role of speaking for women, it seemed obvious enough that white women must also be dislodged from their role of speaking for black women, heterosexual women for lesbians, and middle-class women for those in the working class. The search for authenticity – what Kathleen Jones sees as the dead-end pursuit of that experience which will ground one's authority – then makes it difficult for anyone to represent an experience not identical to her own and, taken to this extreme, renders dialogue virtually impossible. Most feminists have resisted this deadening conclusion, but the problems of authenticity rarely propel them back to the purer regions of a politics of ideas. Indeed, recent contributions have reframed the question of authenticity very much in terms of achieving equality of presence.

[...]

# 29

# JUSTICE AND THE POLITICS OF DIFFERENCE

## Iris Marion Young

[...]

Group differences are manifest not only in different needs, interests, and goals, but also in different social locations and experiences. People in different groups often know about somewhat different institutions, events, practices, and social relations, and often have differing perceptions of the same institutions, relations, or events. For this reason members of some groups are sometimes in a better position than members of others to understand and anticipate the probable consequences of implementing particular social policies. A public that makes use of all such social knowledge in its differentiated plurality is most likely to make just and wise decisions.

I should allay several possible misunderstandings of what this principle of group representation means and implies. First, the principle calls for specific representation of social groups, not interest groups or ideological groups. By an interest group I mean any aggregate or association of persons who seek a particular goal, or desire the same policy, or are similarly situated with respect to some social effect – for example, they are all recipients of acid rain caused by Ohio smokestacks. Social groups usually share some interests, but shared interests are not sufficient to constitute a social group. A social group is a collective of people who have affinity with one another because of a set of practices or way of life; they differentiate themselves from or are differentiated by at least one other group according to these cultural forms.

From Iris Marion Young, *Justice and the Politics of Difference* (Princeton University Press, Princeton, NJ, 1990), pp. 186–9.

By an ideological group I mean a collective of persons with shared political beliefs. Nazis, socialists, feminists, Christian Democrats, and anti-abortionists are ideological groups. The situation of social groups may foster the formation of ideological groups, and under some circumstances an ideological group may become a social group. Shared political or moral beliefs, even when they are deeply and passionately held, however, do not themselves constitute a social group.

A democratic polity should permit the expression of all interests and opinions, but this does not imply specific representation for any of them. A democratic public may wish to provide representation for certain kinds of interests or political orientations; most parliamentary systems, for example, give proportional representation to political parties according to the number of votes they poll. The principle of group representation that I am arguing for here, however, refers only to social groups.

Second, it is important to remember that the principle calls for specific representation only of oppressed or disadvantaged groups. Privileged groups are already represented, in the sense that their voice, experience, values, and priorities are already heard and acted upon. The faces of oppression [. . .] provide at least beginning criteria for determining whether a group is oppressed and therefore deserves representation. Once we are clear that the principle of group representation refers only to oppressed social groups, then the fear of an unworkable proliferation of group representation should dissipate.

Third, while I certainly intend this principle to apply to representative bodies in government institutions, its application is by no means restricted to that sphere. In earlier chapters I have argued that social justice requires a far wider institutionalization of democracy than currently obtains in American society. Persons should have the right to participate in making the rules and policies of any institution with authority over their actions. The principle of group representation applies to all such democratized publics. It should apply, for example, to decisionmaking bodies formed by oppressed groups that aim to develop policy proposals for a heterogeneous public. Oppressed groups within these groups should have specific representation in such autonomous forums. The Black caucus should give specific representation to women, for example, and the women's caucus to Blacks.

This principle of group representation, finally, does not necessarily imply proportional representation, in the manner of some recent discussions of group representation [. . .]. Insofar as it relies on the principle of 'one person one vote,' proportional representation retains the assumption that it is primarily individuals who must be represented in decisionmaking bodies. Certainly they must, and various forms of proportional representation, including proportional representation of groups or parties, may sometimes be an important vehicle for representing individuals equally. With the principle I argue for here, however, I am concerned with the representation of group experience, perspectives, and interests. Proportional representation of group members may sometimes be too little or too much to accomplish that aim. A system of proportional group representation in state and federal government in the United States might result in no seats for American Indians, for example. Given the specific circumstances and deep oppression of Indians as a group, however, the principle would certainly require that they have a specific voice. Allocating strictly half of all places to women, on the other hand, might be more than is necessary to give women's perspectives an empowered voice, and might make it more difficult for other groups to be represented.

A principle of group representation has been implicitly and sometimes explicitly asserted in several contemporary social movements struggling against oppression and domination. In response to the anger and criticism that women, Blacks, gays and lesbians, American Indians, and others have leveled against traditionally unitary radical groups and labor unions, many of them have implemented some form of group representation in their decisionmaking bodies. Some political organizations, unions, and feminist groups have formal caucuses for Blacks, Latinos, women, gay men and lesbians, disabled people, and old people, whose perspectives might be silenced without explicit representation. Frequently these organizations have procedures for giving the caucuses a voice in organization-wide discussion and caucus representation in decisionmaking. Some organizations also require representation of members of disadvantaged groups in leadership bodies.

At the height of efforts to occupy nuclear power construction sites, for example, many anti-nuclear power actions and organizations responded to criticisms by feminists or people of color that the movement was dominated by straight white men. Social group affinity groups formed and were generally encouraged, providing solidarity and representation to formerly invisible groups. The National Women's Studies Association, to take another example, has a complex and effective system of representation for group caucuses in its decisionmaking bodies.

The idea of a Rainbow Coalition expressed a heterogeneous public with forms of group representation. The traditional coalition corresponded to the idea of a unified public that transcends particular differences of experience and concerns. In traditional coalitions diverse groups work together for specific ends which they agree interest or affect them all in a similar way, and they generally agree that the differences of perspective, interests, or opinion among them will not surface in the public statements and actions of the coalition. This form ideally suits welfare state interest-group politics. In a Rainbow Coalition, by contrast, each of the constituent groups affirms the presence of the others as well as the specificity of their experience and perspective on social issues [. . .]. In the Rainbow public Blacks do not simply tolerate the participation of gays, labor activists do not grudgingly work alongside peace movement veterans, and none of these paternalistically concede to feminist participation. Ideally, a Rainbow Coalition affirms the presence and supports the claims of each of the oppressed groups or political movements constituting it, and arrives at a political program not by voicing some 'principles of unity' that hide difference, but rather by allowing each constituency to analyze economic and social issues from the perspective of its experience. This implies that each group maintains significant autonomy, and requires provision for group representation. Unfortunately, the promise of the Jesse Jackson campaign to launch a viable grassroots organization expressing these Rainbow Coalition ideals has not been fulfilled.

A principle of representation for oppressed or disadvantaged groups has been implemented most frequently in organizations and movements that challenge politics as usual in welfare capitalist society. Some more mainstream organizations, however, also have implemented this principle in some form. The National Democratic Party has had rules requiring representation of women and people of color as delegates, and many state Democratic parties have had similar rules. Many nonprofit agencies call for representation of specific groups, such as women, Blacks, Latinos, and disabled people, on their boards of directors. In a program that some of them call 'valuing difference,' some corporations have instituted limited representation of oppressed social groups in corporate discussions. One can imagine such a principle of group representation extended to other political contexts. Social justice would be enhanced in many American cities, for example, if a citywide school committee formally and explicitly represented Blacks, Hispanics, women, gay men and lesbians, poor and working-class people, disabled people, and students.

Some might object that implementing a principle of group representation in governing bodies would exacerbate conflict and divisiveness in public life, rendering decisions even more difficult to reach. Especially if groups have veto power over policies that fundamentally and uniquely affect members of their group, it seems likely, it might be claimed, that decisionmaking would be stalled. This objection presupposes that group differences imply essential conflicts of interest. But this is not so; groups may have differing perspectives on issues, but these are often compatible and enrich everyone's understanding when they are expressed. To the extent that group differences produce or reflect conflict, moreover, group representation would not necessarily increase such conflict and might decrease it. If their differences bring groups into conflict, a just society should bring such differences into the open for discussion. Insofar as structured relations of privilege and oppression are the source of the conflict, moreover, group representation can change those relations by equalizing the ability of groups to speak and be heard. Thus group representation should mitigate, though not eliminate, certain kinds of conflict. If, finally, the alternative to stalled decisionmaking is a unified public that makes decisions ostensibly embodying the general interest which systematically ignore, suppress, or conflict with the interests of particular groups, then stalled decisionmaking may sometimes be just.

# 30

# THE ILLUSION OF UNIVERSAL SUFFRAGE

## Michael Bakunin

Men once believed that the establishment of universal suffrage would guarantee the freedom of the peoples. That, alas, was a great illusion, and the realization of that illusion has led in many places to the downfall and demoralization of the radical party. The radicals did not wish to deceive the people – or so the liberal papers assure us – but in that case they were certainly themselves deceived. They were genuinely convinced when they promised the people freedom through universal suffrage, and inspired by that conviction they were able to arouse the masses and overthrow the established aristocratic governments. Today, having learnt from experience and power politics, they have lost faith in themselves and in their own principles and in that way they have sunk into defeat and corruption.

Yet the whole thing seemed so natural and so simple; once legislative and executive power emanated directly from a popular election, must it not become the pure expression of the people's will, and could that will produce anything other than freedom and well-being among the populace?

The whole deception of the representative system lies in the fiction that a government and a legislature emerging out of a popular election must or even can represent the real will of the people. Instinctively and inevitably the people expect two things: the greatest possible material prosperity combined with the greatest freedom of movement and action: that means the best organization of popular economic interests, and the complete absence of any kind of power or

From Michael Bakunin, 'The Illusion of Universal Suffrage', in George Woodcock (ed.), *The Anarchist Reader* (Fontana/Collins, London, 1977), pp. 108–10. Originally published in 1907.

political organization – since all political organization is destined to end in the negation of freedom. Such are the basic longings of the people.

The instincts of the rulers, whether they legislate or execute the laws, are – by the very fact of their exceptional position – diametrically opposite. However democratic may be their feelings and their intentions, once they achieve the elevation of office they can only view society in the same way as a schoolmaster views his pupils, and between pupils and masters equality cannot exist. On one side there is the feeling of superiority that is inevitably provoked by a position of superiority; on the other side, there is the sense of inferiority which follows from the superiority of the teacher, whether he is exercising an executive or a legislative power. Whoever talks of political power talks of domination; but where domination exists there is inevitably a somewhat large section of society that is dominated, and those who are dominated quite naturally detest their dominators, while the dominators have no choice but to subdue and oppress those they dominate.

This is the eternal history of political power, ever since that power has appeared in the world. This is what also explains why and how the most extreme of democrats, the most raging rebels, become the most cautious of conservatives as soon as they attain to power. Such recantations are usually regarded as acts of treason, but that is an error; their main cause is simply the change of position and hence of perspective ...

In Switzerland, as elsewhere, the ruling class is completely different and separate from the mass of the governed. Here, as everywhere, no matter how egalitarian our political constitution may be, it is the bourgeoisie who rule, and it is the people – workers and peasants – who obey their laws. The people have neither the leisure nor the necessary education to occupy themselves with government. Since the bourgeoisie have both, they have, in fact if not by right, exclusive privilege. Thus, in Switzerland as elsewhere, political equality is merely a puerile fiction, a lie.

But how, separated as they are from the people by all the economic and social circumstances of their existence, can the bourgeoisie express, in laws and in government, the feelings, ideas and wishes of the people? It is impossible, and daily experience in fact proves that, in legislation as well as government, the bourgeoisie is mainly directed by its own interests and prejudices, without any great concern for those of the people.

It is true that all our legislators, as well as all the members of cantonal governments, are elected, directly or indirectly, by the people. It is true that on election day even the proudest of bourgeoisie, if they have any political ambitions, are obliged to pay court to Her Majesty, the Sovereign People ... But once the elections are over, the people return to their work and the bourgeoisie to their profitable businesses and political intrigues. They neither meet nor recognize each other again. And how can one expect the people, burdened by their work and ignorant for the most part of current problems, to supervise the political actions of their representatives? In reality, the control exercised by voters on their elected representatives is a pure fiction. But since, in the representative system, popular control is the only guarantee of the people's freedom, it is quite evident that such freedom in its turn is no more than a fiction.

# 31

# PARLIAMENTARY ISOLATION

## Pierre-Joseph Proudhon

I entered the National Assembly with the timidity of a child, with the ardour of a neophyte. Assiduous, from nine o'clock in the morning, at the meetings of bureaux and committees, I did not quit the Assembly until the evening, and then I was exhausted with fatigue and disgust. As soon as I set foot in the parliamentary Sinai, I ceased to be in touch with the masses; because I was absorbed by my legislative work, I entirely lost sight of the current of events. I knew nothing, either of the situation of the national workshops, or the policy of the government, or of the intrigues that were growing up in the heart of the Assembly. One must have lived in that isolator which is called a National Assembly to realize how the men who are most completely ignorant of the state of the country are almost always those who represent it ... Most of my colleagues of the left and the extreme left were in the same perplexity of mind, the same ignorance of daily facts. One spoke of the national workshops only with a kind of terror, for fear of the people is the sickness of all those who belong to authority; the people, for those in power, are the enemy.

From Pierre-Joseph Proudhon, 'Parliamentary Isolation', in George Woodcock (ed.), *The Anarchist Reader* (Fontana/Collins, London, 1977), pp. 110–11. Originally written 1849.

# SECTION 4
# MAJORITY RULE

# MAJORITY RULE
# INTRODUCTION

Along with representation, the problem of majority rule has been one of the most perplexing in the history of democratic thought and practice. If democracy means rule of the people, how is this to be translated into particular decisions? This becomes a particular problem when 'the people' is not a homogeneous bloc, but is divided in its wishes and preferences. If majority rule is the best procedural device to arrive at decisions in such circumstances, then how can the minority be free if the decision arrived at is not the one they prefer?

The extract from *Rousseau* given here shows his hankering after unanimity, which, he suggests, would be the sign either of a common interest which all citizens aspire to, or, on the other hand, a symptom of acclamation of a dictator. Rousseau has a solution to the question of the freedom of the minority, though it may be questioned whether it is a valid one. He suggests that those who find themselves in the minority were mistaken about the common interest. Hence he arrives at the paradoxical conclusion that those in the minority did not 'really' want their own opinion to have won, because it was in contradiction with the general will, though this can only be ascertained after all citizens have voted. Being free thus involves accepting the majority opinion even though it was not the opinion members of the minority initially held.

There are two key issues raised in the problem of majority voting. If it is the only way of coming to a decision when there is no unanimity then how can it be justified? The extract by *Wollheim* suggests that the outcome of a decision apparently taken following this procedure may be a decision which does not command the support of the majority of citizens. Majority rule as a procedure may thus violate those very democratic principles on which it is supposedly based.

The second issue is the danger that democracy may end up in a new form of tyranny, that of the tyranny of the majority, in which the rights of the individuals comprising the minority are ignored or violated. As expressed in the extracts of *John Stuart Mill* and *Alexis de Tocqueville* reproduced here, their fear was that the coming of democracy would produce a form of dictatorship. Popular sovereignty could give rise to democratic despotism and unlimited sovereignty would be the result. The minority would turn out an oppressed group of citizens. Mill's reflections over the problems of majority rule reveal his concern that majority opinion could lead to the effective 'disenfranchisement of minorities'. His concerns are highly relevant to the workings of contemporary democracy. A government may emerge which does not reflect majority opinion. The workings of the first-past-the-post electoral system in contemporary Britain makes this still a possibility. Furthermore, Mill is worried that the workings of electoral or democratic politics may produce a politics of the lowest common denominator, in which the candidate is a person 'without any distinctive peculiarity, any known opinions except the shibboleth of the party'. Mill gives as an example of this the selection of Presidential candidates in the US, but contemporary British politics may furnish equally striking examples (Frank Dobson as candidate for Mayor of London in the elections of May 2000?). The remedy which Mill proposes is stronger representation for minority opinion. In sections of his book *On Representative Government* not excerpted here, he calls for a system of proportional representation to achieve this end.

The contemporary political philosopher *Giovanni Sartori* seeks to provide analysis of the complexities of the majority – minority relationship. Majority dominance and the role of the minority involve rights of minorities to oppose legislation once it has been enacted, as well as the rights of minorities to be involved in the voting process itself. Both are to be distinguished from the more general societal sense of 'tyranny of the majority' which liberals like de Tocqueville saw as leading to creeping cultural conformism and mediocrity in society at large.

Are there any solutions to these problems arising out of the majority principle? *Dahl*'s idea of 'polyarchy' notes the danger of the polarisation of democracy, if some groups feel that their way of life is 'severely menaced' by the actions of other segments of the population. Rather than majority versus minority he suggests a fluctuating system of 'polyarchy' in which diverse coalitions of minority groups come together on particular issues. In such a situation the likelihood of a solid majority confronting a permanent and hence alienated minority is greatly reduced.

# 32

# THE SOCIAL CONTRACT

## Jean-Jacques Rousseau

### CHAPTER II
#### VOTING

It may be seen, from the last chapter, that the way in which general business is managed may give a clear enough indication of the actual state of morals and the health of the body politic. The more concert reigns in the assemblies, that is, the nearer opinion approaches unanimity, the greater is the dominance of the general will. On the other hand, long debates, dissensions, and tumult proclaim the ascendancy of particular interests and the decline of the State.

This seems less clear when two or more orders enter into the constitution, as patricians and plebeians did at Rome; for quarrels between these two orders often disturbed the comitia, even in the best days of the Republic. But the exception is rather apparent than real; for then, through the defect that is inherent in the body politic, there were, so to speak, two States in one, and what is not true of the two together is true of either separately. Indeed, even in the most stormy times, the *plebiscita* of the people, when the senate did not interfere with them, always went through quietly and by large majorities. The citizens having but one interest, the people had but a single will.

At the other extremity of the circle, unanimity recurs; this is the case when the citizens, having fallen into servitude, have lost both liberty and will. Fear and flattery then change votes into acclamation; deliberation ceases, and only

From Jean-Jacques Rousseau, *The Social Contract and Discourses*, trans. and intro. G. D. H. Cole (Everyman's Library: Dent, London/Dutton, New York, 1968), Book IV, chapter II, pp. 87–9. Originally written 1762.

worship or malediction is left. Such was the vile manner in which the senate expressed its views under the emperors. It did so sometimes with absurd precautions. Tacitus observes that, under Otho, the senators, while they heaped curses on Vitellius, contrived at the same time to make a deafening noise, in order that, should he ever become their master, he might not know what each of them had said.

On these various considerations depend the rules by which the methods of counting votes and comparing opinions should be regulated, according as the general will is more or less easy to discover, and the State more or less in its decline.

There is but one law which, from its nature, needs unanimous consent. This is the social compact; for civil association is the most voluntary of all acts. Every man being born free and his own master, no one, under any pretext whatsoever, can make any man subject without his consent. To decide that the son of a slave is born a slave is to decide that he is not born a man.

If then there are opponents when the social compact is made, their opposition does not invalidate the contract, but merely prevents them from being included in it. They are foreigners among citizens. When the State is instituted, residence constitutes consent; to dwell within its territory is to submit to the Sovereign.

Apart from this primitive contract, the vote of the majority always binds all the rest. This follows from the contract itself. But it is asked how a man can be both free and forced to conform to wills that are not his own. How are the opponents at once free and subject to laws they have not agreed to?

I retort that the question is wrongly put. The citizen gives his consent to all the laws, including those which are passed in spite of his opposition, and even those which punish him when he dares to break any of them. The constant will of all the members of the State is the general will; by virtue of it they are citizens and free. When in the popular assembly a law is proposed, what the people is asked is not exactly whether it approves or rejects the proposal, but whether it is in conformity with the general will, which is their will. Each man, in giving his vote, states his opinion on that point; and the general will is found by counting votes. When therefore the opinion that is contrary to my own prevails, this proves neither more nor less than that I was mistaken, and that what I thought to be the general will was not so. If my particular opinion had carried the day I should have achieved the opposite of what was my will; and it is in that case that I should not have been free.

This presupposes, indeed, that all the qualities of the general will still reside in the majority: when they cease to do so, whatever side a man may take, liberty is no longer possible.

In my earlier demonstration of how particular wills are substituted for the general will in public deliberation, I have adequately pointed out the practicable methods of avoiding this abuse; and I shall have more to say of them later on. I have also given the principles for determining the proportional number of votes for declaring that will. A difference of one vote destroys equality; a single opponent destroys unanimity; but between equality and unanimity, there are several grades of unequal division, at each of which this proportion may be fixed in accordance with the condition and the needs of the body politic.

There are two general rules that may serve to regulate this relation. First, the more grave and important the questions discussed, the nearer should the opinion that is to prevail approach unanimity. Secondly, the more the matter in hand calls for speed, the smaller the prescribed difference in the numbers of votes may be allowed to become: where an instant decision has to be reached, a majority of one vote should be enough. The first of these two rules seems more in harmony with the laws, and the second with practical affairs. In any case, it is the combination of them that gives the best proportions for determining the majority necessary.

# 33

# A PARADOX IN THE THEORY OF DEMOCRACY

## Richard Wollheim

[...]

We might put the difference between the ancient and modern conceptions of Democracy like this: in both cases Democracy is the rule of the people; but in the classical theory the people is identified with a section, or part of the population, whereas in modern theory the people is identified with the population as a whole.

Immediately a problem arises: if Democracy means the rule of the people *as a whole*, how can it be realized? For in any modern state the people is bound to be both *numerous* and *diverse*, and either of these characteristics by itself – let alone the conjunction of the two – surely must make a group of individuals incapable of effective rule. In antiquity, or at any rate in the political theory of antiquity, the problem does not arise. For the *demos* of the Greek city-state was, in the first place, relatively small: and, secondly, it was, or was supposed to be, united in interest, and therefore uniform in desire or want.

One solution to this problem is to suggest a return to the Greek conditions: or the suggestion is, rather, that the conditions which hold for the Greek *demos* should be made to hold for the population of a modern democracy. This population should, in the first place, be considerably reduced in size. And when it is no longer numerous, it will automatically cease to be diverse. Or if any diversity remains, this diversity will be purely phenomenal or apparent. This

From Richard Wollheim, 'A Paradox in the Theory of Democracy', in P. Laslett and W. G. Runciman (eds), *Philosophy, Politics and Society*, 2nd series (Blackwell, Oxford, 1962), chapter 4, pp. 72–3.

solution – which can roughly be equated with Rousseau's ideal of 'legitimate rule' – is obviously unacceptable. The restriction upon population is Utopian: and the 'true' or 'real' uniformity that it advocates, which is consistent with any degree of conscious diversity, is worthless.

Another solution consists in weakening the criteria attached to the notion of effective rule. For if we mean by 'ruling' 'devising and composing laws' – as the Greeks did – then it is clearly impossible for a numerous and diverse population to exercise collective rule. One answer, as we have seen, is that we should bring it about that the population in a Democracy is neither numerous nor diverse. Another answer is that we should mean something different by 'ruling': or that in elucidating Democracy we should employ a different concept of 'rule'. And it is this second answer that is, explicitly or implicitly, incorporated in most modern democratic theories. If modern theory insists that in a democracy the people in the sense of the whole population, not just a section of the population, should rule, it also insists that the people should rule in the sense not of devising or initiating legislation but of choosing or controlling it. And the significance of this is that it permits a people to rule despite its size and its diversity.

[...]

# 34

# REPRESENTATIVE GOVERNMENT

## John Stuart Mill

### CHAPTER VII
#### OF TRUE AND FALSE DEMOCRACY; REPRESENTATION OF ALL, AND REPRESENTATION OF THE MAJORITY ONLY

It has been seen, that the dangers incident to a representative democracy are of two kinds: danger of a low grade of intelligence in the representative body, and in the popular opinion which controls it; and danger of class legislation on the part of the numerical majority, these being all composed of the same class. We have next to consider, how far it is possible so to organize the democracy, as, without interfering materially with the characteristic benefits of democratic government, to do away with these two great evils, or at least to abate them, in the utmost degree attainable by human contrivance.

The common mode of attempting this is by limiting the democratic character of the representation, through a more or less restricted suffrage. But there is a previous consideration which, duly kept in view, considerably modifies the circumstances which are supposed to render such a restriction necessary. A completely equal democracy, in a nation in which a single class composes the numerical majority, cannot be divested of certain evils; but those evils are greatly aggravated by the fact, that the democracies which at present exist are not equal, but systematically unequal in favour of the predominant class. Two very different ideas are usually confounded under the name democracy. The pure idea of

From John Stuart Mill, 'Considerations on Representative Government', in J. S. Mill, *Three Essays* (Oxford University Press, Oxford, London and New York, 1975), chapter VII, pp. 247–52. Originally written 1861.

democracy, according to its definition, is the government of the whole people by the whole people, equally represented. Democracy as commonly conceived and hitherto practised, is the government of the whole people by a mere majority of the people, exclusively represented. The former is synonymous with the equality of all citizens; the latter, strangely confounded with it, is a government of privilege, in favour of the numerical majority, who alone possess practically any voice in the State. This is the inevitable consequence of the manner in which the votes are now taken, to the complete disfranchisement of minorities.

The confusion of ideas here is great, but it is so easily cleared up, that one would suppose the slightest indication would be sufficient to place the matter in its true light before any mind of average intelligence. It would be so, but for the power of habit; owing to which the simplest idea, if unfamiliar, has as great difficulty in making its way to the mind as a far more complicated one. That the minority must yield to the majority, the smaller number to the greater, is a familiar idea; and accordingly men think there is no necessity for using their minds any further, and it does not occur to them that there is any medium between allowing the smaller number to be equally powerful with the greater, and blotting out the smaller number altogether. In a representative body actually deliberating, the minority must of course be overruled; and in an equal democracy (since the opinions of the constituents, when they insist on them, determine those of the representative body) the majority of the people, through their representatives, will outvote and prevail over the minority and their representatives. But does it follow that the minority should have no representatives at all? Because the majority ought to prevail over the minority, must the majority have all the votes, the minority none ? Is it necessary that the minority should not even be heard? Nothing but habit and old association can reconcile any reasonable being to the needless injustice. In a really equal democracy, every or any section would be represented, not disproportionately, but proportionately. A majority of the electors would always have a majority of the representatives; but a minority of the electors would always have a minority of the representatives. Man for man, they would be as fully represented as the majority. Unless they are, there is not equal government, but a government of inequality and privilege: one part of the people rule over the rest: there is a part whose fair and equal share of influence in the representation is withheld from them; contrary to all just government, but above all, contrary to the principle of democracy, which professes equality as its very root and foundation.

The injustice and violation of principle are not less flagrant because those who suffer by them are a minority; for there is not equal suffrage where every single individual does not count for as much as any other single individual in the community. But it is not only a minority who suffer. Democracy, thus constituted, does not even attain its ostensible object, that of giving the powers of government in all cases to the numerical majority. It does something very different: it gives them to a majority of the majority; who may be, and often are, but a minority of the whole. All principles are most effectually tested by extreme cases. Suppose then, that, in a country governed by equal and universal suffrage, there is a contested election in every constituency, and every election is carried by a small majority. The Parliament thus brought together represents little more than a bare majority of the people. This Parliament proceeds to legislate, and adopts important measures by a bare majority of itself. What guarantee is there that these measures accord with the wishes of a majority of the people? Nearly half the electors, having been outvoted at the hustings; have had no influence at all in the decision; and the whole of these may be, a majority of them probably are, hostile to the measures, having voted against those by whom they have been carried. Of the remaining electors, nearly half have chosen representatives who, by supposition, have voted against the measures. It is possible, therefore, and not at all improbable, that the opinion which has prevailed was agreeable only to a minority of the nation, though a majority of that portion of it, whom the institutions of the country have erected into a ruling class. If democracy means the certain ascendancy of the majority, there are no means of insuring that, but by allowing every individual figure to tell equally in the summing up. Any minority left out, either purposely or by the play of the machinery, gives the power not to the majority, but to a minority in some other part of the scale.

The only answer which can possibly be made to this reasoning is, that as different opinions predominate in different localities, the opinion which is in a minority in some places has a majority in others, and on the whole every opinion which exists in the constituencies obtains its fair share of voices in the representation. And this is roughly true in the present state of the constituency; if it were not, the discordance of the House with the general sentiment of the country would soon become evident. But it would be no longer true if the present constituency were much enlarged; still less, if made co-extensive with the whole population; for in that case the majority in every locality would consist of manual labourers; and when there was any question pending, on which these classes were at issue with the rest of the community, no other class could succeed in getting represented anywhere. Even now, is it not a great grievance, that in every Parliament a very numerous portion of the electors, willing and anxious to be represented, have no member in the House for whom they have voted? Is it just that every elector of Marylebone is obliged to be represented by two nominees of the vestries, every elector of Finsbury or Lambeth by those (as is generally believed) of the publicans? The constituencies to which most of the highly educated and public spirited persons in the country belong, those of the large towns, are now, in great part, either unrepresented or misrepresented. The electors who are on a different side in party politics from the local majority, are unrepresented. Of those who are on the same side, a large proportion are misrepresented; having been obliged to accept the man who had the greatest number of supporters in their political party, though his opinions may differ from theirs on every other point. The state of things is, in some respects, even worse than if the minority were not allowed to vote at all; for then, at least the majority might have a member who would represent their own best mind: while now, the necessity of not dividing the party, for fear of letting in its opponents, induces all to vote either for the first person who presents himself wearing their colours, or for the one brought forward by their local leaders; and these, if we pay them the compliment, which they very seldom deserve, of supposing their choice to be unbiassed by their personal interests, are compelled, that they may be sure of mustering their whole strength, to bring forward a candidate whom none of the party will strongly object to – that is, a man without any distinctive peculiarity, any known opinions except the shibboleth of the party. This is strikingly exemplified in the United States; where, at the election of President, the strongest party never dares put forward any of its strongest men, because every one of these, from the mere fact that he has been long in the public eye, has made himself objectionable to some portion or other of the party, and is therefore not so sure a card for rallying all their votes, as a person who has never been heard of by the public at all until he is produced as the candidate. Thus, the man who is chosen, even by the strongest party, represents perhaps the real wishes only of the narrow margin by which that party outnumbers the other. Any section whose support is necessary to success, possesses a veto on the candidate. Any section which holds out more obstinately than the rest, can compel all the others to adopt its nominee; and this superior pertinacity is unhappily more likely to be found among those who are holding out for their own interest, than for that of the public. The choice of the majority is therefore very likely to be determined by that portion of the body who are the most timid, the most narrow-minded and prejudiced, or who cling most tenaciously to the exclusive class-interest; in which case the electoral rights of the minority, while useless for the purposes for which votes are given, serve only for compelling the majority to accept the candidate of the weakest or worst portion of themselves.

That, while recognizing these evils, many should consider them as the necessary price paid for a free government, is in no way surprising: it was the opinion of all the friends of freedom, up to a recent period. But the habit of passing them over as irremediable has become so inveterate, that many persons seem to have lost the capacity of looking at them as things which they would be glad to remedy if they could. From despairing of a cure, there is too often but one step to denying the disease; and from this follows dislike to having a remedy proposed, as if the proposer were creating a mischief instead of offering relief from one. People are so inured to the evils, that they feel as if it were unreasonable, if not wrong, to complain of them. Yet, avoidable or not, he must be a purblind lover of liberty on whose mind they do not weigh; who would not rejoice at the discovery that they could be dispensed with. Now, nothing is more certain, than that the virtual blotting-out of the minority is no necessary or natural consequence of freedom; that, far from having any connexion with democracy, it is diametrically opposed to the first principle of democracy, representation in proportion to numbers. It is an essential part of democracy that minorities should be adequately represented. No real democracy, nothing but a false show of democracy, is possible without it.

# 35

# DEMOCRACY IN AMERICA

## Alexis de Tocqueville

### 7

#### THE OMNIPOTENCE OF THE MAJORITY IN THE UNITED STATES AND ITS EFFECTS

*The natural strength of the majority in democracies. Most of the American constitutions have artificially increased this natural strength. How? Pledged delegates. Moral power of the majority. View of its infallibility. Respects for its rights. What increases it in the United States.*

The absolute sovereignty of the will of the majority is the essence of democratic government, for in democracies there is nothing outside the majority capable of resisting it.

Most American constitutions have sought further artificially to increase this natural strength of the majority.

Of all political powers, the legislature is the one most ready to obey the wishes of the majority. The Americans wanted the members of the legislatures to be appointed *directly* by the people and for a *very short* term of office so that they should be obliged to submit not only to the general views but also to the passing passions of their constituents.

The members of both houses have been chosen from the same class and appointed in the same way, so that the activity of the legislative body is almost as quick and just as irresistible as that of a single assembly.

From Alexis de Tocqueville, *Democracy in America*, trans. G. Lawrence, eds J. P. Meyer and Max Lerner (Harper & Row, New York, 1966; Collins/Fontana Library, London, 1968), Vol. I, pp. 304–17. Originally written 1835.

Having constituted the legislature in this way, almost all the powers of government were concentrated in its hands.

At the same time as the law increased the strength of naturally powerful authorities, it increasingly weakened those that were by nature feeble. It gave the representatives of the executive neither stability nor independence, and by subjecting them completely to the caprices of the legislature, deprived them of what little influence the nature of democratic government might have allowed them to enjoy.

In several states the majority elected the judges, and in all they depended in a way on the legislature, whose members had the right annually to fix their salaries.

Custom has gone even beyond the laws.

A custom is spreading more and more in the United States which will end by making the guarantees of representative government vain; it frequently happens that the electors, when they nominate a deputy, lay down a plan of conduct for him and impose some positive obligations on him which he cannot avoid. It is as if, with tumult threatening, the majority were deliberating in the market-place.

In America several particular circumstances also tend to make the power of the majority not only predominant but irresistible.

The moral authority of the majority is partly based on the notion that there is more enlightenment and wisdom in a numerous assembly than in a single man, and the number of the legislators is more important than how they are chosen. It is the theory of equality applied to brains. This doctrine attacks the last asylum of human pride; for that reason the minority is reluctant in admitting it and takes a long time to get used to it. Like all powers, and perhaps more than any other of them, the power of the majority needs to have proved lasting to appear legitimate. When it is beginning to establish itself, it enforces obedience by constraint; it is only when men have long lived under its laws that they begin to respect it.

The idea that the majority has a right based on enlightenment to govern society was brought to the United States by its first inhabitants; and this idea, which would of itself be enough to create a free nation, has by now passed into mores and affects even the smallest habits of life.

Under the old monarchy the French took it as a maxim that the king could do no wrong, and when he did do wrong, they thought the fault lay with his advisers. This made obedience wonderfully much easier. One could grumble against the law without ceasing to love and respect the lawgiver. The Americans take the same view of the majority.

The moral authority of the majority is also founded on the principle that the interest of the greatest number should be preferred to that of those who are fewer. Now, it is easy to understand that the respect professed for this right of the greatest number naturally grows or shrinks according to the state of the parties. When a nation is divided between several great irreconcilable interests, the privilege of the majority is often disregarded, for it would be too unpleasant to submit to it.

If there existed in America one class of citizens whom the legislators were trying to deprive of certain exclusive privileges possessed for centuries and wanted to force them down from a high station to join the ranks of the crowd, it is probable that that minority would not easily submit to its laws.

But as men equal among themselves came to people the United States, there is as yet no natural or permanent antagonism between the interests of the various inhabitants.

There are states of society in which those who are in the minority cannot hope to win the majority over, for to do so would involve abandoning the very aim of the struggle in which they are engaged against it. An aristocracy, for instance, could not become a majority without giving up its exclusive privileges, and if it did let them go, it would no longer be an aristocracy.

In the United States, political questions cannot arise in such general and absolute fashion, and all the parties are ready to recognise the rights of the majority because they all hope one day to profit themselves by them.

Hence the majority in the United States has immense actual power and a power of opinion which is almost as great. When once its mind is made up on any question, there are, so to say, no obstacles which can retard, much less halt, its progress and give it time to hear the wails of those it crushes as it passes.

The consequences of this state of affairs are fate-laden and dangerous for the future.

### How in America the Omnipotence of the Majority Increases the Legislative and Administrative Instability Natural to Democracies

*How the Americans increase the legislative instability natural to democracies by changing their legislators every year and by giving them almost limitless power. The same effect on the administration. In America the drive toward social improvements is infinitely greater but less continuous than in Europe.*

I have spoken before of the vices natural to democratic government, and every single one of them increases with the growing power of the majority.

To begin with the most obvious of all:

Legislative instability is an ill inherent in democratic government because it is the nature of democracies to bring new men to power. But this ill is greater or less according to the power and means of action accorded to the legislator.

In America the lawmaking authority has been given sovereign power. This authority can carry out anything it desires quickly and irresistibly, and its representatives change annually. That it is to say, just that combination has been chosen which most encourages democratic instability and allows the changing wishes of democracy to be applied to the most important matters.

Thus American laws have a shorter duration than those of any other country in the world today. Almost all American constitutions have been amended within the last thirty years, and so there is no American state which has not modified the basis of its laws within that period.

As for the laws themselves, it is enough to glance at the archives of the various states of the Union to realise that in America the legislator's activity never slows down. Not that American democracy is by nature more unstable than any other, but it has been given the means to carry the natural instability of its inclinations into the making of laws.

The omnipotence of the majority and the rapid as well as absolute manner in which its decisions are executed in the United States not only make the law unstable, but have a like effect on the execution of the law and on public administrative activity.

As the majority is the only power whom it is important to please, all its projects are taken up with great ardour; but as soon as its attention is turned elsewhere, all these efforts cease; whereas in free European states, where the administrative authority has an independent existence and an assured position, the legislator's wishes continue to be executed even when he is occupied by other matters.

Much more zeal and energy are brought to bear in America on certain improvements than anywhere else.

In Europe an infinitely smaller social force is employed, but more continuously.

A few years ago some pious people undertook to make the state of the prisons better. The public was roused by their exhortations, and the reform of criminals became a popular cause.

New prisons were then built. For the first time the idea of reforming offenders as well as punishing them penetrated into the prisons. But that happy revolution in which the public co-operated with such eagerness and which the simultaneous efforts of the citizens rendered irresistible could not be accomplished in a moment.

Alongside the new penitentiaries, built quickly in response to the public's desire, the old prisons remained and housed a great number of the guilty. These seemed to become more unhealthy and more corrupting at the same rate as the new ones became healthy and devoted to reform. This double effect is easily understood: the majority, preoccupied with the idea of founding a new establishment, had forgotten the already existing ones. Everybody's attention was turned away from the matter that no longer held their master's, and supervision ceased. The salutary bonds of discipline were first stretched and then soon broken. And beside some prison that stood as a durable monument to the gentleness and enlightenment of our age, there was a dungeon recalling the barbarities of the Middle Ages.

### TYRANNY OF THE MAJORITY

*How the principle of the sovereignty of the people should be understood. Impossibility of conceiving a mixed government. Sovereign power must be placed somewhere. Precautions which one should take to moderate its action. These precautions have not been taken in the United States. Result thereof.*

I regard it as an impious and detestable maxim that in matters of government the majority of a people has the right to do everything, and nevertheless I place the origin of all powers in the will of the majority. Am I in contradiction with myself?

There is one law which has been made, or at least adopted, not by the majority of this or that people, but by the majority of all men. That law is justice.

Justice therefore forms the boundary to each people's right.

A nation is like a jury entrusted to represent universal society and to apply the justice which is its law. Should the jury representing society have greater power than that very society whose laws it applies?

Consequently, when I refuse to obey an unjust law, I by no means deny the majority's right to give orders; I only appeal from the sovereignty of the people to the sovereignty of the human race.

There are those not afraid to say that in matters which only concern itself a nation cannot go completely beyond the bounds of justice and reason and that there is therefore no need to fear giving total power to the majority representing it. But that is the language of a slave.

What is a majority, in its collective capacity, if not an individual with opinions, and usually with interests, contrary to those of another individual, called the minority? Now, if you admit that a man vested with omnipotence can abuse it against his adversaries, why not admit the same concerning a majority? Have men, by joining together, changed their character? By becoming stronger, have they become more patient of obstacles? For my part, I cannot believe that, and I will never grant to several that power to do everything which I refuse to a single man.

It is not that I think that in order to preserve liberty one can mix several principles within the same government in such a way that they will be really opposed to one another.

I have always considered what is called a mixed government to be a chimera. There is in truth no such thing as a mixed government (in the sense usually given to the words), since in any society one finds in the end some principle of action that dominates all the others.

Eighteenth-century England, which has been especially cited as an example of this type of government, was an essentially aristocratic state, although it contained within itself great elements of democracy, for laws and mores were so designed that the aristocracy could always prevail in the long run and manage public affairs as it wished.

The mistake is due to those who, constantly seeing the interests of the great in conflict with those of the people, have thought only about the struggle and have not paid attention to the result thereof, which was more important. When a society really does have a mixed government, that is to say, one equally shared between contrary principles, either a revolution breaks out or that society breaks up.

I therefore think it always necessary to place somewhere one social power superior to all others, but I believe that freedom is in danger when that power finds no obstacle that can restrain its course and give it time to moderate itself.

Omnipotence in itself seems a bad and dangerous thing. I think that its exercise is beyond man's strength, whoever he be, and that only God can be omnipotent without danger because His wisdom and justice are always equal to His power. So there is no power on earth in itself so worthy of respect or vested with such a sacred right that I would wish to let it act without control and dominate without obstacles. So when I see the right and capacity to do all given to any authority whatsoever, whether it be called people or king, democracy or aristocracy, and whether the scene of action is a monarchy or a republic, I say: the germ of tyranny is there, and I will go look for other laws under which to live.

My greatest complaint against democratic government as organised in the United States is not, as many Europeans make out, its weakness, but rather its irresistible strength. What I find most repulsive in America is not the extreme freedom reigning there but the shortage of guarantees against tyranny.

When a man or a party suffers an injustice in the United States, to whom can he turn? To public opinion? That is what forms the majority. To the legislative body? It represents the majority and obeys it blindly. To the executive power? It is appointed by the majority and serves as its passive instrument. To the police? They are nothing but the majority under arms. A jury? The jury is the majority vested with the right to pronounce judgment; even the judges in certain states are elected by the majority. So, however iniquitous or unreasonable the measure which hurts you, you must submit.

But suppose you were to have a legislative body so composed that it represented the majority without being necessarily the slave of its passions, an executive power having a strength of its own, and a judicial power independent of the other two authorities; then you would still have a democratic government, but there would be hardly any remaining risk of tyranny.

I am not asserting that at the present time in America there are frequent acts of tyranny. I do say that one can find no guarantee against it there and that the reasons for the government's gentleness must be sought in circumstances and in mores rather than in the laws.

### EFFECT OF THE OMNIPOTENCE OF THE MAJORITY ON THE ARBITRARY POWER OF AMERICAN PUBLIC OFFICIALS

*The freedom which American law leaves to functionaries within the sphere marked out for them. Their power.*

It is important to make the distinction between arbitrary power and tyranny. Tyranny can use even the law as its instrument, and then it is no longer arbitrary; arbitrary power may be used in the interest of the ruled, and then it is not tyrannical.

Tyranny ordinarily makes use of arbitrariness, but it can at need do without it.

In the United States that omnipotence of the majority which favours the legal despotism of the legislator also smiles on the arbitrary power of the magistrate. The majority, being in absolute command both of lawmaking and of the execution of the laws, and equally controlling both rulers and ruled, regards public functionaries as its passive agents and is glad to leave them the trouble of carrying out its plans. It therefore does not enter by anticipation into the details of their duties and hardly takes the trouble to define their rights. It treats them as a master might treat his servants if, always seeing them act under his eyes, he could direct or correct them at any moment.

In general, the law leaves American officials much freer than ours within the sphere marked out for them. Sometimes the majority may even allow them to go beyond that. Assured of the views and strengthened by the support of the greatest number, they then dare to do things which astonish a European, accustomed though he be to the spectacle of arbitrary power. Thus habits form in freedom that may one day become fatal to that freedom.

### THE POWER EXERCISED BY THE MAJORITY IN AMERICA OVER THOUGHT

*In the United States, when the majority has irrevocably decided about any question, it is no longer discussed. Why? Moral authority exercised by the majority over thought. Democratic republics have turned despotism into something immaterial.*

It is when one comes to look into the use made of thought in the United States that one most clearly sees how far the power of the majority goes beyond all powers known to us in Europe.

Thought is an invisible power and one almost impossible to lay hands on, which makes sport of all tyrannies. In our day the most absolute sovereigns in Europe cannot prevent certain thoughts hostile to their power from silently circulating in their states and even in their own courts. It is not like that in America; while the majority is in doubt, one talks; but when it has irrevocably pronounced, everyone is silent, and friends and enemies alike seem to make for its bandwagon. The reason is simple: no monarch is so absolute that he can hold all the forces of society in his hands and overcome all resistance, as a majority invested with the right to make the laws and to execute them can do.

Moreover, a king's power is physical only, controlling actions but not influencing desires, whereas the majority is invested with both physical and moral authority, which acts as much upon the will as upon behaviour and at the same moment prevents both the act and the desire to do it.

I know no country in which, speaking generally, there is less independence of mind and true freedom of discussion than in America.

There is no religious or political theory which one cannot preach freely in the constitutional states of Europe or which does not penetrate into the others, for there is no country in Europe so subject to a single power that he who wishes to speak the truth cannot find support enough to protect him against the consequences of his independence. If he is unlucky enough to live under an absolute government, he often has the people with him; if he lives in a free country, he may at need find shelter behind the royal authority. In democratic countries the aristocracy may support him, and in other lands the democracy. But in a democracy organised on the model of the United States there is only one authority, one source of strength and of success, and nothing outside it.

In America the majority has enclosed thought within a formidable fence. A writer is free inside that area, but woe to the man who goes beyond it. Not that he stands in fear of an *auto-da-fé*, but he must face all kinds of unpleasantness and everyday persecution. A career in politics is closed to him, for he has offended the only power that holds the keys. He is denied everything, including renown. Before he goes into print, he believes he has supporters; but he feels that he has them no more once he stands revealed to all, for those who condemn him express their views loudly, while those who think as he does, but without his courage, retreat into silence as if ashamed of having told the truth.

Formerly tyranny used the clumsy weapons of chains and hangmen; nowadays even despotism, though it seemed to have nothing more to learn, has been perfected by civilisation.

Princes made violence a physical thing, but our contemporary democratic republics have turned it into something as intellectual as the human will it is intended to constrain. Under the absolute government of a single man, despotism, to reach the soul, clumsily struck at the body, and the soul, escaping from such blows, rose gloriously above it; but in democratic republics that is not at all how tyranny behaves; it leaves the body alone and goes straight for the soul. The master no longer says: 'Think like me or you die.' He does say: 'You are free not to think as I do; you can keep your life and property and all; but from this day you are a stranger among us. You can keep your privileges in the township, but they will be useless to you, for if you solicit your fellow citizens' votes, they will not give them to you, and if you only ask for their esteem, they will make excuses for refusing that. You will remain among men, but you will lose your rights to count as one. When you approach your fellows, they will shun you as an impure being, and even those who believe in your innocence will abandon you too, lest they in turn be shunned. Go in peace. I have given you your life, but it is a life worse than death.'

Absolute monarchies brought despotism into dishonour; we must beware lest democratic republics rehabilitate it, and that while they make it more oppressive toward some, they do not rid it of its detestable and degrading character in the eyes of the greatest number.

In the proudest nations of the Old World works were published which faithfully portrayed the vices and absurdities of contemporaries; La Bruyère lived in Louis XIV's palace while he wrote his chapter on the great, and Molière criticised the court in plays acted before the courtiers. But the power which dominates in the United States does not understand being mocked like that. The least reproach offends it, and the slightest sting of truth turns it fierce; and one must praise everything, from the turn of its phrases to its most robust virtues. No writer, no matter how famous, can escape from this obligation to sprinkle incense over his fellow citizens. Hence the majority lives in a state of perpetual self-adoration; only strangers or experience may be able to bring certain truths to the Americans' attention.

We need seek no other reason for the absence of great writers in America so far; literary genius cannot exist without freedom of the spirit, and there is no freedom of the spirit in America.

In Spain the Inquisition was never able to prevent the circulation of books contrary to the majority religion. The American majority's sway extends further and has rid itself even of the thought of publishing such books. One finds unbelievers in America, but unbelief has, so to say, no organ.

One finds governments striving to protect mores by condemning the authors of licentious books. No one in the United States is condemned for works of that sort, but no one is tempted to write them. Not that all the citizens are chaste in their mores, but those of the majority are regular.

In this, no doubt, power is well used, but my point is the nature of the power in itself. This irresistible power is a continuous fact and its good use only an accident.

[...]

# 36

# THE THEORY OF DEMOCRACY REVISITED

## Giovanni Sartori

[...]

### 6.2 The Tyranny of the Majority

We must now disentangle the contexts or settings to which the terms majority and minority are variously applied. The settings that require separate consideration are, at a minimum, three: (*a*) constitutional structures and processes, (*b*) electoral and voting arenas, and (*c*) society at large. Therefore let us say that the majority-minority relation obtains three major, context-embedded, clusters of meaning:

> constitutional
> electoral (voting)
> societal

In the *constitutional context* the concern is about minorities, not majorities. More precisely, the problem that comes to the fore in this context is that the minority or minorities must have the right to oppose, the right of opposition. It is here where the expression "majority rule and minority rights" acquires its most precise meaning and a particular prominence. If the opposition is hampered, harassed, or stamped on, we may thus speak of "tyranny of the majority" in the constitutional meaning of the expression. There is, however, a second constitutional meaning of tyranny of the majority, that which Madison and Jefferson called "elective despotism." What they feared was the despotism of an

From Giovanni Sartori, *The Theory of Democracy Revisited* (Chatham House, Chatham, NJ, 1987), pp. 133–7.

assembly government unrestricted by division of power: an elective body (a parliament, but specifically its lower house) that would concentrate in its hands an unlimited and, by this token, a tyrannical power. That their fear was well justified was shown soon after by the French revolutionary *gouvernement conventionnel*, indeed a perfect incarnation of elective despotism. However, the elective despotism envisaged by Madison and Jefferson does not really bear on the majority–minority relationship but on the principle that undivided power is always an excessive and dangerous power. So, the tyranny of the majority that acquires prominence in the constitutional perspective is the one that bears on *minority rights*, and especially on whether the right of opposition is respected or not.

In the *electoral-voting context* the argument takes an entirely different twist. Here the focus is exclusively on the majority principle, that is, on "majority" understood as a rule of the game. And the argument is, very simply, that whoever votes with the majority (i.e., as most other voters do) is on the winning side. Conversely, whoever votes with the minority (thus failing to join a plurality) is on the losing side: His vote counts for nothing. In voting, then, 'minority' simply denotes those who must submit to the will of the majority (even if a simple plurality). The point therefore is that, in voting, the *minority has no rights:* It consists of those whose vote was lost – period. The implication is that in electoral-voting contexts the expression 'majority tyranny' is inapplicable and meaningless.

To be sure, while each act of voting is a finite, single-shot act, when we cast a vote we may well initiate a *process*, as is especially the case with electoral voting. And while the single voting act should not be confused with the process that it eventually triggers, it should not pass unnoticed that the process not only affects the notion of "winning" but is bound to multiply the number of losers. The winning elector is an elector who gets his candidate elected (or who votes for a party list that obtains, in his constituency, at least one seat). However, if we pass on to consider the ensuing sequel of events, which is a multi-stage process, it is apparent that the elector may win at the constituency level and yet lose at other levels: at the parliamentary level (where his representative may belong to a minority party), and again at the governmental level (when his party is excluded from government). The bearing of the foregoing is twofold. First, it brings out the importance of treating separately the *voting act* from the *voting process*. Second, it bears out the earlier point that we cannot derive a *majority rule* (rulership) from the *majority principle*. One reason for this is that if the majority principle applies at successive levels, a multi-stage processing may well eliminate, one at a time, a sequel of minorities that add up to a majority of the initial voting population, of the demos at large.

Let us now turn to the meaning of "majority" in the third setting, that is, in a society-wide or *societal context*. The social meaning of the term majority is the meaning characteristically attributed to the expression "tyranny of the majority" by Tocqueville and by John Stuart Mill. What troubled Tocqueville and, subsequently, Mill, was the danger of a spiritual tyranny that is, of an extreme and suffocating social conformity. Here the majority–minority relationship is no longer important in itself but in its bearing on, and for, the individual. Consequently the focus shifts onto the relationship of *society to the individual*. The antithesis is between majority versus freedom of the individual, or between majority versus intellectual independence. "The democratic republics make despotism superfluous," said Tocqueville, "because the majority itself draws a formidable ring around thought." And Mill wrote:

> When society itself is the tyrant – society collectively over the separate individuals who compose it ... it practices a social tyranny more formidable than many kinds of political oppression, since ... it leaves fewer means of escape, penetrating much more deeply into the details of life, and enslaving the soul itself. Protection, therefore, against the tyranny of the magistrate is not enough: there needs protection also against the tyranny of prevailing opinion and feeling, against the tendency of society to impose ... its own ideas and practices as rules of conduct on those who dissent from them ... and to compel all characters to fashion themselves on the model of its own.

In the above, reference is made to some kind of substantive majority, hardly to the majority criterion or principle. Also, what Mill described has little to do with a majoritarian tyranny, but rather (in his own wording) with "social tyranny." On either count, his case is not very convincing. I am not saying that collectivities do not control and eventually oppress their individual component members, but that Mill's social tyranny long precedes democracy and does not appear to have much to do with democracy. Small-town and village communities easily suffocate individuality precisely in the way he described; yet this is simply the unpleasant side of "commonality," the drawback overlooked by the idealizations of communes and community life. A puritan community of earlier times was far worse – with respect to what Mill feared and lamented – than anything that he ever saw in his time. Should we, therefore, dismiss Mill's argument? And should we, by implication, dismiss also Tocqueville's case?

I would not go that far. For Tocqueville did have a point when he spoke of tyranny of the majority – one that is missed when his concept is translated as "social tyranny." The point is that the majority principle (note that I have switched to the principle) adds an element of legitimacy, a *right*, to what is otherwise a sheer *fact*, namely, that social conformity exists and entails costs and excesses. This is not quite the argument of Tocqueville. It suggests, however, that there is a reason for bringing the notion of majority to bear on our misgivings about social tyranny. This reason is that "the tendency of society to impose its own ideas and practices," i.e., to impose conformity, finds in the majority principle a principle of legitimization. And if this is our reading (between the lines) of Tocqueville and Mill, then also the social meaning of "tyranny of the majority" deserves to be kept in mind.

Before proceeding further, it is well to recapitulate. First, the majority principle poses the problem of protecting minorities. This is, first and foremost, a constitutional problem. In this context we seek, then, a *limited* majority principle, that is, we seek to delimit and temper its application. Conversely put, if the majority principle is unlimited or absolute, then we have a "tyranny of the majority" in the constitutional meaning of the expression. This qualification does not imply that the issue is confined to constitutional provisions. When we put our mind to the problem of empowering without overpowering, we soon discover that juridical checks alone cannot solve it. This is, however, an additional reason for stressing that a governing majority that crushes the rights of opposition does indeed embody a tyranny of the majority. In this context, then, the mark is well hit.

Second, the majority principle confronts the problem of manufacturing a governmental majority. This is the case when the majority principle applies to the electoral-voting process. In this context, each majority (plurality) test eliminates – level by level – its corresponding minority. In order to fabricate a governmental majority the majority criterion can only perform, on each occasion, as a winner-take-all principle. It follows that the expression "tyranny of the majority" is meaningless in the electoral-voting context. At the end of the process the case may also be that a numerical minority of the citizenry emerges – at the governmental level – as the winning majority. Here, then, a majority is often only the *largest minority*.

Third, the majority principle may aggravate social tyranny (as characterized by John Stuart Mill) by legitimizing it. In this respect the tyranny of the majority feared by Tocqueville and Mill – tyranny over the individual – remains a matter of concern.

At first sight it may seem odd that the founding authors of liberal democracy – Madison, Jefferson, Tocqueville, Mill – were so much more concerned with a tyranny of the majority (in one sense or another) than with a tyranny of the minority. But reflection shows otherwise. Since democracy replaces a tyranny by some minority, and since its rule (principle) is that the majority is always right, it attests to their farsightedness that their attention should shift to the "opposite danger," to the danger inherent in the new principle.

Another noteworthy point is that the analysis of the *principle* does not bear out a substantive *majority rule* of the many, of the multitudes or, if you like, of the masses. The reason for this is not far to seek. When reference is made to an institutionalized body (a government, a parliament, a party), the referent of "majority" is some kind of cohesive and identifiable *operating unit*. But when reference is made, as in the case at hand, to large-scale, dispersed collectivities, the referent of "majority" generally is a set of *ephemeral aggregations*. An electoral majority is largely an artifact of an electoral occasion and thereby largely an artifact of the party system qua system of channelment. As for issue majorities, they tend to dissolve and recompose themselves issue by issue. Bluntly put, the majority of a citizenry – a 'mass majority' – is a process of endless amalgamation and dissolution of myriad groups and individuals. This is not to deny that even a mass majority may coalesce and perform, over time, as an operating unit. However, a mass majority becomes an "operating majority" if, and only if, it acquires some kind of fixity, of over time cohesiveness. For this to happen, a majority of a population must consist of *strong* party or class or racial *identifiers*. In Western democracies this has seldom been the case. Most of the time concrete mass majorities are also intermittent and mobile majorities that cannot sustain or produce a "majority rule" (rulership) in any strong sense of the expression. So, with reference to mass majorities there is little reason to fear a tyranny of the majority; and the point is that from the *majority method* for making decisions one cannot derive that there is any one group that constitutes *the majority* and makes the decisions. The majority method connotes only a mathematical majority; it does not denote an enduring major part of a collectivity.

I noted that the overall design is to avoid giving "all power" to either majorities or minorities. Our analysis goes to show that this is precisely what happens. In particular, along the electoral-voting process concrete majorities produce concrete minorities, which are in turn submitted to the majority criterion – and this all the way from a mass electorate up to a government.

[...]

# 37

# POLYARCHY, PARTICIPATION AND OPPOSITION

## Robert A. Dahl

[...]

Let me call a regime near the lower left corner of figure [1] a closed hegemony. If a hegemonic regime shifts upward, as along path I, then it is moving toward greater public contestation. Without stretching language too far, one could say that a change in this direction involves the liberalization of a regime; alternatively one might say that the regime becomes more competitive. If a regime changes to provide greater participation, as along path II, it might be said to change toward greater popularization, or that it is becoming inclusive. A regime might change along one dimension and not the other. If we call a regime near the upper left corner a competitive oligarchy, then path I represents a change from a closed hegemony to a competitive oligarchy. But a closed hegemony might also become more inclusive without liberalizing, i.e., without increasing the opportunities for public contestation, as along path II. In this case the regime changes from a closed to an inclusive hegemony.

Democracy might be conceived of as lying at the upper right corner. But since democracy may involve more dimensions than the two in figure [1], and since (in my view) no large system in the real world is fully democratized, I prefer to call real world systems that are closest to the upper right corner polyarchies. Any change in a regime that moves it upward and to the right, for example along path III, may be said to represent some degree of democratization. Polyarchies, then, may be thought of as relatively (but incompletely) democratized regimes,

From Robert A. Dahl, *Polyarchy, Participation and Opposition* (Yale University Press, New Haven, CT and London, 1971), pp. 6–9 and 105–10.

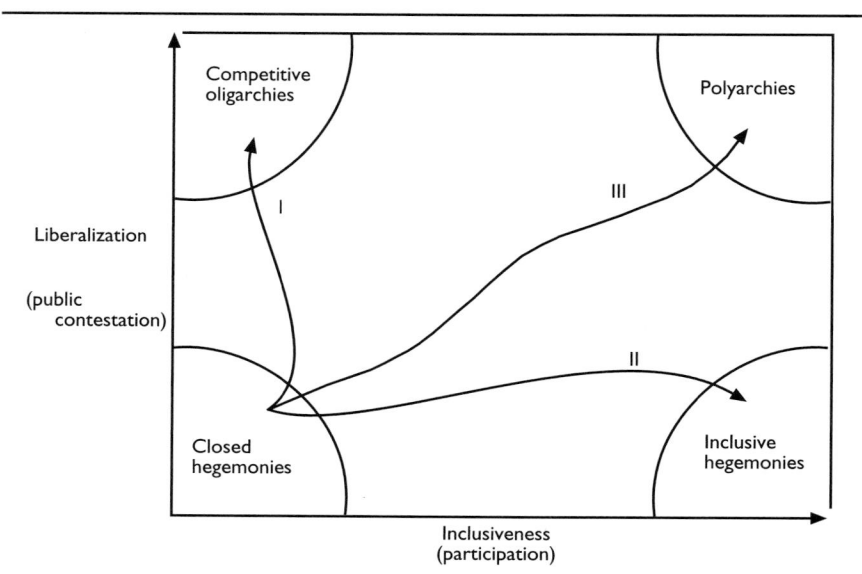

FIGURE [1] Liberalization, Inclusiveness, and Democratization

or, to put it in another way, polyarchies are regimes that have been substantially popularized and liberalized, that is, highly inclusive and extensively open to public contestation.

You will notice that although I have given names to regimes lying near the four corners, the large space in the middle of the figure is not named, nor is it subdivided. The absence of names partly reflects the historic tendency to classify regimes in terms of extreme types; it also reflects my own desire to avoid redundant terminology. The lack of nomenclature does not mean a lack of regimes; in fact, perhaps the preponderant number of national regimes in the world today would fall into the mid-area. Many significant changes in regimes, then, involve shifts within, into, or out of this important central area, as these regimes become more (or less) inclusive and increase (or reduce) opportunities for public contestation. In order to refer to regimes in this large middle area, I shall sometimes resort to the terms near or nearly: a nearly hegemonic regime has somewhat more opportunities for public contestation than a hegemonic regime; a near-polyarchy could be quite inclusive but would have more severe restrictions on public contestation than a full polyarchy, or it might provide opportunities for public contestation comparable to those of a full polyarchy and yet be somewhat less inclusive.

The need to use terms like these later on in this book testifies to the utility of classification; the arbitrariness of the boundaries between "full" and "near" testifies to the inadequacy of any classification. So long as we keep firmly in mind that the terms are useful but rather arbitrary ways of dividing up the space in figure [1], the concepts will serve their purpose.

[...]

7

SUBCULTURES, CLEAVAGE PATTERNS, AND GOVERNMENTAL EFFECTIVENESS

Obviously any system is in peril if it becomes polarized into several highly antagonistic groups. Confronted by severe polarization, competitive regimes are prone to collapse, to a coup d'etat, to civil war: for example, Italy from 1919 to 1923, the first Austrian Republic virtually throughout its brief existence, the Weimar Republic from about 1929 to its demise, the Spanish Republic from 1934 to 1936, and the United States in the decade preceding our Civil War.

In the United States the victors were committed to a more or less inclusive polyarchy, a commitment that for a decade after the end of that war included even the freed slaves. But in other cases, victory went to antidemocratic movements that successfully introduced a hegemonic regime into the country.

There are conflicts, then, that a competitive political system does not manage easily and perhaps cannot handle at all. Any dispute in which a large section of the population of a country feels that its way of life or its highest values are severely menaced by another segment of the population creates a crisis in a competitive system. Whatever the eventual outcome may be, the historical record argues that the system is very likely to dissolve into civil war or to be displaced by a hegemony or both.

Thus any difference within a society that is likely to polarize people into severely antagonistic camps is a cleavage of exceptional importance. Are some countries, then, less likely than others to have competitive regimes and more likely to have hegemonic regimes because, for whatever reason, they are unusually subject to cleavages that are particularly favorable to acute polarization?

Answers to this question are, unfortunately, obscured by the massive impact on social thought of certain dramatic aspects of Marxist thought. For over a century, reflections about polarization and civil war have been dominated, even among non-Marxists, by Marx's conception of polarization around the node of economic classes – working class and bourgeoisie. Yet in the 120 years since the Communist Manifesto was published, no country has developed according to the Marxist model of conflict, nor has any regime, whether hegemonic or competitive, fallen or been transformed because of a clear-cut polarization of working class and bourgeoisie.

A preoccupation with class conflict and often an unarticulated assumption even among sophisticated social theorists that classes are somehow the "real" basis of differences in an industrial society, to which all others are "ultimately" reducible, has tended to deflect attention from other differences that give rise to durable subcultures into which individuals are socialized: these are differences in religion, language, race, or ethnic group, and region.

Differences along these axes, differences that frequently reinforce one another, have obvious, important, and persistent consequences for political life in a great many countries – indeed, it is no exaggeration to say, in most countries in the world. Yet differences of this kind have often been ignored or deprecated as "really" nothing but class differences in disguise, or somehow less "real" than class, or if not less real then surely less enduring, bound to disappear rapidly under the impact of industrialization, urbanization, and mass communications. Yet these differences and the conflicts they engender do not always disappear and may even sharpen with the passage of time, as in contemporary Belgium, Canada, and quite possibly in Britain.

This is not to argue that "class" differences are unimportant. It is to say that economic class is only one factor, often less important than others that can and quite evidently do yield distinct subcultures – ways of life, outlooks, norms, identifications, loyalties, organizations, social structures. What is more, these subcultures are often extraordinarily long-lived not only in the life of an individual (who may change his class identification more readily than his mother tongue or his religion) but also in the life of a society: for over a thousand years, classes and empires have risen and fallen while the linguistic boundaries within what are now Belgium and Switzerland have barely changed.

Presumably because an ethnic or religious identity is incorporated so early and so deeply into one's personality, conflicts among ethnic or religious subcultures are specially fraught with danger, particularly if they are also tied to region. Because conflicts among ethnic and religious subcultures are so easily seen as threats to one's most fundamental self, opponents are readily transformed into a malign and inhuman "they," whose menace stimulates and justifies the violence and savagery that have been the common response of in-group to out-group among all mankind. The junction of ethnic group or religion with regional subcultures creates an incipient nation whose spokesmen clamor for autonomy, and even for independence. Consequently many students of politics have agreed with John Stuart Mill that the boundaries of any country with a representative government must coincide with the boundaries of nationality; a considerable body of experience with multinational states lends impressive support to their argument.

That subcultural pluralism often places a dangerous strain on the tolerance and mutual security required for a system of public contestation seems hardly open to doubt. Polyarchy in particular is more frequently found in relatively homogeneous countries than in countries with a great amount of subcultural pluralism. Perhaps the best evidence for this is to be found in a study by Marie R. Haug that classifies 114 countries according to an index of pluralism and data derived from *A Cross-Polity Survey* by Banks and Textor. Although there have been some changes of regime since the early 1960s, when the data were collected, these can hardly have been so great as to invalidate the general relationships. Comparing the 26 countries where cultural pluralism (in the numerical sense) is negligible with the 34 where it is extreme reveals that:

> Among countries in which subcultural pluralism is negligible, more
> than half are also classified by Banks and Textor as integrated and

homogeneous polities with little or no extreme opposition, communalism, fractionalism, or political nonassimilation (high in political enculturation).

Among these countries, none is classified as a relatively nonintegrated or restrictive polity with a majority or near-majority in extreme opposition, communalized, fractionalized, disfranchised, or politically nonassimilated (low in political enculturation).

Conversely, among countries in which subcultural pluralism is extreme, only 10 percent are high in political enculturation; almost two-thirds are low in political enculturation.

Among countries in which subcultural pluralism is negligible, 60 per cent are also classified by Banks and Textor as having an effective allocation of power to functionally autonomous legislative, executive, and judicial organs (significant horizontal power distribution).

Among these countries, only 18 per cent are classified as having complete dominance of government by one branch or by an extragovernmental agency (negligible horizontal power distribution).

Conversely, among countries in which subcultural pluralism is extreme, only one-third have a significant horizontal power distribution, while in 57 per cent one branch of government is without genuine functional autonomy or two branches have only limited functional autonomy.

[. . .]

# SECTION 5
# CITIZENSHIP

# CITIZENSHIP
## INTRODUCTION

Citizenship is a key concept of democratic theory, for the obvious reason that the 'units' or members of a democratic society are its citizens. But what is a citizen? And what kind of role is citizenship? How active or passive should a citizen be? What are the duties as well as the rights associated with the role of citizen? These questions have been debated in democratic theory ever since the time of the Greek polis, as the first extract from *Aristotle* makes clear. Citizenship raises the question of inclusion and exclusion: who exactly are the citizens, who forms the citizen body, and what exactly should a citizen do?

The modern discussion of citizenship was relaunched by the English sociologist *T. H. Marshall*, in his classic tripartite distinction between civil, political and social citizenship. He saw each of these as successive stages, starting with civil and legal rights, moving on to the political inclusion of wider numbers of people in the democratic process. Finally, for Marshall, came social citizenship, meaning the extension to all citizens of rights to education and housing which were necessary for them to exercise their citizenship capacities.

Contemporary discussions focus on the question of what citizenship would involve in practice. What is required of citizens? The idea of a distinction between active and passive citizens goes back to the French Revolution, as is demonstrated by the extract from the historian *W. H. Sewell*. In the French Revolution, active citizenship, the right to make the laws, was restricted to male property owners. Women and the propertyless were excluded from active citizenship, though as passive citizens they were entitled to security of the person and freedom from arbitrary interference by the state. Clearly, modern democrats reject this division into two categories of citizens and the issue of membership of the democratic order, its rights and responsibilities, is very much a live question for contemporary democratic theory and practice.

Finally, as the extract from *Kymlicka and Norman* suggests, there is renewed interest in the question of what is expected from the citizen in contemporary democracy. Ideas of 'civic republicanism' call for more extended and developed participation in political activity. This definition of the citizen's role poses a challenge to the idea that it is enough to vote once every four or five years to fulfil the criterion of being a 'good citizen'. Is the good citizen one who would live up to Schumpeter's idea of liberal-democracy, and participate only in periodic elections to select the leaders? Or is something more required to be a good citizen? Critics of a more participatory stance warn that demanding too much of the average citizen may demobilise rather than stimulate people to more involvement in the public sphere. These issues are further debated in Section 14 on participation in Part Four below.

# 38

# THE POLITICS

## Aristotle

[...]

A polis or state belongs to the order of 'compounds', in the same way as all other things which form a single 'whole', but a 'whole' composed, none the less, of a number of different parts. This being the case, it clearly follows that we must inquire into the nature of the citizen [i.e. the part] before inquiring into the nature of the state [i.e. the whole composed of such parts]. In other words, a state is a compound made up of citizens; and this compels us to consider who should properly be called a citizen and what a citizen really is. The nature of citizenship, like that of the state, is a question which is often disputed: there is no general agreement on a single definition: the man who is a citizen in a demo-cracy is often not one in an oligarchy.   § 3. We may leave out of consideration those who enjoy the name and title of citizen in some other than the strict sense – for example, naturalized citizens. A citizen proper is not one by virtue of residence in a given place: resident aliens and slaves share a common place of residence [with citizens, but they are not citizens].   § 4. Nor can the name of citizen be given to those who share in civic rights only to the extent of being entitled to sue and be sued in the courts. This is a right which belongs also to aliens who share its enjoyment by virtue of a treaty; though it is to be noted that there are many places where resident aliens do not enjoy even this limited right to the full – being obliged to choose a legal protector [to sue and be sued on their behalf], so that they only share to a limited extent in the common enjoyment of

From Aristotle, *The Politics*, ed. and trans. Ernest Barker (Clarendon Press, Oxford, 1946), Book III, chapter I, pp. 92–5. Originally written *ca.* 335 BC.

the right.   § 5. [We may thus dismiss those who have only the right to sue and be sued from our consideration,] just as we may also dismiss children who are still too young to be entered on the roll of citizens, or men who are old enough to have been excused from civic duties. There is a sense in which the young and the old may both be called citizens, but it is not altogether an unqualified sense: we must add the reservation that the young are undeveloped, and the old super-annuated citizens, or we must use some other qualification; the exact term we apply does not matter, for the meaning is clear.

What we have to define is the citizen in the strict and unqualified sense, who has no defect that has to be made good before he can bear the name – no defect such as youth or age, or such as those attaching to disfranchised or exiled citizens (about whom similar questions have also to be raised and answered).   § 6. The citizen in this strict sense is best defined by the one cri-terion, 'a man who shares in the administration of justice and in the holding of office.' Offices may be divided into two kinds. Some are discontinuous in point of time: in other words, they are of the sort that either cannot be held at all for more than a single term or can only be held for a second term after some definite interval. Others, however, have no limit of time – for example, the office of judge in the popular courts, or the office of a member of the popular assem-bly.   § 7. It may possibly be contended that judges in the courts and members of the assembly are not holders of 'office', and do not share in 'office' by virtue of their position. But it would be ridiculous to exclude from the category of holders of office those who actually hold the most sovereign position in the state; and we may dismiss the contention as trivial, since the argument turns on a word [or rather the absence of one]. The point is that we have no one word to denote the factor common to the judge and the member of the assembly, or to describe the position held by both. Let us, in the interest of a clear analysis, call it 'indeterminate office' [i.e. office held for an indeterminate period].   § 8. On that basis we may lay it down that citizens are those who share in the holding of office as so defined.

Such is the general nature of the definition of citizen which will most satisfactorily cover the position of all who bear the name. [But it still leaves us confronted by difficulties.] Citizenship belongs to a particular class of things where (1) there are different bases on which the thing may depend, (2) these bases are of different kinds and different qualities – one of them standing first, another second, and so on down the series. Things belonging to this particular class, when considered purely as so belonging, have no common denominator whatever – or, if they have one, they have it only to a meagre extent.[1]   § 9. [The different bases of citizenship are different constitutions]; constitutions obvi-ously differ from one another in kind, and some of them are obviously inferior and some superior in quality; for constitutions which are defective and per-verted (we shall explain later in what sense we are using the term 'perverted') are necessarily inferior to those which are free from defects. It follows that [as constitutions differ, so] the citizen under each different kind of constitution must also necessarily be different.    § 10. We may thus conclude that the citizen of our definition [one holding the indeterminate office of judge in a court and member of an assembly] is particularly and especially the citizen of a democracy. Citizens living under other kinds of constitution *may* possibly, but do not necessarily, correspond to the definition. There are some states, for example, in which there is no popular element: such states have no regular meetings of the assembly, but only meetings specially summoned; and [so far as membership of the courts is concerned] they remit the decision of cases to special bodies. In Sparta, for example, the Ephors take cases of contracts (not as a body, but each sitting separately); the Council of Elders take cases of homicide; and some other authority may take other cases.    § 11. Much the same is also true of Carthage, where a number of bodies of magistrates have each the right to decide all cases.

But our definition of citizenship [may still be maintained, in spite of these difficulties, since it] can be amended. We have to note that in constitutions other than the democratic, members of the assembly and the courts do not hold that office for an indeterminate period. They hold it for a limited term; and it is to persons with such a tenure (whether they be many or few) that the citizen's function of deliberating and judging (whether on all issues or only a few) is assigned in these constitutions.    § 12. The nature of citizenship in general emerges clearly from these considerations; and our final definitions will accordingly be: (1) 'he who enjoys the right of sharing in deliberative or judicial office [for any period, fixed or unfixed] attains thereby the status of a citizen of his state', and (2) 'a state, in its simplest terms, is a body of such persons adequate in number for achieving a self-sufficient existence'.

[. . .]

NOTE

1. Applying these general considerations to citizenship, we may say (1) that the 'basis' of citizenship is the constitution; (2) that constitutions are of different 'kinds', with the different kinds of constitutions having different 'qualities'; and (3) that citizenship has therefore differences of quality, so that a common denominator or definition can hardly exist. Considered purely as members of the class of citizens, the citizen under an extreme oligarchy and the citizen under an extreme democracy have little or nothing in common; though if we consider them not as citizens, but as human beings, we may find that they have a common, if meagre, denominator in *that* capacity.

# 39

# CLASS, CITIZENSHIP AND SOCIAL DEVELOPMENT

## T. H. Marshall

[...]

## 2. THE DEVELOPMENT OF CITIZENSHIP TO THE END OF THE NINETEENTH CENTURY

I shall be running true to type as a sociologist if I begin by saying that I propose to divide citizenship into three parts. But the analysis is, in this case, dictated by history even more clearly than by logic. I shall call these three parts, or elements, civil, political and social. The civil element is composed of the rights necessary for individual freedom – liberty of the person, freedom of speech, thought and faith, the right to own property and to conclude valid contracts, and the right to justice. The last is of a different order from the others, because it is the right to defend and assert all one's rights on terms of equality with others and by due process of law. This shows us that the institutions most directly associated with civil rights are the courts of justice. By the political element I mean the right to participate in the exercise of political power, as a member of a body invested with political authority or as an elector of the members of such a body. The corresponding institutions are parliament and councils of local government. By the social element I mean the whole range from the right to a modicum of economic welfare and security to the right to share to the full in the social heritage and to live the life of a civilised being according to the standards prevailing in the society. The institutions most closely connected with it are the educational system and the social services.

From T. H. Marshall, *Citizenship and Social Class and other essays* (Cambridge University Press, Cambridge, 1950), pp. 10–14

In early times these three strands were wound into a single thread. The rights were blended because the institutions were amalgamated. As Maitland said: 'The further back we trace our history the more impossible it is for us to draw strict lines of demarcation between the various functions of the State: the same institution is a legislative assembly, a governmental council and a court of law ... Everywhere, as we pass from the ancient to the modern, we see what the fashionable philosophy calls differentiation.' Maitland is speaking here of the fusion of political and civil institutions and rights. But a man's social rights, too, were part of the same amalgam, and derived from the status which also determined the kind of justice he could get and where he could get it, and the way in which he could take part in the administration of the affairs of the community of which he was a member. But this status was not one of citizenship in our modern sense. In feudal society status was the hall-mark of class and the measure of inequality. There was no uniform collection of rights and duties with which all men – noble and common, free and serf – were endowed by virtue of their membership of the society. There was, in this sense, no principle of the equality of citizens to set against the principle of the inequality of classes. In the medieval towns, on the other hand, examples of genuine and equal citizenship can be found. But its specific rights and duties were strictly local, whereas the citizenship whose history I wish to trace is, by definition, national.

Its evolution involved a double process, of fusion and of separation. The fusion was geographical, the separation functional. The first important step dates from the twelfth century, when royal justice was established with effective power to define and defend the civil rights of the individual – such as they then were – on the basis, not of local custom, but of the common law of the land. As institutions the courts were national, but specialised. Parliament followed, concentrating in itself the political powers of national government and shedding all but a small residue of the judicial functions which formerly belonged to the Curia Regis, that 'sort of constitutional protoplasm out of which will in time be evolved the various councils of the crown, the houses of parliament, and the courts of law'. Finally, the social rights which had been rooted in membership of the village community, the town and the gild were gradually dissolved by economic change until nothing remained but the Poor Law, again a specialised institution which acquired a national foundation, although it continued to be locally administered.

Two important consequences followed. First, when the institutions on which the three elements of citizenship depended parted company, it became possible for each to go its separate way, travelling at its own speed under the direction of its own peculiar principles. Before long they were spread far out along the course, and it is only in the present century, in fact I might say only within the last few months, that the three runners have come abreast of one another.

Secondly, institutions that were national and specialised could not belong so intimately to the life of the social groups they served as those that were local and of a general character. The remoteness of parliament was due to the mere size of its constituency; the remoteness of the courts, to the technicalities of their law and their procedure, which made it necessary for the citizen to employ legal experts to advise him as to the nature of his rights and to help him to obtain them. It has been pointed out again and again that, in the Middle Ages, participation in public affairs was more a duty than a right. Men owed suit and service to the court appropriate to their class and neighbourhood. The court belonged to them and they to it, and they had access to it because it needed them and because they had knowledge of its affairs. But the result of the twin process of fusion and separation was that the machinery giving access to the institutions on which the rights of citizenship depended had to be shaped afresh. In the case of political rights the story is the familiar one of the franchise and the qualifications for membership of parliament. In the case of civil rights the issue hangs on the jurisdiction of the various courts, the privileges of the legal profession, and above all on the liability to meet the costs of litigation. In the case of social rights the centre of the stage is occupied by the Law of Settlement and Removal and the various forms of means test. All this apparatus combined to decide, not merely what rights were recognised in principle, but also to what extent rights recognised in principle could be enjoyed in practice.

When the three elements of citizenship parted company, they were soon barely on speaking terms. So complete was the divorce between them that it is possible, without doing too much violence to historical accuracy, to assign the formative period in the life of each to a different century – civil rights to the eighteenth, political to the nineteenth, and social to the twentieth. These periods must, of course, be treated with reasonable elasticity, and there is some evident overlap, especially between the last two.

[...]

# 40

# LE CITOYEN/LA CITOYENNE

## W. H. Sewell, Jr

[...]

One striking linguistic feature of the summer and autumn of 1792 was the rise of the terms "citoyen" and "citoyenne" as universal forms of address. This usage arose out of the fevered political conjuncture of the time. The term "citoyen" called forth precisely the sort of obsessive patriotism that swept over Paris and parts of the provinces as the new revolutionary French state fought for its existence against the Austrian and Prussian armies and against its real and imagined domestic enemies. As distrust of the King and the "aristocratic conspiracy" mounted, and as the republican movement swelled, the egalitarian designation "citoyen" and "citoyenne" began to replace the "aristocratic" designations "monsieur" and "madame." By the time the insurrection of August 10 had overthrown the monarchy and the National Convention had declared the establishment of a republic, "citoyen" and "citoyenne" had become quasi-official terms of address.

On September 23, 1792, two days after the declaration of the French Republic, Charlier rose in the Convention to demand that "citoyen" become the official designation of all Frenchmen.

> Citoyens, lorsque la Révolution est complètement faite dans les choses, il faut aussi la faire dans les mots. Le titre de *citoyen* doit seul se trouver dans tous les actes émanés de vous. Le mot *Monsieur* et *Sieur*, dérivé de

From W. H. Sewell, Jr, 'Le Citoyen/La Citoyenne: Activity, Passivity and the Revolutionary Conception of Citizenship', in Colin Lucas (ed.), *The Political Culture of the French Revolution* (Pergamon Press, Oxford, 1988), Vol. 2, pp. 113–17.

*monseigneur*, ne doit plus être une qualification en usage. J'en demande la suppression dans toutes les actes de l'état civil ...'

The Convention, which had been discussing another matter at the time of Charlier's intervention, ruled him out of order and continued with the interrupted debate. As far as I know, the term "citoyen" never received the imprimatur of the Convention as the only allowable form of address. Nevertheless, its use became essentially universal in republican speech and in official documents.

Old regime society had recognized a hierarchy of forms of address – ranging downwards from "sire,' "altesse," "excellence," and "monseigneur" to "monsieur" and "madame," to the plainer "le sieur" and "la dame," and finally to simple proper names with no distinguishing appelations (or, in legal documents, the bald designation "le nommé"). Initially, revolutionary language tended toward the general use of "Monsieur" and "Madame." But to the republican sensibility taking shape in 1792, these terms were tainted by their aristocratic derivation and associations. "Monsieur" and "Madame" not only implied the existence of social distinctions but also smacked of fawning and artificial courtly manners. "Monsieur," when used in public discourse, thus seemed to carry private vanities into public life. "Citoyen," by contrast, implied virtue and devotion to the public good. To use Althusser's terminology, it "interpellated" Frenchmen as active participants in the sovereign will. The term "citoyen" reminded them, as it designated them, that they were active and equal members of the sovereign and that as members of the sovereign they were always to place public duty above private satisfactions. The use of "citoyen" as a replacement for "Monsieur" was of course an extension of the term beyond its "sens rigoureux," since it was used not only to designate Frenchmen in their role as members of the sovereign, but also in their private roles in civil society. Indeed, this was one of its major attractions. Unlike "Monsieur," which threatened to contaminate public life with private vanities, "citoyen" was calculated to infuse even private life with salutory public virtues.

But the use of "citoyen" as a universal term of address also had its contradictions and ambiguities. The term "citoyen" clearly had been adopted with French *men* in mind. Yet precisely because the designation was to be universal, to substitute for quotidian usages of "Monsieur" and "Madame" and to apply to all inhabitants of France, it had to have both a masculine form – *le citoyen* – and a feminine form – *la citoyenne*. The term "citoyen" triumphed because it interpellated males as active members of the sovereign who were to think about the public good even in private life. By contrast, the term "citoyenne" was only an afterthought – a kind of unintentional consequence of the adoption of "citoyen." Like "citoyen passif," it was an oxymoron: citoyen implied activity and membership in the sovereign, but the feminine ending implied passivity and exclusion from the public sphere. And like "citoyen passif," it indicated a vulnerable point in the revolutionary project of its creators. The danger of the locution "citoyenne" was, of course, that day after day, in all the routines of social life, it unintentionally interpellated women as active members of the sovereign, as rightful coparticipants in the political life of the nation. It is therefore hardly surprising that some women answered the call.

By the spring of 1793, women were frequently admitted to the popular societies that were constituted by the Sans-Culottes. In July of 1793 the "Société de l'Harmonie Sociale des Sans-Culottes des deux sexes" stated explicitly that "les citoyennes seront admises sans distinction à partager les travaux patriotiques de la Société." But the most spectacular case was the "Société (or club) des citoyennes républicaines révolutionnaires," a popular society made up exclusively of women, whose career has been ably chronicled in several recent works. The *Citoyennes républicaines révolutionnaires* took the universalist implication of the term "citoyenne" literally. Perhaps the most remarkable thing about them as a woman's club is that they did not particularly concern themselves with "women's issues," but discussed and acted on the issues that dominated (male) politics in the same way as men's political clubs did. Nor did they shy away from physical danger. They played a significant role in the insurrection of May 31 to June 2, which purged the Girondins from the Convention – among other things, standing guard at the doors of the Convention and refusing entry to Girondin deputies. This commitment to militant political action was explicitly written into their *règlement*, whose first article stated that the Society's purpose was to join in the armed defense of "la Patrie."

But even for these extraordinarily active and politicized women, the duties of the "citoyenne" were potentially contradictory. This can be seen with particular clarity in an address delivered at a meeting of the *Société des citoyennes républicaines révolutionnaires* by a member of a delegation of "citoyennes" from the Section des Droits de l'homme, which was presenting to the Society a standard to be carried in public demonstrations, ceremonies, and insurrections. In her address, the orator insisted that political activity is the proper duty of the "citoyenne".

> Vous avez rompu un des anneaux de la chaîne des préjugés, il n'existe plus pour vous celui qui, reléguant les femmes dans la sphere étroite de leurs ménages, faisoit de la moitié des individus des êtres passifs et isolés.
>
> Vous voulez tenir votre place dans l'ordre social, la neutralité vous offense, vous humilie. C'est en vain que l'on prétendoit vous distraire des grands intérêts de la Patrie, ils ont remué vos âmes, et désormais vous concourerez à l'utilité commune.
>
> … Et pourquoi les femmes douées de la faculté de sentir, et d'exprimer leurs pensées, verroient-elles prononcer leur exclusion aux affaires publiques? …
>
> Que ce guidon dirige vos pas partout où l'égoisme et l'insouciance enlève des Citoyens à la Patrie, portez dans vos députations cet emblême expressif de l'Egalité; que l'oeil de ses ennemis en soit souvent frappé. Sous

son ombre bienfaisante, venez toutes vous ranger dans les cérémonies publiques; qu'au premier signal du danger, cet étentard révolutionnaire se mêle aux drapeaux tricolores, qu'il mène à la victoire des républicaines dévouées, qui dépouillent la foiblesse de leur sexe devant les périls éminens de la Patrie ...

Republican "citoyennes" must not be passive or neutral; they must send deputations, participate in ceremonies, and join insurrectionary movements when the nation is in peril. "Citoyennes," in all these respects, apparently should be indistinguishable from "citoyens.'

Yet even this call to vigilant activism casts women as the weaker sex. More surprisingly, this militant orator, elsewhere in her speech, seems to characterize the differences between the sexes in a way that normally valorized women's exclusion from political affairs.

... La déclaration des droits est commune à l'un et à l'autre des sexes et la différence consiste dans les devoirs; il en est des publics, il en est de privés. Les hommes sont particulièrement appellés à remplir les premiers, la nature elle-même indiqua la préférence; elle a reparti chez eux une constitution robuste, la force des organes, tous les moyens capables de soutenir des travaux pénibles: qu'aux armées, qu'au sénat, que dans les assemblées publiques, ils occupent préférablement les places, la raison, les convenances le veulent, il faut y céder.

Les femmes au contraire ont pour premières obligations, des devoirs privés, les douces fonctions d'épouses et de mères leur sont confiées, mille objets de détails qu'elles entraînent consument une forte partie de leurs temps, leurs loisirs sont moins fréquens ...

Men and women differ by nature. Men are stronger and women bear children; as a consequence, men are "particulièrement appellés" to fulfill "devoirs publics" and women to fulfill "devoirs privés." All of this is a quite conventional reading of the commands of nature – except that this female orator makes no claim that men possess superior intellectual capacities or an exclusive claim to political rights.

How is this relegation of women to the "douces fonctions d'épouses et de mères" to be reconciled with women's active participation in the public sphere? The orator goes on as follows:

... néanmoins il est possible de concilier, ce qu'exige impérieusement la nature, ce que commande l'amour du bien public. Après avoir vaqué à des occupations indispensables, il est encore des instans, et les femmes citoyennes qui les consacrent dans les Sociétés fraternelles, à la surveillance, à l'instruction ont la douce satisfaction de se voir doublement utiles.

This is, of course, not entirely satisfactory. It implies that women who are also wives and mothers will have precious little chance for political activity – the "mille objets de détails" of their naturally decreed "douces fonctions" will leave them only "des instans" and it is only these rare moments that can be consecrated "à la surveillance, à l'instruction." Hence, only those rare women who remained unmarried – like Claire Lacombe and Pauline Léon, the most prominent leaders of the *Sociétés citoyennes républicaines révolutionnaires* – could hope to devote themselves to public affairs with a zeal comparable to that of men. But avoiding marriage and motherhood could hardly be the proper answer, since the functions of wives and mothers are "exigences impérieuses" of nature. It follows that "citoyennes" could be at best part-time patriots, active in political life only on those occasions when their "premiers obligations" as wives and mothers allowed them sufficient leisure. The sacrifice of private duites and interests to the public good that was implied by the term "citoyen" was impossible to the "citoyenne" – unless she violated the commands of nature and remained unmarried.

The orator from the Section des Droits de l'homme was thus in the uncomfortable position of at once accepting the conventional gender definitions that justified women's exclusion from politics and urging women to continue their seemingly "manly" activism – in other words, of attempting to hold together the passivity and the activity that were simultaneously called forth when women were interpellated by the oxymoron "citoyennes." The orator struggled to avoid this contradiction – for example by characterizing the Society's members as "épouses des Sans-Culottes" (thereby denying the implication that serious political activism would be limited to unmarried women) and by advancing the dubious claim (in view of her stated assumptions) that the Society's militant activism could be pursued purely in wives' and mothers' moments of leisure. She also developed an alternative characterization of the Society and its work in terms more consonant with existing gender-role definitions – as a school where mothers could gain the political knowledge necessary to raise their children as good republicans. "... La Liberté trouve ici une école nouvelle; mères, épouses, enfans y viennent s'instruire, s'exciter mutuellement à la pratique des vertus sociales." But none of these devices could free her discourse from its fundamental trap: as long as "citoyennes" accepted "what nature imperiously requires" of females – as this was understood in the late eighteenth century – their claims to membership in the sovereign were bound to remain precarious.

Just how precarious was demonstrated in October of 1793, when the Convention moved to suppress the *Société des citoyennes républicaines révolutionnaires*. The pretext for the dissolution of the Society was a disturbance touched off when the *citoyennes républicaines révolutionnaires* attempted to force market women to wear the *bonnet rouge*. But the Convention went beyond the particular issue to consider the general question of whether "citoyennes" should be allowed to exercise political rights and to form political associations – that is, whether the "sens rigoureux" of "citoyen" had any application to women. Amar, reporting for the Committee of General Security, answered unhesitatingly in the negative. It is symptomatic of Amar's and the

Jacobins' position that nowhere in his long disquisition about women's role in politics does he utter the term "citoyenne'; women are always referred to as "femmes." His arguments are based on conventional notions about the differences between the sexes – notions similar to those put forth by the orator from the Section des Droits de l'homme, although his version of conventional notions is far more misogynist and the conclusions he draws from them are radically different.

Amar declared that women lack "la force morale et physique" required to exercise political rights – that is to "faire prendre des résolutions relatives à l'intérêt de l'Etat." "Gouverner, c'est régir la chose publique par des lois dont la confection exige des connaissances étendues, une application et un dévouement sans bornes, une impassibilité sévère et l'abnégation de soi-même ..." Women, he went on, are not "susceptible de ces soins et des qualités qu'ils exigent." Not capable of governing, neither should they form political associations.

> Le but des associations populaires est celui-ci: dévoiler les manoeuvres des ennemis de la chose publique, surveiller et les citoyens comme individus, et les fonctionnaires publics, même le corps législatif; exiter le zèle des uns et des autres par l'exemple des vertus républicaines; s'éclairer par des discussions publiques et approfondies sur le défaut ou la réformation des lois politiques. Les femmes peuvent-elles se dévouer à ces utiles et pénibles fonctions? Non, parce qu'elles seraient obligées d'y sacrifier des soins plus importants auxquels le nature les appelle. Les fonctions privées auxquelles sont destinées les femmes par la nature même tiennent à l'ordre général de la societé; cet ordre social résulte de la différence qu'il y a entre l'homme et la femme. Chaque sexe est appelé à un genre d'occupation qui lui est propre; son action est circonscrite dans ce cercle qu'il ne peut franchir, car la nature, qui a posé ces limites à l'homme, commande imperieusement, et ne reçoit aucune loi.

Here we have the familiar imperious commands of nature that assign women to the home and family – but with the difference that the limits commanded by nature are now absolute.

# 41

# THE RETURN OF THE CITIZEN

## Will Kymlicka and Wayne Norman

[…]

In short, we need "a fuller, richer and yet more subtle understanding and practice of citizenship," because "what the state needs from the citizenry cannot be secured by coercion, but only cooperation and self-restraint in the exercise of private power" (Cairns and Williams 1985, p. 43). Yet there is growing fear that the civility and public-spiritedness of citizens of liberal democracies may be in serious decline (Walzer 1992, p. 90).

An adequate conception of citizenship, therefore, seems to require a balance of rights and responsibilities. Where do we learn these virtues? The New Right relies heavily on the market as a school of virtue. But there are other answers to this question.

1. *The left and participatory democracy*. – As we just noted, one of the left's responses to the problem of citizen passivity is to "empower" citizens by democratizing the welfare state and, more generally, by dispersing state power through local democratic institutions, regional assemblies, and judicable rights. However, emphasizing participation does not yet explain how to ensure that citizens participate responsibly – that is, in a public-spirited, rather than self-interested or prejudiced way.

Indeed, as Mulgan notes, "by concentrating too narrowly on the need to devolve power and on the virtues of freedom, issues of responsibility have been pushed to the margins" (Mulgan 1991, pp. 40–41). Empowered citizens may

From Will Kymlicka and Wayne Norman, 'Return of the Citizen: A Survey of Recent Work on Citizenship Theory', *Ethics*, 104, January 1994, pp. 360–7.

use their power irresponsibly by pushing for benefits and entitlements they cannot ultimately afford, or by voting themselves tax breaks and slashing assistance to the needy, or by "seeking scapegoats in the indolence of the poor, the strangeness of ethnic minorities, or the insolence and irresponsibility of modern women" (Fierlbeck 1991, p. 592).

Following Rousseau and J. S. Mill, many modern participatory democrats assume that political participation itself will teach people responsibility and toleration. As Oldfield notes, they place their faith in the activity of participation "as the means whereby individuals may become accustomed to perform the duties of citizenship. Political participation enlarges the minds of individuals, familiarizes them with interests which lie beyond the immediacy of personal circumstance and environment, and encourages them to acknowledge that public concerns are the proper ones to which they should pay attention" (Oldfield 1990b, p. 184).

Many people on the left have tried in this way to bypass the issue of responsible citizenship "by dissolving [it] into that of democracy itself," which in turn has led to the "advocacy of collective decision-making as a resolution to all the problems of citizenship" (Held 1991, p. 23; cf. Pierson 1991, p. 202). Unfortunately, this faith in the educative function of participation seems overly optimistic (Oldfield 1990b, p. 184; Mead 1986, p. 247; Andrews 1991, p. 216).

Hence there is increasing recognition that citizenship responsibilities should be incorporated more explicitly into left-wing theory (Hoover and Plant 1988, pp. 289–91; Vogel and Moran 1991, p. xv; Mouffe 1992). But it seems clear that the left has not yet found a language of responsibility that it is comfortable with, or a set of concrete policies to promote these responsibilities.

2. *Civic republicanism.* – The modern civic republican tradition is an extreme form of participatory democracy largely inspired by Machiavelli and Rousseau (who were in turn enamored with the Greeks and Romans). It is not surprising that the recent upsurge of interest in citizenship has given civic republicans a wider audience.

The feature that distinguishes civic republicans from other participationists, such as the left-wing theorists discussed above, is their emphasis on the intrinsic value of political participation for the participants themselves. Such participation is, in Oldfield's words, "the highest form of human living-together that most individuals can aspire to" (Oldfield 1990a, p. 6). On this view, political life is superior to the merely private pleasures of family, neighborhood, and profession and so should occupy the center of people's lives. Failure to participate in politics makes one a "radically incomplete and stunted being" (Oldfield 1990b, p. 187; cf. Pocock 1992, pp. 45, 53; Skinner 1992; Beiner 1992).

As its proponents admit, this conception is markedly at odds with the way most people in the modern world understand both citizenship and the good life. Most people find the greatest happiness in their family life, work, religion, or leisure, not in politics. Political participation is seen as an occasional, and often burdensome, activity needed to ensure that government respects and supports

221

their freedom to pursue these personal occupations and attachments. This assumption that politics is a means to private life is shared by most people on the left (Ignatieff 1989, pp. 72–73) and right (Mead 1986, p. 254), as well as by liberals (Rawls 1971, pp. 229–30), civil society theorists (Walzer 1989, p. 215), and feminists (Elshtain 1981, p. 327), and defines the modern view of citizenship.

In order to explain the modern indifference to political participation, civic republicans often argue that political life today has become impoverished compared to the active citizenship of, say, ancient Greece. Political debate is no longer meaningful and people lack access to effective participation.

But it is more plausible to view our attachment to private life as a result not of the impoverishment of public life but of the enrichment of private life. We no longer seek gratification in politics because our personal and social life is so much richer than the Greeks'. There are many reasons for this historical change, including the rise of romantic love and the nuclear family (and its emphasis on intimacy and privacy), increased prosperity (and hence richer forms of leisure and consumption), the Christian commitment to the dignity of labor (which the Greeks despised), and the growing dislike for war (which the Greeks esteemed).

Those passive citizens who prefer the joys of family and career to the duties of politics are not necessarily misguided. As Galston has put it, republicans who denigrate private life as tedious and self-absorbed show no delight in real communities of people, and indeed are "contemptuous" of "everyday life" (Galston 1991, pp. 58–63).

3. *Civil society theorists.* – We shall use the label "civil society theorists" to identify a recent development from communitarian thought in the 1980s. These theorists emphasize the necessity of civility and self-restraint to a healthy democracy but deny that either the market or political participation is sufficient to teach these virtues. Instead, it is in the voluntary organizations of civil society – churches, families, unions, ethnic associations, cooperatives, environmental groups, neighborhood associations, women's support groups, charities – that we learn the virtues of mutual obligation. As Walzer puts it, "the civility that makes democratic politics possible can only be learned in the associational networks" of civil society (Walzer 1992, p. 104).

Because these groups are voluntary, failure to live up to the responsibilities that come with them is usually met simply with disapproval rather than legal punishment. Yet because the disapproval comes from family, friends, colleagues, or comrades, it is in many ways a more powerful incentive to act responsibly than punishment by an impersonal state. It is here that "human character, competence, and capacity for citizenship are formed," for it is here that we internalize the idea of personal responsibility and mutual obligation and learn the voluntary self-restraint which is essential to truly responsible citizenship (Glendon 1991, p. 109).

It follows, therefore, that one of the first obligations of citizenship is to participate in civil society. As Walzer notes, "Join the association of your choice" is "not a slogan to rally political militants, and yet that is what civil society requires" (Walzer 1992, p. 106).

The claim that civil society is the "seedbed of civic virtue" (Glendon 1991, p. 109) is essentially an empirical claim, for which there is little hard evidence one way or the other. It is an old and venerable view, but it is not obviously true. It may be in the neighborhood that we learn to be good neighbors, but neighborhood associations also teach people to operate on the "NIMBY" (not in my backyard) principle when it comes to the location of group homes or public works. Similarly, the family is often "a school of despotism" that teaches male dominance over women (Okin 1992, p. 65); churches often teach deference to authority and intolerance of other faiths; ethnic groups often teach prejudice against other races; and so on.

Walzer recognizes that most people are "trapped in one or another subordinate relationship, where the 'civility' they learned was deferential rather than independent and active." In these circumstances, he says, we have to "reconstruct" the associational network "under new conditions of freedom and equality." Similarly, when the activities of some associations "are narrowly conceived, partial and particularist," then "they need political correction." Walzer calls his view "critical associationalism" to signify that the associations of civil society may need to be reformed in the light of principles of citizenship (Walzer 1992, pp. 106–7).

But this may go too far in the other direction. Rather than supporting voluntary associations, this approach may unintentionally license wholesale intervention in them. Governments must of course intervene to protect the rights of people inside and outside the group if these rights are threatened. But do we want governments to reconstruct churches, for example, to make them more internally democratic, or to make sure that their members learn to be independent rather than deferential? And, in any event, wouldn't reconstructing churches, families, or unions to make them more internally democratic start to undermine their essentially uncoerced and voluntary character, which is what supposedly made them the seedbeds of civic virtue?

Civil society theorists demand too much of these voluntary associations in expecting them to be the main school for, or small-scale replica of, democratic citizenship. While these associations may teach civic virtue, that is not their raison d'être. The reason why people join churches, families, or ethnic organizations is not to learn civic virtue. It is, rather, to honor certain values and enjoy certain human goods, and these motives may have little to do with the promotion of citizenship.

Joining a religious or ethnic association may be more a matter of withdrawing from the mainstream of society than of learning how to participate in it. To expect parents, priests, or union members to organize the internal life of their groups to promote citizenship maximally is to ignore why these groups exist in the first place. (Some associations, like the Boy Scouts, are designed to promote citizenship, but they are the exception, not the rule.)

A similar issue arises with theorists of "maternal citizenship," who focus on the family, and mothering in particular, as the school of responsibility and virtue. According to Jean Elshtain and Sara Ruddick, mothering teaches women about the responsibility to conserve life and protect the vulnerable, and these lessons should become the guiding principles of political life as well. For example, mothering involves a "metaphysical attitude" of "holding," which gives priority to the protection of existing relationships over the acquisition of new benefits (Elshtain 1981, pp. 326–27, 349–53; Ruddick 1987, p. 242). This has obvious implications for decisions about war or the environment.

However, some critics argue that mothering does not involve the same attributes or virtues as citizenship and that there is no evidence that maternal attitudes such as "holding" promote democratic values such as "active citizenship, self-government, egalitarianism, and the exercise of freedom" (Dietz 1985, p. 30; Nauta 1992, p. 31). As Dietz puts it, "An enlightened despotism, a welfare-state, a single-party bureaucracy and a democratic republic may all respect mothers, protect children's lives and show compassion for the vulnerable" (Dietz 1992, p. 76).

This criticism parallels that of civil society theories. Both maternal feminists and civil society theorists define citizenship in terms of the virtues of the private sphere. But while these virtues may sometimes be necessary for good citizenship, they are not sufficient, and may sometimes be counterproductive.

4. *Liberal virtue theory.* – Liberals are often blamed for the current imbalance between rights and responsibilities, and not without reason. Liberal theorists in the 1970s and 1980s focused almost exclusively on the justification of rights and of the institutions to secure these rights, without attending to the responsibilities of citizens. Many critics believe that liberals are incapable of righting this imbalance, since the liberal commitment to liberty or neutrality or individualism renders the concept of civic virtue unintelligible (Mouffe 1992).

However, some of the most interesting work on the importance of civic virtue is in fact being done by liberals such as Amy Gutmann, Stephen Macedo, and William Galston. According to Galston, the virtues required for responsible citizenship can be divided into four groups: (i) general virtues: courage, law-abidingness, loyalty; (ii) social virtues: independence, open-mindedness; (iii) economic virtues: work ethic, capacity to delay self-gratification, adaptability to economic and technological change; and (iv) political virtues: capacity to discern and respect the rights of others, willingness to demand only what can be paid for, ability to evaluate the performance of those in office, willingness to engage in public discourse (Galston 1991, pp. 221–24).

It is the last two virtues – the ability to question authority and the willingness to engage in public discourse – which are the most distinctive components of liberal virtue theory. The need to question authority arises in part from the fact that citizens in a representative democracy elect representatives who govern in their name. Hence, an important responsibility of citizens is to monitor those officials and judge their conduct.

The need to engage in public discourse arises from the fact that the decisions of government in a democracy should be made publicly, through free and open discussion. But as Galston notes, the virtue of public discourse is not just the willingness to participate in politics or to make one's views known. Rather, it "includes the willingness to listen seriously to a range of views which, given the diversity of liberal societies, will include ideas the listener is bound to find strange and even obnoxious. The virtue of political discourse also includes the willingness to set forth one's own views intelligibly and candidly as the basis for a politics of persuasion rather than manipulation or coercion" (Galston 1991, p. 227).

Macedo calls this the virtue of "public reasonableness." Liberal citizens must give reasons for their political demands, not just state preferences or make threats. Moreover, these reasons must be "public" reasons, in the sense that they are capable of persuading people of different faiths and nationalities. Hence it is not enough to invoke Scripture or tradition. Liberal citizens must justify their political demands in terms that fellow citizens can understand and accept as consistent with their status as free and equal citizens. It requires a conscientious effort to distinguish those beliefs which are matters of private faith from those which are capable of public defense and to see how issues look from the point of view of those with differing religious commitments and cultural backgrounds (cf. Phillips 1991b, pp. 57–59).

Where do we learn these virtues? Other theorists we have examined relied on the market, the family, or the associations of civil society to teach civic virtue. But it is clear that people will not automatically learn to engage in public discourse or to question authority in any of these spheres, since these spheres are often held together by private discourse and respect for authority.

The answer, according to many liberal virtue theorists, is the system of education. Schools must teach children how to engage in the kind of critical reasoning and moral perspective that defines public reasonableness. As Amy Gutmann puts it, children at school "must learn not just to behave in accordance with authority but to think critically about authority if they are to live up to the democratic ideal of sharing political sovereignty as citizens." People who "are ruled only by habit and authority . . . are incapable of constituting a society of sovereign citizens" (Gutmann 1987, p. 51).

However, this idea that schools should teach children to be skeptical of political authority and to distance themselves from their own cultural traditions when engaging in public discourse is controversial. Traditionalists object to it on the grounds that it inevitably leads children to question tradition and parental or religious authority in private life. And that is surely correct. As Gutmann admits, education for democratic citizenship will necessarily involve "equipping children with the intellectual skills necessary to evaluate ways of life different from that of their parents," because "many if not all of the capacities necessary for choice among good lives are also necessary for choice among good societies" (Gutmann 1987, pp. 30, 40).

Hence, those groups which rely heavily on an uncritical acceptance of tradition and authority, while not strictly ruled out, "are bound to be discouraged by the free, open, pluralistic, progressive" attitudes which liberal education encourages (Macedo 1990, pp. 53–54). This is why groups such as the Amish have sought to remove their children from the school system.

This creates a dilemma for liberals, many of whom wish to accommodate law-abiding groups like the Amish. Some liberals view the demise of such groups as regrettable but sometimes inevitable in a democratic society (Rawls 1975, p. 551; but see Rawls 1988, pp. 267–68). Other liberals, however, want to adjust citizenship education to minimize the impact on parental and religious authority. Galston, for example, argues that the need to teach children how to engage in the public discourse and to evaluate political leaders "does not warrant the conclusion that the state must (or may) structure public education to foster in children skeptical reflection on ways of life inherited from parents or local communities" (Galston 1991, p. 253). However, he admits that is is not easy for schools to promote a child's willingness to question political authority without undermining her "unswerving belief in the correctness" of her parents' way of life.

## REFERENCES

Andrews, G. (ed.), *Citizenship* (Lawrence & Wishart, London, 1991).

Beiner, R., 'Citizenship', in *What's the Matter with Liberalism* (University of California Press, Berkeley, CA, 1992).

Cairns, A. and Williams, C., *Constitutionalism, Citizenship and Society in Canada* (University of Toronto Press, Toronto, 1985).

Dietz, M., 'Citizenship with a Feminist Face: The Problems with Maternal Thinking', *Political Theory*, 13, 1985, pp. 19–35.

Elshtain, J. B., *Public Man, Private Woman: Women in Social and Political Thought* (Princeton University Press, Princeton, NJ, 1981).

Fierlbeck, K., 'Redefining Responsibilities: The Politics of Citizenship in the United Kingdom', *Canadian Journal of Political Science*, 24, 1991, pp. 575–83.

Galston, W., *Liberal Purposes: Goods, Virtues, and Duties in the Liberal State* (Cambridge University Press, Cambridge, 1991).

Glendon, M. A., *Rights Talk: The Impoverishment of Political Discourse* (Free Press, New York, 1991).

Gutman, A., *Democratic Education* (Princeton University Press, Princeton, NJ, 1987).

Heater, D., *Citizenship: The Civic Ideal in World History, Politics and Education* (Longman, London, 1990).

Held, D. [1991], 'Between State and Civil Society: Citizenship', in Andrews, G. (ed.), *Citizenship* (Lawrence & Wishart, London, 1991).

Hoover, K. and Plant, R., *Conservative Capitalism in Britain and the United States* (Routledge, London, 1988).

Ignatieff, M. [1989], 'Citizenship and Moral Narcissism', *Political Quarterly* 60, pp. 63–74, reprinted in Andrews, G. (ed.), *Citizenship* (Laurence & Wishart, London, 1991).

Macedo, S., *Liberal Virtues: Citizenship, Virtue, and Community* (Oxford University Press, Oxford, 1990).

Mead, L., *Beyond Entitlement: The Social Obligations of Citizenship* (Free Press, New York, 1986).

Mouffe, C. (ed.), *Dimensions of Radical Democracy: Pluralism, Citizenship and Community* (Routledge, London, 1992).

Mulgan, G., 'Citizens and Responsibilities' in Andrews, G. (ed.), *Citizenship* (Lawrence & Wishart, London, 1991).

Nauta, L., 'Changing Conceptions of Citizenship', *Praxis International*, 12, 1992, pp. 20–34.

Okin, S. M., 'Women, Equality and Citizenship', *Queen's Quarterly*, 99, 1992, pp. 56–71.

Oldfield, A., *Citizenship and Community: Civic Republicanism and the Modern World* (Routledge, London, 1990a).

Oldfield, A., 'Citizenship: An Unnatural Practice', *Political Quarterly*, 61, 1990b, pp. 177–87.

Phillips, A., *Engendering Democracy* (Polity Press, Cambridge, 1991).

Pierson, C., *Beyond the Welfare State: The New Political Economy of Welfare* (Pennsylvania State University Press, University Park, PA, 1991).

Pocock, J. G. A., 'The Ideal of Citizenship since Modern Times', Queen's Quarterly 99, 1992, pp. 33–55.

Rawls, J., *A Theory of Justice* (Oxford University Press, London, 1971).

Rawls, J., 'Fairness to Goodness', *Philosophical Review* 84, 1975, pp. 536–54.

Rawls, J., 'The Priority of Right and Ideas of the Good', *Philiosophy and Public Affairs* 17, 1988, pp. 251–76.

Ruddick, S., 'Remarks on the Sexual Politics of Reason', in Kittay, E. and Meyers, D. (eds), *Women and Moral Theory* (Rowman & Allanheld, Totowa, NJ, 1987).

Skinner, Q., 'On Justice, the Common Good and the Priority of Liberty', in Mouffe, C. (ed.), *Dimensions of Radical Democracy: Pluralism, Citizenship and Community* (Routledge, London, 1992).

Vogel, U. and Moran, M., *The Frontiers of Citizenship* (St. Martin's Press, New York, 1991).

Walzer, M., 'The Civil Society Argument', in Mouffe, C. (ed.), *Dimensions of Radical Democracy: Pluralism, Citizenship and Community* (Routledge, London, 1992).

# PART THREE
# CRITIQUES OF DEMOCRACY

# SECTION 6
# MARXIST AND SOCIALIST CRITIQUES

# MARXIST AND SOCIALIST CRITIQUES
## INTRODUCTION

We begin our selection of critiques of democracy with statements from socialist and Marxist perspectives. As noted in our general introduction, 'critiques' of democracy can take different forms. There are those who criticise democracy as being undesirable and unattainable, and the critiques that come in Section 7 which follows (Conservative, Elitist and Authoritarian Critiques) fall into this category. The socialist analyses of democracy that make up this section take a different stance. The socialist perspective is not to denigrate the idea of democracy as such, but to maintain that it cannot be realised in the conditions of a capitalist society, or indeed of any form of class-divided or economically unequal society. This is the gist of the analysis of *Marx* put forward in the extract from 'On the Jewish Question'. His argument is that purely political emancipation limited to the achievement of political democracy, important as that is, would not achieve human emancipation. That task would require a social, indeed socialist, revolution, which would go beyond the limits of purely political liberation.

Within the Marxist tradition there has also been vehement criticism of the kind of democracy represented by liberal-democracy. This (liberal-democracy) has been seen as distancing the masses from any genuine form of participation, and as creating representative bodies (parliaments) which exclude and alienate the bulk of the population. The Bolshevik leader *Lenin*, in the extract from 'The State and Revolution', derides parliaments as 'talking shops given over to fooling the common people'. In opposition to liberal-democracy the Marxist tradition has offered the picture of the Paris Commune as a model of socialist democracy. The Paris Commune of March – May 1871 was praised by Marx for its features of the destruction of the standing army and the installation of a political order based on power from below. Delegates rather than representatives, radical forms of decentralisation and the extension of popular participation were all emphasised as central features of this distinct form of state, a more participatory alternative to liberal-democracy. Critics of Marxism, some of whom are to be found in the following section, are sceptical as to whether such a form of Commune-democracy would be appropriate for a complex modern society. Attempts to put it in practice in Russia after the 1917 Bolshevik revolution were certainly not successful. Ideas of doing away with bureaucratic specialists are dismissed by some as Utopian fantasies irrelevant to contemporary politics.

In a different vein, contemporary scholars working in the Marxist tradition emphasise the crucial contradiction in contemporary liberal-democracy between the democratic principle of equality and the inequality stemming from the capitalist economic context of such political systems. They point to the constraints existing within such 'capitalist democracy' upon the popular participation and equality which liberal-democracy proclaims as its guiding principles. The extract from the study by *Miliband* of *Marxism and Politics* points to the importance of universal suffrage, that core democratic right, for the Marxist view of politics. Universal suffrage has been theorised in the Marxist tradition as an essential right in the process of revolution. In the Marxist tradition, political democracy is seen as part, though an indispensable one, of a broader movement of transition from capitalism to socialism. Democratic rights are viewed as essential, but as means to a wider perspective of social emancipation. Some critics of Marxism take the view that this opens up the way for a fatal underestimation of the importance of political rights of democracy. Others, such as Miliband, suggest that it places the politics of what is called 'capitalist democracy' in a different light. Liberal-democratic societies combine political equality in uneasy tension with deep social divisions and economic inequality.

Finally, we reproduce an extract from a more recent theorist sympathetic to Marxist critiques of liberal-democracy. The late political philosopher C. B. *Macpherson* was writing before the collapse of Communism in the USSR and its associated states when he stated that in two-thirds of the world political leaders and their followers have 'concluded that for their countries at least it would be impossible to move towards the ultimate humanistic goals by liberal-democratic methods'. But he is surely right to suggest that ideas of a market or capitalist society with manipulated wants and desires might be in conflict with the emancipatory goals of personal development and social harmony which liberal-democratic theory invokes. The question remains open of whether the intensified market society of contemporary capitalism fosters those qualities and dispositions needed for a cooperative democratic political order. This question is discussed further by those contributors to Section 10 on the market in Part Four.

# 42

# ON THE JEWISH QUESTION

## Karl Marx

[. . .]

The rights of man as *such* are distinguished from the rights of the citizen. Who is the man who is distinct from the citizen? None other than the *member of civil society*. Why is the member of civil society simply called 'man' and why are his rights called the right of man? How can we explain this fact? By the relationship of the political state to civil society, by the nature of political emancipation.

The first point we should note is that the so-called *rights of man*, as distinct from the *rights of the citizen*, are quite simply the rights of the *member of civil society*, i.e. of egoistic man, of man separated from other men and from the community. Consider the most radical constitution, the Constitution of 1793:

*Declaration of the Rights of Man and of the Citizen.*

*Article 2.* 'These rights, etc. (the natural and imprescriptible rights) are: equality, liberty, security, property.'

What is liberty?

*Article 6.* 'Liberty is the power which belongs to man to do anything that does not harm the rights of others', or according to the Declaration of the Rights of Man of 1791: 'Liberty consists in being able to do anything which does not harm others.'

Liberty is therefore the right to do and perform everything which does not harm others. The limits within which each individual can move *without*

From Karl Marx, 'On the Jewish Question', in Karl Marx, *Early Writings*, trans. Rodney Livingstone and Gregor Benton, intro. Lucio Colletti (Penguin Books, Harmondsworth, 1975), pp. 228–34. Originally written in 1843.

harming others are determined by law, just as the boundary between two fields is determined by a stake. The liberty we are here dealing with is that of man as an isolated monad who is withdrawn into himself. Why does Bauer say that the Jew is incapable of acquiring the rights of man?

'As long as he is a Jew the restricted nature which makes him a Jew will inevitably gain the ascendancy over the human nature which should join him as a man to other men; the effect will be to separate him from non-Jews.'

But the right of man to freedom is not based on the association of man with man but rather on the separation of man from man. It is the *right* of this separation, the right of the *restricted* individual, restricted to himself.

The practical application of the right of man to freedom is the right of man to *private property*.

What is the right of man to private property?

*Article 16* (Constitution of 1793): 'The right of *property* is that right which belongs to each citizen to enjoy and dispose *at will* of his goods, his revenues and the fruit of his work and industry.'

The right to private property is therefore the right to enjoy and dispose of one's resources as one wills, without regard for other men and independently of society: the right of self-interest. The individual freedom mentioned above, together with this application of it, forms the foundation of civil society. It leads each man to see in other men not the *realization* but the *limitation* of his own freedom. But above all it proclaims the right of man 'to enjoy and dispose *at will* of his goods, his revenues and the fruit of his work and industry'.

There remain the other rights of man, equality and security.

Equality, here in its non-political sense, simply means equal access to liberty as described above, namely that each man is equally considered to be a self-sufficient monad. The Constitution of 1795 defines the concept of this equality, in keeping with this meaning, as follows:

*Article 3* (Constitution of 1795): 'Equality consists in the fact that the law is the same for everyone, whether it protects or whether it punishes.'

And security?

*Article 8* (Constitution of 1793): 'Security consists in the protection accorded by society to each of its members for the conservation of his person, his rights and his property.'

*Security* is the supreme social concept of civil society, the concept of *police*, the concept that the whole of society is there only to guarantee each of its members the conservation of his person, his rights and his property. In this sense Hegel calls civil society 'the state of need and of reason'.

The concept of security does not enable civil society to rise above its egoism. On the contrary, security is the *guarantee* of its egoism.

Therefore not one of the so-called rights of man goes beyond egoistic man, man as a member of civil society, namely an individual withdrawn into himself, his private interest and his private desires and separated from the community. In the rights of man it is not man who appears as a species-being; on the contrary, species-life itself, society, appears as a framework extraneous to the individuals, as a limitation of their original independence. The only bond which holds them together is natural necessity, need and private interest, the conservation of their property and their egoistic persons.

It is a curious thing that a people which is just beginning to free itself, to tear down all the barriers between the different sections of the people and to found a political community, that such a people should solemnly proclaim the rights of egoistic man, separated from his fellow men and from the community (Declaration of 1791), and even repeat this proclamation at a time when only the most heroic devotion can save the nation and is for that reason pressingly required, at a time when the sacrifice of all the interests of civil society becomes the order of the day and egoism must be punished as a crime. (*Declaration of the Rights of Man*, etc., 1793.) This fact appears even more curious when we observe that citizenship, the *political community*, is reduced by the political emancipators to a mere *means* for the conservation of these so-called rights of man and that the citizen is therefore proclaimed the servant of egoistic man; that the sphere in which man behaves as a communal being [*Gemeinwesen*] is degraded to a level below the sphere in which he behaves as a partial being, and finally that it is man as *bourgeois*, i.e. as a member of civil society, and not man as citizen who is taken as the *real* and *authentic* man.

'The *goal* of all *political association* is the *conservation* of the natural and imprescriptible rights of man' (*Declaration of the Rights of Man* etc., 1791, Article 2). '*Government* is instituted in order to guarantee man the enjoyment of his natural and imprescriptible rights' (*Declaration* etc., 1793, Article 1).

Thus even during the ardour of its youth, urged on to new heights by the pressure of circumstances, political life declares itself to be a mere *means* whose goal is the life of civil society. True, revolutionary practice is in flagrant contradiction with its theory. While, for example, security is declared to be one of the rights of man, the violation of the privacy of letters openly becomes the order of the day. While the '*unlimited* freedom of the press' (Constitution of 1793, Article 122) is guaranteed as a consequence of the right to individual freedom, the freedom of the press is completely destroyed, for 'the freedom of the press should not be permitted when it compromises public freedom'. This therefore means that the right to freedom ceases to be a right as soon as it comes into conflict with *political* life, whereas in theory political life is simply the guarantee of the rights of man, the rights of individual man, and should be abandoned as soon as it contradicts its *goal*, these rights of man. But practice is only the exception and theory is the rule. Even if we were to assume that the relationship is properly expressed in revolutionary practice, the problem still remains to be solved as to why the relationship is set upon its head in the minds of the political emancipators so that the end appears as the means and the means as the end. This optical illusion present in their minds would continue to pose the same problem, though in a psychological and theoretical form.

But there is a straightforward solution.

Political emancipation is at the same time the *dissolution* of the old society on which there rested the power of the sovereign, the political system [*Staatswesen*] as estranged from the people. The political revolution is the revolution of civil society. What was the character of the old society? It can be characterized in one word: *feudalism*. The old civil society had a *directly political* character, i.e. the elements of civil life such as property, family and the mode and manner of work were elevated in the form of seignory, estate and guild to the level of elements of political life. In this form they defined the relationship of the single individual to the *state as a whole*, i.e. his *political* relationship, his relationship of separation and exclusion from the other components of society. For the feudal organization of the life of the people did not elevate property or labour to the level of social elements but rather completed their *separation* from the state as a whole and constituted them as *separate* societies within society. But the functions and conditions of life in civil society were still political, even though political in the feudal sense, i.e. they excluded the individual from the state as a whole, they transformed the particular relationship of his guild to the whole state into his own general relationship to the life of the people, just as they transformed his specific civil activity and situation into his general activity and situation. As a consequence of this organization, the unity of the state, together with the consciousness, the will and the activity of the unity of the state, the universal political power, likewise inevitably appears as the *special* concern of a ruler and his servants, separated from the people.

The political revolution which overthrew this rule and turned the affairs of the state into the affairs of the people, which constituted the political state as a concern of the whole people, i.e. as a real state, inevitably destroyed all the estates, corporations, guilds and privileges which expressed the separation of the people from its community. The political revolution thereby *abolished the political character of civil society*. It shattered civil society into its simple components – on the one hand *individuals* and on the other the *material* and *spiritual elements* which constitute the vital content and civil situation of these individuals. It unleashed the political spirit which had, as it were, been dissolved, dissected and dispersed in the various cul-de-sacs of feudal society; it gathered together this spirit from its state of dispersion, liberated it from the adulteration of civil life and constituted it as the sphere of the community, the *universal* concern of the people ideally independent of those *particular* elements of civil life. A person's *particular* activity and situation in life sank to the level of a purely individual significance. They no longer constituted the relationship of the individual to the state as a whole. Public affairs as such became the universal affair of each individual and the political function his universal function.

But the perfection of the idealism of the state was at the same time the perfection of the materialism of civil society. The shaking-off of the political yoke was at the same time the shaking-off of the bonds which had held in check the egoistic spirit of civil society. Political emancipation was at the same time the emancipation of civil society from politics, from even the *appearance* of a universal content.

Feudal society was dissolved into its foundation [*Grund*], into *man*. But into man as he really was its foundation – into *egoistic* man.

This *man*, the member of civil society, is now the foundation, the presupposition of the *political* state. In the rights of man the state acknowledges him as such.

But the freedom of egoistic man and the acknowledgement of this freedom is rather the acknowledgement of the *unbridled* movement of the spiritual and material elements which form the content of his life.

Hence man was not freed from religion – he received the freedom of religion. He was not freed from property – he received the freedom of property. He was not freed from the egoism of trade – he received the freedom to engage in trade.

The *constitution* of the *political state* and the dissolution of civil society into independent *individuals* – who are related by *law* just as men in the estates and guilds were related by *privilege* – are achieved in *one and the same act*. But man, as member of civil society, inevitably appears as *unpolitical* man, as *natural* man. The rights of man appear as natural rights, for *self-conscious activity* is concentrated upon the *political act*. Egoistic man is the *passive* and merely *given* result of the society which has been dissolved, an object of *immediate certainty*, and for that reason a *natural* object. The *political revolution* dissolves civil society into its component parts without *revolutionizing* these parts and subjecting them to criticism. It regards civil society, the world of needs, of labour, of private interests and of civil law, as the *foundation of its existence*, as a *presupposition* which needs no further grounding, and therefore as its *natural basis*. Finally, man as he is a member of civil society is taken to be the *real* man, *man* as distinct from *citizen*, since he is man in his sensuous, individual and *immediate* existence, whereas *political* man is simply abstract, artificial man, man as an *allegorical, moral* person. Actual man is acknowledged only in the form of the *egoistic* individual and *true* man only in the form of the *abstract citizen*.

Rousseau's description of the abstraction of the political man is a good one:

> Whoever dares to undertake the founding of a people's institutions must feel himself capable of *changing*, so to speak, *human nature*, of transforming each individual, who in himself is a complete and solitary whole, into a *part* of a greater whole from which he somehow receives his life and his being, of substituting a *partial* and *moral existence* for physical and independent existence. He must take *man's own powers away from him* and substitute for them alien ones which he can only use with the assistance of others.

*All* emancipation is *reduction* of the human world and of relationships to *man himself*.

Political emancipation is the reduction of man on the one hand to the member of civil society, the *egoistic, independent* individual, and on the other to the *citizen*, the moral person.

Only when real, individual man resumes the abstract citizen into himself and as an individual man has become a *species-being* in his empirical life, his individual work and his individual relationships, only when man has recognized and organized his *forces propres* as *social forces* so that social force is no longer separated from him in the form of *political* force, only then will human emancipation be completed.

[...]

# 43

# THE CIVIL WAR IN FRANCE

## Karl Marx

[...]

The Paris Commune was, of course, to serve as a model to all the great industrial centres of France. The communal regime once established in Paris and the secondary centres, the old centralized government would in the provinces, too, have to give way to the self-government of the producers. In a rough sketch of national organization which the Commune had no time to develop, it states clearly that the commune was to be the political form of even the smallest country hamlet, and that in the rural districts the standing army was to be replaced by a national militia, with an extremely short term of service. The rural communes of every district were to administer their common affairs by an assembly of delegates in the central town, and these district assemblies were again to send deputies to the national delegation in Paris, each delegate to be at any time revocable and bound by the *mandat impératif* (formal instructions) of his constituents. The few but important functions which still would remain for a central government were not to be suppressed, as has been intentionally mis-stated, but were to be discharged by Communal, and therefore strictly responsible agents. The unity of the nation was not to be broken, but, on the contrary, to be organized by the Communal constitution and to become a reality by the destruction of the state power which claimed to be the embodiment of that unity independent of, and superior to, the nation itself, from which it was but a

From K. Marx, 'The Civil War in France: Address of the General Council', in Karl Marx, *Political Writings*, Vol. 3, *The First International and After*, ed. and intro. David Fernbach (Penguin Books, Harmondsworth, 1974), pp. 210–14. Originally written in 1871.

parasitic excrescence. While the merely repressive organs of the old govern-mental power were to be amputated, its legitimate functions were to be wrested from an authority usurping pre-eminence over society itself, and restored to the responsible agents of society. Instead of deciding once in three or six years which member of the ruling class was to misrepresent the people in parliament, universal suffrage was to serve the people, constituted in communes, as individual suffrage serves every other employer in the search for the workmen and managers in his business. And it is well known that companies, like indi-viduals, in matters of real business generally know how to put the right man in the right place, and, if they for once make a mistake, to redress it promptly. On the other hand, nothing could be more foreign to the spirit of the Commune than to supersede universal suffrage by hierarchic investiture.

It is generally the fate of completely new historical creations to be mistaken for the counterpart of older and even defunct forms of social life, to which they may bear a certain likeness. Thus, this new Commune, which breaks the modern state power, has been mistaken for a reproduction of the medieval communes, which first preceded, and afterwards became the substratum of, that very state power. The Communal constitution has been mistaken for an attempt to break up into a federation of small states, as dreamt of by Montesquieu and the Girondins, that unity of great nations which, if originally brought about by political force, has now become a powerful coefficient of social production. The antagonism of the Commune against the state power has been mistaken for an exaggerated form of the ancient struggle against over-centralization. Peculiar historical circumstances may have prevented the clas-sical development, as in France, of the bourgeois form of government, and may have allowed, as in England, to complete the great central state organs by corrupt vestries, jobbing councillors, and ferocious poor-law guardians in the towns, and virtually hereditary magistrates in the counties. The Communal constitution would have restored to the social body all the forces hitherto absorbed by the state parasite feeding upon, and clogging the free movement of, society. By this one act it would have initiated the regeneration of France. The provincial French middle class saw in the Commune an attempt to restore the sway their order had held over the country under Louis Philippe, and which, under Louis Napoleon, was supplanted by the pretended rule of the country over the towns. In reality, the Communal constitution brought the rural producers under the intellectual lead of the central towns of their districts, and these secured to them, in the working men, the natural trustees of their interests. The very existence of the Commune involved, as a matter of course, local municipal liberty, but no longer as a check upon the, now superseded, state power. It could only enter into the head of a Bismarck, who, when not engaged on his intrigues of blood and iron, always likes to resume his old trade, so befitting his mental calibre, of contributor to *Kladderadatsch* (the Berlin *Punch*), it could only enter into such a head, to ascribe to the Paris Commune aspirations after that caricature of the old French municipal organization of

1791, the Prussian municipal constitution which degrades the town governments to mere secondary wheels in the police machinery of the Prussian state.

The Commune made that catchword of bourgeois revolutions, cheap government, a reality, by destroying the two greatest sources of expenditure – the standing army and state functionarism. Its very existence presupposed the non-existence of monarchy, which, in Europe at least, is the normal incumbrance and indispensable cloak of class rule. It supplied the republic with the basis of really democratic institutions. But neither cheap government nor the 'true republic' was its ultimate aim; they were its mere concomitants.

The multiplicity of interpretations to which the Commune has been subjected, and the multiplicity of interests which construed it in their favour, show that it was a thoroughly expansive political form, while all previous forms of government had been emphatically repressive. Its true secret was this. It was essentially a working-class government, the produce of the struggle of the producing against the appropriating class, the political form at last discovered under which to work out the economical emancipation of labour.

Except on this last condition, the Communal constitution would have been an impossibility and a delusion. The political rule of the producer cannot coexist with the perpetuation of his social slavery. The Commune was therefore to serve as a lever for uprooting the economical foundations upon which rests the existence of classes, and therefore of class rule. With labour emancipated, every man becomes a working man, and productive labour ceases to be a class attribute.

It is a strange fact. In spite of all the tall talk and all the immense literature, for the last sixty years, about emancipation of labour, no sooner do the working men anywhere take the subject into their own hands with a will, than up rises at once all the apologetic phraseology of the mouthpieces of present society with its two poles of capital and wage slavery (the landlord now is but the sleeping partner of the capitalist), as if capitalist society was still in its purest state of virgin innocence, with its antagonism still undeveloped, with its delusions still unexploded, with its prostitute realities not yet laid bare. The Commune, they exclaim, intends to abolish property, the basis of all civilization! Yes, gentlemen, the Commune intended to abolish that class property which makes the labour of the many the wealth of the few. It aimed at the expropriation of the expropriators. It wanted to make individual property a truth by transforming the means of production, land and capital, now chiefly the means of enslaving and exploiting labour, into mere instruments of free and associated labour. But this is communism, 'impossible' communism! Why, those members of the ruling classes who are intelligent enough to perceive the impossibility of continuing the present system – and they are many – have become the obtrusive and full-mouthed apostles of cooperative production. If cooperative production is not to remain a sham and a snare; if it is to supersede the capitalist system; if united cooperative societies are to regulate national production upon a common plan, thus taking it under their own control, and putting an end to the constant anarchy and periodical convulsions which are the fatality of capitalist production – what else, gentlemen, would it be but communism, 'possible' communism?

The working class did not expect miracles from the Commune. They have no ready-made utopias to introduce *par décret du peuple*. They know that in order to work out their own emancipation, and along with it that higher form to which present society is irresistibly tending by its own economical agencies, they will have to pass through long struggles, through a series of historic processes, transforming circumstances and men. They have no ideals to realize, but to set free the elements of the new society with which old collapsing bourgeois society itself is pregnant. In the full consciousness of their historic mission, and with the heroic resolve to act up to it, the working class can afford to smile at the coarse invective of the gentlemen's gentlemen with the pen and inkhorn, and at the didactic patronage of well-wishing bourgeois doctrinaires, pouring forth their ignorant platitudes and sectarian crotchets in the oracular tone of scientific infallibility.

When the Paris Commune took the management of the revolution in its own hands; when plain working men for the first time dared to infringe upon the governmental privilege of their 'natural superiors', and, under circumstances of unexampled difficulty, performed their work modestly, conscientiously, and efficiently – performed it at salaries the highest of which barely amounted to one fifth of what, according to high scientific authority, is the minimum required for a secretary to a certain metropolitan school board – the old world writhed in convulsions of rage at the sight of the red flag, the symbol of the republic of labour, floating over the Hôtel de Ville.

[...]

# 44

# THE STATE AND REVOLUTION

## Vladimir Ilich Lenin

[…]

Democracy for an insignificant minority, democracy for the rich – that is the democracy of capitalist society. If we look more closely into the machinery of capitalist democracy, we see everywhere, in the "petty" – supposedly petty – details of the suffrage (residential qualification, exclusion of women, etc.), in the technique of the representative institutions, in the actual obstacles to the right of assembly (public buildings are not for "paupers"!), in the purely capitalist organisation of the daily press, etc., etc. – we see restriction after restriction upon democracy. These restrictions, exceptions, exclusions, obstacles for the poor seem slight, especially in the eyes of one who has never known want himself and has never been in close contact with the oppressed classes in their mass life (and nine out of ten, if not ninety-nine out of a hundred, bourgeois publicists and politicians come under this category); but in their sum total these restrictions exclude and squeeze out the poor from politics, from active participation in democracy.

Marx grasped this *essence* of capitalist democracy splendidly when, in analysing the experience of the Commune, he said that the oppressed are allowed once every few years to decide which particular representatives of the oppressing class shall represent and repress them in parliament!

But from this capitalist democracy – that is inevitably narrow and stealthily pushes aside the poor, and is therefore hypocritical and false

From Vladimir Ilich Lenin, 'The State and Revolution', in *Selected Works* (Lawrence & Wishart, London, 1969), chapter 9, pp. 326–9. Originally written in 1917.

through and through – forward development does not proceed simply, directly and smoothly, towards "greater and greater democracy", as the liberal professors and petty-bourgeois opportunists would have us believe. No, forward development, i.e., development towards communism, proceeds through the dictatorship of the proletariat, and cannot do otherwise, for the *resistance* of the capitalist exploiters cannot be *broken* by anyone else or in any other way.

And the dictatorship of the proletariat, i.e., the organisation of the vanguard of the oppressed as the ruling class for the purpose of suppressing the oppressors, cannot result merely in an expansion of democracy. *Simultaneously* with an immense expansion of democracy, which *for the first time* becomes democracy for the poor, democracy for the people, and not democracy for the moneybags, the dictatorship of the proletariat imposes a series of restrictions on the freedom of the oppressors, the exploiters, the capitalists. We must suppress them in order to free humanity from wage slavery, their resistance must be crushed by force; it is clear that there is no freedom and no democracy where there is suppression and where there is violence.

Engels expressed this splendidly in his letter to Bebel when he said, as the reader will remember, that "the proletariat needs the state, not in the interests of freedom but in order to hold down its adversaries, and as soon as it becomes possible to speak of freedom the state as such ceases to exist."

Democracy for the vast majority of the people, and suppression by force, i.e., exclusion from democracy, of the exploiters and oppressors of the people – this is the change democracy undergoes during the *transition* from capitalism to communism.

Only in communist society, when the resistance of the capitalists has been completely crushed, when the capitalists have disappeared, when there are no classes (i.e., when there is no distinctions between the members of society as regards their relation to the social means of production), *only* then "the state . . . ceases to exist", and "*it becomes possible to speak of freedom*". Only then will a truly complete democracy become possible and be realised, a democracy without any exceptions whatever. And only then will democracy begin to *wither away*, owing to the simple fact that, freed from capitalist slavery, from the untold horrors, savagery, absurdities and infamies of capitalist exploitation, people will gradually *become accustomed* to observing the elementary rules of social intercourse that have been known for centuries and repeated for thousands of years in all copy-book maxims. They will become accustomed to observing them without force, without coercion, without subordination, *without the special apparatus* for coercion called the state.

The expression "the state *withers away*" is very well chosen, for it indicates both the gradual and the spontaneous nature of the process. Only habit can, and undoubtedly will, have such an effect; for we see around us on millions of occasions how readily people become accustomed to observing the necessary rules of social intercourse when there is no exploitation, when there is nothing that arouses indignation, evokes protest and revolt, and creates the need for *suppression*.

And so in capitalist society we have a democracy that is curtailed, wretched, false, a democracy only for the rich, for the minority. The dictatorship of the proletariat, the period of transition to communism, will for the first time create democracy for the people, for the majority, along with the necessary suppression of the exploiters, of the minority. Communism alone is capable of providing really complete democracy, and the more complete it is, the sooner it will become unnecessary and wither away of its own accord.

In other words, under capitalism we have the state in the proper sense of the word, that is, a special machine for the suppression of one class by another, and, what is more, of the majority by the minority. Naturally, to be successful, such an undertaking as the systematic suppression of the exploited majority by the exploiting minority calls for the utmost ferocity and savagery in the matter of suppressing, it calls for seas of blood, through which mankind is actually wading its way in slavery, serfdom and wage labour.

Furthermore, during the *transition* from capitalism to communism suppression is *still* necessary, but it is now the suppression of the exploiting minority by the exploited majority. A special apparatus, a special machine for suppression, the "state", is *still* necessary, but this is now a transitional state. It is no longer a state in the proper sense of the word; for the suppression of the minority of exploiters by the majority of the wage slaves of *yesterday* is comparatively so easy, simple and natural a task that it will entail far less bloodshed than the suppression of the risings of slaves, serfs or wage-labourers, and it will cost mankind far less. And it is compatible with the extension of democracy to such an overwhelming majority of the population that the need for a *special machine* of suppression will begin to disappear. Naturally, the exploiters are unable to suppress the people without a highly complex machine for performing this task, but *the people* can suppress the exploiters even with a very simple "machine", almost without a "machine", without a special apparatus, by the simple *organisation of the armed people* (such as the Soviets of Workers' and Soldiers' Deputies, we would remark, running ahead).

Lastly, only communism makes the state absolutely unnecessary, for there is *nobody* to be suppressed — "nobody" in the sense of a *class*, of a systematic struggle against a definite section of the population. We are not utopians, and do not in the least deny the possibility and inevitability of excesses on the part of *individual persons*, or the need to stop *such* excesses. In the first place, however, no special machine, no special apparatus of suppression, is needed for this; this will be done by the armed people themselves, as simply and as readily as any crowd of civilised people, even in modern society, interferes to put a stop to a scuffle or to prevent a woman from being assaulted. And, secondly, we know that the fundamental social cause of excesses, which consist in the violation of the rules of social intercourse, is the exploitation of the people, their want and their poverty. With the removal of this chief cause, excesses will inevitably begin to "*wither away*". We do not know how quickly and in what succession, but we do know they will wither away. With their withering away the state will also *wither away.*

# 45

# MARXISM AND POLITICS

## R. Miliband

[...]

Indeed, Marx in *The Class Struggles in France* wrote of the bourgeois republic of 1848 that it 'could be nothing other than the perfected and most purely developed rule of the whole bourgeois class ... *the synthesis of the Restoration and the July monarchy*'. Also, a recurrent theme in Marx's writings on the subject is how repressive and brutal this form of state can turn as soon as its upholders and beneficiaries feel themselves to be threatened by the proletariat. With the June days in Paris, the Republic, Marx wrote in the same text, appeared 'in its pure form, as the state whose avowed purpose it is to perpetuate the rule of capital and the slavery of labour'; and 'bourgeois rule, freed from all fetters, was inevitably transformed, all at once, into bourgeois terrorism'. In the same vein, Marx wrote in *The Civil War in France* more than two decades later that the treatment meted out to the Communards by the government of Thiers showed what was meant by 'the victory of order, justice and civilization': 'The civilization and justice of bourgeois order comes out in its lurid light whenever the slaves and drudges of that order rise against their masters. *Then this civilisation and justice stand forth as undisguised savagery and lawless revenge*'.

But when this has been said, it remains true that Marx and Engels saw considerable virtues in bourgeois democratic regimes *as compared with other forms of class domination*, and notably with Bonapartism, to which Marx in particular devoted much attention. Twenty years of his life, the years of his

From R. Miliband, *Marxism and Politics* (Oxford University Press, 1977), pp. 76–80.

intellectual maturity, were spent in the shadow, so to speak, of this form of dictatorship; and just as capitalist Britain served as Marx's laboratory for the analysis of the political economy of capitalism, so did France under Louis Bonaparte serve him between 1851 and 1871 as a frame of reference for one kind of capitalist politics.

The Bonapartist state was distinguished by an extreme inflation and concentration of executive power, personified in one individual, and nullifying the legislative power. This executive power, Marx wrote in *The Eighteenth Brumaire of Louis Bonaparte*, possessed 'an immense bureaucratic and military organisation, an ingenious and broadly based state machinery, and an army of half a million officials alongside the actual army, which numbers a further half million'; and he further described this state machinery as 'this frightful parasitic body, which surrounds the body of French society like a caul and stops up all its pores ...'

There is, in Marx's writings on the Bonapartist state, a strong sense of the life of 'civil society' being stifled and suppressed in ways which the class state of bourgeois democratic regimes cannot in 'normal' circumstances adopt – a sense epitomized in his description of France after the *coup d'état* of December 2: '... all classes fall on their knees, equally mute and equally impotent, before the rifle butt.'

Closely related to this, and crucially important in the approach of Marx and Engels to the bourgeois republican form of state, as compared with other forms of bourgeois state power, was their belief that the former provided the working class with opportunities and means of struggle which it was precisely the purpose of the latter to deny them. One of the most specific and categorical statements connected with this issue occurs in *The Class Struggles in France*:

> The most comprehensive contradiction in the Constitution (of the Second Republic) consists in the fact that it gives political power to the classes whose social slavery it is intended to perpetuate: proletariat, peasants and petty bourgeoisie. And it deprives the bourgeoisie, the class whose old social power it sanctions, of the political guarantees of this power. It imposes on the political rule of the bourgeoisie democratic conditions which constantly help its enemies towards victory and endanger the very basis of bourgeois society. It demands from the one that it should not proceed from political emancipation to social emancipation and from the other that it should not regress from social restoration to political restoration.

The main feature of the bourgeois democratic regimes on which Marx and Engels fastened was universal suffrage. Still in *The Class Struggles in France*, Marx pointed to the problem which this presented, or could present, to the bourgeoisie:

But does the Constitution still have any meaning the moment that the content of this suffrage, this sovereign will, is no longer bourgeois rule? Is it not the duty of the bourgeoisie to regulate the franchise so that it demands what is reasonable, its rule? By repeatedly terminating the existing state power and by creating it anew from itself does not universal suffrage destroy all stability; does it not perpetually call all existing powers into question; does it not destroy authority; does it not threaten to elevate anarchy itself to the level of authority?

Marx himself answered that the moment must arrive when universal suffrage was no longer compatible with bourgeois rule, and that this moment had indeed arrived in France with the elections of 10 March 1850. The bourgeoisie was now forced to repudiate universal suffrage, he said, and to confess: 'Our dictatorship has existed hitherto by the will of the people; it must now be consolidated against the will of the people.' Nevertheless, he also noted, 'universal suffrage had fulfilled its mission, the only function it can have in a revolutionary period. The majority of the people had passed through the school of development it provided. It had to be abolished – by revolution or by reaction'.

There are many different questions which this conjures up and which will be discussed in Chapter VI. But it may be useful at this point to pursue a little further the issue of universal suffrage and bourgeois democracy as it appeared to Marx and Engels.

Marx himself always held fast to the view that the suffrage, in so far as it helped to sharpen the contradictions of bourgeois society and provided a 'school of development' of the working class, offered definite but limited possibilities to the revolutionary movement.[1] On the other hand, he also described 'the general suffrage' in class society as 'abused either for the parliamentary sanction of the Holy State Power, or a play in the hands of the ruling classes, only employed by the people to sanction (choose the instruments of) parliamentary class rule once in many years', instead of being adapted, as he thought it would have been by the Commune, 'to its real purpose, to choose by the communes their own functionaries of administration and initiation'.

The question of the suffrage and its uses is also connected with that of the 'transition to socialism'; and Marx, as noted earlier, was willing to allow that there might be some isolated cases where that transition would be achieved by non-violent means, and therefore presumably through electoral means made available by the suffrage. But he was clearly very sceptical about such a process, and took it for granted that it would not be the common pattern. 'The workers' he said in a speech after the last Congress of the First International in 1872, 'will have to seize political power one day in order to construct the new organisation of labour; they will have to overthrow the old politics which bolster up the old institutions'. But 'we do not claim', he went on, 'that the road leading to this goal is the same everywhere':

We know that heed must be paid to the institutions, customs and traditions of the various countries, and we do not deny that there are countries, such as America and England, and if I was familiar with its institutions, I might include Holland, where the workers may attain their goal by peaceful means. That being the case, we must recognize that in most continental countries the lever of the revolution will have to be force; a resort to force will be necessary one day in order to set up the rule of labour.

The weight of the argument is unmistakably on the non-peaceful side of the line. The case of Engels is a little more complicated, the complication arising from pronouncements made in the course of developments, notably the growth of German Social Democracy, which postdate Marx's death. By far the most important such pronouncement is Engels's famous Introduction of 1895 to Marx's *Class Struggles in France*. That Introduction was subjected to some expurgation before it was published in *Vorwärts*, the main organ of the German Social Democratic Party; and Engels strongly complained to Kautsky that the expurgated version made him appear as a 'peaceful worshipper of legality *quand même*'. But even though Engel had every right to complain that the editing of his text was misleading, the fact remains that the unexpurgated version unquestionably shows a major shift of emphasis from earlier pronouncements of Marx and Engels on the question of the suffrage and its uses. Engels emphatically denied that he was in any way suggesting that 'our foreign comrades' should 'in the least renounce their right to revolution'. But he went on to say that 'whatever may happen in other countries, the German Social-Democracy occupies a special position and therewith, at least in the immediate future, has a special task'.

This 'special task' was to maintain and preserve the growth of German Social Democracy and its electoral support:

> Its growth proceeds as spontaneously, as steadily, as irresistibly, and at the same time as tranquilly as a natural process. All government intervention has proved powerless against it. We can count even today on two and a quarter million voters. If it continues in this fashion, by the end of the century we shall conquer the greater part of the middle strata of society, petty bourgeois and small peasants, and grow into the decisive power in the land, before which all other powers will have to bow, whether they like it or not. To keep this growth going without interruption until it of itself gets beyond the control of the prevailing governmental system, not to fritter away this daily increasing shock force in vanguard skirmishes, but to keep it intact until the decisive day, that is our main task.

Engels's reference to 'the decisive day' suggests that he had by no means given up the notion that a revolutionary break might yet occur. So does his reference a little later in the text to the likelihood that the powers-that-be would themselves be forced to break through the 'fatal legality' under which Social Democracy thrived, and which it therefore was its bounden duty to maintain. But the shift of emphasis from an earlier perspective is nevertheless quite clear; and whatever Engels himself may have thought, his rejection of notions of 'overthrow', even if bound up with specific conjunctural circumstances, was sufficiently decisive to give considerable encouragement to a much more positive view of what was possible under bourgeois democracy than had earlier been envisaged by Marx and Engels.

[...]

## NOTE

1. In an article on the Chartists published in the *New York Daily Tribune* of 25 August 1852, Marx went as far as the following: '... universal suffrage is the equivalent for political power for the working class of England, where the proletariat forms the large majority of the population, where, in a long, though underground, civil war, it has gained a clear consciousness of its position as a class, and where even the rural districts know no longer any peasants, but only landlords, industrial capitalists (farmers) and hired labourers. The carrying of universal suffrage in England would, therefore, be a far more socialistic measure than anything which has been honoured with the name on the Continent' ('The Chartists' in SE, p. 264). Both he and Engels came, particularly after the passage of the Second Reform Act of 1867, to take a rather less sanguine view of the workings of universal suffrage. (See K. Marx and F. Engels, *On Britain* (Moscow, 1953), *passim*.)

## REFERENCES

*SE* = Karl Marx, 'Surveys from Exile', in Karl Marx, *Political Writings*, Vol. 2, ed. and intro. David Fernbach (Penguin Books, Harmondsworth, 1973).

Marx, K. and Engels, F. *On Britain* (Progress Publishers, Moscow, 1953).

# 46

# DEMOCRATIC THEORY, ESSAYS IN RETRIEVAL

## C. B. Macpherson

[...]

I will risk the generalization that the changes in the liberal-democratic *state*, since the introduction of the democratic franchise, have been less fundamental than the changes in the society and economy. By changes in the state I am thinking in the first place of changes in the ways governments are chosen and authorized. It is true that very considerable changes in the ways governments were chosen and authorized did come with the introduction of democratic franchise. As electorates increased in size, party organization became more important and party discipline stronger. Hence, the responsiveness of elected representatives to their constituencies diminished, as did the responsiveness of governments to elected representatives. But these are not changes in the liberal-democratic state, they are changes as between the pre-democratic liberal state and the liberal-democratic state. Apart from these there have been no great changes in the mechanism of choosing and authorizing governments, unless the proliferation and institutionalization of pressure groups as part of the standard method of determining government policy be so considered. When we turn to what governments do with their power there is a more noticeable change. But here we move into the area of changes in the society and economy. For it is these changes which have called forth the regulatory and welfare state.

When we look at changes in the society and the economy, two changes stand out: the decline of pure competition and the rise of the welfare state. The two

From C. B. Macpherson, 'Post-Liberal-Democracy', *Democratic Theory: Essays in Retrieval* (Clarendon Press, Oxford, 1973), pp. 180–4.

changes may be summed up as a move away from a relatively unregulated free enterprise economy to a system more heavily managed and guided both by large private economic organizations and by the state.

These changes have become most striking in the last few decades. They are not confined to the last few decades, of course. But the cumulative effect of welfare measures, of monetary and fiscal policies designed to prevent depressions and maintain full employment, of control and direction of foreign trade and home production, and all the rest, has given our market economies quite a different look even since the 1930s. Equally important has been the change in scale of the productive units. The move has been from markets in which no producer or supplier could make prices, to markets in which prices are increasingly made by firms or groups of firms who can do so, and who are sometimes able to enlist governments or groups of governments in their arrangements.

This is familiar enough. And it throws us back to the question mentioned at the beginning of this paper: how much has capitalism changed? Are we in an era of post-capitalism? I do not think we are. The change is not as great as some would suggest. It all depends, of course, on how you prefer to define capitalism. If you define it as a system of free enterprise with no government interference, then of course our present heavily regulated system is not capitalism. But I find it very unhistorical to equate capitalism with *laissez-faire*. I think it preferable to define capitalism as the system in which production is carried on without authoritative allocation of work or rewards, but by contractual relations between free individuals (each possessing some resource be it only his own labour-power) who calculate their most profitable courses of action and employ their resources as that calculation dictates.

Such a system permits a great deal of state interference without its essential nature being altered. The state may, as states commonly do, interfere by way of differential taxes and subsidies, control of competition and of monopoly, control of land use and labour use, and all kinds of regulation conferring advantages or disadvantages on some kinds of production or some categories of producers. What the state does thereby is to alter the terms of the equations which each man makes when he is calculating his most profitable course of action. Some of the data for the calculation are changed, but this need not affect the mainspring of the system, which is that men do act as their calculation of net gain dictates. As long as prices still move in response to these calculated decisions, and as long as prices still elicit the production of goods and determine their allocation, we may say that the essential nature of the system has not changed.

One may grant that the regulatory role of the modern state, and the transfer payments involved in the welfare state, are not a contradiction of capitalism, but may still argue that capitalism has been transformed into something else by its other most obvious novelty. This is the rise of the modern corporation to a point where a few firms, whose behaviour is less competitive than (to use Schumpeter's fine word) 'corespective', can make prices and dominate markets, and whose decisions are said to be determined less by desire to maximize profits than to build empires and to grow. The appearance of this phenomenon does indeed cast doubts on the justifying theory implicit in neo-classical economics, for in these conditions there is no reason to believe that the corporations' price-making decision will maximize production or utilities. But it does not alter the basic nature of the system. The driving force is after all still maximization of profit, for it is only by accumulating profit that the corporation can continue to grow and to build empires. The only thing that is different is the time-span over which maximum profit is reckoned.

Our present managed economy, managed both by the state and by the price-making corporation, is not, in my view, to be regarded as a transcendence of capitalism. It is still capitalism. But it has made nonsense of the justifying theory that capitalism maximizes social utility. And so, to the extent that modern liberal-democratic theory has reverted to the maximizing justification, that theory is further out of step than it was in the days of more nearly pure competition.

On the extent to which the welfare state has diminished the old inequality of opportunity and increased the chances for fuller development of individual personality, there will be differences of opinion. Improvements in the general level of health and literacy should, other things being equal, improve the quality of life for the great mass of individuals. But other things are not equal. For the very system of production which has afforded the welfare state has brought other changes. It has, necessarily, organized the work process in such a way that, for most people, their productive labour cannot be itself regarded as a fulfilment or development of their capacities. Fulfilment and development of individual capacities become, therefore, increasingly a matter of the development and satisfaction of wants for all kinds of material and, in the broadest sense, aesthetic or psychic goods.

But here again the system has changed things. For the market system, based on and demanding competition and emulation, creates the wants which it satisfies. The tastes and wants which people learn to satisfy as they rise above bare subsistence are, as we have seen, tastes and wants created by the productive system itself. And as the system increasingly moves away from a pattern of widespread competition between many producers (when it was still possible to think of it in terms of consumer sovereignty) to a pattern of competition for power between fewer and larger corporate units and groupings, which are increasingly able to control prices and products, the tendency of the system to create the wants which it satisfies will become stronger. There is no reason to expect that the wants and tastes which it satisfies will reflect or permit that full development of the individual personality which is the liberal-democratic criterion of the good society.

On balance, then, the changes in the liberal-democratic society seem to have made the justifying theory less, rather than more, adequate. When the changes in the society are taken in conjunction with the changes in the theory, the theory seems less fitted to the society than was the case at the beginning of the liberal-democratic period. One of the changes in the society has gone in the opposite direction from the change in theory. That is, while the theory since Mill has come to rely more heavily on the maximizing of utilities justification, the society has moved towards a more managed system whose claim to maximize utilities can no longer be granted. The other main change in the society has not made up for this, has not provided a way out of the central difficulty of the original liberal-democratic theory. That is to say, the change to the welfare state and the managed market cannot be counted on to provide an improvement in the quality of life as judged by the liberal-democratic criterion. We can only count on the manufacture and control of tastes.

All this by itself would be enough to indicate that we do need a new theory, sufficiently different from what we have now to merit the description 'post-liberal-democratic'. But there is a further reason why such a theory is needed, and this may suggest the direction in which a new theory is to be sought.

## IV

There has been in the last fifty years, and most strikingly in the last twenty, a change of tastes and wants quite different from the one we have noticed within liberal-democratic societies. The change I am thinking of is not a change in our tastes, but a change, on the world scale, of the taste of the aggregate of those who count, of those whose power can have reactions on us. Fifty years ago the world was almost the preserve of the Western liberal-democratic capitalist societies. Their economies were triumphant, and so were their theories. Since then, two-thirds of the world has rejected the liberal-democratic market society, both in practice and in theory. From Lenin to Nkruma and Sékou Touré, the value system of the West has been spurned, either in the name of Marxism or in the name of a Rousseauian populist general-will theory. It is true that all three ideologies assert much the same ultimate value – the development and realization of the creative capacities of the individual. It is the mediate principle of liberal democracy that the other two ideologies reject – the mediate principle that the ultimate human values can be achieved by, and only by, free enterprise in both political and economic life, only by the free party system and the capitalist market system. In the other two-thirds of the world the leaders, with willing enough followers and even positively willing followers, have concluded that for their countries at least it would be impossible to move towards the ultimate humanistic goals by liberal-democratic methods. They have perhaps seen more clearly than we have the dilemma of liberal-democratic theory, and the doubtful adequacy of liberal-democratic society even in the most advanced conditions.

It is time we reflected, more seriously than we have generally done, on their reading of our society. It is time we gave some thought as to whether it is any longer possible for us to move towards our goal within the pattern of the market society. The system of managed capitalism into which we are headed will have to compete steadily from now on with non-capitalist systems. The competition will be in the degree of satisfaction each provides for its members. At present we are well above the other systems in the extremely important psychic satisfaction of individual liberty. But it is possible that our curve is going down, and probable that theirs will come up.

We need a revolution in democratic consciousness if we are to avoid being caught up ourselves in the backwash of the revolutions in the rest of the world. We need to give up the myth of maximization. We need to inquire soberly whether competitive, maximizing behaviour is any longer rational for us, in any ethical or expedient sense, or whether the very high level of material productivity that we now command can be made to subserve the original liberal-democratic vision. We should be considering whether we have been asking the wrong question all this time, in asking, as we have done, how to hold on to the liberty we have got – the liberty of possessive individualists – while moving a little towards more equality. Perhaps we should be asking, instead, whether meaningful liberty can much longer be had without a much greater measure of equality than we have hitherto thought liberty required.

We should not shrink from either the populist teaching of Rousseau or the radical teaching of Marx. Neither will suit us, but we may have more to learn from them than we think. It may even be – if the economists present will permit me an intertemporal comparison of utilities – that the utility of Marxism as a means of understanding the world is increasing over time.

# SECTION 7
# CONSERVATIVE, ELITIST AND
# AUTHORITARIAN CRITIQUES

# CONSERVATIVE, ELITIST AND AUTHORITARIAN CRITIQUES INTRODUCTION

As noted in our general introduction, for much of human history democracy has been criticised and denounced as an ineffective, illegitimate and unjustifiable form of government. Such voices are by no means absent today, even in a situation where democracy seems to command universal assent and approbation. Defenders of the democratic ideal need to be aware of these critiques, and to be able to counter them, for they do raise fundamental questions about the bases on which democracy is justified.

This section therefore contains a range of writings expressing scepticism or even hostility to the democratic ideal from different positions. We start this section of anti-democratic writings with an extract from *Plato*. In his *Republic* he criticises democracy and the character of the 'democratic man'. Both are seen as expressing an attitude of mind where people do what they want, follow their impulses and hence lack any discipline or self-control. The life of the democratic man 'is subject to no order or restraint'.

Such a disparaging attitude towards democracy was echoed by conservative theorists writing at the time of the French Revolution of 1789, which they denounced as showing the power of the mob. For a thinker such as Burke, in the extract featured below, democracy meant mob rule, and in turn this brought with it anarchy. Human beings, he argued, required sovereignty, an ordered hierarchy, without which property would not be safe, social continuity could not endure, and the wisdom of experienced politicians would count for nothing. The masses might not know their own interest best: as Burke put it, 'the will of the many, and their interest, must very often differ; and great will be the difference when they make an evil choice'. Hence conservative thinkers pose the question of whether human beings are capable of being democratic citizens.

Some of these classic conservative criticisms of democracy are echoed by conservatives today, such as the contemporary philosopher *Roger Scruton*. He speaks of democracy as a 'contagion', and questions its legitimacy. Democracy seems to have weaker foundations than conservatism, which is based on established usage, whereas democracy reflects the passing whims of the people at a particular time. Democratic choice is made under highly artificial circumstances, and there is no guarantee that popular choice will in fact be a wise one.

From a much more extreme perspective, fascist thinkers like the Italian fascist leader *Mussolini* take this critique further. Fascism denies the equality of people which is one of the fundamentals of democracy. It affirms the need for leadership, the inevitable domination of the passive masses by the great leader. Mussolini offered a perverted view of democracy, claiming that leadership backed up by the mass was what fascism offered, 'organised, centralised, authoritarian democracy'. He thus seeks democratic backing for authoritarian politics. Similarly, the German political thinker (and sympathiser with Nazism) *Carl Schmitt* affirmed that the basis of political action was the distinction between friend and foe. This idea of bonding as an 'in-group' versus an 'out-group' suggests a politics of hostility, intolerance and inevitable conflict. It is at odds with ideas of democratic community and respect for others. Yet such ideas, often appearing in the form of extreme nationalism (see Section 11 on nationalism and democracy in Part Four below) have frequently been used to mobilise mass support for anti-democratic ends. They raise the possibility, deeply worrying to a democrat, that democracy can degenerate into populist authoritarianism. The 'people's choice' might be for dictatorial leaders, or for politics of demagogic xenophobia, as witnessed by popular support for radical right-wing movements in contemporary Europe (such as the FPÖ and its leader Jörg Haider in Austria).

Another set of critiques of democracy seeks to establish the impracticability of democracy as a means of decision-taking. Those thinkers commonly referred to as 'elitists' make this kind of argument. *Max Weber* and *Robert Michels* point to the need for leadership, and argue that popular power cannot be sustained. Democracy will inevitably give way to the domination of the few over the many. This tendency is what Michels termed the 'iron law of oligarchy'. He saw its exemplification in the mass political parties of modern society, like the German Social-Democratic Party (SPD) in the period before the First World War. Popular sovereignty could never be achieved, and the masses, elevated by democratic theory to the highest governing role, in reality could only 'constitute the pedestal of an oligarchy'.

If Weber and Michels are right, then democracy in any genuine sense is impossible. A less pessimistic perspective is held out by the political theorist *Giovanni Sartori*. He accepts Michels' law of oligarchy, though in a milder form, as a 'bronze' rather than an 'iron' law. Yet Sartori suggests that this need not rule out democracy, if we interpret democracy less stringently. The masses, though politically inactive, become the arbiter in the contest for power between the competing elites, 'the organised minorities of the politically active'. This is the idea of the competitive theory of democracy, usually attributed to Schumpeter, whose classic revision of democratic theory has been excerpted in Part One above.

In this section of our Reader *Schumpeter* appears again as a sceptical analyst of the capacities of the citizen. Schumpeter suggests that while most people are competent judges and perfectly rational in their limited sphere of professional interest, 'the typical citizen drops down to a lower level of mental performance as soon as he enters the political field'. If Schumpeter is right to say that citizens become 'infantile' and emotional in any sphere beyond that of their 'real interests', narrowly defined, then how can a democratic society exist? Such a position certainly casts doubt on the more optimistic claims made by some democratic theorists that participation and autonomy develop the capacities of citizens, and bring them to a higher level. Perhaps the challenge for democratic theory today is to suggest ways in which the scepticism of elitist and 'realist' theories of democracy is too corrosive. There is evidence of movements and ideas which can sustain degrees of popular involvement, and lead to the enhancement of citizen capacities which democratic theory proclaims.

# 47

# THE REPUBLIC

## Plato

[...]

Democracy, I suppose, should come next. A study of its rise and character should help us to recognize the democratic type of man and set him beside the others for judgement.

Certainly that course would fit in with our plan.

If the aim of life in an oligarchy is to become as rich as possible, that insatiable craving would bring about the transition to democracy. In this way: since the power of the ruling class is due to its wealth, they will not want to have laws restraining prodigal young men from ruining themselves by extravagance. They will hope to lend these spendthrifts money on their property and buy it up, so as to become richer and more influential than ever. We can see at once that a society cannot hold wealth in honour and at the same time establish a proper self-control in its citizens. One or the other must be sacrificed.

Yes, that is fairly obvious.

In an oligarchy, then, this neglect to curb riotous living sometimes reduces to poverty men of a not ungenerous nature. They settle down in idleness, some of them burdened with debt, some disfranchised, some both at once; and these drones are armed and can sting. Hating the men who have acquired their property and conspiring against them and the rest of society, they long for a revolution. Meanwhile the usurers, intent upon their own business, seem

From *The Republic of Plato*, trans., intro. and notes F. M. Cornford (Clarendon Press, Oxford, 1941), pp. 274–80. Originally written ca. 375 BC.

unaware of their existence; they are too busy planting their own stings into any fresh victim who offers them an opening to inject the poison of their money; and while they multiply their capital by usury, they are also multiplying the drones and the paupers. When the danger threatens to break out, they will do nothing to quench the flames, either in the way we mentioned, by forbidding a man to do what he likes with his own, or by the next best remedy, which would be a law enforcing a respect for right conduct. If it were enacted that, in general, voluntary contracts for a loan should be made at the lender's risk, there would be less of this shameless pursuit of wealth and a scantier crop of those evils I have just described.

Quite true.

But, as things are, this is the plight to which the rulers of an oligarchy, for all these reasons, reduce their subjects. As for themselves, luxurious indolence of body and mind makes their young men too lazy and effeminate to resist pleasure or to endure pain; and the fathers, neglecting everything but money, have no higher ideals in life than the poor. Such being the condition of rulers and subjects, what will happen when they are thrown together, perhaps as fellow-travellers by sea or land to some festival or on a campaign, and can observe one another's demeanour in a moment of danger? The rich will have no chance to feel superior to the poor. On the contrary, the poor man, lean and sunburnt, may find himself posted in battle beside one who, thanks to his wealth and indoor life, is panting under his burden of fat and showing every mark of distress. 'Such men', he will think, 'are rich because we are cowards'; and when he and his friends meet in private, the word will go round: 'These men are no good: they are at our mercy.'

Yes, that is sure to happen.

This state, then, is in the same precarious condition as a person so unhealthy that the least shock from outside will upset the balance or, even without that, internal disorder will break out. It falls sick and is at war with itself on the slightest occasion, as soon as one party or the other calls in allies from a neighbouring oligarchy or democracy; and sometimes civil war begins with no help from without.

Quite true.

And when the poor win, the result is a democracy. They kill some of the opposite party, banish others, and grant the rest an equal share in civil rights and government, officials being usually appointed by lot.

Yes, that is how a democracy comes to be established, whether by force of arms or because the other party is terrorized into giving way.

Now what is the character of this new régime? Obviously the way they govern themselves will throw light on the democratic type of man.

No doubt.

First of all, they are free. Liberty and free speech are rife everywhere; anyone is allowed to do what he likes.

Yes, so we are told.

That being so, every man will arrange his own manner of life to suit his pleasure. The result will be a greater variety of individuals than under any other constitution. So it may be the finest of all, with its variegated pattern of all sorts of characters. Many people may think it the best, just as women and children might admire a mixture of colours of every shade in the pattern of a dress. At any rate if we are in search of a constitution, here is a good place to look for one. A democracy is so free that it contains a sample of every kind; and perhaps anyone who intends to found a state, as we have been doing, ought first to visit this emporium of constitutions and choose the model he likes best.

He will find plenty to choose from.

Here, too, you are not obliged to be in authority, however competent you may be, or to submit to authority, if you do not like it; you need not fight when your fellow citizens are at war, nor remain at peace when they do, unless you want peace; and though you may have no legal right to hold office or sit on juries, you will do so all the same if the fancy takes you. A wonderfully pleasant life, surely, for the moment.

For the moment, no doubt.

There is a charm, too, in the forgiving spirit shown by some who have been sentenced by the courts. In a democracy you must have seen how men condemned to death or exile stay on and go about in public, and no one takes any more notice than he would of a spirit that walked invisible. There is so much tolerance and superiority to petty considerations; such a contempt for all those fine principles we laid down in founding our commonwealth, as when we said that only a very exceptional nature could turn out a good man, if he had not played as a child among things of beauty and given himself only to creditable pursuits. A democracy tramples all such notions under foot; with a magnificent indifference to the sort of life a man has led before he enters politics, it will promote to honour anyone who merely calls himself the people's friend.

Magnificent indeed.

These then, and such as these, are the features of a democracy, an agreeable form of anarchy with plenty of variety and an equality of a peculiar kind for equals and unequals alike.

All that is notoriously true.

Now consider the corresponding individual character. Or shall we take his origin first, as we did in the case of the constitution?

Yes.

I imagine him as the son of our miserly oligarch, brought up under his father's eye and in his father's ways. So he too will enforce a firm control over all such pleasures as lead to expense rather than profit – unnecessary pleasures, as they have been called. But, before going farther, shall we draw the distinction between necessary and unnecessary appetites, so as not to argue in the dark?

Please do so.

There are appetites which cannot be got rid of, and there are all those which it does us good to fulfil. Our nature cannot help seeking to satisfy both these kinds; so they may fairly be described as necessary. On the other hand, 'unnecessary' would be the right name for all appetites which can be got rid of by early training and which do us no good and in some cases do harm. Let us take an example of each kind, so as to form a general idea of them. The desire to eat enough plain food – just bread and meat – to keep in health and good condition may be called necessary. In the case of bread the necessity is twofold, since it not only does us good but is indispensable to life; whereas meat is only necessary in so far as it helps to keep us in good condition. Beyond these simple needs the desire for a whole variety of luxuries is unnecessary. Most people can get rid of it by early discipline and education; and it is as prejudicial to intelligence and self-control as it is to bodily health. Further, these unnecessary appetites might be called expensive, whereas the necessary ones are rather profitable, as helping a man to do his work. The same distinctions could be drawn in the case of sexual appetite and all the rest.

Yes.

Now, when we were speaking just now of drones, we meant the sort of man who is under the sway of a host of unnecessary pleasures and appetites, in contrast with our miserly oligarch, over whom the necessary desires are in control. Accordingly, we can now go back to describe how the democratic type develops from the oligarchical. I imagine it usually happens in this way. When a young man, bred, as we were saying, in a stingy and uncultivated home, has once tasted the honey of the drones and keeps company with those dangerous and cunning creatures, who know how to purvey pleasures in all their multitudinous variety, then the oligarchical constitution of his soul begins to turn into a democracy. The corresponding revolution was effected in the state by one of the two factions calling in the help of partisans from outside. In the same way one of the conflicting sets of desires in the soul of this youth will be reinforced from without by a group of kindred passions; and if the resistance of the oligarchical faction in him is strengthened by remonstrances and reproaches coming from his father, perhaps, or his friends, the opposing parties will soon be battling within him. In some cases the democratic interest yields to the oligarchical: a sense of shame gains a footing in the young man's soul, and some appetites are crushed, others banished, until order is restored.

Yes, that happens sometimes.

But then again, perhaps, owing to the father's having no idea how to bring up his son, another brood of desires, akin to those which were banished, are secretly nursed up until they become numerous and strong. These draw the young man back into clandestine commerce with his old associates, and between them they breed a whole multitude. In the end, they seize the citadel of the young man's soul, finding it unguarded by the trusty sentinels which keep watch over the minds of men favoured by heaven. Knowledge, right principles, true thoughts, are not at their post; and the place lies open to the assault of false and presumptuous notions. So he turns again to those lotus-eaters and now throws in his lot with them openly. If his family send reinforcements to the support of his thrifty instincts, the impostors who have seized the royal fortress shut the gates upon them, and will not even come to parley with the fatherly counsels of individual friends. In the internal conflict they gain the day; modesty and self-control, dishonoured and insulted as the weaknesses of an unmanly fool, are thrust out into exile; and the whole crew of unprofitable desires take a hand in banishing moderation and frugality, which, as they will have it, are nothing but churlish meanness. So they take possession of the soul which they have swept clean, as if purified for initiation into higher mysteries; and nothing remains but to marshal the great procession bringing home Insolence, Anarchy, Waste, and Impudence, those resplendent divinities crowned with garlands, whose praises they sing under flattering names: Insolence they call good breeding, Anarchy freedom, Waste magnificence, and Impudence a manly spirit. Is not that a fair account of the revolution which gives free rein to unnecessary and harmful pleasures in a young man brought up in the satisfaction only of the necessary desires?

Yes, it is a vivid description.

In his life thenceforward he spends as much time and pains and money on his superfluous pleasures as on the necessary ones. If he is lucky enough not to be carried beyond all bounds, the tumult may begin to subside as he grows older. Then perhaps he may recall some of the banished virtues and cease to give himself up entirely to the passions which ousted them; and now he will set all his pleasures on a footing of equality, denying to none its equal rights and maintenance, and allowing each in turn, as it presents itself, to succeed, as if by the chance of the lot, to the government of his soul until it is satisfied. When he is told that some pleasures should be sought and valued as arising from desires of a higher order, others chastised and enslaved because the desires are base, he will shut the gates of the citadel against the messengers of truth, shaking his head and declaring that one appetite is as good as another and all must have their equal rights. So he spends his days indulging the pleasure of the moment, now intoxicated with wine and music, and then taking to a spare diet and drinking nothing but water; one day in hard training, the next doing nothing at all, the third apparently immersed in study. Every now and then he takes a part in politics, leaping to his feet to say or do whatever comes into his head. Or he will set out to rival someone he admires, a soldier it may be, or, if the fancy takes him, a man of business. His life is subject to no order or restraint, and he has no wish to change an existence which he calls pleasant, free, and happy.

That well describes the life of one whose motto is liberty and equality.

Yes, and his character contains the same fine variety of pattern that we found in the democratic state; it is as multifarious as that epitome of all types of

# 48

# REFLECTIONS ON THE REVOLUTION IN FRANCE

## Edmund Burke

[...]

It is said, that twenty-four millions ought to prevail over two hundred thousand. True; if the constitution of a kingdom be a problem of arithmetic. This sort of discourse does well enough with the lamp-post for its second: to men who *may* reason calmly, it is ridiculous. The will of the many, and their interest, must very often differ; and great will be the difference when they make an evil choice. A government of five hundred country attornies and obscure curates is not good for twenty-four millions of men, though it were chosen by eight and forty millions; nor is it the better for being guided by a dozen of persons of quality, who have betrayed their trust in order to obtain that power. At present, you seem in every thing to have strayed out of the high road of nature. The property of France does not govern it. Of course property is destroyed, and rational liberty has no existence. All you have got for the present is a paper circulation, and a stock-jobbing constitution: and as to the future, do you seriously think that the territory of France, upon the republican system of eighty-three independent municipalities (to say nothing of the parts that compose them) can ever be governed as one body, or can ever be set in motion by the impulse of one mind? When the National Assembly has completed its work, it will have accomplished its ruin. These commonwealths will not long bear a state of subjection to the republic of Paris. They will not bear that this one body should monopolize the captivity of the king, and the dominion over the assembly

From Edmund Burke, *Reflections on the Revolution in France*, ed. Conor Cruise O'Brien (Harmondsworth, Penguin, 1968), pp. 141–2 and 190–5. Originally written 1790.

calling itself National. Each will keep its own portion of the spoil of the church to itself; and it will not suffer either that spoil, or the more just fruits of their industry, or the natural produce of their soil, to be sent to swell the insolence, or pamper the luxury of the mechanics of Paris. In this they will see none of the equality, under the pretence of which they have been tempted to throw off their allegiance to their sovereign, as well as the antient constitution of their country. There can be no capital city in such a constitution as they have lately made. They have forgot, that when they framed democratic governments, they had virtually dismembered their country. The person whom they persevere in calling king, has not power left to him by the hundredth part sufficient to hold together this collection of republics. The republic of Paris will endeavour indeed to compleat the debauchery of the army, and illegally to perpetuate the assembly, without resort to its constituents, as the means of continuing its despotism. It will make efforts, by becoming the heart of a boundless paper circulation, to draw every thing to itself; but in vain. All this policy in the end will appear as feeble as it is now violent.

[. . .]

The consecration of the state, by a state religious establishment, is necessary also to operate with an wholesome awe upon free citizens; because, in order to secure their freedom, they must enjoy some determinate portion of power. To them therefore a religion connected with the state, and with their duty towards it, becomes even more necessary than in such societies, where the people by the terms of their subjection are confined to private sentiments, and the management of their own family concerns. All persons possessing any portion of power ought to be strongly and awefully impressed with an idea that they act in trust; and that they are to account for their conduct in that trust to the one great master, author and founder of society.

This principle ought even to be more strongly impressed upon the minds of those who compose the collective sovereignty than upon those of single princes. Without instruments, these princes can do nothing. Whoever uses instruments, in finding helps, finds also impediments. Their power is therefore by no means compleat; nor are they safe in extreme abuse. Such persons, however elevated by flattery, arrogance, and self-opinion, must be sensible that, whether covered or not by positive law, in some way or other they are accountable even here for the abuse of their trust. If they are not cut off by a rebellion of their people, they may be strangled by the very janissaries kept for their security against all other rebellion. Thus we have seen the king of France sold by his soldiers for an encrease of pay. But where popular authority is absolute and unrestrained, the people have an infinitely greater, because a far better founded confidence in their own power. They are themselves, in a great measure, their own instruments. They are nearer to their objects. Besides, they are less under responsibility to one of the greatest controlling powers on earth, the sense of fame and estimation. The share of infamy that is likely to fall to the lot of each individual in public acts, is small indeed; the operation of opinion being in the inverse ratio to the number of those who abuse power. Their own approbation of their own acts has to them the appearance of a public judgment in their favour. A perfect democracy is therefore the most shameless thing in the world. As it is the most shameless, it is also the most fearless. No man apprehends in his person he can be made subject to punishment. Certainly the people at large never ought: for as all punishments are for example towards the conservation of the people at large, the people at large can never become the subject of punishment by any human hand. It is therefore of infinite importance that they should not be suffered to imagine that their will, any more than that of kings, is the standard of right and wrong.

They ought to be persuaded that they are full as little entitled, and far less qualified, with safety to themselves, to use any arbitrary power whatsoever; that therefore they are not, under a false shew of liberty, but, in truth, to exercise an unnatural inverted domination, tyrannically to exact, from those who officiate in the state, not an entire devotion to their interest, which is their right, but an abject submission to their occasional will; extinguishing thereby, in all those who serve them, all moral principle, all sense of dignity, all use of judgment, and all consistency of character, whilst by the very same process they give themselves up a proper, a suitable, but a most contemptible prey to the servile ambition of popular sycophants or courtly flatterers.

When the people have emptied themselves of all the lust of selfish will, which without religion it is utterly impossible they ever should, when they are conscious that they exercise, and exercise perhaps in an higher link of the order of delegation, the power, which to be legitimate must be according to that eternal immutable law, in which will and reason are the same, they will be more careful how they place power in base and incapable hands. In their nomination to office, they will not appoint to the exercise of authority, as to a pitiful job, but as to an holy function; not according to their sordid selfish interest, nor to their wanton caprice, nor to their arbitrary will; but they will confer that power (which any man may well tremble to give or to receive) on those only, in whom they may discern that predominant proportion of active virtue and wisdom, taken together and fitted to the charge, such, as in the great and inevitable mixed mass of human imperfections and infirmities, is to be found.

When they are habitually convinced that no evil can be acceptable, either in the act or the permission, to him whose essence is good, they will be better able to extirpate out of the minds of all magistrates, civil, ecclesiastical, or military, any thing that bears the least resemblance to a proud and lawless domination.

But one of the first and most leading principles on which the commonwealth and the laws are consecrated, is lest the temporary possessors and life-renters in it, unmindful of what they have received from their ancestors, or of what is due to their posterity, should act as if they were the entire masters; that they should not think it amongst their rights to cut off the entail, or commit waste on the inheritance, by destroying at their pleasure the whole original fabric of their society; hazarding to leave to those who come after them, a ruin instead of an habitation – and teaching these successors as little to respect their contrivances, as they had themselves respected the institutions of their forefathers. By this unprincipled facility of changing the state as often, and as much, and in as many ways as there are floating fancies or fashions, the whole chain and continuity of the commonwealth would be broken. No one generation could link with the other. Men would become little better than the flies of a summer.

And first of all the science of jurisprudence, the pride of the human intellect, which, with all its defects, redundancies, and errors, is the collected reason of ages, combining the principles of original justice with the infinite variety of human concerns, as a heap of old exploded errors, would be no longer studied. Personal self-sufficiency and arrogance (the certain attendants upon all those who have never experienced a wisdom greater than their own) would usurp the tribunal. Of course, no certain laws, establishing invariably grounds of hope and fear, would keep the actions of men in a certain course, or direct them to a certain end. Nothing stable in the modes of holding property, or exercising function, could form a solid ground on which any parent could speculate in the education of his offspring, or in a choice for their future establishment in the world. No principles would be early worked into the habits. As soon as the most able instructor had completed his laborious course of institution, instead of sending forth his pupil, accomplished in a virtuous discipline, fitted to procure him attention and respect, in his place in society, he would find every thing altered; and that he had turned out a poor creature to the contempt and derision of the world, ignorant of the true grounds of estimation. Who would insure a tender and delicate sense of honour to beat almost with the first pulses of the heart, when no man could know what would be the test of honour in a nation, continually varying the standard of its coin? No part of life would retain its acquisitions. Barbarism with regard to science and literature, unskilfulness with regard to arts and manufactures, would infallibly succeed to the want of a steady education and settled principle; and thus the commonwealth itself would, in a few generations, crumble away, be disconnected into the dust and powder of individuality, and at length dispersed to all the winds of heaven.

To avoid therefore the evils of inconstancy and versatility, ten thousand times worse than those of obstinacy and the blindest prejudice, we have consecrated the state, that no man should approach to look into its defects or corruptions but with due caution; that he should never dream of beginning its reformation by its subversion; that he should approach to the faults of the state as to the wounds of a father, with pious awe and trembling solicitude. By this wise prejudice we are taught to look with horror on those children of their country who are prompt rashly to hack that aged parent in pieces, and put him into the kettle of magicians, in hopes that by their poisonous weeds, and wild incantations, they may regenerate the paternal constitution, and renovate their father's life.

quip of Defoe, that the streets of London are full of 'stout fellows that would spend the last drop of their blood against Popery, that do not know whether it be a man or a horse', a remark amply illustrated, not only in such minor madnesses as the Priestley Riots of 1791, but in the whole tradition of the free-born English trouble-maker.)

The defects of democracy are easy to catalogue, but hard to weigh against the defects of every other arrangement. The social fragmentation presaged by de Tocqueville is as elusive as it is virulent, while the supposed legitimacy of the democratic process is a conception of permanent and vivid appeal. Should a politician wish to dispel for a moment this collective hallucination he must represent himself as opposed, not to democracy, but to some local or specialized form of it – proportional representation, say, or the single-chamber parliament, or the plebiscite. But these specialized forms exemplify the same principle that he must also claim to be defending, the principle that, in matters of government, it is the opinion of the governed that confers legitimacy upon what is done. It might be possible to argue against the use of a referendum, on the grounds that twenty million people ought not to be asked to make a momentous decision concerning a matter about which all of them know nothing (for example, whether to join or not to join the European Economic Community). It might be possible to argue against proportional representation, on the grounds that it will generate a parliament that is weak, irresolute and peppered with crackpots. But all such arguments rely on a principle that denies the basis of democracy. For they assert that popular opinion is a legitimate guide only in so far as it is authorized by government. Hence the legitimacy of government cannot be conferred merely by democratic choice.

It is for some such reason that, when Burke first tried, in his great essay on the French Revolution, to locate the principle of constitution, he could not see total franchise as a necessary part of it, or as having anything to do with the legitimacy of rule. And it is quite possible that even now the constitutional essence of our country would remain unaffected were the franchise to be confined to people of position, education, wealth or power – to those, in other words, with a self-conscious interest in the fortunes of the nation. When Disraeli suddenly snatched from the Liberals the banner of electoral reform, it was certainly not because he had regarded universal suffrage as a Tory principle. The gesture was strategic and opportune. It also satisfied his sense that conservatives reside as much at the bottom as at the top of the social scale, and that it is in the middle class, with its contempt for the prejudice of others, that liberalism finds its natural home.

The extent of the ensuing commitment to democracy should not, however, be underrated. It survives in the doctrine (given increasing rhetorical impetus at every general election) of the 'mandate', the doctrine that a party programme is a kind of promise to the people, and that election success is tantamount to a contractual bond to honour it. (If the programme contains more than one such 'promise', then a party may obtain a majority from an electorate all of whom had voted in a minority on the issue which most concerned them. To whom, then, is it fulfilling its obligation? This is no curious exception, but in all probability wholly normal. The view of electoral success as creating a quasi-contractual obligation is therefore nonsense.)

The commitment to democracy can be seen too in the recent Conservative Party report on the future of the House of Lords, in which it is taken for granted that the Upper House stands in need of reform simply *because* of the undemocratic process whereby it is filled. This argument, taken seriously, would lead to the subversion of any institution (such as school, hospital, college, monastery) which depended for its health on a privilege to govern arising independently of the 'mandate' of its members. (Indeed, the recent Bullock report on industrial democracy has prepared the ground for the subversion of private business in just such a way.) The underlying idea is again the profoundly anti-conservative one, that legitimacy can reside only in contractual or quasi-contractual agreement, and not in established usage. Hence, it is thought, the only legitimate government, or procedure, is one that has been 'chosen' or consented to by its subjects. Yet as soon as one considers the highly artificial circumstances of democratic choice, one must see that this 'choice' presupposes in its turn that the citizen should recognize some prior legitimacy in establishment. When a citizen votes, his choice lies between a small number of parties, none of which would be in a position to attract his vote had they not already been incorporated into the political order. Their right to form into parties, and to regiment their members, is a right of establishment, determined independently of the will of the electorate, and necessary if the citizen is to have any clear idea of what he is *doing* when he casts his vote. Once in parliament, a member, rightly subject to the discipline of party, ceases to represent his constituents in any matter of state. He is part of the apparatus of state. What he does is determined by the established interests that seek expression through his party, and not by any 'promises' that he once made at the hustings. Democracy is simply one means of gaining power, and so of freeing oneself from the immediate demands of the multitude. Moreover, it may be no more obviously satisfactory than any other means, and certainly not possessed of some *a priori* legitimacy which its rivals lack. What are called election 'promises' are no such thing; they can be revoked at will, and were given in exchange for nothing more than a favour born from constraint. It is impossible for a politician to think that he is bound by them or that his presence in parliament is made legitimate just because a sufficient vote was cast in support of him (for reasons which will have nothing in common other than the citizen's sense of the established style and authority of his chosen party). If we were to think that this process – of constraining people to choose between two independently constituted powers – were sufficient in itself to confer legitimacy, then any form of banditry could be legitimate tomorrow. Legitimacy, however, must be more *concretely* constituted. Consider those many institutions (school, church, university) where there *must* be a principle of authority (as legitimate power) and where there *cannot* be democratic procedure without the immediate collapse of the institution.

No conservative, then, is likely to think that democracy is an essential axiom of his politics, even though he is likely to value an independent thing which is often confused with it, which is the individual's ability to participate in government, and at the same time to avoid the encroachments of arbitrary, unconstituted power. This ability, exemplified in the entire course of English history, pre-existed democracy, and lay, indeed, from the beginning, implicit in the common law of our Saxon ancestors.

[...]

# 50

# THE DOCTRINE OF FASCISM

## Benito Mussolini

[...]

After Socialism, Fascism attacks the whole complex of democratic ideologies and rejects them both in their theoretical premises and in their applications of practical manifestations. Fascism denies that the majority, through the mere fact of being a majority, can rule human societies; it denies that this majority can govern by means of a periodical consultation; it affirms the irremediable, fruitful and beneficent inequality of men, who cannot be levelled by such a mechanical and extrinsic fact as universal suffrage. By democratic regimes we mean those in which from time to time the people is given the illusion of being sovereign, while true effective sovereignty lies in other, perhaps irresponsible and secret, forces. Democracy is a regime without a king, but with very many kings, perhaps more exclusive, tyrannical and violent than one king even though a tyrant. This explains why Fascism, although before 1922 for reasons of expediency it made a gesture of republicanism, renounced it before the March on Rome, convinced that the question of the political forms of a State is not pre-eminent today, and that studying past and present monarchies, past and present Republics it becomes clear that monarchy and republic are not to be judged *sub specie aeternitatis*, but represent forms in which the political evolution, the history, the tradition, the psychology of a given country are manifested. Now Fascism overcomes the antithesis between monarchy and republic which retarded the movements of democracy, burdening the former

From Benito Mussolini, 'The Doctrine of Fascism', in Adrian Lyttelton (ed.), *Italian Fascisms from Pareto to Gentile* (Jonathan Cape, London, 1973), pp. 49–50. Originally written 1932.

with every defect and defending the latter as the regime of perfection. Now it has been seen that there are inherently reactionary and absolutistic republics, and monarchies that welcome the most daring political and social innovations.

'Reason, Science', said Renan (who was inspired before Fascism existed) in one of his philosophical Meditations, 'are products of humanity, but to expect reason directly from the people and through the people is a chimera. It is not necessary for the existence of reason that everybody should know it. In any case, if such an initiation should be made, it would not be made by means of base democracy, which apparently must lead to the extinction of every difficult culture, and every higher discipline. The principle that society exists only for the prosperity and the liberty of the individuals who compose it does not seem to conform with the plans of nature, plans in which the species alone is taken into consideration and the individual seems to be sacrificed. It is strongly to be feared lest the last word of democracy thus understood (I hasten to say that it can also be understood in other ways) would be a social state in which a degenerate mass would have no other care than to enjoy the ignoble pleasures of vulgar men.'

Thus far Renan. Fascism rejects in democracy the absurd conventional lie of political equalitarianism clothed in the dress of collective irresponsibility and the myth of happiness and indefinite progress. But if democracy can be understood in other ways, that is, if democracy means not to relegate the people to the periphery of the State, then Fascism could be defined as an 'organized, centralized, authoritarian democracy'.

[...]

# 51

# THE CONCEPT OF THE POLITICAL

## Carl Schmitt

[...]

The specific political distinction to which political actions and motives can be reduced is that between friend and enemy. This provides a definition in the sense of a criterion and not as an exhaustive definition or one indicative of substantial content. Insofar as it is not derived from other criteria, the antithesis of friend and enemy corresponds to the relatively independent criteria of other antitheses: good and evil in the moral sphere, beautiful and ugly in the aesthetic sphere, and so on. In any event it is independent, not in the sense of a distinct new domain, but in that it can neither be based on any one antithesis or any combination of other antitheses, nor can it be traced to these. If the antithesis of good and evil is not simply identical with that of beautiful and ugly, profitable and unprofitable, and cannot be directly reduced to the others, then the antithesis of friend and enemy must even less be confused with or mistaken for the others. The distinction of friend and enemy denotes the utmost degree of intensity of a union or separation, of an association or dissociation. It can exist theoretically and practically, without having simultaneously, to draw upon all those moral, aesthetic, economic, or other distinctions. The political enemy need not be morally evil or aesthetically ugly; he need not appear as an economic competitor, and it may even be advantageous to engage with him in business transactions. But he is, nevertheless, the other, the stranger; and it is sufficient for his nature that he is, in a specially intense way, existentially

From Carl Schmitt, *The Concept of the Political*, trans., intro. and notes George Schwab (University of Chicago Press, Chicago, 1996), pp. 26–7.

something different and alien, so that in the extreme case conflicts with him are possible. These can neither be decided by a previously determined general norm nor by the judgment of a disinterested and therefore neutral third party.

Only the actual participants can correctly recognize, understand, and judge the concrete situation and settle the extreme case of conflict. Each participant is in a position to judge whether the adversary intends to negate his opponent's way of life and therefore must be repulsed or fought in order to preserve one's own form of existence. Emotionally the enemy is easily treated as being evil and ugly, because every distinction, most of all the political, as the strongest and most intense of the distinctions and categorizations, draws upon other distinctions for support. This does not alter the autonomy of such distinctions. Consequently, the reverse is also true: the morally evil, aesthetically ugly or economically damaging need not necessarily be the enemy; the morally good, aesthetically beautiful, and economically profitable need not necessarily become the friend in the specifically political sense of the word. Thereby the inherently objective nature and autonomy of the political becomes evident by virtue of its being able to treat, distinguish, and comprehend the friend-enemy antithesis independently of other antitheses.

# 52

# ECONOMY AND SOCIETY

## Max Weber

[...]

### 2. DIRECT DEMOCRACY AND RULE BY NOTABLES

We are primarily interested in "domination" insofar as it is combined with "administration." Every domination both expresses itself and functions through administration. Every administration, on the other hand, needs domination, because it is always necessary that some powers of command be in the hands of somebody. Possibly the power of command may appear in a rather innocent garb; the ruler may be regarded as their "servant" by the ruled, and he may look upon himself in that way. This phenomenon occurs in its purest form in the so-called, "*immediately democratic*" administration ["direct democracy"].

This kind of administration is called democratic for two reasons which need not necessarily coincide. The first reason is that it is based upon the assumption that everybody is equally qualified to conduct the public affairs. The second: that in this kind of administration the scope of power of command is kept at a minimum. Administrative functions are rotated, or determined by drawing lots, or assigned for short periods by election. All important decisions are reserved to the common resolution of all; the administrative functionaries have only to prepare and carry out the resolutions and to conduct "current business" in accordance with the directives of the general assembly. This type of

From Max Weber, *Economy and Society: An Outline of Interpretive Sociology*, eds Guenther Roth and Claus Wittich (Bedminster Press, New York, 1968), vol. III, pp. 948–52.

administration can be found in many private associations, in certain political communities such as the Swiss *Landesgemeinden* or certain townships in the United States, or in universities (insofar as the administration lies in the hands of the rector and the deans), as well as in numerous other organizations of a similar kind. However modest the administrative function may be, some functionary must have some power of command, and his position is thus always in suspense between that of a mere servant and that of master. It is against the very development of the latter that the "democratic" limits of his position are directed. However, "equality" and "minimization" of the dominant powers of functionaries are also found in many aristocratic groups as against the members of their own ruling layer. Illustrations are afforded by the aristocracy of Venice, Sparta or that of the full professors of a German university. They all have been using those same "democratic" forms of rotation of office, drawing lots, or short-term election.

Normally this kind of administration occurs in organizations which fulfill the following conditions:

1) the organization must be local or otherwise limited in the number of members; 2) the social positions of the members must not greatly differ from each other; 3) the administrative functions must be relatively simple and stable; 4) however, there must be a certain minimum development of training in objectively determining ways and means. This latter requirement exists, for instance, in the direct democratic administrations in Switzerland and the United States just as it existed in the Russian *mir* within the confines of its traditional scope of business. We do not look, however, upon this kind of administration as the historical starting point of any typical course of development but rather as a marginal type case, which lends itself well as the starting point of investigation. Neither taking turns nor drawing lots nor election are "primitive" forms of picking the functionaries of an organization.

Wherever it exists, direct democratic administration is unstable. With every development of economic differentiation arises the probability that administration will fall into the hands of the wealthy. The reason is not that they would have superior personal qualities or more comprehensive knowledge, but simply that they can afford to take the time to carry on the administrative functions cheaply or without any pay and as part-time jobs. Those, however, who are forced to work for a living would have to sacrifice time, which means income, and the more intense labor grows, the more intolerable does this sacrifice become. The bearers of that superiority are thus not simply those who enjoy high incomes but rather those who have an income without personal labor or derive it from intermittent labor. Under otherwise equal conditions a modern manufacturer can thus get away from his work less easily and is correspondingly less available for administrative functions than a land-owner or a medieval merchant patrician, both of whom have not had to work uninterruptedly. For the same reason the directors of the great university clinics and institutes are the least suited to be rectors; although they have plenty of administrative experience, their time is too much occupied with their regular work. Hence in the measure in which those who have to work are becoming unable to get away from it, direct democratic administration will tend to turn into rule by notables (*honoratiores*).

We have already met the type as that of the bearer of a special social honor connected with the mode of living. Here we now encounter another indispensable requirement, viz., that capacity to take care of social administration and rule as an honorific duty which derives from economic position. Hence we shall tentatively define *honoratiores* as follows:

Persons who, *first*, are enjoying an income earned without, or with comparatively little, labor, or at least of such a kind that they can afford to assume administrative functions in addition to whatever business activities they may be carrying on; and who, *second*, by virtue of such income, have a mode of life which attributes to them the social "prestige" of a status honor and thus renders them fit for being called to rule.

Frequently such rule by *honoratiores* has developed in the form of deliberating bodies in which the affairs to be brought before the community are discussed in advance; such bodies easily come to anticipate the resolutions of the community or to eliminate them and thus to establish, by virtue of their prestige, a monopoly of the *honoratiores*. The development of the rule by *honoratiores* in this way has existed a long time in local communities and thus particularly in the neighborhood association. Those *honoratiores* of olden times had a character quite different, however, from those who emerge in the rationalized direct democracy of the present. The original qualification was old age. In all communities which orient their social conduct toward tradition, i.e., toward convention, customary law or sacred law, the elders are, so to speak, the natural *honoratiores* not only because of their prestige of wider experience, but also because they know the traditions. Their consent, advance approval (προβούλευμα), or ratification (*auctoritas*) guarantees the properness of a resolution as against the supernatural powers just as it is the most effective decision in a case of dispute. Where all members of a community are in about the same economic position, the "elders" are simply those oldest in the household, the clan, or the neighborhood.

However, the relative prestige of age within a community is subject to much change. Wherever the food resources are scarce, he who can no longer work is just a burden. Also where war is a chronic state of affairs, the prestige of the older men is liable to sink below that of the warriors and there often develops a democratic bias of the younger groups against the prestige of old age (*sexagenarios de ponte*). The same development occurs in periods of economic or political revolution, whether violent or peaceful, and also where the practical power of religious ideas and thus the veneration of a sacred tradition is little developed or on the decline. The prestige of old age is preserved, on the other hand, wherever the objective usefulness of experience or the subjective power of tradition are estimated highly.

Where the elders are deposed, power normally accrues not to youth but to the bearers of some other kind of social prestige. In the case of economic or status differentiation the councils of elders (γερουσία, *senatus*) may retain its name, but *de facto* it will be composed of *honoratiores* in the sense discussed above, i.e., "economic" *honoratiores*, or bearers of status honor whose power ultimately is also based upon their wealth.

On the other hand, the battle cry that a "democratic" administration must be obtained or preserved may become a powerful tool of the poor in their fight against the *honoratiores*, but also of economically powerful groups which are not admitted to status honor. In that case democratic administration becomes a matter of struggle between political parties, especially since the *honoratiores*, by virtue of their status prestige and the dependency on them of certain groups, can create for themselves "security troops" from among the poor. As soon as it is thus made the object of a struggle for power, direct democratic administration loses its specific feature, the undeveloped state of domination. A political party, after all, exists for the very purpose of fighting for domination in the specific sense, and it thus necessarily tends toward a strict hierarchical structure, however carefully it may be trying to hide this fact.

Something similar to this social alienation of the members, who lived in substantially the same manner in the marginal case of "pure" democracy, occurs where the group grows beyond a certain size or where the administrative function becomes too difficult to be satisfactorily taken care of by anyone whom rotation, the lot, or election may happen to designate. The conditions of administration of mass structures are radically different from those obtaining in small associations resting upon neighborly or personal relationships. As soon as mass administration is involved, the meaning of democracy changes so radically that it no longer makes sense for the sociologist to ascribe to the term the same meaning as in the case discussed so far.

The growing complexity of the administrative tasks and the sheer expansion of their scope increasingly result in the technical superiority of those who have had training and experience, and will thus inevitably favor the continuity of at least some of the functionaries. Hence, there always exists the probability of the rise of a special, perennial structure for administrative purposes, which of necessity means for the exercise of rule. As mentioned before, this structure may be one of *honoratiores*, acting as equal "colleagues," or it may turn out to be "monocratic," so that all functionaries are integrated into a hierarchy culminating in one single head.

### 3. Organizational Structure and the Bases of Legitimate Authority

The predominance of the members of such a structure of domination rests upon the so-called "law of the small number." The ruling minority can quickly reach understanding among its members; it is thus able at any time quickly to initiate that rationally organized action which is necessary to preserve its position of power. Consequently it can easily squelch any action of the masses

(*Massen- oder Gemeinschaftshandeln*) threatening its power as long as the opponents have not created the same kind of organization for the planned direction of their own struggle for domination. Another benefit of the small number is the ease of secrecy as to the intentions and resolutions of the rulers and the state of their information; the larger the circle grows, the more difficult or improbable it becomes to guard such secrets. Wherever increasing stress is placed upon "official secrecy," we take it as a symptom of either an intention of the rulers to tighten the reins of their rule or of a feeling on their part that their rule is being threatened. But every domination established as a continuing one must in some decisive point be *secret rule*.

Generally speaking, however, the specific arrangements for domination, as they are established by association, show the following characteristics:

A circle of people who are accustomed to obedience to the orders of *leaders* and who also have a personal interest in the continuance of the domination by virtue of their own participation and the resulting benefits, have divided among themselves the exercise of those functions which will serve the continuation of the domination and are holding themselves continuously ready for their exercise. (This is what is meant by "organization.") Those leaders who do not derive from grant by others the powers of command claimed and exercised by them, we shall call *masters;* while the term *apparatus* shall mean the circle of those persons who are holding themselves at the disposal of the master or masters in the manner just defined.

[...]

# 53

# POLITICAL PARTIES

## Robert Michels

[...]

The sociological phenomena whose general characteristics have been discussed in this chapter and in preceding ones offer numerous vulnerable points to the scientific opponents of democracy. These phenomena would seem to prove beyond dispute that society cannot exist without a "dominant" or "political" class, and that the ruling class, while its elements are subject to a frequent partial renewal, nevertheless constitutes the only factor of sufficiently durable efficacy in the history of human development. According to this view, the government, or, if the phrase be preferred, the state, cannot be anything other than the organization of a minority. It is the aim of this minority to impose upon the rest of society a "legal order," which is the outcome of the exigencies of dominion and of the exploitation of the mass of helots effected by the ruling minority, and can never be truly representative of the majority. The majority is thus permanently incapable of self-government. Even when the discontent of the masses culminates in a successful attempt to deprive the bourgeoisie of power, this is after all, so Mosca contends, effected only in appearance; always and necessarily there springs from the masses a new organized minority which raises itself to the rank of a governing class.

Thus the majority of human beings, in a condition of eternal tutelage, are predestined by tragic necessity to submit to the dominion of a small minority, and must be content to constitute the pedestal of an oligarchy.

From Robert Michels, *Political Parties: A Sociological Study of the Oligarchical Tendencies of Modern Democracy*, trans. Eden and Cedar Paul (Free Press, New York/Collier Macmillan, London, 1962), chapter 2, pp. 353–6.

The principle that one dominant class inevitably succeeds to another, and the law deduced from that principle that oligarchy is, as it were, a preordained form of the common life of great social aggregates, far from conflicting with or replacing the materialist conception of history, completes that conception and reinforces it. There is no essential contradiction between the doctrine that history is the record of a continued series of class struggles and the doctrine that class struggles invariably culminate in the creation of new oligarchies which undergo fusion with the old. The existence of a political class does not conflict with the essential content of Marxism, considered not as an economic dogma but as a philosophy of history; for in each particular instance the dominance of a political class arises as the resultant of the relationships between the different social forces competing for supremacy, these forces being of course considered dynamically and not quantitatively.

The Russian socialist Alexandre Herzen, whose chief permanent claim to significance is found in the psychological interest of his writings, declared that from the day in which man became accessory to property and his life a continued struggle for money, the political groups of the bourgeois world underwent division into two camps: the owners, tenaciously keeping hold of their millions; and the dispossessed, who would gladly expropriate the owners, but lack the power to do so. Thus historical evolution merely represents an uninterrupted series of oppositions (in the parliamentary sense of this term), "attaining one after another to power, and passing from the sphere of envy to the sphere of avarice."

Thus the social revolution would not effect any real modification of the internal structure of the mass. The socialists might conquer, but not socialism, which would perish in the moment of its adherents' triumph. We are tempted to speak of this process as a tragicomedy in which the masses are content to devote all their energies to effecting a change of masters. All that is left for the workers is the honor "of participating in government recruiting." The result seems a poor one, especially if we take into account the psychological fact that even the purest of idealists who attains to power for a few years is unable to escape the corruption which the exercise of power carries in its train. In France, in working-class circles, the phrase is current, *homme élu, homme foutu.* The social revolution, like the political revolution, is equivalent to an operation by which, as the Italian proverb expresses it: "Si cambia il maestro di cappella, ma la musica è sempre quella."

Fourier defined modern society as a mechanism in which the extremest individual license prevailed, without affording any guarantee to the individual against the usurpations of the mass, or the mass against the usurpations of the individual. History seems to teach us that no popular movement, however energetic and vigorous, is capable of producing profound and permanent changes in the social organism of the civilized world. The preponderant elements of the movement, the men who lead and nourish it, end by undergoing a gradual detachment from the masses, and are attracted within the orbit of the "political class." They perhaps contribute to this class a certain number of "new ideas," but they also endow it with more creative energy and enhanced practical intelligence, thus providing for the ruling class an ever-renewed youth. The "political class" (continuing to employ Mosca's convenient phrase) has unquestionably an extremely fine sense of its possibilities and its means of defense. It displays a remarkable force of attraction and a vigorous capacity for absorption which rarely fail to exercise an influence even upon the most embittered and uncompromising of its adversaries. From the historical point of view, the anti-romanticists are perfectly right when they sum up their scepticism in such caustic phraseology as this: "What is a revolution? People fire guns in a street; that breaks many windows; scarcely anyone profits but the glaziers. The wind carries away the smoke. Those who stay on top push the others under ... It is worth the suffering to turn up so many good paving stones which otherwise could not be moved!" Or we may say, as the song runs in *Madame Angot*: "It's not worth the bother to change the government!" In France, the classic land of social theories and experiments, such pessimism has struck the deepest roots.

# 54

# ANTI-ELITISM REVISITED

## Giovanni Sartori

[...]

### THE IRON LAW OF OLIGARCHY

There still remains a fundamental objection – Michels's 'iron law of oligarchy' – that questions the very possibility of democracy, thereby confronting us with the preliminary problem of how and where we should search to find it. It is true that Michels did not propound a general theory of democracy. He concentrated his attention on the *political party*, and the original title of his most important work, which was written in 1910, was *The Sociology of the Political Party in Modern Democracy*. Nonetheless the conclusions that one can draw from his analysis are undoubtedly crucial to the entire problem of democracy, and this for two reasons.

The first is that a democratic system is, in actual operation, a party system. As Kelsen put it, 'modern democracy is founded entirely on political parties; the greater the application of the democratic principle the more important the parties'. Political parties have indeed become such an essential element that a number of authors perceive democracy not simply as a party system but as a 'party-cracy' (*partitocrazia*), meaning that the locus of power is actually shifted from government and parliament to party directorates. Nor is this all. The phenomenology of parties has a paradigmatic significance. For if the democratic way of life springs from the voluntary creation of small and free communities *inter pares*, parties, too, are formed as voluntary associations and

From Giovanni Sartori, 'Anti-Elitism Revisited', *Government and Opposition*, 13 (1), 1978, pp. 67–71.

are, in fact, their typical political expression in a large-scale democratic system. From this point of view, then, parties become the type of political organism that most closely resemble, or should resemble, the prototype of every authentic political democracy.

There is no doubt that Michels put his finger on a strategic point. Furthermore, and even more tellingly, he dealt with the question of organization, and there is no field of human endeavour, nowadays, that does not seek to enlarge and to perfect its organization. 'Organization' is indeed a crucial element and dimension of our lives. From all points of view, therefore, we cannot underestimate the importance of his conclusion, which is, in a nutshell, that organization destroys democracy and turns it into oligarchy: 'He who says organization, says tendency to oligarchy ... The machinery of organization ... completely inverts the position of the leader in respect to the masses ... Wherever organization is stronger, we observe a smaller degree of applied democracy.'

According to Michels, this is an 'iron law', a process that can neither be averted nor stopped. It is inevitable that every party seeks the greatest possible number of members, and it is inevitable, therefore, that 'opinion parties' gradually turn into 'organization parties'. And since the power of the leader increases as the need for organization grows, all party organization tends to become oligarchical. Michels ended his classic study with the following assertion:

> The existence of headship is an inherent phenomenon of all forms of social life. It is not incumbent on science to find out if it be a good or an evil ... However, there is great scientific as well as practical value in establishing the fact that every system of leadership/rulership is incompatible with the most essential postulates of democracy.

Many criticisms can be made of Michels's diagnosis. In the first place, he speaks of oligarchy and organization without ever clearly defining these concepts. In this connection I have pointed out that Michels may well have an iron law of *bureaucracy*, but only a 'bronze law' (by no means iron-clad) of oligarchy. In any event, the gist of this line of criticism is that since there are many different types of organization, we cannot conclude, without qualification, that all are necessarily oligarchies incompatible with democracy. In the second place, Michels's field of observation is too limited, being chiefly restricted to the German Social Democratic Party. In the third place, he is not justified in passing from the premise, 'Parties are not democratic', to the conclusion 'Democracy is not democratic'. The proof he adduces is too narrow for the breadth of his conclusion.

Notwithstanding all this, Michels's law by and large still holds, if only as a 'bronze law'. For the first objection can be met by observing that the basic argument about organization is a generalization which, vague as it is, does touch on a persistent and persisting trend. The second objection can be answered by saying that Michels's case, the pre-1914 German Social Democratic Party, is always relevant to the large mass parties of Europe, which are hardly more democratic in origin and form. And the third objection has been handled by pointing out that if we extend the investigation to cover all the organized sectors of political activity, especially including the trade unions, we shall probably not find in the other organizations more democracy than Michels found in political parties; and, if so, the conclusion that 'democracy leads to oligarchy' stands.

It can be seen that I take Michels's argument seriously. However, I consider it to be exemplary of how we may seek democracy without ever finding it. If we agree to measure democracy by comparing its organizational forms with the prototype of voluntary associations, it will be hard to prove that Michels is mistaken. But can we proceed from a face-to-face democracy to a nationwide democratic form as if the two things were comparable and belonged to the same continuum? Michels conceives democracy à la Rousseau, just as the democratic critics of our democracies do. As far as the formulation of the problem is concerned, Michels is no different from Proudhon, Marx or Bakunin. They all refer to the matrix of voluntary associations, and using this yardstick come to the conclusion that the political democracy under which we live has no organized form that corresponds to that model.

At this point, the prophecies run counter to one another. Along one path, the future belongs to democracy but its advent is postponed to the day that all the organized superstructures that repress it – above all the state – have been dismantled. Along the other path the superstructures are, if anything, destined to grow and, therefore, democracy is for ever unrealizable. In the first case we consider it possible to enlarge to infinity the prototype of voluntary associations and to convert it into that gigantic self-operating collective entity of which Marx and the anarchists dreamed. In the second case, we recognize that in the process of enlargement the prototype is distorted, and so we conclude that large-scale democracy is purely utopian. However, while the prophecies are at odds, their premise, insofar as it impinges upon the present, is the same: our so-called democracies are apocryphal.

The two camps join forces, in their practical impact, in the same negation because both Michels and the perfectionist, the pessimist and the optimist, are looking for democracy with the same lantern. And the trouble lies in the lantern. That the light of the lantern is poor is blatantly revealed by the fact that it sheds no light on the difference between our allegedly false democracies and actual non-democracies. Neither Marx nor Michels perceives, and is less able to explain, this difference. They are unable to explain it because they never grasped how a large-scale democracy is actually produced. Their mistake lies in making a *similarity test without simile*, I mean, a similarity test applied to a non-reproducible case. They seek democracy in structures and not in interactions. They want to find it immobilized *in*, within something, instead of seeking it *between*, as a dynamic *among* groups and organizations. To be sure, structures are important. But their critical importance lies, with respect to how a macro-democracy comes about, in their interplay. If this point is missed, then we shall always land at where democracy is dead or cannot be, and never arrive at where democracy is alive and exists.

Michels sought democracy *inside* the large organization. But organization is, after all, a response to some 'bigness', to something that otherwise gets out of hand. And the bigger the organism, the more it requires definite and hierarchical structures. So, we organize in order to create not a democratic form but a body that is primarily orderly and efficient which is an entirely different thing. Hence our problem begins at the point where Michels left off. Instead of looking inside an organization, let us observe the relations, in the world of politics, between separate and competing organizations.

Why do they compete? Evidently because they seek allies from the outside, as their strength comes from the numbers that follow them. And how do they compete? Clearly, by promising benefits and advantages to their followers. The consequence is that the unorganized majority of the politically inactive becomes the arbiter in the contest among the organized minorities of the politically active. So, no matter how oligarchic the organization of each minority is when examined from within, nonetheless the result of the competition between them is democracy. More pointedly put, an all-encompassing democracy (representative democracy) *results from* the fact that the *power* of deciding between the competitors is in the hands of the *demos*.

[...]

# CAPITALISM, SOCIALISM AND DEMOCRACY

## Joseph A. Schumpeter

[...]

In the realm of public affairs there are sectors that are more within the reach of the citizen's mind than others. This is true, first, of local affairs. Even there we find a reduced power of discerning facts, a reduced preparedness to act upon them, a reduced sense of responsibility. We all know the man – and a very good specimen he frequently is – who says that the local administration is not his business and callously shrugs his shoulders at practices which he would rather die than suffer in his own office. High-minded citizens in a hortatory mood who preach the responsibility of the individual voter or taxpayer invariably discover the fact that this voter does not feel responsible for what the local politicians do. Still, especially in communities not too big for personal contacts, local patriotism may be a very important factor in "making democracy work." Also, the problems of a town are in many respects akin to the problems of a manufacturing concern. The man who understands the latter also understands, to some extent, the former. The manufacturer, grocer or workman need not step out of his world to have a rationally defensible view (that may of course be right or wrong) on street cleaning or town halls.

Second, there are many national issues that concern individuals and groups so directly and unmistakably as to evoke volitions that are genuine and definite enough. The most important instance is afforded by issues involving immediate and personal pecuniary profit to individual voters and groups of voters, such as

From Joseph A. Schumpeter, *Capitalism, Socialism and Democracy* (Unwin University Books, George Allen & Unwin, London, 1943), pp. 260–3.

direct payments, protective duties, silver policies and so on. Experience that goes back to antiquity shows that by and large voters react promptly and rationally to any such chance. But the classical doctrine of democracy evidently stands to gain little from displays of rationality of this kind. Voters thereby prove themselves bad and indeed corrupt judges of such issues,[1] and often they even prove themselves bad judges of their own long-run interests, for it is only the short-run promise that tells politically and only short-run rationality that asserts itself effectively.

However, when we move still farther away from the private concerns of the family and the business office into those regions of national and international affairs that lack a direct and unmistakable link with those private concerns, individual volition, command of facts and method of inference soon cease to fulfill the requirements of the classical doctrine. What strikes me most of all and seems to me to be the core of the trouble is the fact that the sense of reality[2] is so completely lost. Normally, the great political questions take their place in the psychic economy of the typical citizen with those leisure-hour interests that have not attained the rank of hobbies, and with the subjects of irresponsible conversation. These things seem so far off; they are not at all like a business proposition; dangers may not materialize at all and if they should they may not prove so very serious; one feels oneself to be moving in a fictitious world.

This reduced sense of reality accounts not only for a reduced sense of responsibility but also for the absence of effective volition. One has one's phrases, of course, and one's wishes and daydreams and grumbles; especially, one has one's likes and dislikes. But ordinarily they do not amount to what we call a will – the psychic counterpart of purposeful responsible action. In fact, for the private citizen musing over national affairs there is no scope for such a will and no task at which it could develop. He is a member of an unworkable committee, the committee of the whole nation, and this is why he expends less disciplined effort on mastering a political problem than he expends on a game of bridge.[3]

The reduced sense of responsibility and the absence of effective volition in turn explain the ordinary citizen's ignorance and lack of judgment in matters of domestic and foreign policy which are if anything more shocking in the case of educated people and of people who are successfully active in non-political walks of life than it is with uneducated people in humble stations. Information is plentiful and readily available. But this does not seem to make any difference. Nor should we wonder at it. We need only compare a lawyer's attitude to his brief and the same lawyer's attitude to the statements of political fact presented in his newspaper in order to see what is the matter. In the one case the lawyer has qualified for appreciating the relevance of his facts by years of purposeful labor done under the definite stimulus of interest in his professional competence; and under a stimulus that is no less powerful he then bends his acquirements, his intellect, his will to the contents of the brief. In the other case, he has not taken the trouble to qualify; he does not care to absorb the information or to apply to it the canons of criticism he knows so well how to handle; and he is impatient of long or complicated argument. All of this goes to show that without the initiative that comes from immediate responsibility, ignorance will persist in the face of masses of information however complete and correct. It persists even in the face of the meritorious efforts that are being made to go beyond presenting information and to teach the use of it by means of lectures, classes, discussion groups. Results are not zero. But they are small. People cannot be carried up the ladder.

Thus the typical citizen drops down to a lower level of mental performance as soon as he enters the political field. He argues and analyzes in a way which he would readily recognize as infantile within the sphere of his real interests. He becomes a primitive again. His thinking becomes associative and affective. And this entails two further consequences of ominous significance.

First, even if there were no political groups trying to influence him, the typical citizen would in political matters tend to yield to extra-rational or irrational prejudice and impulse. The weakness of the rational processes he applies to politics and the absence of effective logical control over the results he arrives at would in themselves suffice to account for that. Moreover, simply because he is not "all there," he will relax his usual moral standards as well and occasionally give in to dark urges which the conditions of private life help him to repress. But as to the wisdom or rationality of his inferences and conclusions, it may be just as bad if he gives in to a burst of generous indignation. This will make it still more difficult for him to see things in their correct proportions or even to see more than one aspect of one thing at a time. Hence, if for once he does emerge from his usual vagueness and does display the definite will postulated by the classical doctrine of democracy, he is as likely as not to become still more unintelligent and irresponsible than he usually is. At certain junctures, this may prove fatal to his nation.[4]

Second, however, the weaker the logical element in the processes of the public mind and the more complete the absence of rational criticism and of the rationalizing influence of personal experience and responsibility, the greater are the opportunities for groups with an ax to grind. These groups may consist of professional politicians or of exponents of an economic interest or of idealists of one kind or another or of people simply interested in staging and managing political shows. The sociology of such groups is immaterial to the argument in hand. The only point that matters here is that, Human Nature in Politics being what it is, they are able to fashion and, within very wide limits, even to create the will of the people. What we are confronted with in the analysis of political processes is largely not a genuine but a manufactured will. And often this artefact is all that in reality corresponds to the *volonté générale* of the classical doctrine. So far as this is so, the will of the people is the product and not the motive power of the political process.

The ways in which issues and the popular will on any issue are being manufactured is exactly analogous to the ways of commercial advertising. We find the same attempts to contact the subconscious. We find the same technique of creating favorable and unfavorable associations which are the more effective the less rational they are. We find the same evasions and reticences and the same trick of producing opinion by reiterated assertion that is successful precisely to the extent to which it avoids rational argument and the danger of awakening the critical faculties of the people. And so on. Only, all these arts have infinitely more scope in the sphere of public affairs than they have in the sphere of private and professional life. The picture of the prettiest girl that ever lived will in the long run prove powerless to maintain the sales of a bad cigarette. There is no equally effective safeguard in the case of political decisions. Many decisions of fateful importance are of a nature that makes it impossible for the public to experiment with them at its leisure and at moderate cost. Even if that is possible, however, judgment is as a rule not so easy to arrive at as it is in the case of the cigarette, because effects are less easy to interpret.

But such arts also vitiate, to an extent quite unknown in the field of commercial advertising, those forms of political advertising that profess to address themselves to reason. To the observer, the anti-rational or, at all events, the extra-rational appeal and the defenselessness of the victim stand out more and not less clearly when cloaked in facts and arguments. We have seen above why it is so difficult to impart to the public unbiased information about political problems and logically correct inferences from it and why it is that information and arguments in political matters will "register" only if they link up with the citizen's preconceived ideas.

[. . .]

## NOTES

1. The reason why the Benthamites so completely overlooked this is that they did not consider the possibilities of mass corruption in modern capitalism. Committing in their political theory the same error which they committed in their economic theory, they felt no compunction about postulating that "the people" were the best judges of their own individual interests and that these must necessarily coincide with the interests of all the people taken together. Of course this was made easier for them because actually though not intentionally they philosophized in terms of bourgeois interests which had more to gain from a parsimonious state than from any direct bribes.

2. William James' "pungent sense of reality." The relevance of this point has been particularly emphasized by Graham Wallas.

3. It will help to clarify the point if we ask ourselves why so much more intelligence and clear-headedness show up at a bridge table than in, sav. political discussion among non-politicians. At the bridge table we have a definite task; we have rules that discipline us; success and failure are clearly defined; and we are prevented from behaving irresponsibly because every mistake we make will not only immediately tell but also be immediately allocated to us. These conditions, by their failure to be fulfilled for the political behavior of the ordinary citizen, show why it is that in politics he lacks all the alertness and the judgment he may display in his profession.

4. The importance of such bursts cannot be doubted. But it is possible to doubt their genuineness. Analysis will show in many instances that they are induced by the action of some group and do not spontaneously arise from the people. In this case they enter into a (second) class of phenomena which we are about to deal with. Personally, I do

believe that genuine instances exist. But I cannot be sure that more thorough analysis would not reveal some psycho-technical effort at the bottom of them.

Society is indeed a contract. Subordinate contracts for objects of mere occasional interest may be dissolved at pleasure – but the state ought not to be considered as nothing better than a partnership agreement in a trade of pepper and coffee, callico or tobacco, or some other such low concern, to be taken up for a little temporary interest, and to be dissolved by the fancy of the parties. It is to be looked on with other reverence; because it is not a partnership in things subservient only to the gross animal existence of a temporary and perishable nature. It is a partnership in all science; a partnership in all art; a partnership in every virtue, and in all perfection. As the ends of such a partnership cannot be obtained in many generations, it becomes a partnership not only between those who are living, but between those who are living, those who are dead, and those who are to be born. Each contract of each particular state is but a clause in the great primaeval contract of eternal society, linking the lower with the higher natures, connecting the visible and invisible world, according to a fixed compact sanctioned by the inviolable oath which holds all physical and all moral natures, each in their appointed place. This law is not subject to the will of those, who by an obligation above them, and infinitely superior, are bound to submit their will to that law. The municipal corporations of that universal kingdom are not morally at liberty at their pleasure, and on their speculations of a contingent improvement, wholly to separate and tear asunder the bands of their subordinate community, and to dissolve it into an unsocial, uncivil, unconnected chaos of elementary principles. It is the first and supreme necessity only, a necessity that is not chosen but chooses, a necessity paramount to deliberation, that admits no discussion, and demands no evidence, which alone can justify a resort to anarchy. This necessity is no exception to the rule; because this necessity itself is a part too of that moral and physical disposition of things to which man must be obedient by consent or force; but if that which is only submission to necessity should be made the object of choice, the law is broken, nature is disobeyed, and the rebellious are outlawed, cast forth, and exiled, from this world of reason, and order, and peace, and virtue, and fruitful penitence, into the antagonist world of madness, discord, vice, confusion, and unavailing sorrow.

# THE MEANING OF CONSERVATISM

## Roger Scruton

[...]

### DEMOCRACY

Let us begin with the contagion of democracy, now raging so wildly that it is possible to mistake its high flush of fever for the light of health. De Tocqueville wrote of this disease that it 'not only makes each man forget his forefathers, but it conceals from him his descendants and separates him from his contemporaries; it ceaselessly throws him back on himself alone and threatens finally to confine him entirely in the solitude of his own heart'. That is a strong way of putting it, and one that reflects the bitterness spread by the French Revolution in the hearts of all its descendants. But it contains a truth. The constitution that we have inherited has been slowly, and comparatively recently, subject to the democratic principle, not on account of popular pressure so much as of political faction. It is hard to know whether unenfranchised citizens are happier or unhappier than their fellows; hard to know whether they lament their state, or rather borrow their lamentations from others whose interest is not franchise but power, hard to know whether the right to vote would be missed by the populace were it now to be removed from them. Naturally people have rioted in the cause of franchise, as in every other cause that has seemed to spell the instant remedy for present evils. But outbreaks of agitation, whether in Bristol or Barcelona, Moscow or Tehran, show nothing about the value of what is called for, and nothing about its lasting popularity. (In all such matters one must remember the

From Roger Scruton, *The Meaning of Conservatism*, 2nd edn (Macmillan, London, 1984), pp. 53–6.

# SECTION 8
# FEMINIST CRITIQUES

# FEMINIST CRITIQUES
# INTRODUCTION

As we have seen, some critiques of liberal democracy intend not so much to reject its basic principles as to question whether the realities of power in society allow for their adequate realisation. In this way, the Marxist critique of liberal democracy serves to illuminate the actual 'rule of capital'. In a similar vein, the feminist critique highlights the actual oppression of women by men and the impact of gender inequality on the construction of democratic theory and practice.

Feminism identifies and describes a form of power, that of patriarchy, which has all too often fallen outside the remit of democracy. Patriarchal power, it argues, is evident, and indeed widespread, throughout our political and social institutions. Male domination of these institutions results in a profound, and usually concealed, gender inequality. This actual inequality is then seen to undermine the fundamental democratic principle of political equality.

Gender inequality has taken many forms. Historically, women have been assumed to be adequately represented by men who owned their property, their children and even their person. It has also resulted in systematic exclusion from participation, relegation to a domestic realm assumed to be non-political, and a history of democratic thought that either ignores women altogether or presents them in a series of distorted images.

The first significant theoretical analysis of women's claim for equal rights was penned by *Mary Wollstonecraft*. In *A Vindication of the Rights of Woman* (1792), Wollstonecraft both states the case for women's oppression and argues against natural sexual difference. At the time, Rousseau's ideas on women were influential, and so Wollstonecraft directly attacks his position. This critique began a strand of feminist democratic theory, which was to clarify a number of fundamental tensions within liberal-democracy itself.

The fruits of this process are evident in our first selection here by *Coole*, which explores the ways in which women have been treated in the male canon of democratic thought. Her exposition of Rousseau's attitude to women serves to introduce us to a series of emergent problems in social contract and liberal-democratic thought.

Women, of course, were excluded from political participation in all democracies until the early twentieth century. Yet even when they were granted the vote, they continued to struggle with a pervasive social and economic inequality which effectively undermined their newly acquired rights. In attempting to analyse the ways in which this undermining occurs, feminism sought greater clarification of liberal democracy's distinction between the private and the public spheres and its tension between universalism and difference.

In liberal democracy, the public sphere is the arena of collective decision-making and the political struggle over power. The private is an arena of individual freedom, a domestic and non-political realm, one in which the state should generally refrain from interfering. Feminism argues that the realities of patriarchal power are such that this division effectively becomes a gendered one, with women relegated, both socially and economically, to the private sphere, and men systematically favoured in the public. Efforts to restrict democracy to the public sphere therefore deny the importance of women's work and lives, and pretend that the private sphere is not a site of power.

The growth of the women's movement in the 1960s, here described by *Rowbotham*, saw a series of attempts to overcome the problems presented by this gendered distinction, and to invent alternative methods of representing women's interests in the political process.

Finally, the feminist critique of liberal democracy has served to clarify the tension between the universalism of democracy's principles and the real differences between people. The claim to universal rights, for example, as well as that of impartiality, are quite intentionally abstract and general. One of liberal democracy's strengths, then, is precisely its blindness to difference.

The feminist critique, however, shows these apparently universal ideals to be, in fact, particular. As *Mendus* shows, the abstract individual which forms the basic unit of liberal-democracy has always been a man, an actor in the public sphere, a male property accumulator. Thus claims of universalism and impartiality serve to mask a significant gender bias. Universalism is thereby seen to be ideological, and to be underplaying the real differences between men and women. As a result, women, all too often, are seen as inadequate men.

Feminist critics such as Mendus, Phillips and Mouffe therefore seek a participatory democracy that celebrates, rather than ignores, gender difference. They raise serious problems with liberal-democracy's distinctions between the private and the public, the universal and the particular, and the ways in which the politics of everyday personal interactions is covered up. They seek to extend the boundaries of the political to other sites where power really does operate in our society and thereby to deepen democracy in our everyday lives.

# 56

# VINDICATION OF THE RIGHTS OF WOMAN

## Mary Wollstonecraft

[...]

But should it be proved that woman is naturally weaker than man, whence does it follow that it is natural for her to labour to become still weaker than nature intended her to be? Arguments of this cast are an insult to common sense, and savour of passion. The *divine right* of husbands, like the divine right of kings, may, it is to be hoped, in this enlightened age, be contested without danger; and though conviction may not silence many boisterous disputants, yet, when any prevailing prejudice is attacked, the wise will consider, and leave the narrow-minded to rail with thoughtless vehemence at innovation.

The mother who wishes to give true dignity of character to her daughter must, regardless of the sneers of ignorance, proceed on a plan diametrically opposite to that which Rousseau has recommended with all the deluding charms of eloquence and philosophic sophistry, for his eloquence renders absurdities plausible, and his dogmatic conclusions puzzle, without convincing, those who have not ability to refute them.

Throughout the whole animal kingdom every young creature requires almost continual exercise, and the infancy of children, conformable to this intimation, should be passed in harmless gambols that exercise the feet and hands, without requiring very minute direction from the head, or the constant attention of a nurse. In fact, the care necessary for self-preservation is the first natural exercise of the understanding as little inventions to amuse the present moment unfold

From Mary Wollstonecraft, *A Vindication of the Rights of Woman*, ed. and intro. Miriam Brody Kamnick (Penguin Books, Harmondsworth, 1975), pp. 127–40. Originally written in 1792.

the imagination. But these wise designs of nature are counteracted by mistaken fondness or blind zeal. The child is not left a moment to its own direction – particularly a girl – and thus rendered dependent. Dependence is called natural.

To preserve personal beauty – woman's glory – the limbs and faculties are cramped with worse than Chinese bands, and the sedentery life which they are condemned to live, whilst boys frolic in the open air, weakens the muscles and relaxes the nerves. As for Rousseau's remarks, which have since been echoed by several writers, that they have naturally, that is, from their birth, independent of education, a fondness for dolls, dressing, and talking, they are so puerile as not to merit a serious refutation. That a girl, condemned to sit for hours together listening to the idle chat of weak nurses, or to attend at her mother's toilet, will endeavour to join the conversation, is, indeed, very natural; and that she will imitate her mother or aunts, and amuse herself by adorning her lifeless doll, as they do in dressing her, poor innocent babe! is undoubtedly a most natural consequence. For men of the greatest abilities have seldom had sufficient strength to rise above the surrounding atmosphere; and if the pages of genius have always been blurred by the prejudices of the age, some allowance should be made for a sex, who, like kings, always see things through a false medium.

In this manner, may the fondness for dress, conspicuous in woman, be easily accounted for, without supposing it the result of a desire to please the sex on which they are dependent. The absurdity, in short, of supposing that a girl is naturally a coquette, and that a desire connected with the impulse of nature to propagate the species, should appear even before an improper education has, by heating the imagination, called it forth prematurely, is so unphilosophical, that such a sagacious observer as Rousseau would not have adopted it, if he had not been accustomed to make reason give way to his desire of singularity, and truth to a favourite paradox.

Yet thus to give a sex to mind was not very consistent with the principles of a man who argued so warmly, and so well, for the immortality of the soul. But what a weak barrier is truth when it stands in the way of an hypothesis! Rousseau respected – almost adored virtue – and yet he allowed himself to love with sensual fondness. His imagination constantly prepared inflammable fuel for his inflammable senses; but, in order to reconcile his respect for self-denial, fortitude, and those heroic virtues, which a mind like his could not coolly admire, he labours to invert a law of nature, and broaches a doctrine pregnant with mischief, and derogatory to the character of supreme wisdom.

His ridiculous stories, which tend to prove that girls are *naturally* attentive to their persons, without laying any stress on daily example, are below contempt. And that a little miss should have such a correct taste as to neglect the pleasing amusement of making O's, merely because she perceived that it was an ungraceful attitude, should be selected with the anecdotes of the learned pig.[1]

I have, probably, had an opportunity of observing more girls in their infancy than J. J. Rousseau. I can recollect my own feelings, and I have looked steadily around me; yet, so far from coinciding with him in opinion respecting the first dawn of the female character, I will venture to affirm, that a girl, whose spirits have not been damped by inactivity, or innocence tainted by false shame, will always be a romp, and the doll will never excite attention unless confinement allows her no alternative. Girls and boys, in short, would play harmlessly together, if the distinction of sex was not inculcated long before nature makes any difference. I will go further, and affirm, as an indisputable fact, that most of the women, in the circle of my observation, who have acted like rational creatures, or shown any vigour of intellect, have accidentally been allowed to run wild, as some of the elegant formers of the fair sex would insinuate.

The baneful consequences which flow from inattention to health during infancy and youth, extend further than is supposed – dependence of body naturally produces dependence of mind; and how can she be a good wife or mother, the greater part of whose time is employed to guard against or endure sickness? Nor can it be expected that a woman will resolutely endeavour to strengthen her constitution and abstain from enervating indulgences, if artificial notions of beauty, and false descriptions of sensibility, have been early entangled with her motives of action. Most men are sometimes obliged to bear with bodily inconveniences, and to endure, occasionally, the inclemency of the elements; but genteel women are, literally speaking, slaves to their bodies, and glory in their subjection.

I once knew a weak woman of fashion, who was more than commonly proud of her delicacy and sensibility. She thought a distinguishing taste and puny appetite the height of all human perfection, and acted accordingly. I have seen this weak sophisticated being neglect all the duties of life, yet recline with self-complacency on a sofa, and boast of her want of appetite as a proof of delicacy that extended to, or, perhaps, arose from, her exquisite sensibility; for it is difficult to render intelligible such ridiculous jargon. Yet, at the moment, I have seen her insult a worthy old gentlewoman, whom unexpected misfortunes had made dependent on her ostentatious bounty, and who, in better days, had claims on her gratitude. Is it possible that a human creature could have become such a weak and depraved being, if, like the Sybarites, dissolved in luxury, everything like virtue had not been worn away, or never impressed by precept, a poor substitute, it is true, for cultivation of mind, though it serves as a fence against vice?

Such a woman is not a more irrational monster than some of the Roman emperors, who were depraved by lawless power. Yet, since kings have been more under the restraint of law, and the curb, however weak, of honour, the records of history are not filled with such unnatural instances of folly and cruelty, nor does the despotism that kills virtue and genius in the bud, hover over Europe with that destructive blast which desolates Turkey, and renders the men, as well as the soil, unfruitful.

Women are everywhere in this deplorable state; for, in order to preserve their innocence, as ignorance is courteously termed, truth is hidden from them, and they are made to assume an artificial character before their faculties have acquired any strength. Taught from their infancy that beauty is woman's sceptre, the mind shapes itself to the body, and roaming round its gilt cage, only seeks to adore its prison. Men have various employments and pursuits which engage their attention, and give a character to the opening mind; but women, confined to one, and having their thoughts constantly directed to the most insignificant part of themselves, seldom extend their views beyond the triumph of the hour. But were their understanding once emancipated from the slavery to which the pride and sensuality of man and their short-sighted desire, like that of dominion in tyrants, of present sway, has subjected them, we should probably read of their weaknesses with surprise. I must be allowed to pursue the argument a little further.

Perhaps, if the existence of an evil being were allowed, who, in the allegorical language of Scripture, went about seeking whom he should devour, he could not more effectually degrade the human character, than by giving a man absolute power.

This argument branches into various ramifications. Birth, riches, and every extrinsic advantage that exalt a man above his fellows, without any mental exertion, sink him in reality below them. In proportion to his weakness, he is played upon by designing men, till the bloated monster has lost all traces of humanity. And that tribes of men, like flocks of sheep, should quietly follow such a leader, is a solecism that only a desire of present enjoyment and narrowness of understanding can solve. Educated in slavish dependence, and enervated by luxury and sloth, where shall we find men who will stand forth to assert the rights of man, or claim the privilege of moral beings, who should have but one road to excellence? Slavery to monarchs and ministers, which the world will be long in freeing itself from, and whose deadly grasp stops the progress of the human mind, is not yet abolished.

Let not men then in the pride of power, use the same arguments that tyrannic kings and venal ministers have used, and fallaciously assert that woman ought to be subjected because she has always been so. But, when man, governed by reasonable laws, enjoys his natural freedom, let him despise woman, if she do not share it with him; and, till that glorious period arrives, in descanting on the folly of the sex, let him not overlook his own.

Women, it is true, obtaining power by unjust means, by practising or fostering vice, evidently lose the rank which reason would assign them, and they become either abject slaves or capricious tyrants. They lose all simplicity, all dignity of mind, in acquiring power, and act as men are observed to act when they have been exalted by the same means.

It is time to effect a revolution in female manners – time to restore to them their lost dignity – and make them, as a part of the human species, labour by reforming themselves to reform the world. It is time to separate unchangeable morals from local manners. If men be demi-gods, why let us serve them! And if the dignity of the female soul be as disputable as that of animals – if their reason does not afford sufficient light to direct their conduct whilst unerring instinct is denied – they are surely of all creatures the most miserable! and, bent beneath the iron hand of destiny, must submit to be a *fair defect* in creation. But to justify the ways of Providence respecting them, by pointing out some irrefragable reason for thus making such a large portion of mankind accountable and not accountable, would puzzle the subtilest casuist.

The only solid foundation for morality appears to be the character of the Supreme Being; the harmony of which arises from a balance of attributes; – and, to speak with reverence, one attribute seems to imply the *necessity* of another. He must be just, because He is wise; He must be good, because He is omnipotent. For to exalt one attribute at the expense of another equally noble and necessary, bears the stamp of the warped reason of man – the homage of passion. Man, accustomed to bow down to power in his savage state, can seldom divest himself of this barbarous prejudice, even when civilization determines how much superior mental is to bodily strength; and his reason is clouded by these crude opinions, even when he thinks of the Deity. His omnipotence is made to swallow up, or preside over His other attributes, and those mortals are supposed to limit His power irreverently, who think that it must be regulated by His wisdom.

I disclaim that specious humility which, after investigating nature, stops at the Author. The High and Lofty One, who inhabiteth eternity, doubtless possesses many attributes of which we can form no conception; but Reason tells me that they cannot clash with those I adore – and I am compelled to listen to her voice.

It seems natural for man to search for excellence, and either to trace it in the object that he worships, or blindly to invest it with perfection, as a garment. But what good effect can the latter mode of worship have on the moral conduct of a rational being? He bends to power; he adores a dark cloud, which may open a bright prospect to him, to burst in angry, lawless fury, on his devoted head – he knows not why. And, supposing that the Deity acts from the vague impulse of an undirected will, man must also follow his own, or act according to rules, deduced from principles which he disclaims as irreverent. Into this dilemma have both enthusiasts and cooler thinkers fallen, when they laboured to free men from the wholesome restraints which a just conception of the character of God imposes.

It is not impious thus to scan the attributes of the Almighty: in fact, who can avoid it that exercises his faculties? For to love God as the fountain of wisdom, goodness, and power, appears to be the only worship useful to a being who wishes to acquire either virtue or knowledge. A blind unsettled affection may, like human passions, occupy the mind and warm the heart, whilst, to do justice, love mercy, and walk humbly with our God, is forgotten. I shall pursue this subject still further, when I consider religion in a light opposite to that recommended by Dr Gregory, who treats it as a matter of sentiment or taste.

To return from this apparent digression. It were to be wished that women would cherish an affection for their husbands, founded on the same principle that devotion ought to rest upon. No other firm base is there under heaven – for let them beware of the fallacious light of sentiment; too often used as a softer phrase for sensuality. It follows then, I think, that from their infancy women should either be shut up like Eastern princes, or educated in such a manner as to be able to think and act for themselves.

Why do men halt between two opinions, and expect impossibilities? Why do they expect virtue from a slave, from a being whom the constitution of civil society has rendered weak, if not vicious?

Still I know that it will require a considerable length of time to eradicate the firmly rooted prejudices which sensualists have planted; it will also require some time to convince women that they act contrary to their real interest on an enlarged scale, when they cherish or affect weakness under the name of delicacy, and to convince the world that the poisoned source of female vices and follies, if it be necessary, in compliance with custom, to use synonymous terms in a lax sense, has been the sensual homage paid to beauty: – to beauty of features; for it has been shrewdly observed by a German writer, that a pretty woman, as an object of desire, is generally allowed to be so by men of all descriptions; whilst a fine woman, who inspires more sublime emotions by displaying intellectual beauty, may be overlooked or observed with indifference, by those men who find their happiness in the gratification of their appetites. I foresee an obvious retort – whilst man remains such an imperfect being as he appears hitherto to have been, he will, more or less, be the slave of his appetites; and those women obtaining most power who gratify a predominant one, the sex is degraded by a physical, if not by a moral necessity.

This objection has, I grant, some force; but while such a sublime precept exists, as, 'Be pure as your heavenly Father is pure'; it would seem that the virtues of man are not limited by the Being who alone could limit them; and that he may press forward without considering whether he steps out of his sphere by indulging such a noble ambition. To the wild billows it has been said, 'Thus far shalt thou go, and no farther; and here shall thy proud waves be stayed.' Vainly then do they beat and foam, restrained by the power that confines the struggling planets in their orbits, matter yields to the great governing Spirit. But an immortal soul, not restrained by mechanical laws and struggling to free itself from the shackles of matter, contributes to, instead of disturbing, the order of creation, when, co-operating with the Father of spirits, it tries to govern itself by the invariable rule that, in a degree, before which our imagination faints, the universe is regulated.

Besides, if women be educated for dependence, that is, to act according to the will of another fallible being, and submit, right or wrong, to power, where are we to stop? Are they to be considered as vicegerents allowed to reign over a small domain, and answerable for their conduct to a higher tribunal, liable to error?

It will not be difficult to prove that such delegates will act like men subjected by fear, and make their children and servants endure their tyrannical oppression. As they submit without reason, they will, having no fixed rules to square their conduct by, be kind, or cruel, just as the whim of the moment directs; and we ought not to wonder if sometimes, galled by their heavy yoke, they take a malignant pleasure in resting it on weaker shoulders.

But, supposing a woman, trained up to obedience, be married to a sensible man, who directs her judgement without making her feel the servility of her subjection, to act with as much propriety by this reflected light as can be expected when reason is taken at secondhand, yet she cannot ensure the life of her protector; he may die and leave her with a large family.

A double duty devolves on her; to educate them in the character of both father and mother; to form their principles and secure their property. But, alas! she has never thought, much less acted for herself. She has only learned to please[2] men, to depend gracefully on them; yet, encumbered with children, how is she to obtain another protector – a husband to supply the place of reason? A rational man, for we are not treading on romantic ground, though he may think her a pleasing docile creature, will not choose to marry a *family* for love, when the world contains many more pretty creatures. What is then to become of her? She either falls an easy prey to some mean fortune-hunter, who defrauds her children of their paternal inheritance, and renders her miserable; or becomes the victim of discontent and blind indulgence. Unable to educate her sons, or impress them with respect, – for it is not a play on words to assert, that people are never respected, though filling an important station, who are not respectable, – she pines under the anguish of unavailing impotent regret. The serpent's tooth enters into her very soul, and the vices of licentious youth bring her with sorrow, if not with poverty also, to the grave.

This is not an overcharged picture; on the contrary, it is a very possible case, and something similar must have fallen under every attentive eye.

I have, however, taken it for granted, that she was well disposed, though experience shows, that the blind may as easily be led into a ditch as along the beaten road. But supposing, no very improbable conjecture, that a being only taught to please must still find her happiness in pleasing; what an example of folly, not to say vice, will she be to her innocent daughters! The mother will be lost in the coquette, and, instead of making friends of her daughters, view them with eyes askance, for they are rivals – rivals more cruel than any other, because they invite a comparison, and drive her from the throne of beauty, who has never thought of a seat on the bench of reason.

It does not require a lively pencil, or the discriminating outline of a caricature, to sketch the domestic miseries and petty vices which such a mistress of a family diffuses. Still she only acts as a woman ought to act, brought up according to Rousseau's system. She can never be reproached for being masculine, or turning out of her sphere; nay, she may observe another of his grand rules, and, cautiously preserving her reputation free from spot, be reckoned a good kind of woman. Yet in what respect can she be termed good? She abstains, it is true, without any great struggle, from committing gross crimes; but how does she fulfil her duties? Duties! in truth she has enough to think of to adorn her body and nurse a weak constitution.

With respect to religion, she never presumed to judge for herself; but conformed, as a dependent creature should, to the ceremonies of the Church which she was brought up in, piously believing that wiser heads than her own have settled that business; and not to doubt is her point of perfection. She therefore pays her tithe of mint and cumin – and thanks her God that she is not as other women are. These are the blessed effects of a good education! These are the virtues of man's helpmate![3]

I must relieve myself by drawing a different picture.

Let fancy now present a woman with a tolerable understanding, for I do not wish to leave the line of mediocrity, whose constitution, strengthened by exercise, has allowed her body to acquire its full vigour; her mind, at the same time, gradually expanding itself to comprehend the moral duties of life, and in what human virtue and dignity consist.

Formed thus by the discharge of the relative duties of her station, she marries from affection, without losing sight of prudence, and looking beyond matrimonial felicity, she secures her husband's respect before it is necessary to exert mean arts to please him and feed a dying flame, which nature doomed to expire when the object became familiar, when friendship and forbearance take place of a more ardent affection. This is the natural death of love, and domestic peace is not destroyed by struggles to prevent its extinction. I also suppose the husband to be virtuous; or she is still more in want of independent principles.

Fate, however, breaks this tie. She is left a widow, perhaps, without a sufficient provision; but she is not desolate! The pang of nature is felt; but after time has softened sorrow into melancholy resignation, her heart turns to her children with redoubled fondness, and anxious to provide for them, affection gives a sacred heroic cast to her maternal duties. She thinks that not only the eye sees her virtuous efforts from whom all her comfort now must flow, and whose approbation is life; but her imagination, a little abstracted and exalted by grief, dwells on the fond hope that the eyes which her trembling hand closed, may still see how she subdues every wayward passion to fulfil the double duty of being the father as well as the mother of her children. Raised to heroism by misfortunes, she represses the first faint dawning of a natural inclination, before it ripens into love, and in the bloom of life forgets her sex – forgets the pleasure of an awakening passion, which might again have been inspired and returned. She no longer thinks of pleasing, and conscious dignity prevents her from priding herself on account of the praise which her conduct demands. Her children have her love, and her brightest hopes are beyond the grave, where her imagination often strays.

I think I see her surrounded by her children, reaping the reward of her care. The intelligent eye meets hers, whilst health and innocence smile on their chubby cheeks, and as they grow up the cares of life are lessened by their grateful attention. She lives to see the virtues which she endeavoured to plant on principles, fixed into habits, to see her children attain a strength of character sufficient to enable them to endure adversity without forgetting their mother's example.

The task of life thus fulfilled, she calmly waits for the sleep of death, and rising from the grave, may say – 'Behold, Thou gavest me a talent, and here are five talents.'

I wish to sum up what I have said in a few words, for I here throw down my gauntlet, and deny the existence of sexual virtues, not excepting modesty. For man and woman, truth, if I understand the meaning of the word, must be the same; yet the fanciful female character, so prettily drawn by poets and novelists, demanding the sacrifice of truth and sincerity, virtue becomes a relative idea, having no other foundation than utility, and of that utility men pretend arbitrarily to judge, shaping it to their own convenience.

Women, I allow, may have different duties to fulfil; but they are *human* duties, and the principles that should regulate the discharge of them, I sturdily maintain, must be the same.

To become respectable, the exercise of their understanding is necessary, there is no other foundation for independence of character; I mean explicitly to say that they must only bow to the authority of reason, instead of being the *modest* slaves of opinion.

In the superior ranks of life how seldom do we meet with a man of superior abilities, or even common acquirements? The reason appears to me clear, the state they are born in was an unnatural one. The human character has ever been formed by the employments the individual, or class, pursues; and if the faculties are not sharpened by necessity, they must remain obtuse. The argument may fairly be extended to women; for, seldom occupied by serious business, the pursuit of pleasure gives that insignificancy to their character which renders the society of the *great* so insipid. The same want of firmness, produced by a similar cause, forces them both to fly from themselves to noisy pleasures, and artificial passions, till vanity takes place of every social affection, and the characteristics of humanity can scarcely be discerned. Such are the blessings of civil governments, as they are at present organized, that wealth and female softness equally tend to debase mankind, and are produced by the same cause; but allowing women to be rational creatures, they should be incited to acquire virtues which they may call their own, for how can a rational being be ennobled by anything that is not obtained by its *own* exertions?

## NOTES

1. 'I once knew a young person who learned to write before she learned to read, and began to write with her needle before she could use a pen. At first, indeed, she took it into her head to make no letter than the O: this letter she was constantly making of all sizes, and always the wrong way. Unluckily, one day, as she was intent on this employment, she happened to see herself in the looking-glass; when, taking a dislike to the constrained attitude in which she sat while writing, she threw away her pen, like another Pallas, and determined against making the O any more. Her brother was also

equally averse to writing; it was the confinement, however, and not the constrained attitude, that most disgusted him.' – ROUSSEAU'S *Emilius*.

2. In the union of the sexes, both pursue one common object, but not in the same manner. From their diversity in this particular, arises the first determinate difference between the moral relations of each. The one should be active and strong, the other passive and weak; it is necessary the one should have both the power and the will, and that the other should make little resistance.

'This principle being established, it follows that woman is expressly formed to please the man: if the obligation be reciprocal also, and the man ought to please in his turn, it is not so immediately necessary: his great merit is in his power, and he pleases merely because he is strong. This, I must confess, is not one of the refined maxims of love; it is, however, one of the laws of nature, prior to love itself.

'If woman be formed to please and be subjected to man, it is her place, doubtless, to render herself agreeable to him, instead of challenging his passion. The violence of his desires depends on her charms; it is by means of these she should urge him to the exertion of those powers which nature hath given him. The most successful method of exciting them, is, to render such exertion necessary by resistance; as, in that case, self-love is added to desire, and the one triumphs in the victory which the other is obliged to acquire. Hence arise the various modes of attack and defence between the sexes; the boldness of one sex and the timidity of the other; and, in a word, that bashfulness and modesty with which nature hath armed the weak in order to subdue the strong.' – ROUSSEAU'S *Emilius*.

I shall make no other comment on this ingenious passage than just to observe, that it is the philosophy of lasciviousness.

3. 'O how lovely,' exclaims Rousseau, speaking of Sophia, 'is her ignorance! Happy is he who is destined to instruct her! She will never pretend to be the tutor of her husband, but will be content to be his pupil. Far from attempting to subject him to her taste, she will accommodate herself to his. She will be more estimable to him, than if she was learned, he will have a pleasure in instructing her.' – ROUSSEAU'S *Emilius*.

I shall content myself with simply asking, how friendship can subsist when love expires, between the master and his pupil.

# 57

# WOMEN IN POLITICAL THEORY

## Diana Coole

[...]

Okin argues that Rousseau's views on women 'violate all the major principles of his ethics and social theory'. Examples of such violation abound. Rousseau demands equality and autonomy among male citizens but authority and heteronomy in the family. He sees that men cannot be free while they depend on the economic or arbitrary power of other men yet he deliberately fosters women's dependence on husbands, from provision of their daily bread to choice of their religion and judgement of their virtue. He looks back to the originally free and self-sufficient natural man whose liberty is to be recaptured in civil life, yet the natural woman he idealizes is the dependent being of the patriarchal family. He advises male citizens to suppress their private interests on behalf of the General Will, yet he would imprison women in the particularity of domestic life. He sees in men a limitless drive to self-improvement through development of their rational capacities, yet defines women according to natural functions which yield them moral and psychological qualities of a fixed and limited type. In short, if Rousseau's political thinking is inspired by Locke, his sexual beliefs are closer to Aristotle.

The characteristics ascribed to women rob them of the credentials for citizenship: they lack the right sort of reason, autonomy, judgement, sense of justice and ability to consent. We have already seen that Locke probably doubted women's rational qualifications for active political membership but

From Diana Coole, *Women in Political Theory. From Ancient Misogyny to Contemporary Feminism*, 2nd edn (Harvester-Wheatsheaf, Hemel Hempstead, 1993), pp. 85–92.

that this only resulted from a lack of opportunity to develop their faculties. Rousseau returns to more traditional claims regarding innate sexual differences here. Although women do have reason, he writes in *Emile*, it is of a practical nature. Woman lacks the accuracy or attention for success in the sciences; she cannot appreciate genius. For abstract and speculative truths, principles and axioms, generalizations as such, are beyond her grasp. Of course, the education that Rousseau advises makes this a self-fulfilling prognosis, but it is of obvious significance in the political sphere where it is just that reasoning of which he finds women incapable, which is required to discern the General Will.

In order for the General Will to emerge, individuals must not only reason but they must do so independently. Should their thoughts be too influenced by others' beliefs or interests, then the delicate balancing of individual differences will degenerate into clusters of particularity. Yet it is impossible to imagine Rousseau's women making any impartial assessment of the public good, since they have been raised to make no independent judgement: their guide is always the question 'what will others think of me?' Appearance is for them everything. They lack a capacity to penetrate to, or articulate, truth. In any case, confinement in the home surely denies to Sophy and her sisters the breadth of vision which they need to evaluate public issues. The 'genuine mother of a family', Rousseau insists, 'is no woman of the world, she is almost as much of a recluse as the nun in her convent' She has her sights fixed on the well-being of her particular family, not on the world outside. She is not therefore predisposed to considerations of impersonal justice and Rousseau goes so far as to suggest that this is a natural limitation: 'woman is made to submit to man and to endure even injustice at his hands. You will never bring young lads to this; their feelings rise in revolt against injustice; nature has not fitted them to put up with it.'

Finally, it is evident that women cannot give the sort of consent needed in the polity – or, what comes to the same thing, they are incapable of withdrawing consent and so of making its grant meaningful. In the family, their duty is to arouse their husband's desire only to control it through a natural modesty which men lack. It is left to men to interpret the real message that might be at odds with more overt expressions:

> Why do you consult their words when it is not their mouths that speak? Consult their eyes, their colour, their breathing, their timid manner, their slight resistance, that is the language nature gave them for your answer. The lips always say no, and rightly so; but the tone is not always the same, and that cannot lie. Has not a woman the same needs as a man, but without the same right to make them known?

She who says 'no' when she means 'yes', whose real language is that of the body rather than of the mind and who responds to passion by camouflaging rather than transcending it, is hardly a candidate for the General Will.

Thanks to all these lacunae in their reason, autonomy, judgement and consent, women are thus as unsuited to the ideals of citizenship as are the unreconstructed males of the *Second Discourse*. The only difference is that their shortcomings are natural and hence immutable. It might be argued, of course, that it is in their very feminine qualities (whether natural or acquired) that women are uniquely well equipped for the sort of communitarian politics Rousseau envisaged. Separated from property acquisition, they are rarely avaricious and inspired by self-gain; used to servicing infantile and virile dependants, they are well practised in putting the needs of others before their own; lacking strength, they are used to extending persuasion rather than force. And it is indeed because he recognizes such virtues that Rousseau does ultimately find women indispensable to the just state. But the role they yield remains for him indirect and largely implicit. It is next necessary, then, to examine the purpose which sexual differences played in his political philosophy as a whole.

Despite the dichotomies that Rousseau insisted upon between women and men in the ideal state, he was nevertheless unable to sever them completely. It is in the family that new male citizens are reproduced. Moreover, nature, which remains for Rousseau an ideal realm, primitive yet undefiled and authentic, is associated with the family and woman. Indeed the rural family remains for him something of a utopian model: the Golden Age in which it is the primary social unit is one where the conflicts and miseries of modernity might be avoided. It is therefore both impossible and inadvisable to insulate the private and public spheres too definitively, as Rousseau is well aware. Accordingly, the plan for woman's education is 'crucial to Rousseau's vision of the good society'. Why is this?

The ideal woman is for Rousseau, as his critics have frequently noted, simultaneously madonna and whore. But this schizoid picture is also applied to women as a whole, dividing them into two classes: those who, like Sophy, remain naturally good and domesticated, and those who eschew their natural duties in order to emulate men and take up positions in the public world. It is this division which accounts for the apparent inconsistency with which Rousseau discusses women's influence on men. In his Dedication to the *Second Discourse*, for example, he eulogizes the influence which Geneva's female inhabitants exert, implying that it is they who teach civic virtue to the Republic's male citizens.

> Amiable and virtuous daughters of Geneva, it will be always the lot of your sex to govern ours. Happy are we, so long as your chaste influence, solely exercised within the limits of conjugal union, is exerted only for the glory of the state and the happiness of the public ... It is your task to perpetuate, by your insinuating influence and your innocent and amiable rule, a respect for the laws of state, and harmony among the citizens.

In the *Letter to M. D'Alembert*, on the other hand, Rousseau condemns the introduction of theatre to Geneva on the grounds that it will encourage the sexes to mingle in public, allowing women's influence to render men weak and effeminate while distracting them from their public duties.

This apparent hiatus is resolved once we recognize that Rousseau refers in the two pieces to his different types of woman. He values Genevan women precisely because their seclusion, which he fears the theatre will destroy, places them in the virtuous category. A note in his *First Discourse* clarifies his position: he is 'far from thinking that the ascendency which women have obtained over men is an evil in itself. It is a present which nature has made for the good of mankind. If better directed, it might be productive of as much good, as it is now of evil.' It is her public profile that corrupts contemporary woman, to render sinister a power that is naturally beneficial. But what is the relationship between sexual segregation and woman's moral mission? To answer this, it is necessary to return to the *Discourse on Inequality* once again.

When we first encounter primitive individuals, they exhibit two tendencies: a diluted self-interest concerned with self-preservation (*amour de soi*) and compassion (*pitié*), which is a sort of pre-reflective empathy with the suffering of others. It is because these instincts bind one another in a broad equilibrium that the natural state is a peaceful yet progressive one. Development, however, enflames these incipient passions. The mother's tenderness for her offspring is claimed as an early example of the natural virtue of compassion, out of which social virtues like generosity, friendship and eventually civic virtue itself, will emerge. The first step in its enhancement occurs precisely in the reproductive domain, where conjugal love and paternal affection are sparked by cohabitation. But unfortunately self-love is also enhanced as the proliferation of property and produce transforms gentle self-regard into an avaricious and aggressive *amour propre*.

The initial psychological equilibrium seems to imply a more gender-neutral human type than had Hobbes's portrayal of insatiable egoists, and there is no sense at this stage of masculine or feminine natures. However, the passions unfold at the same time as the sexual division of labour and it seems to follow that they will now disaggregate along sexual lines. The woman who tends her children will enrich her compassion and it is she who is responsible, according to *Emile*, for inciting paternal affection. And since it is private property which is especially associated with the degeneration of *amour de soi* into *amour propre*, while it is men who go 'abroad in search of their common subsistence', we would expect the male half of the species to strengthen its self-regard disproportionately. In other words, beings who were first androgynous in their sentiments now evolve gendered personalities as the dyadic disposition, which was originally so well balanced, splits. Its two halves can no longer bind one another and so one part flourishes in a distorted manner, varying according to sex. It follows that if social beings are to reclaim their natural equilibrium on a moral level, the two qualities must be resynthesized.

One means by which this might be achieved would be for individuals of both sexes to redevelop the quality they lack and this would imply integrated personalities sharing domestic and civic tasks. Rousseau's solution, however, is to fuse members of the two sexes in a marital unity such that the different qualities can again complement and bind one another; they become virtually one person. Thus he describes the woman as the eye and the man the hand; they 'are so dependent on one another that the man teaches the woman what to see while she teaches him what to do'. There is nevertheless a constant danger that one sex will imitate the other and then the balance will be destroyed. This is why Rousseau counsels sexual segregation outside the home, fearing both men who become effeminate when they are consumed with winning a woman's love and women who compete with men in intellectual endeavours.

Ideally, then, Rousseau believes that mutual dependence will limit the excesses of both sexes. The male uses his strength to rule but also his reason, thereby defusing the particularity to which woman's compassion inclines her. But the woman uses the love which that compassion incites, to temper her husband's competitiveness and coldness, reminding him of the sentimental bonds that unite persons. This is why the female's domestic domain evinces an ethic so different from the public world where 'unbridled passions' of rich and poor have 'suppressed the cries of natural compassion and the still feeble voice of justice, and filled men with avarice, ambition and vice'.

Rousseau's preference for female seclusion in the home is thus twofold. First, it prevents women from taking their particular powers into the public realm, where they would be inappropriate. As he writes in the *Letter to M. D'Alembert*, 'Love is the empire of the fair. Here they must give the law, because in the order of nature, resistance belongs to them, and man cannot surmount this resistance, but at the expense of his liberty.' Because women's natural modesty is always better able to control their sexual desire than men's reason can their own, infatuated males are at a woman's mercy. If her powers are unleashed outside marriage they are destructive because they entice citizens away from the masculine world of generality and abstract reason, infecting it with rampant desires for particular persons and encouraging illicit relationships. But second, women must also be kept out of public in order to safeguard their natural qualities. Those who participate in the public realm of men themselves quickly develop *amour propre* and then not only do they fail in their guardianship of the compassionate side of human nature, but they use their advantages in the sphere of love to dominate men rather than to assuage them. It is because women are associated through their relationship with their young with a natural compassion, that they must be protected by confinement in the domestic world, where they are awarded a crucial role in sustaining the sentiments which are required for civic virtue. Without their compassion, a regenerating social contract would remain inconceivable. This is perhaps why Rousseau places such great store on the strength of the original mother – child bond: 'when mothers deign to nurse their children, then will be a reform in morals; natural feeling will revive in every heart; there will be no lack of citizens for the state; this first step by itself will restore mutual affection'.

To be good citizens, individuals must not only obey the law as a set of formal instructions; they must identify with it because they see in it an expression of the community, of which they are a part. They must therefore empathize with others and it is just this feeling which women teach. Ironically, it is from their mothers that men first learn the sentiments necessary to patriotism, fraternity and discernment of the General Will. Thus Rousseau asks: 'can devotion to the state exist apart from the love of those near and dear to us? Can patriotism thrive except in the soil of that miniature fatherland, the home? Is it not the good son, the good husband, the good father, who makes the good citizen?' As part of a romantic reaction against the Enlightenment, Rousseau believed that sentiment as well as reason must guide justice. Yet we now see that these two attributes tended to be contributed by the different sexes, united through marriage. Without domestic virtue, in short, there could be no civic virtue; the conventional state does ultimately require a foundation in nature and this can only come from the family. Such a conclusion at first seems to contradict Rousseau's denial in Chapter 2 of *The Social Contract*, that the state can originate in the family. However, he is merely reiterating here the Lockean case against patriarchy and this does not conflict with the impression *Emile* conveys, that the natural sentiments engendered in the family during the child's immaturity are a prerequisite to the virtues that citizen will require. It is natural feeling, not natural authority, which allows the family still to underpin the state; if it cannot legitimize it, it can facilitate it.

There are further civic implications of women's domestic confinement for Rousseau. The family provides a place where particularity and passion can be safely expressed because they are defused there. The wife who services her husband encourages such expressions but then safeguards them such that they never cross the domestic threshold to invade that public realm where they would be so threatening. Even within the home, marriage, as Mary O'Brien says, 'purifies the passions of particularity, thus making the private realm truly ethical' and less of a threat to the universality required of citizen-husbands. In a similar vein, Carole Pateman contends that within 'the shelter of domestic life, women impose an order, a social pattern, and thus give meaning to the natural world of birth and death and other physical processes, of dirt and raw materials'. Yet because women mediate for men between nature and society, they are always tainted by the process and represent a constant threat to social order. Finally, Lynda Lange suggests that 'the nature of Rousseau's ideal state makes the refuge of the home a virtual necessity for the citizen. Because the demands of citizenship are so stringent, it would be appalling to imagine everyone called to that status'. Again, then, the domestic realm plays an important role as that arena in which private passions are safely indulged and discharged.

If women were active in the polity, the differentiations without which justice and liberty could not endure for Rousseau, would collapse. Compassion/self-love, particularity/generality, love/law, personal/impersonal, natural/conventional are all for him oppositions which are simultaneously sustained and harmonized only as long as women and men maintain their diffuse identities in an intimate relationship. The moral complicity of the sexes, who together fuse the originally balanced virtues, is embodied in a family – state dyad. This explains why Rousseau, despite his paranoid denunciation of factions in *The Social Contract*, fails to cite the family as one of those manifestations of particularity that would threaten the state. It is indispensable to it.

In conclusion, I do not think that Rousseau's enchantment with the Ancients can be overemphasized here. In essence he adopts Aristotle's view that women should be excluded from citizenship but accepts, with him, that they might provide its preconditions. In propounding a rather Aristotelian notion of civic virtue, he grants to women an indispensable moral and emotional mission. As he says of the Greek use of slaves, there 'are some unhappy circumstances in which we can only keep our liberty at others' expense'. Like his predecessor Rousseau distinguishes between beneficiaries and others according to their supposedly natural functions, on the basis of which he ascribes to them an appropriate type of reason and virtue. He imputes to women the typically Greek virtues of fidelity and modesty. He recognizes, like Plato, that the virtues of family life are needed in the just state even while they threaten it, but he must eschew the Platonic/Spartan attempt to overcome the sexual division of function and to collapse the family into the state, otherwise the necessary tensions will not be sustained. His preferred solution, to seclude women in the home and to segregate the sexes even there, is rather that of Aristotle and of classical Athens.

It was Hegel who would take up the mantle of this sexual conservatism; it is to Mary Wollstonecraft that we must now turn for its radical critique. We can discern in her engagement with Rousseau a further rehearsal of that ancient debate between Plato and Aristotle regarding woman's real nature and public role.

Mary Wollstonecraft's *A Vindication of the Rights of Woman* (1792) was by no means the first feminist appeal to be published, for the question of women's place in society had been in the air since the English Civil War, but it was probably the first sustained argument in English for women's rights. In this book Wollstonecraft combined natural rights arguments inherited from Locke with utilitarian claims concerning the social benefits of sexual equality. This involved her in a direct confrontation with Rousseau's image of natural sexual difference, yet the ideal which the utility of women's improved status was to serve often came close to Rousseau's own vision of citizenship.

As a young woman, Wollstonecraft had set up a school in Stoke Newington, where she was befriended by a group of radical dissenters who 'worshipped reason and Locke'. It was through these acquaintances that she met Thomas Paine and her future husband, the anarchist William Godwin. Tomalin suggests that Paine, engaged in writing his *Rights of Man*, may have suggested to Mary that she write a book on women's rights. However, her first *Vindication* was a defence *Of the Rights of Men*, written in opposition to Burke's conservative

*Reflections on the Revolution in France* (1790). Always committed to the revolutionary attack on privilege, it is not surprising that Wollstonecraft should have discerned a parallel between aristocratic and patriarchal abuses which alerted her to inconsistencies in the liberal position.

Wollstonecraft was fully aware of the radical implications of natural rights theories. If all individuals are born free and equal bearers of such rights, then it is 'both inconsistent and unjust' to exclude women from their enjoyment: reason itself demands 'JUSTICE for one half of the human race' (Wollstonecraft, *A Vindication of the Rights of Woman* pp. 11, 13). She thus demands that women share in the 'rights of man' in being accorded civil, and even political, rights. But she realizes, too, that the argument must be applied to relations in the family: the '*divine* right of husbands, like the divine right of kings, may, it is hoped, in this enlightened age, be contested without danger' (p. 46).

In order to establish her rights claim, Wollstonecraft needed to refute Rousseau's description of women as possessing reason and virtue that naturally differed from men's. For the Lockean tradition associated both virtue and rights with the capacity for moral and rational agency, and if women could be shown defective here, their sex might legitimately be used as a criterion for excluding them from equal rights with men. Accordingly, Wollstonecraft issues her challenge: 'if women are to be excluded, without having a voice, from a participation of the natural rights of mankind, prove first, to ward off the charge of injustice and inconsistency, that they want reason' (pp. 11f). It is such a contention that she sets out to refute.

In order to overturn Rousseau's depiction of the natural woman, Wollstonecraft makes use of the argument that Rousseau had himself launched against Hobbes: that in deducing the essential being stripped of its acquired characteristics, he had not gone far enough. The 'crude inferences' he makes are in fact drawn from the eighteenth-century Frenchwoman, raised from infancy only to please men (p. 90). While she shares Rousseau's distaste for the females who ignore their motherly duties, Wollstonecraft equally condemns those who emulate Sophy. The behaviour prescribed for the latter is not natural because it is insincere and it is not moral because it rests on falsehood. She sees both types of woman as the creation of poor education and patriarchal culture, which encourage development of the senses at the expense of reason and wrongly identify ignorance with innocence. Femininity as described by Rousseau is, in short, an artificial construct; resocialize women in the same manner as men and their essential humanity will reveal itself.

[...]

# 58

# FEMINISM AND DEMOCRACY

## Sheila Rowbotham

[...]

When the feminist movement reappeared in the late 1960s it seemed as if it was not linked to any previous organizational forms. It appeared to be using political assumptions which were quite unlike either those of liberal feminism or the working-class women's organizations of earlier eras.

After nearly two decades the wheel has turned several circles. The contours of similarity and contrast appear somewhat differently. It is possible to see more clearly the changed social circumstances which brought so many young women in most of the developed capitalist countries to contest their feminine destiny. The expansion of education hurtled a generation beyond the confines of their mothers' world into the male sphere of public affairs and work. Yet these social changes were not accompanied by shifts to greater social provision for children. So young mothers who had been educated for equality found themselves tied to the home when they had children. Geographical mobility cut them off from kinship networks which could have provided some assistance. Housing intensified this isolation. 'The captive wife' was discovered before the women's liberation movement emerged. She might not have anyone to talk to, but she could aspire to a fridge, a washing machine and tranquillizers like Serenid D. The market for domestic goods was flourishing, but there was no equivalent development of social provision to meet women's needs as carers and domestic workers.

From Sheila Rowbotham, 'Feminism and Democracy', in David Held and Christopher Pollitt (eds), *New Forms of Democracy* (Sage, London, 1986), pp. 85–6.

The emphasis on consumption also affected the beauty industry. Here again there was an incongruence. While the adverts played on young women's anxieties about desirability, the political message was that equality had been achieved. The existence of a form of contraceptive technology which could be relied upon to be effective – before the health hazards of the pill were widely known – meant that control over fertility was no longer a gamble. Yet even amidst the optimism of the pill there were increasing numbers of young single mothers dependent on the state for welfare. There was moreover a clash in attitudes towards women's sexuality. One morality demanded virginity, another sexual proficiency, imaginative performance and the untroubled achievement of orgasm [. . .].

It is perhaps not surprising that young women facing these contradictory versions of what women should be like, which, with differing emphases were also prevalent in North America and Europe, began to seek their own definitions. It was hard to find a language that carried them into the arena of politics [. . .]. Their aspirations could not be expressed in terms of political democracy. The vote after all had been won. Nor did they completely coincide with the arguments for economic equality which working-class women in the trade unions were expressing. They were to involve widening the definitions of democracy to include domestic inequality, identity, control over sexuality, challenge to cultural representation, community control over state welfare and more equal access to public resources. Strangely enough this has been a process of looking backwards as well as forwards and discovering many lost trails which had been silted over in women's past struggles. Historical recognition emerged which signposted ways in which feminists had wanted much more of democracy than the vote – not only in the capitalist countries but in the Third World as well [. . .].

But the political concepts used by women's liberation were to be found in more recent movements. The new movement drew on ideas current in civil rights, black power, the American new left, the student movement and the May events in France in 1968.

Already in these earlier movements it is possible to find extended meanings of democracy which have come to be associated with feminism. These are the idea that 'the personal is political', which involves challenging the boundaries of concepts of politics, the assumption that democratic control has to be extended not only to the workplace but to the circumstances of everyday life, and the conviction that the *forms* of actions chosen contribute to the result, and should consequently seek to prefigure an alternative [. . .].

It is not to diminish women's liberation as a movement to say that it drew on ideas which existed in other social movements as well as rejecting the male domination that was present in these. Feminism developed often as a challenge to the way these movements failed to live up to their own democratic ideals in relation to women. Women turned the men's rhetoric towards their own inequality, both in the public politics of radical movements and in personal life.

The recognition of political derivations is in fact a useful corrective to the danger, which is always there in considering feminism, of fostering an artificially contained sphere of thought which is presented as having no dynamic interaction. This, of course, leaves 'politics in general' still a male sphere.

The women's movement put the political concepts of the earlier radical movements to a sustained test in practice. The attempt to understand how they have served us – for well or ill – and where the difficulties have arisen is of relevance not only for feminism but for other political movements

[...]

# 59

# LOSING THE FAITH, FEMINISM AND DEMOCRACY

## Susan Mendus

[...]

The belief that democratic theory condones undemocratic practice is not confined to feminist theorists. John Dunn has argued that there are 'two distinct and developed democratic theories loose in the world today – one dismally ideological and the other fairly blatantly utopian'. On the dismally ideological account democracy is simply the least bad mechanism for securing a measure of responsibility on the part of the governors to the governed. By contrast, the blatantly utopian account envisages a society in which all social arrangements represent the interests of all people. The former constitutes a practical proposal, but hardly an inspiring one; the latter may be inspiring, but it is hardly practical. Despairing of finding anything which can reflect democracy's status as both a high ideal and a practical proposal, Dunn concludes that 'today, in politics, democracy is the *name* for what we cannot have – yet cannot cease to want' [...]. On Dunn's analysis the grounds for scepticism about democracy lie largely in the circumstances of modern life: the social and economic differentiation which are characteristic of the modern world necessarily generate inequalities which fit ill with the democratic ideal of political equality. Connectedly, the sheer size of modern states creates a rift between the individual and the community which makes it impossible for individuals to perceive the state as a focus of common good. Thus, democracy is not attainable in large, modern, postindustrial societies: as an ideal, it promises human fulfilment and human

From Susan Mendus, 'Losing the Faith: Feminism and Democracy', in J. Dunn (ed.), *Democracy: The Unfinished Journey, 508 BC to AD 1993* (Oxford University Press, Oxford, 1992), pp. 208–16.

freedom, but in the modern world this promise cannot be met and democracy has therefore become at best a method of curbing the excesses of rulers, and at worst an idle, or even a utopian dream.

But if Dunn fears that democracy cannot exist, given the nature of modern states, feminists note with some chagrin that democracy never did exist even prior to the growth of modern states: Carole Pateman briskly dismisses the subject, claiming that 'for feminists, democracy has never existed; women never have been and still are not admitted as full and equal members in any country known as a "democracy"' [...]. Put together, the two accounts are deeply unsettling: Dunn tells us that without small states and an undifferentiated public there cannot be democracy. Feminists tell us that even when there were small states and an undifferentiated public, still there never was democracy. For feminists, the facts of history – the denial of the vote to women, their historical confinement to a domestic realm, their incorporation within the interests of their husbands – prove beyond doubt that for women democracy has never existed. For them, therefore, Dunn's lament is not even a lament for times past, but only a reflection on what might have been but in fact never was.

Why was there never democracy for women, and why is there still no democracy for women? A number of modern writers implicitly assume that it is because women have historically been denied equality under the law and the formal, political right to vote. For example, Robert Dahl recognizes that almost all the major writers in the democratic tradition excluded women from their theories, but he implies that this is merely evidence of the fact that philosophers are children of their time, and that the problem may be solved simply by rewriting references to 'all men' as 'all men and women' or 'all adults'. Thus, indicating that all is now well, he writes: 'In most countries women gained the suffrage only in this century, and in a few only after the Second World War. In fact, not until our own century did democratic theory and practice begin to reflect a belief that all (or virtually all) adults should be included in the demos as a matter of right' [...]. And this completes his discussion of the role of women in modern democratic states.

Dahl's optimism is grounded in his recognition that women are now formally equal citizens, and in his belief that this formal equality need not be fatally undermined by social and economic inequalities. He accepts the general claim that political equality is compromised by lack of economic power, but argues that this should not lead to the pessimistic conclusion that democracy is 'something we cannot have yet cannot cease to want'. Rather, it suggests the more robust conclusion that the pursuit of democracy includes the removal of social and economic inequalities. He writes:

> Though the idea of equal opportunity is often so weakly interpreted that it is rightly dismissed as too undemanding, when it is taken in its fullest sense it is extraordinarily demanding – so demanding, indeed, that the criteria for the democratic process would require a people committed to it to

institute measures well beyond those that even the most democratic states have hitherto brought about. [...]

For Dahl, therefore, inequality is a practical problem which admits of practical solutions. Since it is a widespread and intransigent problem, there will be no 'quick fix', but there can be progress, and in tracing that progress Dahl does not see the need to make reference to any special feature of women's position beyond the recognition that they are, in general, amongst those who suffer from a lack of social and economic power. By implication, he denies that women constitute a special and intransigent problem for democratic theory. They are simply a specific example of a quite general, but remediable, problem, the problem of how to ensure that social and economic inequalities do not undermine the formal equality of the vote.

Many feminists dissent: although agreeing that there are practical problems, they also insist that, in the case of women, the problems have a theoretical origin which goes beyond mere social and economic inequality. Women, they argue, are different not simply because they lack economic and social power, but because historically they have been explicitly excluded from the category of citizen in the democratic state. So we might agree that democracy depends upon enlarging the economic power of those who are citizens, but so long as women (along with children, animals, and the insane) were excluded from that category, the question of enlarging their economic and social power frequently failed to arise. Indeed, women's economic power was normally identified with the economic power of their husbands, and the fact that wives themselves owned nothing was (and often still is) conveniently forgotten. Again, it is important to be clear about the status of this objection: usually, it is taken as simply a reflection on the historical facts of democratic societies, but it also contains the seeds of a criticism of democratic theory itself. The criticism may be made explicit by considering Dahl's two interpretations of what he calls 'the principle of inclusion' in democratic theory. This principle is the principle which dictates who shall count as a citizen in the democratic state, and therefore who shall have a say in determining the laws of the state.

Dahl notes that historically philosophers have vacillated between a contingent and a categorical principle of inclusion: thus, some urge that all adult members of a state are also, and thereby, citizens (the categorical criterion); others claim that only those who are qualified to rule may be citizens (the contingent claim). He concedes that the contingent criterion has been the most popular in the history of political philosophy, but urges that the categorical criterion is the appropriate one for modern democratic states. There should be no question of individuals having to prove their fitness to rule. The criterion for being a full citizen is simply that one is an adult member of the state in question. This, and this alone, justifies according rights of citizenship.

There is, however, a worrying tension between the assumptions inherent in the demand for increased social and economic equality and the assumptions inherent in the demand for a categorical criterion of citizenship. For the former recognizes that if citizenship is to be meaningful, more than formal equality is required, whereas the latter is content with a formal criterion for being or becoming a citizen. The danger is that acceptance of the categorical principle of inclusion, with its requirement that we ignore differences between people at the formal level, may lead to minimizing differences between people in framing social policy. Most importantly, it may lead to an understanding of difference, specifically women's differences, as disadvantage, disability, or deviance. If difference is the problem at the level of inclusion, then the removal of difference may be thought to be the solution at the level of social policy.

Thus, to provide a concrete example, pregnancy is often treated as akin to illness, and maternity leave as a special case of sick-leave. Pregnant women are then equated with men who are ill or temporarily disabled, and the attempt to attain 'equality' for them rests on the assumption that they are, in effect, disabled men. By this strategy, inequalities are certainly reduced because women attain something by way of maternity benefit, and something is surely better than nothing. But the importance of the practical benefits should not disguise the fact that the theoretical assumptions of the strategy are assimilationist and patriarchal. Women attain a degree of equality only by conceding that the differences between themselves and men are differences which carry the implication of female inferiority. Moreover, this is not simply a complaint about the practical arrangements governing pregnancy and childbirth; it is a more general concern about the unspoken assumptions of many democratic theorists, specifically their assumption that equality is to be attained via the removal or minimization of disadvantage, where what counts as disadvantage is held to be clear and uncontroversial, but is in fact determined by reference to a model which is intrinsically male.

Considerations of this sort highlight the fact that for women lack of social and economic power is only half the story: it is not simply bad luck that women, in general, lack economic power. It is the male model of normality which *guarantees* that that will be so. Iris Marion Young expresses the point forcefully:

> In my view an equal treatment approach to pregnancy and childbirth is inadequate because it either implies that women do not have any right to leave and job security when having babies, or assimilates such guarantees under the supposedly gender-neutral category of 'disability' ... Assimilating pregnancy and disability tends to stigmatize these processes as 'unhealthy'. [...]

It is for this reason that many feminists have found it difficult to retain faith in democracy and democratic theory. And, as we have seen, the loss of faith occurs at several levels: historically, feminists are aware that the denial of difference at the level of inclusion has rarely been observed. Most philosophers have noted differences between men and women, and have argued that these differences support the exclusion of women from even the rights of formal political equality. More recently, feminists have drawn attention to the fact that even where the categorical criterion has been employed, it has not been accompanied by any strenuous efforts to remove the social and economic disadvantages suffered by women, and therefore formal political equality has been undermined by practical social and economic inequality. Finally, and most importantly, many feminists now doubt whether the denial or removal of difference is even an acceptable aim for political theory and practice. Again, the doubts arise on two levels. Anne Phillips has argued that the individualistic character of modern philosophy makes it inadequate for feminist purposes. She notes:

> The anti-discrimination that informs much contemporary liberalism implies removing obstacles that block an individual's path and then applauding when that individual succeeds. The problem is still perceived in terms of previous *mis*treatment, which judged and dismissed people because they had deviated from some prejudiced norm. The answer is presented in terms of treating them just as people instead. [...]

Where difference is interpreted as deviance or disadvantage, the response to it is to implement social policy which will minimize the effects of that disadvantage *in the specific case*. This individualistic response has been countered by the demand that what is required is recognition of *group* disadvantage. Far from asserting that it should not matter whether we are men or women, this strategy insists that men and women do have different degrees of power and that therefore policies should be implemented which take account of this fact and guarantee increased power to women as a group.

The second response is rather different. It denies that difference is always to be construed as disadvantage and, in the case of women, urges a restructuring of both political theory and political practice in such a way as to celebrate at least some differences. In other words, it denies that all difference is disability, and it objects to the strategy whereby the 'disadvantages' of pregnancy and childbirth are mitigated by assimilating them to male illness. So, where democratic theory characteristically urges that we should assume that everyone is the same, feminists urge a recognition that men and women are different. Similarly, where democratic theorists have urged that, in decisions about social policy, we should aim to minimize the disadvantages which spring from difference, feminists ask why such normal states as pregnancy should be categorized as disadvantages at all.

For feminists, therefore, losing the faith has been losing faith in the ability of doctrines of equality, understood as doctrines which advocate the minimization of difference, to deliver a political theory which will be sensitive to the realities of women's lives. The solution to this problem lies in a rewriting of democratic theory in such a way as to ensure that it acknowledges and incorporates difference. Most importantly, it lies in a recognition that, in the case of women, the disadvantages which spring from difference are themselves politically significant. They are disadvantages inherent in not being male. So democratic theory falls at the first hurdle because it in fact employs a male, rather than a gender-neutral, standard by which to decide what counts as disadvantage.

The proposed solution is not without its dangers: oppressed and disadvantaged groups have long used a doctrine of equality as their most important single weapon, and have appealed to such concepts as 'common humanity' in their attempts to attain political and legal rights. Moreover, they have vigorously denied the significance of difference in political contexts, and urged that differences between them and other, more advantaged, groups should be ignored in the distribution of political *rights*. It is therefore a discomfiting about-face for feminist theorists now to insist on a politics of difference; and to pin their faith in the possibility that difference may be acknowledged, not construed as disadvantage.

To what extent do feminists wish to attack democratic ideals, and to what extent do they wish to reconstruct them? Is their argument that we should substitute an acceptance of difference for the demand for equality, or that the demand for equality itself requires a full and sensitive recognition of the practical significance of difference?

### REVISING THE FAITH

Some critics have argued that feminists do indeed reject the ideal of equality, and that they do so because they wrongly assume that equality is at odds with the recognition of difference. Thus, Richard Norman writes: 'Equality does not require the elimination of difference. Sexual equality, in particular, does not require a denial of the inescapable biological facts of sexual difference, and leaves open what further differences might follow from these' [...]. Certainly some feminists have spoken of equality in dismissive terms, and have urged that we should pay less attention to it. Virginia Held, for example says:

> Occasionally, for those who give birth, equality will be an important concept as we strive to treat children fairly and have them treat each other with respect. But it is normally greatly overshadowed by such other concerns as that the relationship between ourselves and our children and each other be trusting and considerate. [...]

But this is simply the point that equality is not the only concept in moral and political life. It is not the complaint that equality necessarily conflicts with difference. And more generally, when feminists express reservations about equality, it is because they recognize that democratic theory itself has interpreted it as requiring the elimination or minimization of difference. In general, it is not feminists who urge that equality and difference are incompatible concepts; it is democratic theory which does that by its insistence on a specific understanding of equality – as something to be attained by the minimization of difference. The crucial debate in contemporary feminism is the debate between those who urge that sex should become irrelevant and those who believe that sex should not provide the basis for inequality. Neither of these strategies involves rejecting equality. Rather, the dispute is about how equality is to be attained.

However, the strategic problem is acute in the case of women for the simple reason that, unlike social and economic differences, sexual difference cannot be removed by social policy in quite the simple way which the theory requires. Where inequalities of power spring simply from social and economic inequalities, there is some hope of removing them by seeking to minimize them – though the task would be difficult. But where inequalities of power spring from sex, it may be morally undesirable, or even impossible, to attempt to remove them by this approach. Of course, such strategies have been used, and with great success, by early feminists in their attempt to secure equal legal and political rights for women. But feminists are now sceptical about such attempts, fearing that ultimately they leave for women only the possibility of assimilation into a male world. Speaking about her own 'assimilation' feminism, Simone de Beauvoir said: 'the modern woman accepts masculine values: she prides herself on thinking, taking action, working, creating, on the same terms as men; instead of seeking to disparage them, she declares herself their equal' [. . .]. But the price of this form of feminism is high for, as Simone de Beauvoir herself concedes, it is incompatible with child care and mothering. This not only means that, for many women, it will be difficult, if not impossible, to 'win the game', it also means accepting the rules of the game – where those rules dictate that pregnancy is an illness and child care a disadvantage.

What is needed, therefore, is a way of conceptualizing difference which renders it compatible with equality, but also, and crucially, does not simply increase social differentiation. Yet more radically, what is needed is a recognition that in much traditional democratic theory the concepts of equality, difference, and disadvantage are themselves gender-biased: they assume a standard of normality which is inherently male.

What are the possibilities of re-conceptualizing in this way? How can democratic states revise the ideal in a way which acknowledges difference as both ineliminable and valuable? At this stage, it is worth emphasizing that it is not only feminists who should have a strong interest in this question. Modern states are characterized by the heterogeneity of the people who inhabit them. Unlike fifth-century Athens, or Rousseau's ideal state, they are not gatherings of the like-minded, gentlemen's clubs writ large, where those who deviate may be excluded or required to conform. The denial of citizenship to all but white males is no longer an option, nor is the easy assumption that newcomers must earn their right to citizenship by becoming 'like us'. Difference is not going to go away, nor is it something for which those who are different feel disposed to apologize. Against this background, the insistence that equality is to be preserved via the minimization of difference, or via assimilation itself appears utopian and the complaint that the differentiation of modern life militates against democracy may elicit the response: 'so much the worse for democracy'.

[...]

# PART FOUR
# CONTEMPORARY ISSUES

# SECTION 9
# RATIONAL CHOICE

# RATIONAL CHOICE
## INTRODUCTION

One of the classic concerns of politics is always the question of what, in a given situation, we should do. However we answer this question, most of us assume that there should be some rational basis for our collective judgment. In a democracy, this rational basis is precisely the free and informed choices of individuals. Our answer to the question, 'what should we do?' must therefore arise from a consultation with the people. The collective judgement, or social choice, that results from this process of consultation should accurately reflect the individual choices collected by elections. The social choice is, therefore, an aggregation of a great number of individual judgements. The rational basis for the social choice is thus its accurate reflection of individual choices.

As the selection by *Amartya Sen* shows, however, there have always been concerns that whatever voting system we use to aggregate individual choices into a social choice inevitably involves some distortion of those individual choices. In a first-past-the-post voting system, for example, those who voted for the loser find their individual choices rated less highly than those who voted for the winner. Similarly, where there are more than two candidates, it is possible that a winner might emerge with more votes cast against them (i.e. for the other two candidates) than for them. In these cases, the social choice does not accurately reflect individual choices. If this is so, then there can be no such thing as a neutral voting system. Whichever one we use will distort the relation between individual and social choice in some way.

This problem received a full mathematical investigation in the work of the economist *Kenneth Arrow*. His 'impossibility theorem' showed that whatever voting system is used, social choice can never reflect individual choices with perfect accuracy. A non-technical passage from Arrow is included below. To prove his impossibility theorem, he imported a series of assumptions about individual action from the discipline of economics. Economic actors are assumed to be rational, in the sense of always selecting what is best for themselves. Rationality is thereby seen to mean self-interest and the efficiency of means towards some given end. These methodological assumptions are made explicit in the selection from *Downs*.

What has now become known as Rational Choice, or Social Choice, Theory thus makes a series of methodological assumptions about the rationality of individual action in order to explain and deepen our understanding of the actual functioning of democracy. Of particular importance to our current concerns are the resulting attempts to explain why people participate in politics.

In the selections included here by *Brian Barry*, we find presented a debate over how best to rationally analyse participation. Barry explores the theories of Downs, Riker and Olson in such a way as to show the strengths and weaknesses of Rational Choice explanations.

At issue here, then, are a series of profound methodological questions for the study of democracy. Should we seek to provide a rational explanation for participation, for example, which relies so heavily on assumptions imported from the analysis of the market? Put in this way, we can see that the question of how best to explain and study democracy turns on the comparative nature of the market and democracy on the one hand, and the validity and efficacy of economic assumptions on the other. In our subsequent section on the market we further explore the relation of democracy and the market.

# THE POSSIBILITY OF SOCIAL CHOICE

## Amartya Sen

"A camel," it has been said, "is a horse designed by a committee." This might sound like a telling example of the terrible deficiencies of committee decisions, but it is really much too mild an indictment. A camel may not have the speed of a horse, but it is a very useful and harmonious animal – well coordinated to travel long distances without food and water. A committee that tries to reflect the diverse wishes of its different members in designing a horse could very easily end up with something far less congruous: perhaps a centaur of Greek mythology, half a horse and half something else – a mercurial creation combining savagery with confusion.

The difficulty that a small committee experiences may be only greater when it comes to decisions of a sizeable society, reflecting the choices "of the people, by the people, for the people." That, broadly speaking, is the subject of "social choice," and it includes within its capacious frame various problems with the common feature of relating social judgments and group decisions to the views and interests of the individuals who make up the society or the group. If there is a central question that can be seen as the motivating issue that inspires social choice theory, it is this: how can it be possible to arrive at cogent aggregative judgments about the society (for example, about "social welfare," or "the public interest," or "aggregate poverty"), given the diversity of preferences, concerns, and predicaments of the different individuals *within* the society? How can we find any rational basis for making such aggregative judgements as "the

From Amartya Sen, 'The Possibility of Social Choice', *American Economic Review*, 89 (3), June 1999, pp. 349–51.

society prefers this to that," or "the society should choose this over that," or "this is socially right"? Is reasonable social choice at all possible, especially since, as Horace noted a long time ago, there may be "as many preferences as there are people"?

## I. SOCIAL CHOICE THEORY

In this lecture, I shall try to discuss some challenges and foundational problems faced by social choice theory as a discipline. The immediate occasion for this lecture is, of course, an award, and I am aware that I am expected to discuss, in one form or another, my own work associated with this event (however immodest that attempt might otherwise have been). This I will try to do, but it is, I believe, also a plausible occasion to address some general questions about social choice as a discipline – its content, relevance, and reach – and I intend to seize this opportunity. The Royal Swedish Academy of Sciences referred to "welfare economics" as the general field of my work for which the award was given, and separated out three particular areas: social choice, distribution, and poverty. While I have indeed been occupied, in various ways, with these different subjects, it is social choice theory, pioneeringly formulated in its modern form by Arrow (1951), that provides a general approach to the evaluation of, and choice over, alternative social possibilities (including inter alia the assessment of social welfare, inequality, and poverty). This I take to be reason enough for primarily concentrating on social choice theory in this Nobel lecture.

Social choice theory is a very broad discipline, covering a variety of distinct questions, and it may be useful to mention a few of the problems as illustrations of its subject matter (on many of which I have been privileged to work). When would *majority rule* yield unambiguous and consistent decisions? How can we judge how well a *society as a whole* is doing in the light of the disparate interests of its different members? How do we measure *aggregate poverty* in view of the varying predicaments and miseries of the diverse people that make up the society? How can we accommodate *rights and liberties* of persons while giving adequate recognition to their preferences? How do we appraise social valuations of public goods such as the *natural environment*, or *epidemiological security*? Also, some investigations, while not directly a part of social choice theory, have been helped by the understanding generated by the study of group decisions (such as the causation and prevention of *famines and hunger*, or the forms and consequences of *gender inequality*, or the demands of *individual freedom* seen as a "social commitment"). The reach and relevance of social choice theory can be very extensive indeed.

## II. ORIGINS OF SOCIAL CHOICE THEORY AND CONSTRUCTIVE PESSIMISM

How did the subject of social choice theory originate? The challenges of social decisions involving divergent interests and concerns have been explored for a long time. For example, Aristotle in ancient Greece and Kautilya in ancient

India, both of whom lived in the fourth century B.C., explored various constructive possibilities in social choice in their books respectively entitled *Politics* and *Economics*.

However, social choice theory as a systematic discipline first came into its own around the time of the French Revolution. The subject was pioneered by French mathematicians in the late eighteenth century, such as J. C. Borda (1781) and Marquis de Condorcet (1785), who addressed these problems in rather mathematical terms and who initiated the formal discipline of social choice in terms of voting and related procedures. The intellectual climate of the period was much influenced by European Enlightenment, with its interest in reasoned construction of social order. Indeed, some of the early social choice theorists, most notably Condorcet, were also among the intellectual leaders of the French Revolution.

The French Revolution, however, did not usher in a peaceful social order in France. Despite its momentous achievements in changing the political agenda across the whole world, in France itself it not only produced much strife and bloodshed, it also led to what is often called, not inaccurately, a "reign of terror." Indeed, many of the theorists of social coordination, who had contributed to the ideas behind the Revolution, perished in the flames of the discord that the Revolution itself unleashed (this included Condorcet who took his own life when it became quite likely that others would do it for him). Problems of social choice, which were being addressed at the level of theory and analysis, did not wait, in this case, for a peacefully intellectual resolution.

The motivation that moved the early social choice theorists included the avoidance of both instability and arbitrariness in arrangements for social choice. The ambitions of their work focused on the development of a framework for rational and democratic decisions for a group, paying adequate attention to the preferences and interests of all its members. However, even the theoretical investigations typically yielded rather pessimistic results. They noted, for example, that majority rule can be thoroughly inconsistent, with $A$ defeating $B$ by a majority, $B$ defeating $C$ also by a majority, and $C$ in turn defeating $A$, by a majority as well.

A good deal of exploratory work (often, again, with pessimistic results) continued in Europe through the nineteenth century. Indeed, some very creative people worked in this area and wrestled with the difficulties of social choice, including Lewis Carroll, the author of *Alice in Wonderland* (under his real name, C. L. Dodgson, 1874, 1884).

When the subject of social choice was revived in the twentieth century by Arrow (1951), he too was very concerned with the difficulties of group decisions and the inconsistencies to which they may lead. While Arrow put the discipline of social choice in a structured – and axiomatic – framework (thereby leading to the birth of social choice theory in its modern form), he deepened the pre-existing gloom by establishing an astonishing – and apparently pessimistic – result of ubiquitous reach.

Arrow's (1950, 1951, 1963) "impossibility theorem" (formally, the "General Possibility Theorem") is a result of breathtaking elegance and power, which showed that even some very mild conditions of reasonableness could not be simultaneously satisfied by any social choice procedure, within a very wide family. Only a dictatorship would avoid inconsistencies, but that of course would involve: (1) in politics, an extreme sacrifice of participatory decisions, and (2) in welfare economics, a gross inability to be sensitive to the heterogeneous interests of a diverse population. Two centuries after the flowering of the ambitions of social rationality, in Enlightenment thinking and in the writings of the theorists of the French Revolution, the subject seemed to be inescapably doomed. Social appraisals, welfare economic calculations, and evaluative statistics would have to be, it seemed, inevitably arbitrary or unremediably despotic.

Arrow's "impossibility theorem" aroused immediate and intense interest (and generated a massive literature in response, including many other impossibility results). It also led to the diagnosis of a deep vulnerability in the subject that overshadowed Arrow's immensely important *constructive* program of developing a systematic social choice theory that could actually work.

[...]

# 61

# SOCIAL CHOICE AND INDIVIDUAL VALUES

## Kenneth J. Arrow

[...]

If we continue the traditional identification of rationality with maximization of some sort (to be discussed at greater length below), then the problem of achieving a social maximum derived from individual desires is precisely the problem which has been central to the field of welfare economics. There is no need to review the history of this subject in detail. There has been controversy as to whether or not the economist *qua* economist could make statements saying that one social state is better than another. If we admit meaning to interpersonal comparisons of utility, then presumably we could order social states according to the sum of the utilities of individuals under each, and this is the solution of Jeremy Bentham, accepted by Edgeworth and Marshall. Even in this case we have a choice of different mathematical forms of the social utility function in terms of individual utilities; thus, the social utility might be the sum of the individual utilities or their product or the product of their logarithms or the sum of their products taken two at a time. So, as Professor Bergson has pointed out, there are value judgments implicit even at this level. The case is clearly much worse if we deny the possibility of making interpersonal comparisons of utility. It was on the latter grounds that Professor Robbins so strongly attacked the concept that economists could make any policy recommendations, at least without losing their status as economists and passing over into the realm of ethics. On the other hand, Mr. Kaldor and, following him, Professor Hicks have

From Kenneth J. Arrow, *Social Choice and Individual Values*, 2nd edn (Yale University Press, New Haven, CT and London, 1963), pp. 3–5.

argued that there is a meaningful sense in which we can say that one state is better than another from an economic point of view, even without assuming the reality of interpersonal comparison of utilities. The particular mechanism by which they propose to accomplish the comparison of different social states, the compensation principle, will be examined in more detail in Chapter IV.

The controversy involves a certain confusion between two levels of argument. There can be no doubt that, even if interpersonal comparison is assumed, a value judgment is implied in any given way of making social choices based on individual utilities; so much Bergson has shown clearly. But, given these basic value judgments as to the mode of aggregating individual desires, the economist should investigate those mechanisms for social choice which satisfy the value judgments and should check their consequences to see if still other value judgments might be violated. In particular, he should ask the question whether or not the value judgments are consistent with each other, i.e., do there exist any mechanisms of social choice which will in fact satisfy the value judgments made? For example, in the voting paradox discussed above, if the method of majority choice is regarded as itself a value judgment, then we are forced to the conclusion that the value judgment in question, applied to the particular situation indicated, is self-contradictory.

In the matter of consistency, the question of interpersonal comparison of utilities becomes important. Bergson considers it possible to establish an ordering of social states which is based on indifference maps of individuals, and Samuelson has agreed. On the other hand, Professor Lange, in his discussion of the social welfare function, has assumed the interpersonal measurability of utility, and elsewhere he has insisted on the absolute necessity of measurable utility for normative social judgments. Professor Lerner similarly has assumed the meaningfulness of an interpersonal comparison of intensities of utility in his recent work on welfare economics.

[...]

# 62

# AN ECONOMIC THEORY OF DEMOCRACY

## Anthony Downs

Throughout the world, governments dominate the economic scene. Their spending determines whether full employment prevails; their taxes influence countless decisions; their policies control international trade; and their domestic regulations extend into almost every economic act.

Yet the role of government in the world of economic theory is not at all commensurate with this dominance. True, in each separate field of economics, recent thought has fruitfully concentrated upon the impact of government on private decision-making, or the share of government in economic aggregates. But little progress has been made toward a generalized yet realistic behavior rule for a rational government similar to the rules traditionally used for rational consumers and producers. As a result, government has not been successfully integrated with private decision-makers in a general equilibrium theory.

This thesis is an attempt to provide such a behavior rule for democratic government and to trace its implications. In pursuing these ends, we do not pretend to solve all the problems which have been frustrating analysis in this field. However, we hope to start toward a solution of some and to formulate a reasonable evasion of others which are intrinsically insoluble.

### I. THE MEANING OF RATIONALITY IN THE MODEL
### A. THE CONCEPT OF RATIONALITY IN ECONOMIC THEORY

Economic theorists have nearly always looked at decisions as though they were made by rational minds. Some such simplification is necessary for the prediction

From Anthony Downs, *An Economic Theory of Democracy* (Harper & Row, New York, 1957), pp. 3–7.

of behavior, because decisions made at random, or without any relation to each other, do not fall into any pattern. Yet only if human actions form some pattern can they ever be forecast or the relations between them subject to analysis. Therefore economists must assume an ordering of behavior takes place.

There is no *a priori* reason to suppose that this ordering is rational, i.e., reasonably directed toward the achievement of conscious goals. Nevertheless, economic theory has been erected upon the supposition that conscious rationality prevails, in spite of acid assertions to the contrary by men like Thorstein Veblen and John Maurice Clark. Since our model is *ex definitione* one concerning rational behavior, we also make this assumption.

As a result, the traditional methods of prediction and analysis are applicable in our model. If a theorist knows the ends of some decision-maker, he can predict what actions will be taken to achieve them as follows: (1) he calculates the most reasonable way for the decision-maker to reach his goals, and (2) he assumes this way will actually be chosen because the decision-maker is rational.

Economic analysis thus consists of two major steps: discovery of the ends a decision-maker is pursuing, and analysis of which means of attaining them are most reasonable, i.e., require the least input of scarce resources. In carrying out the first step, theorists have generally tried to reduce the ends of each economic agent to a single goal, so that one most efficient way to attain it can be found. If multiple goals are allowed, means appropriate to one may block attainment of another; hence no unique course can be charted for a rational decision-maker to follow. To avoid this impasse, theorists posit that firms maximize profits and consumers maximize utility. Any other goals which either possess are considered deviations that qualify the rational course toward the main goal.

In such analysis, the term *rational* is never applied to an agent's ends, but only to his means. This follows from the definition of *rational* as efficient, i.e., maximizing output for a given input, or minimizing input for a given output. Thus, whenever economists refer to a "rational man" they are not designating a man whose thought processes consist exclusively of logical propositions, or a man without prejudices, or a man whose emotions are inoperative. In normal usage all of these could be considered rational men. But the economic definition refers solely to a man who moves toward his goals in a way which, to the best of his knowledge, uses the least possible input of scarce resources per unit of valued output.

To clarify this definition, let us consider an example of behavior which is rational only in the economic sense. Assume that a monk has consciously selected as his goal the achievement of a state of mystical contemplation of God. In order to attain his goal, he must purge his mind of all logical thoughts and conscious goal-seeking. Economically speaking, this purging is quite rational, even though it would be considered irrational, or at least nonrational, by any of the noneconomic definitions of rationality.

Economic rationality can also be formally defined in another manner. A rational man is one who behaves as follows: (1) he can always make a decision when confronted with a range of alternatives; (2) he ranks all the alternatives facing him in order of his preference in such a way that each is either preferred to, indifferent to, or inferior to each other; (3) his preference ranking is transitive; (4) he always chooses from among the possible alternatives that which ranks highest in his preference ordering; and (5) he always makes the same decision each time he is confronted with the same alternatives. All rational decision-makers in our model – including political parties, interest groups, and governments – exhibit the same qualities.

Rationality thus defined refers to processes of action, not to their ends or even to their success at reaching desired ends. It is notorious that rational planning sometimes produces results greatly inferior to those obtained by sheer luck. In the long run, we naturally expect a rational man to outperform an irrational man, *ceteris paribus*, because random factors cancel and efficiency triumphs over inefficiency. Nevertheless, since behavior in our model cannot be tested by its results, we apply the terms *rational* or *irrational* only to processes of action, i.e., to means. Of course, some intermediate ends are themselves means to ultimate goals. The rationality of the former we can judge, but evaluation of the latter is beyond our scope.

## B. THE NARROW CONCEPT OF RATIONALITY IN THE PRESENT STUDY

However, even though we cannot decide whether a decision-maker's ends are rational, we must know what they are before we can decide what behavior is rational for him. Furthermore, in designating these ends, we must avoid the tautological conclusion that every man's behavior is always rational because (1) it is aimed at some end and (2) its returns must have outweighed its costs in his eyes or he would not have undertaken it.

To escape this pitfall, we focus our attention only upon the economic and political goals of each individual or group in the model. Admittedly, separation of these goals from the many others which men pursue is quite arbitrary. For example, a corporation executive may work for a higher income because he enjoys working as well as to gain more purchasing power; hence, viewing the latter as his only real motive is erroneous as well as arbitrary. Nevertheless, this is a study of economic and political rationality, not of psychology. Therefore, even though psychological considerations have a legitimate and significant place in both economics and political science, we bypass them entirely except for a brief mention in Chapter 2.

Our approach to elections illustrates how this narrow definition of rationality works. The political function of elections in a democracy, we assume, is to select a government. Therefore rational behavior in connection with elections is behavior oriented toward this end and no other. Let us assume a certain man prefers party A for political reasons, but his wife has a tantrum whenever he fails to vote for party B. It is perfectly rational *personally* for this man to vote for party B if preventing his wife's tantrums is more important to him than having A win instead of B. Nevertheless, in our model such behavior is considered irrational because it employs a political device for a nonpolitical purpose.

Thus we do not take into consideration the whole personality of each individual when we discuss what behavior is rational for him. We do not allow for the rich diversity of ends served by each of his acts, the complexity of his motives, the way in which every part of his life is intimately related to his emotional needs. Rather we borrow from traditional economic theory the idea of the rational consumer. Corresponding to the infamous *homo economicus* which Veblen and others have excoriated, our *homo politicus* is the "average man" in the electorate, the "rational citizen" of our model democracy.

Because we allow this political man to be uncertain about the future, he will not appear to be as much of a calculating-machine-brained character as was the utilitarians' economic man. Nevertheless, he remains an abstraction from the real fullness of the human personality.

[...]

# 63

# POLITICAL PARTICIPATION AS RATIONAL ACTION

## Brian Barry

### 1 THE DECISION TO VOTE: DOWNS AND RIKER

Let us begin by examining the 'economic' approach to a simple question: why do people involve themselves in political activity? There are three advantages in studying this question. First, it is hardly possible to deny its importance for the understanding of politics. Second, an 'economic' style of analysis is able to show that the question is not as easy to answer as one might at first glance suppose, and that some answers which appeal to common sense are fallacious. Thus, the power of the 'economic' approach to clarify thought can be illustrated, even though its claims to produce interesting deductions that are also true must be judged more dubious. And, third, in following the attempts of economic theorists to answer the question 'why participate?', we can see in a relatively clear form some of the conceptual difficulties about the definition and scope of the 'economic' approach that have up to this point been skated over.

Two treatments of the question will be discussed in this chapter: first, Anthony Downs's analysis of the decision to vote (as against not voting) in his book *An Economic Theory of Democracy* (1957), and then Mancur Olson's more general theory of rational participation in 'collective action', as set out in his book *The Logic of Collective Action* (1965). We shall be returning to Downs in Chapter V in order to examine in detail his theory of the

From Brian Barry, *Sociologists, Economists and Democracy* (Collier Macmillan, London/ Macmillan, Toronto, 1970), chapter II, pp. 13–16 and 24–32.

workings of party competition. All we need do now, therefore, is present the minimum outline necessary to make intelligible our discussion of the decision to vote.

Downs constructs a theory of politics in which there are, basically, only two kinds of actor. There are the parties, and there are the voters. The internal processes of the parties are abstracted from by the assumption that they consist of single-minded teams, and a further assumption is that they are dedicated to only one object, namely winning elections. 'The politicians in our model never seek office as a means of carrying out particular policies; their only goal is to reap the rewards of holding office *per se*' (Downs, page 28). There is a clear analogy with the conception of the profit-maximising entrepreneur of classical economic theory. The voters correspond to the consumers. But, whereas there is not much point in asking why consumers do *anything* with their money (as against throwing it away), it is a perfectly serious question why voters should use their vote.[1] For one has to make some effort in order to cast a vote, yet what is the benefit to be derived from so doing? If we wish to apply an 'economic' analysis, an obvious line to take is that with which Downs begins: the value of voting is the value of the expected effect it would have in changing what would otherwise happen.

But what are the components of this calculation? When there are only two parties, the matter is fairly simple. The citizen faced with the question whether it is worth voting or not first computes his 'party differential', that is, how much better off he would be (not necessarily in purely financial terms) if his preferred party won the election, and he then multiplies it by the probability that his vote for that party will change the result of the election so that his party wins instead of losing. Obviously, this means that he has to reckon the probability of the election's turning on a single vote, and in an electorate of millions this probability is so small that the value of voting will be infinitesimal, even for someone who has a large party differential.[2] Thus, it seems to follow that rational citizens would not vote if there are costs involved – and it always takes time and energy to cast a vote. But in fact it is notorious that many people do vote. Even low turnouts of, say, 25% are, on this analysis, clearly inconsistent with rationality.

In a recent article, Riker has criticised Downs as if this were his last word on the subject. He says that 'it is certainly no explanation to assign a sizeable part of politics to the mysterious and inexplicable world of the irrational' (Riker, 1968, page 25). And he then proposes an amendment to the theory. But the 'amendment' is in essence the same as one put forward by Downs himself, though Downs describes it as a factor increasing the reward of voting and Riker counts it as a reduction of the cost.[3] Riker says that this reward consists of satisfactions such as 'compliance with the ethic of voting', 'affirming allegiance to the political system', 'affirming a partisan preference', 'deciding, going to the polls etc.', and 'affirming one's efficacy in the political system' (Riker, page 28).

Now it may well be true that much voting can be accounted for in this way, and one can of course formally fit it into an 'economic' framework by saying that people get certain 'rewards' from voting. But this *is* purely formal.[4] And it forces us to ask what really is the point and value of the whole 'economic' approach. It is no trick to restate all behaviour in terms of 'rewards' and 'costs'; it may for some purposes be a useful conceptual device, but it does not in itself provide anything more than a set of empty boxes waiting to be filled. The power of the 'economic' method is that, in appropriate kinds of situation, it enables us, operating with simple premises concerning rational behaviour, to deduce by logic and mathematics interesting conclusions about what will happen. Whether a situation is 'appropriate' or not depends on the extent to which other factors can safely be ignored.

Thus, the classical model of 'competitive equilibrium' in a market does approximate what happens in various 'real world' situations especially where profit-maximising traders make a living by dealing in some homogeneous commodity. But in a situation where, for example, all the participants believe in a 'just price' which is independent of supply and demand, the 'competitive equilibrium' model of price-determination will have no application. Again, we can bring this formally within the 'economic' framework by saying that the people get 'satisfaction' from keeping to the 'just price', or we can simply say that they are maximising subject to a 'constraint'. (Government controls are often dealt with in this way in economic analysis.) But neither of these devices helps very much. The point is that explanatory attention must shift to the question how people came to believe in a 'just price', how the belief is transmitted and maintained, and what determines the level of price which is believed right for each commodity. In other words, there are no interesting deductions to be drawn from the interaction of given 'tastes' in a market; the price can simply be read off from the universal 'taste' for a certain price. The question is how that taste arises, and this is a question that cannot be answered within the 'economic' framework.

The relevance of this example to voting decisions will, I hope, be clear. Riker says that people vote because they derive satisfaction from voting for reasons entirely divorced from the hope that it will bring about desired results. This may well be true but it does not leave any scope for an economic model to come between the premises and the phenomenon to be explained. Instead, the question shifts back to: 'Why do some people have this kind of motivation more strongly than others?'

[...]

We shall take this up by following the argument of *The Logic of Collective Action* by Mancur Olson, Jr. (1965). This is the only book fit to rank with Downs' *Economic Theory of Democracy*, as an exemplar of the virtues of the 'economic' approach to political analysis. Both books, as may be expected in pioneering works, suffer from obscurities and ambiguities which become apparent on close examination. But it is greatly to their advantage that, unlike so many books on political and sociological theory, they stimulate and repay this degree of careful attention.

The discussion so far will enable us to present Olson's central point very quickly, for it is essentially a generalization of the idea that the reward of voting (in rational 'economic' terms) is the party differential times the probability that one vote will alter the outcome of the election. Olson's argument is intended to apply wherever what is at stake is a 'public good', that is, a benefit which cannot be deliberately restricted to certain people, such as those who helped bring it into existence. A potential beneficiary's calculation, when deciding whether to contribute to the provision of such a benefit, must take the form of seeing what the benefit would be to him and discounting it by the probability that his contribution would make the difference between the provision and the non-provision of the benefit. Where there are large numbers of potential beneficiaries, and especially when none of them stands to gain a lot, Olson argues that the total contribution made to the provision of the benefit will be much less than it would be if the beneficiaries were all rolled into one person who did the best possible for himself. In many cases, he suggests, there will simply be no contributions at all.

An excellent example of a 'public good' is a state policy – for instance, a particular piece of legislation on tariffs or the labelling of consumer goods. Someone who stands to be benefited by this legislation will not automatically be advantaged by paying to support a lobby in its favour. He has to ask not whether an extra pound spent on campaigning will bring in more than a pound's worth of benefit to the potential beneficiaries taken all together, but whether an extra pound contributed by him will bring in more than a pound's worth of benefit to him. And on this basis he often will not contribute. He will not reason: 'If everyone fails to contribute, we'll all be worse off than if we all contribute, so I'll contribute'. For whether all, some or none of the others contribute will not be affected by whether or not he does, and it is therefore irrelevant to ask what would happen if they all acted on the same principle as himself.

Of course, where the beneficiaries form a small group in close contact with one another, the assumption that the decisions are independent of one another cannot be upheld. The members of the group can say to one another 'I won't contribute unless everyone else does', and, by making mutual threats of this kind, get the rate of contributions above what it would otherwise be. Even in quite small groups, however, this round of threats may be pretty hollow if some of the potential beneficiaries obviously could not afford *not* to contribute because they stand to gain so much. So the basic logic of self-interest may still show through. Thus, Olson has argued (Olson, 1966) that, insofar as N.A.T.O. can be regarded as providing a 'public good' to the member countries – defence against 'Communist aggression' – one would expect from the theory that the bigger countries (especially the U.S.A.) would contribute more than in proportion to their G.N.P., and the smallest countries less than in proportion, and this is in fact the case.

There are, then, two general results if people apply an individually rational calculation to the decision whether to contribute to the provision of a public good. First, the total contribution will be 'too low'; and, second, the contribution of the greatest beneficiaries will be disproportionately high. The latter will tend to come about in conditions of independent decision as well as in the interdependent case discussed. Suppose the total benefit is £1,000, and that one potential beneficiary stands to gain £100 while 90 others stand to gain £10 each. The first man should think it worth spending £25 on promoting the benefit even if nobody else co-operates, provided he thinks that this expenditure has a better than one in four chance of bringing about the benefit. But it would not pay any of the others to contribute £2 10s. unless he thought that £2 10s. had one chance in four of bringing the benefit about.[5]

### 4 APPLICATION OF OLSON'S THEORY

The bulk of Olson's short book consists of applications of the basic ideas to various kinds of social organization. His analysis has a destructive and a constructive side. The destructive part consists of pointing out that a common explanation of organizations providing 'public goods' to the members is fallacious. This is the explanation that it pays them to belong because by contributing to it they help it to succeed and thus increase the benefits to themselves. The question is whether the contribution that the individual makes increases the benefit *he* gets enough to make it worth while, and where there are many beneficiaries the discounted pay-off from the organisation's success is unlikely to be significant. The fallacy arises from treating 'the beneficiaries' as if they were a single individual deciding how to allocate his resources to the best advantage. Thus one must reject all conventional explanations of the existence of trade unions or pressure groups in terms of the self-interest of members stemming directly from the collective benefits provided. Similarly, if Marx's theory of class was intended to move from an assumption of individual self-interest to the 'rationality' of pursuing one's *class* interests once one realises what they are, then, Olson argues, it breaks down in precisely the same way.

The constructive side of Olson's work lies in his insistence that wherever we do find an organisation providing a public good and supported by the beneficiaries we must look for, and will normally find, motives other than the provision of the public good keeping people contributing to the organisation. Olson calls these 'selective incentives': that is to say, they are benefits which (unlike the public good) can be provided for members and effectively withheld from non-members, thus providing a particular gain to offset the cost of belonging.[6] Olson suggests that trade unions do not gain members by preaching their advantages to the working class as a whole, or even to all the workers in a particular industry, but by providing selective incentives. These may in the earlier stages be such things as sickness and death benefits but, once established, the union may succeed in getting a 'closed shop' (i.e. make union membership a condition of employment enforced by the firm) or bring about the same result by informal social pressures. Another possibility is that the function of representing individual workers who have grievances against management may be to some degree a selective incentive offered by the union to its members. Again, Olson argues that pressure groups do not rely for membership on showing that they are doing a good job in promoting measures to benefit all members (since these would equally well benefit potential members who do not join) but, as predicted by his theory, their staffs tend to devote a great deal of energy to providing specific benefits – information and other services – on an individual basis to members.

How convincing are these applications of the basic idea? Let us divide this into two questions, one involving its application to the arguments of other writers, and the other involving its use in explaining actual social phenomena. It seems to me quite clear that Olson has succeeded in finding arguments in various writers which make sense only if one supplies the premise that it is in an individual's interest to support collective action that would be to his interests. Thus, D. B. Truman, in his influential book *The Governmental Process* (Truman, 1951), really does seem to claim that wherever there is a common interest among people similar in some respect we have what he calls a latent group, and this group will be transformed from latency to actuality if its common interests are infringed. This is, of course, a very comforting notion for one who supports a group-dominated polity (as does Truman) because it suggests that if there are interests with no organisation this must show that they are being adequately catered for already. Olson is surely right to argue against this that 'latent groups' are latent not because there is no collective action that would advance the interest but because conditions are unpropitious for getting it organised.[7]

The difficulty which a highly intelligent man can have in extricating himself from the fallacy attacked by Olson – moving from collective interest to individual interest without specifying selective sanctions – may be illustrated by referring to a recent lecture by the German sociologist, Ralf Dahrendorf (1967). In this, he repudiates what he claims to have been his earlier assumption that quasi-groups (defined as a category of person with a shared interest in something's happening) have a natural tendency to become actual, organised groups. I am not at all sure that his earlier theory (in Dahrendorf, 1959) was definite enough to have committed him to this (or to anything else) but that is not the present point. What I wish to show is that Dahrendorf fails, in the lecture, to free himself from the fallacy exposed by Olson.

The idea he puts forward is that, starting from an axiom of self-interest, we can deduce the circumstances under which energy will be put into collective action, namely that it will be at a maximum when there is little scope for advancement by individual action. Collective action among the working class has declined, Dahrendorf asserts, and the explanation is that it is now possible to find self-fulfilment by, say, taking a holiday in Italy. But, on Olson's analysis, it is doubtful whether joining in collective action aimed at the benefit of the working class as a whole would ever be in the interests of an individual, if we are thinking (as Dahrendorf apparently is) of the benefit as simply the value to the individual of the result of the collective action. Dahrendorf would probably have been on a better tack had he argued that the *selective* incentives offered by being a prominent member of an organisation have declined in value because other sources of gratification have become available and also because the status gained in a local community from being, say, a Chapel Elder or a Labour Party officer, has less currency in a more mobile society with a more centralised status-hierarchy.

Turning to Olson's examples of successful and unsuccessful organisations, I think one has to say that he tends to pick the cases which support his thesis rather than start by sampling the universe of organisations of a certain type within certain spatio-temporal boundaries. This is especially significant in the matter of explaining the levels of success of different organisations. Olson seems on fairly safe ground when he suggests (with examples) that an organisation which starts offering selective incentives at a certain point in its history will find that recruitment increases. But can we hope to explain the generally higher levels of unionism in Britain than in the U.S.A. by saying that there are more selective incentives? Can we explain the variations in union membership between industries by selective incentives? And can we explain the rise of mass unionism in Britain in the 1880s and the decline in union membership after 1926 by this means? On the face of it, these seem more related to such things as the perceived prospects for the success of collective action: the 'new unionism' was reinforced by successful industrial action, while the fiasco of the General Strike led to disillusionment. Likewise, the more similar the positions of a large number of workers are, the more they are likely to see a chance for collective betterment by unionism [...]. Yet these are precisely the kinds of consideration that are ruled out by Olson, on the grounds that it is not rational for anyone to incur a cost where the increased amount of a public good that will thereby come to him personally is negligible.

## 5 PARTICIPATION IN COLLECTIVE ACTION: SOME EXPLANATIONS

We thus arrive at a somewhat curious position. Downs tries to argue for the discounted value of the additional collective benefit (in this case the prospect of averting the collapse of the system) as an adequate explanation of voting. Olson, on the other hand, in accounting for membership of trade unions and pressure groups, dismisses the extra bit of collective benefit as an inadequate motive and insists on 'selective incentives'. The actual situation seems to be the same in both cases. In neither case would the marginal bit of collective benefit normally be sufficient to motivate an economically 'rational' person. Here Downs is wrong and Olson right. But, equally, in both cases a belief in the efficacy of the process does look as if it is related to participation, though not necessarily via an ill-calculated judgment of private self-interest. Whatever the reason why a person may attach himself to a cause, more enthusiasm for its pursuit is likely to be elicited if it looks as if it has a chance of succeeding than if it appears to be a forlorn hope. Nobody likes to feel that he is wasting his time, and that feeling may be induced by contributing to a campaign which never looks as if it has a chance.[8] Thus, it has been suggested that extreme right-wing political groups flourish in California and certain other states not so much because the sentiments are so much commoner as because the political structure (especially the weakness of party organisations) makes it more likely that intervention will produce results [...]. In a similar vein, Banfield has argued that the fragmented decision-making structure in Chicago makes it easier for citizen groups to modify policy and thus encourages their activity (Banfield, 1961).

Finally, a 'sense of duty' appears to be an important factor in voting, and perhaps it is in some voluntary associations too. To take a pure case, it is difficult to see what 'selective incentive' or personal benefit comes about from sending a cheque to Oxfam. It is, of course, true and important that organisations providing selective incentives (e.g. shops) and those raising money coercively to provide public goods (e.g. the government) succeed in getting hold of a lot more of our incomes. But the example shows that other factors must be allowed for somewhere.

Now, as we have already seen, we can fit anything into a loosely 'economic' framework, if we are sufficiently hospitable to different kinds of 'reward' and 'cost'. Thus, we could say that the sense of guilt at not contributing to some altruistic organisation provides a 'selective incentive', since the guilt is obviously not incurred if one contributes. Or, where an organisation is expected to provide collective benefits for its members (but, by definition, not exclusively to its members), a man might be said to feel the pangs of conscience if he shares in the benefits without contributing time or money to the organisation himself. It is interesting to notice that this is a moral position, in that it does not reflect pure self-interest, though at the same time it depends on the belief that one will benefit personally from the activities of the organisation.[9] A difficulty here is that sentiments of reciprocity are probably most likely to arise in face-to-face groups, and it is in these that social sanctions (a straightforward selective incentive) are most likely to be applied and to be effective. This implies that behaviour alone will often not enable us to infer the actor's motivation. But there are still two kinds of evidence. One is what people say, and the other is how they act when the non-co-operative move would remove them from the reach of the group's available sanctions. Examples, from armies in the Second World War, may be found for both. Thus, survey data on soldiers' attitudes for the U.S.A. and information on desertion rates in the closing stages of the war for Germany both bear out the point. [...] In both cases it can be concluded that unwillingness to let down 'buddies' seems to be a large component of 'morale', that is to say preparedness for fighting.

An alternative 'moral' position which might lead to participation in collective action would be a simple utilitarian one. On this basis someone might argue in a certain instance that the increment of benefits (or incremental probability of benefit) produced by his contribution would be greater than the cost incurred by himself, so there would be a net benefit (not to himself, of course, but to the human race as a whole) if he contributed. Olson himself argues, contrary to this, that even if a man's intentions were wholly altruistic it would not be rational to join an organisation producing collective benefits. 'Even if the member of a large group were to neglect his own interests entirely, he still would not rationally contribute toward the provision of any collective or public good, since his own contribution would not be perceptible' (Olson, 1956, page 64). This is surely absurd. If each contribution is literally 'imperceptible' how can all the contributions together add up to anything? Conversely, if a hundred thousand members count for something, then each one contributes on the average a hundred-thousandth. If it is rational for workers in an industry to wish for a closed shop, thus coercing everyone to join the union, this must mean that the total benefits brought by the union are greater than its total costs. (Otherwise it would be better not to have the union.) But if this is so, it must mean that anyone who wished purely to maximise the gains of workers in the industry would join the union voluntarily.

It should be clear that this is not inconsistent with the basic point of Olson's that we have accepted. Suppose, for example, that (up to some point) for every pound spent on a public good a thousand people will derive ten pounds'-worth of benefit each. An altruist (who might or might not be one of the potential beneficiaries) would clearly find a good use for his funds here. But it would not *pay* one of the potential beneficiaries to contribute, because the benefit *to him* from giving a pound would be only one new penny (ten pounds divided by a thousand).[10]

[...]

## NOTES

1. Of course, a consumer may decide to defer expenditure on consumption and save money instead, but this course is not open to a voter. If you fail to vote in one election you have lost that vote for ever – you do not get an extra vote next time.
2. Even if we relax the assumption of a single national electorate, and allow for constituencies, the citizen still has to guess (i) what is the chance of his constituency being won by a single vote, and (ii) even if it were, how likely it is that a single seat more for his party would make any great difference. Of course, we could suppose that politicians are sensitive to the narrowness of their majority in popular votes as such (and this was apparently true of Churchill in 1951 and Kennedy in 1960) but even so, one vote is still not likely to make a noticeable difference (cf. Riker, 1968, pages 40–2).
3. Another point which Riker presents as original is that a rational voter's decision will be partly a function of how close he expects the election to be, and not simply of the size of the electorate. In fact, Downs makes this observation quite explicitly on page 244. Riker also describes the idea as 'non-obvious' (page 38). Its non-obviousness is not, perhaps, obvious.

4. Insofar as it includes voting as a purely expressive act, not undertaken with any expectation of changing the state of the world, it fails to fit the minimum requirements of the means – end model of rational behaviour.

5. As it stands, this analysis is somewhat weak in that it argues from the amount that each actor would contribute if he were the only contributor to the amount he would actually contribute. But of course the question a potential beneficiary must ask is what his contribution would do at the margin. But in order to know where the margin is he has to know the decisions of everyone else, and their decisions in turn depend on everyone else's. So the answer is strictly indeterminate. But we can say that, if campaign funds (etc.) bring decreasing returns, the amount each person would contribute if he were the only contributor gives us the *maximum* total contribution possible. We can also say that if the biggest beneficiary commits himself first, then the next biggest, and so on, the tendency for the biggest beneficiaries to pay disproportionately will be increased. It must be admitted, though, that Olson does not seem to appreciate the way in which assumptions of this kind are needed to make his 'proof' work.

6. The word 'benefits', here, as normally in economic analysis, includes the absence of costs. Thus, for example, if a man would be ostracised or physically molested for not joining a trade union, we can say that belonging to the union provides the benefit of *not* having these unpleasant things happen.

7. For a development of this argument at a theoretical level, see Barry, 1965, Chapters 14 and 15. A full-scale treatment of the theme, with much supporting evidence drawn from the history of the U.S.A. is McConnell, 1966.

8. There is, of course, in addition to this the combative satisfaction of being on the winning side, but this takes on a high value only if one previously had doubts about one's own side winning. So this reinforces the tendency for cases where the issue is in doubt to produce more activity, though it would lead us to expect a bias towards the side with the better chances.

9. Goldthorpe *et al.* seem to me to neglect this point in their discussion of the motives for joining a trade union. They contrast 'moral conviction' with a belief that 'union membership pays', but the latter belief needs to be broken down into conceptions of individual and collective benefit (Goldthorpe, 1968, page 98; Table 39 on page 97). Notice that this is not just a matter of finding out more exactly what people think, but of having, as an observer, a clear idea of the structure of the situation and its implications for distinguishing between self-interested behaviour and 'principled' or altruistic behaviour. The informant might not think of his behaviour explicitly as altruistic, though objectively it is.

10. It may be noted that the same analysis can be applied to Downs's calculus of voting. If someone adopts a utilitarian position he may well think it worth voting, either to increase the chance of one party winning or to protect the system. (Cf. Barry, 1965, pages 328–30.)

## REFERENCES

Banfield, E. C., *Political Influence* (Free Press, New York, 1961).

Barry, B., *Political Argument* (Routledge & Kegan Paul, London, 1965).

Dahrendorf, R., *Class and Class Conflict in Industrial Society* (Stanford University Press, Stanford, CA, 1959).

Dahrendorf, R., *Conflict after Class: New Perspectives on the Theory of Social and Political Conflict*, 3rd Noel Buxton Lecture at the University of Essex (Longmans, London, 1967).

Goldthorpe, J. H., Lockwood, D., Bechhofer, F. and Platt, J., *The Affluent Worker: Industrial Attitudes and Behaviour*, Cambridge Studies in Sociology No. 1 (Cambridge University Press, Cambridge, 1968).

McConnell, G., *Private Power and American Democracy* (Alfred A. Knopf, New York, 1966).

Olson, M. Jr, *The Logic of Collective Action: Public Goods and the Theory of Groups* (Harvard University Press, Cambridge, MA, 1965).

Olson, M. Jr and Zeckhauser, R., 'An Economic Theory of Alliances', *Review of Economics and Statistics* 48, 1966, pp. 266–79.

Riker, W. H. and Ordeshook, P. C., 'A Theory of the Calculus of Voting', *American Political Science Review*, 62, 1968, pp. 25–42.

Truman, D. B., *The Governmental Process* (Alfred A. Knopf, New York, 1951).

# SECTION 10
# THE MARKET

# THE MARKET
# INTRODUCTION

As we saw with the Marxist critique of liberal democracy, the nature of the relationship between the 'free' market and democracy is a contentious one. While Marxists claim that capitalism hinders democracy, others see the market as affording a model of information exchange and action coordination that assists democracy. In this section, we present selections which, particularly following upon the work of Hayek, stress the profoundly democratic nature of the market itself. Crucial to any investigation of the compatibility of the market and democracy is the role of democratic state intervention in the market.

The opening selection from *Hayek* describes the functioning of the market in terms of a 'spontaneous order' throughout which knowledge is widely dispersed. According to Hayek, it is precisely the dispersed and decentralised nature of knowledge in a market that enables individuals to be autonomous and free. Where governments, and even democratic governments, seek to centrally operate or control markets, we find not only a significant loss of efficiency, but also a loss of liberty.

The selection from *Friedman* makes the case for free markets more strongly still, claiming that the market is the most appropriate mechanism for the coordination of action, one which should therefore be widely utilised throughout society. Once again, by stressing the extraordinary capacities of markets to derive effectiveness from diversity and the absence of central authority, we arrive at the conclusion that democratic governments should be primarily conceived as umpires upon private exchanges. Here then, the market is seen as an important counterweight to the possible centralisation of political power.

In the selection from *Beetham*, we are provided with an overview of the debate surrounding the relation between the market and democracy. Beetham argues that while there are a number of ways in which capitalism indeed functions as a limitation upon democracy, these limitations also afford significant democratic gains. He then considers socialist accounts of the relation between the market and democracy and concludes that these place even greater limits on democracy.

The final selection from *Wainwright* considers the implications of Hayek's account of dispersed knowledge for the development of self-managed firms and other initiatives in an 'economic democracy'. Wainwright's concern is to accept the account of decentralised knowledge offered by Hayek in his analysis of markets. She then seeks to extend his insights in order to inspect the possibilities they afford for democratic innovation. Wainwright advocates a thorough democratisation of knowledge in our society, particularly knowledge that so successfully circulates within a market, and which all too often eludes even minimal democratic guidance.

# 64

# THE FATAL CONCEIT:
# THE ERRORS OF SOCIALISM

## F. A. Hayek

[...]

### HOW WHAT CANNOT BE KNOWN CANNOT BE PLANNED

Where has the discussion of our last two chapters brought us? The doubts Rousseau cast on the institution of several property became the foundation of socialism and have continued to influence some of the greatest thinkers of our century. Even as great a figure as Bertrand Russell defined liberty as the 'absence of obstacles to the realisation of our desires' (1940: 251). At least before the obvious economic failure of Eastern European socialism, it was widely thought by such rationalists that a centrally planned economy would deliver not only 'social justice' [...], but also a more efficient use of economic resources. This notion appears eminently sensible at first glance. But it proves to overlook the facts just reviewed: that the totality of resources that one could employ in such a plan *is simply not knowable to anybody*, and therefore can hardly be centrally controlled.

Nonetheless, socialists continue to fail to face the obstacles in the way of fitting separate individual decisions into a common pattern conceived as a 'plan'. The conflict between our instincts, which, since Rousseau, have become identified with 'morality', and the moral traditions that have survived cultural evolution and serve to restrain these instincts, is embodied in the separation now often drawn between certain sorts of ethical and political philosophy on the one hand and economics on the other. The point is not that whatever

From F. A. Hayek, *The Fatal Conceit: The Errors of Socialism*, ed. W. W. Bartley (Routledge, London, 1988), pp. 85–8.

economists determine to be efficient is therefore 'right', but that economic analysis can elucidate the usefulness of practices heretofore thought to be right – usefulness from the perspective of any philosophy that looks unfavourably on the human suffering and death that would follow the collapse of our civilisation. It is a betrayal of concern for others, then, to theorise about the 'just society' without carefully considering the economic consequences of implementing such views. Yet, after seventy years of experience with socialism, it is safe to say that most intellectuals outside the areas – Eastern Europe and the Third World – where socialism has been tried remain content to brush aside what lessons might lie in economics, unwilling to wonder whether there might not be a *reason* why socialism, as often as it is attempted, never seems to work out as its intellectual leaders *intended*. The intellectuals' vain search for a truly socialist community, which results in the idealisation of, and then disillusionment with, a seemingly endless string of 'utopias' – the Soviet Union, then Cuba, China, Yugoslavia, Vietnam, Tanzania, Nicaragua – should suggest that there might be something about socialism that does not conform to certain facts. But such facts, first explained by economists more than a century ago, remain unexamined by those who pride themselves on their rationalistic rejection of the notion that there could be any facts that transcend historical context or present an insurmountable barrier to human desires.

Meanwhile, among those who, in the tradition of Mandeville, Hume, and Smith, did study economics, there gradually emerged not only an understanding of market processes, but a powerful critique of the possibility of substituting socialism for them. The advantages of these market procedures were so contrary to expectation that they could be explained only retrospectively, through analysing this spontaneous formation itself. When this was done, it was found that decentralised control over resources, control through several property, leads to the generation and use of more information than is possible under central direction. Order and control extending beyond the immediate purview of any central authority could be attained by central direction only if, contrary to fact, those local managers who could gauge visible and potential resources were *also* currently informed of the constantly changing relative importance of such resources, and could then communicate full and accurate details about this to some central planning authority in time for it to tell them what to do in the light of all the other, different, concrete information it had received from other regional or local managers – who of course, in turn, found themselves in similar difficulties in obtaining and delivering any such information.

Once we realise what the task of such a central planning authority would be, it becomes clear that the commands it would have to issue could not be derived from the information the local managers had recognised as important, but could only be determined through direct dealings among individuals or groups controlling clearly delimited aggregates of means. The hypothetical assumption, customarily employed in theoretical descriptions of the market process (descriptions made by people who usually have no intention of supporting socialism), to the effect that all such facts (or 'parameters') can be assumed to be known to the explaining theorist, obscures all this, and consequently produces the curious deceptions that help to sustain various forms of socialist thinking.

The order of the extended economy is, and can be, formed only by a wholly different process – from an evolved method of communication that makes it possible to transmit, not an infinite multiplicity of reports about particular facts, but merely certain abstract properties of several particular conditions, such as competitive prices, which must be brought into mutual correspondence to achieve overall order. These communicate the different rates of substitution or equivalence that the several parties involved find prevailing between the various goods and services whose use they command. Certain quantities of any such objects may prove to be equivalents or possible substitutes for one another, either for satisfying particular human needs or for producing, directly or indirectly, means to satisfy them. Surprising as it may be that such a process exists at all, let alone that it came into being through evolutionary selection without being deliberately designed, I know of no efforts to refute this contention or discredit the process itself – unless one so regards simple declarations that all such facts can, somehow, be known to some central planning authority. [...]

Indeed the whole idea of 'central control' is confused. There is not, and never could be, a single directing mind at work; there will always be some council or committee charged with designing a plan of action for some enterprise. Though individual members may occasionally, to convince the others, quote particular pieces of information that have influenced their views, the conclusions of the body will generally not be based on common knowledge but on agreement among several views based on different information. Each bit of knowledge contributed by one person will tend to lead some other to recall yet other facts of whose relevance he has become aware only by his being told of yet other circumstances of which he did not know. Such a process thus remains one of making use of dispersed knowledge (and thus simulates trading, although in a highly inefficient way – a way usually lacking competition and diminished in accountability), rather than unifying the knowledge of a number of persons. The members of the group will be able to communicate to one another few of their distinct reasons; they will communicate chiefly conclusions drawn from their respective individual knowledge of the problem in hand. Moreover, only rarely will circumstances really be the same for different persons contemplating the same situation – at least in so far as this concerns some sector of the extended order and not merely a more or less self-contained group.

Perhaps the best illustration of the impossibility of deliberate 'rational' allocation of resources in an extended economic order without the guidance by prices formed in competitive markets is the problem of allocating the current supply of liquid capital among all the different uses whereby it could increase the final product. The problem is essentially how much of the currently accruing productive resources can be spared to provide for the more distant future as against present needs. Adam Smith was aware of the representative character of this issue when, referring to the problem faced by an individual owner of such capital, he wrote: 'What is the species of domestick industry which his capital can employ, and of which the produce is likely to be of the greatest value, every individual, it is evident, can, in his local situation, judge much better than any statesman or lawgiver can do for him' (1776/1976).

> If we consider the problem of the use of all means available for investment in an extended economic system under a single directing authority, the first difficulty is that no such determinate aggregate quantity of capital available for current use can be known to anyone, although of course this quantity is limited in the sense that the effect of investing either more or less than it must lead to discrepancies between the demand for various kinds of goods and services. Such discrepancies will not be self-correcting but will manifest themselves through some of the instructions given by the directing authority proving to be impossible of execution, either because some of the goods required will not be there or because some materials or instruments provided cannot be used due to the lack of required complementary means (tools, materials, or labour). None of the magnitudes that would have to be taken into account could be ascertained by inspecting or measuring any 'given' objects, but all will depend on possibilities among which other persons will have to choose in the light of knowledge that they possess at the time. An approximate solution of this task will become possible only by the interplay of those who can ascertain particular circumstances which the conditions of the moment show, through their effects on market prices, to be relevant. The 'quantity of capital' available then proves, for example, what happens when the share of current resources used to provide for needs in the more distant future is greater than what people are prepared to spare from current consumption in order to increase provision for that future, i.e., their willingness to save.

Comprehending the role played by the transmission of information (or of factual knowledge) opens the door to understanding the extended order. Yet these issues are highly abstract, and are particularly hard to grasp for those schooled in the mechanistic, scientistic, constructivist canons of rationality that dominate our educational systems – and who consequently tend to be ignorant of biology, economics, and evolution. I confess that it took me too a long time from my first breakthrough, in my essay on 'Economics and Knowledge' (1936/48), through the recognition of 'Competition as a Discovery Procedure' (1978: 179–190), and my essay on 'The Pretence of Knowledge' (1978: 23–34), to state my theory of the dispersal of information, from which follows my conclusions about the superiority of spontaneous formations to central direction.

[...]

# 65

# CAPITALISM AND FREEDOM

## Milton Friedman

[...]

Historical evidence speaks with a single voice on the relation between political freedom and a free market. I know of no example in time or place of a society that has been marked by a large measure of political freedom, and that has not also used something comparable to a free market to organize the bulk of economic activity.

Because we live in a largely free society, we tend to forget how limited is the span of time and the part of the globe for which there has ever been anything like political freedom: the typical state of mankind is tyranny, servitude, and misery. The nineteenth century and early twentieth century in the Western world stand out as striking exceptions to the general trend of historical development. Political freedom in this instance clearly came along with the free market and the development of capitalist institutions. So also did political freedom in the golden age of Greece and in the early days of the Roman era.

History suggests only that capitalism is a necessary condition for political freedom. Clearly it is not a sufficient condition. Fascist Italy and Fascist Spain, Germany at various times in the last seventy years, Japan before World Wars I and II, tzarist Russia in the decades before World War I – are all societies that cannot conceivably be described as politically free. Yet, in each, private enterprise was the dominant form of economic organization. It is therefore

From Milton Friedman, *Capitalism and Freedom* (University of Chicago Press, Chicago and London, 1962), pp. 9–16.

clearly possible to have economic arrangements that are fundamentally capitalist and political arrangements that are not free.

Even in those societies, the citizenry had a good deal more freedom than citizens of a modern totalitarian state like Russia or Nazi Germany, in which economic totalitarianism is combined with political totalitarianism. Even in Russia under the Tzars, it was possible for some citizens, under some circumstances, to change their jobs without getting permission from political authority because capitalism and the existence of private property provided some check to the centralized power of the state.

The relation between political and economic freedom is complex and by no means unilateral. In the early nineteenth century, Bentham and the Philosophical Radicals were inclined to regard political freedom as a means to economic freedom. They believed that the masses were being hampered by the restrictions that were being imposed upon them, and that if political reform gave the bulk of the people the vote, they would do what was good for them, which was to vote for laissez faire. In retrospect, one cannot say that they were wrong. There was a large measure of political reform that was accompanied by economic reform in the direction of a great deal of laissez faire. An enormous increase in the well-being of the masses followed this change in economic arrangements.

The triumph of Benthamite liberalism in nineteenth-century England was followed by a reaction toward increasing intervention by government in economic affairs. This tendency to collectivism was greatly accelerated, both in England and elsewhere, by the two World Wars. Welfare rather than freedom became the dominant note in democratic countries. Recognizing the implicit threat to individualism, the intellectual descendants of the Philosophical Radicals – Dicey, Mises, Hayek, and Simons, to mention only a few – feared that a continued movement toward centralized control of economic activity would prove *The Road to Serfdom*, as Hayek entitled his penetrating analysis of the process. Their emphasis was on economic freedom as a means toward political freedom.

Events since the end of World War II display still a different relation between economic and political freedom. Collectivist economic planning has indeed interfered with individual freedom. At least in some countries, however, the result has not been the suppression of freedom, but the reversal of economic policy. England again provides the most striking example. The turning point was perhaps the "control of engagements" order which, despite great misgivings, the Labour party found it necessary to impose in order to carry out its economic policy. Fully enforced and carried through, the law would have involved centralized allocation of individuals to occupations. This conflicted so sharply with personal liberty that it was enforced in a negligible number of cases, and then repealed after the law had been in effect for only a short period. Its repeal ushered in a decided shift in economic policy, marked by reduced reliance on centralized "plans" and "programs", by the dismantling of many controls, and by increased emphasis on the private market. A similar shift in policy occurred in most other democratic countries.

The proximate explanation of these shifts in policy is the limited success of central planning or its outright failure to achieve stated objectives. However, this failure is itself to be attributed, at least in some measure, to the political implications of central planning and to an unwillingness to follow out its logic when doing so requires trampling rough-shod on treasured private rights. It may well be that the shift is only a temporary interruption in the collectivist trend of this century. Even so, it illustrates the close relation between political freedom and economic arrangements.

Historical evidence by itself can never be convincing. Perhaps it was sheer coincidence that the expansion of freedom occurred at the same time as the development of capitalist and market institutions. Why should there be a connection? What are the logical links between economic and political freedom? In discussing these questions we shall consider first the market as a direct component of freedom, and then the indirect relation between market arrangements and political freedom. A by-product will be an outline of the ideal economic arrangements for a free society.

As liberals, we take freedom of the individual, or perhaps the family, as our ultimate goal in judging social arrangements. Freedom as a value in this sense has to do with the interrelations among people; it has no meaning whatsoever to a Robinson Crusoe on an isolated island (without his Man Friday). Robinson Crusoe on his island is subject to "constraint," he has limited "power," and he has only a limited number of alternatives, but there is no problem of freedom in the sense that is relevant to our discussion. Similarly, in a society freedom has nothing to say about what an individual does with his freedom; it is not an all-embracing ethic. Indeed, a major aim of the liberal is to leave the ethical problem for the individual to wrestle with. The "really" important ethical problems are those that face an individual in a free society – what he should do with his freedom. There are thus two sets of values that a liberal will emphasize – the values that are relevant to relations among people, which is the context in which he assigns first priority to freedom; and the values that are relevant to the individual in the exercise of his freedom, which is the realm of individual ethics and philosophy.

The liberal conceives of men as imperfect beings. He regards the problem of social organization to be as much a negative problem of preventing "bad" people from doing harm as of enabling "good" people to do good; and, of course, "bad" and "good" people may be the same people, depending on who is judging them.

The basic problem of social organization is how to co-ordinate the economic activities of large numbers of people. Even in relatively backward societies, extensive division of labor and specialization of function is required to make effective use of available resources. In advanced societies, the scale on which co-ordination is needed, to take full advantage of the opportunities offered by modern science and technology, is enormously greater. Literally millions of people are involved in providing one another with their daily bread, let alone with their yearly automobiles. The challenge to the believer in liberty is to reconcile this widespread interdependence with individual freedom.

Fundamentally, there are only two ways of co-ordinating the economic activities of millions. One is central direction involving the use of coercion – the technique of the army and of the modern totalitarian state. The other is voluntary co-operation of individuals – the technique of the market place.

The possibility of co-ordination through voluntary co-operation rests on the elementary – yet frequently denied – proposition that both parties to an economic transaction benefit from it, *provided the transaction is bi-laterally voluntary and informed*.

Exchange can therefore bring about co-ordination without coercion. A working model of a society organized through voluntary exchange is a *free private enterprise exchange economy* – what we have been calling competitive capitalism.

In its simplest form, such a society consists of a number of independent households – a collection of Robinson Crusoes, as it were. Each household uses the resources it controls to produce goods and services that it exchanges for goods and services produced by other households, on terms mutually acceptable to the two parties to the bargain. It is thereby enabled to satisfy its wants indirectly by producing goods and services for others, rather than directly by producing goods for its own immediate use. The incentive for adopting this indirect route is, of course, the increased product made possible by division of labor and specialization of function. Since the household always has the alternative of producing directly for itself, it need not enter into any exchange unless it benefits from it. Hence, no exchange will take place unless both parties do benefit from it. Co-operation is thereby achieved without coercion.

Specialization of function and division of labor would not go far if the ultimate productive unit were the household. In a modern society, we have gone much farther. We have introduced enterprises which are intermediaries between individuals in their capacities as suppliers of service and as purchasers of goods. And similarly, specialization of function and division of labor could not go very far if we had to continue to rely on the barter of product for product. In consequence, money has been introduced as a means of facilitating exchange, and of enabling the acts of purchase and of sale to be separated into two parts.

Despite the important role of enterprises and of money in our actual economy, and despite the numerous and complex problems they raise, the central characteristic of the market technique of achieving co-ordination is fully displayed in the simple exchange economy that contains neither enterprises nor money. As in that simple model, so in the complex enterprise and money-exchange economy, co-operation is strictly individual and voluntary *provided*: (*a*) that enterprises are private, so that the ultimate contracting parties are individuals and (*b*) that individuals are effectively free to enter or not to enter into any particular exchange, so that every transaction is strictly voluntary.

It is far easier to state these provisos in general terms than to spell them out in detail, or to specify precisely the institutional arrangements most conducive to their maintenance. Indeed, much of technical economic literature is concerned with precisely these questions. The basic requisite is the maintenance of law and order to prevent physical coercion of one individual by another and to enforce contracts voluntarily entered into, thus giving substance to "private". Aside from this, perhaps the most difficult problems arise from monopoly – which inhibits effective freedom by denying individuals alternatives to the particular exchange – and from "neighborhood effects" – effects on third parties for which it is not feasible to charge or recompense them. These problems will be discussed in more detail in the following chapter.

So long as effective freedom of exchange is maintained, the central feature of the market organization of economic activity is that it prevents one person from interfering with another in respect of most of his activities. The consumer is protected from coercion by the seller because of the presence of other sellers with whom he can deal. The seller is protected from coercion by the consumer because of other consumers to whom he can sell. The employee is protected from coercion by the employer because of other employers for whom he can work, and so on. And the market does this impersonally and without centralized authority.

Indeed, a major source of objection to a free economy is precisely that it does this task so well. It gives people what they want instead of what a particular group thinks they ought to want. Underlying most arguments against the free market is a lack of belief in freedom itself.

The existence of a free market does not of course eliminate the need for government. On the contrary, government is essential both as a forum for determining the "rules of the game" and as an umpire to interpret and enforce the rules decided on. What the market does is to reduce greatly the range of issues that must be decided through political means, and thereby to minimize the extent to which government need participate directly in the game. The characteristic feature of action through political channels is that it tends to require or enforce substantial conformity. The great advantage of the market, on the other hand, is that it permits wide diversity. It is, in political terms, a system of proportional representation. Each man can vote, as it were, for the color of tie he wants and get it; he does not have to see what color the majority wants and then, if he is in the minority, submit.

It is this feature of the market that we refer to when we say that the market provides economic freedom. But this characteristic also has implications that go far beyond the narrowly economic. Political freedom means the absence of coercion of a man by his fellow men. The fundamental threat to freedom is power to coerce, be it in the hands of a monarch, a dictator, an oligarchy, or a momentary majority. The preservation of freedom requires the elimination of such concentration of power to the fullest possible extent and the dispersal and distribution of whatever power cannot be eliminated – a system of checks and balances. By removing the organization of economic activity from the control of political authority, the market eliminates this source of coercive power. It enables economic strength to be a check to political power rather than a reinforcement.

Economic power can be widely dispersed. There is no law of conservation which forces the growth of new centers of economic strength to be at the expense of existing centers. Political power, on the other hand, is more difficult to decentralize. There can be numerous small independent governments. But it is far more difficult to maintain numerous equipotent small centers of political power in a single large government than it is to have numerous centers of economic strength in a single large economy. There can be many millionaires in one large economy. But can there be more than one really outstanding leader, one person on whom the energies and enthusiasms of his countrymen are centered? If the central government gains power, it is likely to be at the expense of local governments. There seems to be something like a fixed total of political power to be distributed. Consequently, if economic power is joined to political power, concentration seems almost inevitable. On the other hand, if economic power is kept in separate hands from political power, it can serve as a check and a counter to political power.

[...]

# 66

# LIBERAL DEMOCRACY AND THE LIMITS OF DEMOCRATIZATION

## David Beetham

[...]

At first sight the questions of how much the state should do, and who can or should control it, would seem to belong in quite different theoretical domains. Surely the extent and the distribution of political power are two separate issues? Yet both liberals and socialists have argued that they are connected. Among the many issues in contention between them about the organization of economic life (justice, freedom, efficiency), not least is its implications for democracy. The liberal contention is that representative democracy has to be capitalist democracy, because only capitalism ensures the necessary limitation of state power that enables it to be democratically controlled. It is possible to distinguish a number of different arguments here, two about private property, two about the market, and a more general one about the pluralism of power. I shall set them out in propositional form to facilitate analysis and comparison.

L1 If the state owns and controls all productive property, it will be able to deny resources and even a livelihood to those campaigning against its policies. Political opposition requires secure access to the means of organizing, campaigning and disseminating information, and such access can only be guaranteed by the institution of private property.

L2 A system of socialized property of whatever kind will necessarily have to outlaw private ownership of the means of production, and, for its own

From David Beetham, 'Liberal Democracy and the Limits of Democratization', in D. Held (ed.), *Prospects for Democracy: North, South, East, West* (Polity, Cambridge, 1993), pp. 49–52.

survival, prevent political parties emerging which might campaign for its restitution. Socialism's tendency towards single-party rule is thus no historical aberration, whereas capitalism's ability to tolerate forms of social ownership in its midst (cooperatives, collective welfare organizations, and so on) provides a secure basis for multi-party competition.

L3 If the state takes over the task of economic coordination from the market, replacing its voluntary and lateral relations with a compulsory hierarchy of administrative planning, it will create a bureaucratic monster that no one can control, and stifle all independent initiative within society.

L4 From the standpoint of the citizen, the market is experienced as a much more democratic device than the polity, since it allows maximum individual choice and power to the consumer, in comparison with the monopolistic and insensitive provision of the public sector, where collective choices necessarily disregard minority preferences. Democracy therefore requires that the scope of the latter be restricted to an absolute minimum.

L5 The political liberties intrinsic to democracy depend upon a plurality of power centres capable of checking one another, among which the separation of power between the political and economic spheres, and within each, such as capitalism guarantees, is the most critical.

These propositions, taken together, do not entail that capitalism always produces political democracy, only that it is necessary to it; and more careful liberals will make this distinction clear. 'History suggests only that capitalism is a necessary condition for political freedom', writes Milton Friedman; 'clearly it is not a sufficient condition ...' In other words, there can be both capitalist democracies and capitalist dictatorships; but there can only be socialist dictatorships. On this view a fourth quartile (socialist democracy) is necessarily a historically empty category.

To each of these liberal propositions can be counterposed a corresponding socialist assertion.

S1 Private ownership makes democratization of the workplace impossible, since management must account to its shareholders rather than to its workers. The subordination of the latter in a key area of their lives is not only a major infringement of autonomy; it also discourages its exercise at the wider political level.

S2 Capitalism's 'tolerance' of socialist experiments in its midst is very limited, since they are forced to operate under conditions which hamper their effectiveness. The historical record shows that, if a socialist movement or party gathers sufficient support to threaten the interests of private property, capitalists will back a dictatorship to eliminate the threat.

S3 Leaving key economic decisions to market forces is to surrender a crucial sphere of collective self-determination to the haphazard play of private choices and to powerful institutions that owe no accountability to the public at large.

S4 Exercising choice in the consumer market depends upon income derived from the capital and labour markets, and here the character of the market is to intensify the inequalities of resource that people bring to it. The freer the market, the more repressive the state has to be to control the dissatisfactions of market losers.

S5 Capitalist society's pluralism is a highly constrained one, given the many modes of capitalism's integration into the state. Socialist pluralism would be more diverse, since it would not be tied to class conflict at the point of production.

Each of the ten propositions above merits a volume of commentary in itself, but I shall confine myself to making a few points that can be drawn from a comparison between them. First, although the liberal and socialist theses can be said to correspond to one another, they are not symmetrical. Whereas the thrust of the socialist five is that socialism is necessary to the *full* realization of democracy, the liberal case is that capitalism is necessary to the preservation of any democracy *at all*. In keeping with the characteristically sceptical temper of liberalism comes the advice to democrats to limit their ambitions: half a loaf is better than none.

Secondly, however, it is evident that not all liberalism's propositions carry the same weight against different versions of socialism. While all five can be arrayed against a command economy of the Soviet type, only one (L2) has any force against a form of market socialism with diversified social ownership. On the other hand, social democrats for their part can appeal to proposition S4 against neo-liberals to argue that, whatever other conditions democracy needs, it cannot be secure without a substantial welfare state. The balance sheet, in other words, is more complex than appears at first sight.

Thirdly, one of socialism's own propositions (the second part of S2) underlines what has proved a key historical dilemma for democratic socialists: whenever they have successfully mobilized popular support against private property, they have jeopardized the existence of representative democracy through the threat of capitalist reaction. Although the prospect of such support looks highly improbable in socialism's present nadir, it would be foolish to exclude the re-emergence of such support for ever, given that the end of the communist experiment does not signal the end of the problems of capitalism which gave it its initial impetus, least of all in the developing world. It is not enough, therefore, for socialists to show how a future socialist society might *guarantee* as well as extend democracy. They must also provide a credible strategy for realizing such a society within the framework of liberal democratic institutions.

It is this dilemma of transition, in conclusion, that justifies those strategies of economic democratization that work with the grain of private property rather than against it. Creating special representative bodies at the regional and national level to control the investment of pension funds on the one side; requiring a percentage of profits in individual firms to be set aside as shares for the collective control of employees on the other: these could provide the basis for a thoroughgoing democratization of economic life. The former would give workers the control over their own property that they now patently lack; the latter would ensure a progressive accumulation of ownership rights to accompany codetermination within enterprises. Unlike liberal proposals for wider share-ownership, however, such rights would have a crucial collective as well as individual dimension and would give the idea of a 'property-owning democracy' a more genuinely democratic content through the equalization of control over collective decisions they would bring.

[. . .]

# 67

# ARGUMENTS FOR A NEW LEFT

## Hilary Wainwright

[. . .]

SELF-MANAGEMENT AND ECONOMIC REGULATION

This returns us to the need to scrutinize the model classically set out by John Stuart Mill and developed more recently by David Prychitko: the combination of workers' self-management and the market. The importance of this view for the argument of this book is this: that the widespread implicit challenge, 'on the ground', to the presumption that the private entrepreneur has all the appropriate economic knowledge to revive the economy and must therefore be allowed a free hand, is a pragmatic belief in the knowledge and capacity for self-management of many of the recently elected factory committees. In itself, it does not provide an economic strategy, but it is an approach in dissonance with both the old orthodoxy and the new. Its starting point is appropriate: with those in these collapsing economies who have the practical knowledge about production.

Does the thesis of the social character of economic knowledge that I argued against Hayek, provide any clues as to mechanisms of co-ordination in an economy based on workers' self-management of the enterprise? Mill's view of knowledge and of the formation of individual capacities for knowledge was very different to that of Hayek. Mill's developmental and educational view of democracy implies a recognition of the social character of knowledge in the sense of an individual's knowledge being shaped to a significant extent by social

From Hilary Wainwright, *Arguments for a New Left: Answering the Free-Market Right* (Blackwell, Oxford and Cambridge, MA, 1994), pp. 146–9.

institutions. This understanding gave Mill's liberalism very different foundations to that of Hayek. Indeed, Hayek argues, along with others more sympathetic to Mill's position, that in driving his view of democracy to its logical
conclusion, in the second edition of *The Principles of Political Economy*, Mill
ended up arguing for socialism.

Mill, like Hayek, warned against the possibility of an overbearing, despotic
state if the market were regulated. He was also, however, against any political
and economic system which deprives individuals of a 'potential voice in their
own destiny', on the grounds that this undermines the basis of human dignity.
For Mill, 'the highest and harmonious expansion of individual capacities'
depends on peoples' active involvement in determining the conditions of their
existence. Moreover, Mill believed that when people participate in the resolution of social problems affecting themselves or a wider collectivity, energies are
unleashed which enhance the likelihood of imaginative solutions and successful
strategies. Participation in social and public life undercuts passivity and
increases general prosperity 'in proportion to the amount and variety of the
personal energies enlisted in promoting it.' What a contrast to Hayek's notion
that 'all man's mind can effectively comprehend are the facts of the narrow
circle of which he is the centre'.

Mill's developmental view of individual capacities does not, however, lead
him on to a radically distinct view of the knowledge problem involved in
economic co-ordination. His case for the market is mainly a case against economic monopoly, for both political and economic reasons. Competition is, in
his view, necessary for innovation and therefore economic progress. His
justification of the market was essentially based on the importance of competition and therefore economic pluralism. Whatever the adequacy of his analysis in
his own day, in present circumstances, where the threat of monopoly comes not
only from the state but also from concentrations of economic power produced
by the private market, a new question is posed for anyone who shares Mill's
belief in workers' self-management and in an egalitarian pluralism. The question is whether there are mechanisms of economic co-ordination and regulation
which allow an element of competition between self-managed enterprises, and
which at the same time promote social and environmental goals arising from
society-wide democratic processes in economic affairs. Or, putting it negatively,
can both market pressures and the rampant enterprise egoism that historically
has tended to undermine the practice of self-management be contained other
than exclusively through the state – and hence ineffectively, given the state's
inadequate knowledge? How would such non-state social mechanisms require
the support and resources of a democratic state? What would such a state need
to be like to provide the appropriate support?

### THE SOCIAL ORGANIZATION OF ECONOMIC KNOWLEDGE

Studies of the workings of actually existing market economies and of the
practices of the institutions and economic agents which shape them indicate

that the way that knowledge is distributed and organized is central to the way that existing economic arrangements reproduce themselves. The social distribution and organization of economic knowledge is being discovered as a vital economic variable. For some time there has been a recognition of the role of informal networks, social connections and, more recently, of inter-enterprise systems of direct co-ordination. This is acknowledgement, in the reproduction of a capitalist economy, of social relations that are neither market nor plan, neither the haphazard outcome of individual activity nor the design of an all-knowing central authority. The importance of many of these informal institutions lies above all in their role in sharing knowledge, in making established economic actors more knowing and consequently more powerful. In this chapter I want to argue that central to a variety of trade union and community based challenges to the present economic order are efforts to democratize and socialize economic knowledge. I will argue further that they illustrate the emergence of means of socializing the market through mechanisms embedded in independent democratic associations sharing practical knowledge, rather than the state – though these mechanisms, to be sustained, would need the support of the state institutions. This alliance between public institutions and independent associations would in turn lead to a process of democratising the former and making them more responsive.

Over the last twenty years or so a distinct feature of radical workplace and local organizing has been the creation – initially *ad hoc* but in many cases increasingly formally organized – of popularly based networks, especially on an international or at least continental scale, where no adequate means exists of political co-ordination on the left. Trade union committees, health and safety projects, initiatives for socially responsible fair trade, lesbian and gay movements, women's and other campaigning groups with a common interest, have found ways of associating without losing their autonomy. One of the prime purposes of making the connections, in the course of a variety of immediate practical tasks, has been to gather, share and accumulate knowledge which makes resistance more effective in reaching its target. To achieve this over a sustained period they have sometimes been supported by local or regional governments or, more recently, the EC; otherwise they have obtained funding from trade unions, sympathetic foundations and Church organizations.

[...]

# SECTION 11
# NATIONALISM

# NATIONALISM
# INTRODUCTION

---

The relationship between nationalism and democracy is one of the most pressing and troubled ones of contemporary politics, in both theory and practice. Nationalism and democracy seem to exist in a paradoxical relationship: at one and the same time they seem complementary, and yet contradictory. Nationalism and democracy in its modern form emerged simultaneously: ideas of the nation as a body of citizens determining their own fate, inhabiting a common territory, went together with democratic ideas of popular sovereignty. As *Ghia Nodia* observes in the extract reproduced in this section, '"Nation" is another name for "We the People"'. Nodia stresses that nationalism provides the emotional or non-rational basis for a democratic community. It offers a criterion for deciding on who are the members of the democratic community, and demarcates those who are citizens from those who are outside the boundaries of the citizen body.

Nationalism is also essentially bound up with ideas of autonomy, which we have seen (in Part One of this Reader) is a core concept of democracy. When extended from the individual to the national collective, the idea of national self-determination invokes the idea of a group of people, sharing a common history, culture and democratic rights, ruling themselves, free from foreign rule and internal tyranny. As *David Miller* argues in his study *On Nationality,* part of which appears below, the idea of national self-determination is an expression of collective autonomy. He implies that the trust and feelings of reciprocity involved in a single national community can offer a strong basis for a genuinely democratic community. National solidarity could function as a powerful reinforcement for a democratic society.

While these arguments stress the compatibility of nationalism and democracy, it is clear that nationalism and the national idea can take many forms, some of which undermine rather than reinforce democratic community. Ethnic nationalism has been witnessed in the phenomenon of 'ethnic cleansing', as recently seen in ex-Yugoslavia. If the state is made the vehicle of one ethnic group, nationalism restricts citizenship rights to members of this group, often excluding minority ethnic and national groups from the bounds of the citizenship community. How can these two faces of nationalism be reconciled?

In the course of his study of socialism and nationalism, *John Schwarzmantel* argues for a distinction between two concepts of the nation. He contrasts a citizenship-based or democratic view of the nation with a more ethnic form of nationalism. His argument is that the former is quite compatible with ideas of democratic community, and also with socialism. Ethnic nationalism, on the other hand, tends to be exclusive and to elevate the nation to the position of supreme focus of identity. In both respects it may threaten democracy.

There are thus two problem areas in the relationship between nationalism and democracy, which can be labelled as 'internal' and 'external' respectively. The former deals with the danger that nationalism can harness state power to one cultural, ethnic or national group, and result in exclusion and social closure. A democratic society could become intolerant of the cultural identities of minority groups, or remain wedded to one culturally relative set of assumptions, say those of North America and Western Europe. These issues are dealt with in Sections 12 and 13 on multiculturalism and non-Western perspectives below.

As for the 'external' challenges, some theorists hold that the historical association of democracy and the nation-state has now been superseded in an age of globalisation. They suggest that adequate conceptualisations of democracy can only be developed in a framework that goes beyond the nation-state.

# 68

# NATIONALISM AND DEMOCRACY

## Ghia Nodia

### THE LOGIC OF DEMOCRACY

At the core of democracy is the principle of popular sovereignty, which holds that government can be legitimated only by the will of those whom it governs. This general principle has to be distinguished from democratic *procedures*, which are intended as devices for discerning what the people really will. The main procedure is, of course, elections. Other sets of procedures help to safeguard democracy by restraining elected rulers through such measures as the separation of powers, limits on reelection, special requirements for constitutional amendments, and so on.

Democracy is supposed to be a highly *rational* enterprise. Its debt to the rationalist philosophical tradition can be easily seen in the notion of the social contract, which conceives of society as the construct of free and calculating individuals bent on maximizing their own interests. Democracy is a system of rules legitimated by the will of the people; it is presumed that the people will generally choose what seems to be in their best interest.

Thus anything that seems insufficiently rational, be it irrationalist philosophy or irrational human sentiments, is commonly understood as contrary to the idea of democracy. Nationalism is only one example of an "irrational" phenomenon that supposedly cuts against the democratic grain. By arguing that there is a

From Ghia Nodia, 'Nationalism and Democracy', in L. Diamond and Marc F. Plattner (eds), *Nationalism, Ethnic Conflict and Democracy* (Johns Hopkins University Press, Baltimore, MD and London, 1994), pp. 5–7.

necessary and positive link between nationalism and democracy, I am of course flying in the face of this common understanding.

To see how a nonrational phenomenon like nationalism can be vital to the democratic enterprise, it is helpful to compare this enterprise to a game. Democracy, like any game, consists of rules whose validity depends solely on the willingness of a certain community (the players, or citizens) to observe them. This analogy corresponds well to both of the aspects of democracy that we mentioned: the principle of popular sovereignty, and the fact that this sovereignty can meaningfully express itself only insofar as a specific set of rules (the constitution and laws) is created in its name. Popular sovereignty consists in the claim that "We the People" are going to play only by rules that we ourselves freely choose. Such rules (unlike the rules of games) are usually thought to have some independent moral value, which may in turn be grounded on certain religious beliefs ("In God We Trust"). But the concrete manner of *interpreting* those universal values (or God's will) depends on individual believers – on "We the People." Thus does democracy differ in principle from political systems (whether traditional or modern) where some ruling elite interprets the divine will (or an equivalent, like Marx's "laws" of historical development) and hands down rules accordingly.

This "game-like" aspect of democracy supposedly shows it to be completely rational. If we push the analogy further, however, we uncover nonrational aspects of the democratic enterprise. In addition to rules, a game also requires a community of players and a playing field. In games, all these things are wholly conventional and arbitrary, but this is not the case with the democratic enterprise. Democratic laws ("the rules") may be consensual products of rational decision making, but the composition and territory of the polity (the "players" and the "playing field") in which these laws will have force cannot be defined that way. Democracy, of course, has standard categories (citizenship and borders) for defining the players and the playing field. But the criteria for deciding just who is a citizen and just where the borders are cannot be derived from any logic intrinsic to the democratic enterprise.

Successful democracy presupposes the setting of these questions, whether or not the logic of rational democratic action has any inner resources for solving them. It is true that the democratic principle of self-determination and the democratic procedure of voting may help to facilitate their resolution, but the logic of democracy itself provides no specific criteria to guide one's vote or identify just which people and territories are to be included in the polity. Why should or should not a given group of people in a given area join or secede from some larger political entity?

Since the idea of democracy is universal, it would only be logical for the principle of popular sovereignty to be embodied in a worldwide polity. But this assumes that the democratic transition should be worldwide in the first place, and that the people themselves want it that way. History bears out neither of these assumptions. Democracy has always emerged in distinct communities;

there is no record anywhere of free, unconnected, and calculating individuals coming together spontaneously to form a democratic social contract *ex nihilo*. Whether we like it or not, nationalism is the historical force that has provided the political units for democratic government. "Nation" is another name for "We the People."

[...]

# 69

# ON NATIONALITY

## David Miller

[...]

Finally, we must consider the case for national self-determination as an expression of collective autonomy. This argument is more speculative than the other two because it appeals to a contestable view of the person. It supposes that people have an interest in shaping the world in association with others with whom they identify. This interest can be pursued in various forms – for instance in enterprises in an economic setting – so it is not tied exclusively to national self-determination. But, given the many important ways in which states are able to impress their will on both their physical and social environments, being a participant in such a collective undertaking is likely to represent a significant form of collective autonomy.

This argument must immediately be qualified in several respects. People appear to vary a great deal in the value they attach to collective autonomy, just as they differ in the importance they attach to national identity. For some people it is enough to be in control of their personal lives. The idea of taking part in some collective enterprise which sets its stamp on the world has little appeal. So we are dealing here with a human interest that is widely shared but far from universal. Next, the quest for collective autonomy may take unacceptable forms, forms that are damaging to personal liberty. People may come to regard dictatorial leaders or authoritarian states as the embodiment of collective purposes, and sacrifice their own personal interests in the name of illusory

From David Miller, *On Nationality* (Clarendon Press, Oxford, 1995), pp. 88–91.

'self-determination'. This lies at the heart of the critique of 'positive liberty' delivered by Isaiah Berlin. Collective autonomy may also be illusory for a different reason, namely that the state faces an external environment in which powerful economic and political forces effectively determine most of what it purports to control (for example, the chief parameters of the economy). Here, then, claims for national self-determination would be claims for a kind of autonomy that cannot, in fact, be achieved.

These qualifications show that appeals to the value of collective autonomy must be made with some care. In particular, autonomy of this kind requires more than that the state should coincide with the nation; it requires that what the state does should correspond to what we might call the popular will. The best guarantee of this is that the state should be democratic in form, with its decisions reflecting the judgements of its citizens as to what should be done. From this point of view, the historical association between ideas of democracy and ideas of national self-determination is hardly accidental: only a democratic state can ensure that the self-determination we are talking about is genuinely *national*, as opposed to the self-determination of a class or a governing clique. But it would be too strong to say that national self-determination strictly requires democracy. Provided there is indeed a genuine convergence in aims and interests between the population at large and those making decisions on their behalf, the interest in collective autonomy may be satisfied. We should see demands for self-determination in a colonial context in this light. It was not absurd for people to expect that they would have a greater sense of control over their destinies when ruled by local oligarchies than when ruled by imperial powers, even if in many cases these expectations have been frustrated.

I have been looking so far at nationalist reasons for valuing national self-determination. As I noted earlier, the thesis that a nation should want its own state is at one level tautological, since the ambition to be politically self-determining is built in to the very idea of nationhood. What we have seen, however, is that this ambition flows naturally from other aspects of nationality. It is *conceivable* that someone should accept that national identities are valuable, and that nationality carries with it special obligations to compatriots, but find no value in nations being autonomous political units, but we can now see why this is such an unlikely position to hold.

So let me now reverse the direction of the argument and ask why states, or more generally political authorities, are likely to function most effectively when they embrace just a single national community. The arguments here all appeal to the political consequences of solidarity and cultural homogeneity. They focus on the important role played by trust in a viable political community. Much state activity involves the furthering of goals which cannot be achieved without the voluntary co-operation of citizens. For this activity to be successful, the citizens must trust the state, and they must trust one another to comply with what the state demands of them. Let me give a couple of examples. One concerns the provision of public goods such as a clean and healthy environment.

The state can do certain things directly – it can fine polluters, for instance – but to achieve real results it must also very often rely on education and exhortation. Since adhering to the rules the state proposes will usually have costs, each person must be confident that the others will generally comply – and this involves mutual trust. For another example, consider state grants or concessions to particular groups within the population, say financial support to an industry hard hit by changes in the terms of trade, or special funding for local authorities with inner-city problems. These dispensations are made on the understanding that other sections of the community would qualify for similar favourable treatment in the event that they too faced new and unforeseen difficulties. Such a practice cannot evolve if each sectional group jealously guards its own interests and insists that each dispensation should be strictly egalitarian. Again, what is needed is mutual confidence which allows you to sanction aid to group G on this occasion with the assurance that group G will give you its reciprocal support when it is your turn to ask for help.

Now a state might attempt to diminish its reliance on mutual trust by restricting its role to that of a night-watchman, merely presiding over a market economy in which outcomes depend on separate individuals pursuing their own interests. Yet, quite apart from the question whether this is a viable possibility for a state in the late twentieth century, certain kinds of trust are still required to support the ground rules of a market: individuals must have confidence in one another to deal fairly, to keep contracts, and to refrain from using their industrial or financial muscle to oblige the state to intervene in the market on their behalf.

[…]

# 70

# TWO CONCEPTS OF THE NATION

## John Schwarzmantel

TAKING THE NATION SERIOUSLY

The argument will now be put forward that socialist perspectives on the nation need to be different from what they have been in the past. The discussion starts again from the distinction between nation in the *primary* (ethnic) sense, and nation in the *secondary* (political) sense. It has to be admitted that 'traditional' nationalism, of what was called [...] the organic cultural sort, based on a 'primary' concept of the nation, has been a much more powerful force than socialists were willing to recognize. The reasons for this appeal of nationalism have to be understood. Historically speaking, each primary nation wanted the protection of the state for its own culture. Taking a favourable view of nationalism, one could say that it has encapsulated values of autonomy and self-respect: each national group wanted to be self-determining, and this meant having its own state. This is the basis of the political idea of national self-determination, which has been such a powerful demand in the modern world.

Nationalism can be seen to have a positive side, in the aspiration for a world of diversity in which different national groups (primary nations, culture groups) each enjoy the protection of their own state. It was argued in some optimistic versions of the nationalist credo, like that of Herder, that the world would be a better place because of this variety. There would be no monotonous uniformity, but each nation, with its own state, would contribute something to a world

From John Schwarzmantel, *Socialism and the Idea of the Nation* (Harvester-Wheatsheaf, Hemel Hempstead, 1991), pp. 210–14.

enriched by the diversity of languages and national cultures. Each nation would respect the value and autonomy of other nations, and this would be guaranteed by the state structure – a world of nation-*states*, each state acting as an umbrella to allow the free flourishing of a particular national culture. Such a picture was presented by the classical 'moderate' nationalist perspective of the 1848 variety.

The force of this nationalist vision, its attractive element, resided in the values of autonomy and respect for a particular culture, indeed by extension for all cultures, and in the recognition that individuals are born into a particular national group. Such national cultures need 'space', literally and metaphorically, in which to develop. Furthermore, each individual person is inconceivable, except in a totally abstract sense, as a social being apart from or outside of such a cultural group, which therefore needs protecting.

This does, of course, present too rosy a picture of nationalism. The problem has been, historically speaking, that one of the ways in which ethnic groups (primary nations) asserted their autonomy was at the expense of other ethnic groups that happened to be living in the same geographical area. Some of the most disastrous episodes of modern history and politics found, and still do find, expression in pathological and aggressive forms of nationalism. Such forms stem from the fact that one way of asserting the originality and independence of a national group has been a xenophobic opposition and hostility to other cultures. Ethnic and cultural nationalism has certainly taken aggressive forms far removed from the harmonious world of nations envisaged in the democratic and republican nationalism of the 1848 tradition.

Nevertheless, the possibility of a reconciliation between socialism and some forms of nationalism can be defended. There are certain values in the nationalist perspective which can be reconciled with a socialist world-view. Let us return to the fundamental distinction between culture or ethnic-based nationalism, contrasted with a citizenship-based or democratic view of the nation, each seeing the nation in a different way. While the first view of the nation has certainly been most effective, historically speaking, the second can provide the basis for a nationalism of a different kind. This would preserve some of the values of nationalism (ideas of autonomy and self-determination), yet would not have the aggressive and anti-democratic tendencies manifested by some, though not all, kinds of the first form of nationalism. The argument put forward here is that socialism has to take seriously some of the values encapsulated in nationalism, and that it can do so by developing a perspective based on what is here distinguished as the *secondary* view of the nation.

As far as socialism is concerned, at the risk of some oversimplification one can say that two perspectives are possible with regard to nationalism. The first is an *instrumental* or *tactical* one. It means using nationalism and allying with nationalist movements where they seem to fit in with socialist aims, or to bypass and ignore such movements where they do not. In either case nationalism is regarded as fundamentally incompatible with a socialist perspective. Nationalism is often seen as 'false consciousness', and as such inherently irreconcilable with socialism. The second perspective, which we could call an 'internal' one, would yield a less 'external' view of the nation. It would seek to understand the core values which lie at the heart of nationalism, though they may find expression in different ways. Accepting this latter perspective, it could be argued that what lies at the heart of nationalism and secures its appeal is the respect for a particular cultural tradition which as such as constitutive of the nation. There seems to be no reason why this idea should necessarily clash with socialist perspectives of whatever kind – whether evolutionary or more radical – unless one of two positions is maintained which both exclude any attempt at reconciliation.

In the one position, class is made the sole focus of loyalty irrespective of any national setting. In the other position the nation is presented in its most demanding and almost dominant form, as an ethnic and cultural group with its own state demanding exclusive loyalty and cohesion overriding all individual and sub-group loyalties. The *integral nationalism* of Maurras and the *Action Française*, for example, maintained such a position, yet this is by no means true of all forms of nationalism. Similarly, with regard to the first position, class as the sole focus of loyalty, historically, as we have seen [...], class loyalty has often gone hand in hand with a sense of national identity. There seems no *a priori* reason to assume that there is a *zero-sum* position in which a greater degree of national loyalty necessarily and in all situations diminishes class solidarity or socialist feeling. As E. P. Thompson notes in a recent review, writing of the relationship between nationalism and internationalism, it is an error to assume that there is 'some limited quantum of political energy, like an account out of which nationalist or internationalist sentiment must be drawn, and an excessive draft of one must necessarily involve a deficit in the other'.

The conclusion is that there is no necessary reason why socialism should not take up some of the themes of nationalism based on citizenship or on political organization. Indeed, we argue here that the failure to take nationalism seriously, or the way in which it has been understood in predominantly *instrumental* terms, has been damaging to the Left. Nationalism exists, and remains powerful, for reasons which should be clear from what was said above. These reasons have to do with respect for and autonomy of a cultural and ethnic group, protection for the nation within which people come to acquire their particular identity through language. The fact that this demand for national and cultural autonomy has taken disastrously brutal and aggressive forms does not entail that socialists should have no truck with nationalism of any kind. The sentiment of nationalism exists and can be exploited in different ways. It can and has taken anti-democratic and authoritarian forms. But it has also, historically, taken the form of a democratic community sharing a national territory within which democratic rights are secured, free from outside oppression.

Thus in this 'secondary' sense of the nation ideas of a national community and a socialist community can go together. The socialist view could be a view of the nation as a community of citizens. This is a *political*, rather than an *ethnic* concept of the nation. To illustrate this 'secondary' concept of the nation the example was given of the United States of America. There, it could be said, citizens of the United States come from a whole host of different ethnic and cultural backgrounds, white Anglo-Saxon Protestants (WASP), Italian, Jewish, Hispanic, or whatever. Despite this heterogeneous background, they are members of a political community, the American nation, sharing common political rights, at least in theory. Indeed it is those citizenship rights, their shared possession, that define the nation. It would be wrong to say that this secondary (or political) concept of the nation does not involve a shared culture. There exists a common political culture, expressed in loyalty to the flag, rites and emblems of citizenship which bind the society together. This shared political culture then coexists with a range of ethnic cultures (primordial loyalties), with forms of cultural pluralism. Yet these latter are 'private', are not constitutive of the nation, any more than religious affiliation or any other group membership. There is a shared 'civic culture', one could say, with an ideology of citizenship that constitutes the American nation. Then beneath that layer, there is the range of private ethnic and cultural affiliations forming civil society, the private sphere.

Nationalism has been effective because of the idea of the nation as an ethnic community. Socialists cannot accept this concept of the nation, though they can recognize the reasons for its appeal. It is argued here that they must therefore reject the primary or ethnic concept of the nation, but oppose to it an alternative idea of the nation, which is different from the way in which the nation has been defined by nationalists. The difference resides both in the criteria of national identity, and in the fact that the nation is not seen as the sole or overriding focus of loyalty. The nation is the unit embracing all those who share common political and indeed social rights. It has nothing to do with common ethnic affiliation, and this concept of the nation is in no way incompatible with forms of internationalism. Furthermore, the nation is seen in a pluralistic way, i.e. it is seen as one group or social unit to which people feel attachment, but not the *only* focus of loyalty. National identification is compatible with identification with other units, of a social or class kind, of a regional kind, and of a supranational kind. In this sense we may call it a pluralistic form of nationalism.

[...]

# SECTION 12
# MULTICULTURALISM

# MULTICULTURALISM
# INTRODUCTION

This section could equally well be entitled 'democracy and difference'. It raises crucial questions about the membership of the democratic community, and representation of different groups within it. These are some of the most troubling issues in democratic politics today. Broadly speaking, they raise the question of whether the supposedly universal and individualist model of liberal-democracy has a 'hidden agenda' that privileges one particular culture, that of white male heterosexual individuals. In a society that is increasingly diverse, how can different interests and indeed different cultural and sexual perspectives find representation? Does this involve strategies of group representation that break with the predominantly individualist basis of representation of liberal-democracy? And is there, in contemporary democracies, an implicit but powerful 'racial contract' that oppresses and marginalises people of colour, even if formally they share the status of citizens?

The theme of exclusion is highlighted in the extract by the Canadian philosopher *Charles Taylor*. He notes how the 'challenge of new arrivals' raises crucial problems for democracy. Democratic societies are now necessarily multicultural, and the assimilationist strategy, in which newcomers downplayed their particular identity in order to integrate into the host culture, is no longer acceptable. Rather than a 'Jacobin' policy of denying difference, democratic societies have to accept the existence of a variety of cultural and ethnic groups affirming their identity and particularity, sometimes in association with a widespread diaspora of co-nationals. This then raises problems of how these various groups are to be represented in a democratic polity. It casts doubt on whether the classical liberal individualist model of representation is appropriate.

This is the issue discussed by another Canadian political philosopher, *Will Kymlicka*, in his important study of multicultural citizenship. He suggests an ideal of group representation to cope with the problems of difference and diversity. However, group representation itself raises problems, which Kymlicka highlights. Should groups be represented in proportion to their numbers in the population as a whole? Or is that not enough, and would a larger number of representatives be necessary in some cases to ensure not merely representation, but *effective* representation? Kymlicka discusses the possibility of 'mirror representation', in which different groups would be represented through the presence in the legislature of representatives who were members of different cultural and ethnic groups. However, he also suggests a model of accountability, in which representatives might not themselves be members of the group in question but would be held accountable to represent those groups. In either case, group representation and its problems has replaced an individualist model of representation.

The US philosopher *Iris Marion Young* provides a further critique of the assimilationist model and stresses the importance of recognising difference. She argues that an assimilationist model imposes one group's norms as (falsely) universal, as a standard in relation to which other groups are seen as deviant and 'Other'. Democratic politics has to overcome the oppression of a variety of groups, among which she singles out 'women, Blacks, Hispanics, gay men and lesbians, old people'. Instead of assimilationist perspectives, she advocates 'puncturing the universalist claim to unity'. This would involve a positive sense of group difference and of particular identities.

Among the various differences in contemporary democratic societies, those of racial difference and exclusion continue to be most problematic. Finally in this section we reproduce an extract from *Charles Mills'* text *The Racial Contract*. Mills argues that contemporary liberal-democracies constitute a 'racial polity', where there is a 'colour coded configuration' of power that undermines the formal equality of all citizens. These democracies are systems of white privilege, he argues, that implicitly deny to non-whites the effective exercise of citizenship rights.

The extracts in this section thus raise a number of questions fundamental for democracy. In the first place they question whether a democratic society requires a shared culture, and what the nature of this shared culture might be. If this is increasingly impossible and undesirable in the contemporary conditions of multicultural societies, how can problems of marginalisation and exclusion be avoided? And are the democratic ideals proclaimed in these societies culturally specific, the product of local histories and white-dominated traditions that claim a false universality? This last issue raises the topic of non-Western perspectives on democracy, which forms the subject of the following section.

# 71

# THE DYNAMICS OF DEMOCRATIC EXCLUSION

## Charles Taylor

### New Arrivals and New Attitudes

I hope I have made somewhat clear what I mean by the dynamic of exclusion in democracy. We might describe it as a temptation to exclude that arises not from narrow sympathies or historic prejudice, but from the requirement of democratic rule itself for a high degree of mutual understanding, trust, and commitment. This can make it hard to integrate outsiders, and lead to the drawing of a line around the original community. But it can also lead us to what I have called "inner exclusion," the creation of a common identity based upon a rigid formula of politics and citizenship, one that refuses to accommodate any alternatives and imperiously demands the subordination of other aspects of citizens' identities.

It is clear that these two modes are not mutually exclusive. Societies based on inner exclusion may come to turn away outsiders as well – as the strength of France's Front National clearly shows – while societies whose main historical challenge has been the integration of outsiders may have recourse to inner exclusion in an attempt to create some unity amid all their diversity.

The present drama of English Canada (or Canada outside Quebec) illustrates this only too well. Over the past ten years, attitudes in English Canada have become steadily more rigid toward any possible accommodation of Quebec's desire to have a different status than other provinces. This is partly due to

From Charles Taylor, 'The Dynamics of Democratic Exclusion', *Journal of Democracy*, 19 (4), 1998, pp. 148–50.

age-old Canadian angst about national identity, but it is also partly due to a sense of fragmentation that some Canadians feel as a consequence of the rapid diversification of Canada's population, a sense of fragmentation that is often heightened rather than diminished by Quebec's affirmation of difference. Canada's tragedy is that just at the moment when it is becoming more and more necessary to do something about Quebec's status in the federation, it is also becoming politically less and less possible to do anything meaningful.

This growing rigidity is visible, for example, in the insistence that all provinces be treated identically. This kind of uniformity is, in fact, very foreign to Canada's history, but it now seems to many to offer the only way to recreate trust and common understanding among diverse regions, some of whom bear a grudge against others. This rigidity will make it difficult to accommodate not only Quebec, but also aboriginal groups who are calling for new modes of self-rule.

Now, an obvious fact about our era is that the challenge of the new arrival is becoming generalized and multiplied in all democratic societies. The scope and rate of international migration are making all societies increasingly "multicultural." At the same time, the "Jacobin" response to this challenge – insistence upon a rigorous assimilation to a formula involving fairly intense inner exclusion – is becoming less and less sustainable.

This last point is not easy to explain, but it seems to me an undeniable fact. There has been a subtle switch in the mindset of our civilization, probably coinciding with the 1960s. The idea that one ought to suppress one's difference for the sake of fitting in to the dominant mold has been considerably eroded. Feminists, cultural minorities, homosexuals, and religious groups all demand that the reigning formula be modified to accommodate them, rather than the other way around.

At the same time, there has been another change, possibly connected to the first, though it certainly has its own roots. Immigrants no longer feel the imperative to assimilate in the same way. Most of them still want to assimilate substantively to the societies they have entered, and they certainly want to be accepted as full members. But now they frequently want to do so at their own pace and in their own way, and in the process they reserve the right to alter the host society even as they assimilate to it.

The case of Hispanics in the United States is very telling in this regard. It is not that they do not want to become English-speaking Americans. They see obvious advantages in doing so, and they have no intention of foregoing them. Nonetheless, they frequently demand schools and services in Spanish because they want to make this process as painless for themselves as they can, and because they wish to retain as much of their original culture as they can. They will all eventually learn English, but they will also alter somewhat the prevailing sense of what it means to be an American, just as earlier waves of immigrants have done. The difference is that Hispanics now seem to be consciously operating with a sense of their eventual role in codetermining the culture, whereas with earlier immigrants this sense arose only retrospectively.

The difference between the earlier near-total success of France in assimilating East Europeans and its present difficulty with North Africans may reflect many other factors – for example, greater cultural and religious differences, and the collapse of full employment – but I believe that it also reflects the new attitude among immigrants. The earlier sense of unalloyed gratitude toward the countries of refuge and opportunity, which seemed to make any affirmation of difference quite unjustified and out of place, has been replaced by a view that seems to evoke the old doctrine, central to many religions, that the earth has been given to human beings in common. A given territory does not unqualifiedly belong to the people born in it, so it is not simply theirs to give. In return for entry, one is not morally bound to accept every condition they seek to impose.

Two new features arise from this shift. First, the notion I attributed to Hispanics in the United States – the idea that the culture they are joining is in continual evolution, and that they have a chance to codetermine its future – has become widespread. This, instead of simple one-way assimilation, is increasingly becoming the (often unspoken) understanding behind the act of immigration.

Second, the long-established tendency of certain immigrant groups to function morally, culturally, and politically as a 'diaspora' has not only intensified but come to be regarded as fully 'normal.' This has been going on for a long time – think, for instance, of the "Polonia" in all the countries of exile. But whereas it once was frowned upon by many people in the receiving society, who muttered darkly about "dual loyalties," this kind of behavior is coming to be widely accepted. Today one may think of oneself and be regarded as, say, a Canadian in good standing while remaining heavily involved in the fate of one's country of origin.

[...]

# 72

# MULTICULTURAL CITIZENSHIP

## Will Kymlicka

### 3. Evaluating Group Representation

I have tried to show that group representation has important continuities with existing practices of representation in liberal democracies, and, while the general idea of mirror representation is untenable, there are two contextual arguments which can justify limited forms of group representation under certain circumstances – namely, overcoming systemic disadvantage and securing self-government. These arguments provide grounds for thinking that group representation can play an important if limited role within the system of representative democracy. However, any proposal for group-based representation must answer a number of difficult questions. [...] I want to flag some of these questions, to indicate the sorts of issues that need to be addressed when developing or evaluating any specific proposal for group representation.

*Which groups should be represented?* How do we decide which groups, if any, should be entitled to group-based representation? Many critics of group representation take this to be an unanswerable question, or rather that any answer to it will be arbitrary and unprincipled. The result will be an unlimited escalation of demands for political recognition and support, and bitter resentment amongst those groups whose demands are denied. Since there is no way to stop this 'torrent of new demands on the part of previously marginalized

From Will Kymlicka, *Multicultural Citizenship: A Liberal Theory of Minority Rights* (Clarendon Press, Oxford, 1995), pp. 144–9.

groups', it is better to reject all claims for group representation (Galston 1991: 142; cf. Glazer 1983: 227–9).

But the arguments above suggest that there are ways of drawing principled distinctions between various groups. Groups have a claim to representation if they meet one of two criteria: (1) are the members of the group subject to systemic disadvantage in the political process? or (2) do the members of the group have a claim to self-government?

Of these two criteria, self-government is the easier to apply. As I noted [. . .], self-government rights are typically demanded by national minorities. In Canada, for example, Aboriginals and the Québécois are seen as having rights of self-government. In the United States, the clearest examples of groups with recognized rights of self-government are Puerto Rico, Indian tribes, the Chamorros of Guam, and other Pacific Islanders.

The criteria of systemic disadvantage are more complicated. Many groups claim to be disadvantaged in some respect, even though they may be privileged in others, and it is not clear how one measures overall levels of disadvantage. According to Iris Young, there are five forms of oppression: exploitation, marginalization, powerlessness, cultural imperialism, and 'random violence and harassment motivated by group hatred or fear' (I. Young 1989: 261; 1990: 40). She adds that 'Once we are clear that the principle of group representation refers only to oppressed social groups, then the fear of an unworkable proliferation of group representation should dissipate' (I. Young 1990: 187).

However, her list of 'oppressed groups' in the United States would seem to include 80 per cent of the population. She says that 'in the United States today, at least the following groups are oppressed in one or more of these ways: women, blacks, Native Americans, Chicanos, Puerto Ricans and other Spanish-speaking Americans, Asian Americans, gay men, lesbians, working-class people, poor people, old people, and mentally and physically disabled people' (I. Young 1989: 261). In short, everyone but relatively well-off, relatively young, able-bodied, heterosexual white males.

Even then, it is hard to see how this criterion would avoid an 'unworkable proliferation', since each of these groups has subgroups that might claim their own rights. In the case of Britain, for example, the category of 'black' people obscures deep divisions between the Asian and Afro-Caribbean communities, each of which in turn comprises a wide variety of ethnic groups. As Phillips asks, given the almost endless capacity for fragmentation, 'What in this context then counts as "adequate" ethnic representation?' (A. Phillips 1992: 89; cf. Minow 1991: 286).

On the other hand, as Young observes, a large number of political parties and trade unions have allowed group representation for many years without entering an escalating spiral of increasing demands and resentment (I. Young 1989: 187–9; A. Phillips 1991: 65). And, as I noted earlier, we already have some experience with the issue of identifying disadvantaged groups in the context of affirmative action programmes. Yet the problem is formidable – and certainly none of the proposals for group representation to date has addressed it in a satisfactory way. This is one reason why alternative reform schemes are preferable, if they are available and effective. However, the problem of identifying disadvantaged groups is not unique to issues of political representation, and it may not be avoidable in a country committed to redressing injustice.

It is important to note that not all historically disadvantaged groups are in favour of the group representation strategy. Many immigrant groups prefer to work within existing political parties to make them more inclusive, rather than trying to get guaranteed seats in legislation. The option of refusing group representation must of course be available to each group. The additional visibility which comes with group representation carries risks as well as benefits, and each group should be free to evaluate these considerations in light of its own circumstances.

*How many seats should a group have?* If certain groups do need group representation, how many seats should they have? There are two common answers to this question that are often conflated, but which should be kept distinct, since they lead in different directions.

One view is that a group should be represented in proportion to its numbers in the population at large. For example, Canada's National Action Committee on the Status of Women (NAC) proposed that women be guaranteed 50 per cent of Senate seats, which is essentially their proportional electoral representation. The second view is that there should be a threshold number of representatives, sufficient to ensure that the group's views and interests are effectively expressed. The first view follows naturally from a commitment to the general principle of mirror representation. But, as I noted earlier, most proponents of group representation wish to avoid the principle of mirror representation. And once we drop that principle, it is not clear why proportional representation is preferable to a threshold level of representation.

For example, Anne Phillips rejects the underlying premiss of mirror representation that one has to be a member of a particular group in order to understand or represent that group's interests. But she goes on to say that 'in querying the notion that *only* the members of particular disadvantaged groups can understand or represent their interests [one] might usefully turn this question round and ask whether such understanding or representation is possible without the presence of *any* members of the disadvantaged groups?' (Phillips 1994: 89 n. 12). Phillips's argument is that, without a threshold number of seats, others will not be able to understand, and so be able to represent, the interests of a disadvantaged group.

Applying this criterion of a threshold number of seats may lead to different results from the criterion of proportional electoral representation. In the case of women, the threshold number of seats necessary to present women's views effectively is arguably less than the proportional number of seats. The president of NAC defended the guarantee of 50 per cent Senate seats for women on the ground that this would ensure women a 'place at the table' (Rebick and Day

1992) – that is, she demanded proportional representation, but defended it in terms of the need for threshold representation. But does having a place at the table require having 50 per cent of the places at the table?

In other cases, however, the threshold number of seats necessary for effective representation may be greater than the proportional number of seats. Evidence suggests that if there are only one or two members from a marginalized or disadvantaged group in a legislative assembly or committee, they are likely to be excluded, and their voices ignored (Guinier 1991a: 1434–7). Yet proportional representation for some disadvantaged groups, such as racial minorities or immigrant groups, will only amount to such token representation. The number of seats necessary for effective presentation of their views, therefore, may exceed the number of seats required for proportional electoral representation.

The choice between proportional and threshold representation may depend on the nature of the decision-making process – i.e. whether the legislative body has adopted consensual, consociational, super-majority, or other kinds of compromise decision-making rules, as opposed to simple majority voting rules. The more consensual the process, the more threshold representation may be sufficient.

*How are group representatives held accountable?* What mechanisms of accountability can be put in place to ensure that the legislators who hold reserved seats in fact serve the interests of the groups they are supposed to represent? How do we ensure that their 'representatives' are in fact accountable to the group?

Here again we need to distinguish two very different answers. The Maori model in New Zealand involves setting up a separate electoral list for the Maori, so that some legislators are elected solely by Maori voters. This model of group representation does not try to specify the characteristics of the candidate – indeed, it would be possible, however unlikely, that Maori voters might elect a white MP. What matters, on this model, is not who is elected, but how they are elected – that is, they are elected by, and hence accountable to, the Maori.

This is similar to the practice of drawing constituency boundaries so that they largely coincide with a 'community of interest'. It is safe to assume that these communities use their electoral strength to elect 'one of their own'. But they can, and sometimes do, elect someone who is not a member of their group. This does not undermine the value of accommodating communities of interest, because the justification for this practice is not mirror representation (which could be secured by a lottery or random sample). The justification is rather to promote the representation of the group's interests by making a legislator accountable to the community. Thus many defenders of redistricting in the USA insist that they are more interested in accountability than mirror representation:

> affirmative gerrymandering is, in my view, misconceived if it is seen as a mechanism to guarantee that blacks will be represented by blacks, Hispanics by Hispanics, and whites by whites; rather, the proper use of

affirmative gerrymandering is to guarantee that important groups in the population will not be substantially impaired in their ability to elect representatives of *their choice*. (Grofman 1982: 98)

The Maori model attempts to provide the same sort of accountability to smaller or more territorially dispersed groups.

In many proposals for group representation, however, there are no separate electoral lists or gerrymandered constituencies. These proposals focus on the characteristics of the candidates, rather than the characteristics of the electorate. For example, the NAC proposal required that 50 per cent of Senators in Canada be women, but they would be chosen by the general electorate, which contains as many men as women. And while the NAC proposal would guarantee a proportional number of seats for racial minorities, these Senators would also be chosen by the general electorate, which is predominantly white.

In this model, group representation means having legislators who belong to one's group, even though they are not elected by one's group. But it is unclear in what sense this is a form of *representation*, for there are no mechanisms in this model for establishing what each group wants, or for ensuring that the 'representatives' of the group act on the basis of what the group wants. The representative is not accountable to the group, and so may simply ignore the views of that group. Indeed, given that the group's 'representatives' are chosen by the general electorate, it might be unwise for representatives to act in ways that upset the sentiments of the members of the dominant groups. As Phillips puts it, 'Accountability is always the other side of representation, and, in the absence of procedures for establishing what any group wants or thinks, we cannot usefully talk of their political representation' (Phillips 1992: 86–8).

This suggests that there is an asymmetry between the problem of exclusion and the solution of inclusion (Phillips 1995). That is, it may be reasonable to conclude that a group which falls far short of its proportional electoral representation is therefore 'under-represented', particularly if the group has been subject to historical discrimination or disadvantage. But it does not follow that reversing this exclusion through guaranteed seats ensures that the group's interests or perspectives are then 'represented'. The idea that the presence of women legislators, for example, would *by itself* ensure the representation of women's interests, even in the absence of any electoral accountability, only makes sense if one thinks that there is 'some fundamental unity between women, some essential set of experiences and interests that can be represented by any of the sex' (Phillips 1995). But this is implausible, not only in the case of women, but also in the case of ethnic, national, or racial minorities, given the heterogeneity of interests and perspectives within each of these groups.

So here again we have conflicting models, based on conflicting ideals. The Maori model guarantees that some representatives are solely accountable to Maori voters, although it does not guarantee that the representatives are themselves Maori – that is, it does not guarantee that the representative 'mirrors' the electorate. The NAC model guarantees that representatives mirror important groups in the electorate, but it does not guarantee that the representatives are accountable to the group they mirror. Of course, many proponents of guaranteed representation for disadvantaged groups believe in the need for accountability, and would like to find some way of making sure that representatives are accountable to the groups they are supposed to represent. But to date, the ideals of mirror representation and democratic accountability have not yet been adequately integrated.

[. . .]

## REFERENCES

Galston, W., *Liberal Purposes: Goods, Virtues, and Duties in the Liberal State* (Cambridge University Press, Cambridge, 1991).

Glazer, N., *Ethnic Dilemmas: 1964–1982* (Harvard University Press, Cambridge, MA, 1983).

Grofman, B., 'Should Representatives Be Typical of Their Constituents?', in B. Grofman et al. (eds), *Representation and Redistricting Issues* (D. C. Heath & Co., Lexington, MA, 1982).

Guinier, L., 'No Two Seats: The Elusive Quest for Political Equality', *Virginia Law Review*, 49 (2), 1991, pp. 237–65.

Minow, M., 'From Class Action to Miss Saigon: The Concept of Representation in the Law', *Cleveland State Law Review*, 39, 1991, pp. 269–300.

Phillips, A., *Engendering Democracy* (Polity Press, Cambridge, 1991).

Phillips, A., 'Democracy and Difference: Some Problems for Feminist Theory', *Political Quarterly*, 63 (1), 1992, pp. 79–90.

Phillips, A., 'Dealing with Difference: A Politics of Ideas or a Politics of Presence?', *Constellations*, 1 (1), 1994, pp. 74–91.

Phillips, A., *The Politics of Presence: Issues in Democracy and Group Representation* (Oxford University Press, Oxford, 1995).

Rebick, J. and Day, S., 'A Place at the Table: The New Senate Needs Gender Equality, Minority Representation', *Ottawa Citizen*, 11 September 1992.

Young, I. M., 'Polity and Group Difference: A Critique of the Ideal of Universal Citizenship', *Ethics*, 99 (2), 1989, pp. 250–74.

Young, I. M., *Justice and the Politics of Difference* (Princeton University Press, Princeton, NJ, 1990).

# 73

# JUSTICE AND THE POLITICS OF DIFFERENCE

## Iris Marion Young

EMANCIPATION THROUGH THE POLITICS OF DIFFERENCE

Implicit in emancipatory movements asserting a positive sense of group difference is a different ideal of liberation, which might be called democratic cultural pluralism (cf. Laclau and Mouffe, 1985, pp. 166–71; Cunningham, 1987, pp. 186–99; Nickel, 1987). In this vision the good society does not eliminate or transcend group difference. Rather, there is equality among socially and culturally differentiated groups, who mutually respect one another and affirm one another in their differences. What are the reasons for rejecting the assimilationist ideal and promoting a politics of difference?

As I discussed [. . .], some deny the reality of social groups. For them, group difference is an invidious fiction produced and perpetuated in order to preserve the privilege of the few. Others, such as Wasserstrom, may agree that social groups do now exist and have real social consequences for the way people identify themselves and one another, but assert that such social group differences are undesirable. The assimilationist ideal involves denying either the reality or the desirability of social groups.

Those promoting a politics of difference doubt that a society without group differences is either possible or desirable. Contrary to the assumption of modernization theory, increased urbanization and the extension of equal formal rights to all groups has not led to a decline in particularist affiliations. If

From Iris Marion Young, *Justice and the Politics of Difference* (Princeton University Press, Princeton, NJ, 1990), pp. 163–7.

anything, the urban concentration and interactions among groups that modernizing social processes introduce tend to reinforce group solidarity and differentiation (Rothschild, 1981; Ross, 1980; Fischer, 1982). Attachment to specific traditions, practices, language, and other culturally specific forms is a crucial aspect of social existence. People do not usually give up their social group identifications, even when they are oppressed.

Whether eliminating social group difference is possible or desirable in the long run, however, is an academic issue. Today and for the foreseeable future societies are certainly structured by groups, and some are privileged while others are oppressed. New social movements of group specificity do not deny the official story's claim that the ideal of liberation as eliminating difference and treating everyone the same has brought significant improvement in the status of excluded groups. Its main quarrel is with the story's conclusion, namely, that since we have achieved formal equality, only vestiges and holdovers of differential privilege remain, which will die out with the continued persistent assertion of an ideal of social relations that make differences irrelevant to a person's life prospects. The achievement of formal equality does not eliminate social differences, and rhetorical commitment to the sameness of persons makes it impossible even to name how those differences presently structure privilege and oppression.

Though in many respects the law is now blind to group differences, some groups continue to be marked as deviant, as the Other. In everyday interactions, images, and decisions, assumptions about women, Blacks, Hispanics, gay men and lesbians, old people, and other marked groups continue to justify exclusion, avoidance, paternalism, and authoritarian treatment. Continued racist, sexist, homophobic, ageist, and ableist institutions and behavior create particular circumstances for these groups, usually disadvantaging them in their opportunity to develop their capacities. Finally, in part because they have been segregated from one another, and in part because they have particular histories and traditions, there are cultural differences among social groups – differences in language, style of living, body comportment and gestures, values, and perspectives on society.

Today in American society, as in many other societies, there is widespread agreement that no person should be excluded from political and economic activities because of ascribed characteristics. Group differences nevertheless continue to exist, and certain groups continue to be privileged. Under these circumstances, insisting that equality and liberation entail ignoring difference has oppressive consequences in three respects.

First, blindness to difference disadvantages groups whose experience, culture, and socialized capacities differ from those of privileged groups. The strategy of assimilation aims to bring formerly excluded groups into the mainstream. So assimilation always implies coming into the game after it is already begun, after the rules and standards have already been set, and having to prove oneself according to those rules and standards. In the assimilationist strategy, the privileged groups implicitly define the standards according to which all will be measured. Because their privilege involves not recognizing these standards as culturally and experientially specific, the ideal of a common humanity in which all can participate without regard to race, gender, religion, or sexuality poses as neutral and universal. The real differences between oppressed groups and the dominant norm, however, tend to put them at a disadvantage in measuring up to these standards, and for that reason assimilationist policies perpetuate their disadvantage. Later [...] I shall give examples of facially neutral standards that operate to disadvantage or exclude those already disadvantaged.

Second, the ideal of a universal humanity without social group differences allows privileged groups to ignore their own group specificity. Blindness to difference perpetuates cultural imperialism by allowing norms expressing the point of view and experience of privileged groups to appear neutral and universal. The assimilationist ideal presumes that there is a humanity in general, an unsituated group-neutral human capacity for self-making that left to itself would make individuality flower, thus guaranteeing that each individual will be different. As I argued in Chapter 4, because there is no such unsituated group-neutral point of view, the situation and experience of dominant groups tend to define the norms of such a humanity in general. Against such a supposedly neutral humanist ideal, only the oppressed groups come to be marked with particularity; they, and not the privileged groups, are marked, objectified as the Others.

Thus, third, this denigration of groups that deviate from an allegedly neutral standard often produces an internalized devaluation by members of those groups themselves. When there is an ideal of general human standards according to which everyone should be evaluated equally, then Puerto Ricans or Chinese Americans are ashamed of their accents or their parents. Black children despise the female-dominated kith and kin networks of their neighborhoods, and feminists seek to root out their tendency to cry, or to feel compassion for a frustrated stranger. The aspiration to assimilate helps produce the self-loathing and double consciousness characteristic of oppression. The goal of assimilation holds up to people a demand that they "fit," be like the mainstream, in behavior, values, and goals. At the same time, as long as group differences exist, group members will be marked as different – as Black, Jewish, gay – and thus as unable simply to fit. When participation is taken to imply assimilation the oppressed person is caught in an irresolvable dilemma: to participate means to accept and adopt an identity one is not, and to try to participate means to be reminded by oneself and others of the identity one is.

A more subtle analysis of the assimilationist ideal might distinguish between a conformist and a transformational ideal of assimilation. In the conformist ideal, status quo institutions and norms are assumed as given, and disadvantaged groups who differ from those norms are expected to conform to them. A transformational ideal of assimilation, on the other hand, recognizes that institutions as given express the interests and perspective of the dominant groups. Achieving assimilation therefore requires altering many institutions and practices in accordance with neutral rules that truly do not disadvantage or stigmatize any person, so that group membership really is irrelevant to how persons are treated. Wasserstrom's ideal fits a transformational assimilation, as does the group-neutral ideal advocated by some feminists (Taub and Williams, 1987). Unlike the conformist assimilationist, the transformational assimilationist may allow that group-specific policies, such as affirmative action, are necessary and appropriate means for transforming institutions to fit the assimilationist ideal. Whether conformist or transformational, however, the assimilationist ideal still denies that group difference can be positive and desirable; thus any form of the ideal of assimilation constructs group difference as a liability or disadvantage.

Under these circumstances, a politics that asserts the positivity of group difference is liberating and empowering. In the act of reclaiming the identity the dominant culture has taught them to despise (Cliff, 1980), and affirming it as an identity to celebrate, the oppressed remove double consciousness. I am just what they say I am – a Jewboy, a colored girl, a fag, a dyke, or a hag – and proud of it. No longer does one have the impossible project of trying to become something one is not under circumstances where the very trying reminds one of who one is. This politics asserts that oppressed groups have distinct cultures, experiences, and perspectives on social life with humanly positive meaning, some of which may even be superior to the culture and perspectives of mainstream society. The rejection and devaluation of one's culture and perspective should not be a condition of full participation in social life.

Asserting the value and specificity of the culture and attributes of oppressed groups, moreover, results in a relativizing of the dominant culture. When feminists assert the validity of feminine sensitivity and the positive value of nurturing behavior, when gays describe the prejudice of heterosexuals as homophobic and their own sexuality as positive and self-developing, when Blacks affirm a distinct Afro-American tradition, then the dominant culture is forced to discover itself for the first time as specific: as Anglo, European, Christian, masculine, straight. In a political struggle where oppressed groups insist on the positive value of their specific culture and experience, it becomes increasingly difficult for dominant groups to parade their norms as neutral and universal, and to construct the values and behavior of the oppressed as deviant, perverted, or inferior. By puncturing the universalist claim to unity that expels some groups and turns them into the Other, the assertion of positive group specificity introduces the possibility of understanding the relation between groups as merely difference, instead of exclusion, opposition, or dominance.

The politics of difference also promotes a notion of group solidarity against the individualism of liberal humanism. Liberal humanism treats each person as an individual, ignoring differences of race, sex, religion, and ethnicity. Each person should be evaluated only according to her or his individual efforts and achievements. With the institutionalization of formal equlity some members of formerly excluded groups have indeed succeeded, by mainstream standards.

Structural patterns of group privilege and oppression nevertheless remain. When political leaders of oppressed groups reject assimilation they are often affirming group solidarity. Where the dominant culture refuses to see anything but the achievement of autonomous individuals, the oppressed assert that we shall not separate from the people with whom we identify in order to "make it" in a white Anglo male world. The politics of difference insists on liberation of the whole group of Blacks, women, American Indians, and that this can be accomplished only through basic institutional changes. These changes must include group representation in policymaking and an elimination of the hierarchy of rewards that forces everyone to compete for scarce positions at the top.

Thus the assertion of a positive sense of group difference provides a standpoint from which to criticize prevailing institutions and norms. Black Americans find in their traditional communities, which refer to their members as "brother" and "sister," a sense of solidarity absent from the calculating individualism of white professional capitalist society. Feminists find in the traditional female values of nurturing a challenge to a militarist world-view, and lesbians find in their relationships a confrontation with the assumption of complementary gender roles in sexual relationships. From their experience of a culture tied to the land American Indians formulate a critique of the instrumental rationality of European culture that results in pollution and ecological destruction. Having revealed the specificity of the dominant norms which claim universality and neutrality, social movements of the oppressed are in a position to inquire how the dominant institutions must be changed so that they will no longer reproduce the patterns of privilege and oppression.

[...]

REFERENCES

Laclau, E. and Mouffe, C., *Hegemony and Socialist Strategy* (Verso, London, 1985).
Cunningham, F., *Democratic Theory and Socialism* (Cambridge University Press, Cambridge, 1987).
Nickel, J., 'Equal Opportunity in a Pluralistic Society', in Ellen Frankel Paul et al. (eds), *Equal Opportunity* (Blackwell, Oxford, 1987).
Rothschild, J., *Ethnopolitics* (Columbia University Press, New York, 1981).
Ross, J., 'Introduction' to Jeffrey Ross and Ann Baker Cottrell (eds), *The Mobilization of Collective Identity* (University Press of America, Lanham, MD, 1980).
Fischer, C., *To Dwell among Friends: Personal Networks in Town and City* (University of Chicago Press, Chicago, 1982).

# 74

# THE RACIAL CONTRACT

## Charles W. Mills

[...]

The Racial Contract [...] underwrites the social contract, is a visible or hidden operator that restricts and modifies the scope of its prescriptions. But since there is both synchronic and diachronic variation, there are many different versions or local instantiations of the Racial Contract, and they evolve over time, so that the effective force of the social contract itself changes, and the kind of cognitive dissonance between the two alters. (This change has implications for the moral psychology of the white signatories and their characteristic patterns of insight and blindness.) The social contract is (in its original historical version) a specific discrete event that founds society, even if (through, e.g., Lockean theories of tacit consent) subsequent generations continue to ratify it on an ongoing basis. By contrast the Racial Contract is *continually being rewritten* to create different forms of the racial polity.

A global periodization, a timeline overview of the evolution of the Racial Contract, would highlight first of all the crucial division between the time before and the time after the institutionalization of global white supremacy. (Thus Janet Abu-Lughod's book about the thirteenth-century/fourteenth-century medieval world system is titled *Before European Hegemony*.) The time after would then be further subdivided into the period of formal, juridical white supremacy (the epoch of the European conquest, African slavery, and European colonialism, overt white racial self-identification, and the largely undisputed

From Charles W. Mills, *The Racial Contract* (Cornell University Press, Ithaca, NY and London, 1997), pp. 72–8.

hegemony of racist theories) and the present period of de facto white supremacy, when whites' dominance is, for the most part, no longer constitutionally
and juridically enshrined but rather a matter of social, political, cultural, and
economic privilege based on the legacy of the conquest.

In the first period, the period of de jure white supremacy, the Racial Contract
was explicit, the characteristic instantiations – the expropriation contract, the
slave contract, the colonial contract – making it clear that whites were the
privileged race and the egalitarian social contract applied only to them.
(Cognitively, then, this period had the great virtue of social transparency: white
supremacy was *openly* proclaimed. One didn't have to look for a *sub*text,
because it was there in the text itself.) In the second period, on the other hand,
the Racial Contract *has written itself out of formal existence.* The scope of the
terms in the social contract has been formally extended to apply to everyone, so
that "persons" is no longer coextensive with "whites." What characterizes *this*
period (which is, of course, the present) is tension between continuing de facto
white privilege and this *formal* extension of rights. The Racial Contract
continues to manifest itself, of course, in unofficial local agreements of various
kinds (restrictive covenants, employment discrimination contracts, political
decisions about resource allocation, etc.). But even apart from these, a crucial
manifestation is simply *the failure to ask certain questions,* taking for granted as
a status quo and baseline the existing color-coded configurations of wealth,
poverty, property, and opportunities, the pretence that formal, juridical equality is sufficient to remedy inequities created on a foundation of several hundred
years of racial privilege, and that challenging that foundation is a transgression
of the terms of the social contract. (Though actually – in a sense – it *is*, insofar as
the Racial Contract is the real meaning of the social contract.)

*Globally*, the Racial Contract effects a final paradoxical norming and racing
of space, a *writing out* of the polity of certain spaces as conceptually and
historically irrelevant to European and Euro-world development, so that these
raced spaces are categorized as disjoined from the path of civilization (i.e., the
European project). Fredric Jameson writes: "Colonialism means that a significant structural segment of the economic system as a whole is now located
elsewhere, beyond the metropolis, outside of the daily life and existential
experience of the home country . . . Such spatial disjunction has as its immediate
consequence the inability to grasp the way the system functions as a whole." By
the social contract's decision to remain in the space of the European nation-
state, the connection between the development of this space's industry, culture,
civilization, and the material and cultural contributions of Afro-Asia and the
Americas is denied, so it seems as if this space and its denizens are peculiarly
rational and industrious, differentially endowed with qualities that have
enabled them to dominate the world. One then speaks of the "European
miracle" in a way that conceives this once marginal region as sui generis, conceptually severing it from the web of spatial connections that made its development possible. *This* space actually comes to have the character it does because

of the pumping exploitative causality established between it and those *other* conceptually invisible spaces. But by remaining within the boundaries of the European space of the abstract contract, it is valorized as unique, inimitable, autonomous. Other parts of the world then disappear from the white contractarian history, subsumed under the general category of risible non-European space, the "Third World," where for reasons of local folly and geographical blight the inspiring model of the self-sufficient white social contract cannot be followed.

*Nationally*, within these racial polities, the Racial Contract manifests itself in white resistance to anything more than the *formal* extension of the terms of the abstract social contract (and often to that also). Whereas before it was denied that nonwhites *were* equal persons, it is now pretended that nonwhites *are* equal abstract persons who can be fully included in the polity merely by extending the scope of the moral operator, without any fundamental change in the arrangements that have resulted from the previous system of explicit de jure racial privilege. Sometimes the new forms taken by the Racial Contract are transparently exploitative, for example, the "jim crow" contract, whose claim of "separate but equal" was patently ludicrous. But others – the job discrimination contract, the restrictive covenant – are harder to prove. Employment agencies use subterfuges of various kinds: "In 1990, for example, two former employees of one of New York City's largest employment agencies divulged that discrimination was routinely practiced against black applicants, though concealed behind a number of code words. Clients who did not want to hire blacks would indicate their preference for applicants who were "All American." For its part the agency would signal that an applicant was black by reversing the initials of the placement counselor." Similarly, a study of how "American apartheid" is maintained points out that whereas in the past realtors would have simply refused to sell to blacks, now blacks "are met by a realtor with a smiling face who, through a series of ruses, lies, and deceptions, makes it hard for them to learn about, inspect, rent, or purchase homes in white neighborhoods ... Because the discrimination is latent, however, it is usually unobservable, even to the person experiencing it. One never knows for sure." Nonwhites then find that race is, paradoxically, both everywhere and nowhere, structuring their lives but not formally recognized in political/moral theory. But in a racially structured polity, the only people who can find it psychologically possible to deny the centrality of race are those who are racially privileged, for whom race is invisible precisely because the world is structured around them, whiteness as the ground against which the figures of other races – those who, unlike us, are raced – appear. The fish does not see the water, and whites do not see the racial nature of a white polity because it is natural to them, the element in which they move. As Toni Morrison points out, there are contexts in which claiming racelessness is itself a racial act.

Contemporary debates between nonwhites and whites about the centrality or peripherality of race can thus be seen as attempts respectively to point out, and deny, the existence of the Racial Contract that underpins the social contract. The frustrating problem nonwhites have always had, and continue to have, with mainstream political theory is not with abstraction *itself* (after all, the "Racial Contract" is itself an abstraction) but with an *idealizing* abstraction that abstracts *away* from the crucial realities of the racial polity. The shift to the hypothetical, ideal contract encourages and facilitates this abstraction, since the eminently *non*ideal features of the real world are not part of the apparatus. There is then, in a sense, no conceptual point-of-entry to start talking about the fundamental way in which (as all nonwhites know) race structures one's life and affects one's life chances.

The black law professor Patricia Williams complains about an ostensible neutrality that is really "racism in drag," a system of "racism as status quo" which is "deep, angry, eradicated from view" but continues to make people "avoid the phantom as they did the substance," "defer[ring] to the unseen shape of things." The black philosophy professor Bill Lawson comments on the deficiencies of the conceptual apparatus of traditional liberalism, which has no room for the peculiar post-Emancipation status of blacks, simultaneously citizens and noncitizens. The black philosopher of law Anita Allen remarks on the irony of standard American philosophy of law texts, which describe a universe in which "all humans are paradigm rightsholders" and see no need to point out that the actual U.S. record is somewhat different. The retreat of mainstream normative moral and political theory into an "ideal" theory that ignores race merely rescripts the Racial Contract as the invisible writing between the lines. So John Rawls, an American working in the late twentieth century, writes a book on justice widely credited with reviving postwar political philosophy in which not a single reference to American slavery and its legacy can be found, and Robert Nozick creates a theory of justice in holdings predicated on legitimate acquisition and transfer without more than two or three sentences acknowledging the utter divergence of U.S. history from this ideal.

The silence of mainstream moral and political philosophy on issues of race is a sign of the continuing power of the Contract over its signatories, an illusory color blindness that actually entrenches white privilege. A genuine transcendence of its terms would require, as a preliminary, the acknowledgement of its past and present existence and the social, political economic, psychological, and moral implications it has had both for its contractors and its victims. By treating the present as a somehow neutral baseline, with its given configuration of wealth, property, social standing, and psychological willingness to sacrifice, the idealized social contract renders permanent the legacy of the Racial Contract. The ever-deepening abyss between the First World and the Third World, where millions – largely nonwhite – die of starvation each year and many more hundreds of millions – also largely nonwhite – live in wretched poverty, is seen as unfortunate (calling, certainly, for the occasional charitable contribution) but unrelated to the history of transcontinental and intracontinental racial exploitation.

Finally, the Racial Contract evolves not merely by altering the relations between whites and nonwhites but by shifting the criteria for who *counts* as white and nonwhite. (So it is not merely that relations between the respective populations change but that the population boundaries themselves change also.) Thus – at least in my preferred account of the Racial Contract (again, other accounts are possible) – race is *debiologized*, making explicit its political foundation. *In a sense, the Racial Contract constructs its signatories as much as they construct it.* The overall trend is toward a limited expansion of the privileged human population through the "whitening" of the previously excluded group in question, though there may be local reversals.

[...]

# SECTION 13
# BEYOND THE WEST

# BEYOND THE WEST
## INTRODUCTION

Moving on from the problems of multiculturalism and 'difference', we come to the related question of whether democracy is genuinely a universal idea. Those who argue that it is not universal suggest that the democratic ideal is a product of a particular and relatively local environment, Western Europe and North America. Hence attempts to apply democracy to other parts of the world are disguised attempts at cultural imperialism, and come up against obstacles of non-Western religious and cultural traditions inimical to democracy. A more nuanced version of this argument would suggest that liberal-democracy in its Western form needs at the very least adaptation to the quite different conditions of non-Western societies. Some theorists suggest, furthermore, that these non-Western traditions offer alternative perspectives on democracy that can enrich and develop the all too limited and culturally circumscribed version on offer in the West.

These are all important and contested issues. They are particularly significant in the light of ongoing attempts to spread and assist the process of democratisation worldwide, and to monitor the progress of democracy in a global context.

We start our selections illustrating these issues with a robust defence by *Amartya Sen* of the claim that democracy is a universal value. He suggests that democracy rests on a number of values which are universal in appeal and scope. These values are those of the intrinsic importance of political participation, the instrumental function of keeping governments accountable to their citizens, and finally the role of democracy in stimulating exchange of ideas and the understanding of what our needs are. Sen is critical of attempts to distinguish between a 'Western' culture of democracy and Islamic or non-Western cultures reputedly at odds with the democratic ideal. He points out the lack of evidence, historical and contemporary, for such an antithesis.

A similar, though in some ways different, perspective is defended by *B. Parekh*. He suggests that democracy can indeed flourish in non-Western parts of the world, but it may be a form of democracy less marked by liberalism, which he sees as marked by its Western origins and particularity. If democracy is to be encouraged throughout the world, then it has to be open to cultural diversity and recognition of autonomy. This may involve accepting as democratic the diverse practices of particular cultures and groups, and thus abandoning ideas of uniformity, of one single pattern of democratic politics. In this way liberalism might, paradoxically, show its strength by accepting as legitimate non-liberal forms of democratic rule.

The questions of whether non-Western societies are receptive or hostile to the spread of democratic ideas, and whether these ideas are marked – and limited – by cultural particularity, are further considered by the remaining extracts in this section.

As the extracts by both *Silverstein* and *Nathan* suggest, and as Sen observes in his article, struggles for democratic freedoms witnessed in a wide range of countries in Asia and Africa give ample evidence that democracy is as much sought after and fought for in developing countries of the 'South' as in the developed countries of the 'North'. Silverstein comments on the synthesis between Burmese traditions of Buddhism and Western ideas of liberalism, as witnessed in the struggle of the Burmese democratic activist Daw Aung San Suu Kyi. In a text written in 1986, before the Tiananmen Square demonstrations of 1989, and their subsequent repression, Andrew Nathan describes the struggles of the democratic movement in (and outside) China, and the difficulties faced in the Chinese context. These difficulties stem, he suggests, from 'China's century-long obsession with political order and national strength'.

These extracts taken together suggest both the universal appeal of the democratic idea, and the difficulties of realising it worldwide, in societies whose cultural traditions are at odds with some central strands of the tradition of democratic theorising. That tradition involves ideas of the autonomy of the individual, the secularisation of political power, and the tolerance of a wide variety of different lifestyles and religious practices. While the spread of ideas and practices of democracy may to some extent be encouraged by the phenomenon of globalisation, the claims of democracy to be universal come into conflict with more local or particular traditions of thought and behaviour.

# 75

# DEMOCRACY AS A UNIVERSAL VALUE

## Amartya Sen

### THE ARGUMENT FROM CULTURAL DIFFERENCES

There is also another argument in defense of an allegedly fundamental regional contrast, one related not to economic circumstances but to cultural differences. Perhaps the most famous of these claims relates to what have been called "Asian values." It has been claimed that Asians traditionally value discipline, not political freedom, and thus the attitude to democracy must inevitably be much more skeptical in these countries. I have discussed this thesis in some detail in my Morgenthau Memorial Lecture at the Carnegie Council on Ethics and International Affairs.

It is very hard to find any real basis for this intellectual claim in the history of Asian cultures, especially if we look at the classical traditions of India, the Middle East, Iran, and other parts of Asia. For example, one of the earliest and most emphatic statements advocating the tolerance of pluralism and the duty of the state to protect minorities can be found in the inscriptions of the Indian emperor Ashoka in the third century B.C.

Asia is, of course, a very large area, containing 60 percent of the world's population, and generalizations about such a vast set of peoples is not easy. Sometimes the advocates of "Asian values" have tended to look primarily at East Asia as the region of particular applicability. The general thesis of a contrast between the West and Asia often concentrates on the lands to the east of

From Amartya Sen, 'Democracy as a Universal Value', *Journal of Democracy*, 10 (3), 1999, pp. 13–16.

Thailand, even though there is also a more ambitious claim that the rest of Asia is rather "similar." Lee Kuan Yew, to whom we must be grateful for being such a clear expositor (and for articulating fully what is often stated vaguely in this tangled literature), outlines "the fundamental difference between Western concepts of society and government and East Asian concepts" by explaining, "when I say East Asians, I mean Korea, Japan, China, Vietnam, as distinct from Southeast Asia, which is a mix between the Sinic and the Indian, though Indian culture itself emphasizes similar values."

Even East Asia itself, however, is remarkably diverse, with many variations to be found not only among Japan, China, Korea, and other countries of the region, but also *within* each country. Confucius is the standard author quoted in interpreting Asian values, but he is not the only intellectual influence in these countries (in Japan, China, and Korea for example, there are very old and very widespread Buddhist traditions, powerful for over a millennium and a half, and there are also other influences, including a considerable Christian presence). There is no homogeneous worship of order over freedom in any of these cultures.

Furthermore, Confucius himself did not recommend blind allegiance to the state. When Zilu asks him 'how to serve a prince,' Confucius replies (in a statement that the censors of authoritarian regimes may want to ponder), "Tell him the truth even if it offends him." Confucius is not averse to practical caution and tact, but does not forgo the recommendation to oppose a bad government (tactfully, if necessary): "When the [good] way prevails in the state, speak boldly and act boldly. When the state has lost the way, act boldly and speak softly."

Indeed, Confucius provides a clear pointer to the fact that the two pillars of the imagined edifice of Asian values, loyalty to family and obedience to the state, can be in severe conflict with each other. Many advocates of the power of "Asian values" see the role of the state as an extension of the role of the family, but as Confucius noted, there can be tension between the two. The Governor of She told Confucius, "Among my people, there is a man of unbending integrity: when his father stole a sheep, he denounced him." To this Confucius replied, "Among my people, men of integrity do things differently: a father covers up for his son, a son covers up for his father – and there is integrity in what they do."

The monolithic interpretation of Asian values as hostile to democracy and political rights does not bear critical scrutiny. I should not, I suppose, be too critical of the lack of scholarship supporting these beliefs, since those who have made these claims are not scholars but political leaders, often official or unofficial spokesmen for authoritarian governments. It is, however, interesting to see that while we academics can be impractical about practical politics, practical politicians can, in turn, be rather impractical about scholarship.

It is not hard, of course, to find authoritarian writings within the Asian traditions. But neither is it hard to find them in Western classics: one has only to reflect on the writings of Plato or Aquinas to see that devotion to discipline is not a special Asian taste. To dismiss the plausibility of democracy as a universal value because of the presence of some Asian writings on discipline and order would be similar to rejecting the plausibility of democracy as a natural form of government in Europe or America today on the basis of the writings of Plato or Aquinas (not to mention the substantial medieval literature in support of the Inquisitions).

Due to the experience of contemporary political battles, especially in the Middle East, Islam is often portrayed as fundamentally intolerant of and hostile to individual freedom. But the presence of diversity and variety *within* a tradition applies very much to Islam as well. In India, Akbar and most of the other Moghul emperors (with the notable exception of Aurangzeb) provide good examples of both the theory and practice of political and religious tolerance. The Turkish emperors were often more tolerant than their European contemporaries. Abundant examples can also be found among rulers in Cairo and Baghdad. Indeed, in the twelfth century, the great Jewish scholar Maimonides had to run away from an intolerant Europe (where he was born), and from its persecution of Jews, to the security of a tolerant and urbane Cairo and the patronage of Sultan Saladin.

Diversity is a feature of most cultures in the world. Western civilization is no exception. The practice of democracy that has won out in the *modern* West is largely a result of a consensus that has emerged since the Enlightenment and the Industrial Revolution, and particularly in the last century or so. To read in this a historical commitment of the West – over the millennia – to democracy, and then to contrast it with non-Western traditions (treating each as monolithic) would be a great mistake. This tendency toward oversimplification can be seen not only in the writings of some governmental spokesmen in Asia, but also in the theories of some of the finest Western scholars themselves.

As an example from the writings of a major scholar whose works, in many other ways, have been totally impressive, let me cite Samuel Huntington's thesis on the clash of civilizations, where the heterogeneities *within* each culture get quite inadequate recognition. His study comes to the clear conclusion that "a sense of individualism and a tradition of rights and liberties" can be found in the West that are "unique among civilized societies." Huntington also argues that "the central characteristics of the West, those which distinguish it from other civilizations, antedate the modernization of the West." In his view, "The West was West long before it was modern." It is this thesis that – I have argued – does not survive historical scrutiny.

For every attempt by an Asian government spokesman to contrast alleged "Asian values" with alleged Western ones, there is, it seems, an attempt by a Western intellectual to make a similar contrast from the other side. But even though every Asian pull may be matched by a Western push, the two together do not really manage to dent democracy's claim to be a universal value.

## WHERE THE DEBATE BELONGS

I have tried to cover a number of issues related to the claim that democracy is a universal value. The value of democracy includes its *intrinsic importance* in human life, its *instrumental role* in generating political incentives, and its *constructive function* in the formation of values (and in understanding the force and feasibility of claims of needs, rights, and duties). These merits are not regional in character. Nor is the advocacy of discipline or order. Heterogeneity of values seems to characterize most, perhaps all, major cultures. The cultural argument does not foreclose, nor indeed deeply constrain, the choices we can make today.

Those choices have to be made here and now, taking note of the functional roles of democracy, on which the case for democracy in the contemporary world depends. I have argued that this case is indeed strong and not regionally contingent. The force of the claim that democracy is a universal value lies, ultimately, in that strength. That is where the debate belongs. It cannot be disposed of by imagined cultural taboos or assumed civilizational predispositions imposed by our various pasts.

# 76

# THE CULTURAL PARTICULARITY OF LIBERAL DEMOCRACY

## Bhikhu Parekh

[. . .]

In short, the liberal principle of individuation and other liberal ideas are culturally and historically specific. As such a political system based on them cannot claim universal validity.

The non-liberal but not necessarily illiberal societies we are discussing cherish and wish to preserve their ways of life. Like most pre-modern societies they are communally orientated and believe that their members' 'rights' may be legitimately restricted in the larger interest of the traditional way of life. Most of them allow freedom of speech and expression, but not the freedom to mock and ridicule their sacred texts, practices, beliefs and rituals. They restrict the right to property and to trade and commerce lest it should undermine the ethos of social solidarity and the ethic of communal obligation lying at the basis of their ways of life. They restrict travel, immigration and the freedom to buy and sell land for basically the same reasons. Liberals find such restrictions unacceptable, but most members of traditional societies do not. Unless we assume that liberalism represents the final truth about human beings, we cannot indiscriminately condemn societies that do not conform to it. This is particularly so today when the liberal societies are themselves beginning to wonder if they have not carried individualism too far, and how they can create genuine communities without which individuals lack roots and stability. Community implies shared values and a common way of life, and is incompatible with the

From Bhikhu Parekh, 'The Cultural Particularity of Liberal Democracy', in D. Held. (ed.), *Prospects for Democracy: North, South, East, West* (Polity, Cambridge, 1993), pp. 169–75.

more or less unrestrained rights of its members to do as they please. It is striking that many a communitarian theorist has suggested restrictions on pornography, freedom of expression and immigration that are not very different from those characteristic of traditional societies.

It is, of course, true that some traditional societies have grossly outrageous practices and customs which obviously need to be changed, preferably by internal and, when necessary, by a judiciously applied external pressure. The question we are considering, however, is not how to improve their ways of life but whether they must adopt, and be condemned for refusing to adopt, liberal democratic institutions. It is difficult to see how this question can be answered in the affirmative. As long as their forms of government are acceptable to their people and meet the basic conditions of good government, to which I shall return later, they must be at liberty to work out their political destiny themselves.

We have so far talked about cohesive communities. We may now briefly consider multi-communal societies; that is, societies which comprise several cohesive and self-conscious communities each seeking to preserve its traditional way of life. Several third world countries belong to this category. Neither the Athenian model, which presupposes a community, nor the liberal model, which presupposes none, applies to such multi-communal societies, with the result that the theoretical problems raised by their experiences have received little attention in much of western democratic theory.

The point will become clear if we look at the case of India, one of the most ethnically and religiously diverse societies in the world. The colonial state in India left the long-established communities more or less alone, accepted their 'laws' and practices, and superimposed on them a minimal body of mainly criminal laws. Unlike its European counterpart, it permitted a plurality of legal systems and shared its 'sovereignty' with the autonomous and largely self-governing communities.

Post-independence India only partially rationalized the colonial state and remains a highly complex polity. It has a uniform body of criminal but not civil laws. Muslims continue to be governed by their own personal laws, which the state enforces but with which it does not interfere. The tribals too are governed by their separate laws, and the state has committed itself to making no changes in the practices and laws of the Christians without their explicit consent and approval. The Parsis are subject to the same civil laws as the rest of non-Muslim Indians, but the interpretation and application of the laws is in some cases left to their *panchayats* or community councils. Thus the ordinary civil courts will hear a Parsi divorce case, but leave it to the Parsi *panchayat* to decide on the machinery of reconciliation and the amount of alimony. The Indian state is thus both an association of individuals and a community of communities, recognizing both individuals and communities as bearers of rights. The criminal law recognizes only individuals, whereas the civil law recognizes most minority communities as distinct legal subjects. This makes India a liberal democracy of a very peculiar kind.

It is tempting to say, as many Indian and foreign commentators have said, that the Indian state is too 'deeply embedded' in society and too 'plural' and 'chaotic' to be considered a properly constituted state or a state in the 'true' sense of the word. But such a view is obviously too superficial and ethnocentric to be satisfactory. There is no reason why we should accept the view that the modern western constitution of the state is the only true or proper one, and deny India and other non-western societies the right to indigenize the imported institution of the state and even to evolve their own alternative political formations. Rather than insist that the state *must* be autonomous and separate from society, and then set about finding ways of restoring it to the people, we might argue that it should not be separated from society in the first instance. And rather than insist that the state *must* have a uniform legal system, we might argue that it should be free to allow its constituent communities to retain their different laws and practices, so long as these conform to clearly laid down and nationally accepted principles of justice and fairness. Thus the law might require that a divorced wife must be provided for, but leave the different communities free to decide whether the husband, his family, or his community as a whole should arrange for her maintenance, so long as the arrangments are foolproof and not open to abuse and arbitrary alternation. If the multi-communal polities are to hold together and to avoid the all too familiar eruptions of inter- and intra-communal violence, they need to be extremely sensitive to the traditions, values and levels of development of their constituent communities, and may find the institutions and practices developed in socially homogeneous liberal societies deeply subversive.

Like the concepts of the individual, right, property and so on, such institutions as elections, multiple political parties, the separation of powers and the abstract state too cannot be universalized. Elections of the western type impose a crushing financial burden on poor countries and encourage the all too familiar forms of corruption. In an ethnically and religiously diverse society lacking shared values, or in a society unused to discussing its differences in public and articulating them in neat ideological terms, elections might also prove deeply divisive, generate artificial ideological rigidities, release powerful aggressive impulses and channel them into dangerous and unaccustomed directions. Such societies might be better off sticking to or evolving consensual and less polarized ways of selecting their governments and conducting their affairs. What is true of elections is equally true of other liberal democratic institutions and practices.

This is not to say that liberal democratic institutions have no value for non-western societies, rather that the latter have to determine the value themselves in the light of their cultural resources, needs and circumstances, and that they cannot mechanically transplant them. As a matter of fact, many third world countries have tried all manner of political experiments, some successful and others disastrous. Thanks to the profoundly mistaken belief, partly self-induced and partly encouraged by western governments and developmental experts, that their experiments were 'deviations' from the 'true' liberal democratic model and symptomatic of their immaturity and backwardness, they often undertook them without much zeal and self-confidence and abandoned them prematurely. Their political predicament is very like their linguistic predicament. They abandoned their traditional languages, which they well knew how to speak, in favour of the 'proper' and 'respectable' languages of their colonial rulers, which they could never adequately master.

It would appear that the democratic part of liberal democracy, consisting in such things as free elections, free speech and the right to equality, has proved far more attractive outside the west and is more universalizable than the liberal component. Millions in non-western societies demand democracy, albeit in suitably indigenized forms, whereas they tend to shy away from liberalism as if they instinctively felt it to be subversive of what they most valued and cherished. This is not because it leads to capitalism, for many of them welcome the latter, but because the third world countries feel that the liberal view of the world and way of life is at odds with their deepest aspirations and self-conceptions. As they understand it, liberalism breaks up the community, undermines the shared body of ideas and values, places the isolated individual above the community, encourages the ethos and ethic of aggressive self-assertion, rejects traditional wisdom and common sense in the name of scientific reason, and weakens the spirit of mutual accommodation and adjustment. Non-western societies wonder why they cannot import such western technology and expertise as they need while rejecting some of its liberal values and suitably indigenizing some of its democratic practices. They might be proved wrong and may suffer as a result. But forcing them into the standard liberal democratic mould is not without its heavy human cost either.

To reject the universalist claims of liberal democracy is not to endorse the crude relativist view that a country's political system is its own business and above criticism, and that western experiences have no relevance outside the west. In an increasingly interdependent world every country's internal affairs impinge on others and are a matter of general concern. The dissidents, the oppressed minorities and the ill-treated masses the world over appeal to international public opinion for support, and we cannot respond to them without the help of general principles to guide our judgements and actions. Thanks to the widening of our moral consciousness, we feel morally concerned about human suffering even when our help is not directly asked for. And thanks to the increasing demystification of the modern state, we are beginning to realize that its citizens are not its property, that it is accountable to humankind for the way it treats them, and that it must be opened up to external scrutiny. All this calls for a body of moral and political principles that are both universally valid and capable of accommodating cultural diversity and autonomy. We need to work out the minimum conditions or principles of good government and leave different countries free to evolve their own appropriate forms of government compatible with these regulative principles.

Since we cannot here pursue this large and complex question, a few general remarks will have to suffice. Universally valid regulative principles cannot be laid down by western governments, let alone by a philosopher, both because they are bound to be infected by an ethnocentric bias and because they can have no authority over the rest of humankind. It is easy to be prescriptive, but such prescriptions have no meaning and force unless they resonate in the lives of, and evoke sympathetic responses in the minds of, those affected by them. The principles of good government can be genuinely universal (in their scope and content) *and* binding only if they are freely negotiated by all involved and grounded in a broad global consensus. It would be wholly naive to imagine that all governments and all men and women everywhere will ever agree on them. What we can legitimately hope and strive for is a broad cross-cultural consensus commanding varying degrees of universal support. As individuals and groups in different parts of the world invoke it in their internal struggles, and as the rest of the world responds to them, the consensus acquires depth and vitality, becomes an acceptable political currency, strikes roots in popular consciousness, and acquires new adherents. This is broadly how almost all our moral principles have evolved and acquired authority. And this is also how the 1948 United Nations Declaration of Human Rights has acquired its current appeal. A pious statement of good intentions when first formulated in the aftermath of the second world war, it was increasingly invoked by the leaders of colonial struggles for independence and oppressed minorities, and over time became an important part of domestic and international morality.

The UN Declaration is a complex document and articulated at three different levels. First, it lays down the general principles every government should satisfy. Secondly, it translates these principles into the language of rights and lists different kinds of rights. Thirdly, it lays down institutions and practices that alone in its view can guarantee and protect these rights. The last two parts of it have a liberal democratic bias, the second part because of its use of the language of rights and the kinds of rights it stresses, and the third because the recommended institutions and practices presuppose and are specific to liberal democracy.

As for the general principles of the UN Declaration, they fall into two categories. Some are distinctly liberal and culturally specific; for example, the more or less unlimited right to freedom of expression and to private property, and the insistence that marriages must be based on the 'free and full consent' of the intending spouses. Other principles relate to vital human interests valued in almost all societies and have a genuinely universal core, such as respect for human life and dignity, equality before the law, equal protection of the law, fair trial and the protection of minorities. Liberalism does, of course, deeply cherish and place great value on these principles, but they are not unique to it. They were found in classical Athens and Rome and many a medieval kingdom, are emphasized in the sacred texts of all great religions, and were widely practised in many non-western societies. Indeed the record of some non-western societies in such areas as respect for human life and the protection of minorities, including Jews, is not only as good as but even better than that of the liberal west.

Evidence that the second category of principles laid down by the UN Declaration commands considerable universal support is threefold. First, the UN Declaration was signed by a large number of governments representing different cultures, geographical areas and political systems. Secondly, when the newly liberated Asian and African countries joined the UN they demanded amendments to its Declaration, which were accepted after much debate and embodied in the two International Covenants of 1966. The latter documents rejected the right to property and to full compensation in the event of nation-alization, toned down the individualistic basis of the 1948 Declaration, and endorsed the occasional need to suspend individual rights in the national interest. However they not only left untouched but even strengthened what I have called the genuinely universal principles of the 1948 Declaration. Thirdly, people the world over have frequently appealed to these principles in their struggles against repressive governments. For their part the latter have almost invariably preferred to deny the existence of unacceptable practices rather than shelter behind relativism and cultural autonomy. In their own different ways both parties are thus beginning to accept the principles as the basis of good government, conferring on them the moral authority they otherwise cannot have. In other words, the principles are increasingly becoming 'a common standard of achievement for all peoples and nations' as the UN Declaration itself had hoped. As such they provide a most valuable basis for a freely negotiated and constantly evolving consensus on universally valid principles of good government.

Within the limits set by these principles, different countries should remain free to determine their own appropriate forms of government. They may choose liberal democracy, but if they do not their choice deserves respect and even encouragement. After all, liberals have always held, and rightly, that diversity is the precondition of progress and choice, and that truth can only emerge from a peaceful competition between different ways of life.

# 77

# THE IDEA OF FREEDOM IN BURMA

## J. Silverstein

I think it is important for every people to work for the preservation of their culture and religion. At the same time it must be remembered that a progressive nation should move with the times and avoid bigoted and narrow-minded attitudes.

In these words Daw Aung San Suu Kyi expressed the unity in Burmese culture of the two traditions of freedom she had come to know through her education, her own reflection, and travel and living abroad. As a child growing up in Burma, she gained a deep understanding of Buddhism, Burmese traditions, and the Western liberal ideas which were part of modern Burmese culture and the Burmese language; from her education in India and England, her experiences of living and working in several areas of the world and her postgraduate studies in Japan, she acquired an extensive intellectual experience which broadened and deepened her perspective on the thought and culture of modern Burma.

The synthesis of the two traditions is clearly expressed in her essay 'In Quest of Democracy'. Writing in 1988, at the time of the peaceful revolution in Burma and its suppression by the military, she found nothing new in the rhetoric of the opponents of freedom and democracy, who questioned the ability of the people to judge what is best for the nation and condemned the liberal ideas drawn from

From J. Silverstein, 'The Idea of Freedom in Burma and the Political Thought of Daw Aung San Suu Kyi', in David Kelly and Anthony Reid (eds), *Asian Freedoms: The Idea of Freedom in East and Southeast Asia* (Cambridge University Press, Cambridge, 1998), pp. 198–202.

the West as un-Burmese. She argued that even without the sophisticated techniques and methods of political and economic analysis common in the West, the Burmese could find answers to the terrible political and socio-economic conditions in Burma by turning to the words of the Buddha on the causes of decline and decay – 'failure to recover that which has been lost, omission to repair that which has been damaged, disregard for the need of a reasonable economy and the elevation to leadership of men without morality or learning' – and applying them to their situation. Put in modern terms, she said: 'when democratic rights had been lost to military dictatorship sufficient efforts had not been made to regain them, moral and political values had been allowed to deteriorate without concerted attempts to save the situation, the economy had been badly managed, and the country had been ruled by men without integrity and wisdom.' For her, the 1988 peaceful revolution was an attempt by the people to act as the Buddha taught and take back their right to rule and reverse the process of decline.

For Aung San Suu Kyi, the contradiction between Buddhism and dictatorship begins with the question about the nature of man. Buddhism, she argued, places the highest value on man, who alone has the ability to attain the supreme state of Buddhahood. 'Each man has in him the potential to realize the truth through his own will and endeavor and to help others to realize it.' But under despotic rule man is valued least, as a 'faceless, mindless – and helpless – mass to be manipulated at will'. Reflecting on this contradiction, she observed: 'It is a puzzlement to the Burmese how concepts which recognize the inherent dignity and the equal and inalienable rights of human beings, which accept that all men are endowed with reason and conscience and which recommend a universal spirit of brotherhood, can be inimical to indigenous values. 'If man is endowed with reason and has the innate ability to realise his potential, then the political system and social environment must allow him freedom to pursue that end. For Aung San Suu Kyi, only in a democratic society can man truly exercise his freedom. Democracy, she argues, acknowledges the right to differ as well as the duty to settle differences peacefully. Under democracy, 'protest and dissent can exist in healthy counterpart with orthodoxy and conservatism, contained by a general recognition of the need to balance respect for individual rights with respect for law and order'.

The idea of law and order, she wrote, is frequently misused as an excuse for oppression. In Burmese, the idea is officially expressed as *nyein-wut-pi-pyar* (quiet-crouched-crushed-flattened). A prominent Burmese writer drew the conclusion that 'the whole made for an undesirable state of affairs, one which militated against the emergence of an alert, energetic, progressive citizenry'. For Aung San Suu Kyi, law must be equated with justice, and order with the discipline of a people satisfied that justice has been done. For her this could only exist where the people's elected representatives make the laws and the administrators have no power to set them aside and replace them with new arbitrary decrees. Drawing on Buddhist precepts, she wrote that the concept of law was based on *dhamma* ('righteousness or virtue'), not on the power to impose harsh and inflexible rules on a defenceless people. Noting that the teachings of the Buddha centre on universal values of truth, righteousness and loving kindness and that Burmese associated peace and security with coolness and shade, she found the modern liberal democratic idea of rule under law in a Burmese poem:

> The shade of the tree is cool indeed
> The shade of parents is cooler
> The shade of teachers is cooler still
> The shade of the ruler is yet more cool
> But coolest of all is the shade of Buddha's teachings.

Towards the end of her essay on democracy, Daw Aung San Suu Kyi wrote that 'in their quest of democracy the people of Burma explore not only the political theories and practices of the world outside their country but also the spiritual and intellectual values that have given shape to their own environment'.

Implicit in her writing and speeches is the idea that freedom is a universal idea – an idea which was given modern approval in the Universal Declaration of Human Rights which the United Nations adopted in 1948. As she noted, the Burma delegation to the world body voted for it with no reservations when it was adopted by the General Assembly. The vote was consistent with the thought and goals of the nation's founding fathers at the Anti-Fascist People's Freedom League pre-convention meeting, the constituent assembly, and the language included in the constitution for an independent Burma. She referred frequently to the Declaration as a universal standard for all people, and maintained that until its content was inscribed in the basic law of the land and upheld by the government and respected by those with power, the nation and its people were not free.

But freedom is more than constitutional guarantees and institutional arrangements. It also is psychological. In an address which, because of her imprisonment, she could not deliver to the European Parliament in response to being awarded the Sakharov Prize for Freedom of Thought, she spoke to the peoples of Burma, who have lived under corrupt military rule since 1962, when she wrote that, as important as the traditional ideas of freedom are, man is not truly free if he lives in fear. 'It is not power that corrupts but fear. Fear of losing power corrupts those who wield it and fear of the scourge of power corrupts those who are subject to it.' Fear, Aung San Suu Kyi wrote, stifles and slowly destroys all sense of right and wrong. Fear contributes to corruption; 'where fear is rife corruption in all forms becomes entrenched.'

> The quintessential revolution is that of the spirit, born of an intellectual conviction of the need for change in those mental attitudes and values which shape the course of a nation's development ... It is not enough merely to call for freedom, democracy and human rights. There has to be a united determination to persevere in the struggle, to make sacrifices in the

name of enduring truths, to resist the corrupting influences of desire, ill will, ignorance and fear.

Daw Aung San Suu Kyi has demonstrated her courage in the face of threat and has shown that she will not be intimidated or made fearful. It is her model of courage which has sustained the people who have looked to her for leadership since 26 August 1988, when, for the first time, she stepped forward and became their instant leader. She recalled something her father said in an earlier time of troubles:

> Democracy is the only ideology which is consistent with freedom. It is also an ideology that promotes and strengthens peace. It is therefore the only ideology that promotes and strengthens peace. It is therefore the only ideology we should aim for.

She said that was the reason why she was taking part in the struggle for freedom and democracy.

The ideas and thoughts of Daw Aung San Suu Kyi are not offered as an example of those of a scholar or reflective thinker working in the abstract. Rather, she is an example of a special person who, because of her name and family, gained an immediate audience; but it was her words and ideas, which the people understood and related to, that vaulted her into the leadership of Burma's revolution against authoritarian rule. Despite the military's effort to isolate and erase her presence from the mind of the public, she continues to hold its loyalty because of her courage and because the message she continues to deliver is in the mainstream of Burmese culture and tradition.

Freedom in modern Burma is not contrary to tradition; it has been part of it from the very start. Burma was not frozen in time in the face of the British military victories and the imposition of colonial rule. The Burmese learned new meanings for freedom from the British and other Western sources and incorporated those new meanings into their own beliefs and values. By the end of the Second World War, the emergent élite spoke of freedom and democracy to an audience who understood and freely followed in the direction it led.

But Burma was not destined to have an easy transition from authoritarian rule to political freedom; even after independence in 1948, several rebellions erupted, challenging the democracy and authority of the constitution.

The military's seizure of power in 1962 met virtually no organised opposition in the Burman heartland until 1988; but during that period the rulers' efforts to root out the nascent and imperfectly formed democracy of their predecessors and create a totalitarian dictatorship with a population of 'rice-eating robots' failed because the memory of and desire for freedom remained alive in the minds of the people. The student-led peaceful revolution provided the means to release those pent-up memories, and the speeches of Daw Aung San Suu Kyi reacquainted them with the meaning of freedom and rekindled their desire to recover it. The peaceful revolutionaries and their new leader were effective because freedom was part of the Burmese tradition which the military dictators tried to erase and failed.

# 78

# CHINESE DEMOCRACY

## Andrew J. Nathan

[. . .]

The most eloquent evidence for the democrats' thesis that power will continue to be abused so long as it remains uncontrolled has been the treatment of those who propounded it: the democracy movement has been effectively crushed within China. In 1981, Fu Yuehua, leader of the Peking petitioners' demonstrations, was released from prison but transferred to a labor camp. Liu Qing, the editor of *April Fifth Forum* who had been sent for three years of labor reeducation for distributing the transcript of Wei Jingsheng's trial, was sentenced in 1982 to another seven years after he smuggled out a camp diary that was published in the West. His brother and a colleague were arrested for assisting him. Xu Wenli, another editor of *April Fifth Forum* and a strong backer of Deng Xiaoping among the democrats, was sentenced to fifteen years' imprisonment; Wang Xizhe, the independent Marxist theorist of Canton, to fourteen years; and He Qiu, former editor of *People's Road*, to ten years, all for counter-revolutionary propaganda or incitement. Late one night in August 1983, teams of police and militiamen appeared on the streets of Shanghai and other cities, carrying lists and knocking on doors. An estimated 100,000 suspected criminals were arrested nationwide in this and a second sweep in October. Most were sentenced to labor reeducation in border areas, their urban residence permits revoked so that they would have to stay in the borderlands after their sentences had expired. According to interviews, a number of former activists were swept

From Andrew J. Nathan, *Chinese Democracy* (I. B. Tauris, London, 1986), pp. 230–2.

into the net. By 1984, Wei Jingsheng had served the first five years of his fifteen-year sentence in solitary confinement in a prison near Peking; according to Amnesty International, his mental health had seriously deteriorated.

Ren Wanding, the founder of the China Human Rights League, was freed from prison in 1983. His term had been extended to four years because of his failure to make a satisfactory self-criticism. Other activists, especially those who were given labor reeducation terms, must also have been released, although reliable word of this has seldom reached the outside world. All have remained silent.

Chinese advocates of democracy today face a difficult prospect. At one time many activists believed that the advance of legal codification and the people's congress system would permit their movement to prosper. But these activists obviously overestimated the tolerance of the reformers whose support they thought they had. Other democrats dreamed that Deng's economic reforms would fail, thereby bringing about a Polish-style workers' rebellion which would force the regime to permit some form of political pluralism (a possibility that apparently also worried some of the leaders for a time). But the success of the economic reforms to date has made this scenario appear increasingly unlikely. Some activists (and foreigners) now hope that the development of the economy will cause a kind of natural political evolution – that the government will loosen its control of the economy, accommodate more and more ideas from the West, and yield to the demands for freedom of a rising technical and managerial class. Judging from the experience of the developed socialist economies of Europe, such economically induced change may include greater legal protection for individuals, enhanced intellectual and cultural tolerance, and a consultative style of decision-making – the types of evolution that are in fact occurring in Deng's China. But there is little prospect that the party will adopt, voluntarily or under pressure, either of the two conditions that the radical democrats identified as essential for authentic democracy: free elections and an independent press. (The government may adopt a law permitting privately owned publications, but if so these would certainly be kept under effective government supervision.)

The democracy movement persists in the open only overseas. A government-funded Chinese student, Wang Bingzhang, after completing a combined M.D.-Ph.D. program at McGill University, announced in New York in November 1982 that he was staying in the West to continue the movement that had been suppressed at home. Together with a number of other Chinese in the U.S. and Canada, he launched a magazine called *China Spring*, which analyzes events in China and publishes theoretical discussions of democracy and reform, some of them purportedly sent by contributors living in China. The magazine's platform includes political pluralism and an independent press. In December 1983, the group held its "first international representative conference" in New York, attended by fifty-three delegates from around the world. Adopting the name "Chinese Alliance for Democracy," the organization claimed chapters in Hong

Kong, Japan, Australia, France, West Germany, Holland, Belgium, and Mauritius, as well as in thirteen U.S. and Canadian cities, and an underground network in China.

Nonetheless, support for pluralist democracy among Chinese both at home and abroad seems if anything weaker today than when the democracy movement emerged. Even those who agree with the democrats' analysis that overconcentration of power is at the root of China's political problems fear the disorder they believe would flow from any weakening of party control. Most intellectuals appear to accept the party's claim that political order in their country requires leaders with strong authority. They hold to the old view that, because of China's feudal tradition and peasant backwardness, institutional change is useless until the culture is reformed. Many who speak this way seem unaware of how their words echo back through history: to the judgment of Liang Qichao that China was fit only for enlightened despotism; to the political passivity and cultural reformism of dispirited liberals of the 1920s and 1930s; to the tutelage theory of the Guomindang.

Never seriously addressed in the course of the democracy controversy was the feasibility, as distinct from the desirability, of pluralist democracy in China. Proponents might have pointed to the relative success of pluralism in other countries with approximately China's level of development, such as India; or to the apparent compatibility of robust political rights and freedoms with political stability and economic growth in other settings with Confucian cultural traditions, such as twentieth-century Japan and even, to some extent, contemporary Taiwan. They might have argued that even though China is still backward, conditions for pluralism are much more promising now than during the abortive experiment of the early republic, because there is a strong government to guarantee political order and a better-educated population that is also becoming better off economically.

Like the early Liang Qichao and other reformers in China's tradition of Confucian optimism, however, the democrats seemed to see institutional change as needing only to be ordained to be successful. Confucius once said, "Is virtue a thing remote? If I desire to be virtuous, virtue will be at hand." To the democrats, pluralist reform was similarly a matter of making up one's mind as to its desirability, and so they concentrated on demonstrating the benefits of their proposed reforms, as if this were all that was needed to make the case for adopting them. By default, they left the task of evaluating their ideas' practicality to those who feared, in the pessimistic tradition of the later Liang and other conservatives, that society was still too backward to allow the people to hold real power. In the end, the democrats may have had the better of the theoretical argument that democracy cannot perform its functions without competitive elections and an independent press. But so far, China's century-long obsession with political order and national strength has made it impossible for most other Chinese, even non-Marxists, to share their vision of change.

# SECTION 14
# PARTICIPATION

# PARTICIPATION
# INTRODUCTION

While it may be true, as Dunn says,[1] that 'we are all democrats today', there is significantly less agreement when it comes to the question of participation. As we have seen throughout this Reader, some theorists highlight the threat posed to democracy by excessive participation, while others claim that the present level of participation is insufficient to provide the political system with legitimacy. In the former 'realist' camp we can identify the conservative and elitist critics of liberal-democracy, though clearly this is a thread that runs throughout the development of democracy since Plato's time. Against them, 'participatory' theorists voice concern over the low levels of political participation in the liberal democracies. Such theorists are keen to assert that there can be more political participation, and that this does not necessarily result in a loss of effectiveness.

In this section, we explore how political participation is to be conceived. We begin with a selection from *Parry and Moyser*, which sets out the two opposing camps. Whether we take a realist or a participatory approach to political participation, it is clear from this selection that participation is a complex process, and one that is all too often directly equated with democracy. In fact, not only is participation of many different types, it is also only one of a series of components of democracy.

In the selection from *Barber*, we find a spirited call for a radical increase in participatory activity throughout our society. Barber argues that a more participatory politics, which he refers to as 'Strong Democracy' can deliver a viable and effective government and a reconstruction of political community. These issues are further taken up by *Pitkin and Shumer*. Here, we receive an account of recent developments in participatory democracy, both theoretical and practical, and a full discussion of the problems and prospects of such an approach.

Lest we forget just how demanding of citizens the participatory vision really is, we here include a selection from *Walzer*. Walzer highlights not only the time and effort required to sit in meetings, but also the many ways in which participatory groups can construct their own disciplinary culture, every bit as exclusionary as the one they seek to oppose.

One area where scholars have made significant attempts to address participation, as we have already seen in Section 9 on rational choice, is in the area of non-participation, or apathy. Both 'realist' and 'participatory' theorists of democracy acknowledge that in many liberal-democratic systems levels of participation are lower than they might be. Yet the attention given to apathy is also, in part, a reaction to the widespread use of economic methods in the explanation of participation. As we saw, in the section on Rational Choice above, such methods are rather better at explaining why people do not participate than they are at why they do.

In the selection from *Berelson et al.*, we find an early study of voting which was strongly influenced by economic and rational choice methods, and which, in turn, influenced subsequent discussions of apathy. Berelson concludes that though the populace is largely apathetic about politics, this is a good thing for the stability of the system as a whole.

*Pateman* analyses Berelson's findings, as well as those of Dahl. Her conclusion is that the orientation taken by these studies to the system as a whole tends to determine their findings before they have begun. At the heart of such approaches, she argues, is the fear that the populace might overcome their apathy and thereby destabilise democracy. We should not, therefore, be surprised that these early studies tend to applaud the level of participation already in existence, and to conceive of themselves as having provided a profound empirical critique of the classic ideals of democracy.

## NOTE

1. J. Dunn, *Western Political Theory in the Face of the Future* (Cambridge University Press, Cambridge, 1979), p. 1.

# 79

# MORE PARTICIPATION, MORE DEMOCRACY?

## Geraint Parry and George Moyser

In any attempt to measure the extent of democracy, the degree of popular political participation must constitute one of the indices. Democracy meant originally the 'rule', or 'power', of 'the people'. To put it at its most simplistic, a regime in which the people exercised no part in rule could not qualify as 'democratic' (although some may have claimed that it did). But, conversely, should one conclude that the more the people participate in politics, the more democratic the system of government? Unfortunately, things are not so simple.

The definition of democracy as the power of the people is derived from its Greek original. This fact, however obvious, may still alert one to the difficulties in taking popular participation as a measure of democratization, not least because of the discontinuities between the ancient and modern experiences of 'democracy' (see Farrar, 1988; Finley, 1973; Held, 1987). The prime political discontinuity is that in Athens the term 'power' of the people meant something that it cannot mean in the modern world. The 'people', meaning the citizens, exercised control over policy by *direct* acts of will in the assembly. In addition, the citizens had the opportunity to be chosen, by lot, to carry out the executive tasks of government. Clearly citizen participation in the modern world is very far removed from this. As John Dunn puts it: 'in no modern state do its members, male or female, decide what

From Geraint Parry and George Moyser, 'More Participation, More Democracy?', in David Beetham (ed.), *Defining and Measuring Democracy* (Sage, London, 1994), pp. 44–7.

is in fact done, or hold their destiny in their own hands. They do not, because they cannot' (1992: vi).

Thus democracy as the 'power' of the people has to be attenuated to 'rule' of the people or to some rather weaker term which captures the elements we associate with modernity – institutionalized popular influence, procedures of accountability. In the era when something to be called democracy was reinvented (even if termed 'republic'), the claim advanced in its favour was its superiority to the direct popular forms of the ancient world rather than any element of continuity (Wokler, 1994). This is seen in Federalist Paper 63, where one element in the 'most advantageous superiority' of the American system lay in 'the total exclusion of the people in their collective capacity' from any share in government. It is not, in fact, that popular participation is being totally excluded – in republican terminology it is one of the elements in mixed government. But this participation is to be mediated through political leaders who, with relative rapidity, became professionalized (Pizzorno, 1970).

Citizen participation thus ceased to be the *paramount* indicator of democracy. It has been joined by several others – the competitiveness of élites, the representativeness of representation, the control of bureaucracy, the independence of the judiciary, freedoms of various kinds. Thus when Dahl opened his treatment of democratization in *Polyarchy* (1971) he employed two broad indicators. One was, indeed, participation – measured by the right to take part in elections and office. The other was 'public contestation' (competition for office and political support). This is taken to be a measure of 'liberalization' (Dahl, 1971: 1–9). Each element, Dahl suggests, is possible in the absence of the other. Political contestation may increase without a corresponding increase in participation, thereby creating competitive oligarchies such as existed in nineteenth-century Europe. Equally, participation in elections may be provided without increasing political choice. It is only when liberalization occurs in tandem with participation that one can speak of democratization (or of the emergence of polyarchies, since Dahl would add a range of other indicators for full democratization to be identified). Thus, in isolating participation as an indicator of democracy, no claim is being advanced that it is *the* indicator. Indeed, the significance to be attached to participation, or to various forms of participation, turns very much on the conception of democracy which is held.

A broad distinction can be drawn between a 'participatory' or 'radical' conception and a 'realist' conception which places its stress on political leadership, accountability and representation (see Nordlinger, 1981:207; Sartori, 1987:39–55). In distinguishing these two dispositions, one is doing some disservice to the nuances of various theorists by putting into a single camp writers who do differ in various ways. To place Pateman, Gould and Barber into the 'participatory' school is not to deny significant differences in emphasis. The same is true for such 'realists' as Schumpeter, Sartori and Nordlinger. Nevertheless, the distinction between the approaches will serve the purpose of suggesting how conceptions of democracy can result in contrasting evaluations of participation.

The participatory democrats may trace a genealogy from ancient models of citizenship or, within modern thought, from Rousseau or from J. S. Mill and G. D. H. Cole. None believes that existing democracies live up to their ideals of participatory citizenship. Indeed, contemporary institutions serve, rather, to discourage such ideals and so participationists look for changes in the structures of politics to widen citizen involvement. People would not only go to the polls but would also attend party meetings, take part in referendums and even 'participate' in the executive arm of government and the workplace. The process of taking part becomes integral to democracy. Deliberation, the search for consensus, the desire to encourage the reticent or the less privileged to have their say, the educative effects of involvement – all are valued in different ways (see Barber, 1984; Pateman, 1970:42). For all, the decisive test of a democracy is its capacity to encourage its population to play an active role in its government.

This is not the case for the realists. Sartori, for example, contends that democracy is 'the by-product of a competitive method of leadership recruitment' (1987:152). The search for indicators of democracy will start with the competition between political leaders. It will not end there because competition is not itself democracy but produces democracy. It does so because the leaders can only win the competition by appealing to the people. Hence democracy 'still results from the sheer fact that the *power* of deciding between the competitors is in the hands of the demos' (Sartori, 1987:151; original emphasis). Thus the index of democratization would also be sought for in some, probably qualitative, account of the '*responsiveness* of the leaders to the led' (Sartori, 1987: 156; original emphasis; but see also below).

The popular input required is at once all important yet minimal. It is all important in that elections constitute the decisive point in democracy. It is minimal in that the ordinary citizen is asked to do little more than turn out on election day. Indeed, Schumpeter (1952) would go so far as positively to discourage citizens from intervening between elections. They are urged to respect a division of labour between themselves and the professional politicians. In short, for Sartori and Schumpeter, participation, apart from voting, is not taken to be a key indicator of democracy. Representation or élite responsiveness would be more relevant.

### PARTICIPATION AS A MULTIPLE INDICATOR

That one theory should pay special attention to one mode of participation – voting – and virtually none to others is a reminder of the multidimensionality of 'participation'. This has been stressed by most studies of participation since the work of the Verba and Nie team (Parry et al., 1992; Verba and Nie, 1972; Verba et al., 1978). The various modes of taking part in politics – voting, party campaigning, group activity, contacting representatives and officials, protesting

**Table [1]**  *Five modes of political participation and associated levels of activity (N = c. 1,570)*

| Activity | % **Yes/At least once** | % **Often/Now and then** |
|---|---|---|
| (A) *Contacting*: | | |
| Member of parliament | 9.7 | 3.4 |
| Civil servant | 7.3 | 3.1 |
| Councillor | 20.7 | 10.3 |
| Town hall | 17.4 | 8.9 |
| Media | 3.8 | 1.6 |
| (B) *Groups*: | | |
| Organized group | 11.2 | 6.7 |
| Informal group | 13.8 | 6.4 |
| Issue in group | 4.7 | 2.3 |
| (C) *Protest*: | | |
| Attend protest meeting | 14.6 | 6.1 |
| Organize petition | 8.0 | 2.1 |
| Sign petition | 63.3 | 39.9 |
| Block traffic | 1.1 | 0.3 |
| Protest march | 5.2 | 2.1 |
| Political strike | 6.5 | 2.3 |
| Political boycott | 4.3 | 2.3 |
| (D) *Party campaigning*: | | |
| Fund[-]raising | 5.2 | 4.3 |
| Canvasing | 3.5 | 2.6 |
| Clerical work | 3.5 | 2.4 |
| Attend party rally | 8.6 | 4.9 |
| (E) *Voting*: | | |
| Local | 86.2[1] | 68.8[2] |
| National (% voted 1983) | 82.5 | |
| European (% voted 1984) | 47.3 | |

1. % some or more
2. % most or all

– have a number of different characteristics, not least their effects on political outcomes. Hence there is a strong argument for treating each mode of participation as a distinct indicator of democratization. For Britain, which will serve as an illustration, some idea of the broad participatory modes and their specific activity levels is given in Table [1].

## REFERENCES

Barber, B., *Strong Democracy* (University of California Press, Berkeley, 1984).

Dahl, R., *Polyarchy: Participation and Opposition* (Yale University Press, New Haven, CT and London, 1971).

Dunn, J., *Democracy: The Unfinished Journey 508 BC to AD 1993* (Oxford University Press, Oxford, 1992).

Farrar, C., *The Origins of Democratic Thinking* (Cambridge University Press, Cambridge, 1988).

Finley, M., *Democracy Ancient and Modern* (Chatto & Windus, London, 1973).

Held, D., *Models of Democracy* (Polity Press, Cambridge, 1987).

Nordlinger, E., *On the Autonomy of the Democratic State* (Harvard University Press, Cambridge, MA, 1981).

Parry, G. and Moyser, G., *Political Participation and Democracy in Britain* (Cambridge University Press, Cambridge, 1992).

Pateman, C., *Participation and Democratic Theory* (Cambridge University Press, Cambridge, 1970).

Pizzorno, A., 'An Introduction to the Theory of Political Participation', *Social Science Information*, 9 (5), 1970, pp. 29–61.

Sartori, G., *The Theory of Democracy Revisited*, 2 vols (Chatham House, Chatham, NJ, 1987).

Schumpeter, J. A., *Capitalism, Socialism and Democracy* (Allen & Unwin, London, 1966).

Verba, S. and Nie, N., *Participation in America: Political Democracy and Social Equality* (Harper & Row, New York, 1972).

Verba, S., Nie, N. and Kim J.-O., *Participation and Political Equality* (Cambridge University Press, Cambridge, 1978).

Wokler, R., 'Democracy's Mythical Ordeals: The Procrustean and Promethean Paths to Popular Self-Rule', in Moran, M. and Parry, G. (eds), *Democracy and Democratization* (Routledge, London, 1994), pp. 21–46.

# 80

# STRONG DEMOCRACY

## Benjamin R. Barber

STRONG DEMOCRACY: POLITICS IN THE PARTICIPATORY MODE

The future of democracy lies with strong democracy – with the revitalization of a form of community that is not collectivistic, a form of public reasoning that is not conformist, and a set of civic institutions that is compatible with modern society. Strong democracy is defined by politics in the participatory mode: literally, it is self-government by citizens rather than representative government in the name of citizens. Active citizens govern themselves directly here, not necessarily at every level and in every instance, but frequently enough and in particular when basic policies are being decided and when significant power is being deployed. Self-government is carried on through institutions designed to facilitate ongoing civic participation in agenda-setting, deliberation, legislation, and policy implementation (in the form of "common work"). Strong democracy does not place endless faith in the capacity of individuals to govern themselves, but it affirms with Machiavelli that the multitude will on the whole be as wise as or even wiser than princes and with Theodore Roosevelt that "the majority of the plain people will day in and day out make fewer mistakes in governing themselves than any smaller body of men will make in trying to govern them."

Considered as a response to the dilemmas of the political condition, strong democracy can be given the following formal definition: *strong democracy in*

From Benjamin R. Barber, *Strong Democracy: Participatory Politics for a New Age* (University of California Press, Berkeley, Los Angeles and London, 1984), pp. 150–5.

*the participatory mode resolves conflict in the absence of an independent
ground through a participatory process of ongoing, proximate self-legislation
and the creation of a political community capable of transforming dependent
private individuals into free citizens and partial and private interests into public
goods.*

The crucial terms in this strong formulation of democracy are *activity,
process, self-legislation, creation*, and *transformation*. Where weak democracy
eliminates conflict (the anarchist disposition), represses it (the realist disposition), or tolerates it (the minimalist disposition), strong democracy *transforms
conflict*. It turns dissensus into an occasion for mutualism and private interest
into an epistemological tool of public thinking.

Participatory politics deals with public disputes and conflicts of interest by
subjecting them to a never-ending process of deliberation, decision, and action.
Each step in the process is a flexible part of ongoing procedures that are
embedded in concrete historical conditions and in social and economic actual-
ities. In place of the search for a prepolitical independent ground or for an
immutable rational plan, strong democracy relies on participation in an evolving
problem-solving community that creates public ends where there were none
before by means of its own activity and of its own existence as a focal point of the
quest for mutual solutions. In such communities, public ends are neither
extrapolated from absolutes nor "discovered" in a preexisting "hidden consensus." They are literally forged through the act of public participation, created
through common deliberation and common action and the effect that deliberation and action have on interests, which change shape and direction when
subjected to these participatory processes.

Strong democracy, then, seems potentially capable of transcending the
limitations of representation and the reliance on surreptitious independent
grounds without giving up such defining democratic values as liberty, equality,
and social justice. Indeed, these values take on richer and fuller meanings
than they can ever have in the instrumentalist setting of liberal democracy.
For the strong democratic solution to the political condition issues out of a self-
sustaining dialectic of participatory civic activity and continuous community-
building in which freedom and equality are nourished and given political being.
Community grows out of participation and at the same time makes participation
possible; civic activity educates individuals how to think publicly as citizens even
as citizenship informs civic activity with the required sense of publicness and
justice. Politics becomes its own university, citizenship its own training ground,
and participation its own tutor. Freedom is what comes out of this process, not
what goes into it. Liberal and representative modes of democracy make politics
an activity of specialists and experts whose only distinctive qualification,
however, turns out to be simply that they engage in politics – that they encounter
others in a setting that requires action and where they have to find a way to act in
concert. Strong democracy is the politics of amateurs, where every man is
compelled to encounter every other man without the intermediary of expertise.

This universality of participation – every citizen his own politician – is essential, because the "Other" is a construct that becomes real to an individual only when he encounters it directly in the political arena. He may confront it as an obstacle or approach it as an ally, but it is an inescapable reality in the way of and on the way to common decision and common action. *We* also remains an abstraction when individuals are represented either by politicians or as symbolic wholes. The term acquires a sense of concreteness and simple reality only when individuals redefine themselves as citizens and come together directly to resolve a conflict or achieve a purpose or implement a decision. Strong democracy creates the very citizens it depends upon *because* it depends upon them, because it permits the representation neither of *me* nor of *we*, because it mandates a permanent confrontation between the *me* as citizen and the "Other" as citizen, forcing *us* to think in common and act in common. The citizen is by definition a *we*-thinker, and to think of the *we* is always to transform how interests are perceived and goods defined.

This progression suggests how intimate the ties are that bind participation to community. Citizenship is not a mask to be assumed or shed at will. It lacks the self-conscious mutability of a modern social "role" as Goffman might construe it. In strong democratic politics, participation is a way of defining the self, just as citizenship is a way of living. The old liberal notion, shared even by radical democrats such as Tom Paine, was that a society is "composed of distinct, unconnected individuals [who are] continually meeting, crossing, uniting, opposing, and separating from each other, as accident, interest, and circumstances shall direct." Such a conception repeats the Hobbesian error of setting participation and civic activity apart from community. Yet participation without community, participation in the face of deracination, participation by victims or bondsmen or clients or subjects, participation that is uninformed by an evolving idea of a "public" and unconcerned with the nurturing of self-responsibility, participation that is fragmentary, part-time, half-hearted, or impetuous – these are all finally sham, and their failure proves nothing.

It has in fact become a habit of the shrewder defenders of representative democracy to chide participationists and communitarians with the argument that enlarged public participation in politics produces no great results. Once empowered, the masses do little more than push private interests, pursue selfish ambitions, and bargain for personal gain, the liberal critics assert. Such participation is the work of prudent beasts and is often less efficient than the ministrations of representatives who have a better sense of the public's appetites than does the public itself. But such a course in truth merely gives the people all the insignia and none of the tools of citizenship and then convicts them of incompetence. Social scientists and political elites have all too often indulged themselves in this form of hypocrisy. They throw referenda at the people without providing adequate information, full debate, or prudent insulation from money and media pressures and then pillory them for their lack of judgment. They overwhelm the people with the least tractable problems of mass society – busing, inflation, tax structures, nuclear safety, right-to-work legislation, industrial waste disposal, environmental protection (all of which the representative elites themselves have utterly failed to deal with) – and then carp at their uncertainty or indecisiveness or the simple-mindedness with which they muddle through to a decision. But what general would shove rifles into the hands of civilians, hurry them off to battle, and then call them cowards when they are overrun by the enemy?

Strong democracy is not government by "the people" or government by "the masses," because a people are not yet a citizenry and masses are only nominal freemen who do not in fact govern themselves. Nor is participation to be understood as random activity by maverick cattle caught up in the same stampede or as minnow-school movement by clones who wiggle in unison. As with so many central political terms, the idea of participation has an intrinsically normative dimension – a dimension that is circumscribed by citizenship. Masses make noise, citizens deliberate; masses behave, citizens act; masses collide and intersect, citizens engage, share, and contribute. At the moment when "masses" start deliberating, acting, sharing, and contributing, they cease to be masses and become citizens. Only then do they "participate."

Or, to come at it from the other direction, to be a citizen *is* to participate in a certain conscious fashion that presumes awareness of and engagement in activity with others. This consciousness alters attitudes and lends to participation that sense of the *we* I have associated with community. To participate *is* to create a community that governs itself, and to create a self-governing community *is* to participate. Indeed, from the perspective of strong democracy, the two terms *participation* and *community* are aspects of one single mode of social being: citizenship. Community without participation first breeds unreflected consensus and uniformity, then nourishes coercive conformity, and finally engenders unitary collectivism of a kind that stifles citizenship and the autonomy on which political activity depends. Participation without community breeds mindless enterprise and undirected, competitive interest-mongering. Community without participation merely rationalizes collectivism, giving it an aura of legitimacy. Participation without community merely rationalizes individualism, giving it the aura of democracy.

This is not to say that the dialectic between participation and community is easily institutionalized. Individual civic activity (participation) and the public association formed through civic activity (the community) call up two strikingly different worlds. The former is the world of autonomy, individualism, and agency; the latter is the world of sociability, community, and interaction. The world views of individualism and communalism remain at odds; and institutions that can facilitate the search for common ends without sabotaging the individuality of the searchers, and that can acknowledge pluralism and conflict as starting points of the political process without abdicating the quest for a world of common ends, may be much more difficult to come by than a pretty paragraph about the dialectical interplay between individual participation and community. Yet it is just this dialectical balance that strong democracy claims to strike.

[...]

# 81

# ON PARTICIPATION

## Hannah Fenichel Pitkin and Sara M. Shumer

[...]

One day, as Albert Camus puts it, "a slave who has been taking orders all his life suddenly decides that he cannot obey some new command," and he says, "No more!" So one begins, and others join in; together they try to take charge of their lives. Historically, such popular empowerment has appeared both on the large, dramatic scale of revolution, and on the small, everyday, and local scene. It appeared in the sections of the Paris Commune and the "popular societies" and political clubs of the French Revolution, in the soldiers' and workers' soviets of the Russian Revolution, the "fanshen" assemblies of the Chinese Revolution, in the Committees of Correspondence of the American Revolution. Still visible to Tocqueville in the America of the 1830s, it reappeared in the Populist mobilization of the 1880s and 1890s. But it can also be found in Swiss cantons and Yugoslavian factories, in early Israeli kibbutzim, in the "Prague Spring," the literacy campaign of the Nicaraguan revolution, the struggles of Japanese peasants to oppose expansion of the Tokyo airport, at times in the labor movement, the Civil Rights movement, the women's movement. It can begin in some local incident (a bus in Montgomery or a shipyard in Gdansk) and spread to mobilize most of a nation. It can occur among colonized people, among slaves, among the subjects of a ruthless dictator. It is no mere fantasy or utopian absolute, but a relatively familiar recurrent phenomenon, a persistent struggle pursued in the widest variety of ways, under the most diverse and inhospitable

From Hanna Fenichel Pitkin and Sara M. Shumer, 'On Participation', *Democracy*, 2 (4), 1982, pp. 48–53.

circumstances. People find ways of being citizens even when they are excluded from the formal institutions of power.

The romantic, abstracted, and thoroughly unpolitical image of participation offered by recent theorists needs to be corrected by such a list of historical examples, showing that democracy is no dim and distant chimera, confined to the Greek city or the idealistic affinity group, remote from people's needs or presupposing automatic harmony, but a very real, practical human enterprise of the greatest possible political significance, repeatedly undertaken by ordinary people. Such a list of historical examples is, of course, motley, mixing rebellion and revolt with democratic movements, democratic societies, democracy as an established form of government. Few of the instances listed can be said unambiguously to have succeeded. Historically, such efforts have not only aimed at democratizing their societies, but also themselves provided the democratic experience for their participants. At what point and in what ways shall we say that such a movement has failed or ended? Certainly many "failed" movements left both the world and their members significantly transformed in democratic directions.

Nor is it obvious what might be proved by a record of democratic defeats. It might, for instance, be taken as confirming the thesis that democracy is dangerous: as soon as such a movement gives any signs of succeeding, all the resources of established power and privilege will be brought to bear "to destroy it, divert it, buy it, or try in any way to gain effective control over it," as Lawrence Goodwyn has written. Or the record might be taken as indicating how often democrats are misled by bad theoretical formulations, failing to nurture and preserve within their own groups the democracy they seek for their polity as a whole.

Certainly such a review of historical examples reminds us that hope – and the democratic impulse – springs eternal, even in the face of the most forbidding circumstances; and that from small, seemingly harmless beginnings, great and genuinely radical movements can grow. Much of the history of democracy has taken place within movements struggling to transform societies that were themselves far from democratic. The power and radical nature of those movements grew specifically from the liberating, transforming capacity of political action. So the decision of a tired black woman to sit in the front of the bus can become a national drive for human dignity and equality; a self-help cooperative providing credit for poor farmers can become a democratizing national movement; sections of the Paris Commune can, in demanding cheap bread, simultaneously begin developing "a new type of political organization" that will enable people to be "participators in government."

Democratic movements become stronger and potentially more radical as they diversify and reach out to other groups: when workers join with peasants, antinuclear ecologists join with nuclear plant workers and the unemployed, civil rights activists join with blue-collar workers and feminists. Not only do they acquire new members and allies, but they grow more political, and more just. As the group becomes more inclusive, members move beyond scapegoating toward increasing sophistication about the true social causes of their pain, and toward a more principled justification of who should pay what price to relieve it. So members discover their connectedness – and forge new connections – with others, with principle, and with their own capacities. Democrats must be as committed to fostering participatory politics within their movements as they are to the intrinsic value of participation in democratic government.

When people say that democracy is "obviously" not suitable for a large population, they fall captive to an abstract notion of assembling more and more people in one place: "no room can hold them all." But that is not how democratic movements grow, nor how real democratic polities function. Consider the America Tocqueville discovered in the 1830s, a people deeply engaged in democratic self-government: their "most important business" and their greatest pleasure. Take away politics from the American, Tocqueville said, and you rob him of half his existence, leaving a "vast void in his life" and making him "incredibly unhappy." Yet Tocqueville's America was no city-state, nor could its citizens assemble in one place. If size was no bar then to so lively a democratic engagement, it need not be now.

Face-to-face citizen assemblies are indeed essential to democracy, but one single assembly of all is not. Representation, delegation, cooperation, coordination, federation, and other kinds of devolution are entirely compatible with democracy, though they do not constitute and cannot guarantee it. Disillusioned democrats from Robert Michels to Frances Fox Piven and Richard A. Cloward have argued that any large organization and any differentiated leadership necessarily must take the life out of democracy, rigidifying into bureaucratic hierarchy. But formless, spontaneous mobs in the streets disrupting an established order cannot by themselves be a source of enduring change or even enduring challenge. Even if ossification were ultimately inevitable for any democratic engagement, surely the democrat's task would still be to prolong and revitalize the early, militant stage of popular involvement. The point is not to eschew all organization and all differentiated leadership, confining democracy to the local and spontaneous, but to develop those organizational forms and those styles of authority that sustain rather than suppress member initiative and autonomy. From historical examples we know that such forms and styles exist; it has sometimes been done.

Democrats need to think hard – both historically and theoretically – about the circumstances and the institutions by which large-scale collective power can be kept responsible to its participatory foundations. In the new American states, for example, after the disruption of British rule, radicals insisted on unicameral legislatures, weak or collective executives, frequent elections, rotation in office to prevent formation of a class of professional politicians. Most important, representatives were elected by participatory town or country meetings, thus by political bodies with an identity and some experience in collective action, rather than by isolated voters. Consequently, dialogue between representatives and their constituencies was frequent and vigorous; representatives were often instructed and sometimes recalled. But there are many possibilities for vital and fruitful interaction between the local and the national community. Recent resolutions on nuclear disarmament passed by New England town meetings are a promising experiment. All such devices, however, depend ultimately on the character of the citizenry, their love of and skill in exercising freedom; and these, in turn, rest mainly on the direct experience of meaningful local self-government.

Tocqueville argued that what made the American nation democratic was the vitality of direct participation in small and local associations. Face-to-face democracy was the foundation – not a substitute – for representative institutions, federalism, and national democracy. In direct personal participation, Tocqueville observed, people both learn the skills of citizenship and develop a taste for freedom; thereafter they form an active rather than deferential, apathetic, or privatized constituency for state and national representation, an engaged public for national issues. Size is not an insurmountable problem. On the basis of local, face-to-face politics, all sorts of higher and more distant structures of representation and collective power can be erected without destroying democracy – indeed, they can enhance it. Lacking such a basis, no institutional structures or programs of indoctrination can produce democracy.

From the question of size, turn next to that of technology. Has the technological complexity of modern society, requiring specialized expertise, rendered democracy obsolete? Here it is useful to remember that while the technological society may be new, the claims for expertise against democracy are very old at least as old as Plato's *Republic*. The idea that ordinary people are incompetent to deal intelligently with the issues affecting their lives rests now, as it always has, on an overly narrow idea of what constitutes politically relevant knowledge, and a confusion between knowledge and decision.

First off, stupidity knows no class. Maybe most people are foolish, but foolishness is found in all social strata. Education removes some kinds of ignorance, but may entrench or instill others. The cure is not to exclude some but to include as diverse a range of perspectives and experience as possible in political deliberation. Second, expertise cannot solve political problems. Contemporary politics is indeed full of technically complex topics, about which even the educated feel horribly ignorant. But on every politically significant issue of this kind, the "experts" are divided; that is part of what makes the issues political. Though we may also feel at a loss to choose between them, leaving it to the experts is no solution at all.

Finally, while various kinds of knowledge can be profoundly useful in political decisions, knowledge alone is never enough. The political question is what we are to do; knowledge can only tell us how things are, how they work, while a political resolution always depends on what we, as a community, want and think right. And those questions have no technical answer; they require collective deliberation and decision. The experts must become a part of, not an alternative to, the democratic political process.

Technology as such is not the problem for democracy; the problems here are popular deference to experts, and the belief in technology as an irresistible force, an "imperative" beyond human control. Since such deference and fatalism originate in people's experience, which is rooted in social conditions, they may be fought wherever they arise; and that is reason for hope and perseverence. The apathetic oppressed constitute an enormous pool of potential democratic energy. And as the historical examples remind us, even the most oppressed people sometimes rediscover within themselves the capacity to act. Democrats today must seek out and foster every opportunity for people to experience their own effective agency: at work, at school, in family and personal relations, in the community. Democratic citizenship is facilitated by democratic social relations and an autonomous character structure; dependency and apathy must be attacked wherever people's experience centers. Yet such attacks remain incomplete unless they relate personal concerns to public issues, extend individual initiative into shared political action. A sense of personal autonomy, dignity, and efficacy may be requisite for, but must not be confused with, citizenship.

And so we return to the need for direct, personal political participation. As Tocqueville already made clear, not just any kind of small or local group can provide the democratic experience: the point is not gregariousness but politicization.

To support democracy, face-to-face groups must themselves be internally democratic in ways already discussed, must deal with issues that really matter in their members' lives, and must have genuine power to affect the outcomes of those issues. One can experience freedom or learn citizenship no better in a "Mickey Mouse" group where nothing of importance is at stake than in a hierarchical organization.

Tocqueville's America was already big, but many important matters could still be addressed and resolved on the small scale. Confronting the realities of large-scale private power and social problems today requires national and even international organization. Such organization can be democratic, we have argued, if it rests on an active, engaged citizenry. Technology, too, can be democratically handled by such a citizenry. But such a citizenry emerges only from *meaningful* small-scale participation. Is that still a realistic possibility in a society such as ours?

To answer that crucial question, one must distinguish between short- and long-run requirements. In the long run, if we truly want full democracy, there is no doubt that we shall have to change our society and economy in fundamental ways. But in the short run, the right means toward that goal are participatory democratic movements. That such movements can still occur was shown in the 1960s; nothing fundamental has changed since then. Today's democrat must hope that in the brief experience of active participation that follows a flaring up of the democratic impulse, ordinary people, discovering the connections between local problems and national structures, coming up against the repressive power of established privilege, will themselves discover the need for more fundamental changes. We must be prepared to use the impulses toward and the experience of democracy, where they occur and while they last, to produce the social and economic changes that will further facilitate democracy. Each time it is, one might say, a race between the radicalizing and liberating potential of political action, and the dispiriting and paralyzing effects of the repression and political defeat likely to follow.

[...]

# 82

# A DAY IN THE LIFE OF A
# SOCIALIST CITIZEN

## Michael Walzer

[...]

Radicalism and socialism make political activity for the first time an option for all those who relish it and a duty – sometimes – even for those who do not. But what a suffocating sense of responsibility, what a plethora of virtue would be necessary to sustain the participation of everybody all the time! How exhausting it would be! Surely there is something to be said for the irresponsible nonparticipant and something also for the part-time activist, the half-virtuous man (and the most scorned among the militants), who appears and disappears, thinking of Marx and then of his dinner? The very least that can be said is that these people, unlike the poor, will always be with us.

We can assume that a great many citizens, in the best of societies, will do all they can to avoid what Melvin Tumin has called "the merciless masochism of community-minded and self-regulating men and women." While the necessary meetings go on and on, they will take long walks, play with their children, paint pictures, make love, and watch television. They will attend sometimes, when their interests are directly at stake or when they feel like it. But they will not make the full-scale commitment necessary for socialism or participatory democracy. How are these people to be represented at the meetings? What are their rights? These are not only problems of the future, when popular participation has finally been established as the core of political and economic

From Michael Walzer, 'A Day in the Life of a Socialist Citizen', in *Obligations: Essays on Disobedience, War, and Citizenship* (Harvard University Press, Cambridge, MA, 1971), pp. 234–8.

life. They come up in every radical movement; they are the stuff of contemporary controversy.

Many people feel that they ought to join this or that political movement; they do join; they contribute time and energy – but unequally. Some make a full-time commitment; they work every minute; the movement becomes their whole life and they often come to disbelieve in the moral validity of life outside. Others are established outside, solidly or precariously; they snatch hours and sometimes days; they harry their families and skimp on their jobs, but yet cannot make it to every meeting. Still others attend scarcely any meetings at all; they work hard but occasionally; they show up, perhaps, at critical moments, then they are gone. These last two groups make up the majority of the people available to the movement (any movement), just as they will make up the majority of the citizens of any socialist society. Radical politics radically increases the amount and intensity of political participation, but it does not (and probably ought not) break through the limits imposed on republican virtue by the inevitable pluralism of commitments, the terrible shortage of time, and the day-to-day hedonism of ordinary men and women.

Under these circumstances, words like citizenship and participation may actually describe the enfranchisement of only a part, and not necessarily a large part, of the movement or the community. Participatory democracy means the sharing of power among the activists. Socialism means the rule of the men with the most evenings to spare. Both imply, of course, an injunction to the others: join us, come to the meetings, participate! Sometimes young radicals sound very much like old Christians, demanding the severance of every tie for the sake of politics. "How many Christian women are there," John Calvin once wrote, "who are held captive by their children!" How many "community people" miss meetings because of their families! But there is nothing to be done. Ardent democrats have sometimes urged that citizens be legally required to vote: that is possible, though the device is not attractive. Requiring people to attend meetings, to join in discussions, to govern themselves: that is not possible, at least not in a free society. And if they do not govern themselves, they will, willy-nilly, be governed by their activist fellows. The apathetic, the occasional enthusiasts, the part-time workers: all of them will be ruled by full-timers, militants, and professionals.

But if only some citizens participate in political life, it is essential that they always remember and be regularly reminded that they are ... only some. This is not easy to arrange. The militant in the movement, for example, does not represent anybody; it is his great virtue that he is self-chosen, a volunteer. But since he sacrifices so much for his fellowmen, he readily persuades himself that he is acting in their name. He takes their failure to put in an appearance only as a token of their oppression. He is certain he is their agent, or rather, the agent of their liberation. He is not in any simple sense wrong. The small numbers of participating citizens in the U.S. today, the widespread fearfulness, the sense of impotence and irrelevance: all these are signs of social sickness. Self-government is an important human function, an exercise of significant talents and energies, and the sense of power and responsibility it brings is enormously healthy. A certain amount of commitment and discipline, of not-quite-merciless masochism, is socially desirable and efforts to evoke it are socially justifiable.

But many of the people who stay away from meetings do so for reasons that the militants do not understand or will not acknowledge. They stay away not because they are beaten, afraid, uneducated, lacking confidence and skills (though these are often important reasons), but because they have made other commitments; they have found ways to cope short of politics; they have created viable subcultures even in an oppressive world. They may lend passive support to the movement and help out occasionally, but they will not work, nor are their needs and aspirations in any sense embodied by the militants who will.

The militants represent themselves. If the movement is to be democratic, the others must *be represented*. The same thing will be true in any future socialist society: participatory democracy has to be paralleled by representative democracy. I am not sure precisely how to adjust the two; I am sure that they have to be adjusted. Somehow power must be distributed, as it is not today, to groups of active and interested citizens, but these citizens must themselves be made responsible to a larger electorate (the membership, that is, of the state, movement, union, or party). Nothing is more important than that responsibility; without it we will only get one or another sort of activist or *apparatchik* tyranny. And that we have already.

Nonparticipants have rights; it is one of the dangers of participatory democracy that it would fail to provide any effective protection for these rights. But nonparticipants also have functions; it is another danger that these would not be sufficiently valued. For many people in America today, politics is something to watch, an exciting spectacle, and there exists between the activists and the others something of the relation of actor and audience. Now for any democrat this is an unsatisfactory relation. We rightly resent the way actors play upon and manipulate the feelings of their audiences. We dislike the aura of magic and mystification contrived at on stage. We would prefer politics to be like the new drama with its alienation effects and its audience participation. That is fair enough. But even the new drama requires its audience, and we ought not to forget that audiences can be critical as well as admiring, enlightened as well as mystified. More important, political actors, like actors in the theater, need the control and tension imposed by audiences, the knowledge that tomorrow the reviews will appear, tomorrow people will come or not come to watch their performance. Too often, of course, the reviews are favorable and the audiences come. That is because of the various sorts of collusion which presently develop between small and co-opted cliques of actors and critics. But in an entirely free society, there would be many more political actors and critics than ever before, and they would, presumably, be self-chosen. Not only the participants, but also the nonparticipants, would come into their own. Alongside the democratic politics of shared work and perpetual activism, there would arise the open and leisurely culture of part-time work, criticism, second-guessing, and burlesque. And into this culture might well be drawn many of the alienated citizens of today. The modes of criticism will become the forms of their participation and their involvement in the drama the measure of their responsibility.

It would be a great mistake to underestimate the importance of criticism as a kind of politics, even if the critics are not always marked, as they will not be, by "republican virtue." It is far more important in the political arena than in the theater. For activists and professionals in the movement or the polity do not simply contrive effects; their work has more palpable results. Their policies touch us all in material ways, whether we go or do not go to the meetings. Indeed, those who do not go may well turn out to be more effective critics than those who do: no one who was one of its "first guessers" can usefully second-guess a decision. That is why the best critics in a liberal society are men-out-of-office. In a radically democratic society they would be men who stay away from meetings, perhaps for months at a time, and only then discover that something outrageous has been perpetrated that must be mocked or protested. The proper response to such protests is not to tell the laggard citizens that they should have been active these past many months, not to nag them to do work that they do not enjoy and in any case will not do well, but to listen to what they have to say. After all, what would democratic politics be like without its kibitzers?

# 83

# VOTING: A STUDY OF
# OPINION FORMATION IN
# A PRESIDENTIAL CAMPAIGN

## Bernard R. Berelson, Paul F. Lazarsfeld,
## and William N. McPhee

[...]

Political theory written with reference to practice has the advantage that its categories are the categories in which political life really occurs. And, in turn, relating research to problems of normative theory would make such research more realistic and more pertinent to the problems of policy. At the same time, empirical research can help to clarify the standards and correct the empirical presuppositions of normative theory. As a modest illustration, this concluding chapter of the volume turns to some of the broad normative and evaluative questions implied in this empirical study.

### REQUIREMENTS FOR THE INDIVIDUAL

Perhaps the main impact of realistic research on contemporary politics has been to temper some of the requirements set by our traditional normative theory for the typical citizen. "Out of all this literature of political observation and analysis, which is relatively new," says Max Beloff, "there has come to exist a picture in our minds of the political scene which differs very considerably from that familiar to us from the classical texts of democratic politics."

Experienced observers have long known, of course, that the individual voter was not all that the theory of democracy requires of him. As Bryce put it:

From Bernard R. Berelson, Paul F. Lazarsfeld and William N. McPhee, *Voting: A Study of Opinion Formation in a Presidential Campaign* (University of Chicago Press, Chicago and London, 1954), pp. 306–15.

How little solidity and substance there is in the political or social beliefs of nineteen persons out of every twenty. These beliefs, when examined, mostly resolve themselves into two or three prejudices and aversions, two or three prepossessions for a particular party or section of a party, two or three phrases or catch-words suggesting or embodying arguments which the man who repeats them has not analyzed.

While our data do not support such an extreme statement, they do reveal that certain requirements commonly assumed for the successful operation of democracy are not met by the behavior of the "average" citizen. The requirements, and our conclusions concerning them, are quickly reviewed.

*Interest, discussion, motivation.* – The democratic citizen is expected to be interested and to participate in political affairs. His interest and participation can take such various forms as reading and listening to campaign materials, working for the candidate or the party, arguing politics, donating money, and voting. In Elmira the majority of the people vote, but in general they do not give evidence of sustained interest. Many vote without real involvement in the election, and even the party workers are not typically motivated by ideological concerns or plain civic duty.

If there is one characteristic for a democratic system (besides the ballot itself) that is theoretically required, it is the capacity for and the practice of discussion. "It is as true of the large as of the small society," says Lindsay, "that its health depends on the mutual understanding which discussion makes possible; and that discussion is the only possible instrument of its democratic government." How much participation in political discussion there is in the community, what it is, and among whom – these questions have been given answers in an earlier chapter. In this instance there was little true discussion between the candidates, little in the newspaper commentary, little between the voters and the official party representatives, some within the electorate. On the grass-roots level there was more talk than debate, and, at least inferentially, the talk had important effects upon voting, in reinforcing or activating the partisans if not in converting the opposition.

An assumption underlying the theory of democracy is that the citizenry has a strong motivation for participation in political life. But it is a curious quality of voting behavior that for large numbers of people motivation is weak if not almost absent. It is assumed that this motivation would gain its strength from the citizen's perception of the difference that alternative decisions made to him. Now when a person buys something or makes other decisions of daily life, there are direct and immediate consequences for him. But for the bulk of the American people the voting decision is not followed by any direct, immediate, visible personal consequences. Most voters, organized or unorganized, are not in a position to foresee the distant and indirect consequences for themselves, let alone the society. The ballot is cast, and for most people that is the end of it. If their side is defeated, "it doesn't really matter."

*Knowledge.* – The democratic citizen is expected to be well informed about political affairs. He is supposed to know what the issues are, what their history is, what the relevant facts are, what alternatives are proposed, what the party stands for, what the likely consequences are. By such standards the voter falls short. Even when he has the motivation, he finds it difficult to make decisions on the basis of full information when the subject is relatively simple and proximate; how can he do so when it is complex and remote? The citizen is not highly informed on details of the campaign, nor does he avoid a certain misperception of the political situation when it is to his psychological advantage to do so. The electorate's perception of what goes on in the campaign is colored by emotional feeling toward one or the other issue, candidate, party, or social group.

*Principle.* – The democratic citizen is supposed to cast his vote on the basis of principle – not fortuitously or frivolously or implusively or habitually, but with reference to standards not only of his own interest but of the common good as well. Here, again, if this requirement is pushed at all strongly, it becomes an impossible demand on the democratic electorate.

Many voters vote not for principle in the usual sense but "for" a group to which they are attached – their group. The Catholic vote or the hereditary vote is explainable less as principle than as a traditional social allegiance. The ordinary voter, bewildered by the complexity of modern political problems, unable to determine clearly what the consequences are of alternative lines of action, remote from the arena, and incapable of bringing information to bear on principle, votes the way trusted people around him are voting. A British scholar, Max Beloff, takes as the "chief lesson to be derived" from such studies:

> Election campaigns and the programmes of the different parties have little to do with the ultimate result which is predetermined by influences acting upon groups of voters over a longer period ... This view has now become a working hypothesis with which all future thinking on this matter will have to concern itself. But if this is admitted, then obviously the picture of the voter as a person exercising conscious choice between alternative persons and alternative programmes tends to disappear.

On the issues of the campaign there is a considerable amount of "don't know" – sometimes reflecting genuine indecision, more often meaning "don't care." Among those with opinions the partisans *agree* on most issues, criteria, expectations, and rules of the game. The supporters of the different sides disagree on only a few issues. Nor, for that matter, do the candidates themselves always join the issue sharply and clearly. The partisans do not agree over-whelmingly with their own party's position, or, rather, only the small minority of highly partisan do; the rest take a rather moderate position on the political considerations involved in an election.

*Rationality.* – The democratic citizen is expected to exercise rational judgment in coming to his voting decision. He is expected to have arrived at his principles by reason and to have considered rationally the implications and alleged consequences of the alternative proposals of the contending parties. Political theorists and commentators have always exclaimed over the seeming contrast here between requirement and fulfilment. Even as sensible and hard-minded an observer as Schumpeter was extreme in his view:

> Even if there were no political groups trying to influence him, the typical citizen would in political matters tend to yield to extra-rational or irrational prejudice and impulse. The weakness of the rational processes he applies to politics and the absence of effective logical control over the results he arrives at would in themselves suffice to account for that. Moreover, simply because he is not "all there," he will relax his usual moral standards as well and occasionally give in to dark urges which the conditions of private life help him to repress.

Here the problem is first to see just what is meant by rationality. The term, as a recent writer noted, "has enjoyed a long history which has bequeathed to it a legacy of ambiguity and confusion ... Any man may be excused when he is puzzled by the question how he ought to use the word and particularly how he ought to use it in relation to human conduct and politics." Several meanings can be differentiated.

It is not for us to certify a meaning. But even without a single meaning – with only the aura of the term – we can make some observations on the basis of our material. In any rigorous or narrow sense the voters are not highly rational; that is, most of them do not ratiocinate on the matter, e.g., to the extent that they do on the purchase of a car or a home. Nor do voters act rationally whose "principles" are held so tenaciously as to blind them to information and persuasion. Nor do they attach efficient means to explicit ends.

The fact that some people change their minds during a political campaign shows the existence of that open-mindedness usually considered a component of rationality. But among whom? Primarily among those who can "afford" a change of mind, in the sense that they have ties or attractions on both sides – the cross-pressured voters in the middle where rationality is supposed to take over from the extremes of partisan feeling. But it would hardly be proper to designate the unstable, uninterested, uncaring middle as the sole or the major possessor of rationality among the electorate. As Beloff points out: "It is likely that the marginal voter is someone who is so inadequately identified with one major set of interests or another and so remote, therefore, from the group-thinking out of which political attitudes arise, that his voting record is an illustration, not of superior wisdom, but of greater frivolity."

The upshot of this is that the usual analogy between the voting "decision" and the more or less carefully calculated decisions of consumers or businessmen or courts, incidentally, may be quite incorrect. For many voters political preferences may better be considered analogous to cultural tastes – in music, literature, recreational activities, dress, ethics, speech, social behavior. Consider the parallels between political preferences and general cultural tastes. Both have their origin in ethnic, sectional, class, and family traditions. Both exhibit stability and resistance to change for individuals but flexibility and adjustment over generations for the society as a whole. Both seem to be matters of sentiment and disposition rather than "reasoned preferences." While both are responsive to changed conditions and unusual stimuli, they are relatively invulnerable to direct argumentation and vulnerable to indirect social influences. Both are characterized more by faith than by conviction and by wishful expectation rather than careful prediction of consequences. The preference for one party rather than another must be highly similar to the preference for one kind of literature or music rather than another, and the choice of the same political party every four years may be parallel to the choice of the same old standards of conduct in new social situations. In short, it appears that a sense of fitness is a more striking feature of political preference than reason and calculation.

II

If the democratic system depended solely on the qualifications of the individual voter, then it seems remarkable that democracies have survived through the centuries. After examining the detailed data on how individuals misperceive political reality or respond to irrelevant social influences, one wonders how a democracy ever solves its political problems. But when one considers the data in a broader perspective – how huge segments of the society adapt to political conditions affecting them or how the political system adjusts itself to changing conditions over long periods of time – he cannot fail to be impressed with the total result. Where the rational citizen seems to abdicate, nevertheless angels seem to tread.

The eminent judge, Learned Hand, in a delightful essay on "Democracy: Its Presumptions and Reality," comes to essentially this conclusion.

> I do not know how it is with you, but for myself I generally give up at the outset: The simplest problems which come up from day to day seem to me quite unanswerable as soon as I try to get below the surface ... My vote is one of the most unimportant acts of my life; if I were to acquaint myself with the matters on which it ought really to depend, if I were to try to get a judgment on which I was willing to risk affairs of even the smallest moment, I should be doing nothing else, and that seems a fatuous conclusion to a fatuous undertaking.

Yet he recognizes the paradox – somehow the system not only works on the most difficult and complex questions but often works with distinction. "For, abuse it as you will, it gives a bloodless measure of social forces – bloodless, have you thought of that? – a means of continuity, a principle of stability, a relief from the paralyzing terror of revolution."

Justice Hand concludes that we have "outgrown" the conditions assumed in traditional democratic theory and that "the theory has ceased to work." And yet, the system that has grown out of classic democratic theory and, in this country, out of quite different and even elementary social conditions, does continue to work – perhaps even more vigorously and effectively than ever.

That is the paradox. *Individual voters* today seem unable to satisfy the requirements for a democratic system of government outlined by political theorists. But the *system of democracy* does meet certain requirements for a going political organization. The individual members may not meet all the standards, but the whole nevertheless survives and grows. This suggests that where the classic theory is defective is in its concentration on the *individual citizen*. What are undervalued are certain collective properties that reside in the electorate as a whole and in the political and social system in which it functions.

The political philosophy we have inherited, then, has given more consideration to the virtues of the typical citizen of the democracy than to the working of the *system* as a whole. Moreover, when it dealt with the system, it mainly considered the single constitutive institutions of the system, not those general features necessary if the institutions are to work as required. For example, the rule of law, representative government, periodic elections, the party system, and the several freedoms of discussion, press, association, and assembly have all been examined by political philosophers seeking to clarify and to justify the idea of political democracy. But liberal democracy is more than a political system in which individual voters and political institutions operate. For political democracy to survive, other features are required: the intensity of conflict must be limited, the rate of change must be restrained, stability in the social and economic structure must be maintained, a pluralistic social organization must exist, and a basic consensus must bind together the contending parties.

Such features of the system of political democracy belong neither to the constitutive institutions nor to the individual voter. It might be said that they form the atmosphere or the environment in which both operate. In any case, such features have not been carefully considered by political philosophers, and it is on these broader properties of the democratic political system that more reflection and study by political theory is called for. In the most tentative fashion let us explore the values of the political system, as they involve the electorate, in the light of the foregoing considerations.

## REQUIREMENTS FOR THE SYSTEM

Underlying the paradox is an assumption that the population is homogeneous socially and should be homogeneous politically: that everybody is about the same in relevant social characteristics; that, if something is a political virtue (like interest in the election), then everyone should have it; that there is such a thing as "the" typical citizen on whom uniform requirements can be imposed. The tendency of classic democratic literature to work with an image of "the" voter was never justified. For, as we will attempt to illustrate here, some of the most important requirements that democratic values impose on a system require a voting population that is not homogeneous but heterogeneous in its political qualities.

The need for heterogeneity arises from the contradictory functions we expect our voting system to serve. We expect the political system to adjust itself and our affairs to changing conditions; yet we demand too that it display a high degree of stability. We expect the contending interests and parties to pursue their ends vigorously and the voters to care; yet, after the election is over, we expect reconciliation. We expect the voting outcome to serve what is best for the community; yet we do not want disinterested voting unattached to the purposes and interests of different segments of that community. We want voters to express their own free and self-determined choices; yet, for the good of the community, we would like voters to avail themselves of the best information and guidance available from the groups and leaders around them. We expect a high degree of rationality to prevail in the decision; but were all irrationality and mythology absent, and all ends pursued by the most coldly rational selection of political means, it is doubtful if the system would hold together.

In short, our electoral system calls for apparently incompatible properties – which, although they cannot all reside in each individual voter, can (and do) reside in a heterogeneous electorate. What seems to be required of the electorate as a whole is a *distribution* of qualities along important dimensions. We need some people who are active in a certain respect, others in the middle, and still others passive. The contradictory things we want from the total require that the parts be different. This can be illustrated by taking up a number of important dimensions by which an electorate might be characterized.

## Involvement and Indifference

How could a mass democracy work if all the people were deeply involved in politics? Lack of interest by some people is not without its benefits, too. True, the highly interested voters vote more, and know more about the campaign, and read and listen more, and participate more; however, they are also less open to persuasion and less likely to change. Extreme interest goes with extreme partisanship and might culminate in rigid fanaticism that could destroy democratic processes if generalized throughout the community. Low affect toward the election – not caring much – underlies the resolution of many political problems; votes can be resolved into a two-party split instead of fragmented into many parties (the splinter parties of the left, for example, splinter because their advocates are *too* interested in politics). Low interest provides maneuvering room for political shifts necessary for a complex society in a period of rapid change. Compromise might be based upon sophisticated awareness of costs and returns – perhaps impossible to demand of a mass society – but it is more often induced by indifference. Some people are and should be highly interested in politics, but not everyone is or needs to be. Only the doctrinaire would deprecate the moderate indifference that facilitates compromise.

[...]

# 84

# PARTICIPATION AND DEMOCRATIC THEORY

## Carole Pateman

[...]

In Schumpeter's theory of democracy, participation has no special or central role. All that is entailed is that enough citizens participate to keep the electoral machinery – the institutional arrangements – working satisfactorily. The focus of the theory is on the minority of leaders. 'The electoral mass', says Schumpeter, 'is incapable of action other than a stampede' (p. 283),[1] so that it is leaders who must be active, initiate and decide, and it is competition between leaders for votes that is the characteristically democratic element in this political method.

There is no doubt about the importance of Schumpeter's theory for later theories of democracy. His notion of a 'classical theory', his characterisation of the 'democratic method' and the role of participation in that method have all become almost universally accepted in recent writing on democratic theory. One of the few places where more recent theorists differ slightly from Schumpeter is over the question of whether a basic 'democratic character' is necessary for democracy and whether the existence of that character depends on the working of the democratic method. We shall now consider four well-known examples of recent work on democratic theory; those of Berelson, Dahl, Sartori and Eckstein. There is more emphasis on the stability of the political system in these works than in Schumpeter, but the theory of democracy common to them all is one descended directly from Schumpeter's attack on the 'classical' theory of democracy.

From Carole Pateman, *Participation and Democratic Theory* (Cambridge University Press, Cambridge, 1970), pp. 5–10.

In Chapter 14 of *Voting* (1954), which is called 'Democratic Theory and Democratic Practice', Berelson's theoretical orientation, a functionalist one, is very different from that of Schumpeter, but he has the same aim.[2] He sets out to examine the implications for 'classical' democratic theory of a 'confrontation' with the empirical evidence to be found in the previous chapters of the book. For the purpose of this confrontation he adopts Schumpeter's strategy of presenting a model of the 'classical theory' – or, more accurately, a model of the qualities and attitudes that this theory is asserted to require on the part of individual citizens – and this procedure reveals that 'certain requirements commonly assumed for the successful operation of democracy are not met by the behaviour of the "average citizen"'.[3] For example, 'the democratic citizen is expected to be interested and to participate in political affairs' but 'in Elmira the majority of the people vote but in general they do not give evidence of sustained interest' (1954, p. 307). Nevertheless, despite this and all the other deficiencies in democratic practice, Western democracies have survived; so we are faced with a paradox,

> *Individual voters* today seem unable to satisfy the requirements for a democratic system of government outlined by political theorists. But the *system of democracy* does meet certain requirements for a going political organisation. The individual members may not meet all the standards, but the whole nevertheless survives and grows (p. 312, Berelson's italics).

The statement of this paradox enables us to see, according to Berelson, the mistake made by the 'classical' writers, and to see why their theory does not give us an accurate picture of the working of existing democratic political systems. 'Classical' theory, he argues, concentrated on the individual citizen, virtually ignoring the political system itself, and where it did deal with the latter, it considered specific institutions and not those 'general features necessary if the institutions are to work as required'. Berelson lists the conditions necessary 'if political democracy is to survive' as follows: intensity of conflict must be limited, the rate of change restrained, social and economic stability maintained, and a pluralist social organisation and basic consensus must exist.[4]

According to Berelson, the earlier theorists also assumed that a politically homogeneous citizenry was required in a democracy (homogeneous that is in attitudes and behaviour). In fact what is required, and happily, what is found, is heterogeneity. This heterogeneity is necessary because we expect our political system to perform 'contradictory functions' but, despite this, the system works: it works because of the way in which qualities and attitudes are distributed among the electorate; this distribution enables the contradictions to be resolved while the stability of the system is also maintained. Thus the system is both stable and flexible, for example, because political traditions in families and ethnic groups and the long-lasting nature of political loyalties contribute to stability, whereas, 'the voters least admirable when measured against individual requirements contribute most when measured against the aggregate requirement for flexibility ... they may be the least partisan and the least interested voters, but they perform a valuable function for the entire system'.[5]

In short, limited participation and apathy have a positive function for the whole system by cushioning the shock of disagreement, adjustment and change.

Berelson concludes by arguing that his theory is not only realistic and descriptively accurate but that it also includes the values that 'classical' theory ascribed to individuals. He says that the existing distribution of attitudes among the electorate 'can perform the functions and incorporate the same values ascribed by some theorists to each individual in the system as well as to the constitutive political institutions'! This being so we should not, therefore, reject the normative content of the older theory – that is presumably the account of attitudes required by individual citizens – but this content should be revised to fit in with present realities.[6]

Berelson's theory provides us with a clear statement of some of the main arguments of recent work in democratic theory. For example, the argument that a modern theory of democracy must be descriptive in form and focus on the ongoing political system. From this standpoint we can see that high levels of participation and interest are required from a minority of citizens only and, moreover, the apathy and disinterest of the majority play a valuable role in maintaining the stability of the system as a whole. Thus we arrive at the argument that the amount of participation that actually obtains is just about the amount that is required for a stable system of democracy.

Berelson does not explicitly consider what characteristics are required for a political system to be described as 'democratic', given that maximum participation by all citizens is not one of them. An answer to this question can be found in two studies by Dahl, *A Preface to Democratic Theory* (1956) and *Hierarchy, Democracy and Bargaining in Politics and Economics* (1956a), and it is an answer that closely follows Schumpeter's definition.

Dahl does not 'confront' theory and fact in the same way as Berelson; indeed, Dahl seems very uncertain about whether there is, or is not, such a thing as the 'classical theory of democracy'. At the beginning of *A Preface to Democratic Theory* he remarks that 'there is no democratic theory – there are only democratic theories'.[7] In the earlier paper, however, he had written that 'classical theory is demonstrably invalid in some respects' (1965a, p. 86). Certainly Dahl regards the theories that he criticises in *A Preface to Democratic Theory* (the 'Madisonian' and the 'Populist') as inadequate for the present day and his theory of democracy as polyarchy – the rule of multiple minorities – is presented as a more adequate replacement for these, as an explanatory, modern theory of democracy.

Dahl offers a list of the defining characteristics of a democracy and these, following Schumpeter's argument that democracy is a political method, are a list of 'institutional arrangements' that centre on the electoral process (1956, p. 84). Elections are central to the democratic method because they provide the mechanism through which the control of leaders by non-leaders can take place;

'democratic theory is concerned with the processes by which ordinary citizens exert a relatively high degree of control over leaders' (p. 3). Dahl, like Schumpeter, emphasises that more should not be put into the notion of 'control' than is realistically warranted. He points out that contemporary political writings emphasise that the democratic relationship is only one of a number of social control techniques that in fact co-exist in modern democratic polities and this diversity must be taken account of in a modern theory of democracy (1956a, p. 83). Nor is it any use putting forward a theory that requires maximum participation from ordinary people for 'control' to take place when we know that most tend to be disinterested and apathetic about politics, and Dahl puts forward the hypothesis that a relatively small proportion of individuals in any form of social organisation will take up decision-making opportunities.[8] It is, therefore, on the other side of the electoral process, on the competition between leaders for the votes of the people, that 'control' depends; the fact that the individual can switch his support from one set of leaders to another ensures that leaders are 'relatively responsive' to non-leaders. It is this competition that is the specifically democratic element in the method, and the value of a democratic (polyarchical) system over other political methods lies in the fact that it makes possible an extension of the number, size and diversity of the minorities that can bring their influence to bear on policy decisions, and on the whole political ethos of the society (1956, pp. 133–4).

The theory of polyarchy may also give us 'a satisfactory theory about political equality' (1956, p. 84). Once again we must not ignore political realities. Political equality must not be defined as equality of political control or power for, as Dahl notes, the lower socio-economic status groups, the majority, are 'triply barred' from such equality by their relatively greater inactivity, their limited access to resources, and – in the United States – by 'Madison's nicely contrived system of constitutional checks' (1956, p. 81). In a modern theory of democracy 'political equality' refers to the existence of universal suffrage (one man, one vote) with its sanction through the electoral competition for votes and, more importantly, to the fact of equality of opportunity of access to influence over decision makers through inter-electoral processes by which different groups in the electorate make their demands heard. Officials not only listen to the various groups, but 'expect to suffer in some significant way if they do not placate the group, its leaders or its most vociferous members' (p. 145).

Another aspect of Dahl's theory that is of particular interest is his discussion of the social prerequisites for a polyarchical system. A basic prerequisite is a consensus on norms, at least among leaders. (The necessary and sufficient, institutional conditions for polyarchy can be formulated as norms (1956, pp. 75–6).) This consensus depends on 'social training' which, in turn, depends on the existing amount of agreement on policy choices and norms, so that an increase or decrease in one element will affect the others (p. 77). The social training takes place through the family, schools, churches, newspapers, etc., and Dahl distinguishes three kinds of training: reinforcing, neutral and negative. He argues that 'it is reasonable to suppose that these three kinds of training operate on members of most, if not all, polyarchical organisations and perhaps on members of many hierarchical organisations as well' (1956, p. 76). Dahl does not say what the training consists of, nor does he offer any suggestions as to which kind of training is likely to be produced by which kind of control system, but he does remark that its efficacy will depend on the existing, 'deepest predispositions of the individual' (p. 82). Presumably, 'effective' social training would be a training which would develop individual attitudes that support the democratic norms; on the other hand, Dahl argues that no single 'democratic character' is required, as suggested by earlier theorists, because this is unrealistic in the face of the 'blatant fact' that individuals are members of diverse kinds of social control systems. What is required is personalities that can adapt to different kinds of roles in different control systems (1956a, p. 89), but Dahl gives no indication how training to produce this kind of personality aids the consensus on *democratic* norms.

Finally, Dahl puts forward an argument about the possible dangers inherent in an increase in participation on the part of the ordinary man. Political activity is a prerequisite of polyarchy, but the relationship is an extremely complex one. The lower socio-economic groups are the least politically active and it is also among this group that 'authoritarian' personalities are most frequently found. Thus, to the extent that a rise in political activity brought this group into the political arena, the consensus on norms might decline and hence polyarchy decline. Therefore, an increase over the existing amount of participation could be dangerous to the stability of the democratic system (1956, Ch. 3. App. E).

[...]

## NOTES

1. [See Joseph A. Schumpeter, *Capitalism, Socialism and Democracy* (Unwin University Books, George Allen & Unwin, London, 1943) – Eds.]
2. See also Berelson (1952). For some criticisms of the functionalist aspects of Berelson's theory see Duncan and Lukes (1963).
3. Berelson (1954, p. 307). Berelson, in common with almost all other writers who talk of 'classical' democratic theory, does not say from *which* writers his model is drawn. In the earlier article he remarks of the composite set of attitudes he draws up, that 'while not all of them may be required in any single political theory of democracy, all of them are mentioned in one or another theory' (1952, p. 314). But, again, no names are given.
4. (1954, pp. 312–13). The specific connection between these conditions and democracy is not made clear; the first three would seem to be required, almost tautologically, for *any* political system to continue. Berelson adds that he is going to continue by exploring 'the values' of the political system. In fact what he does it to look at the 'requirements of the system'; see the section heading on p. 313.
5. (1954. p. 316). It is difficult to see why Berelson calls the items he cites 'contra-dictory'. Certainly they might be empirically difficult to obtain at the same time, but it is possible to have, and not illogical to ask for, both stability and flexibility or to have voters who express free, self-determined choices, at the same time making use of the best information and guidance from leaders (see pp. 313–14).

6. (1954, pp. 322–3). The exclamation mark is well placed in the passage quoted, which verges on the nonsensical.
7. (1956, p. 1). But he also refers at least once to 'traditional theory' (p. 131). However, cf. Dahl (1966) where he says there never was a classical theory of democracy.
8. (1956a, p. 87). See also (1956, pp. 81 and 138).

## REFERENCES

Berelson, B. R., 'Democratic Theory and Public Opinion', *Public Opinion Quarterly*, 16 (3), 1952, pp. 331–30.

Berelson, B. R., Lazarsfeld, P. F. and McPhee, W. N., *Voting: A Study of Opinion Formation in a Presidential Campaign* (University of Chicago Press, Chicago, and London, 1954).

Dahl, R. A., *A Preface to Democratic Theory* (University of Chicago Press, Chicago and London, 1956).

Dahl, R. A., 'Hierarchy, Democracy and Bargaining in Politics and Economics', in Eulau, H., Eldersveld, S. and Janowitz, M. (eds), *Political Behaviour* (Free Press, Glencoe, IL, 1956a).

Dahl, R. A., 'Further Reflections on the "Elitist Theory of Democracy"', *American Political Science Review*, LX (2), 1966, pp. 296–306.

Duncan, G. and Lukes, S., 'The New Democracy', *Political Studies*, XI (2), 1963, pp. 156–7.

# SECTION 15
# CIVIL SOCIETY

# CIVIL SOCIETY
# INTRODUCTION

The concept of civil society has recently regained importance as a central focus of debate in democratic theory and practice. Originally of eighteenth-century origin, the term was used by theorists of the Scottish Enlightenment like Adam Ferguson in his *Essay on the History of Civil Society* of 1767. In that usage the concept referred to an individualist market society, marked by the devotion of individuals to productive and trading activities rather than the warlike marauding characteristic of pre-modern social formations. In recent years, however, the idea of 'civil society' has undergone a rebirth, and is used in a somewhat different sense. As the extract from *Cohen and Arato* makes clear, civil society in their eyes refers to an area of public activity distinct from both the state and the market. This area involves a range of groups and associations, including families. Cohen and Arato see this field of civil society as essential for a healthy democratic society. It permits participation and communicative interaction of individuals. They argue that this field of social life is supplementary to, rather than a replacement of, the political institutions of representative democracy. Like Putnam in the extract which follows, Cohen and Arato trace this use of the idea to de Tocqueville, who in his study of *Democracy in America* saw an active associational life as the hallmark of democratic society.

In his frequently-cited article 'Bowling Alone', the American social scientist *Robert Putnam* suggests that the associations of civil society can create 'social capital', a set of social practices which involve civic engagement and ideas of reciprocity. The implication is that such a network of civic involvement is necessary for an effective democracy. However, as the title 'Bowling Alone' suggests, Putnam argues that present-day American society is characterised by a reduction in citizens' activity in these associations, with a possible consequent decline in the quality of American democracy.

A further development of 'civil society' arguments is made by the British academic *Paul Hirst* in his study of 'Associational democracy'. He presents a vision of voluntary organisations which would be the primary bases for democracy. He proposes a model of democracy in which 'self-governing associations [would] perform public functions', hence reducing the burden on, and the power of, the central state. While these associations would supplement rather than replace representative democracy, the picture presented is of a society in which it is through those groups, rather than through a centralised state, that democracy is primarily achieved. A self-governing civil society is the primary factor, the state becomes secondary in importance, with its main task supervising and regulating the voluntary associations of civil society.

Civil society is thus a central theme of contemporary democratic debate. It is seen as the basis for citizen involvement and participation, and also viewed as the site for democratic action against the old-style Communist systems which sought to monopolise all political power in the hands of the one-party state. For many theorists, civil society and the associative network it comprises is the locus of democracy, a bastion against an all-powerful state, and as de Tocqueville said, citizen associations are the 'schools for democracy', instilling habits of civic virtue and public spirit into their members. This raises the question of whether civil society can in fact sustain the participation required of citizens of modern democracy (see Section 14 on Participation above).

There is also one further problem which deserves mention. Do contemporary theorists paint too rosy a picture of civil society as the seedbed of participatory and public-spirited citizens? More sceptical observers suggest that this depends upon the internal structure and degree of democracy which prevails in the groups that make up civil society. These groups might themselves be subject to elitist or oligarchic tendencies, noted by some of the elite theorists cited in Part Two above. Furthermore, in some of its manifestations civil society can take highly 'uncivil' forms. Groups can develop an intense sense of particularity and loyalty to their own association. This could assist some tendencies hostile to democracy, emphasising partial loyalties (say those of ethno-nationalism or cultural particularism) which might undermine a sense of common civic identification. Some of these issues are discussed in Sections 11 and 12 on Nationalism and Multiculturalism.

# 85

# CIVIL SOCIETY AND POLITICAL THEORY

## Jean L. Cohen and Andrew Arato

[...]

On the pluralist analysis, a highly articulated civil society with cross-cutting cleavages, overlapping memberships of groups, and social mobility is the presupposition for a stable democratic polity, a guarantee against permanent domination by any one group and against the emergence of fundamentalist mass movements and antidemocratic ideologies. Moreover, a civil society so constituted is considered to be capable of acquiring influence over the political system through the articulation of interests that are "aggregated" by political parties and legislatures and brought to bear on political decision making, itself understood along the lines of the elite model of democracy.

Although we use many of the terms of this analysis in our work on civil society, our approach differs in several key respects from that of the pluralists. First, we do not accept the view that the "civic culture" most appropriate to a modern civil society is one based on civil privatism and political apathy. As is well known, the pluralists value involvement in one's family, private clubs, voluntary associations, and the like as activities that deflect from political participation or activism on the part of citizens. It is this which allegedly makes for a stable democratic polity. Moreover, it makes no difference to this model what the internal structure of the institutions and organizations of civil society is. Indeed, in their haste to replace "utopian (participatory democratic) principles" with realism, the pluralists tend to

From Jean L. Cohen and Andrew Arato, *Civil Society and Political Theory* (MIT Press, Cambridge, MA and London, 1992), pp. 19–24.

consider attempts to apply the egalitarian norms of civil society to social institutions as naive.

We do not share this view. Instead, we build upon the thesis of one of the most important predecessors of the pluralist approach, Alexis de Tocqueville, who argued that without *active* participation on the part of citizens in *egalitarian* institutions and civil associations, as well as in politically relevant organizations, there will be no way to maintain the democratic character of the political culture or of social and political institutions. Precisely because modern civil society is based on egalitarian principles and universal inclusion, experience in articulating the political will and in collective decision making is crucial to the reproduction of democracy.

This, of course, is the point that is always made by participation theorists. Our approach differs from theirs in arguing for more, not less, structural differentiation. We take seriously the normative principles defended by radical democrats, but we locate the genesis of democratic legitimacy and the chances for direct participation not in some idealized, dedifferentiated polity but within a highly differentiated model of civil society itself. This shifts the core problematic of democratic theory away from descriptive and/or speculative models to the issue of the relation and channels of influence between civil and political society and between both and the state, on the one side, and to the institutional makeup and internal articulation of civil society itself, on the other. Moreover, we believe that the democratization of civil society – the family, associational life, and the public sphere – necessarily helps open up the framework of political parties and representative institutions.

Indeed, these concerns open the way to a dynamic conception of civil society, one that avoids the apologetic thrust of most pluralist analyses. Far from viewing social movements as antithetical to either the democratic political system or to a properly organized social sphere (the pluralists' view), we consider them to be a key feature of a vital, modern, civil society and an important form of citizen participation in public life. Yet we do not see social movements as prefiguring a form of citizen participation that will or even ought to substitute for the institutional arrangements of representative democracy (the radical democratic position). In our view, social movements for the expansion of rights, for the defense of the autonomy of civil society, and for its further democratization are what keep a democratic political culture alive. Among other things, movements bring new issues and values into the public sphere and contribute to reproducing the consensus that the elite/pluralist model of democracy presupposes but never bothers to account for. Movements can and should supplement and should not aim to replace competitive party systems. Our conception of civil society thus retains the normative core of democratic theory while remaining compatible with the structural presuppositions of modernity. Finally, while we also differentiate the economy from civil society, we differ from the pluralists in that we do not seal off the borders between them on the basis of an allegedly sacrosanct freedom of contract or property right. Nor do we seek to "reembed" the economy in society. Instead, on our analysis, the principles of civil society can be brought to bear on economic institutions within what we call economic society. The question here, as in the case of the polity, is what channels and receptors of influence do, can, and ought to exist. Indeed, we are able to pose such questions on the basis of our model without risking the charges of utopianism or antimodernism so frequently and deservedly leveled against worker-based versions of radical democracy.

It is also our thesis that the tensions between rights-oriented liberalism and, at least, democratically oriented communitarianism can be considerably diminished if not entirely overcome on the basis of a new theory of civil society. While the idea of rights and of a democratic political community derive from distinct traditions in political philosophy, today they belong to the same political culture. They need not be construed as antithetical, although on an empirical level the rights of an individual may conflict with majority rule and "the public interest," necessitating a balancing between the two sides. Nor is it necessary to view these as based on two conflicting sets of principles or presuppositions, such that one could accommodate the first set only insofar as it is instrumental to the achievement or preservation of the other. On the contrary, we contend that what is best in rights-oriented liberalism and democratically oriented communitarianism constitutes two mutually reinforcing and partly overlapping sets of principles. Two steps are necessary to argue this thesis and to transcend the relevant antinomies. First, one must show that there is a philosophical framework that can provide a political ethic able to redeem the normative claims of both rights-oriented liberalism and radical democracy. Second, one must revise the conception of civil society as the private sphere, shared by both theoretical paradigms, in order to grasp the institutional implications of such an ethic.

We also defend the principles of universality and autonomy to which the rights thesis is wed, but we deny that this commits us either to the liberal notion of neutrality or to an individualist ontology. The communitarians are right: Much of liberal theory, especially the contract tradition from Hobbes to Rawls, has relied on either one or both of these principles. However, the Habermasian theory of discourse ethics, on which we rely, provides a way to develop conceptions of universality and autonomy that are free of such presuppositions. On this theory, universality does not mean neutrality with respect to a plurality of values or forms of life but rather refers, in the first instance, to the metanorms of symmetric reciprocity that are to act as regulative principles guiding discursive processes of conflict resolution and, in the second instance, to those norms or principles to which all those who are potentially affected can agree. The procedure of universalization defended here involves an actual rather than a hypothetical dialogue. It does not require that one abstract from one's concrete situation, need interpretations, or interests in order to engage in an unbiased moral testing of principles. Instead, it requires that these be freely articulated. It also requires that all those potentially affected by institutionalized norms (laws or policies) be open to a multiplicity of perspectives. Accordingly, universality is a regulative principle of a discursive process in and through which participants reason together about which values, principles, need-interpretations merit being institutionalized as common norms. Thus, the atomistic disembodied individual allegedly presupposed by procedural (deontological) ethics is most emphatically not the basis of this approach. Assuming that individual and collective identities are acquired through complex processes of socialization that involve both internalizing social norms or traditions, and developing reflective and critical capacities vis-à-vis norms, principles, and traditions, this theory has at its core an intersubjective, interactive conception of both individuality and autonomy. It is thus able to accommodate the communitarian insights into the social core of human nature without abandoning the ideas of either universality or moral rights. Indeed, discourse ethics provides a philosophical basis for democratic legitimacy that presupposes valid rights, even if not all of these rights are derivable from it.

While it is of course individuals who have rights, the concept of rights does not have to rest on philosophical or methodological individualism, nor, for that matter, on the idea of negative liberty alone. Although most liberal and communitarian theorists have assumed that such a conception of freedom and of individualism is presupposed by the very concept of rights, we believe that only some rights involve primarily negative liberty while none requires a philosophically atomistic conception of individuality. It is here that a revised conception of civil society, together with a new theory of rights, must enter into the analysis. For every theory of rights, every theory of democracy, implies a model of society. Unfortunately, communitarians and liberals also agree that the *societal* analogue of the rights thesis is a civil society construed as the private sphere, composed of an agglomeration of autonomous but egoistic, exclusively self-regarding, competitive, possessive individuals whose negative liberty it is the polity's task to protect. It is their assessments and not their analysis of this form of society that diverge.

But this is only one possible version of civil society and certainly not the only one that can be "derived" from the rights thesis. Only if one construes property to be not simply a key right but the core of the conception of rights – only, that is, if one places the philosophy of possessive individualism at the heart of one's conception of civil society and then reduces civil to bourgeois society – does the rights thesis come to be defined in this way. If, however, one develops a more complex model of civil society, recognizing that it has public and associational components as well as individual, private ones, and if, in addition, one sees that the idea of moral autonomy does not presuppose possessive individualism, then the rights thesis begins to look a bit different. In short, rights do not only secure negative liberty, the autonomy of private, disconnected individuals. They also secure the autonomous (freed from state control) *communicative interaction* of individuals with one another in the public and private spheres of civil society, as well as a new relation of individuals to the public and the political spheres of society and state (including, of course, citizenship rights). Moral rights are thus not by definition apolitical or antipolitical, nor do they constitute an exclusively private domain with respect to which the state must limit itself. On the contrary, the rights to communication, assembly, and association, among others, constitute the public and associational spheres of civil society as spheres of *positive freedom* within which agents can collectively debate issues of common concern, act in concert, assert new rights, and exercise influence on political (and potentially economic) society. Democratic as well as liberal principles have their locus here. Accordingly, some form of differentiation of civil society, the state, and the economy is the basis for both modern democratic and liberal institutions. The latter presuppose neither atomistic nor communal but rather associated selves. Moreover, on this conception the radical opposition between the philosophical foundations and societal presuppositions of rights-oriented liberalism and democratically oriented communitarianism dissolves. This conception of civil society does not, of course, solve the question of the relation between negative and positive liberty, but it does place this issue within a common societal and philosophical terrain. It is on this terrain that we learn how to compromise, take reflective distance from our own perspective so as to entertain others, learn to value difference, recognize or create anew what we have in common, and come to see which dimensions of our traditions are worth preserving and which ought to be abandoned or changed.

[...]

# 86

# BOWLING ALONE

## Robert D. Putnam

Many students of the new democracies that have emerged over the past decade and a half have emphasized the importance of a strong and active civil society to the consolidation of democracy. Especially with regard to the postcommunist countries, scholars and democratic activists alike have lamented the absence or obliteration of traditions of independent civic engagement and a widespread tendency toward passive reliance on the state. To those concerned with the weakness of civil societies in the developing or postcommunist world, the advanced Western democracies and above all the United States have typically been taken as models to be emulated. There is striking evidence, however, that the vibrancy of American civil society has notably declined over the past several decades.

Ever since the publication of Alexis de Tocqueville's *Democracy in America*, the United States has played a central role in systematic studies of the links between democracy and civil society. Although this is in part because trends in American life are often regarded as harbingers of social modernization, it is also because America has traditionally been considered unusually "civic" (a reputation that, as we shall later see, has not been entirely unjustified).

When Tocqueville visited the United States in the 1830s, it was the Americans' propensity for civic association that most impressed him as the key to their unprecedented ability to make democracy work. "Americans of all

From Robert D. Putnam, 'Bowling Alone: America's Declining Social Capital', in Larry Diamond and Marc F. Plattner (eds), *The Global Resurgence of Democracy*, 2nd edn (Johns Hopkins University Press, Baltimore, MD and London, 1998), pp. 290–2.

ages, all stations in life, and all types of disposition," he observed, "are forever forming associations. There are not only commercial and industrial associations in which all take part, but others of a thousand different types – religious, moral, serious, futile, very general and very limited, immensely large and very minute ... Nothing, in my view, deserves more attention than the intellectual and moral associations in America."

Recently, American social scientists of a neo-Tocquevillean bent have unearthed a wide range of empirical evidence that the quality of public life and the performance of social institutions (and not only in America) are indeed powerfully influenced by norms and networks of civic engagement. Researchers in such fields as education, urban poverty, unemployment, the control of crime and drug abuse, and even health have discovered that successful outcomes are more likely in civically engaged communities. Similarly, research on the varying economic attainments of different ethnic groups in the United States has demonstrated the importance of social bonds within each group. These results are consistent with research in a wide range of settings that demonstrates the vital importance of social networks for job placement and many other economic outcomes.

Meanwhile, a seemingly unrelated body of research on the sociology of economic development has also focused attention on the role of social networks. Some of this work is situated in the developing countries, and some of it elucidates the peculiarly successful "network capitalism" of East Asia. Even in less exotic Western economies, however, researchers have discovered highly efficient, highly flexible "industrial districts" based on networks of collaboration among workers and small entrepreneurs. Far from being paleoindustrial anachronisms, these dense interpersonal and interorganizational networks undergird ultramodern industries, from the high tech of Silicon Valley to the high fashion of Benetton.

The norms and networks of civic engagement also powerfully affect the performance of representative government. That, at least, was the central conclusion of my own 20-year, quasi-experimental study of subnational governments in different regions of Italy. Although all these regional governments seemed identical on paper, their levels of effectiveness varied dramatically. Systematic inquiry showed that the quality of governance was determined by longstanding traditions of civic engagement (or its absence). Voter turnout, newspaper readership, membership in choral societies and football clubs – these were the hallmarks of a successful region. In fact, historical analysis suggested that these networks of organized reciprocity and civic solidarity, far from being an epiphenomenon of socioeconomic modernization, were a precondition for it.

No doubt the mechanisms through which civic engagement and social connectedness produce such results – better schools, faster economic development, lower crime, and more effective government – are multiple and complex. While these briefly recounted findings require further confirmation and perhaps qualification, the parallels across hundreds of empirical studies in a dozen disparate disciplines and subfields are striking. Social scientists in several fields have recently suggested a common framework for understanding these phenomena, a framework that rests on the concept of *social capital*. By analogy with notions of physical capital and human capital – tools and training that enhance individual productivity – "social capital" refers to features of social organization such as networks, norms, and social trust that facilitate coordination and cooperation for mutual benefit.

For a variety of reasons, life is easier in a community blessed with a substantial stock of social capital. In the first place, networks of civic engagement foster sturdy norms of generalized reciprocity and encourage the emergence of social trust. Such networks facilitate coordination and communication, amplify reputations, and thus allow dilemmas of collective action to be resolved. When economic and political negotiation is embedded in dense networks of social interaction, incentives for opportunism are reduced. At the same time, networks of civic engagement embody past success at collaboration, which can serve as a cultural template for future collaboration. Finally, dense networks of interaction probably broaden the participants' sense of self, developing the "I" into the "we," or (in the language of rational-choice theorists) enhancing the participants" "taste" for collective benefits.

[...]

# 87

# ASSOCIATIVE PRINCIPLES AND DEMOCRATIC REFORM

## Paul Hirst

THREE PRINCIPLES OF ASSOCIATIONALIST POLITICAL ORGANIZATION

PRIMARY ASSOCIATIONS AS DEMOCRATIC GOVERNANCE

The conception that voluntary self-governing associations become the primary means of democratic governance of economic and social affairs involves two processes. First, that the state should cede functions to such associations, and create the mechanisms of public finance whereby they can undertake them. Second, that the means to the creation of an associative order in civil society are built-up, such as alternative sources of mutual finance for associative economic enterprises, agencies that aid voluntary bodies and their personnel to conduct their affairs effectively, and so on. This is not intended to be a once-and-for-all change, but a gradual process of supplementation, proceeding as fast as the commitment to change by political forces and the capacity to accept tasks by voluntary associations allows. This development can be seen in two ways, as a necessary means of reforming representative democracy, and as a desirable method of organizing economic and social affairs in and of itself.

The principal aim of an associative supplement to representative democracy is to reduce both the scale and the scope of the affairs of society that are administered by state agencies overseen by representative institutions. Existing legislatures and elected government personnel are hopelessly overburdened by the sheer size of modern bureaucratic big government, and the multiplicity of the functions of social provision and regulation undertaken by modern states.

From Paul Hirst, *Associative Democracy: New Forms of Economic and Social Governance* (Polity Press, Cambridge, 1994), pp. 21–6.

The result is to undermine representative democracy, weakening accountability to the people through their representatives of both policy-making and the delivery of services. Associational governance would lessen the tasks of central government to the extent that greater accountability both of the public power and of the devolved associationally-governed activities would be possible.

Economic liberals have attempted to address these problems of accountability and the scale of government by reducing the activities performed by the state, reducing both public provision and public regulation of the wider society. They have sought to privatize and to deregulate activities, but in doing so they have typically handed these activities over to undemocratic and unaccountable bodies, either quasi-public bureaucratic agencies or hierarchically-managed business corporations. Associative democracy is not like economic liberalism, although both advocate that the state should shed certain functions. Associationalism does not aim to reduce either social provision or economic governance, but to change their form of organization. It devolves the performance and administration of public functions to voluntary bodies that are accountable both to their members and to the public power. What would conventionally be regarded as 'private' agencies undertake public functions, but, unlike the agencies created by economic liberal reforms, they are accountable to those for whom the service or activity is provided. The administration of such voluntary bodies is doubly answerable: directly to their membership through their members' rights to participate in, and to exit from, associations and, for the performance of publicly-funded activities, to common political institutions composed of elected representatives and appointed officials like judges or inspectors. Associative democracy aims at a manageable and accountable state, but not an under-governed society. Associationalism does not strip down and diminish the public sphere as economic liberalism does, but actually revitalizes it and extends it.

Associationalists are not the only critics of the present balance between state and civil society, this too is the concern of thoughtful liberal democrats. Thus Noberto Bobbio and Robert Dahl, without doubt the two most accomplished contemporary democratic theorists, argue that democracy is endangered when the pluralism and autonomy of civil society is threatened by unaccountable hierarchically-controlled power. The problem for classical liberal democrats is that democratic government based on accountability to the individual citizen means little if the great bulk of economic affairs are controlled by large privately-owned corporations, and if the great bulk of other social affairs are controlled by state bureaucracies. The space for real democratic government is then small, and 'civil society' becomes vestigial, confined to marginal groups and peripheral areas of social life with little influence over the real decision-makers. If the dominant bureaucratic institutions persist unreformed, then the role of democracy is reduced in the case of companies to shareholders (at least nominally) electing directors and, in the case of the state, to individual citizens electing representatives who have formal direction of public administrative agencies. The problem here for Bobbio and Dahl is unaccountable bureaucracy and the excessive influence of certain groups, not the form and functions of the liberal democratic state.

Noberto Bobbio in *The Future of Democracy* (1987) contends that democracy has stopped short of the 'two great blocks of descending and hierarchical power in every complex society, big business and public administration. And as long as these blocks hold out against the pressures exerted from below, the democratic transformation of society cannot be said to be complete' (p. 57). For Bobbio the acid test of democracy is not just '"who votes" but "where" they can vote' (p. 56). The central contention in Robert Dahl's' *A Preface to Economic Democracy* (1985) is that effective democracy requires both the widespread diffusion of property and the sturdy economic independence of a substantial portion of the citizens. Excessive control of the economy either by the state or by a small number of private agencies is a threat to the plural society that is the foundation of political democracy. Democracy does not require capitalism, but a market society and a substantial number of autonomous economic units. The concentration of corporate power threatens democracy both because it increases the capacity for influence on government of a small number of unaccountable private bodies, and because it reduces the independence of the citizens, the majority of whom may be employees of such companies. Dahl's answer is the development of a worker-owned cooperative sector as a way of checking the unhealthy concentration of corporate control over the economy, and therefore the polity, that has developed in this century.

These are powerful arguments, and they help to make the associationalist case, but both writers stop well short of advocating associationalism. The reason is that both remain committed to a vision of a liberal-democratic state that is at once a self-governing political community and answerable to its citizens. It is difficult to see how liberal democracy can be restored in an omnicompetent state that is no longer able to function as the sole locus of economic and social regulation, however. Neither Bobbio or Dahl proposes the associationalisation of social provision and the pluralization of the state, but nothing less will suffice to correspond to the complexity of the levels of governance developing in the modern world, and to restore choice and control over their affairs to the citizens themselves. Moreover, if corporate power were as secure and overwhelming as Dahl and Bobbio seem to think, then the prospects for any radical reform would be grim, however, [...] the large-scale corporation is by no means the inevitable form of organization of economic activity, and hence arguments for the reform of corporate governance and the promotion of alternative means of economic regulation have acquired a new legitimacy.

Modern societies are pluralistic as far as the objectives and beliefs of individuals and the social groups they join are concerned, but not in their dominant forms of service provision and administration. Associationalism aims to make provision correspond more fully to this pluralism. Voluntary associations would thus progressively take over an increasing range of social and public functions and would be answerable in the first instance to their own memberships through their processes of self-government for the administration of these activities. Members would choose the organization they wished to perform a given function for them. [...] [T]here would be a variety of associations embodying different conceptions of how the activity or service should be performed. Associative reform would thus gradually change the primary role of government from that of a service provider to a means of ensuring that services were adequately provided and the rights of citizens and associations protected. That is a task representative democratic institutions could perform, given a significant measure of decentralization. The public power would serve both as a mechanism to raise and approve public funds for voluntary bodies to carry out specified social functions and as a means of ensuring that such funds were properly spent, and acceptable standards of service delivered by the voluntary bodies. The representative democratic institutions would have a more limited set of tasks to do than at present in supervising government bureaucracies, not least because associations' members would police and control them themselves, but, in consequence, they would have a greater capacity to carry out those tasks than do overburdened supervisory institutions in omnicompetent public service states. Such states seek to perform simultaneously two contradictory tasks, to provide services and to police the provision of these services.

Associationalism would alter the balance of the public and the private spheres. At present, participation in the public sphere is declining because modern large-scale mass democracies and bureaucratic states are remote, minimize participation, and are ineffective at providing the services citizens require. At the same time the private sphere has shrunk under the dual pressures of state intervention and compulsion, and of corporate power over employees and consumers. Associative democracy by 'publicizing' the private sphere, through democratically-controlled voluntary associations, would not trespass on individuals' liberties, but would enhance them by providing citizens with greater control of their affairs in the economy and in welfare. The point is that unless civil society is given certain 'political' attributes through self-governing associations that perform public functions, then it will be difficult to preserve its autonomy, squeezed as it has been by hierarchical administration. Associative reform would not threaten liberal freedoms by increasing the scope of social governance through voluntary associations, since those associations are independent and self-governing. Thus it is quite unlike totalitarian schemes of compulsory political mobilization of voluntary bodies, or authoritarian corporatist schemes to bureaucratize civil society and to compel individuals to be represented through collective agencies.

One reason why liberal democratic theorists have not adopted associative ideas is because they still see the state as the central political community. Voluntary associations are regarded in modern liberal democratic theory primarily in terms of their role as the social foundation of a pluralistic politics, that

# SECTION 16
# DELIBERATION

# DELIBERATION
# INTRODUCTION

The growing interest in civil society is, as we have seen, an expansion of our understanding of democracy. No longer do we assume democracy to be merely an arrangement for the making of decisions at the level of the state. Now we understand it as also pertaining to different sites within society, within associations and groups, in meetings and, following the feminist critique, even within families. Increasingly, our expectations of political participation are being expanded, not only in regard to where it might take place, but also to the forms it might take. As we have seen in Section 14 on Participation, some theorists of democracy have pointed out the limitations of seeing democratic participation merely in terms of voting and competition between elites, as Schumpeter did. Instead, theorists are now focusing on the quality of information and the formation of individual preferences that are fed into the process of decision-making. Democracy, it is here suggested, involves open discussion, and an interactive search for an answer to the question: what should we do? What is crucial is, therefore, the deliberation that precedes the making of a decision.

Theorists who are currently exploring deliberative democracy claim that democracy is indeed the only defensible source of political legitimacy. Yet they stress that the way it provides legitimacy is not so much via the granting of individual consent. Rather, it is by virtue of its capacity to enable and benefit from what Kant called 'the public use of reason'. Individuals engage in discussion about political matters, and thus gain information and form their preferences. It is this process of deliberation that provides a decision with legitimacy, though it only does so when that deliberation is fair and open. Theorists have therefore concentrated their efforts on articulating the nature of fair deliberation, on the ways in which it provides legitimacy and on ways in which institutional arrangements might be put in place to allow for an increase in such deliberation.

In our first selection, *Blaug* reviews the wide range of current activity in the area of deliberative democracy and highlights the strengths and weaknesses of the various approaches on offer. *Manin* then takes up the issue of precisely how it is that deliberation provides for legitimacy in decision-making. His analysis of how preferences are formed in deliberation raises again the question of methodology. When approached by a methodology derived from the market, he argues, we tend to miss the importance of the moment of deliberation, and to downplay its role in our existing democratic institutions.

When we consider the problem of how deliberative democracy is to achieve institutional form, we need to clarify where, in a society, we expect this to take place. In his encyclopedia article, *Habermas* identifies a sphere of public deliberation which covers parts of both civil society and the state. By tracking the evolution of the public sphere over time, Habermas shows the ways in which it has, historically, provided political decision-making with the vital input of public reason and deliberation.

The theoretical analysis of deliberation, and the identification of a public sphere in which this variously occurs, still requires translation into institutional form. This issue is taken up directly by *Fishkin*, who seeks to outline a political culture in which deliberation is maximized and where it is as fair as possible. Fishkin thus extends the notion of deliberative legitimacy in the public sphere into the political forms that might arise in a 'self-reflective society'.

# 88

# NEW DEVELOPMENTS IN DELIBERATIVE DEMOCRACY

## Ricardo Blaug

### REPUBLICAN DELIBERATIVE THEORIES

Theories of this type base their moral claim for more deliberation on a communitarian view of individual identity and collective ways of life. Contra liberalism, they hold that questions of identity are bound up with traditions and communities in such a way as to remain outside a simple aggregation of revealed preferences and the language of individual rights. Only in deliberation with others can we choose the way of life we want to share. Only in interaction can we rise above our individual interests and discover a common good.

Republican theories justify their moral claim for free deliberation by appealing to values which they find already present in our political culture (Eder, 1992). By carefully inspecting our traditions and shared understandings (Beiner, 1989), they identify common values, such as autonomy and mutual respect, which constitute hitherto untapped moral resources for a deepening of democracy. In this way, deliberative theories of the republican type seek to privilege increased participation as a way of life, incorporating both ethical and political questions.

This contextual mode of justification, and the common values it locates within our political culture, also provides criteria for distinguishing between fair and unfair debate. Thus, many republican theorists have called for the deliberative input into politics to be more open and reflective (Barber, 1984), and less distorted by the structures of power (Fishkin, 1992). Following Arendt,

From Ricardo Blaug, 'New Developments in Deliberative Democracy', *Politics*, 16 (2), 1996, pp. 72–6.

some have described fair debate not as a cool and rational assessment but as a combative process of self-revelation and display (Villa, 1992). Such a process considers not just private interests and their adjudication, but the common good, collective identities and intersubjective understandings. Deliberation, therefore, not only changes preferences (Sunstein, 1991), but constitutes the only means by which people can learn to be responsible citizens (Warren, 1992).

Republican deliberative theory is realistic in the sense that it attends carefully to the traditions, communities and contexts of meaning in which deliberation actually takes place. It also tries to address the need for efficiency and the pressures of the world of action. In some theories, this takes the form of a claim that deliberation gives rise to more efficient decisions (Barber, 1984; Miller, 1992), while others have attempted to design practical institutions that would bolster the legitimacy of the liberal state (Fishkin, 1992; Hirst, 1994). Importantly, recent republican suggestions for institutional reform have moved beyond their more usual call for economic democracy and have concentrated instead on the spaces of civil society (Keane, 1988). This rediscovery of civil society can be seen as an attempt to overcome the criticism of republican theory so effectively levelled by feminism: that it upholds a false distinction between the public and the private spheres (Phillips, 1991). The result has been new theories of citizenship (Kimlicka and Nelson, 1994), social movements (Melucci, 1989; Offe, 1985), secondary associations (Hirst, 1994), functional demarchies (Burnheim, 1985) and deliberative opinion polls (Fishkin, 1992, pp. 81ff). These suggested institutional reforms are not so far from those presently in existence as to be impossible or overly utopian. The way republican positions understand justification: that it is reducible to a particular context of meaning, raises the possibility that significant moral resources for deliberation exist within our own political culture. This then allows them to suggest improvements to liberal institutions which would restore their claim to legitimacy while at the same time preserving their efficiency.

Yet republican theories of deliberative democracy are at the same time hampered by the mode of justification they employ. While our political culture undoubtedly contains hitherto untapped moral resources which might support an increase in deliberation, it is also shot through with values like familial privatism, possessive individualism and the instrumental rationality of the market, all of which act directly against such an increase. Also, the 'fact of pluralism' in modernity suggests that no single community or consensus of values can be located which, when internally unpacked, might support such a polity. There is not one way of life that can be privileged. To suggest that there is shows a lack of attention to the many differences among us.

Political decisions certainly involve questions of identity and the good, but they also involve questions of justice (Habermas, 1994, p. 4). When two conceptions of the good confront one another, we must make appeal to some external criteria if we are to rationally adjudicate between them. The need for extra-contextual criteria also arises when we try to assess the fairness of a deliberative process. The threat here is that the appeal to tradition cannot support a valid distinction between a merely empirical consensus and a rational one (Ferrara, 1989). It could not, for example, question the legitimacy of Hitler's 1933 electoral victory. In conditions where unfairness is the tradition, an appeal to criteria outside that tradition is required in order to show that it is unjust. Theories of this type, therefore, having conflated questions of identity and the good life with those of justice and politics, are unable to locate the critical power required to adjudicate between competing moral claims. The appeal to extant values within our political culture can, in this way, degenerate into a mere approbation of the status quo. While there is nothing necessarily conservative about confining moral claims to contexts alone, such a mode of justification certainly holds this danger (Passerin d'Entrèves, 1988).

## Postmodern Deliberative Theories

Against the republican claim that moral validity is internal to particular cultures, postmodern deliberative theories reject the notion of moral validity altogether. For them, knowledge and truth are merely configurations of power, and history is strewn with the bodies of those sacrificed in the name of the 'morally right.' There are, therefore, no criteria which might enable us to rationally distinguish between right and wrong (Lyotard and Thébaud, 1985, p. 25). Their argument for an increase of deliberation turns, not on the conditions of legitimacy, but on those of illegitimacy. Where power is the central constituent of knowledge and identity, anything less than the total inclusion of all voices, the complete fairness of procedure and the celebration of difference, is open to criticism.

This denial of the very possibility of justification means that postmodern theories do not concern themselves with abstract notions of fairness, nor do they see tradition as supplying normative validity (Connolly, 1991). Instead, they concentrate firmly on the details of actual discursive practices. In focusing on the conditions of illegitimacy, such theories tend to be particularly strong in their disclosure of insidious exclusionary practices which render discursive practices unfair (Foucault, 1981). This approach highlights the importance of configurations of knowledge and power in the production of individual and collective identities, and successfully complicates the relation of the private to the public sphere. It characterises deliberation as an aesthetic and agonistic activity (Lyotard, 1984), and sees the deepening of democracy in terms of a multiplication of diversity (Mouffe, 1993).

Yet the absence of normative criteria places significant constraints on postmodern attempts to articulate a viable deliberative politics. First, it precludes any rational justification for resisting the abuses of power. To resist is to take up an aesthetic posture, which, no matter how compelling, cannot articulate why it is to be undertaken (Habermas, 1987, p. 284). Second, the absence of normative criteria makes it very difficult to move beyond an investigation of the modes of illegitimacy in order to guide our political actions. Where knowledge is the slave of power, there can be no *reasons* to act in a certain way, nor can one course of action be more legitimate than another. Postmodern deliberative theorists are thus more comfortable with the critique of existing practices than they are in suggesting ways in which power might be exercised legitimately. Mouffe, for example, though adamant that democracy must be radicalised, is unable to offer concrete ways in which such a project might be actualised in a practical yet legitimate form (Kymlicka and Nelson, 1994, p. 369). This apparent weakness is an expression of what White has called postmodernism's 'responsibility to other,' which it favours over political theory's more traditional 'responsibility to act' (White, 1991, pp. 20–23).

Postmodern deliberative theory is realistic in that it attends to the details of existing practices, yet its mode of justification makes it incoherent as a political project (Benhabib, 1994, ft. 15, p. 47). Unable to justify any form of power, or to rationally distinguish between gradations of illegitimacy, it does not address the question of how we are to balance fair deliberation and the need for efficient action.

### UNIVERSALIST DELIBERATIVE THEORIES

The third type of theory concentrates its efforts on the articulation of a universal ideal of deliberative fairness. It then attempts to apply this ideal to the real world in order to assess the fairness of particular instances of communication (Cohen, 1991; Manin, 1987).

Perhaps the most articulate example of this tactic is that of Jürgen Habermas. He argues that successful communication relies on certain universal assumptions about the way we use speech acts. Similarly, when we question and debate one another's positions, we cannot avoid making appeal to a universal notion of fair procedure. This ideal of fairness does not raise some utopian dream, nor does it tell participants in a debate what the outcome of their deliberation should be. Rather, it reconstructs the sense in which any decision can be said to be legitimate: that the deliberative procedure by which it was reached included all, allowed all to raise questions and was not distorted by relations of power or the pressures of time (Habermas, 1990).

What is particularly helpful in Habermas's position is the rigour with which he derives the moral grounding for deliberative fairness. Here, the justificatory claim is fully articulated, and the conditions of democratic legitimacy are clearly spelled out. The result is a theory of great critical power. Able to distinguish between mere agreement and rational consensus, and to point to fine gradations of illegitimacy, such a position breaks from the theoretical constrictions of the first two types considered above. It can give arguments for deepening a democracy and for resisting the distortions of power. It can give reasons for defending those few deliberative spaces left to us and for increasing the fairness of those deliberations.

Yet it does so at some cost. The degree of abstraction required to posit a universal norm of communicative fairness moves Habermasian theory so far from actual contexts of meaning that he tends to gloss over the importance of rhetoric, persuasion and other aesthetic components of collective judgment (Coole, 1995). This tendency is accentuated by his strongly Kantian distinction between questions of justice and those of the good life, which gives rise to a devaluation of the role of ethical questions in the making of practical decisions. Also, there is some concern, among both detractors and adherents, that the critical power available from a universalist morality might be used to simply select a political programme and bully those who disagree into accepting it (White, 1980).

While the critical power afforded by universalist theories has caused some anxiety (Estlund, 1993), the level of their abstraction has resulted in disappointment. Such theories tend to generate only the most general and tentative institutional designs. Examples are discursive fora (Dryzek, 1990), self-limiting public spheres operating at the periphery of the state (Habermas, 1992; 1994) and an account of the rights individuals required in order to deliberate freely (Arato and Cohen, 1992; Ingram, 1993). Once again, such suggestions are directed at the spaces of civil society, yet they are more nebulous than those put forward by republican theorists. Habermas has been careful to point out that only when his ideal of deliberative fairness is met *half-way* by the real identities, motivations and circumstances of actual participants do we begin to understand what is involved in justifying particular institutions (Habermas, 1990, p. 109). For this reason, he insists his universalist theory cannot be used to preselect particular institutional arrangements (Habermas, 1992).

In concentrating on the theoretical grounds for deliberation, this third type of theory is generally stronger on normative questions than on pragmatic ones. Yet there clearly is a moral difference between an exclusionary democracy and one that is less so (Benhabib, 1992). This moral difference is not a matter of tradition, nor of personal taste. Habermas in particular gives us the conceptual tools to understand why one is better than another.

## CONCLUSION

The way the new theories attempt to justify deliberative fairness affects the kind of problems they encounter when trying to cross over into questions of practice. The three conceptions of justification considered above each have their respective strengths and weaknesses. Yet if a deliberative politics is to be both legitimate and realistic, their gains must somehow be brought together. A fully adequate deliberative theory would need to be both normative and empirical, utopian and realistic. It would need to be attentive to the exigencies of the real world and the available motivations and ethical resources currently available, as are those of the republican type. It would require sensitivity to the many subtle power distortions we confront in actual practices, and to the complex relation of private to public concerns, as are those of the postmodern type. At the same time, the call for an increase in fair deliberation requires a coherent justification, which only universalist theories can provide. If the pressures of the real world inevitably result in the distortion of deliberative fairness, then the need for moral criteria becomes still more acute. Faced with having to select between a range of actions, all of which are imperfectly fair in some way, participants in deliberation must make hard choices. They need the critical power of a normative criterion in order to morally distinguish between gradations of illegitimacy.

[...]

## REFERENCES

Arato, A. and Cohen, J., *Civil Society and Political Theory* (MIT Press, Cambridge, MA, 1992).

Barber, B., *Strong Democracy* (University of California Press, Berkeley, 1984).

Beiner, R., 'Do We Need a Philosophical Ethics? Theory, Prudence, and the Primacy of Ethos', *The Philosophical Forum*, 20 (3), 1989, pp. 230–43.

Benhabib, S., *Situating the Self* (Polity Press, Cambridge, 1992).

Benhabib, S., 'Deliberative Rationality and Models of Democratic Legitimacy', *Constellations*, 1 (1), 1994, pp. 26–52.

Burnheim, J., *Is Democracy Possible?* (Polity Press, Cambridge, 1985).

Cohen, J., 'Deliberation and Democratic Legitimacy', in Hamlin, A. and Pettit, P. (eds), *The Good Polity: Normative Analysis of the State* (Blackwell, Oxford, 1991), pp. 17–34.

Connolly, W., *Identity/Difference: Democratic Negotiations of Political Paradox* (Cornell University Press, Ithaca, NY, 1991).

Coole, D., 'Habermas and the Question of Alterity', in Passerin d'Entrèves, M. and Benhabib, S. (eds), *Habermas and the Unfinished Project of Modernity: Critical Essays on The Philosophical Discourse of Modernity* (Polity Press, Cambridge, 1995).

Dryzek, J. S., *Discursive Democracy: Politics, Policy, and Political Science*, Cambridge University Press, Cambridge, 1990).

Eder, K., 'Politics and Culture: On the Sociological Analysis of Political Participation', in Honneth, A., McCarthy, T., Offe, C. and Wellmer, A. (eds), *Cultural-Political Interventions in the Unfinished Project of Enlightenment* (MIT Press, Cambridge, MA, 1992), pp. 95–120.

Ferrara, A., (1989) 'Universalisms: Procedural, Contextual and Prudential', *Philosophy and Social Criticism*, 14 (3/4), 1989, pp. 243–69.

Fishkin, J. S., *The Dialogue of Justice: Toward a Self-Reflective Society* (Yale University Press, New Haven, CT, 1992).

Foucault, M., *The History of Sexuality*, vol. 1 (Penguin, Harmondsworth, 1981).

Habermas, J., *The Philosophical Discourse of Modernity* (Polity Press, Cambridge, 1987).

Habermas, J., *Moral Consciousness and Communicative Action* (Polity Press, Cambridge, 1990).

Habermas, J., 'Further Reflections on the Public Sphere', in Calhoun, C. (ed.), *Habermas and the Public Sphere* (MIT Press, Cambridge, MA, 1992), pp. 421–61.

Habermas, J., 'Three Models of Democracy', *Constellations*, 1 (1), 1994, pp. 1–10.

Hirst, P., *Associative Democracy* (Polity Press, Cambridge, 1994).

Ingram, D., 'The Limits and Possibilities of Communicative Ethics for Democratic Theory', *Political Theory*, 21 (2), 1993, pp. 294–321.

Keane, J., (1988) 'Introduction', in Keane, J. (ed.), *Civil Society and the State* (Verso, London, 1988), pp. 1–32.

Kymlicka, W. and Nelson, W., 'Return of the Citizen: A Survey of Recent Work on Citizenship Theory', *Ethics*, 104, 1994, pp. 352–81.

Lyotard, J.-F., *The Postmodern Condition: A Report on Knowledge* (University of Minnesota Press, Minneapolis, 1984).

Lyotard, J.-F. and Thébaud, J.-L., *Just Gaming* (Manchester University Press, Manchester, 1985), p. 25.

Manin, B., 'On Legitimacy and Political Deliberation', *Political Theory*, 15 (3), 1987, pp. 338–68.

Melucci, A., *Nomads of the Present* (Hutchinson Radius, London, 1989).

Miller, D., (1992) 'Deliberative Democracy and Social Choice', *Political Studies*, XL, Special Issue, 1992, pp. 54–67.

Mouffe, C., *The Return of the Political* (Verso, London, 1993).

Offe, C., 'New Social Movements: Challenging the Boundaries of Institutional Politics', *Social Research*, 52 (4), 1985, pp. 817–68.

Passerin d'Entrèves, M., 'Aristotle or Burke? Some Comments on H. Schnädelbach's "What is Neo-Aristotelianism?"', *Praxis International*, 7 (3/4), 1988, pp. 238–45.

Phillips, A., *Engendering Democracy* (Polity Press, Cambridge, 1991).

Villa, D. A., 'Beyond Good and Evil: Arendt, Nietzsche, and the Aestheticization of Political Action', *Political Theory*, 20 (2), 1992, pp. 274–308.

White, S. K., 'Reason and Authority in Habermas: A Critique of the Critics', *American Political Science Review*, 74, pp. 1007–17.

White, S. K., (1991) *Political Theory and Postmodernism* (Cambridge University Press, Cambridge, 1991), pp. 20–8.

# 89

# ON LEGITIMACY AND
# POLITICAL DELIBERATION

## B. Manin

[...]

In fact, what must be criticized in Rawls's and Rousseau's theories is not their neglect of the collective dimension, but the assumption that individuals in society, in particular, those having to make a political decision, possess an already formed will, already know exactly what they want, and at most only need to apply their criteria of evaluation to the proposed solutions. This criticism can be conducted in accordance with the principles of individualism. We need not argue that individuals, when they begin to deliberate political matters, know nothing of what they want. They know what they want in part: they have certain preferences and some information, but these are unsure, incomplete, often confused and opposed to one another. The process of deliberation, the confrontation of various points of view, helps to clarify information and to sharpen their own preferences. They may even modify their initial objectives, should that prove necessary.

It is, therefore, necessary to alter radically the perspective common to both liberal theories and democratic thought: the source of legitimacy is not the predetermined will of individuals, but rather the process of its formation, that is, deliberation itself. An individual's liberty consists first of all in being able to arrive at a decision by a process of research and comparison among various solutions. As political decisions are characteristically imposed on *all*, it seems reasonable to seek, as an essential condition for legitimacy, the deliberation of

From B. Manin, 'On Legitimacy and Political Deliberation', *Political Theory*, August 1987, pp. 351–9.

*all* or, more precisely, the right of all to participate in deliberation. We must, therefore, challenge the fundamental conclusion of Rousseau, Sieyès, and Rawls: a legitimate decision does not represent the *will* of all, but is one that results from the *deliberation of all*. It is the process by which everyone's will is formed that confers its legitimacy on the outcome, rather than the sum of already formed wills. The deliberative principle is both individualistic and democratic. It implies that *all* participate in the deliberation, and in this sense the decision made can reasonably be considered as emanating from the people (democratic principle). The decision also proceeds from the liberty of individuals: those individuals deliberate together, form their opinions through deliberation, and at the close of the process each opts freely for one solution or another (individualistic and liberal principle). We must affirm, at the risk of contradicting a long tradition, that legitimate law is the *result of general deliberation*, and not the *expression of the general will*.

There is a double dimension to the process of deliberation; it is simultaneously collective and individual. It is individual in the sense that everyone reasons for himself, finding arguments, and weighing them. Because the aim of the deliberative process is to broaden the participants' information and enable them to discover their own preferences, that process requires a multiplicity of points of view and/or arguments. As the individual listens to arguments formulated by others, he broadens his own point of view and becomes aware of things he had not perceived at the outset. Deliberation requires not only multiple but conflicting points of view because conflict of some sort is the essence of politics. The parties in deliberation will not be content to defend their own positions, but will try to refute the arguments of the positions of which they disapprove. New information emerges as each uncovers the potentially harmful consequences of the other parties' proposals.

Thus deliberation tends to increase information and to pinpoint individuals' preferences. It helps them to discover aspects both of proposed solutions and of their own objectives that they had not perceived earlier. But deliberation is not only a process of discovery: the parties are not satisfied with presenting various and conflicting theses; they also try to persuade each other. They argue. Argumentation is a sequence of propositions aiming to produce or reinforce agreement in the listener. In this sense, it is a discursive and rational process. Yet, in contrast to logical proof, argumentation does not result in a necessary conclusion that the listener cannot reject. A conclusion developed from argumentation is not a necessary proposition. The listener remains free to give his agreement or to withhold it. The listener is free because argumentation does not start from evident premises or from conventional ones. Rather, one starts by taking propositions one assumes are generally accepted by the audience being addressed. In politics, one would argue by assuming certain common values as held by the public at a given moment. Argumentation is, therefore, always relative to its audience. Someone who does not share these values will not be convinced by the arguments presented. Nor are the procedures of linking the propositions logically binding. One may use, for example, arguments by analogy and *a fortiori* arguments. These do not make the passage from one proposition to another strictly necessary. It is, therefore, not said of a conclusion developed from arguments that it is either true or false, but that it simply generates more or less support depending on whether the argument was more or less convincing. Nor is an argument either true or false; it is stronger or weaker. Whatever the force of an argumentation, its conclusion is never strictly necessary. The listener may withhold his approval, and it must even be acknowledged that his refusal to approve a conclusion may have reasons as well. The force of an argumentation is always relative.

One argues in order to try to persuade others. But one tries only to persuade, that is, to produce or reinforce agreement to a proposition, in cases where no proposition imposes itself with unimpeachable and universally recognized force. People need not be persuaded of the truth. In this sense, argumentation differs from a logical demonstration. On the negative side, it differs also from refutation. One piles up several arguments against a thesis, one tries to weaken it because one lacks the refutation that would incontestably destroy it.

Thus argumentation is particularly suited to the nature of political debate, which most frequently consists of a confrontation between opposing norms or values. We must admit, with Weber, that no science can resolve this conflict in a rigorous and necessary manner. However, contrary to Weber's thesis, it does not follow that the choice of values remains ineluctably arbitrary. Some values are more likely than others to win the approval of an audience of reasonable people. It is impossible to *demonstrate* their soundness; they can only be *justified*. A decision or norm is not either true or false. But we are nevertheless not reduced to pure arbitrationess because a norm can be more or less *justified*. The relative force of its justification can only be measured by the amplitude and the intensity of the approval it arouses in an audience of reasonable people.

Political deliberation and argumentation certainly presuppose a relatively reasonable audience. They also require a certain degree of instruction and culture on the part of the public. But they constitute processes of education and of training in themselves. They broaden the viewpoints of citizens beyond the limited outlook of their private affairs. They spread light. Such a concept of deliberation implies that the majority of citizens should be educated, but it is not the kind of pedagogic model in which an enlightened elite is intended to bring the light of science down from its pulpit to a backward people. Rather, the people educate themselves. Certainly, knowledge is not distributed equally, and all speeches will not have the same weight, but because those who are more knowledgeable tend not to be in agreement among themselves, their exchange of opinions, refereed by the public, offers an education without a unique and eminent teacher. J.S. Mill has analyzed this educational function of arguments remarkably well.

In the political sphere, deliberation does not permit us to arrive at necessary and universally admitted truths, but it also does not permit the absolute and incontestable refutation of a norm or a value. It is doubtless possible to show that a policy that was based on given normative principles failed, but most of the time, this failure is not sufficient to refute either the policy in question, or the normative principle from which it was derived. This is so because first of all it is extremely difficult, if not impossible, to discover exactly what in a given policy caused the failure. In order to find that out, it would be necessary to isolate exactly what derived from the initial conditions in which the policy was adopted and what derived from the normative principles themselves. Even supposing that one succeeds in isolating the normative principles that caused the failure, the unhappy outcome does not necessarily prove that this principle should be rejected. One can always argue that it should have been put into practice in another form or to a lesser degree. The planned economy is surely a failure with respect to its own objectives, but for all that, economic planning as a normative principle is not absolutely refuted. A limited nonbinding form of planning may be defended. Ascertaining a failure does not refute a political principle; it merely creates a *presumption* against it. Despite a certain closeness, political deliberation and scientific argumentation remain separated by an irreducible difference. One does not really say that the scientific community *deliberates* when it exchanges conjectures and refutations.

## POLITICAL PLURALISM AND THE MARKET

The process of the formation of the collective will is the essential moment of political decision making. It does not consist in totaling up previously formed intentions or wills. Individual intentions, individual wills are decided progressively in its course. A diversity of points of view and of arguments is an essential condition both for individual liberty (for individuals must have a choice among several parties) and for the rationality of the process (for the exchange of arguments and criticisms creates information and permits comparing the reasons presented to justify each position). However, this perspective differs from that of traditional pluralism. The latter views the pluralism of social groups in light of the model of market competition. Various groups or elites enter into competition to win over the voters just as they would build up a clientele. The competition among parties with respect to the voters is, in this model, analogous to the competition of producers facing consumers. The public chooses in each case.

However, the analogy is misleading. In the marketplace, competition among producers is justified because it favors producers who produce goods at the lowest cost. From the collective point of view, this is rational because these producers use the smallest amount of scarce resources, thus leaving a larger amount available for the production of other goods. This outcome is assured because it is in each consumer's self-interest to select the most competitive producer. Buying goods from that producer will permit him to devote larger resources to other purchases. If the consumer makes a poor choice (i.e., if he does not choose the most efficient producer), he himself is penalized and he (in the purest model) experiences this disadvantage both directly and within a short time.

The same is not true in politics: both the negative and the positive effects of political decisions often make themselves felt only in the long run. The effects are often diffuse and scattered. If a voter chooses poorly, that is, if he opts for the least effective policy for society, the effect on his own position will usually become apparent only after a long time. At that time, the voter would presumably change his original position, but the change would come too late to correct the initial decision in an effective manner. Such a system is bound to engender a succession of chaotic measures rather than real self-regulation. Furthermore, if the voters behave just like consumers in the marketplace, they are apt to choose from among proposed policies those whose consequences they perceive as affecting their particular situation most deeply and clearly. But the consequences that affect them only marginally will tend to be neglected, regardless of their importance for society as a whole. These two reasons (the remoteness in time of the effects and their dispersion) make it impossible to attribute the self-regulating virtues of the economic market to the political one. They also explain the need for political persuasion. Citizens must be persuaded to adopt a policy because they cannot simply choose according to the immediate effects that they perceive themselves. In the *marketplace*, individuals feel the effects of their choice immediately and directly. This cannot be the case in the *forum* where they deliberate political decisions.

Furthermore, individuals entering the marketplace know their needs. They may discover new products they had not looked for a priori, but they choose those that correspond to some sort of previously felt need. On the other hand, when citizens enter the political forum, they do not know exactly what they want or need. The aim of political competition is, therefore, to offer voters not only a range of solutions, among which they may choose according to predetermined needs, but also to enlighten them about their needs, and have them weigh the options presented by the parties. Pluralism, therefore, has a different function in the forum. The market requires not simply *some* diversity as in political pluralism, but rather a *great multiplicity* of agents. In order to be as efficient as possible, competition in the marketplace requires the maximal dispersion of forces. In the model of the perfect competitive market proposed by neoclassic economics, the formation of coalitions among producers or consumers is not permitted. But if the object of the conflict among varying points of view is the forming of the will, then *some* degree of diversity and not an *extreme multiplicity* is necessary.

In fact, political pluralism implies a drastic reduction in the number of proposed solutions. But this is precisely what is required by the nature of deliberation. It is not possible to deliberate everything, or all the possibilities permitted by a given situation. In highly complex systems, the cost of exploring all possibilities, even if that were theoretically possible, would be enormous. Chess players, for example, cannot examine all possible moves with all their consequences; they examine only certain types of moves, and explore only those moves that seem most promising. This situation characterizes deliberation. It is not possible to deliberate all possible outcomes; the range of proposed solutions must by necessity be limited. In the political arena, the limited pluralism of parties is required for effective deliberation. The people, as such, before the intervention of any mediating process, do not have a determined will, but rather offer a multiplicity of incomplete preferences, which are often incoherent. It is only when more well-defined issues are proposed for its deliberation that the influence of the people on the government of their society can become real and effective.

If the parties that specify which issues would come up for collective deliberation had no connection to the bulk of citizens, some kind of deliberative opinion formation would still unfold, but the original definition of these matters would completely escape the control of the ordinary citizens. (This would occur, for example, in the case of closed oligarchies competing between one another to win the support of the mass public.) That is why it is important, in a democratic society, that the parties themselves be set up by the mass of citizens. Under such conditions, the proposed solutions originate in part from the people themselves. But this goal can only be partially attained. It has been known since Michels that political parties are, at least in part, oligarchical. Yet one should not conclude that for that reason they are harmful to democracy. Their essential contribution to democracy comes from the fact that they allow the deliberation by all of matters already relatively determined. The existence of political parties is essential for deliberation. The parties face each other, and the process of argumentation is submitted to the arbitration of all.

## THE DELIBERATIVE PROCESS

Deliberation is freely conducted because each person, who may or may not be convinced by a given argument, does have ultimately a choice between several alternatives. That is why it is necessary that individuals have a genuine choice among different alternatives, all of which should seem realistically possible. If only one solution were proposed, and the citizens were free to choose it or not, their eventual choice would be both unbalanced and misleading as a guide to their preference. There would not even be a real choice because the option would be between the unique solution proposed and the absence of any solution at all. The first term of the choice would have an exaggerated advantage, for it would be too easy to convince people to select it. Yet they would still remain free either to give or to withhold their assent.

In many cases, the different points of view that are presented first to the public's scrutiny and then to its choice are defended by parties or individuals who wish to accede to positions of power. Admittedly, individuals who support a particular point of view are elected, not only the programs themselves. Schumpeter is correct in stressing that democracy is a process that aims to select those who govern. Candidates for positions of power compete with one another and try to collect the greatest number of votes for themselves. Because they wish to exercise political power, in a sense, they act in their own self-interest; and, in accordance with Schumpeter's formula, they may be compared to "entrepreneurs" dealing in votes. Yet we need not deem the programs these entrepreneurs represent and the points of view they advocate as being without importance, as Schumpeter does. Politicians offer simultaneously both their services in governmental functions and a particular point of view concerning the public good. The two elements are indissolubly linked. Experience shows that voters do not make up their minds solely on the basis of written programs or projects explicitly announced by the candidates, but they do take these programs and projects into account. Even when voters decide primarily on the basis of a global, though often confused image they have of the candidates, this image is still related to voters' idea of his or her community good. It may owe more to the personality of the candidate as the voters perceive it than to the expressed declarations about programs, but the "image" still represents some idea of what is admirable, successful, and fit in that country.

Competition among the different points of view of the candidates also encourages each protagonist to make use of those principles and arguments likely to win the largest possible agreement. The process of argumentation takes place before a universal audience, the complete set of citizens. In order to increase its support, each party has an interest in showing that its point of view is *more general* than the others. Therefore, universalism also plays a part here, but it is not assumed at the start. It seems rather to be the ideal term of the process. In truth, no party will ever become an actually universal party; there will always remain opponents; this is the core of political pluralism. Nevertheless the structure of the deliberative system usually makes the protagonists strive to enlarge their points of view and propose more and more general positions. There is a sort of competition for generality. The deliberative process never results in strictly universal proposals; universality remains the unattainable end, but the system provides *an incentive to generalization*.

The deliberative process is brought to a close by a choice – the vote. In the vote, the process of the formation of the wills is finished. The final tabulation lets the people know which solution prevailed, that is, which has won the approval of the largest number. The approval of the greatest number reflects, in that context, the greater strength of one set of arguments compared to others. The process nevertheless institutionalizes the admission that there were also reasons not to desire the solution finally adopted. The minority (or minorities) also had reasons, but these reasons were less convincing. We can now see the justification for the majority principle (it is not a simple necessity of fact). Because it comes at the close of a deliberative process in which everyone was able to take part, choose among several solutions, and remain free to approve or refuse the conclusions developed from the argument, the result carries legitimacy. The decision results from a process in which the minority point of view was also taken into consideration. Although the decision does not conform to all points of view, it is the result of the confrontation between them.

The decisions that will be made by the elected officials will come from the candidates and the points of view that have won a majority. These decisions are legitimate because they are, in the last analysis, the outcome of the deliberative process taking place before the universal audience of all the citizens. These political decisions do not necessarily have to apply to all the citizens; nor do they require the agreement of all the citizens. In the last analysis, and taking into account the mediation that the elected representatives introduce, a political decision is legitimate because it has been able to win the approval of the majority at the conclusion of a process of free confrontation among various points of view. Political decisions dealing with particular objectives (selected social groups, for example) may be legitimate if they satisfy this condition. With respect to the law, the deliberative perspective allows us to drop the requirements of either strict universality of application or unanimity of approval.

[. . .]

# 90

# THE PUBLIC SPHERE:
# AN ENCYCLOPEDIA ARTICLE

## Jürgen Habermas

1. *The Concept.* By "the public sphere" we mean first of all a realm of our social life in which something approaching public opinion can be formed. Access is guaranteed to all citizens. A portion of the public sphere comes into being in every conversation in which private individuals assemble to form a public body. They then behave neither like business or professional people transacting private affairs, nor like members of a constitutional order subject to the legal constraints of a state bureaucracy. Citizens behave as a public body when they confer in an unrestricted fashion – that is, with the guarantee of freedom of assembly and association and the freedom to express and publish their opinions – about matters of general interest. In a large public body this kind of communication requires specific means for transmitting information and influencing those who receive it. Today newspapers and magazines, radio and television are the media of the public sphere. We speak of the political public sphere in contrast, for instance, to the literary one, when public discussion deals with objects connected to the activity of the state. Although state authority is so to speak the executor of the political public sphere, it is not a part of it. To be sure, state authority is usually considered "public" authority, but it derives its task of caring for the well-being of all citizens primarily from this aspect of the public sphere. Only when the exercise of political control is effectively subordinated to the democratic demand that information be accessible to the public, does the political public sphere win an institutionalized influence over the government through

From Jürgen Habermas, 'The Public Sphere: An Encyclopedia Article', *New German Critique*, 3, 1974, pp. 49–55.

the instrument of law-making bodies. The expression "public opinion" refers to the tasks of criticism and control which a public body of citizens informally – and, in periodic elections, formally as well – practices *vis-à-vis* the ruling structure organized in the form of a state. Regulations demanding that certain proceedings be public (*Publizitätsvorschriften*), for example those providing for open court hearings, are also related to this function of public opinion. The public sphere as a sphere which mediates between society and state, in which the public organizes itself as the bearer or public opinion, accords with the principle of the public sphere – that principle of public information which once had to be fought for against the arcane policies of monarchies and which since that time has made possible the democratic control of state activities.

It is no coincidence that these concepts of the public sphere and public opinion arose for the first time only in the eighteenth century. They acquire their specific meaning from a concrete historical situation. It was at that time that the distinction of "opinion" from "opinion publique" and "public opinion" came about. Though mere opinions (cultural assumptions, normative attitudes, collective prejudices and values) seem to persist unchanged in their natural form as a kind of sediment of history, public opinion can by definition only come into existence when a reasoning public is presupposed. Public discussions about the exercise of political power which are both critical in intent and institutionally guaranteed have not always existed – they grew out of a specific phase of bourgeois society and could enter into the order of the bourgeois constitutional state only as a result of a particular constellation of interests.

2. *History*. There is no indication European society of the high middle ages possessed a public sphere as a unique realm distinct from the private sphere. Nevertheless, it was not coincidental that during that period symbols of sovereignty, for instance the princely seal, were deemed "public." At that time there existed a public representation of power. The status of the feudal lord, at whatever level of the feudal pyramid, was oblivious to the categories "public" and "private," but the holder of the position represented it publicly: he showed himself, presented himself as the embodiment of an ever present "higher" power. The concept of this representation has been maintained up to the most recent constitutional history. Regardless of the degree to which it has loosed itself from the old base, the authority of political power today still demands a representation at the highest level by a head of state. Such elements, however, derive from a pre-bourgeois social structure. Representation in the sense of a bourgeois public sphere, for instance the representation of the nation or of particular mandates, has nothing to do with the medieval representative public sphere – a public sphere directly linked to the concrete existence of a ruler. As long as the prince and the estates of the realm still "are" the land, instead of merely functioning as deputies for it, they are able to "re-present"; they represent their power "before" the people, instead of for the people.

The feudal authorities (church, princes and nobility), to which the representative public sphere was first linked, disintegrated during a long process of polarization. By the end of the eighteenth century they had broken apart into private elements on the one hand, and into public on the other. The position of the church changed with the reformation: the link to divine authority which the church represented, that is, religion, became a private matter. So-called religious freedom came to insure what was historically the first area of private autonomy. The church itself continued its existence as one public and legal body among others. The corresponding polarization within princely authority was visibly manifested in the separation of the public budget from the private household expenses of a ruler. The institutions of public authority, along with the bureaucracy and the military, and in part also with the legal institutions, asserted their independence from the privatized sphere of the princely court. Finally, the feudal estates were transformed as well: the nobility became the organs of public authority, parliament and the legal institutions; while those occupied in trades and professions, insofar as they had already established urban corporations and territorial organizations, developed into a sphere of bourgeois society which would stand apart from the state as a genuine area of private autonomy.

The representative public sphere yielded to that new sphere of "public authority" which came into being with national and territorial states. Continuous state activity (permanent administration, standing army) now corresponded to the permanence of the relationships which with the stock exchange and the press had developed within the exchange of commodities and information. Public authority consolidated into a concrete opposition for those who were formerly subject to it and who at first found only a negative definition of themselves within it. These were the "private individuals" who were excluded from public authority because they held no office. "Public" no longer referred to the "representative" court of a prince endowed with authority, but rather to an institution regulated according to competence, to an apparatus endowed with a monopoly on the legal exertion of authority. Private individuals subsumed in the state at whom public authority was directed now made up the public body.

Society, now a private realm occupying a position in opposition to the state, stood on the one hand as if in clear contrast to the state. On the other hand, that society had become a concern of public interest to the degree that the reproduction of life in the wake of the developing market economy had grown beyond the bounds of private domestic authority. *The bourgeois public sphere* could be understood as the sphere of private individuals assembled into a public body, which almost immediately laid claim to the officially regulated "intellectual newspapers" for use against the public authority itself. In those newspapers, and in moralistic and critical journals, they debated that public authority on the general rules of social intercourse in their fundamentally privatized yet publically relevant sphere of labor and commodity exchange.

3. *The Liberal Model of the Public Sphere.* The medium of this debate – public discussion – was unique and without historical precedent. Hitherto the estates had negotiated agreements with their princes, settling their claims to power from case to case. This development took a different course in England, where the parliament limited royal power, than it did on the continent, where the monarchies mediatized the estates. The third estate then broke with this form of power arrangement since it could no longer establish itself as a ruling group. A division of power by means of the delineation of the rights of the nobility was no longer possible within an exchange economy – private authority over capitalist property is, after all, unpolitical. Bourgeois individuals are private individuals. As such, they do not "rule." Their claims to power *vis-à-vis* public authority were thus directed not against the concentration of power, which was to be "shared." Instead, their ideas infiltrated the very principle on which the existing power is based. To the principle of the existing power, the bourgeois public opposed the principle of supervision – that very principle which demands that proceedings be made public (*Publizität*). The principle of supervision is thus a means of transforming the nature of power, not merely one basis of legitimation exchanged for another.

In the first modern constitutions the catalogues of fundamental rights were a perfect image of the liberal model of the public sphere: they guaranteed the society as a sphere of private autonomy and the restriction of public authority to a few functions. Between these two spheres, the constitutions further insured the existence of a realm of private individuals assembled into a public body who as citizens transmit the needs of bourgeois society to the state, in order, ideally, to transform political into "rational" authority within the medium of this public sphere. The general interest, which was the measure of such a rationality, was then guaranteed, according to the presuppositions of a society of free commodity exchange, when the activities of private individuals in the marketplace were freed from social compulsion and from political pressure in the public sphere.

At the same time, daily political newspapers assumed an important role. In the second half of the eighteenth century literary journalism created serious competition for the earlier news sheets which were mere compilations of notices. Karl Bücher characterized this great development as follows: "Newspapers changed from mere institutions for the publication of news into bearers and leaders of public opinion – weapons of party politics. This transformed the newspaper business. A new element emerged between the gathering and the publication of news: the editorial staff. But for the newspaper publisher it meant that he changed from a vendor of recent news to a dealer in public opinion." The publishers insured the newspapers a commercial basis, yet without commercializing them as such. The press remained an institution of the public itself, effective in the manner of a mediator and intensifier of public discussion, no longer a mere organ for the spreading of news but not yet the medium of a consumer culture.

This type of journalism can be observed above all during periods of revolution when newspapers of the smallest political groups and organizations spring up, for instance in Paris in 1789. Even in the Paris of 1848 every half-way eminent politician organized his club, every other his journal: 450 clubs and over 200 journals were established there between February and May alone. Until the permanent legalization of a politically functional public sphere, the appearance of a political newspaper meant joining the struggle for freedom and public opinion, and thus for the public sphere as a principle. Only with the establishment of the bourgeois constitutional state was the intellectual press relieved of the pressure of its convictions. Since then it has been able to abandon its polemical position and take advantage of the earning possibilities of a commercial undertaking. In England, France, and the United States the transformation from a journalism of conviction to one of commerce began in the 1830s at approximately the same time. In the transition from the literary journalism of private individuals to the public services of the mass media the public sphere was transformed by the influx of private interests, which received special prominence in the mass media.

4. *The Public Sphere in the Social Welfare State Mass Democracy*. Although the liberal model of the public sphere is still instructive today with respect to the normative claim that information be accessible to the public, it cannot be applied to the actual conditions of an industrially advanced mass democracy organized in the form of the social welfare state. In part the liberal model had always included ideological components, but it is also in part true that the social pre-conditions, to which the ideological elements could at one time at least be linked, had been fundamentally transformed. The very forms in which the public sphere manifested itself, to which supporters of the liberal model could appeal for evidence, began to change with the Chartist movement in England and the February revolution in France. Because of the diffusion of press and propaganda, the public body expanded beyond the bounds of the bourgeoisie. The public body lost not only its social exclusivity; it lost in addition the coherence created by bourgeois social institutions and a relatively high standard of education. Conflicts hitherto restricted to the private sphere now intrude into the public sphere. Group needs which can expect no satisfaction from a self-regulating market now tend towards a regulation by the state. The public sphere, which must now mediate these demands, becomes a field for the competition of interests, competitions which assume the form of violent conflict. Laws which obviously have come about under the "pressure of the street" can scarcely still be understood as arising from the consensus of private individuals engaged in public discussion. They correspond in a more or less unconcealed manner to the compromise of conflicting private interests. Social organizations which deal with the state act in the political public sphere, whether through the agency of political parties or directly in connection with the public administration. With the interweaving of the public and private realm, not only do the political

authorities assume certain functions in the sphere of commodity exchange and social labor, but conversely social powers now assume political functions. This leads to a kind of "refeudalization" of the public sphere. Large organizations strive for political compromises with the state and with each other, excluding the public sphere whenever possible. But at the same time the large organizations must assure themselves of at least plebiscitary support from the mass of the population through an apparent display of openness (*demonstrative Publizität*).

The political public sphere of the social welfare state is characterized by a peculiar weakening of its critical functions. At one time the process of making proceedings public (*Publizität*) was intended to subject persons or affairs to public reason, and to make political decisions subject to appeal before the court of public opinion. But often enough today the process of making public simply serves the arcane policies of special interests; in the form of "publicity" it wins public prestige for people or affairs, thus making them worthy of acclamation in a climate of non-public opinion. The very words "public relations work" (*Oeffentlichkeitsarbeit*) betray the fact that a public sphere must first be arduously constructed case by case, a public sphere which earlier grew out of the social structure. Even the central relationship of the public, the parties and the parliament is affected by this change in function.

Yet this trend towards the weakening of the public sphere as a principle is opposed by the extension of fundamental rights in the social welfare state. The demand that information be accessible to the public is extended from organs of the state to all organizations dealing with the state. To the degree that this is realized, a public body of organized private individuals would take the place of the now-defunct public body of private individuals who relate individually to each other. Only these organized individuals could participate effectively in the process of public communication; only they could use the channels of the public sphere which exist within parties and associations and the process of making proceedings public (*Publizität*) which was established to facilitate the dealings of organizations with the state. Political compromises would have to be legitimized through this process of public communication. The idea of the public sphere, preserved in the social welfare state mass democracy, an idea which calls for a rationalization of power through the medium of public discussion among private individuals, threatens to disintegrate with the structural transformation of the public sphere itself. It could only be realized today, on an altered basis, as a rational reorganization of social and political power under the mutual control of rival organizations committed to the public sphere in their internal structure as well as in their relations with the state and each other.

# 91

# THE DIALOGUE OF JUSTICE:
# TOWARD A SELF-REFLECTIVE SOCIETY

## J. S. Fishkin

[...]

Explicit manipulation imposes penalties, not only on particular individuals, but also, when carried out systematically, on entire societies. In the interests of maintaining those in power, such societies blind themselves to the possibility of self-improvement or self-reflective re-examination. Within our framework, their practices cannot satisfy the conditions for solving the legitimacy problem because any consensus supporting them must be suspect. Any such consensus has not passed the test of self-reflective political dialogue, a test that could give us confidence in the kind of scrutiny it has survived.

Thus far, we have focused only on explicit manipulation. However, public dialogue can be subjected to strong manipulation without any recourse to coercion or penalties. Crucial voices may fail to achieve an effective hearing without it being necessary for any voices to be silenced. The same result may follow without anyone being penalized for speaking: if the relevant voices do not wish to speak, if they do not have an opportunity to be heard, or if the relevant audiences have learned not to listen. In these three main ways, effects similar to those of explicit manipulation may be achieved without any penalties actually being imposed or threatened against anyone within the sphere of political culture. In this sense, avoiding explicit manipulation is not enough to guarantee meaningful freedom of political culture.

From J. S. Fishkin, *The Dialogue of Justice: Toward a Self-Reflective Society* (Yale University Press, New Haven, CT, 1992), pp. 155–65.

To cover these cases, a second form of strong manipulation needs to be specified. Because it concerns the structure of communication, rather than explicit acts of manipulation, I will call it *structural manipulation*. In some ways it may seem misleading to call it manipulation at all, since it may well occur without anybody consciously playing the role of manipulator. But just as some situations may be structured in a coercive manner without anybody consciously playing the role of coercer, some situations may be structured in a manner that has the effect of manipulation, without anyone consciously playing the role of manipulator. With this terminological caveat in mind, we can define structural manipulation.

The basic idea is that *effective voice must be given to interests across every significant cleavage in the society*. When this effective voice is denied, then the political dialogue has been subjected to structural manipulation. An effective voice is one that is widely disseminated and that people are prepared to, and capable of, substantially evaluating on its merits (rather than merely on the basis of the source). The difficulty, of course, is that it is not clear, at least at first glance, how such an effective voice can be guaranteed.

Note, first, that whatever the difficulties of implementation, the criterion at least gives us a notion of what voices are crucial to the dialogue's being self-reflective rather than suspect. Second, the strategy for achieving a self-reflective political culture will often be *indirect*. It will focus on altering background conditions for the development of practices and preferences. It need not be the direct result of policy choice. Clearly, in this case, structural manipulation will only be avoided when the background conditions are adjusted, in an ongoing society, so that a culture of *participatory civility* has been achieved. In such a culture, people will participate and listen (and be capable of listening) on the merits.

Setting aside, for the moment, the issue of background conditions, let us consider the dangers of strong manipulation. Manipulated debate in either of our two senses deserves to be distrusted. What confidence can we have in any political proposition when critics of it have been silenced? Or when crucial interests, reflecting any of the main cleavages in the society, have been shut out? If there is a consensus, under such conditions of manipulation, it must be suspect. It is suspect because we cannot know how it would generally be evaluated if the challenging voices had not been suppressed.

When crucial interests or contrary voices are suppressed, the claim of political institutions to make rational demands upon us has been compromised. It is compromised because, within our framework, the claim to rationality depends upon those institutions and practices being supported by a consensus that *survives* unmanipulated self-scrutiny. We cannot know how a consensus would survive contrary voices if there are none. We cannot know whether, if some crucial interest had been given effective voice, support across a main cleavage might have disappeared. We cannot know the degree to which acts of manipulation (or the toleration of structural manipulation) are self-serving.

The capacity of the system (and those acting within it) to evaluate itself has been severely impaired.

The claim of the political practices to survive rational evaluation is only vindicated when threatening voices and crucial interests obtain the requisite hearing. After such a hearing, if we should conclude that the contrary arguments are mistaken, or even ridiculous, we are likely to have benefited from them, nonetheless. We would then get what Mill called "the clearer perception and livelier impression of truth, produced by its collision with error."

Most important, if the dialogue takes place free of strong manipulation, any consensus that survives has a basis for making a rational claim upon us. Strong manipulation would rob us of one of the necessary conditions for reasonably having confidence in those propositions. While Mill's argument was only formulated to deal with what we have called explicit manipulation, his general point is relevant: "There is the greatest difference between presuming an opinion to be true, because, with every opportunity for contesting it, it has not been refuted, and assuming its truth for the purpose of not permitting its refutation. Complete liberty of contradicting and disproving our opinion is the very condition which justifies us in assuming its truth for purposes of action; and on no other terms can a being with human faculties have any rational assurance of being right."

I will rely on this basic insight of Mill's in the argument for liberty of political culture. However, by the "complete liberty of contradicting and disproving our opinion," we mean something more demanding than the liberties of thought and discussion defended in Mill's essay.

Nevertheless, Mill's insight here is central and far-reaching. It permits a different slant than the one commonly taken on what we have been calling the legitimacy problem. Instead of arguing that liberty of thought and discussion are instrumental to truth, in general, and that truth, in general, is instrumental to utility, we are arguing that liberty of political culture is necessary if we are to have any confidence in certain particular political "truths," and that having confidence in just those particular political "truths" is part of the solution to the legitimacy problem.

As I noted earlier, political practices that can justifiably determine obligations of all members provide a basis for solving the legitimacy problem. But members are obligated to support political practices only if they are of a kind that it is reasonable for them to accept. I am taking the position here that, at least within ideal theory, it is reasonable to accept only political practices that have passed a certain test of rationality – of self-critical re-examination. That test is that the consensus about them must survive the self-reflective scrutiny of what we have been calling unmanipulated debate. Once the debate is manipulated, then the political practices protected by such manipulation are suspect in their rationality. If the practices are suspect, then it is no longer reasonable in the same way for us to accept them. As a matter of expediency, under less-than-ideal conditions, we may well be forced to accept them. But the claim of the system to provide a full solution to the legitimacy problem would have been undermined.

According to the ideal proposed here, a political culture is "self-reflective" when it provides the collective conditions for its own rational self-evaluation. We should be suspicious of the self-evaluation of any other form of political culture. The hand of the state is heavy on most citizens – demanding moral deference in the name of allegiance and patriotism. The latter qualities may be admirable, even in a self-reflective political culture – but only when care is taken to separate them from unthinking obedience and from the surrendering of self-critical capacities.

A self-reflective political culture defines certain far-reaching conditions of liberty, conditions under which a society's members are free from all forms of strong manipulation of their conscientious political views. That this require-ment is distinctive can be seen from comparing it to the most common formulation of liberty of political thought and discussion. Consider what might be called a minimal, or laissez-faire, construction: no significant coercive inter-ference with the liberty of individuals to express political opinions, hold political beliefs, or associate voluntarily together for those same purposes. By "no significant" coercive interference, I do not mean to rule out time, place, and manner restrictions used sparingly enough so as not to affect the basic character of political debate.

The laissez-faire view is a close cousin to the one developed here. The most obvious connection is that coercive interferences with political expression, belief, or association will count as explicit manipulations of the political culture in the sense defined earlier. Penalties imposed on people (individually or col-lectively) for expressing or holding certain beliefs will either silence voices in the debate through sheer coercion or silence them through intimidation and self-censorship (conducted under threat of coercion). The requirement that a self-reflective political culture forgo explicit manipulation is sufficient, by itself, to yield significant liberties.

Of course, it is not enough that the state refrain from acts of coercion intended to silence people. If the state fails to protect individuals or groups from third-party efforts to intimidate or silence political expression or the holding of certain political beliefs, the same problem of explicit manipulation arises. Vigilante groups may silence unpopular views as effectively as may official action. Less obviously, job discrimination based on political belief or political expression may have equally devastating effects. If I am threatened with firing, or if I am denied the equal consideration I am entitled to in the job market because my ideological views (irrelevant to the job at issue) prompt employment discrimination, my liberty to express and/or hold political opin-ions has been interfered with, coercively.

However, this minimal, or laissez-faire, construction is clearly insufficient to bring about a self-reflective political culture. Consider the possibility raised forcefully by C. E. Lindblom that democratic systems are vulnerable to "circularity": "It may be that people are indoctrinated to demand ... to buy and to vote for ... nothing other than what a decision-making elite is already disposed to grant them. The volitions that are supposed to guide leaders are formed by the same leaders." The key to what Lindblom calls "indoctrination" is its "lopsided" character. It is "not the mutual persuasion of liberal democratic aspiration but a lopsided, sometimes nearly unilateral persuasion by business, governmental and political leadership directed at ordinary citizens who do not themselves easily command, as leaders do, the services of printing and broadcasting."

There is no need for us here to enter the fierce empirical debate about the extent to which this kind of circularity applies to the U.S. or to any other major Western democracy. At the very least, it is, theoretically, a troubling possibility, one that is clearly compatible with the minimal, laissez-faire construction of political liberties. Without any resort to coercive interference in political expression, belief, or association, it is possible for some groups to speak, as it were, so loudly and so much as to deny an effective hearing to contrary voices.

Hence, the negative guarantees embodied in the minimal, laissez-faire conception do not, by any means, ensure the conditions for a self-reflective political culture. They do block the coercive interference that could be achieved by explicit manipulation. However, those guarantees do nothing to prevent the other form of strong manipulation discussed above: they do nothing to ensure an effective hearing for other crucial voices, voices representing interests across the main cleavages in the society.

Somehow, the possibility of structural manipulation has to be ruled out without the remedy itself taking the objectionable form of strong manipulation. The kind of liberty guaranteed by the laissez-faire view would protect individuals, groups, or institutions acting voluntarily, but in concert, so as to drown out all opposing voices. Instead of employing the blunt tool of coercion to silence voices in the chorus that would otherwise predominate, the state should attempt to create forums and positive incentives for political dialogue – particularly for crucial interests that would not otherwise achieve an effective hearing. In this sense, a more activist liberty of political culture is required.

But is not intervening actively in this way itself a form of manipulation by the state? While it might be labeled manipulation by some, it is not a form of strong manipulation in the sense defined here. No voices are suppressed, no crucial interests are shut out of the dialogue. If the state intervenes to create forums or positive incentives for the expression of opposing views, it is not attempting to manufacture consensus around a preferred conclusion. Rather, it is preventing us from adopting views prematurely, before there has been an airing of contrasting voices and of crucial interests.

The term *intervention* should not be misunderstood. I use it only to distinguish the activist conception from the merely laissez-faire, or minimal, conception of liberty of political culture. It does not imply that the government should follow every debate and intervene directly to balance out the dialogue based on its judgment of predominant messages about any particular issue. Not only is such a system not required; it would be extremely unlikely to operate well or to facilitate the goal of a self-reflective political culture. The very fact that public debate was known to be under official scrutiny, for whatever putative reasons, would likely have a chilling effect on the more extreme forms of dissent or criticism. As a matter of institutional design, we should distrust efforts by public officials to explicitly manage or control the content of political dialogue. On any realistic construction, they have too much at stake for their self-interest not to affect the results, covertly if not insidiously. This caution should be applied even if their mandate were to free dialogue from all forms of strong manipulation, both explicit and structural. Rather, the strategy should be to create certain general practices in the operation of the media and of the public spaces open for political debate. Over the long term, these practices should be designed to facilitate the openness of forums and positive incentives in those forums for opposing views and for the representation of crucial interests.

But why limit these general interventions to positive incentives and other adjustments in background conditions? If a self-reflective political culture is so important, why not just threaten or coerce everyone to participate so as to produce one? There are two obvious objections. First, we cannot expect to achieve a form of political culture untarnished by strong manipulation by threatening people with coercive penalties whose application, in many cases, will constitute strong manipulation in the explicit sense. Second, our goal is a political culture that is self-reflective in its political dialogue. By "dialogue" I mean the expression of conscientious, reasoned debate on grounds sincerely believed to be valid and appropriate by its participants. As a matter of institutional design, it is unrealistic to expect coercion, threats, and intimidation to produce much conscientious debate in this sense. Apart from some principled resistance, this kind of brute interference is likely to produce only cynical or self-serving efforts to avoid whatever penalties are feared.

Let us attempt to formulate, in greater detail, what is distinctive about the activist conception of liberty of political culture. Unlike the laissez-faire conception, the activist conception is not merely negative. It does not consist entirely in prohibitions on interferences with the holding or expressing of political beliefs (or of people associating together for either purpose). While the activist conception gives a major role to such guarantees, sole reliance on them would leave the system vulnerable to "circularity," indoctrination, and patterns by which the interests of certain groups or institutions prompt them to drown out their opposition, effectively shutting crucial interests out of the continuing dialogue. For this reason, I have posited the need for incentives, forums, and forms of access for political dissent if a self-reflective political culture is to be achieved – if, in other words, the political culture is to become significantly self-critical as a result of unmanipulated debate.

Of course, this goal may strike some people, at the outset, as bizarre. Why should critics even be permitted, much less encouraged, by official design? A common view is that the state can pursue its goals more efficiently if meddlesome critics are out of the way. But without critics – and the self-reflective political culture they help create – one must be suspicious of the state's goals and of the processes by which those goals have been determined in the first place.

Of course, agonized self-reflection is no substitute for action. But the prescription for a self-reflective political culture does not preclude a design for political institutions permitting swift action when circumstances require it. Of necessity, criticism will often be retrospective rather than prospective. In any case, we have said very little thus far about the structure of political decision making. The self-reflective argument is not intended to produce a blueprint for the best liberal institutions. Rather, it is meant to single out certain distinctive features of an ideal liberal state – features that would permit a full solution to the legitimacy problem.

Suppose, however, that all forms of strong manipulation are eliminated but no criticisms of the system result. Political theorists and social planners finally think up the perfect system and get it adopted. Our definition of a self-reflective political culture requires that it be consistently self-critical through unmanipulated debate. Suppose that unmanipulated debate produces no criticism. Are we then in the position of claiming that such a system must be worse precisely because it is so perfect as to be beyond criticism?

With Mill, I assume that the empirical concomitant of significant freedom of thought is diversity of opinion on the full range of questions touching on our definition of the political. Hence, perfect agreement that a system was beyond criticism would in itself constitute powerful evidence that meaningful freedom of thought had not been achieved.

Hence, without suppression of freedom of thought, we can assume that there will always be critical voices which could be given an opportunity to contribute to self-reflective dialogue, to the system's capacity to examine itself. If we do away with both forms of strong manipulation, then these conscientious criticisms can get aired. If the consensus supporting the system's political practices can maintain itself in the face of the resulting self-critical examination, then that consensus has a reasonable claim to authority over us.

[...]

# SECTION 17
# THE FUTURE OF DEMOCRACY

# THE FUTURE OF DEMOCRACY
## INTRODUCTION

As the various sections on contemporary issues have shown, there is a tremendous vitality to current debates about democracy. This is despite, or perhaps because of, increasing external pressures in the form of globalised markets and serious internal disagreements that go all the way from basic principles to the institutional forms appropriate for their practical enactment. These debates are also being acted out in practice. Across the world, in what has been called the 'associational revolution', there is an extraordinary level of democratic activity, whether in civic groups, protest movements and non-governmental organisations. At the same time, there is also significant experimentation in the existing institutions of liberal-democracies, particularly in the area of devolution, regional and local government.

One important theme which runs through all this activity is that of decentralisation. A large part of the hopes for democracy in the future turn on whether a decentralised democratic system can both involve the people more meaningfully and preserve the stability and effectiveness of existing representational structures.

This section presents a range of expectations for the future of democracy. Such aspirations are, at the same time, attempts to show the resources that are currently available for change and how changes might be brought about. First, *Mouffe* explores the meaning and prospects of democracy in a postmodern world in which concepts can no longer claim to be certain or objective. Her call for a decentralised and radical democracy arises from her concern to celebrate the many differences among us, and sends us back to a politics based, once again, on civic virtues.

*Epstein* then takes up these suggestions and analyses them in the light of practical developments. In so doing, she raises a series of problems with the continuing liberal division between politics and economics, and argues further that current conditions are right for a recombination of socialism and decentralised democracy. A quite different hope is voiced by *Stewart*. He outlines a series of practical and concrete innovations that are being tried out in the area of local government in order to increase participation, deliberation and decentralisation. Finally, *Hague and Loader* explore the possible impact the new information and computer technologies might have on democracy.

# 92

# RADICAL DEMOCRACY: MODERN OR POST-MODERN?

## Chantal Mouffe

[...]

Recent attempts by neoliberals and neoconservatives to redefine concepts such as liberty and equality and to disarticulate the idea of liberty from that of democracy demonstrate how within the liberal democratic tradition different strategies can be pursued, making available different kinds of intimations. Confronted by this offensive on the part of those who want to put an end to the articulation that was established in the nineteenth century between liberalism and democracy and who want to redefine liberty as nothing more than an absence of coercion, the project of radical democracy must try to defend democracy and to expand its sphere of applicability to new social relations. It aims to create another kind of articulation between elements of the liberal democratic tradition, no longer viewing rights in an individualist framework but as "democratic rights." This will create a new hegemony, which will be the outcome of the articulation of the greatest possible number of democratic struggles.

What we need is a hegemony of democratic values, and this requires a multiplication of democratic practices, institutionalizing them into ever more diverse social relations, so that a multiplicity of subject-positions can be formed through a democratic matrix. It is in this way – and not by trying to provide it with a rational foundation – that we will be able not only to defend democracy

From Chantal Mouffe, 'Radical Democracy: Modern or Post-modern?', in A. Ross (ed.), *Universal Abandon? The Politics of Postmodernism* (University of Edinburgh Press, Edinburgh, 1988), pp. 41–4.

but also to deepen it. Such a hegemony will never be complete, and anyway, it is not desirable for a society to be ruled by a single democratic logic. Relations of authority and power cannot completely disappear, and it is important to abandon the myth of a transparent society, reconciled with itself, for that kind of fantasy leads to totalitarianism. A project of radical and plural democracy, on the contrary, requires the existence of multiplicity, of plurality, and of conflict, and sees in them the *raison d'être* of politics.

### RADICAL DEMOCRACY, A NEW POLITICAL PHILOSOPHY

If the task of radical democracy is indeed to deepen the democratic revolution and to link together diverse democratic struggles, such a task requires the creation of new subject-positions that would allow the common articulation, for example, of antiracism, antisexism, and anticapitalism. These struggles do not spontaneously converge, and in order to establish democratic equivalences, a new "common sense" is necessary, which would transform the identity of different groups so that the demands of each group could be articulated with those of others according to the principle of democratic equivalence. For it is not a matter of establishing a mere alliance between given interests but of actually modifying the very identity of these forces. In order that the defense of workers' interests is not pursued at the cost of the rights of women, immigrants, or consumers, it is necessary to establish an equivalence between these different struggles. It is only under these circumstances that struggles against power become truly democratic.

Political philosophy has a very important role to play in the emergence of this common sense and in the creation of these new subject-positions, for it will shape the "definition of reality" that will provide the form of political experience and serve as a matrix for the construction of a certain kind of subject. Some of the key concepts of liberalism, such as rights, liberty, and citizenship, are claimed today by the discourse of possessive individualism, which stands in the way of the establishment of a chain of democratic equivalences.

I have already referred to the necessity of a concept of democratic rights, rights which, while belonging to the individual, can only be exercised collectively and presuppose the existence of equal rights for others. But radical democracy also needs an idea of liberty that transcends the false dilemma between the liberty of the ancients and the moderns and allows us to think individual liberty and political liberty together. On this issue, radical democracy shares the preoccupations of various writers who want to redeem the tradition of civic republicanism. This trend is quite heterogeneous, and it is therefore necessary to draw distinctions among the so-called communitarians who, while they all share a critique of liberal individualism's idea of a subject existing prior to the social relations that form it, have differing attitudes toward modernity. On the one hand, there are those like Michael Sandel and Alasdair MacIntyre, inspired mainly by Aristotle, who reject liberal pluralism in the name of a politics of the common good; and, on the other hand, those like Charles Taylor and Michael Walzer, who, while they criticize the epistemological presuppositions of liberalism, try to incorporate its political contribution in the area of rights and pluralism.[1] The latter hold a perspective closer to that of radical democracy, whereas the former maintain an extremely ambiguous attitude toward the advent of democracy and tend to defend premodern conceptions of politics, drawing no distinctions between the ethical and the political which they understand as the expression of shared moral values.

It is probably in the work of Machiavelli that civic republicanism has the most to offer us, and in this respect the recent work of Quentin Skinner is of particular interest. Skinner shows that in Machiavelli one finds a conception of liberty that, although it does not postulate an objective notion of the good life (and therefore is, according to Isaiah Berlin, a "negative" conception of liberty), nevertheless includes ideals of political participation and civic virtue (which, according to Berlin, are typical of a "positive" conception of liberty). Skinner shows that the idea of liberty is portrayed in the *Discourses* as the capacity for individuals to pursue their own goals, their "humors" (*humori*). This goes together with the affirmation that in order to ensure the necessary conditions for avoiding coercion and servitude, thereby rendering impossible the use of this liberty, it is indispensable for individuals to fulfill certain public functions and to cultivate required virtues. For Machiavelli, if one is to exercise civic virtue and serve the common good, it is in order to guarantee oneself a certain degree of personal liberty which permits one to pursue one's own ends.[2] We encounter in this a very modern conception of individual liberty articulated onto an old conception of political liberty, which is fundamental for the development of a political philosophy of radical democracy.

But this appeal to a tradition of civic republicanism, even in the privileging of its Machiavellian branch, cannot wholly provide us with the political language needed for an articulation of the multiplicity of today's democratic struggles. The best it can do is provide us with elements to fight the negative aspects of liberal individualism while it remains inadequate to grasp the complexity of politics today. Our societies are confronted with the proliferation of political spaces which are radically new and different and which demand that we abandon the idea of a unique constitutive space of the constitution of the political, which is particular to both liberalism and civic republicanism. If the liberal conception of the "unencumbered self" is deficient, the alternative presented by the communitarian defenders of civic republicanism is unsatisfactory as well. It is not a question of moving from a "unitary unencumbered self" to a "unitary situated self"; the problem is with the very idea of the unitary subject. Many communitarians seem to believe that we belong to only one community, defined empirically and even geographically, and that this community could be unified by a single idea of the common good. But we are in fact always multiple and contradictory subjects, inhabitants of a diversity of communities (as many, really, as the social relations in which we participate and the subject-positions they define), constructed by a variety of discourses and precariously and temporarily sutured at the intersection of those subject-positions. Thus the importance of the postmodern critique for developing a political philosophy aimed at making possible a new form of individuality that would be truly plural and democratic. A philosophy of this sort does not assume a rational foundation for democracy, nor does it provide answers, in the way of Leo Strauss, to questions concerning the nature of political matters and the best regime. On the contrary, it proposes to remain within the cave and, as Michael Walzer puts it, "to interpret to one's fellow citizens the world of meanings that we share."[3] The liberal democratic tradition is open to many interpretations, and the politics of radical democracy is but one strategy among others. Nothing guarantees its success, but this project has set out to pursue and deepen the democratic project of modernity. Such a strategy requires us to abandon the abstract universalism of the Enlightenment, the essentialist conception of a social totality, and the myth of a unitary subject. In this respect, far from seeing the development of postmodern philosophy as a threat, radical democracy welcomes it as an indispensable instrument in the accomplishment of its goals.

## NOTES

1. I refer here to the following studies: Michael Sandel, *Liberalism and the Limits of Justice* (Cambridge: Cambridge University Press, 1982); Alasdair MacIntyre, *After Virtue* (Notre Dame, Ind.: University of Notre Dame Press, 1984); Charles Taylor, *Philosophy and the Human Sciences*, Philosophical Papers, 2 (Cambridge: Cambridge University Press, 1985); Michael Walzer, *Spheres of Justice* (New York: Basic Books, 1983).
2. Quentin Skinner, 'The Idea of Negative Liberty: Philosophical and Historical Perspectives,' in *Philosophy in History*, eds. R. Rorty, J. B. Schneewind, and Q. Skinner (Cambridge: Cambridge University Press, 1984).
3. Walzer, *Spheres of Justice*, xiv.

# 93

# RADICAL DEMOCRACY AND CULTURAL POLITICS: WHAT ABOUT CLASS? WHAT ABOUT POLITICAL POWER?

## Barbara Epstein

[...]

The term "radical democracy" has a set of positive connotations: it is associated with the social movements of the seventies and eighties, in particular feminism, gay and lesbian rights, environmentalism, and multiculturalism; it suggests a politics oriented more toward cultural than toward political or economic struggles; and it is associated with decentralization and has vaguely anarchist, or at least anti-bureaucratic, overtones. It suggests grassroots politics, diversity, a playful political practice that is not bound by rigid structures but is continually in the process of transformation. All of these aspects of the politics suggested by "radical democracy" are genuinely appealing.

However, there are also serious problems associated with the adoption of this term, and I believe that the problems outweigh the advantages. To state the problems briefly before exploring them in more detail: the term radical democracy is anchored in the "new social movements," a category that did not entirely fit the map of social change activism even at the moment when it was most useful – roughly the mid-seventies to the mid-eighties – and which is considerably less relevant to social movements of the mid-nineties than it was to those a decade or so ago. The "new social movements" are a thin basis for a left perspective for the nineties. If one regards radical democracy as rooted not in the particular kinds of movements described by new social movement theory

From Barbara Epstein, 'Radical Democracy and Cultural Politics: What about Class? What about Political Power?', in D. Trend (ed.), *Radical Democracy: Identity, Citizenship and the State* (Routledge, London, 1996), pp. 128–37.

but associated simply with the range of existing movements, then this is an even thinner basis for a radical perspective. If the left has nothing more to contribute than to refer to the current map of social activism, it has little reason to exist. Furthermore, current activism includes as much on the right as on the left; in fact, the term "radical" is easily appropriated by the right.

The turn toward radical democracy involves a turn away from class as a key category of left politics, and also a loss of interest in politics or the question of who controls states (and other governing institutions) and what policies they produce. The shift away from class and state power is understandable, given the disappointing record of left politics in both arenas, but it is a big mistake, especially at a moment when class polarization is proceeding rapidly both in the United States and internationally, and when economic globalization is raising the question of who will hold power and what those who hold it will do with it. For the last ten years or so, much of the intellectual left has celebrated cultural and political marginality. The left, especially the intellectual left, is in danger of becoming entirely irrelevant to the major shifts that are taking place nationally and internationally. This essay will trace at least some of the political and intellectual currents that have led to the current rejection of class (and of the issue of state power), argue that these currents should be seen critically rather than being made the basis for left politics, and try to suggest more promising directions.

New social movement theory is an intellectual tendency that presents an analysis of contemporary social movements while at the same time identifying with those social movements, and in effect prescribing particular directions for radical politics. First developed by continental social analysts such as Alain Touraine, Alberto Melucci, and others in the seventies and early eighties, new social movement theory sharply distinguished between "old" and "new" social movements.[1] The "old" social movements were those organized around class, especially the working class; they were concerned with political power and with economic structures, or issues of economic redistribution. The concept of "old" social movements carried a flavor of communism or of social democracy; it referred to the movements that set the tone for radical politics, in Europe at least, from the mid-nineteenth century through the thirties. The "new" social movements, according to the theoretical model, were organized not around class but around other kinds of identities; these movements were not interested in political power or in economic restructuring, but rather in cultural change, in the transformation of values and of everyday life. "New" social movements were anti-hierarchical as opposed to bureaucratic. Internally highly democratic, they were concerned with the defense and construction of community, and of particular identities. These were presented both as descriptions of emerging forms of social movement practice, and as prescriptions for a form of radicalism appropriate to Western society, at least, in the late twentieth century.

Particularly in its claim to describe a form of radicalism appropriate to late twentieth-century Western society, new social movement theory interacted with two other strands of theory, both of which were taking hold in Europe, especially France and Germany, at roughly the same time: Fordist/post-Fordist theory, and poststructuralism. Fordist analysis suggested that the form of capitalism that was based on the compromise between capital and labor, a welfare state, and massive assembly-line production of commodities had gone into crisis, and that more decentralized or fragmented forms were emerging not only in the realm of production but in politics and the organization of social life. This analysis could be seen to have implications for the arena of culture. An economy driven by consumption and a social order held together by a capital-labor compromise required a high level of consent, making culture a crucial arena of struggle. The stable structures and bureaucratic organizations of Fordist society had helped to inculcate discipline; as these broke down, culture became an increasingly important arena both of the inculcation of ideologies of social control, and of protest. Though Fordist theory was developed by people who in many cases remained close to Marxism, and new social movement theory was generally associated with an anti-Marxist stance, the two came together in suggesting that the era of class politics based on struggles at the point of production was over, and that new movements were likely to be locally based, decentralized, and focused on issues of culture and daily life.[2]

New social movement theory, enhanced by Fordist theory, also intersected in some respects with poststructuralism, which though based in France was gaining wide influence elsewhere by the late seventies and eighties. On the whole, the circles in which new social movement theory was being developed were quite distinct from poststructuralist or postmodernist circles. Despite the fact that leading poststructuralist theorists looked back on May '68 as a key moment in their lives, poststructuralism was considerably more remote from actual social movements than new social movement theory, which required interaction with actual movements. Poststructuralism did, however, reinforce certain aspects of new social movement theory. Poststructuralism's emphasis on language overlapped with the new social movement emphasis on culture. Its emphasis on the unstable, fragmentary, and fleeting, its rejection of unity and coherence either as reality or as goal reinforced the emphasis on decentralization and spontaneity as qualities of social movements. Poststructuralism's rejection of universal values as "totalizing" was absorbed into the discussion of new social movements. In fact, the leading theorists of new social movements had never claimed that new social movements rejected universal values; for Touraine, for instance, the leading characteristic of such movements was that they presented a new set of values as those that should govern society. But as poststructuralism and new social movement theory have been absorbed into left intellectual discourse, the distinctions between them have tended to be forgotten.[3]

The problem is not that new social movement theory has become overlaid with poststructuralist aesthetic preferences but that even from the mid-seventies to the mid-eighties – the high point of actual "new social movements" – the fit between the theory and the social movement reality was never very close, and that in the nineties there are few social movements that fit the "new social movement" model. New social movement theory was inspired by the amalgam of oppositional youth movements that gained strength in Western Europe, especially West Germany, in the late seventies. The anti-nuclear movement – opposition to US-imposed nuclear weapons, and also to nuclear power plants – was at the center of this movement culture; it was infused as well with feminism, pacifism, anarchism, a network of alternative institutions, and efforts to construct a viable counter-culture. This movement culture impressed students of social movements and other left-leaning intellectuals because of its size (at least in some areas), its attractive style (the efforts to build community, the renunciation of machismo and authoritarianism), and its fit with the new theories of capitalism that were being advanced at the time.

Even when the new social movements were flourishing in Western Europe, many movements and organizations did not fit this model. One respect in which the theory was broadly borne out was that the organized working class had ceased to be the main basis of movements for social change. But this did not mean that all or even most collective efforts for social change fit the anti-bureaucratic, anarchist-oriented model described by the theory. Through the seventies and eighties more conventionally organized movements, oriented toward elections and policy reform rather than broad cultural change, continued to exist; as the counter-culture began to decline (or at least to become detached from social protest) in the mid- to late eighties, it was these more conventional organizations that were able to retain popular support around concerns such as peace and the environment.[4]

In the United States there has been even less cohesion between new social movement theory and the actual shape of movements for social change. Over the same time period when new social movements were flourishing in Western Europe, there were a few movements in the United States that more or less fit the same model: for instance, the nonviolent direct action movement, which addressed, in turn, nuclear power, nuclear arms, and United States intervention in Central America. Each phase of the movement, after a series of dramatic mass mobilizations, went into decline; in the mid-eighties the movement as a whole came to an end. Ecofeminism, which shared the same approach to politics, had a brief life as an activist social movement and then retreated into the academy and became a branch of theory. Radical Christian activism (expressed, for instance, in the Sanctuary movement), which fit much of the "new social movement" model, also flourished in the early eighties and attracted many activists not associated with the churches; it continues to exist but has to a large degree lost its former mass character.[5]

Some gay and lesbian organizations of the seventies and eighties fit the description of new social movements; this is perhaps the arena in which the "new social movement" impulse has best survived into the nineties, especially in the form of ACT UP and Queer Nation. But much of the gay and lesbian movement has become strongly, and quite effectively, oriented toward the electoral arena. Through the seventies and the eighties there were many movements and organizations organized around issues of identity – race, gender, sexuality – and by virtue of addressing these issues contributed to a transformation of culture. But they did not necessarily participate in the more specific cultural radicalism that new social movement theory described, and that the concept of radical democracy presumes.

In the nineties there is still an arena of countercultural activism, oriented toward cultural transformation and infused with an anarchist or anti-state sensibility (Earth First!, for instance). But it is no longer possible to describe "new social movements" as a growing tendency. As in Europe, in many arenas – such as the women's movement, the environmental movement, and movements of groups of color – more conventional organizations continued to function through the seventies and eighties, and remain strong today. Meanwhile, different (that is, new but not "new") forms of grassroots social activism are emerging. Perhaps the most promising grassroots movement is the toxics/ environmental justice movement, the overlapping networks of local groups opposed to chemical contamination and protesting the particular exposure of communities of color to such hazards. These groups exhibit some of the characteristics associated with new social movements: they are locally based and democratic. The movement as a whole is not organized around class (though it is composed mostly of people at the lower ends of the economic ladder, since these are the people most exposed to toxics). Race and gender are major issues for this movement, due to its focus on environmental racism, the large and growing numbers of people of color within its ranks, and the fact that it is overwhelmingly a movement of women. But it is not a movement that is about identity. Groups within the movement often find themselves opposing the state, or more precisely, agencies of the state.[6]

Toxics/environmental justice groups are not culturally radical, except in the broad sense that the demand for a livable environment is a critique of prevailing values. They are also not anarchist. They do not want less state power, but do want more effective regulation on behalf of the public. The toxics/environmental justice movement is not primarily concerned with issues of production, but it has not entirely left these issues aside: experienced activists argue that ultimately it will be necessary to go beyond struggles against particular local toxic dumps and facilities and demand that production be transformed to eliminate toxic hazards at their point of origin.

The above thumbnail description of the toxics/environmental justice movement is not intended to suggest that this is the new model of social movements for the nineties and beyond. It is more likely that this will be one among many forms that social movements will take. But this description does highlight certain differences. The new social movements of the seventies and eighties (and beyond, to the extent that they still exist) have been made up overwhelmingly of young people, and in most cases of young people of middle class status or at least origin. The age range within toxics/environmental justice groups is much broader, with older people playing a much larger role; it is skewed toward people for whom economic constraints are a bigger issue. Its constituencies, though diverse, are much more distant from university and related intellectual cultures. This is not to argue that there is some necessary connection between these constituencies and a grassroots politics that regards both the state and issues of production as important terrains of struggle. Broad popular constituencies can be associated with any number of political positions – including, for instance, the Christian right, or anti-abortion. But it does suggest that the ascendancy of the "new social movements" have been more tied to a particular moment, in particular national contexts, and to a constituency of a particular age, class, and cultural orientation than theorists of the movements believed at the time.

Radical democracy has been associated not only with the new social movements, via new social movement theory, but also with poststructuralism, especially as it has been expressed in the realm of social analysis. It is important to stress though that radical democracy has not been *equated* with poststructuralism; some of those who invoke it, such as Cornel West, have explicitly dissociated themselves from aspects of the poststructuralist perspective;[7] occasionally it is used by people whose concerns are quite different from those of poststructuralism (for Bogdan Denitch, for instance, "radical democracy" is imbued with something like a social democratic perspective).[8] Nevertheless, on the whole what might be called "the discourse of radical democracy" is strongly influenced by a poststructuralist mindset. One of the consequences of this is the absence of class from that discourse.

Ernesto Laclau and Chantal Mouffe's book, *Hegemony and Socialist Strategy*, has done more than any other single piece of work to set the terms for the discussion of cultural politics, or radical democracy.[9] This may be particularly the case in the United States, where their book was widely read and taken by many as the authoritative statement of the implications of poststructuralism (or postmodernism, the term that was then more widely in use) for radical politics. The book was also received with a certain amount of relief among those who wanted to engage in poststructuralist analysis and at the same time lay claim to radical politics. The appearance of a poststructuralist tour de force with "socialist strategy" in its title seemed to establish the connection between the two.

The book presents a thoughtful critique of Marxism, including an appreciation of some aspects of the Marxist tradition. Laclau and Mouffe argue that the fundamental flaw in Marxism, its essentialist element, is its equation between the working class and socialist politics, the claim that there is an innate or automatic relationship between the working class and socialism. Laclau and Mouffe want to argue instead for a contingent concept of politics, one in which there is no given relationship between a particular class position and a particular political stance: every political position, in their view, is constructed, negotiated on the terrain of shifting alliances and changing struggles, among many social actors.

Laclau and Mouffe do not entirely castigate Marxism. They argue that both Lenin and Gramsci introduced concepts of class coalition, and also more complex conceptions of political consciousness, according to which no one political path is predetermined. They note that Gramsci's concept of hegemony introduced an indeterminacy to the relation between class and political position: in Gramsci's view, creating a progressive or socialist bloc required ideological struggle and the construction of alliances among various classes and sections of classes. Emphasizing Gramsci's view of politics as a terrain of ideological struggle, they portray him as a forerunner of a poststructuralist perspective in which politics becomes entirely contingent, entirely detached from class position. What Laclau and Mouffe leave out is that for Gramsci there remained a profound connection between class and politics. The working class, in Gramsci's view, might not attain a socialist politics easily. For long periods most workers might hold other political views; the working class would not be able to win socialism alone. But for Gramsci socialism remained the most authentic expression of the interests of the working class. In his view socialism could not be achieved unless the majority of the working class, especially its most politically active members, came to support it.

In *Hegemony and Socialist Strategy* Laclau and Mouffe give their readers a choice between a reductionist version of Marxism, in which class position determines politics, and a poststructuralist or "constructionist" position according to which there is no relation between class and politics at all. This leaves out a middle option (held by most Marxist theorists): that working class people may be conservative, and people of wealthier classes – even capitalists – may be politically radical, but economic and social position remains a kind of baseline for politics. Working class people may vote against social services if they become convinced that it is supported out of their taxes and going to people other than themselves. But the fact remains that people on the lower economic rungs need social services more than those above them. Societies in which the working class is highly organized, and in which there are labor parties, tend to have much more extensive welfare states than societies in which these are weak or absent – prime example of the latter being the United States. Another way of making the same point: it is hard to imagine a situation in which a socialist program, proposed by the capitalist class, is defeated by working class opposition.

Radical democracy suggests a politics that is detached from issues of the state as well as from class. This is partly a heritage of the new social movements, which tended to avoid the arena of electoral politics, especially on the national level. The avoidance of the state also reflects the influence of Michel Foucault, and a particular reading of his approach to power. In the arena of cultural radicalism, Foucault's critique of the repression hypothesis, his argument that power is productive (of social relations, identities, resistance, and so forth) has been taken very seriously; meanwhile his recognition that power is also repressive tends to be forgotten.[10] Foucault, used in this way, has become the point of reference for a large and influential theoretical literature, especially in queer and feminist theory, that equates radical politics with play, parody, and the subversion or reversal of existing cultural forms, that is not concerned with social repression and finds efforts to either understand it or confront it uninteresting.[11] This reading of Foucault is of a piece with the current tendency to oppose the cultural to the political and economic realms, and to claim a superior place for cultural politics, not on grounds of efficacy but of aesthetic sophistication.

Foucault's influence has reinforced the turn away from the state as an arena of struggle in another way as well, at least among those who take his work to be the new foundation of radical analysis. In *Discipline and Punish* Foucault describes the repressive effects of state power and traces its changing character over the centuries, arguing that while the state at one time employed spectacular displays of force and violence to ensure its will, it has evolved into a much more sophisticated instrument, resting on surveillance, discipline-instilling habits of subordination, and the creation of subjects who participate in the state's project of social control.[12] This portrait captures the increasingly sophisticated, and insidious, forms of social control that we find ourselves subject to. But it leaves out the possibility of positive social intervention on the part of the state. Capitalism means class polarization and immiseration at the lower levels of society: if the state fails to intervene, suffering increases. There is a long history of popular, and left, struggles to reorient state power, to incorporate popular forces into the state and transform it to whatever degree possible into an instrument of social welfare. Foucault's view of the state as consisting of technologies of intrusive control leaves no room for the fact that in industrial societies people, especially poor people, need social services. In his view of the state as a concentrated location of disciplinary power, there is no room for struggles on the terrain of state power.

Though the term radical democracy can be used in many ways, on the whole the discourse of radical democracy has been framed by the assumptions of cultural politics, by the view that the object of radical politics is to take control of discourse. This is to some extent a sign of cynicism, or resignation, after repeated defeats on other terrains. Dick Flacks has argued that the United States left has failed where it set out to succeed – on the terrain of political power – while it has succeeded where it did not intend to, on the terrain of culture. He points out that in the United States the left has never managed to organize a party with any hope of taking power, but that it has created many enclaves of alternative culture and has had some influence on mainstream culture as well.[13] It is as if cultural politics (and, on the whole, radical democracy) takes this description of history as a proscription for action.

Though class struggle has never come anywhere near bringing socialism, and the left has never approached the point of taking power, there have been real accomplishments. Principles of workers' rights, civil rights (in relation not only to race but also to gender, sexual orientation, and other social categories), and the responsibilities of the state in relation to social welfare have all been won through struggle and have had lasting implications for the quality of most people's lives. A retreat into the arena of discourse does nothing to address the erosion of these rights. The orientation of cultural radicalism toward the deconstruction of the concept of "rights" is politically extremely dangerous. It is true that rights are not given but constructed through struggle. The implication of this, for the left at least, should be to defend and extend them.

In a recent article, Arif Dirlik addresses the relation between cultural radicalism, specifically postcolonialism, and global shifts in the organization of capital. Dirlik argues that "postcolonialism" is the moment when intellectuals from nations of what would until recently have been called the Third World arrive in the universities of the First World and begin to speak in the vocabulary of poststructuralism, celebrating cultural diversity and rejecting categories of capitalism and class. Dirlik situates this in the shift between two forms of international capitalism. The old form, now on the way out, was firmly tied to national states, grounded first of all in the United States and secondly in Western Europe. This (Fordist) capitalist order, he points out, was culturally conservative: it was dominated by white male elites who regarded challenges from others as threats to their power. The emerging, multinational form of international capitalism is oriented toward the United States and the West as a whole, but never quite puts its feet down anywhere. The new elites recognize their need to make room for a range of cultures and therefore the value of a multiplicity of voices, especially elite voices from the parts of what used to be the Third World in which multinational capital operates or hopes to operate. As long as such elites do not point to the global capitalist order that has created their privileged status, their voices are welcome.[14]

The nineties is a very poor time for the left to turn aside from issues of class and state power – of who has it and what they do with it. This is a period of accelerating class polarization, in the US and also globally. In the United States it is impossible to take our understanding of race, gender, or questions of social division and disintegration further without acknowledging the fact of class polarization. The majority, including the overwhelming majority of people of color and large numbers of women, are being pushed down the economic ladder, and many are losing the few protections or benefits they once were able to claim from the state. On a global scale, a different version of the same points holds: some nations in the category once referred to as the Third World are being drawn into the circuits of multinational capital and subjected to the same pressures toward internal class polarization while others are being left aside, to starve. The realm of politics, nationally and internationally, is where decisions are being made about how globalization will be shaped and what restrictions will be placed on it. Standing aside from this arena means leaving it to the right.

The contest between two forms of international capitalism (and the fact that multinational capital is winning, and that the globalization of capital is proceeding rapidly) poses an awkward situation for the left, and for social movements generally. What positions should the left, or progressive social movements, take on the issue of free trade? On international conventions that reduce the scope of national sovereignty? Should national boundaries be strengthened, or allowed to become more permeable? There is a certain pull toward strengthening the boundaries of the nation: how else is it possible to exert any control over capital? How are progressive social policies possible if capital is free to move at will? But reinforcing national boundaries means ignoring the impact of globalizing capital, placing obstacles in the way of the waves of migration forced by the reorganization of economies and environmental degradation. There is also a pull from the side of multinational capitalism: it is much more sophisticated; it invites cultural diversity; and it makes room for (and even gives financial support to) many discourses, including the discourse of cultural radicalism. It is more fun.

The danger for the left is allowing itself to be caught up in the contest between declining and ascendant forms of capitalism; for culturally oriented intellectuals, the danger is confusing the ascendant form of capitalism with radicalism. Following Dirlik I would argue that we have to focus our attention on the transformation of international capital and on the question of class. We have to develop political principles and initiatives that point toward a progressive alternative to the existing choices. In the United States, the two-party system is on the verge of collapse; entering a Democratic Party that is in the process of disintegrating is not a good idea, except possibly as part of a larger strategy. It is likely that third parties will begin to be formed; it would make sense for the left to be part of this process. But the prior question is not whether people on the left should turn their efforts toward a third party, but what its politics would be.

I am suggesting a politics involving, on the national level, demands for an improved welfare system and a state more accountable to the needs of the people, especially those on the lower economic levels of society. I think we should revive our commitment to democratic socialism, not as a goal for the foreseeable future but as a vision, a moral reference point for a more modest program for the present. We need international movements around questions of labor, the environment, and human rights. There is a need for coordinated national and international structures enforcing international standards on these issues. It is unrealistic to think of world government (and also frightening to speculate on who would run it, given the weakness of movements of the left and the strength of multinational capital). It is more realistic to think of international agreements based on conceptions of human rights and environmental protection.

Rejecting the idea that culture is the main arena of struggle and that subversion lies at the margins of society does not have to mean going back to the authoritarian structures of the Communist movement or the domination of social movements by white men. An updated social democratic politics would have to be internally democratic. It would have to address questions of whose agendas are to be included, who will shape the coalitions and frame the demands. It would have to find forms that would enable full expression for all of the overlapping groups that form the potential basis for a progressive politics: working class people, groups of color, women, sexual and other cultural minorities. It would have to find ways of incorporating the recognition that none of these groups speak with one voice. Such a movement – perhaps involving one or more parties, and networks of groups and organizations of various kinds – would also have to be majoritarian: whites, men as well as women, would have to have a legitimate place.

Perhaps the term radical democracy can be stretched to incorporate something like the above politics. Some people use the term to suggest that we need to go beyond a narrow identity politics; this is certainly compatible with the approach that I am outlining. So is the aim of constructing a movement based on a wide range of democratic grass-roots groups. But if we want to pose a credible challenge to the right, I think we need to also put forward a program that addresses questions of inequality and power, of how resources are used and who decides.

## NOTES

1. See Alain Touraine, *The Post-Industrial Society: Tomorrow's Social History: Conflict and Culture in the Programmed Society* (New York: Random House, 1971); Alberto Melucci, *Nomads of the Present: Social Movements and Individual Needs in Contemporary Society* (Philadelphia: Temple University Press, 1989), 'The New Social Movements: A Theoretical Approach,' *Social Science Information* 19, no. 12 (1980), 'The Symbolic Challenge of Contemporary Movements,' *Social Research* 52, no. 4 (Winter 1985): 789–816; Claus Offe, 'New Social Movements: Challenging the Boundaries of Institutional Movements,' *Social Research* (Winter 1985); Jean Cohen, 'Rethinking Social Movements,' *Berkeley Journal of Sociology* (1983): 97–98.
2. See Joachim Hirsch, 'The Fordist Security State and the New Social Movements,' *Kapitalstate* 10–11 (1983): 75–87; Michel Aglietta, *Capitalist Regulation: the US Experience* (London: Verso, 1979); and 'Phases of US Capitalist Expansion,' *New Left Review* 110 (1978).
3. Alain Touraine, 'An Introduction to the Study of Social Movements,' *Social Research*, 52 (1985): 749–787.
4. On the peace movement in Western Europe, and the inadequacy of new social movement theory in relation to it, see Thomas R. Rochon, 'The West European Peace Movement and the Theory of New Social Movements,' in Russell J. Dalton and Manfred Kuechler, *Challenging the Political Order: New Social and Political Movements in Western Democracies* (New York: Oxford University Press, 1990). On the institutionalization of the new social movements in Germany and elsewhere see Margit Mayer and Roland Roth, 'New Social Movements and the Transformation to Post-Fordist Society,' in *Social Movements and Cultural Politics*, Marcy Darnovsky, Barbara Epstein and Richard Flacks, eds. (Temple University Press, forthcoming).
5. On social movements in the United States in relation to new social movement theory, see Carl Boggs, *Social Movements and Political Power: Emerging Forms of Radicalism in the West* (Philadelphia: Temple University Press, 1986), and Margit Mayer, 'Social Movement Research and Social Movement Practice: the U.S. Pattern,' in *Research on Social Movements*, ed. Dieter Rucht (Boulder and San Francisco: Westview, 1991).

6. For accounts of the toxics/environmental justice movements, see Andrew Szasz *Ecopopulism: Toxic Waste and the Movement for Environmental Justice* (Minnesota: University of Minnesota Press, 1994); Robert Gottlieb, *Forcing the Spring: the Transformation of the American Environmental Movement* (Washington, DC: Island Press, 1994); *Confronting Environmental Racism: Voices from the Grassroots*, ed. Robert D. Bullard (Boston: South End Press, 1993); and *Toxic Struggles: The Theory and Practice of Environmental Justice*, ed. Richard Hofrichter (Philadelphia: New Society Publishers, 1993).

7. Cornel West, 'Race and Social Theory,' in *Keeping Faith: Philosophy and Race in America* (New York: Routledge, 1993).

8. Bogdan Denitch, 'A Foreign Policy for Radical Democrats,' in this volume.

9. Laclau and Mouffe, *Hegemony and Socialist Strategy*. On related questions, see the following exchange: Norman Geras, 'Post-Marxism?' *New Left Review* 163 (1987): 40–82, and Laclau and Mouffe, 'Post Marxism without Apologies,' *New Left Review* 160 (1987): 79–106.

10. Michel Foucault, *The History of Sexuality*, volume one (New York: Pantheon, 1986).

11. For examples of this approach, see Judith Butler, *Gender Trouble* (New York: Routledge, 1990); Eve Kosofsky Sedgwick, *Epistemology of the Closet* (Berkeley: University of California Press, 1990).

12. Michel Foucault, *Discipline and Punish: The Birth of the Prison* (New York: Pantheon, 1977).

13. Richard Flacks, *Making History: The American Left and the American Mind* (New York: Columbia University Press, 1988).

14. Arif Dirlik, 'The Postcolonial Aura in the Age of Global Capitalism,' *Critical Inquiry* vol. 20, no. 2 (Winter 1994): 328–56.

# 94

# THINKING COLLECTIVELY IN THE PUBLIC DOMAIN

## John Stewart

The case for a public domain based on public learning is grounded in the government of uncertainty. The need for public learning has always been present, but has recently been highlighted by the transformations of our times. Economic, technological, social and environmental changes now pose problems imperfectly understood, which require us to search for a response.

In *Management for the Public Domain: Enabling the Learning Society*, Stewart Ranson and I argue that the polities of the post-war era neglected the need for public learning. It was assumed too readily that government understood the problems faced and could deliver a solution through reliance on professional expertise. A system of government was built for certainty, which required no place for public learning and hence for an active citizenship.

In reaction, attempts were made to establish the neo-liberal polity, although never so successfully as its advocates sought. There was no concern for public learning, because the market would spontaneously produce responses to perceived needs. It is now realised that markets do not replace the need for public learning, but reveal it in the problems they create and in the issues they cannot resolve. The reality of the government of uncertainty has now replaced the apparent government of certainty or the assumption that the market will resolve public problems.

Reconstituting the public domain as an arena for public learning must involve the public as citizens, otherwise it merely reconstitutes the government

From John Stewart, 'Thinking Collectively in the Public Domain', *Soundings*, 4 Autumn 1996, pp. 213–23.

of certainty in new forms. The argument for a public domain based on public learning is in effect an argument for strengthening the democratic base through active citizenship.

The British system of government is based on representative democracy, but on an attenuated conception of representation. It is as if the act of being elected constitutes the representative without the need for any further action, beyond making oneself available through surgeries to hear individual problems. This is a passive concept of being a representative, rather than an active process of representing or re-presenting the views of those represented.

The passive concept of representation leaves little or no place for participatory democracy or the active involvement of citizens in the process of government. There is a tendency therefore to see representative democracy and participatory democracy as opposed. Given an active process of representation, however, representative democracy requires and is strengthened by participatory democracy; and by participatory democracy more is meant than collecting the views of individual citizens. It involves informing, discussing and listening. Participatory democracy makes the role of the elected representative more important.

The public do not and will not speak with one voice, but with many voices, making different demands. Within any area there are many communities, and lines of conflict as well as cooperation. The development of participatory democracy, if successful, should extend the range of voices beyond those normally heard. The importance of discussion in participatory democracy is to establish an awareness of different positions, to test them against other and wider concerns and to see whether, through discussion, new positions can be reached which can reconcile differences, or at least explore how far they can be reconciled. It is the role of the elected representative to aid that process, and in the end, if required, to balance and to judge differing views.

If there has been an attenuated conception of representative democracy, there has also been an attenuated conception of citizenship. In the welfare state, the role of citizen was that of elector, but beyond that little more than client. In the neo-liberal polity the Citizens' Charter as an expression of a market philosophy defines the citizen as customer, and in so doing limits the role of citizens or even their concerns. Even if I am not a customer of education, as a citizen I have views on education and a right to express them, as I have a duty to listen to others.

The attenuated state of democracy has led to and is constrained by a centralist culture. While many countries have come to appreciate that one cannot govern a complex and changing society in the certainty of centralism, centralisation has proceeded apace in Britain, weakening local government. Geographical and organisational distance separate central government and citizen.

Of course it will be said that citizens are apathetic. Examples will be quoted of attempts to involve citizens that have failed. The low turnout in local elections will be quoted in confirmation of that apathy. But too often attempts to involve citizens are on the organisation's terms. Little attempt is made to work with the grain of how people behave. Old tired forms of public meeting are hardly likely to generate public involvement. New approaches have to be developed based on an understanding of the reality of people's attitudes and behaviour.

## INNOVATION IN DEMOCRATIC PRACTICE

There is a need for innovation in democratic practice. While much has changed in policy and management, there has been little innovation in democratic practice. For example, while concern has been widely expressed about local electoral turnout, there has been no attempt to improve it. Even the notice that announces the election remains as unreadable as it was when the design was first laid down many years ago. In New Zealand local authorities have the option to hold the election by post and now all authorities do so, because of the improvement in turnout. In Europe elections are held at the weekend. These are organisational changes, and do not necessarily deal with the real weaknesses of local democracy. They are indications, however, of the general lack of innovation in British democratic practice.

In two publications on innovation in democratic practice, I have set out a wide number of approaches that could be developed to enhance citizen participation. Public bodies should recognise the need to develop citizen participation, and develop a repertoire of approaches to nurture the habit of citizenship.

## THE INFORMED CITIZEN

This article takes as its main illustration of the possibilities a family of approaches that are designed to find the informed views of a representative group of citizens. These are not the only approaches, and the range of possibilities will also be discussed.

There are three main defining characteristics of the approaches on which this article concentrates. They involve a group of citizens deliberately chosen as a representative sample of citizens generally, as the modern equivalent of the Athenian principle of selection by lot. In that way people from all sections of the population are involved, avoiding the danger that only the articulate and the joiners take part. They also ask from citizens not a continuing involvement, impossible to sustain, but a particular commitment over a limited period of time.

The approaches ensure that citizens only give their views after hearing about the issue in depth, with an opportunity to question and challenge. There is a fundamental difference between these approaches and opinion polls, which can be merely a device for obtaining the uninformed and often unconsidered views of citizens. Recently the Local Government Commission for England sought citizens' views on local government reorganisation in most counties. Generally they showed opinions were divided, although there was a tendency to favour 'no change' in many areas. However, on one issue there was general agreement; about 80 per cent on average said they knew nothing or very little about the issues on which they were giving their view. One might consider that that robbed their views of some of their value.

These approaches also ensure that the citizens involved have discussed the issues amongst themselves. Democracy, if it is to be meaningful, must be more than a recording system for individual views. It should involve discourse in which citizens explore views together, test ideas, seek agreement, yet become aware of difference. These approaches bring deliberation by citizens into the process of government. As Fishkin has argued:

> The distinction between the inclinations of the moment and public opinions that are refined by 'sedate reflection' is an essential part of any adequate theory of democracy. Political equality without deliberation is not of much use, for it amounts to nothing more than the power without the opportunity to think about how that power could be exercised.

Although the numbers involved are small they are a microcosm of the citizenry at large.

## CITIZENS' JURIES

Citizens' juries are an example of these approaches. Citizens' juries were developed independently in Germany, where are they called planning cells, and in the United States. A group of citizens representing the general public meet together to explore a policy issue or to discuss a particular decision. Witnesses present information and jurors ask questions. They then deliberate amongst themselves before making their conclusions public.

Normally in Germany and the United States citizens' juries last about four to five days. In that time, it has been found that citizens develop a good under-standing of the issues involved, and effective discussion develops. Jurors find it a rewarding experience and can become advocates for its further development.

Citizens' juries are not used as decision-making bodies. They are a source of advice and guidance for decision-makers on issues on which they seek to learn the views of informed citizens. Normally the decision-maker will easily learn the views of interested parties, at least if they belong to groups having ease of access to government. They can learn through opinion polls the, too often, uninformed views of citizens. They do not readily have access to the informed views of citizens.

There are issues on which elected representatives are uncertain how to proceed. They may be unconvinced by the professional advice they receive, but be uncertain of the public's attitude. They may be aware of conflicts of views between interested parties or the pressure of particular parties, and will wish to know what the views of the public generally would be if informed about the issue. In fields of policy where new issues are arising they may seek ideas from an informed public.

In all these circumstances and others, decision-makers may seek the views of a citizens' jury. In Germany where the use of citizens' juries is more developed, Professor Peter Dienel and the Research Institute for Public Participation and Planning Procedures at the University of Wuppertal accept commissions from local authorities, the Länder and federal government. The authority commissioning the citizens' jury does not undertake to accept its views. It will however undertake to consider the views expressed and to respond to them. This emphasises that the role of the citizens' juries is not decision-making, but to inform decision-making, in the same way as participatory democracy generally has been presented as informing, not replacing, representative democracy.

Citizens' juries were used to consider designs for development in and around Cologne City Square, and led to reconsideration of the proposals of the council's professional advisers. One wonders whether some town centre developments in Britain would have survived appraisal by citizens' juries. In Grevelsburg a citizens' jury examined alternative approaches to traffic problems in a historic town centre. Citizens' juries have also been used to explore broader policy issues on which they may well produce guidelines rather than specific recommendations. In Germany they have considered the social consequences of new technology and in Greater New Haven in the United States they have explored the problems of at-risk children.

The phrase 'citizens' juries' commands attention and connects the development with an established tradition involving citizens in the process of government. It can mislead however, because the process differs from the formality of courts of law – and indeed the phrase is not used in Germany. There is no judge, but rather a moderator whose role is to facilitate discussion and certainly not to maintain quasi-legal procedures. The jury does not have to reach agreement, but only record its different views if agreement is not reached. Importance is attached to discussion which can take place throughout the process. In Germany, with juries of 25, some of the discussion takes place in groups of five, before coming back to the wider group. The emphasis is on informality in easing discussion.

One of the main problems with citizens' juries is to avoid bias and ensure the integrity of the process. In Germany and America (at the Jefferson Centre in Minneapolis, where Ned Crosby originated the phrase) this is the responsibility of the independent centres who organise the citizens' juries, and whose reputation depends upon the integrity of the process. While the sponsoring organisation will specify the issue to be the subject of the jury, the charge (or way the issue is posed) will be determined by the organisers. They will control the selection of the jury and seek to secure it as a representative group. The organisers will also select the witnesses and control the information provided.

Citizens' juries naturally involve costs, particularly since some form of payment is made to jurors. Costs can vary from £10,000 up to over £100,000, when multiple juries are involved. Equivalent costs may be involved in other means of investigating issues, including of course opinion surveys. Citizens' juries should be seen as one means of investigating public issues through the exercise of citizenship.

Since the publication of the Institute of Public Policy Research's work on Citizens' Juries there has been considerable interest in their potential in local authorities. The Local Government Management Board has sponsored a series of pilot projects. Over forty authorities expressed interest in the projects and six were chosen to proceed. The issues covered include the impact of new technology, drugs issues and the improvement of a specific area of a town.

There has also been interest in health authorities. This is seen as, in part, a means of enhancing their own accountability, as concern with the accountability of appointed boards has grown. The Institute of Public Policy Research and the King's Fund are supporting a number of citizens' juries in health authorities focusing on such issues as health rationing.

These citizens' juries in this country are being undertaken as this article is being written. There will be evaluations of their success and their impact on authorities. For the purpose of this article they have been used as an example of innovation in democratic practice. Citizen involvement can take different forms. Citizens' juries are not *the* approach to building participatory democracy, but *an* approach amongst a repertoire of approaches designed to find the informed views of citizens. Here, more briefly, are several others.

## DELIBERATIVE OPINION POLLS

Deliberative opinion polls also seek the informed views of citizens. However, while citizens' juries take as their starting point the jury system and then modify it, the deliberative opinion poll takes as its starting point the opinion poll and seeks to overcome its weakness. Fishkin, its main advocate, has argued, 'An ordinary opinion poll models what the public thinks, given how little it knows. A deliberative opinion poll models what the public would think, if it had a more adequate chance to think about the questions at issue.'

Deliberative opinion polls differ from citizens' juries in that they involve larger numbers and can involve less time and less intense discussion. They differ from normal opinion polls in that opinions will be tested after the participants have had an opportunity to hear witnesses, ask questions and discuss the issue, although for the purpose of comparison views may also have been tested at the outset of the process.

Fishkin piloted a deliberative opinion poll on issues of law and order in Britain through Channel Four television and the *Independent* newspaper. In January of this year a National Issues convention was held in the United States which included a deliberative opinion poll based on six hundred voters selected as a representative sample of the American population. They discussed key issues facing America, including the economy, America's role in the world and the state of the family.

## CITIZENS' PANELS

Citizens' panels are representative panels of citizens called together as sounding boards. In 1993 eight health panels, each consisting of twelve people selected to be a representative sample of the population, were set up by the Somerset Health Commission to discuss the values that should guide health resource allocation decisions. The panels held four meetings over the following year. At the first meeting panel members were asked to bring their own health issues. At the succeeding meeting they discussed issues raised by the health authorities. These included whether the health authority should pay for coronary artery by-pass operations for people who smoke, and whether certain treatments should be given at all. The topics chosen were issues being actively considered by the authorities.

There is an emphasis on deliberation: 'An important rationale of our approach to consultation was that those involved should have the opportunity to explore issues in some depth. Most people need a period of listening to the views of others and talking about issues themselves in order to clarify their thoughts on any complex questions.' After discussion, panel members complete a series of decision sheets, in effect voting on the issue. The research team organising the project prepared reports for the health authority on the panels, using the discussion to convey the flavour of the panel meeting as well as the results from the decision sheets. The panels are continuing with four members of the panels replaced at each meeting.

The same principle has been suggested for a local authority, but with a panel of 200 to 300, to meet once a month, as a sounding board for the authority, again with a number changing each month. The panel would again be a representative panel ensuring that sections of the public were represented from whom the authority rarely heard views.

## CONSENSUS CONFERENCES

Consensus conferences are another variant. They were designed to incorporate public interests and concerns into processes of science policy-making, which has often been seen as a matter for experts but increasingly raises ethical or environmental issues. This approach was developed in Denmark and a consensus conference was organised in Britain by the Science Museum in London on plant biotechnology.

Simon Joss and John Durant define consensus conferences as 'a forum in which a group of lay people put questions about a scientific or technological subject of controversial political and social interest to experts, listen to the experts' answers, then reach a consensus about this subject and finally report their findings at a press conference'.

In Denmark, subjects have included air pollution, childlessness, food irradiation and electronic identity cards, and the cost has been £35,000 to £50,000 per conference. The procedure is well-established in that country, and differs from citizens' juries in having a less representative method of selection, based on written applications. More time is spent in preparation, and the emphasis on consensus is an important difference. Consensus conferences are a variation on the theme of the informed citizen.

## A RANGE OF INNOVATION

These are not the only possible innovations. Other examples include:

- mediation groups which bring together groups which are in conflict over, for example, environmental issues, to see if through discussion differences can be reconciled or at least reduced
- new forms of public meetings designed to enable discussion in groups, rather than to structure meetings around platform and audience
- community forums in which authorities can reach out to diverse communities, remembering that as well as communities of place there are communities of interest
- stakeholder conferences in which all interested in an issue can be brought together in a variety of forms of discussion designed to identify areas for action
- teledemocracy which as time passes can have an increasing role in providing access for the public and involving the public
- involvement of citizens in scrutiny panels, village appraisal, environmental assessments.

All of these can enhance participatory democracy and strengthen representative democracy. There is also a case for direct democracy on specific issues. There is more of a tradition of referenda at local level than is often appreciated. There is a long history of referenda on libraries, local licensing options, Sunday opening of cinemas and private bills. Although most of these are in the past, the right of electors to call parish polls remains and what are, in effect, referenda have been instituted by the Conservative government for parents on options for grant maintained status and for tenants on the transfer of local authority housing stock. Some local authorities have recently held referenda on local issues such as the Sunday opening of leisure centres. The use of referenda on issues of community concern that lie outside the main framework of party political divides can be an exercise in citizenship, encouraging public discussion.

## TOWARDS DECENTRALISATION

Strengthening democracy and public learning requires a learning government. The capacity of central government to constitute the basis for a learning system of government is limited. Many tiers in organisational hierarchies separate ministers from action and impact. Central government cannot easily encompass diversity of circumstance and achieve diversity in response. Yet learning comes from a recognition of diversity of need, diversity of aspiration and diversity of response. From uniformity one may learn little except of the scale of one's failure. One learns from diversity, of relative success and relative failure. A central government can achieve learning if it uses the diversity of local government as its base.

Participation is built more easily at local level than at national level and the evidence is that citizens are more ready to participate at that level. A commitment to the strengthening of participatory democracy is a commitment to decentralisation within the system of government, both to local authorities and within local authorities. Within local government, too, decentralisation and more effective local democracy involves a commitment to strengthen participatory democracy, through innovation in democratic practice for which a repertoire of approaches is being and can be developed.

In that repertoire citizens' juries are one example of a family of approaches constituting a public arena for discourse based on a representative sample of citizens. In that public arena, discourse can constitute the public domain for public learning and active citizenship.

# 95

# DIGITAL DEMOCRACY:
# AN INTRODUCTION

## Barry N. Hague and Brian D. Loader

There exists a growing body of thought that articulates the belief that recent developments in information and communications technologies (ICTs) contain within them the potential to facilitate 'quantum leaps in the field of democratic politics' (Becker 1998: 343). For Becker, these amount to no less than a paradigm shift in the process of the understanding of democratic governance.

A variety of models, experiments and initiatives are emerging in response to the challenge of (re)invigorating democratic institutions and practice by utilising ICTs. These initiatives are variously grouped in the literature under the umbrella of 'electronic democracy', 'teledemocracy' and 'cyberdemocracy'. The term 'digital democracy' is preferred here since it is the bringing together of existing electronic technologies through developments in digital data transfer that unleashes the potential of ICTs. At present, the notion of digital democracy can refer to a fairly wide range of technological applications including televised 'people's parliaments' or citizens' juries, e-mail access to electronic discussion groups, and public information kiosks (DEMOS 1997). It is not the aim of this collection to provide a comprehensive coverage of such initiatives; this task is left to other authors. Neither is it intended to provide detailed accounts of competing models of democracy, their relative merits and the underlying conditions required for their realisation (see Held 1987). Still less is the collection intended to join arms with either the cyber-libertarian vision of a digital utopia (Barlow

From Barry N. Hague and Brian D. Loader, 'Digital Democracy: An Introduction', in Barry N. Hague and Brian D. Loader (eds), *Digital Democracy: Discourse and Decision Making in the Information Age* (Routledge, London, 1999), pp. 3–10.

1996) or the technophobic distopian nightmares of a surveillance society (Davies 1996). Both of these scenarios lean too much towards technological determinism. It is important to recognise that new ICT applications, whether directed at enhancing democracy or not, emerge out of the 'dialectical interaction between technology and society' (Castells 1997: 5); they are subject to 'social shaping' (Kubicek *et al.* 1997) and, as such, they will be influenced by such factors as technological precedent, culture (political or otherwise), legal frameworks, etc., and will emerge through the activities of human agents, constrained as they are by existing power relations.

The aims of this book, then, are as follows. First, to address the question of what a 'strong democracy' based on extensive use of ICTs might look like. Second, to explore the likely effects of alternative underlying social, economic and political conditions on the 'digital democracy' we actually achieve. Third, to draw together international case study material with a view to separating the rhetoric from the reality concerning the current impacts of ICTs on democratic practice. Fourth, to draw lessons from this case study material concerning barriers to the realisation of 'digital democracy', the pursuit of alternative 'agendas', and the emergence of unintended consequences from the application of ICTs. Before elaborating upon these aims, let us briefly rehearse the justifications for such a project.

### DIGITAL DEMOCRACY: WHY THE INTEREST?

The major justifications for (re)visiting democratic practice in the light of an emergent Information Age are twofold. The first concerns a growing perception that current political institutions, actors and practice in advanced liberal democracies are in a frail condition and are held in poor public regard. The second concerns a belief that the current period of rapid social, economic and political change, which may signal an emergent Information Age, provides opportunities hitherto unavailable to rethink and, if necessary, radically overhaul or replace those institutions, actors and practice.

Representative models of democracy have come to characterise many twentieth-century societies. It is only by conceding a great deal of their power, runs the argument, to a smaller number of politicians whose job it is to represent their common interests that citizens can live in a democratic society at all. Conversely, its opponents have argued that elected representatives often do not represent the 'will of the people' and are prone to elitism (Michels 1962). More recently, politicians have become tarnished with allegations of sleaze, corruption, self-seeking behaviour and sound-bite politics that may have produced widespread disillusionment and apathy amongst citizens and particularly the young (Wilkinson and Mulgan 1995). It is against this background that we have to assess where the notion of digital democracy fits in.

The second reason why a focus on 'digital democracy' is apposite concerns the notion that society is undergoing a paradigmatic shift. Castells quotes palaeontologist Stephen J. Gould thus:

> The history of life, as I read it, is a series of stable states, punctuated at rare intervals by major events that occur with great rapidity and help to establish the next stable era ... [A]t the end of the twentieth century, we are living through one of these rare intervals in history. An interval characterised by transformation of our 'material culture' by the works of a new technological paradigm organised around information technologies.
>
> (Castells 1997: 29)

It is the assumption here that such an interval may indeed be in progress and, furthermore, that it is during such periods of upheaval that the potential for human agency in the shaping of our collective future is at its greatest (cf. Hoggett 1990). It is for this reason that deliberation on the likely and desired future shape of our political institutions and practice, and the potential role of ICTs therein, is paramount. Contributions to the debate are to be sought from and between various academic disciplines and fields (including political science, sociology, public administration, economics, law, information management and computer science) as well as from public servants, ICT professionals and lay enthusiasts, and the wider citizenry. It is hoped that this edited collection makes an important, if modest, contribution to this end.

## A VISION OF 'STRONG DEMOCRACY'

There are already a number of competing conceptions of democracy, and it is not entirely clear whether electronic democracy is being put forward as a different variant. Typically, debate in recent years has tended to focus upon a kind of continuum, with participatory democracy (Pateman 1970) at one end of the scale and representative democratic models at the other. Participatory democracy has been seen to be the closest approximation to direct democracy, with its exhortation to involve the public in decision-making processes. Its critics have pointed out that examples of such participatory behaviour tend to be rather limited to a few instances of local politics and workplace groups. Furthermore, its advocates have often paid less attention to those who do not wish constantly to embrace political debate and action. Moreover, the size and complexity of modern nation-states has meant that the citizen has little realistic opportunity (or perhaps desire) to influence their environment beyond the village pump.

Is there something qualitatively different about digital democracy that gives it a new conceptual status? As we have seen, at present the notion of digital democracy is used to refer to a range of technological applications and experiments. Whilst such experiments are useful for improving existing representative democratic institutions, and the huge increase in local, regional and state government web-sites should be welcomed as attempts to improve the citizen – government interface, they do not seem to us to constitute an entirely new democratic system. As is frequently the case, ICTs are often used to augment existing practice rather than revolutionise institutions.

It is assumed here, however, that the evangelists of the internet have something more in mind when they extol the virtues of digital democracy, which suggests that power will transfer to the *demos* once they are armed with ICTs. In its extreme form, the internet is conceived as an electronic forum comprising a vast network of liberated and equal citizens of the world capable of debating all facets of their existence without fear of control from national sovereign authorities (Barlow 1996). The limitations of this cyber-libertarian approach have been dealt with elsewhere (Loader 1997). It is worth reminding ourselves, however, of the key features of interactive media that are claimed to offer the potential for the development of a new variety of democracy:

- Interactivity – users may communicate on a many-to-many reciprocal basis.
- Global network – communication is not fettered by nation-state boundaries.
- Free speech – net users may express their opinions with limited state censorship.
- Free association – net users may join virtual communities of common interest.
- Construction and dissemination of information – net users may produce and share information that is not subject to official review or sanction.
- Challenge to professional and official perspectives – state and professional information may be challenged.
- Breakdown of nation-state identity – users may begin to adopt global and local identities.

Whilst all of these features raise important questions for empirical study and debate, their existence seems somewhat restricted at the present time. Welcome though existing initiatives are, democracy is about more than voting or providing better public information to the citizen: electronic plebiscites and public information kiosks are simply not sufficient conditions to affirm the existence of digital democracy. Democracy has at its heart self-determination, participation, voice and autonomy. It is a political culture that includes a wide range of realms for self-development and mutual collective expression.

If an enhanced form of digital democracy is to emerge, it would seem reasonable to speculate, on the basis of the foregoing discussion, that it is likely to be a hybrid democratic model containing elements of both participatory and representative forms of democracy. The concept of 'democratic autonomy' developed by David Held (1996) is useful in developing this line of argument. Held's model, like the argument presented in this chapter, is predicated upon an inclusive definition of politics:

> politics is a phenomenon found in and between all groups, institutions and societies, cutting across public and private life. It is expressed in all the activities of co-operation, negotiation and struggle over the use and distribution of resources. It is involved in all the relations, institutions

and structures which are implicated in the activities of production and reproduction in the life of societies.

(Held 1996: 310)

If we accept this inclusive definition of politics, then 'strong democracy' must offer the opportunity for the 'participation of citizens in all those decisions concerning issues which impinge upon and are important to them (i.e. us)' (ibid.). The practical achievement of such a state must involve a symbiotic relationship between both representative and participatory democratic forms and, for Held, requires that democracy be 'reconceived as a double-sided phenomenon: concerned on the one hand, with the *re*-form of state power and, on the other hand, with the restructuring of civil society' (ibid.: 316).

Held's 'principle of autonomy' requires the protection of individual rights and, hence, makes some form of constitutional government, overseen by elected representatives, necessary. The challenge is to reform such government so as to circumscribe its power to impinge upon individual autonomy whilst retaining the authority to uphold it, and to make its business accountable to all citizens. At the same time, the 'principle of autonomy' requires that '[people] should be able to participate in a process of debate and deliberation, open to all on a free and equal basis, about matters of pressing public concern' (ibid.: 302).

From the foregoing discussion, certain questions, which are open to empirical investigation, begin to emerge in relation to the role of ICTs in the creation of 'strong democracy':

- To what extent might ICTs facilitate more accountable government (national and local)?
- To what extent might ICTs be used to create a more informed (about the business of government) citizenry?
- To what extent might ICTs facilitate citizen participation in decision making concerning affairs of state?
- To what extent might ICTs facilitate participation by citizens in 'debate and deliberation', on a 'free and equal basis', concerning affairs of state?
- To what extent might ICTs facilitate participation by citizens in 'debate and deliberation', on a 'free and equal basis', within civil society?
- To what extent might ICTs facilitate citizen participation, on a 'free and equal basis', in collective decision making concerning issues that impinge upon them within civil society?

Each of the contributors to this book addresses one or more of the above questions. The chapters in Part II are concerned primarily with developments relating to the democratisation of the state. Those in Part III focus upon developments in civil society. A common theme for each of the chapters is a concern with the potential for ICTs, often but not exclusively focused upon the interactive characteristics of the internet, to foster more deliberative, discursive, democratic forms. This reflects, we feel, a mutual recognition of the centrality of what Robert Putnam (1993a) calls 'social capital', which promotes civic engagement and interaction between citizens concerning matters of common concern – to any notion of 'strong democracy'.

Two further themes that emerge throughout the book, and which are central to the prospects for 'strong democracy', are those concerning access to and ownership and control of those ICTs holding potential for democratic reform, and it is to these that we now turn.

## THE QUESTION OF ACCESS

Consideration of the potential of ICTs to facilitate the creation of 'strong democracy' inevitably raises concerns over access. Typically, such concerns, particularly as expressed by governments, have focused on broadening access to ICT hardware and software and providing widely available basic training in their use (the British government-sponsored 'IT for All' and 'Computers Don't Bite' initiatives provide good examples). As important and welcome as these considerations and the initiatives that flow from them are, we feel that the question of access raises a range of issues that move beyond a concern with physical access to ICTs

## ACCESS TO ICTS

Naturally, the question of who has access to the latest ICTs, and who does not, is an important one. The potential of ICTs to facilitate 'strong democracy' must be seriously questioned if people are systematically denied access on the basis of economic status, gender, geographic location, educational attainment, and so on. Advocates of the emancipatory potential of the internet, for example, would do well to remember that it remains the domain of a relatively elite association of mainly white, male, professional people from advanced societies (Holderness 1998). Of course, it might be argued that the exponential growth of connectivity means that the unconnected 'information poor' will become an increasingly small group that can be targeted and prioritised through state-sponsored initiatives. This would, however, be somewhat to miss the point. It is highly likely that the achievement of mass connectivity will coincide with the creation of a commercially dominated (and owned?) 'global digital high-bandwidth network'. By the time such a network is in place, the technological paradigm that will both constrain the types of activity and interactivity that are possible in cyberspace and, more fundamentally, provide the conceptual tools with which we seek to understand and shape cyberspace, may already be entrenched. Traffic around this network may bear little resemblance to the anarchic, global commons so beloved of internet enthusiasts today [...]. As Castells states with his usual perceptiveness, 'while governments and futurologists speak of wiring classrooms, doing surgery at a distance and tele-consulting the Encyclopaedia Britannica, most of the actual construction of the new system focuses on "video-on-demand", tele-gambling and VR theme parks' (1997: 366).

Accepting our previous argument that the potential for human agency in the shaping of tomorrow's technologies is at present relatively strong, it becomes of paramount importance, to anyone genuinely concerned with 'strong democracy', that all citizens are exposed to the current capabilities of ICTs and are encouraged to consider whether and how they might be utilised to the betterment of their individual and collective lives. This is where state-sponsored initiatives to broaden access, like those mentioned earlier, can be found wanting. Such initiatives have been conceived and implemented in a very 'top down' manner. The underlying logic would appear to run along the following lines: ICTs are a good thing *per se*; those who can access and have the skills to utilise these ICTs will gain obvious advantages (primarily economic) for themselves and will be more useful (primarily economically) to society; better drag as many people as possible along to their nearest training provider, overcome their groundless fears and equip them with some basic computing skills. What is missing here is any attempt to ground awareness raising and training regarding ICTs in the everyday experience of individuals and communities and to allow them to decide for themselves what use ICTs may be to them.

[...]

## REFERENCES

Barlow, J. P., 'Declaration of the Independence of Cyberspace', *Cyber-Rights Electronic List*, 8 February 1996.

Becker, T., 'Governance and Electronic Innovation: A Clash of Paradigms', *Information, Communication and Society*, 1 (3), 1998, pp. 339–43.

Davies, S., *Big Brother: Britain's Web of Surveillance and the New Technological Order* (Pan Books, London, 1996).

Castells, M., *The Rise of the Network Society* (Blackwell, Oxford, 1996).

Pateman, C., *Participation and Democratic Theory* (Cambridge University Press, Cambridge, 1970).

Held, D., *Models of Democracy* (Polity Press, Cambridge, 1987).

Held, D., *Models of Democracy* (Polity Press, Cambridge, 1996).

Hoggett, P., *Modernisation, Political Strategies and the Welfare State* (SAUS, Bristol, 1990).

Holderness, M., 'Who Are the World's Information Poor?', in Holderness, M. (ed.), *The Cyberspace Divide: Equality, Agency and Policy in the Information Society* (Routledge, London, 1998).

Kubicek, H., Dutton, W. H. and Williams, R. (eds), *The Social Shaping of Information Superhighways* (Campus Verlag, Frankfurt, 1997).

Loader, B. D. (ed.) *The Governance of Cyberspace: Politics, Technology and Global Restructuring* (Routledge, London, 1997).

Michels, R., *Political Parties: A Sociological Study of the Oligarchical Tendencies of Modern Democracy* (Collier, New York, 1962).

# BIBLIOGRAPHY

(Where works are listed which have been extracted in this Reader, the editions cited are those used in the compilation of this Reader.)

PART ONE: TRADITIONAL AFFIRMATIONS OF DEMOCRACY

CLASSIC TEXTS

Aristotle, *The Politics*, ed. and trans. Ernest Barker (Oxford University Press, London, Oxford and New York, 1976).

Constant, B., *Political Writings*, ed. B. Fontana (Cambridge University Press, Cambridge, 1988).

Hobbes, T., *Leviathan*, ed. C. B. Macpherson (Penguin Books, Harmondsworth, 1968).

Locke, J., *Two Treatises of Government*, ed. P. Laslett (Cambridge University Press, Cambridge, 1988).

Machiavelli, N., *The Discourses*, ed. and intro. Bernard Crick (Penguin Books, Harmondsworth, 1970).

Madison, J., Hamilton, A. and Jay, J., *The Federalist Papers*, ed. Isaac Kramnick (Penguin Books, Harmondsworth, 1987).

Mill, J., *Political Writings*, ed. Terence Ball (Cambridge University Press, Cambridge, 1992).

Mill, J. S., 'Considerations on Representative Government', in Mill, J. S., *Three Essays* (Oxford University Press, London, Oxford and New York, 1975).

Paine, T., *The Rights of Man*, ed. H. Collins (Penguin Books, Harmondsworth, 1969).

*Puritanism and Liberty. Being the Army Debates (1647–9) from the Clarke Manuscripts*, selected and edited with an introduction by A. S. P. Woodhouse (Dent, London, 1974).

Rousseau, J.-J., *The Social Contract* and *Discourses*, trans. and intro. G. D. H. Cole (Everyman's Library: Dent, London/Dutton, New York, 1968).

Schumpeter, J. A., *Capitalism, Socialism and Democracy* (George Allen & Unwin, London, 1943).

Thucydides, *History of the Peloponnesian War*, trans. Rex Warner, intro. and notes M. I. Finley (Penguin Books, Harmondsworth, 1983).

Tocqueville, A. de, *Democracy in America*, eds J. P. Mayer and Max Lerner, 2 vols (Collins, Fontana Library, 1968).


GENERAL WORKS ON DEMOCRACY (CONTEMPORARY WRITINGS)

Arato, A. (ed.), special issue on 'Prospects for Democracy', *Social Research*, 66 (3), Fall 1999.

Axtmann, R., *Liberal Democracy into the Twenty-First Century. Globalization, Integration and the Nation-State* (Manchester University Press, Manchester and New York, 1996).

Beetham, D., *Democracy and Human Rights* (Polity Press, Cambridge, 1999).

Beetham, D. and Boyle, K., *Introducing Democracy. 80 Questions and Answers* (Polity Press, Cambridge, 1995).

Benhabib, S. (ed.), *Democracy and Difference. Contesting the Boundaries of the Political* (Princeton University Press, Princeton, NJ, 1996).

Birch, A. H., *The Concepts and Theories of Modern Democracy* (Routledge, London and New York, 1993).

Bobbio, N., *The Future of Democracy* (Polity Press, Cambridge, 1987).

Bobbio, N., *Democracy and Dictatorship. The Nature and Limits of State Power* (Polity Press, Cambridge, 1989).

Burnheim, J., *Is Democracy Possible?* (Polity Press, Cambridge, 1985).

Dahl, R. A., *Democracy and Its Critics* (Yale University Press, New Haven, CT and London, 1989).

Diamond, L. and Plattner, M. F. (eds), *The Global Resurgence of Democracy*, 2nd edn (Johns Hopkins University Press, Baltimore, MD and London, 1996).

Duncan, G. (ed.), *Democracy and the Capitalist State* (Cambridge University Press, Cambridge, 1989).

Dunn, J. (ed.), *Democracy. The Unfinished Journey 508 BC to AD 1993* (Oxford University Press, Oxford, 1992).

Elshtain, J. B., *Democracy on Trial* (Basic Books, New York, 1995).

Held, D. (ed.), *Prospects for Democracy: North, South, East, West* (Polity Press, Cambridge, 1993).

Held, D., *Models of Democracy*, 2nd edn (Polity Press, Cambridge, 1996).

Hirst, P. and Khilnani, S. (eds), *Reinventing Democracy* (Blackwell, Oxford, 1996).

Holden, B., *Understanding Liberal Democracy*, 2nd edn (Harvester-Wheatsheaf, Hemel Hempstead, 1993).

Holmes, S., *Passions and Constraints. On the Theory of Liberal Democracy* (University of Chicago Press, Chicago and London, 1995).

Huntington, S. P., *The Third Wave. Democratization in the Late Twentieth Century* (University of Oklahoma Press, Norman and London, 1991).

Isaac, J. C., *Democracy in Dark Times* (Cornell University Press, Ithaca, NY and London, 1998).

Katz, R. S., *Democracy and Elections* (Oxford University Press, New York and Oxford, 1997).

Lakoff, S., *Democracy. History, Theory, Practice* (Westview Press, Boulder, CO and Oxford, 1996).

Lijphart, A., *Democracies. Patterns of Majoritarian and Consensus Government in Twenty-One Countries* (Yale University Press, New Haven, CT and London, 1984).

Macpherson, C. B., *The Real World of Democracy* (Clarendon Press, Oxford, 1966).

Macpherson, C. B., *Democratic Theory: Essays in Retrieval* (Clarendon Press, Oxford, 1973).

Macpherson, C. B., *The Life and Times of Liberal Democracy* (Oxford University Press, Oxford, London, New York, 1977).

Mahr, A. and Nagle, J. D, *Democracy and Democratization* (Sage, London, 1999).

Resnick, P., *Twenty-First Century Democracy* (McGill-Queen's University Press, Montreal, Kingston, Buffalo and London, 1997).

Sartori, G., *The Theory of Democracy Revisited*, 2 vols (Chatham House, Chatham, NJ, 1987).

Saward, M., *The Terms of Democracy* (Polity Press, Cambridge, 1998).

Shapiro, I., *Democracy's Place* (Cornell University Press, Ithaca, NY and London, 1996).

Shapiro, I. and Hacker-Cordon, C. (eds), *Democracy's Edges* (Cambridge University Press, Cambridge, 1999).

Shapiro, I. and Hacker-Cordon, C. (eds), *Democracy's Value* (Cambridge University Press, Cambridge, 1999).

Townshend, J., *C. B. Macpherson and the Problem of Liberal Democracy* (Edinburgh University Press, Edinburgh, 2000).

Weale, A., *Democracy* (Macmillan, London, 1999).

## PART TWO: KEY CONCEPTS
### FREEDOM AND AUTONOMY

Berlin, I., *Four Essays on Liberty* (Oxford University Press, Oxford, 1969).

Lindley, R., *Autonomy* (Macmillan, London, 1986).

Pettit, P., *Republicanism. A Theory of Freedom and Government* (Clarendon Press, Oxford, 1997).

Skinner, Q., *Liberty before Liberalism* (Cambridge University Press, Cambridge, 1998).

### EQUALITY

Arneson, R. J., 'Equality', in Goodin, R. E. and Pettit, P. (eds), *A Companion to Contemporary Political Philosophy* (Blackwell, Oxford, 1993).

Dworkin, R., *Sovereign Virtue. The Theory and Practice of Equality* (Harvard University Press, Cambridge, MA and London, 2000).

Lukes, S., 'Equality and Liberty: Must They Conflict?', in D. Held (ed.), *Political Theory Today* (Polity Press, Cambridge, 1991), pp. 48–66.

Phillips, A., *Which Equalities Matter?* (Polity Press, Cambridge, 1999).

### REPRESENTATION

Birch, A., *Representation* (Pall Mall Press, London, 1971).

Burke, E., 'On Representation', in *The Political Philosophy of Edmund Burke*, I. Hampsher-Monk (ed.) (Longman, London, 1987).

Burnheim, J., *Is Democracy Possible?* (Polity Press, Cambridge, 1985).

Manin, B., *The Principles of Representative Government* (Cambridge University Press, Cambridge, 1997).

Pitkin, H. F., *The Concept of Representation* (University of California Press, Berkeley, 1967).

Pitkin, H. F (ed.), *Representation* (Atherton Press, New York, 1969).

### MAJORITY RULE

Guinier, L., *The Tyranny of the Majority. Fundamental Fairness in Representative Democracy* (Free Press, New York, 1995).

Mill, J. S., *On Liberty*, in Mill, J. S., *Three Essays* (Oxford University Press, London, Oxford and New York, 1975).

Spitz, E., *Majority Rule* (Chatham House, Chatham, NJ, 1984).

Tocqeville, A. de, *Democracy in America*, eds J. P. Mayer and Max Lerner, 2 vols (Collins, Fontana Library, London and Glasgow, 1966), Vol. I, Part II, Chapters 7 and 8.

## CITIZENSHIP

Beiner, R. (ed.), *Theorizing Citizenship* (SUNY Press, Albany, NY, 1995).

Benhabib, S., 'Citizens, Residents and Aliens in a Changing World: Political Membership in the Global Era', *Social Research*, 66 (3), Fall 1999, pp. 709–45.

Clark, P. B, *Deep Citizenship* (Pluto Press, London and Chicago, 1996).

Dagger, R., *Civic Virtues. Rights, Citizenship, and Republican Liberalism* (Oxford University Press, New York and Oxford, 1997).

Frazer, E., 'Citizenship Education: Anti-political Culture and Political Education in Britain', *Political Studies*, 48 (1), March 2000, pp. 88–103.

Habermas, J., 'Citizenship and National Identity: Some Reflections on the Future of Europe', *Praxis International*, 12 (1), 1992, pp. 1–19.

Janoski, T., *Citizenship and Civil Society. A Framework of Rights and Obligations in Liberal, Traditional, and Social Democratic Regimes* (Cambridge University Press, Cambridge, 1998).

Kymlicka, W. and Norman, W. (eds), *Citizenship in Diverse Societies* (Oxford University Press, Oxford and New York, 2000).

van Gunsteren, H. R., *A Theory of Citizenship. Organizing Plurality in Contemporary Democracies* (Westview Press, Boulder, CO and Oxford, 1998).

## PART THREE: CRITIQUES
### MARXIST AND SOCIALIST CRITIQUES

Bernstein, E., *The Preconditions of Socialism*, ed. and trans. Henry Tudor (Cambridge University Press, Cambridge, 1993).

Bobbio, N., *Which Socialism?* (Polity Press, Cambridge, 1986).

Callinicos, A., 'Socialism and Democracy', in Held, D. (ed.), *Prospects for Democracy: North, South, East, West* (Polity Press, Cambridge, 1993), pp. 200–12.

'Capitalism, Socialism and Democracy', *Journal of Democracy*, Special Issue, 3 (3), 1992.

Femia, J., *Marxism and Democracy* (Oxford University Press, Oxford, 1983).

Harding, N., 'The Marxist-Leninist Detour', in Dunn, J. (ed.), *Democracy: The Unfinished Journey, 508 BC to AD 1993* (Oxford University Press, Oxford, 1992).

Miliband, R., *Marxism and Politics* (Oxford University Press, Oxford, 1977).

Miliband, R., *Socialism for a Sceptical Age* (Polity Press, Cambridge, 1994).

Therborn, G., 'The Rule of Capital and the Rise of Democracy', *New Left Review*, 103, 1977, pp. 3–42.

### CONSERVATIVE, ELITIST AND AUTHORITARIAN CRITIQUES

Burke, E., *Reflections on the Revolution in France*, ed. Conor Cruise O'Brien (Penguin, Harmondsworth, 1969).

De Maistre, J., *The Works of Joseph de Maistre*, ed. J. Lively (Allen & Unwin, London, 1965).

Michels, R., *Political Parties: A Sociological Study of the Oligarchical Consequences of Modern Democracy*, trans. E. and C. Paul (Dover, New York, 1959).

Parry, G., *Political Elites* (George Allen & Unwin, London, 1969).

Scruton, R., *The Meaning of Conservatism*, 2nd edn (Macmillan, London, 1984).

### FEMINIST CRITIQUES

Butler, J. and Scott, J. W. (eds), *Feminists Theorize the Political* (Routledge, London, 1992).

Ferguson, K. E., *The Feminist Case Against Bureaucracy* (Temple University Press, Philadephia, 1983).

Mendus, S., 'Losing the Faith: Feminism and Democracy', in Dunn, J. (ed.), *Democracy: The Unfinished Journey, 508 BC to AD 1993* (Oxford University Press, Oxford, 1992).

Pateman, C., *The Sexual Contract* (Polity Press, Cambridge, 1988).

Phillips, A., 'Dealing with Difference: A Politics of Ideas or a Politics of Presence?', *Constellations*, 1 (1), 1994, pp. 74–91.

Phillips, A., *Engendering Democracy* (Polity Press, Cambridge, 1991).

Phillips, A., *Democracy and Difference* (Polity Press, Cambridge, 1993).

Sirianni, C., 'Learning Pluralism: Democracy and Diversity in Feminist Organisations', in *Nomos – Democratic Community* ( New York University Press, New York, 1993), pp. 283–312.

Squires, J., *Gender in Political Theory* (Polity Press, Cambridge, 1999).

PART FOUR: CONTEMPORARY ISSUES

RATIONAL CHOICE

Downs, A., *An Economic Theory of Democracy* (Harper & Row, New York, 1957).

Mackay, A. F., *Arrow's Theorem: The Paradox of Social Choice – A Case Study in the Philosophy of Economics* (UMI Books, Ann Arbor, MI, 1996).

Mueller, D. C., *Public Choice II* (Cambridge University Press, Cambridge, 1989).

Olson, M., *The Logic of Collective Action* (Harvard University Press, Cambridge, MA, 1971).

Riker, W. H., *Liberalism Against Populism* (Freeman, San Francisco, 1982).

Riker, W. H. and Ordeshook, P. C., 'A Theory of the Calculus of Voting', *American Political Science Review*, 62 (1), 1968, pp. 25–42.

THE MARKET

Barry, N., 'F. A. Hayek and Market Liberalism', in Tivy, L. (ed.), *Political Thought Since 1945* (Edward Elgar, Aldershot, 1992), pp. 133—50.

Beetham, D., 'Four Theorems about the Market and Democracy', *European Journal of Political Research*, 23, 1993, pp. 187–201.

Bowles, S., Gintis, H. and Gustafsson, B. (eds), *Markets and Democracy: Participation, Accountability and Efficiency* (Cambridge University Press, Cambridge, 1993).

Jackman, R. W., 'On the Relation of Economic Development to Democratic Performance', *American Journal of Political Science*, 17, 1973, pp. 611–21.

Przeworski, A. and Wallenstein, M. 'The Structure of Class Conflicts under Democratic Capitalism', *American Political Science Review*, 76, 1982.

Rueschemyer, D., Stephens, E. H. and Stephens, J. D., *Capitalist Development and Democracy* (Polity Press, Cambridge, 1992).

NATIONALISM AND DEMOCRACY

Alter, P., *Nationalism* (Edward Arnold, London, 1989).

Buchanan, A., *Secession. The Morality of Political Divorce from Fort Sumter to Lithuania and Quebec* (Westview Press, Boulder, CO, San Francisco and Oxford, 1991).

Caney, S., George, D. and Jones, P. (eds), *National Rights, International Obligations* (Westview Press, Boulder, CO and Oxford, 1996).

Diamond, L. and Plattner, M. F. (eds), *Nationalism, Ethnic Conflict, and Democracy* (Johns Hopkins University Press, Baltimore, MD and London, 1994).

Mill, J. S., 'Considerations on Representative Government', in Mill, J. S., *Three Essays* (OUP, London, Oxford and New York, 1975), Chapter XVI 'Of Nationality, as connected with Representative Government'.

Miller, D., *On Nationality* (Clarendon Press, Oxford, 1995).

Periwal, S. (ed.), *Notions of Nationalism* (Central European University Press, Budapest, London and New York, 1995).

Viroli, M., *For Love of Country. An Essay on Patriotism and Nationalism* (Clarendon Press, Oxford, 1995).

## MULTICULTURALISM

Habermas, J., 'Struggles for Recognition in Constitutional States', *European Journal of Philosophy*, 1 (2), 1993, pp. 128–55.

Honneth, A., 'Integrity and Disrespect: Principles of a Conception of Morality Based on a Theory of Recognition', *Political Theory*, 20 (2), 1992, pp. 187–201.

Kymlicka, W., *Multicultural Citizenship* (Clarendon Press, Oxford, 1995).

Lijphart, A., *Democracy in Plural Societies. A Comparative Exploration* (Yale University Press, New Haven, CT and London, 1977).

Taylor, C. et al., *Multiculturalism. Examining the Politics of Recognition* (Princeton University Press, Princeton, NJ, 1994).

## BEYOND THE WEST

Addi, L., 'Political Islam and Democracy: The Case of Algeria', in Hadenius, A. (ed.), *Democracy's Victory and Crisis* (Cambridge University Press, Cambridge, 1996).

Kelly, D. and Reid, A. (eds), *Asian Freedoms. The Idea of Freedom in East and Southeast Asia* (Cambridge University Press, Cambridge, 1998).

Nathan, A. J., *Chinese Democracy* (I. B. Tauris, London, 1986).

Parekh, B., 'The Cultural Particularity of Liberal Democracy', in Held, D. (ed.), *Prospects for Democracy: North, South, East, West* (Polity Press, Cambridge, 1993).

Salame, G., *Democracy without Democrats? The Renewal of Politics in the Muslim World* (I. B. Tauris, London and New York, 1994).

Sen, A., 'Democracy as a Universal Value', *Journal of Democracy*, 10 (3), July 1999, pp. 3–17.

## PARTICIPATION

Almond, G. and Verba, S., *The Civic Culture* (Princeton University Press, Princeton, NJ, 1963).

Bachrach, P. and Botwinick, A., *Power and Empowerment: A Radical Theory of Participatory Democracy* (Temple University Press, Philadelphia, 1992).

Goodin, R. and Dryzek, J., 'Rational Participation: The Politics of Relative Power', *British Journal of Political Science*, 10, 1980, pp. 273–92.

Mansbridge, J. J., *Beyond Adversary Democracy* (Basic Books, New York, 1980).

Milbrath, L. W., *Political Participation: How and Why Do People Get Involved in Politics?* (Rand McNally, Chicago, 1965).

Nie, N. H., Powell, G. B. and Prewitt, K., 'Social Structure and Political Participation', *American Political Science Review*, 63, 1969, pp. 361–78.

Verba, S. and Nie, N. H., *Participation in America* (Harper & Row, New York, 1972).

Verba, S., Schlozman, K. L. and Brady, H. E., *Voice and Equality: Civic Voluntarism in American Politics* (Harvard University Press, Cambridge, MA, 1995).

## CIVIL SOCIETY

Cohen, J. L and Arato, A., *Civil Society and Political Theory* (MIT Press, Cambridge, MA and London, 1992).

Habermas, J., 'Further Reflections on the Public Sphere', in Calhoun, C. (ed.), *Habermas and the Public Sphere* (MIT Press, Cambridge, MA, 1992), pp. 421–61.

Hall, J. A. (ed.), *Civil Society. Theory, History, Comparison* (Polity Press, Cambridge, 1995).

Hirst, P., *Associative Democracy. New Forms of Economic and Social Governance* (Polity Press, Cambridge, 1994).

Keane, J. (ed.), *Civil Society and the State* Verso, London, 1988).

Putnam, R. D., *Making Democracy Work: Civic Traditions in Modern Italy* (Princeton University Press, Princeton, NJ, 1993).

Seligman, A. B., *The Idea of Civil Society* (Princeton University Press, Princeton, NJ, 1992).


## DELIBERATION

Blaug, R., *Democracy, Real and Ideal: Discourse Ethics and Radical Politics* (State University of New York Press, Albany, NY, 1999).

Bohman, J., *Public Deliberation. Pluralism, Complexity, and Democracy* (MIT Press, Cambridge, MA and London, 1996).

Bohman, J. and Rehg, W. (eds), *Deliberative Democracy. Essays on Reason and Politics* (MIT Press, Cambridge, MA and London, 1997).

Duncan, G. and Lukes, S., 'The New Democracy', *Political Studies*, 11 (2), pp. 156–77.

Elster, J. (ed.), *Deliberative Democracy* (Cambridge University Press, Cambridge, 1998).

Fishkin, J. S., *Democracy and Deliberation. New Directions for Democratic Reform* (Yale University Press, New Haven, CT and London, 1991).

Habermas, J., *Moral Consciousness and Communicative Action* (Polity Press, Cambridge, 1992).

Habermas, J., *Between Facts and Norms: Contributions to a Discourse Theory of Law and Democracy* (Polity Press, Cambridge, 1996).

Miller, D., 'Deliberative Democracy and Social Choice', in Held, D. (ed.), *Prospects for Democracy: North, South, East, West* (Polity Press, Cambridge, 1993), pp. 74–92.

Warren, M., 'Democratic Theory and Self-Transformation', *American Political Science Review*, 86 (1), 1992, pp. 8–23.


## THE FUTURE OF DEMOCRACY

Bauman, Z., *In Search of Politics* (Polity Press, Cambridge, 1999).

Budge, I., *The New Challenge of Direct Democracy* (Polity Press, Cambridge, 1996).

Held, D. and Pollitt, C. (eds), *New Forms of Democracy* (Sage, London, 1986).

Kaplan, R. D., 'The Coming Anarchy', *Atlantic Monthly*, 273 (2), 1994, pp. 44–76.

Offe, C., *Contradictions of the Welfare State* (Hutchinson, London, 1984).

Stewart, J., Kendall, L. and Coote, A., *Citizens' Juries* (Institute of Public Policy Research, London, 1994).

Tsagarousianou, R., Tambini, D. and Bryan, C. (eds), *Cyberdemocracy: Technology, Cities and Civic Networks* (Routledge, London, 1997).

# INDEX